A Canadian Myth:
Quebec, Between Canada and the Illusion of Utopia

By the same author:

Anglophobie Made in Québec (in French)
Toute ma vérité (with Carole Devault)
The Informer (with Carole Devault), Fleet Publishers

Other fine books from the same publisher:

The Traitor and The Jew, by Esther Delisle
Zen & the Art of Post-Modern Canada, by Stephen Schecter
The Last Cod Fish, by Pol Chantraine
Seven Fateful Challenges for Canada, by Deborah Coyne
Economics in Crisis, by Louis-Philippe Rochon
Devil's Advocate, by Patrice Dutil
Dead-End Democracy? by Yves Leclerc
Voltaire's Man in America, by Jean-Paul de Lagrave
Judaism: from the religious to the secular, by A.J. Arnold

Canadian Cataloguing in Publication Data
Johnson, William, 1931-
A Canadian myth : Quebec, between Canada and the illusion of utopia
Includes index
ISBN 1-895854-08-3
1. Quebec (Province) - History - Autonomy and independance movements.   2.
Nationalism - Quebec (Province).   3. Federal-provincial relations - Quebec (Province).   4. English-French relations - Quebec (Province).   5. Canada - Politics and
government - 1963-   I Title

FC2925.9.M68J63 1994   971.4'04   C94-941155-8
F1053.2.J63 1994

If you would like to receive our current catalogue and announcements
of new titles, please send your name and address to:
ROBERT DAVIES PUBLISHING,
P.O. Box 702, Outremont, Quebec, Canada H2V 4N6

William Johnson

A Canadian Myth: Quebec, Between Canada and the Illusion of Utopia

Robert Davies Publishing

MONTREAL - TORONTO

The publisher takes this opportunity to thank the Canada Council and
the Ministère de la Culture du Québec for their continuing support.

To Carol Dutcher Bream
Who is present on every page of this book
As she is present in every hour of my life

Table of Contents

Introduction

In the summer of 1831, political philosopher Alexis de Tocqueville stopped off in Lower Canada for ten days, on his way home to France after discovering democracy in America. The cities he saw, especially Montreal, reminded him of provincial cities in France, though he noted a striking difference:

The bulk of the population and the immense majority, everywhere, is French. But it is easy to see that the French are the vanquished people. The rich classes belong for the most part to the English race.[1]

De Tocqueville heard French spoken everywhere; most of the newspapers, however, were published in English, and the signs in front of the shops were in English, even when their owners were francophones. The ruling class, he concluded, was English. But he did not think that would last: "The clergy and much of the enlightened classes are French; they have come to feel strongly about their subordinate position. The French newspapers that I read maintain a constant and lively opposition to *les Anglais*." To the French visitor's regret, the common people, "living a very comfortable material life," had no sense of being a conquered people and gave little support to the polemics of the more "enlightened" in their midst. That, he anticipated, would change, and he expected that, some day, the French and the English of Canada would separate. "I cannot believe that they will ever fuse together, or that there can be an indissoluble union between them. I still hope that the French, in spite of the conquest, will some day manage to form, alone, a fine empire in the New World, while being perhaps more enlightened, more moral, and happier than their fathers."[2]

In the more than sixteen decades since, much indeed has changed. Lower Canada experienced the Rebellion of 1837, the Union, responsible government, Confederation, the Statute of Westminster, and patriation of the constitution. The former colonists, the "conquered people," acquired full and equal political rights, and they helped to fashion one of the most successful countries on earth. The English ruling classes eventually left or were displaced by people speaking French. The "English" of 1831 Lower Canada became the "anglophones" of the 1990s: a multi-ethnic, multi-racial, multi-religious composite of whom fewer than one quarter were of British origin. The omnipresent English signs that de Tocqueville deplored disappeared after a Quebec law banished English from sight.

The "French," too, became diverse, including many of aboriginal, Haitian, North African, Lebanese, and Vietnamese origin. Even among the 82,790 Quebecers who listed themselves as strictly of Irish origin, 64.7 per cent spoke French at home. Three recent francophone premiers of Quebec, all named

Johnson, had an Irish ancestor, as did a mayor of Montreal, Jean Doré, whose great-grandfather was an Irishman by the name of Dawray. There was no longer in Quebec, by the last decade of the twentieth century, a clear polarization between two ethnic groups. The conquerors and the conquered had vanished into history.

And yet, the rift that de Tocqueville sensed has remained, more or less latent, never completely healed. His romantic image of a "liberator," a man who would lead the "French" to independence, has resurfaced periodically since 1837. At times, such as when the Meech Lake constitutional reforms failed to pass, in 1990, it seemed as though the independence of Quebec was imminent, almost inevitable. Parti Québécois leader Jacques Parizeau predicted an independent Quebec by 1995; many across Canada concurred with that prediction, give or take a referendum.

The paradox is striking: quickly, after the rebellion of 1837, most of the former rebels of Lower Canada were back from exile and pardoned, were again elected to the legislature, joined with reformers from Upper Canada to defeat the assimilative objective set by Durham for the Union, won recognition for French as an official language of Canada, won responsible government, and helped create the Dominion of Canada as a "new nationality." And yet a sense of alienation remained.

There were two fundamental sources for the persisting cleavage. The first lay in the ultra-conservative mentality that was fostered by French Canada's intellectual, religious, and political elites after the failure of the Rebellion, and that lasted for more than a century. Despite the pleas of a few, such as the great *patriote* journalist Étienne Parent, the elites steered French Canada toward a life of rural ultra-Catholic isolation, away from the cities, from industry, from *les Anglais,* and from the seductions of the English language, Protestantism, and pluralism. The second lay in the militant British imperialism and English chauvinism that swept through English-speaking Canada from the last decades of the Victorian era up to the First World War. The Fathers of Confederation had protected English and French in the federal Parliament and courts, and in Quebec's government and courts. However, they failed to vest in the constitution French education in other provinces. In the half-century following Confederation, French schooling was struck down or restricted in province after province.

These two sources of alienation played on each other. French-Canadian leaders rejected modernity just when English-speaking Canada was modernizing. Without entrepreneurship or a democratized system of education, most French Canadians were condemned to economic and social inequality, just as Étienne Parent had predicted. That inequality, in turn, practically excluded the French language from command positions in the textile factories, the logging camps, the mines, the pulp mills, and the cities. French Canadians, poorer and less educated on average, and therefore less powerful, were unsuccessful in defending their schools, under attack outside Quebec. The fate of the French minorities became a constant source of outrage, while in Quebec itself the relative poverty of the French Canadians, their subordinate positions in the economy, and the absence of French in positions of command were a constant source of humiliation.

So things remained, until Maurice Duplessis died, in 1959. Up to then, French Quebec, through most of its intelligentsia, had claimed fidelity to the France of the Middle Ages and the seventeenth century, rejecting the liberalism and secularism of the Enlightenment and the 1789 Revolution. As well, the intelligentsia's commitment to a supposed agricultural "vocation" of French Canadians had precluded the acquisitive, entrepreneurial, and innovative attitudes that had taken hold in the United States and Canada, following the earlier example of Britain, the first country to commit itself to capitalism and the Wealth of Nations. But the cultural differences between anglophones and francophones then narrowed considerably with the Quiet Revolution. For French-speaking Quebecers, the 1960s brought, belatedly and simultaneously, the spirit of the French Revolution and the Industrial Revolution.

The Quiet Revolution became two revolutions in one in another sense as well. In the beginning, it represented a commitment to modernize what had become, mostly in spite of the francophone elites, an urban industrial society. But this emphasis on modernization was soon overtaken by a commitment to "national liberation." The year 1960, when Jean Lesage's Liberals came to power, was also the year when seventeen new African states were created out of former colonies. This momentous political transformation of the world map was preceded and accompanied by a powerful literature of mobilization, written by North Africans such as Albert Memmi and Frantz Fanon, and by French intellectuals such as Jean-Paul Sartre and Jacques Berque, and it was adopted by much of the Quebec intelligentsia and applied, literally, to French Quebec. In Quebec's provincial politics, the theme of *libération* was adopted with varying explicitness by the Quebec Liberals, the Union Nationale, and then the Parti Québécois.

The "national liberation" thrust of French Quebec created instability that had repercussions throughout Canada. In 1965, a royal commission commented, "Canada, without being fully conscious of the fact, is passing through the greatest crisis in its history."[3] To cast the Quiet Revolution as a story of national liberation was, at the same time, to cast *les Anglais* implicitly in the role of the enemy against which French Canadians revolted. This scenario shone a more heroic light on recent history than the alternative of portraying the Quiet Revolution as one against the clergy, the misguided francophone elites, and the frozen institutions that had left French Canadians badly prepared for the modern world. "National liberation" also implied that the relative poverty of French Canadians in the past was caused by *les Anglais,* who somehow kept them in a state of bondage. The scenario carried with it an implicit plan of action: it suggested that *les Anglais*, dangerous colonizers that they were, must be kept in future under controlled supervision, by legislation which would apply the coercive power of the state to restrict the use of English. Through use of the state, francophones would be promoted within Quebec's economic power structure.

English-speaking Canadians, who had largely brought the economic development of Quebec to one of the highest levels in the world, were to be considered not as fellow citizens or as partners in building a better country for all, but as historic oppressors, current threats, and despoilers of the dream of a French Quebec. That such a tribalist vision could gain acceptance in a country in which all have equal political rights is an astonishing phenomenon in itself. It can be understood only by reference to the dark family secret of the French Canadian intellectual tradition: the demonization of *les Anglais*. Since the 1840s, the *Anglais* was the skeleton in the closet, treated as a person without faith or country, lusting for money, corrupting French Canadian youth, threatening the rural paradise which was the natural home of French Canadians. The Quiet Revolution, for a brief time, turned its back on the old tribalist tradition, but it soon returned, more virulent than ever, with the discovery that colonization theory justified, in a modern dress, all the old hatreds.

Since the Quiet Revolution, Quebec nationalism has worn two masks: the smiling mask, symbolizing a remarkable outburst of love and creativity, but also the angry mask of 150 years of anglophobia cultivated as a core tradition by the elites of Quebec. Gilles Vigneault composed the words sung by the first figure: *Gens du pays, c'est votre tour de vous laisser parler d'amour.*[4] In this country of the imagination, everyone is linked by words of love. Tensions and antagonisms, clashes of interest and confrontations, have all passed away. A permanent legacy of this face of the Quiet Revolution is the scintillating burst of artistic creativity expressed by Robert Lepage, Carbone 14, La-la-la Human Steps, Les Deux Mondes, Le Cirque du Soleil, and many others.

But Quebec's beloved singer-composer Félix Leclerc revealed in song the darker, more threatening mask in *L'alouette en colère*, in which he took the familiar folk song *Alouette* and turned it into a litany of outrages supposedly perpetrated by English Canada against the Québécois, who are presented as the plucked birds of the familiar chant:

I have a son crushed by the temples of finance which he cannot enter, and by those of words which he cannot leave. I have a son despoiled, as was his father, a drawer of water, hewer of wood, tenant, unemployed in his own land. He has nothing left but a beautiful view of the river and his mother tongue, which they will not recognize. I have a son in revolt, a son humiliated, a son who tomorrow will be an assassin.,

So I took fright and called to the others, Help, someone! The big neighbour came running, armed, gross, a foreigner, to fell my son once and for all, and to crush his spine and his back and his head and his wings, ah . . . My son is in prison and I, I feel in the depths of me, for the first time, despite myself, between flesh and bone, a burning anger.

The national liberation approach fostered a Fortress Quebec mentality. It tended to distance French-speaking Quebecers also from French Canadians living outside Quebec's boundaries, who had previously been considered part of one French-Canadian nationality. The fight for the French language had been, above all, a struggle to win school rights for French Canadians in other provinces. But, as Quebec converted to the new mythology, French Canadians in other provinces became a political embarrassment. They could not be liberated from their colonization. The only large body of French Canadians who could be decolonized, according to accepted theory, and become independent, or at least acquire a kind of national state, was in Quebec. And so the vocabulary was deliberately changed. French-speaking Quebecers were urged to call themselves Québécois rather than French Canadians (the word Québécois had previously applied only to the burghers of Quebec City). The French-speaking minorities were redefined as part of a different nation, now that Quebec was to be a nation to itself.

A group of dissidents, who saw this return to nationalism as reactionary and contrary to the interests of most Quebecers, was given intellectual leadership by Jean Marchand, Gérard Pelletier, and Pierre Trudeau. When "the three doves," as they were called in French, or "three wise men," as they were called in English, were elected to Parliament in 1965, they launched a counter-offensive, in which they appealed directly to the people of Quebec, over the heads of Quebec's political class. They offered an alternative Quiet Revolution: one in which all of Canada was to be made the home of French Canadians, by gaining recognition in the federal government and in all provinces for their language rights. This vision rejected the Fortress Quebec mentality: it proposed, instead, a closer and more respectful partnership between French Canadians and all other Canadians.

The separatist tide receded after Pierre Trudeau became prime minister in 1968. Trudeau rejected national status for the Quebec government, but promoted national status for the French language. It took him more than a decade to achieve his objective. When Quebec, in 1980, rejected in a referendum the dream of a "fine French empire" on the banks of the St. Lawrence, it seemed that, at last, Quebec's and Canada's identity crisis was resolved.

Then Brian Mulroney came to power, in 1984, on a strategy of accommodating Quebec nationalists. Quebec nationalism seemed in remission—if not dead, at least permanently weakened. Even René Lévesque, by the time of his death in 1987, had given up hope of ever seeing Quebec achieve sovereignty.

Mulroney did not invent Quebec nationalism; it was always there, dormant. But what he did, as only a prime minister of Canada who came from Quebec could, was rehabilitate and reactivate it. In 1987, the prime minister and ten premiers set off joyously, triumphantly, on the road to Meech Lake. By 1990, the flags of utopia were flying over Quebec.

What is remarkable, in retrospect, is how little our leaders learned from the national identity crisis of the 1960s and 1970s, when, a new concept of the role of the government, wedding traditional anglophobia to the discovery of the interventionist state, drove Quebec nationalism and threatened the country with secession. It produced the vision of a French ethnic state of Quebec, in which the government was identified with the French majority as its promoter and protector against all people who spoke English, whether in Quebec, in Canada as a whole, or in North America. In this vision, all the important powers of a state need to be concentrated in the Quebec government to fulfill the active role now demanded of the ethnic state. Attempting to accommodate it, as this book will show, can only strengthen separatism, increase regional conflicts, accentuate instability, weaken the country politically and economically, and bring about precisely what well-meaning people sought to avoid: a polarization between Quebec and the rest of Canada.

Quebec separatism, as will be seen, is ultimately based on mythology and illusions. Ultimately, beyond the sound and fury of politics, the single and only permanent antidote to Quebec separatism is demystification. That is the task undertaken by this book.

But first, a word about the author. I was born of a father who was an English-speaking Quebecer and a Franco-Ontarian mother. From my earliest memories, I spoke both English and French. I spent most of my childhood in the province of Quebec and studied for seven years at Collège Jean-de-Brébeuf, where I absorbed the nationalist view of history and the stereotype of *l'Anglais* as the alien to be resisted. All students had to memorize the poetic passage from the novel *Maria Chapdelaine* in which "the voice of the land of Quebec" speaks: "All around us foreigners have come whom we please to call the barbarians. They have taken almost all power, they have acquired almost all the money. But in the land of Quebec, nothing has changed."

When I took a master's degree in French literature at the Université de Montréal in the mid-1950s, I tried to make sense of the anglophobic messages of French-Canadian writing. Later still, I studied sociology at the University of California at Berkeley, and taught it for three years at the University of Toronto before becoming a journalist. Always, Quebec nationalism was the intellectual puzzle that most fascinated me. As both an academic and a journalist, unraveling that mystery was my central preoccupation.

As a political journalist, I covered the Quebec elections of 1976 which brought the PQ to power, and spent the next five years reporting on the Quebec govenment on a daily basis, including its 1980 referendum campaign. By 1990, when Quebec separatism was at its height, I had come to the conclusion that anglophobia—the depiction of *l'Anglais* as the enemy—was the most central and continuous theme of the historiography and the literature of Quebec, and the driving force behind separatism. To prove this thesis—which was not easily acceptable to most

16

right-thinking nationalists—I wrote, in French, a book reviewing the anglophobic motif through 150 years of intellectual production.[5]

The present book is, in a sense, a sequel. It concentrates on the politics of Quebec since 1960 to show, through all the changes that took place during the Quiet Revolution and since, the return of anglophobia, the refuge in the vision of the ethnic state, the role of mythology and illusion in driving political events. In the imminent showdown between two visions of Quebec and of Canada, the key to understanding the plot, the antagonists, and the themes is to understand what happened to the minds, hearts, and sensibilities of Quebecers beginning in 1960.

This book invites you to a voyage of discovery. It takes you on a trip through three and a half decades to see how Quebec evolved from Maurice Duplessis to Jacques Parizeau. In understanding—in demystification—lies the solution to the identity problems that agitate the country. There will be no solution without the understanding that makes people free.

Notes

1. Alexis de Tocqueville, *Oeuvres complètes. Édition définitive publiée sous la direction de J.-P. Mayer.* Vol. 5, *Voyage en Sicile et aux États-Unis* (Paris: Gallimard, 1957), p. 210.
2. Ibid., pp. 210–11.
3. Royal Commission on Bilingualism and Biculturalism, *Preliminary Report* (Ottawa: Queen's Printer, 1965), p. 13.
4. People of our country, now it's your turn to have words of love spoken to you.
5. William Johnson, *Anglophobie made in Québec* (Montreal: Stanké, 1991).

CHAPTER ONE

The Quiet Revolution: The Formation of the Ethnic State

The Quiet Revolution, when it came at last, began as an outbreak of hope. Suddenly, after a century of withdrawal and retreat into the past, Quebec decided to join the modern world. Everything seemed possible. Quebec began to change its institutions rapidly and deeply. The attitudes and values of the people changed even more rapidly. History quickened its pace. Long-standing walls crumbled.

All that it took, it seemed, was a few new leaders with the right ideas. Quebec could be quickly reborn, shedding the backwardness of the past. It could now be whatever it wanted to be, if it had the political will and the right plan.

And yet, no one could have predicted how quickly the changes would come. Quebec's slumber seemed as deep as ever in 1959, until 7 September, when Maurice Duplessis died. His successor, Paul Sauvé, promised to look to the future rather than to the past; his personal watchword was *désormais* (from now on). But Sauvé died within four months, and his nondescript successor, Antonio Barrette, went down to defeat, on 22 June 1960, to Jean Lesage's Liberals. So began a new era.

The slogan for the Liberal campaign had suggested a break with the past: *Il faut que ça change* (things have to change). The words were a repudiation of the long-standing ultra-conservative mind-set in Quebec, which novelist Louis Hémon had immortalized in *Maria Chapdelaine* with the words "*Au pays de Québec, rien ne doit changer*" (in the land of Quebec, nothing must change).

Maurice Duplessis had built his conservative regime on support from the rural areas. A long consensus of the elites held that French Canadians were destined by God for the rural life, the best protector of fundamentalist Catholic virtue and the French language. Duplessis's throne speech of 1958, just two years before the Quiet Revolution was to upset the old equilibrium, still reflected the rural preoccupation, even though 52 per cent of Quebec's population already lived in urban areas of 100,000 or more:[1] "The Union Nationale government has always understood that agriculture is the basic industry of all nations. . . . Moreover, the traditions, the customs, the folklore that give a people its true face are preserved in the countryside."[2] The lieutenant-governor, reading the throne speech written by Duplessis, heralded new "measures destined to favour rural areas. This is, in my opinion, the leading idea guiding the several bills that the government, under the direction of its leader, has presented to the Legislature."

In 1960, in contrast, Lesage came to power with a program conceived for an urban society. The reforms followed fast and furious, taking on a life of their own and reaching far beyond anyone's expectations. The Liberal election program had been extraordinarily detailed. It promised to raise the age of compulsory schooling to sixteen from fourteen, and to make schooling free at all levels, even for university—at a time when almost the only secondary schools were private *collèges* that charged tuition fees; it even promised a royal commission on education. But it offered not the slightest hint that Quebec's church-run system of French education would be replaced within four years by a state-run system. That was still unthinkable. In fact, Lesage solemnly promised that as long as he was premier, Quebec would never set up a ministry of education. But, by 1964, Quebec had a ministry of education for the first time since 1875, when it had been abolished at the insistence of the Catholic bishops, who held that only the church should control education.

Reform of the public administration meant separating the government from the private interests of the ruling party and its friends. The Union Nationale, while in power from 1944 to 1959, had spent $682 million on road construction without ever once calling a bid: contracts went to the regime's favourites, who were expected to show their gratitude in kind.[3]

Under Lesage, road-construction contracts were put out to tender. The civil service was professionalized, the Quebec provincial police reorganized. Lesage introduced the federal system of hospital insurance, which Duplessis had refused, and created a ministry of culture. And the Liberals did in fact raise the age for compulsory schooling to sixteen. When, in 1943, a previous Liberal regime had instituted compulsory schooling for the first time for children aged six to fourteen, Duplessis, as leader of the opposition, and his entire party had voted against the measure.

The new Cabinet quickly impressed the public: it was dubbed *l'équipe du tonnerre,* the dynamite team. It was led by four brilliant figures who lent their distinction to the rest. There was Jean Lesage himself, a handsome man with regular features, silvery hair, a dignified bearing, and a strong tenor voice. Lesage communicated a sense of grandeur, increasingly so over the next few years as the historic contribution of his regime to Quebec was recognized by Quebec's urban elites. He had been a member of Parliament for thirteen years, a federal

Cabinet minister for four, in charge of resources and northern affairs. But the defeat of Louis Saint-Laurent by John Diefenbaker in 1957 tempered his taste for federal politics. After the Diefenbaker landslide of 1958, in which Lesage was re-elected even though Quebec returned fifty Tories, he left Ottawa to win the leadership of the dispirited Quebec Liberals.

Lesage had felt humiliated by the lower levels of education and the poverty of French Canadians. He had said in a speech, which was quoted in the 1960 Liberal election program, "An expanding economy can raise the general standard of living, but we cannot be satisfied with that as an ethnic group, as long as the control and management of that economy continue to remain so tragically out of our hands."

Those words were prophetic of one direction that the Quiet Revolution would soon take. In one of his early speeches as premier, on 10 July 1960, Lesage said that the Quebec government had a duty to protect "the French face of Quebec." Increasingly, over the following years, the province of Quebec was to be transformed into an ethnic state defined by its French-speaking majority.

A second pillar of the Cabinet was Georges-Émile Lapalme, also a former Liberal member of Parliament, and Lesage's immediate predecessor as leader of the provincial Liberals. Somber and sensitive, with heavy horn-rimmed glasses that gave him the aura of a monk, Lapalme had led the Liberals from 1950 until his resignation from the leadership in 1958, but he had made little headway against the Duplessis machine. A cultivated man, idealistic and nationalistic, Lapalme managed to improve the image of the Liberal party, making it possible to attract star candidates by 1960.

Lapalme sensitized the party to the importance of culture and the protection of the French language, at a time when Duplessis dismissed all intellectuals as "piano players" and when Quebec was almost bereft of public libraries and museums. He ensured that the promise to create a ministry of cultural affairs found a place in the 1960 election program, and he served as its first minister from 1961 to 1964.

Paul Gérin-Lajoie, mustachioed, dark, and full of energy, was responsible for two major thrusts of the Lesage government. A Rhodes scholar with an Oxford doctorate in international law, Gérin-Lajoie developed the justification that the Lesage government was to invoke to act as a sovereign state internationally in matters within exclusive provincial areas of jurisdiction, notably education. But it was as minister of youth and then, after 1964, as minister of education, that Gérin-Lajoie made the single most important contribution to the Quiet Revolution. He campaigned tirelessly across the province and finally won acceptance for a truly daring reform of the education system, in which the fragmented patchwork of tiny school boards was amalgamated into a few large boards; public secondary schooling was extended beyond the then customary two years through

21

the construction of large comprehensive high schools; and schools were controlled through a new ministry of education.

But it was René Lévesque, the former radio and television public-affairs star, and now the minister of water and natural resources, who was to remain in public memory as the politician who most changed Quebec. He was actually ugly, though most people who knew him personally or through television soon forgot that. His nose was bulbous, his head half bald: straggly strands partly covered the dome. His forehead was wrinkled, his cheeks were pock-marked, his decaying teeth were yellowed by constant smoking. He had learned to hide his teeth by a smile that was fleeting, the lips remaining closed, a quick grimace. But his blue eyes were beautifully expressive and his entire face extraordinarily animated.

The young Lévesque had had nationalism ingrained in him when he attended a private secondary school, then run by the Jesuits. At the age of fourteen, in 1936, he wrote in the school publication some inspirational thoughts for the feast of Dollard des Ormeaux, the hero of New France who had led a sortie against the Iroquois and whom historian Lionel Groulx was promoting as the model for French-Canadian youth: "Surrounded by Protestants, almost invisible in this immense crowd of 137 million Anglo-Saxons who surround us, we are threatened, not with lightning, but with a slow and subtle penetration. Faced with this peril we have no other defence than struggle—a struggle for life, that is, for survival." He quoted a writer who had said that the French nation had a mission to accomplish in the world, and went on to formulate his opinion—or the opinion of his teachers—of what that collective "mission" would be for French Canadians: "In America, it is we, the sons of this same France, who have the mission: this duty is to project over materialistic America the light of French culture, of the spiritual culture that we alone possess. To do that, we must remain integrally French."

As an adult, Lévesque moved away from the nationalist tradition and specialized in international reporting. But, when he became a politician, he soon returned to a secularized version of the same nationalism that he had been taught as a child. "We must remain integrally French," he wrote as a boy in 1936. Increasingly, that would be his war cry as a politician. His sense of being threatened by an immense throng of "Anglo-Saxons who surround us" would, in later life, become the driving force for constructing a state of Quebec to protect French-speaking Quebecers.

He spoke rapidly, moving both hands before him, juggling words and images, waving his cigarette like a wand, creating atmosphere, generating excitement. And the words were spun into long sentences with clauses springing from clauses, perilous constructions, hard for a reporter to write down. But, somehow, it all seemed to make great sense. Lévesque was a superb communicator. And his words and his hands conjured up a new country to be created.

Despite a voice that was hoarse from childhood, Lévesque had a gift for words that redeemed everything else. Improbably, he became Quebec's foremost public-affairs commentator in the 1950s, when his program, *Point de Mire*, had an enormous audience. And, "miraculously" as he called it, in a kind of epiphany, a fully resonant voice came to him for the first time while he was campaigning for the 1960 Quebec election—the campaign that launched him on his political career. Surely, this miracle was too symbolic to be a coincidence. The long-muffled political leader had found his voice at last.

The first report of the royal commission on education, chaired by Mgr Alphonse-Marie Parent, described Quebecers as pathetically undereducated. Lévesque recalled in his memoirs the impact the report had: "I remember the collective shiver caused by the stunning revelations of the Parent Commission on education. In 1964—scarcely more than 20 years ago—four-fifths of our adults had not gone beyond, nor even in many cases finished, elementary school!"[4]

Lévesque suffered to see the people of Quebec diminished, and, like many of his generation, he held English-speaking Quebecers responsible. What he saw in Quebec was a case of colonialism. French-speaking Quebecers took for granted that they were *"nés pour un p'tit pain"*—born predestined for a small crust of bread.[5] Anglophones, on the other hand, as he described them, were haughty, arrogant, and complacent in their conviction that they should be in command of Quebec's economy.

As minister responsible for water resources and natural resources, Lévesque had many encounters with the province's mining and power companies, and these meetings wounded his pride. He looked at the mining and pulp-and-paper towns and reacted with bitterness to the invidious distinctions that were all too evident.

Serious money was made only in English. All the strategic resources, as we'd call them now, were also in anglophone hands. It was obvious at first glance in those "company towns" that belong to mines and pulp mills, where the finest neighbourhood, neat and clean, shaded, in the most pleasant location, invariably carried a name that was foreign to us. A whole regional parcel of little Upper Westmounts or little Hampsteads where lived not just fortune, but also influence and, above all, control.[6]

Lévesque soon focused on the nationalization of eleven private power companies. He perceived the Québécois as underdeveloped, undersized, and needing a powerful instrument—the state, the Quebec state—to help them deal as equals with English-speaking Canadians.

This change of attitude toward the state was to be the single most significant change wrought by the Quiet Revolution, and Lévesque was its most eloquent preacher. It was not just that the state took over education, hospitals, and welfare institutions from the church. The change was much broader and deeper in people's minds.

The critical change was reflected in Lévesque's oft-quoted sentence, "The state is one of us, it's even the one of us with the biggest muscles."[7] When he used the word *us,* Lévesque was not talking about Canadians, or all Quebecers. He was talking about francophone Quebecers only. And he identified the state with francophones. The state is one of *us.* Just as religions had once been established and institutionalized in the state, now the state of Quebec was to be reorganized progressively to promote the interests of Quebec's majority ethnic group and to inhibit the power, the growth, the ease of operations, and even the visible presence of English-speaking Quebecers.

With that concept of *us* accepted, it followed that the more "muscles" the French-Canadian state had, the more fully it could fulfil its role as ethnic state. Lévesque himself adopted this logic long before he decided to break with federalism altogether. He made his thinking clear in a speech to the Liberal Reform Club in Montreal in January 1964.

For three hundred years we have been here and this is the only part of the world where we can feel at home. A lot of other people can find their place anywhere in the world but there's only one place that we can call home and that's right here.

Quebec is on a road on which there is hardly any way back, a road leading very quickly to as full a measure of self-determination as can be allowed in the world today to a small, compact, and very resistant group of people.[8]

He would, before very long, conclude that Quebec's self-determination could and should cover the entire range of sovereignty.

Lévesque settled on hydro-electric power as the first step in transforming Quebec. But first he had to get together a team to formulate a workable plan. He invited Marcel Bélanger, then a federal civil servant in the ministry of finance, to Quebec to help plan the takeover of the power companies. "Meeting him with the avowed purpose of luring him from Ottawa, I asked him to help us draw up a plan of *décolonisation* in the hydro-electric sector," Lévesque later wrote.[9] What Ontario had done back in 1911 was to be placed, in Quebec, in the ideological context of national liberation.

Lévesque got his experts together, worked up a plan, and eventually convinced Lesage that the Quebec governmment should nationalize the private power companies. The Quebec Cabinet met at a mountain retreat for two days in 1962; on the second day, Lesage announced he would hold a snap election on the issue of expropriation.

The campaign needed a slogan. Four or five people, including Lévesque, tossed ideas back and forth for an evening. Then, suddenly, they had their slogan.

Jean-François Pelletier, one of the best publicists of the day, recalled an expression which he had already used for other purposes: *Maîtres chez nous.* Eureka! We agreed unanimously.

Deep down, though, I could not help but think that this was going a little too far. Masters of an important sector, yes. But masters, period? Masters, so to speak, of everything in sight? That and the decision to ignore two years of administration to focus the campaign on a single spectacular project left me a little uneasy with this hyperbolic slogan—and that unease never left me completely.[10]

Lévesque could have found more significant reasons for unease. *Maîtres chez nous,* masters in our own house, raised disquieting questions: masters over whom? Why must there be masters at all in a common house? Would the state remove one inequality only to impose another? And who is *nous*? Who is not *nous*?

The nationalization itself was not terribly radical. But the tone of the election campaign that followed was that of an attack against English-speaking domination. The Liberals published an election manifesto, which stated on its cover, "The era of economic colonialism is finished in Quebec. Now or never, *maîtres chez nous."* The implication was clear: the colonized were the French Canadians; the colonizers were *les autres, les étrangers, les Anglais.* The manifesto used the word *libération* six times. *Libération* was the word used when France was liberated from the Nazis, and in the Algerian war of decolonization the revolutionary group that organized the armed struggle was called the *Front de Libération Nationale. Libération* was a very strong, martial word to use for the nationalization of a few power companies.

The manifesto even suggested that nationalization of the power companies was only the beginning of a larger liberation: "In Quebec, by becoming masters of this natural wealth, we enter on the path of our economic liberation. A people like ours must use those instruments of economic liberation of which it can avail itself." In speaking of "a people like *ours,"* the manifesto was clearly not embracing all Quebecers. The Anglos owned the power companies. So the election was run as a struggle between *nous* and the Anglos.

The ethnic polarization implied by the Liberal campaign platform suggested that French-speaking Quebecers were not free, even though they constituted 80 per cent of the population of the province and controlled its government. They were not free and—though it was not stated baldly—the Anglos had enslaved them.

Lévesque's own attitude was similar. Never did he acknowledge that the people who had developed the mines, pulp mills, and power companies had done a service to all Quebecers. He implied that the Québécois would have been better off without the Anglos who had taken the initiative for economic development—in fact, that the mines and power companies would have been there without the Anglos, but minus the humiliation. His politics were the politics of resentment.

"We have had enough of being spectators of the activity of the others," the manifesto declared. "We must be active if we wish to survive." The aggressive, hostile tone was particularly evident in the manifesto's final sally. "The time has come for us to attack fundamentally, without delay or hesitation, the exalting task of the economic liberation of Quebec. For this principle, the Quebec Liberal Party puts its existence on the line. Never *chez nous* has a political party fought with such ardour for an ideal." Reflecting on that election campaign years later, Lévesque again used words suggesting an uprising: "This was the *beau risque* of the Lesage government and, at the same time, the beginning of the economic reconquest of Quebec."[11]

Thus was electric power turned into a symbol of the national power of francophone Quebecers. Hydro-Québec became the symbol suggesting that French Canadians are collective giants, able to build huge dams and generate mega-watts of electricity. It was a form of water therapy for people who felt weak and inferior.

Lévesque himself often displayed this attitude of *us versus them*. With few exceptions, his stories involving Anglos put them in the position of the arrogant colonizer. He loved to recount anecdotes in which he featured as the French-Canadian runt turning the tables on the Anglo bully kicking sand in his face. It was a congenial metaphor for his entire political career. During the 1962 election campaign, he recalled, at a party in west-end Montreal, that part of the city where live anglophones with "a tranquil superiority complex," a man waved his brandy glass under his nose and said, "But, Lévesque, how can people like you imagine you can run Shawinigan Water and Power?" "My friend," Lévesque replied, "just wait a little and you will see what you will see." Lévesque then turned that one boor into the very prototype of all English-speaking Montrealers. "People like you," he mused. "Or, rather, people like you people. Exactly the way the British and French had treated the Egyptians a few years earlier: how did 'those people' ever imagine they could operate the Suez Canal?"[12]

Lévesque's view of Quebec as "colonized" led him progressively to opt for "decolonization" in the form of a progressive emancipation from the Canadian federation. At first, the object was *la libération économique*, exemplified by the 1962 campaign to nationalize the power companies. But the movement quickly expanded beyond the economy to focus on politics—from the liberation of a few companies controlled by some English-speaking Quebecers to the liberation of French Quebec from the rest of Canada as represented by the federal government.

"Either Quebec will obtain a really special status—which I am not the expert called on to define—or Quebec will become independent," Lévesque told students at Montreal's Collège Sainte-Marie in May, 1964.[13] This special status, he said, must give the Quebec government fundamental economic, political, social, and cultural powers. This would be so hard to achieve as to seem almost impossible, he continued. And if it could not be achieved, the alternative would be independence. "Despite the risks, independence is possible economically, politically, and humanly," he concluded.

Jean Lesage did not travel so far so fast. But he did travel quickly, and in the same direction. Years later, on 13 January 1980, he reflected back on the Quiet Revolution in an interview with Jean Larin of Radio-Canada. I quote him here at great length because he gives a unique insight into the logic of Quebec governments both then and right down to the present.

First, he recalled an agreement that he reached with Pearson for the federal-provincial conference of 20 April 1964, when Pearson accepted his claim for "special status" by making special accommodations for Quebec in federal programs. At the time, it was called co-operative federalism.

First, we won the right to a tax compensation for all continuing joint-cost programs and for continuing conditional grants. Second, we caused the aborting of the program for student loans. Third, we received tax compensation for school grants. Fourth, our model of a pension plan won out over Ottawa's. . . . At the opening of the conference, we had already won recognition of the principle of opting out and of the principle that equalization payments should be based on the province where the per capita tax revenues were the highest. So, obviously, we had got just about everything we had asked for at the federal-provincial conference of 1960.[14]

As well as withdrawing Quebec from these federal-provincial financial arrangements, Lesage had gone to France in 1964 and, without the presence of the Canadian ambassador, had held discussions with French president Charles de Gaulle. The following year, against international conventions, he had signed an agreement with France without going through the federal government. He was questioned about that agreement by Larin.

Larin: When all is said and done, you were engaged in international relations?

Lesage: Yes, I admit it, I admit it quite openly. We had always preached that our jurisdiction over education was exclusive and that we had sovereignty in the areas of provincial jurisdiction, especially exclusive jurisdictions. We considered, therefore, that it was our right, without going through Ottawa, to sign agreements with foreign countries in the area of education. That was the first step.

We got bolder. And we were changing our position. We had won almost everything that we wanted to win in 1964, and we began to attack the grey areas. We demanded that the residual powers of the constitution should belong to the provinces; we wished to make an inventory of all the grey areas there were—cultural affairs was one of them, and in fact it still is. And from there, we went on the attack to declare our sovereignty, our jurisdiction in the area of culture, and we signed the convention, or agreement, with France in the fall of 1965.

Larin: Without consultations with Ottawa?

Lesage: No, no.

The negotiations between Pearson and Lesage were to be the prototype for negotiations between the federal and Quebec governments ever after. Whatever demands were made initially soon escalated. No settlement was more than temporary. Every gain became the springboard for new demands. As Lesage said when, in 1964, he had got just about everything he had asked for, Quebec "got bolder."

How did it happen that an avowed federalist like Jean Lesage—himself a former minister in the federal government of Louis Saint-Laurent—embarked on such a course of confrontation with Ottawa? The answer is to be found in twin concepts that came to underlie his political action: that francophone Quebecers were an embattled, besieged minority on a continent of hostile, or at least threatening, anglophones; and that French Canadians were weak, poor, without the means to resist their English-speaking neighbours, except for the protection offered by the Quebec government.

Lesage articulated these ideas in a speech on 7 August 1962, in Victoria, at the annual premiers' meeting: "In Canada as a whole, there are about six million French Canadians, of whom some five million live in Quebec. But what is often forgotten is that we are surrounded by 180 million anglophones who do not speak our language."[15] And again, in a speech before the Canadian Chamber of Commerce at the end of 1963: "The Québécois have only one single powerful institution: their government. And now they want to use that instrument to build the new era to which they could not otherwise aspire."[16]

The image of a helpless people whose only hope for salvation is their government, however pathetic and appealing, was false and dangerously misleading. It fostered a siege mentality, just as Quebec seemed ready to emerge from a century-old siege mentality. It asssumed that the Québécois had no partners, no fellow citizens on this continent or elsewhere in the world. They had to look only to themselves, since all others were dangerous. The logical conclusion was precisely the political vision that would be the temptation and the mirage of Quebec's political class for the next three decades: the ethnic state. Whether that state should go all the way to full sovereignty or stop somewhere short of it depended only on practical considerations.

This mind-set was partly a hold-over from that of French-Canadian leaders during the period of Catholic reaction, when their rejection of the modern world and espousal of a rural theocracy really *was* subject to terrible pressure from an alien North America and a secularized France. But the image lost its reality in the 1960s, when Quebec's elites joined the modern world and reformed Quebec's institutions. Old mind-sets change more slowly than do institutions: the new political and intellectual elites retained the traditional separatist mentality, but after 1960 it was applied to politics and to the newly rehabilitated state.

In fact, the Québécois had the tremendous advantage of living in a country with great natural resources and a highly developed infrastructure. They had

French-language newspapers, radio and television stations, book and magazine publishers. They spoke an international, prestigious language and had the support and cultural enrichment of all other French-speaking countries—of France, above all. They benefited from the rapid and inexpensive transfer of technology in North America. They had a federal government in which they exerted great influence and which underwrote their culture as well as their economy. Consider what Radio-Canada, the Canada Council, and the National Film Board have contributed to consolidating and expanding culture in French Quebec. And the economy, even though it was developed mostly by English-speaking entrepreneurs from several countries, benefited all Quebecers and was available for all Quebecers, especially after francophones reformed their institutions and rejected their previous anti-industrial attitudes.

Instead of a realistic assessment that recognized the enormous advantages for French-speaking Quebecers of living in what was then the richest and most dynamic part of the world, Lesage preferred to cultivate the traditional heroic image of the few francophones besieged in their lonely bastion of Quebec, a modern version of Dollard des Ormeaux besieged by the Iroquois. Instead of treating English-speaking Quebecers as partners in the task of modernizing all of Quebec, as fellow citizens sharing the risks and costs of common life, he chose to designate them as threats.

Lesage's isolationist vision had far-reaching political implications. If Quebec was the state, and the only state, of French-speaking Quebecers, if it was their only powerful instrument as they faced an alien and threatening world, then they could not take the risk of surrendering any important power to any other government. The logic of the Quiet Revolution suggested dissolving the Canadian federation to form a confederacy of sovereign states.

Lesage never went all the way to that conclusion. He kept looking for some intermediate solution that was never spelled out. But, as long as he was premier, he kept pushing in one direction only: more power for the Quebec government. He did not ask how Quebecers could best be served. He took it as evident *a priori* that the well-being of the Québécois required ever more power and money for his government. And he spoke increasingly of Quebec as a sovereign or semi-sovereign state. As early as 1962, in his budget speech, Lesage proclaimed the quest for power by Quebec governments as a constant of history.

The vocabulary changes, the style varies according to the time, but the fundamental principle remains the same. In a word, men pass away but the battle for autonomy continues. It stands as a constant in the history of Quebec—the "autonomist constant." And even though the governments of other provinces consented in practice to become the "prefectures" of the federal government, the government of Quebec defended its autonomy just as energetically, maintaining thus the right to existence of a nation of which it is the political expression and of which it remains the principal instrument of economic self-assertion and cultural development.[17]

Proceeding with a vast build-up of the Quebec state, the Lesage government set up an agency for central planning, the Office de Planification et de Développement du Quebec, following France into the new era of a planned economy. Planning was one of the discoveries of the Quiet Revolution, and for a while it was believed that it would deliver economic miracles. The Société Générale de Financement was created to invest in private companies and bring them or keep them under the control of the Québécois. A publicly owned steel company, Sidbec, was to be set up. (It came into being under Lesage's successor, Daniel Johnson.) The government also took over a couple of forestry companies to create Sogefors. It created the Société Québécoise d'Exploration Minière (Soquem) to prospect for mines and, after Lesage was defeated, Soquip, the Société Québécoise d'Initiatives Pétrolières, to explore for oil and natural gas.

Above all, Lesage wanted to create a vast pool of capital that would be under the control of the Quebec government. His solution was the Caisse de Dépôt et Placement (Deposit and Investment Fund), which would control the pension fund of public employees, but in such a way that it was funded long in advance, so that billions of dollars would accumulate for investment. The Caisse eventually became the largest single pool of capital in Canada. The state of Quebec needed big muscles.

It took some time before all these initiatives had their desired effect. But they did, cumulatively, transform Quebec's economy and society. They augmented the publicly owned sector of the economy enormously compared to the private sector. And they progressively replaced English-speaking managers and entrepreneurs with French-speaking managers and entrepreneurs, as later statistics and studies were to demonstrate.

The public sector, including the provincial and municipal governments, schools, colleges, universities, hospitals, and the like, but exclusive of the Crown corporations, increased its share of the gross provincial product from 25.2 per cent, in 1961, to 44.8 per cent in 1975, truly a spectacular leap. The public sector provided a great preserve for francophone managers, who ruled almost alone over what had become about half of Quebec's economy. A Statistics Canada report published in 1973 showed that francophones accounted for only 28.4 per cent of management personnel in Quebec's manufacturing sector and 50 per cent of management in primary industries. But in the public sector, francophones constituted 95.1 per cent of management in the provincial administration and 96.7 per cent of management in municipal administrations. Crown corporations and publicly funded agencies also became instruments for replacing anglophones with francophones, even in the private sector, where the public bodies became increasingly important players.

In 1978, political scientist Pierre Fournier, then at the Université du Québec à Montréal, published a study that showed how effectively the Crown corporations created by the Quiet Revolution had been used as instruments of the ethnic state.[18] The seventeen provincial Crown agencies that Fournier studied had assets of $10 billion in 1975, invested more than $2 billion annually, and had more than 35,000 employees. These agencies included the largest enterprise in the province (Hydro-Québec, with more than 16,000 employees in 1977) and the rapidly growing Caisse de Dépôt et Placement, which managed the money accumulated not only from the Quebec Pension Plan, but also from the pension plans of construction workers, from the provincial medical-insurance program, and from other public insurance and pension funds.[19]

Each of the seventeen agencies deliberately made a contribution to careers specifically for French Canadians. This was true, for instance, for the Société Générale de Financement, which had the mission of investing taxpayers' money to help businesses develop. "The great majority of the SGF's affiliates are French-Canadian companies, and they are the ones that have most benefited from the technical and financial help of the SGF," Fournier wrote. "Only 2 or 3 per cent of the thousand or so cadres at the SGF and its affiliates are not francophones. Moreover, all new appointments among the directors are French Canadians that the SGF went after, mostly from the private sector."

When Hydro-Québec took over Shawinigan Water and Power Co. as part of the nationalizations of 1963, only 12 per cent of the engineers were French-speaking Canadians. That soon changed, Fournier notes: "More than 90 per cent of the management personnel and of the employees are francophones and the language of work is French."

According to Fournier, the Caisse de Dépôt et Placement held shares in Canadian companies worth $638.7 million in 1975. It used its great leverage to have the companies with which it dealt promote francophones. "For the past few years, the Caisse has favoured the appointment of francophones to the boards of large companies. More recently, certain members of the Caisse's executive have begun to accept positions on the boards of directors of private companies." Fournier listed National Cablevision Ltd., Scott-LaSalle Ltd., Prenor Group Ltd., and M. Loeb Ltd. as examples. "In general, it is especially concerns of a nationalist order that seem to guide the Caisse with respect to being represented on boards of directors." The Caisse, according to Fournier, had also "contributed somewhat to francizing St. James Street" via a policy of favouring in the first place local francophone financial houses, then other Montreal firms, and then Toronto firms, "especially if they have a research branch in Montreal."

What Fournier was describing, in great detail, was one dimension of "Québec Inc.," which began to be constructed with the 1962 Quebec election and the nationalization of the private power companies that followed in 1963. It meant fostering with public money companies that already were or could become controlled by francophones. It meant discriminating in favour of francophones against anglophones, and in favour of Quebec-based enterprises against enterprises based elsewhere. Québec Inc. was one important part of building Quebec into an ethnic state for French-speaking Quebecers, long before the language laws, Bill 22 and Bill 101, would conscript the coercive powers of the state to the same objective.

The Caisse de Dépôt had not been created without some difficulty. Prime Minister Pearson planned a Canada-wide pension plan that would be portable, as citizens moved from province to province. Its object was to ensure that older Canadians would be guaranteed a pension anywhere in Canada. Because it was not intended to create a pool of capital for government investment, Pearson planned to fund it on the basis of "pay as you go." The Quebec plan, with its objective of nation-building for francophones, conflicted with the federal plan. After a dramatic confrontation, Pearson backed down and the two leaders came to an agreement. Quebec developed its own plan, and the federal plan was adjusted accordingly.

Lesage was engaged in a constant tug-of-war with Ottawa to wrest control of new areas from the federal government. It involved bluff, bluster, and brinkmanship. And Lester Pearson was always the one who blinked and made the concessions. "For the past month I have lived a terrifying life," Lesage said in the Quebec Legislature in 1964, after the successful confrontation with Pearson over the pension plan. "I have made use of all the means which Providence granted me . . . so that Quebec, at last, could be recognized as a province which has a special status in Confederation, and I have succeeded."[20]

Pearson backed down again when Lesage insisted on Quebec's being exempted from participating in national programs in which Ottawa reimbursed the provinces for half their spending for such purposes as hospital insurance and post-secondary education. These "shared-cost" programs, according to Lesage (and to Maurice Duplessis before him), violated Quebec's autonomy. So a formula was devised to allow Quebec to "opt out" of the programs. Instead of Ottawa turning over money to Quebec to match what Quebec had actually spent, Ottawa gave up collecting a certain percentage of income tax, which Quebec would collect instead. Opting out became one of the cardinal principles of the Quiet Revolution.

So it was that the Quiet Revolution, which began as a modernization of French Quebec's archaic institutions, deviated into a more or less disguised, more or less declared, quiet war of "libération." So it was that an operation of rattrapage—of catching up with the modern, dynamic institutions of North America—turned into an operation in which English-speaking Canadians were held responsible for disastrous choices made in the past by Quebec's elites.

"Quiet Revolution," a descriptive phrase now encrusted in history and in mythology, was misleading. The great changes of the 1960s were primarily an emancipation from the paralyzing institutions established under the control of the anti-modern Catholic church. A better name would have been the Quiet Secularization, except that the ideology of nationalism quickly took over and obscured the true course of events.

Jean Lesage's biographer tells a revealing anecdote. The more conservative members of Lesage's Cabinet feared that the reformers were stripping religion from the schools. One day, Georges-Émile Lapalme and Paul Gérin-Lajoie arrived early in the Cabinet chamber and removed the large crucifix from the wall where it had always hung, presiding over the Cabinet meetings.

When some ministers noticed the missing crucifix, a violent feeling of indignation overcame them. "You see," they said to Lesage, who guessed what had happened. "You see what things have come to in this province? Tomorrow, it will be revolution."

The crucifix was put back in its place and calm returned.[21]

That was the real issue of the Quiet Revolution: freeing the people of Quebec from the heavy cross that they had been forced to carry for far too long. The real struggle was one within French Canadian society, not a struggle between a colonized people and its foreign masters. But Quebec's intellectual and political classes preferred to imagine themselves as taking part in an epic, a dramatic story of national liberation from the clutches of imperialist aliens. It made for sometimes interesting fiction, but for bad politics. Once again, ordinary Quebecers would be made to pay for the ideological infatuations of their leaders.

Lesage's concept of "special status" for the Quebec state had the advantage—and the drawback—of being essentially undefined. The Quebec government was to have special status to assume all kinds of functions as the ethnic instrument of the Québécois. But how special was the status to be? Was there any point of equilibrium at which all new demands would cease? Lesage never faced that question. He was defeated in 1966 by Daniel Johnson, before he defined his constitutional vision more precisely than as the demand for ever more power and money and "special status."

Notes

1. According to the 1961 Census of Canada.
2. Throne speech quoted by Richard Daignault, *Lesage* (Montréal: Libre expression, 1981), p. 166. Daignault's book, while analytically weak, provides a mine of information on which I have drawn.
3. Ibid., p. 121.
4. René Lévesque, *Attendez que je me rappelle . . .* (Montreal: Québec/Amérique, 1986), p. 248.
5. Ibid., p. 227.
6. Ibid., p. 228.
7. "L'État, c'est pourtant l'un des nôtres, avais-je osé dire, c'est même le plus musclé des nôtres." Ibid., p. 230.
8. Quoted in Peter Desbarats, *The State of Quebec* (Toronto, McClelland & Stewart, 1965), p. 99.

9.Lévesque, *Attendez*, p. 229. In 1990, Marcel Bélanger was co-chair of the commission on Quebec's constitutional future.

10.Ibid., p. 239.

11.Ibid., p. 228.

12.Ibid., p. 245.

13.As reported by Jean Sisto in *La Presse*, 11 May 1964.

14.The interview is reproduced in Daignault, *Lesage*, pp. 230–2.

15.Reprinted in ibid., p. 163.

16.Quoted in ibid., p. 171.

17.Quoted in Desbarats, *The State of Quebec*, p. 181.

18.Fournier's study, *Les Sociétés d'État et les Objectifs Économiques du Québec: Une Évaluation préliminaire,* was carried out for the Office de Planification et de Développment du Québec.

19.By 1994, the Caisse managed assets of about $49 billion.

20.Quoted in Graham Fraser, *PQ. René Lévesque and the Parti Québécois* (Toronto: Macmillan of Canada, 1984), p. 34.

21.Daignault, *Lesage*, p. 191.

CHAPTER TWO

Anglophobia: A Cherished Quebec Tradition

It requires a certain audacity to explain the emergence of the Quebec ethnic state in the 1960s by reference to the previous intellectual tradition of French Canada, and to call that tradition anglophobic. And yet, that is the reality. A literary tradition that began in the 1840s and culminated in the 1960s and 1970s portrayed the English-speaking Canadian—and sometimes, by extension, also the Canadian state—as an existential threat, an evil influence, a corrupter, a destroyer, and the cause of all that was wrong with French Canadian society. This negative stereotype was not merely incidental or episodic: it was the most central and constant theme of French-Canadian literature.

The new state envisioned by Jean Lesage and René Lévesque was, to use the word that has gained currency in recent years, a tribal state, and the outgrowth of a tribal tradition. "Tribal" is used when an ethnic group defines itself as being in opposition to other ethnic groups and demands its own state so that it can be be the single dominant group in the society, and can use the power of the state against other ethnic groups. Such was to be the state of Quebec, the object of political desire by provincial politicians for the past three decades.[1]

It began with poet and historian François-Xavier Garneau, the true father of French-Canadian literature—not because he was the first published writer,[2] but because he published in 1840 the first long poem, *Louise, une légende canadienne,* and, far more important, he published in 1845 the first volume of his monumental *Histoire du Canada*, which totally supplanted everything written before.[3] It launched the themes that informed almost all future historiography, inspired a school of patriotic poetry, and suggested the plot of many historical novels. With its publication, French-Canadian literature took on a recognizable form, and Garneau's influence on other writers is discernible even to this day.

French-Canadian literature, by a decisive coincidence, was born shortly after the Rebellion of 1837–38 and after the Union Government was set up in accordance with Lord Durham's recommendations for the precise purpose of

35

assimilating French Canadians and eliminating the French language and culture from the British colony. The circumstances of that birth gave a poignancy and dramatic intensity to writing of that critical period which later generations would be reluctant to forgo, even after French Canada's survival was secured.

In the first shock of reaction to Durham's report, French-Canadian intellectuals despaired. The eminent *Patriote* journalist Étienne Parent, who had been jailed during the Rebellion, at first advocated submission. Further struggle seemed hopeless. Parent, who had been Louis-Joseph Papineau's chief propagandist, and had broken with the fiery orator only when he judged that the latter's leadership would draw the people into an armed adventure, now wrote his saddest words.

We invite our compatriots to make a virtue of necessity and not to struggle foolishly against the inflexible course of events. . . . In the situation in which they find themselves, French Canadians now have no alternative other than to resign themselves with the best grace possible. . . . Oh, it would have been so good to live and die with the hope of maintaining on the banks of the St. Lawrence the nationality of our fathers.[4]

However, Durham's intentions were soon defeated. Louis-Hippolyte Lafontaine formed an alliance with reformers Robert Baldwin and Francis Hinks, giving the representatives of French Canada the balance of power. Though the Act of Union (1840) recognized only English as the language of the Legislature, Lafontaine insisted on speaking French, and he was supported by his English-speaking allies. By 1848, only seven years after the Union came into effect, Governor-General Elgin accepted the principle of responsible government, turning over power to the elected representatives; he asked Lafontaine to form the government. London amended the act to give French official status, and the attempt to assimilate French Canadians in Lower Canada was at an end.

By then, however, the course of literature was set, and its central theme for 150 years would be the epic struggle for the life or death of a people. It would be concerned, overtly or latently, with salvation and damnation. Individual and collective destinies would become metaphors for each other.

Durham had pronounced French Canadians a people without a history or a literature. Garneau gave him the lie: the early history of Canada is as exciting as any other to be found on this continent, he countered. And, from the first pages of his *Histoire du Canada*, he denounced the injustices perpetrated on French Canada, especially "the abolition of their language, and the restriction on their electoral ballot intended to keep them, despite their greater number, in the minority and in subservience."[5] His was a *littérature de combat*, and his history was an act of patriotism. "Happy is the historian who is spared having to carry out such a task for his nation!" he lamented.[6] And yet, what an inspiring undertaking was his. His work placed him among the heroes of New France and French Canada whom he celebrated in his writing. His very writing was a creative act of faith, giving a demoralized people a sustaining national legend:

We believe in the future existence of this people, whose annihilation, sooner or later, some consider an inevitable fate. If I let myself go as they do to such sad thoughts, far from wishing to retrace the events that marked that people's birth and its progress, and to take pleasure in recounting the facts that are to its honour, I would raise my voice only to moan on its tomb.[7]

There was an interesting discrepancy between Garneau's life and his writing. He derived his concept of historiography from the French historian Augustin Thierry, who held that the conflict of "races" was the driving force of history. Garneau's history of Canada was essentially the story of such a conflict. Initially, it opposed the French and the Iroquois, but, throughout, the essential conflict unfolded between the two "races" derived from Europe, French and English. In his own life, though, Garneau experienced more co-operation from than conflict with his English-speaking compatriots. The son of a poor and illiterate peasant, he could not afford to attend a private *collège*. At the age of sixteen, he went to work as an apprentice to notary Archibald Campbell, a cultivated man with a large library. Campbell encouraged the bright young Garneau to read widely among both French and English authors and helped to pay for a trip that he made to the United States, where he was able to observe republican democracy.

As he wrote the several volumes of his history, Garneau had before his eyes the unfolding co-operation between Lafontaine and Baldwin, which was to change the course of Canadian history and give it a direction opposite to that envisaged by Durham. The Lafontaine-Baldwin duality, which was followed by that of Macdonald and Cartier, was the prototype of Canadian national political life.

After the first volume of the *Histoire* was published, Garneau was aided in his work by a grant of money, voted him by the Assembly of the Province of Canada, with its English-speaking majority. Governor-General Elgin made available to him all the correspondence of previous governors from the Conquest until 1828. This hardly exemplified an ineluctable conflict of two "races."

Still, Garneau wrote his history as though only the conflict between the French and English, not their co-operation, was of historical significance. And for him, part of the very splendour of the conflict was that it was waged, on the *Canadien* side, against such hopeless odds: "For 150 years [the *Canadien* people] struggled against English colonies thirty or forty times its number without ever flinching, and the content of this history tells us how it carried out its duty on the battlefield."[8] The terrible odds in the struggle against *les Anglais* was an enduring theme of later literature, as was the parallel theme that French Canadians were a rural people who must cling to all their traditions and not change them, except most cautiously.

Les Canadiens are today a farming people in a hard and severe climate. . . . Let the *Canadiens* be faithful to themselves; let them be wise and persevering, may they not be carried away by the sparkle of social or political novelties. . . . A part of our strength comes from our traditions; let us not leave them or change them, except gradually.[9]

An opposing view was put forward at that very time by Étienne Parent. At first discouraged about the prospects for a French-Canadian nation, he soon changed his mind, and now saw the future of French Canadians threatened by their unwillingness to change, to adopt new techniques. The newcomers were constantly searching for new and better ways of working, according to Parent. But the *Canadiens*, to his regret, seemed to think that their ancestors, when they came from France, had brought with them the last word on everything, and there was no reason ever to do anything differently. Traditions had become sacred.

But, Parent warned, the way of doing things in Europe had improved markedly over the two centuries since the *Canadiens'* ancestors had arrived, while they continued to do things in the same old way. They had to change, or they would be left behind: "Hurry to bring yourselves up to the level of these newcomers; otherwise, you can expect to become the servants of their servants, as several of you are already on the outskirts of the big cities. Hurry to have your children educated."[10]

In a series of public lectures, Parent worried particularly about the prejudice rampant against commerce and industry among French Canadians. "Let us admit it," he said, "we despise industry."[11] No sooner had a man managed to set up a successful shop than he wanted to sell it and have his son become a professional—a doctor, lawyer, notary, or priest. The prejudice against industry and the lack of interest in education would eventually be fatal, Parent admonished. "The means of getting an education have been scarce among us up till now, and if those who have enough money to have their children well educated also despise industry, we will lose industry irrevocably to other hands, and the mass of the population will fall body and soul under the domination and the exploitation of another race."[12]

Unfortunately, Parent's warnings were ignored. The ultra-conservative mentality urged by Garneau prevailed, becoming even stronger in Quebec after Confederation, and his prophecy came true. The intellectual and religious elite almost entirely embraced traditionalism and rural life, rejecting the life of the artisan, the tradesman, the businessman. The only good life was in the country, especially on the farm.

Two novels published in 1846—only three novels had been published earlier in Quebec—both tell the story of a prodigal son who abandons the family farm. One goes off seeking adventure as a *coureur de bois* working for a fur-trading company.[13] The other goes to the city to study law and becomes enamoured of a young *Anglaise*.[14] In both cases, the family of the young man is ruined. In the first novel, the prodigal returns to find the family farm in the hands of—horrors— an *Anglais*. In the second, the *Anglaise*'s rapacious father has thrown his daughter in the hero's path in order to defraud him of his family's inheritance. Both novels

38

end with the prodigal coming to his senses. One gives up adventures in the forest, the other gives up law and the city. Each marries the French-Canadian farm girl who lives nearby, takes up a life of farming, and raises many children.

This formula—a young man abandons the farm and becomes degraded, but is saved at last by a return to the land and the French-Canadian girl living nearby—was followed by other novels over the next century. These books routinely contained a passage describing a hellhole, a den of iniquity, where a French-Canadian youth learned to drink and smoke and swear and brawl and descend into sloth and sin: the city.[15] Often it was *une Anglaise*, a temptress, who lured the French-Canadian boy away from the rural paradise. If he succumbed to her wiles, unless he came back to his senses and abandoned her, he came to a tragic end. The latent message was that to leave the land, to go to the city and work in industry where *les Anglais* were dominant, was to run the risk of losing one's soul, individually and collectively.

The message of earthly paradise on the farm, of decadence and possible damnation in the cities, was also delivered regularly by the clergy, who had enormous influence on the daily lives of the people before 1960. Here is a typical passage in a joint pastoral letter from all the Quebec bishops to be read from the pulpit in all the churches in 1923.

We address ourselves especially to the inhabitants of our countryside, in whom we always have been pleased to recognize the reserves of our religious and national forces. It is there, in contact with the land which roots one in the homeland, in the great fresh air of the fields which tones one's physical and moral vigour, in the grandiose setting of nature which elevates the soul, and in the virtue of sanctifying work which disciplines the energies, it is there that our race drew its strength, it is there that our survival was assured, there that those virtues which are characteristic of our people and have made it the happiest and the most religious people on earth, grew and were strengthened.[16]

In contrast to this mystical, nationalist view of the land, the bishops evoked the infernal dangers of the city, even warning parents that they might be condemning their children to damnation if they moved there.

For the little bit of money that can be earned there more easily, the factory will atrophy the physical vigour of your children; the city, with its promiscuities, its unhealthy attractions, its immodest sights, will exercise over their souls an influence that will be all the more distrastrous because the simplicity of their preceding education will have forearmed them poorly against the fascinating assaults of these novelties.[17]

Other than farm idylls, the only form of fiction that was popular before 1944 was the historical novel. In a rigidly controlled Catholic society, a novel based on sexual passion was simply unthinkable. So was a novel based on class conflicts: it was taken for granted that there were no class distinctions to speak of within

French-Canadian society. In historical novels, the conflict necessary for a plot was provided by the outsider: sometimes the Iroquois, but most often the *Anglais*, who were almost uniformly villains.

For example, in 1866 Napoléon Bourassa, father of the great nationalist politician and journalist Henri Bourassa, published a novel, *Jacques et Marie*, which fictionalized the deportation of the Acadians. (How often the poor Acadians have been deported ever since!) It portrays an English-speaking officer, Lieutenant George Gordon, who proposes an infamous bargain to the beautiful and virtuous Marie Landry, engaged to the brave Jacques Hébert. Gordon offers to spare Marie's parents from deportation if she will submit to his sexual advances. She recoils in horror.

"Ah! An *Anglais!*" she cried out in terror. "Get away! Do not touch me with those hands. They have blood and tears on them—the tears of my father and of my mother! Monster! You have splattered me with them! And though this blood and these tears are stains on you, keep them, keep them eternally, before God and before men! May they judge you and damn you forever! Forever!"[18]

Garneau's vision of ethnic conflict also inspired an entire school of poets, notably Octave Crémazie and Louis Fréchette. The most popular collection of poems in French Canada in the nineteenth century was Fréchette's *La légende d'un peuple*, which offered a series of historical tableaux closely modelled on Garneau's history. The historian's influence is also evident in, among other examples, Octave Crémazie's poem *Le vieux soldat canadien:*

Do you remember the days, old men of my country,
When our fathers, struggling against tyranny,
By their noble efforts saved our future?
Quivering under the yoke of a foreign race,
Despite the oppression, their soul, always proud,
Kept alive the memory of France.[19]

Of course, the "foreign race" were *les Anglais*. In part, this abundant cautionary literature was a warning against the loss of the French language by assimilation to English, but above all was a fear of a loss of religious values. Cleaving to the French language was fostered as a protection for the conservative Catholic faith. As a common saying had it, *Qui perd sa langue, perd sa foi.* When you lose your language, you lose your faith.

Henri Bourassa gave classic formulation to the fusion of language with religion in a celebrated speech he gave in 1910, at an international conference in Montreal to celebrate the Eucharist.

Yes, when Christ was attacked by the Iroquois, when Christ was denied by the English, when Christ was fought by all the world, we confessed Him, and confessed Him in our language. . . .

Providence has wished that the principal group of this French and Catholic colonization should constitute in America a separate corner of the earth, where the social, religious, and political situation most closely approximates that which the church teaches us to be the ideal state of society.[20]

An entire intellectual tradition cautioned French Canadians against admiring, envying, imitating, or even associating with *les Anglais*. Above all, one must never marry them.[21] Lionel Groulx, the historian who had more influence on the thinking of French Canada than anyone else in the twentieth century, espoused Garneau's vision of history as a conflict of "races," but he also had a peculiarly biological view of ethnicity. For him, "races," in the sense of nationalities, pass on from generation to generation a common soul of the nation. That soul must not be impaired by the biological union of people from different nationalities, for such unions result in mongrel offspring. Both biologically and culturally, Groulx believed that foreign influences were to be excluded, or the nation would be degraded.

Groulx expressed his ideas most fully in a novel, *L'appel de la race.*[22] It tells the story of a French-Canadian hero who has made the mistake of marrying an English-speaking woman. Though she actually converts to Catholicism to marry him, he comes to realize that he has betrayed his ancestors and *la race* by marrying her. His children, especially the two who lean toward the English side, are confused and nasty, because the children of a mixed marriage always have two different souls fighting inside them and they can never have an integrated personality.

The hero, who practises law in Ottawa, returns to his native village, where, on the graves of his ancestors, he has a mystical experience and discovers his national soul. When he goes back to Ottawa, he is resolved to restore his children to their French heritage. He removes all traces of English culture (such as books and a painting of General Wolfe) from the family home and begins to associate only with French-speaking people. His wife eventually leaves him (a happy circumstance, which saves him from having to leave her in order to recover fully his French soul). The two of his children who tend to the English side turn against him, but he saves the other two for French culture, and becomes a leading French-Canadian nationalist champion in Ontario. The moral of Groulx's novel is that French Canadians must have as little to do as possible with English-speaking people or non-French culture. Those who have been corrupted by exposure or miscegenation are invited to take heed and restore their French soul.

Groulx conveyed his ideas in an outpouring of essays and books. He summarized his ideological program in a 1921 article in *L'action française:*

Our doctrine can be contained in this brief formula: We wish to reconstitute the fullness of our French life. We wish to rediscover, to recover in its entirety, the ethnic type which France left here and which

150 years of history have shaped. We wish to make an inventory again of those moral and social forces, which, within that ethnic type, were preparing to flower. We wish to prune this type of foreign growths in order to foster in it intensively the original culture, and graft onto it the new virtues which it has acquired since the Conquest.[23]

The most virulently anti-English novel in the rich canon of anti-English literature was also written by a priest. *Menaud, maître-draveur*, by Mgr Félix-Antoine Savard, first appeared in 1937 and was soon recognized as a classic.[24] It tells the story of a master lumberjack named Menaud who feels invaded by the approach of *les Anglais*, who take out a lease on the nearby mountain. He is horrified. The very presence of *les Anglais* on his mountain is sacrilegious.

At the start of the novel, Menaud is approached by nameless, faceless *Anglais* to work for them. He can scarcely contain his rage and hate. For him, to work for *les Anglais* is the ultimate indignity. He meditates obsessively on a quotation from *Maria Chapdelaine*, "All around us, foreigners have come whom we choose to call the barbarians. They have taken almost all power, they have acquired almost all the money. But in the land of Quebec, nothing has changed." He sees that the land has in fact changed: it has been violated by the presence of *l'Anglais*, whom Menaud compares to an animal: "Menaud thought he could see his enemy skulking like a wolf around his house. . . . Since the foreigner had set his paws on it, Memaud thought he could hear the domain of his fathers in pain. . . . The foreigner will soon set his claws on the whole mountain." The land of Quebec is sacred, and for an *Anglais* to occupy any part of it is a desecration. "The places of his mountain, profound and holy as the very sanctuary of the country, would be wholly desecrated." But Menaud will resist the desecration, the intrusion of the foreigner. "Menaud had suffered under the yoke and heard the reproaches of his blood too long to let the foreigner ever sully the inheritance as he had done elsewhere."

Menaud has brought up his son with the revanchist mission of driving out *les Anglais* from the land of Quebec. When the son drowns in an accident while driving logs on the river, Menaud takes up the battle himself. By the end of the novel, he has gone mad and is hiding out in the mountain, wanting to raise a guerrilla war to drive out *les Anglais*. He is mad, but it is a sacred madness.

During the First World War, many French-Canadian men and women moved into cities and towns to work in factories. The abundance of jobs and good wages brought by war disrupted the way of life preached by the traditional ideology. In addition, the cinema invaded every part of Quebec, bringing the alien language and foreign sexual mores, licentiousness and liberalism, into the very heartland. The counter-revolutionary society built in Quebec, especially during the second half of the nineteenth century, was under siege.

In 1902, the chief adviser to the Quebec bishops, Mgr. Louis-Adolphe Pâquet, gave a homily on the occasion of the feast of the patron saint of French Canadians, presenting a classic formulation of the other-worldly vision of French-Canadian society which the religious and intellectual leaders had tried to cultivate. Pâquet spoke of the different vocations that God gave to different peoples. Some were destined for the land, some for industry, some for trade, some for arts and sciences. French Canadians had a vocation as apostles.

This social priesthood reserved for elite people, it is our privilege to be invested with it; this religious and civilizing vocation is, I am convinced, the proper vocation, the special vocation of the French race in America. Let us leave to other nations, which are less idealistic, that feverish mercantilism and that gross materialism that rivets them to matter.[25]

Trade, materialism, and urbanization came rapidly to Quebec during the First World War. A reaction set in during the Depression of the 1930s: the failure of the modern economy seemed to confirm the traditional values once again, and Quebec was the scene of a major back-to-the-land movement. Menaud represented a frantic resistance against modernity, which was embodied by les Anglais, and a violent anger against his own people, who were passive before the invasion of the modern world.

It was only at the end of the Second World War, with the publication of Roger Lemelin's Les Plouffes in 1944 and Gabrielle Roy's Bonheur d'occasion in 1945,[27] that writers at last began to recognize that a majority of French Canadians had moved to Montreal, Trois-Rivières, or Quebec City, and to acknowledge that these urban dwellers also had a story to be told. While novels until then had triumphantly presented rural French-Canadian society as a paradise, threatened only by les Anglais, most novels after 1944 explored the poverty and wretched existence of French-speaking urban dwellers, so different from their rich anglais neighbours'.

The stark contrast between the two societies living side by side in the city aroused anger and a crisis of conscience among Quebec's intellectuals. Earlier, the ultra-conservative religious philosophy that held sway had provided a ready explanation: les Anglais had a vocation for making money, whereas les Canadiens had a vocation for the higher things in life, notably religion, and for heaven in the hereafter. Lionel Groulx had expressed the assuaging thought in poetic language: "We know, thanks be to God, that there are riches and riches; we know that there are some races that are more willing than others to do without gold and silver, and that a church or monastery steeple, despite appearances, rises higher in the heavens than does a factory chimney."[28]

After the Second World War, however, the old religion began to break down and writers reflected on what they saw in the cities. The vocation to be apostles surely did not justify the helpless poverty, vulnerability, ignorance, humiliation, the lack of preparation for city life of Lemelin's Boucher family or Roy's Lacasse family. The new novels also raised the question of why: if it was not God's will, why was the life of French Canadians so much more difficult than the life of

English Canadians? This question dominated Quebec's intellectual life from the end of the Second World War until the Quiet Revolution.

A group of historians, followers of Lionel Groulx, found the explanation for ethnic inequality in a single cause: the Conquest. For Guy Frégault, Maurice Séguin, and Michel Brunet, writing in the 1940s and 1950s, French Canada was a frail child that had been brutally severed from its mother country by the fall of New France and had never recovered from the trauma. A new, alien, and incompatible structure of government and of organization of life was imposed upon French Canadians: that of the English conquerors. Frégault accepted Groulx's view that a national culture is an organic whole that is impaired when foreign elements are introduced. The imposition of the alien structure on frail French Canada explained why French Canadians were much poorer and less well educated than their neighbours in 1945 or 1955, almost two centuries after the Conquest—and despite Confederation, despite all having the same political rights, despite Quebec having a government elected by francophones and headed by francophones, from 1867 to the present, with jurisdiction over education (even though it had surrendered it to the church) and over property and civil rights.

Séguin added to Frégault's basic argument the lesson that he himself had drawn from the occupation of France by the Nazis during the Second World War: the conqueror always despoils the conquered people. Therefore, the answer to the economic problems of French Canadians was to get rid of the occupier—by achieving independence: "Someday, the occasion will arise for the *nation canadienne* to return to the traditions that preceded 1837 and to rid its economy of the paralyzing trusteeship of the Occupier."[29]

Brunet, the most influential historian of the 1950s, also asked how the economic inferiority of the French-Canadian collectivity could be explained. His answer was, "When a society has lost its collective freedom, it is condemned to a state of inferiority in all areas."[30] Brunet postulated that the effect of the Conquest was continued down to the 1950s because in Canada, English-speaking Canadians were the majority, French Canadians the minority. A majority always governs for itself, against the interests of the minority, he stated, without further proof. The majority had its government in Ottawa, and that government acted in the interest of English Canada and against the interest of French Canada. The minority had its own government in Quebec City, and it could rely only on that government to defend the interests of French Canadians. "Canada is an English country, inside which survives a French-Canadian province, which is really an economic and political colony of the English Canadians," Brunet wrote in 1954.

In many ways, this explanation of the backwardness of French Canadians by reference to a single original catastrophe that produced a permanent structure of oppression was convenient. It spared its authors from having to call into question the current, real institutions of French Quebec, such as the clergy-controlled, archaic education system. The explanations offered by Frégault, Séguin, and

Brunet, and largely accepted by educated French Canadians, precluded a serious commitment to a program of reform. There was a single explanation for francophone poverty, and so there was a single solution: independence. Since this was not considered a practical alternative in the 1950s, it could be offered as a utopian dream, a thrilling thought for some indefinite future. But it had little effect on the daily lives of the people. The only practical implication of the doctrine was that French-speaking Quebecers should press for as many jurisdictions as possible to be concentrated in Quebec City rather than Ottawa. The federal government was to be resisted at every turn as the enemy. Provincial autonomy, such as it was defended by Premier Duplessis, was the only course for enlightened francophone Quebecers to pursue.

This was also a much easier, much safer, much less demanding course than to proclaim the need for reform of Quebec's own institutions. A call for reform would have pitted these intellectuals against their own French-Canadian elites, rather than against *les Anglais*. Battling *les Anglais* in literature, designating them as the source of all evil and the cause of all problems, was a time-honoured tradition in French-Canadian intellectual life, and it was perfectly safe. Considered virtuous and patriotic, it had been practised almost continuously since the 1840s, and had led to many splendid careers in literature, the universities, the church, and politics. For instance, the first thoroughly anglophobic novel, *Charles Guérin*, was written by Pierre-Joseph-Olivier Chauveau, who went on to become the first premier of Quebec at Confederation.

But attacking French-Canadian institutions, demanding their reform, could be dangerous. There were many examples over the years of intellectuals who had lost their reputation and their jobs because they had criticized church control over society. Jean-Charles Harvey, a journalist and novelist, was fired from his job as editor-in-chief of the Quebec City daily *Le Soleil* when his free-thinking anti-clerical novel, *Les demi-civilisés,* was published in 1934. The novel was placed on the church's Index of Prohibited Books and Harvey was forced to withdraw it from circulation as a condition for getting a job in the public service; nonetheless, he was fired from his position when the Union Nationale came to power in 1936.

Pierre Trudeau, upon his return from brilliant studies at several outstanding universities, was barred from teaching at the Université de Montréal: "From 1952 to 1960, I was prohibited several times from teaching at the University, because (so it was said) I was anti-clerical and a communist."[31] He was considered anti-clerical because he publicly advocated the separation of church and state at a time when this was still considered heretical, and he proposed the creation of a ministry of education to take over control of education from the church. He was considered a communist because he advocated the use of the Quebec state to improve the lives of the people. "That is what it meant to be a radical before 1960!" he retorted

By 1960, however, times were changing and, tentatively at first, people discovered that it was possible safely to suggest reforms. Soon, in fact, reforms gathered a momentum of their own, and almost everything was called into question. Many assumed that now, the old anglophobia would disappear; *Menaud, Maître-Draveur* would now become quaintly obsolete as Quebec joined the North American liberal consensus. That novel and Lionel Groulx would surely be remembered as vestiges of an era when nationalism and intolerant Catholicism had been fused into a kind of mystical chauvinism that had adhered to the doctrine *extra ecclesiam, nulla salus*—outside the church there is no salvation.

With the Quiet Revolution, most cultural values became common to French and English society in Quebec: all now increasingly accepted pluralism, materialism, secularism, and liberal democracy. As the institutional and moral control of the church waned, French Canadians came to accept birth control, small families, sexual permissiveness, divorce, urban lifestyles, hedonism, and an individualistic conscience. Most of the former reasons for anglophobia, which had been centred around an ultra-conservative Catholic vision of life, were gone.

But a new doctrine replaced the old as the basis for holding *les Anglais* as enemies: the theory of decolonization, as developed by francophone writers reflecting on the struggle between France and its colonies in North Africa. The writings of Albert Memmi, Jacques Berque, Jean-Paul Sartre, and Frantz Fanon had a great impact; their descriptions of the state of colonialism in North Africa were applied indiscriminately to Quebec.

The view of French Quebec as a colony of English Canada became a fighting doctrine, a concept to mobilize anger and opposition. If Quebec was a colony, Quebecers had an imperative duty to decolonize. After the Second World War, former colonies regained their independence one by one, often after a violent uprising: India from Britain, Morocco and Algeria from France. During the Quiet Revolution, the war in Algeria polarized France and served as a model, at least conceptually, for the liberation of Quebec from Canada.

A separatist party, the Rassemblement pour l'Indépendance Nationale (RIN) was founded in 1960 on the concept of Quebec as a colony. This gave the party its central program: national liberation. Its manifesto, published in October 1960, made this clear: "At the present time when, the world over, peoples emancipate themselves from the colonial yoke and nations demand their full independence, French Canada can no longer accept to remain under the economic and political trusteeship of the outsider."[32] English-speaking Canadians were not to be considered fellow citizens of the same country, the same province, the same city. They were *l'étranger,* the outsider, the foreigner, the colonizer, and thus the enemy.

In 1960, the RIN was still a radical movement and fairly marginal. But the Quebec Liberal Party, then governing the province, took up some of the same language, though not quite so explicitly, for the 1962 election.

Nor were the lessons of the RIN and the Liberals lost on the rest of the population. The 1962 election was held on 14 November. Less than four months later, on the night of 7–8 March 1963, incendiary bombs were launched at the armouries of three regiments of the Canadian armed forces in Montreal. The perpetrators left behind three initials that soon became notorious: FLQ. They were copied from the Algerian terrorist movement, the FLN, or Front de Libération Nationale. FLQ, of course, stood for Front de Libération du Québec.

In a communiqué, the new group identified itself as "a revolutionary movement made up of volunteers ready to die for the cause of the political and economic independence of Quebec." Its targets were to be "all the colonial symbols and institutions." The manifesto ended with a call to arms: "Students, workers, peasants, form your own clandestine groups against Anglo-American colonialism. Independence or death!"[33] Most of the bombs that exploded during that first wave of FLQ activity, in 1963, were targeted against mailboxes, bearing the insigna of the Royal Mail, in Westmount, traditional symbol of Anglo dominance.

The FLQ did not greatly affect ordinary life or change appreciably the political or social institutions, but it altered the perceptions and revitalized the imagination of intellectuals and artists by confirming dramatically the vision of Quebec as a colony of English Canada. That vision spread among intellectuals until it became consensual, a matter of conventional wisdom, and the FLQ triggered off trains of thought, romantic adventures, new publications, passionate debates, manifestos, demonstrations, books and more books, television documentaries—and sometimes even a few bombs.

One can grasp the immediate impact of the FLQ by considering its effect on Pierre Maheu, a young man working in a public-relations agency composing advertising copy. He was from Outremont, where the Québécois upper classes lived. He had studied in a *collège classique* and continued his education in French literature at the Université de Montréal. He had read the French existentialist philosopher Jean-Paul Sartre, and swore only by Sartre. Sartre preached that one should become committed, *engagé*. Maheu was all for commitment, but to what? He had no idea. He told an interviewer, "Of course, when my brother said that I had to commit myself, it hurt, because, well, I was for commitment, but somehow it didn't seem to me to apply here in Québec. To me, people here were stupid and it was no use committing yourself to them. All I wanted to do was get out of this place." Maheu felt that he was simply in the wrong time and place. But the bombs changed all that: "Then came the FLQ. My God, I said to myself, history can happen here as well as anywhere else."[34]

The time for making history had at last arrived for Quebec's intellectuals. Maheu got together a group of other people like himself, and they founded a "revolutionary" literary magazine called *Parti pris*. The name was a play on words, meaning "prejudice" or "taking sides." From the start, the magazine

47

rejected bourgeois objectivity and neutrality and committed itself to revolutionary decolonization, independence, and socialism.

Parti pris began publication in the fall of 1963, and it had a powerful impact on college and university campuses. It was brilliantly written, especially by Pierre Maheu himself. Among its contributors were some of the chief literary figures of modern Quebec, including poets Paul Chamberland and Gaston Miron, critic-novelist André Brochu, novelist André Major, filmmaker Denys Arcand (who later acquired fame as the director of *The Decline of the American Empire* and *Jésus of Montréal)*, and poet, Radio-Canada journalist, and future politician Gérald Godin, who was to be a minister in René Lévesque's government.

The power of *Parti pris* came partly from the fact that it applied to Quebec the decolonization doctrines of Sartre, Fanon, Memmi, and Berque. This made Quebec the scene of a great dramatic struggle between good and evil, between the forces of darkness and the children of light. *Parti pris* defined its editorial position in the first issue: "The alienation from which we are suffering and which exists at all levels arises from the fact the we are colonized and exploited."[35]

How could the Québécois be colonized when they had full political rights and controlled the government of Quebec? *Parti pris* had a ready answer. The Quebec government was only a semblance of a government, a "roi nègre" or puppet ruler. The only real government was in Ottawa, and it was controlled by the colonizers. Colonization was most evident in the economy: almost all natural resources and industry were in the hands of English-speaking Canadians or Americans; local francophone entrepreneurs were themselves controlled by foreign capital.

Parti pris scored most effectively when it described the cultural and psychological effects of colonization. Everyone knew that economic power lay largely in the hands of anglophones, but most learned for the first time what a pervasive impact such colonization had on the hearts and souls and sensibilities of the Québécois:

On the cultural level, the degeneration of our language and the bastardization of our people testifies to our alienation; the clerico-bourgeois intellectual "elite" sustains from within our society the power of those who colonize us and exploit us, by encouraging humanist or religious myths that perpetuate and justify our submission.[36]

That hit home. French Canadians had always had a sense of inferiority about their language, especially when it was compared to the French of France. Now, decolonization theory explained why the language had necessarily degenerated, why French Canadians were less educated and less prominent in cultural life: it was because they were alienated, and they were alienated because they were colonized.

Colonization had affected Quebec's entire history. Now that the intense and pervasive religious control of the past was waning, it became evident that the religious and intellectual leaders of Quebec had been profoundly wrong in trying to isolate French Canadians on the land. But that, too, now became understandable and inevitable: all those myths of a rural Catholic messianic mission were themselves the effects of alienation caused by colonization. It was not really the French-Canadian leaders' fault: they could not help themselves, because they were colonized.

And so, ultimately, behind every evil and every woe was the same old enemy: the colonizer, *l'Anglais*. Menaud the lumberjack, who dreamed of driving out *les Anglais,* was now rehabilitated: he hadn't needed to go mad, for he had been right all along. He was wrong only about the name. He raged against *les étrangers*, the outsiders. That was reactionary. But had he used the right name—*les colonisateurs*—he would have been avant-garde. Maheu and *Parti pris* had justified, through a new, exciting, modern doctrine, the same old anglophobia. But now, anglophobia was explained as being a higher form of consciousness, it was the revolution becoming aware of itself. And now, the remedy was at hand, because revolution was on the horizon: "We will soon liberate ourselves from this alienation because Quebec society has entered into a revolutionary period."

Maheu was a brilliant publicist. In a few pages, he provided his readers with an exciting new theory that explained everything about Quebec society and put it at the frontier of history. To acquire a revolutionary conscience, to know the truth about Quebec's reality, did not require years of study. One acquired higher knowledge by reading just a few pages of *Parti pris,* or even just one phrase: Quebec is a colony.

Parti pris inspired a school of novels, poems, and plays that explored the lower depths—murderers and thugs and other losers—in the name of exposing the Québécois' fallen state. Often, the authors wrote in *joual*, the popular language of uneducated people, full of blasphemous expressions and anglicisms. To write in this way was also considered a political act.

Perhaps the most perfect expression of the *Parti pris* vision and its glorification of the FLQ was Marcel Dubé's play *Les Beaux Dimanches,*[37] first performed in 1965. It has remained the most popular play by one of Quebec's most popular playwrights, and was performed as recently as May, 1994, at Ottawa's National Arts Centre.[38]

The play bears a striking resemblance to Federico Fellini's 1960 film *La Dolce Vita.* Dubé portrayed four middle-class couples spending a Sunday together. As they reveal themselves, their lives are empty, loveless, boring, hypocritical. This is a post-Catholic Québécois society. The characters no longer attend Sunday mass, or do so only for appearances. As in Fellini's classic, the age of faith provides the background, but now only its dead forms remain. Alcohol and extra-marital flirtations provide the titillation to while away the empty hours. There is even a strip-tease scene, as there was in *La Dolce Vita.* The great difference, though, is that *La Dolce Vita* presented corrupt Italian bourgeois society as decadent after a previous age of heroic faith, while *Les Beaux Dimanches* presents Quebec's professional class in 1965 as suffering from an inability to love and inability to feel passion after two hundred years of colonization by the *Anglais* masters and the oppressive religion enforced by the colonizers' obsequious accomplices, the priests, nuns, and brothers.

There is hope in Dubé's play, unlike Fellini's film. The younger generation has been awakened to the reality of Quebec. Some young people have chosen terrorism as the path of national liberation. Others, equally determined, press for Quebec's independence through legal means. The young will not end up corrupt, cynical, compromised, and empty, as their parents have. The new generation shows the courage to strike at the root of the "radical evil" that has corrupted Quebec for more than two centuries.

The play becomes, in its most memorable scene, a lesson on interpreting Quebec's history according to classic decolonization theory. The protagonist, Olivier, a physician, gives a soliloquy that goes on, in the printed text, for ten pages, explaining why he and his friends lead such dead lives. It all started in 1763, when New France became the prize of the English.

The women began to carry in their wombs childen who had been conceived without joy, without love, by men who were guilt-ridden and castrated. The bourgeois, the *curés*, formed an alliance after they had quickly discovered which way lay their profit. Once allied, they concluded pacts of loyalty toward the occupier. . . . For things to last, the recipe was at hand: cultivate fear and ignorance while forming alliances with the new masters and their money.[39]

There is another way of reading the play: it provides a classic instance of the totalitarian mentality as it has been analyzed by French philosopher Bernard-Henri Lévy. In several books, Lévy has explored the fascination of so many of France's intellectuals of the first half of the twentieth century with totalitarianism of the left or the right, with communism or fascism. As he describes the totalitarian mentality, it includes, first of all, the judgment that a society is "sick" with a "radical ill," which can be cured only by the equivalent of a surgical operation. The source of the evil is identified—it is the Jews or capitalism or certain foreign influences. There is the cult of "purity," of a brave new society in which all the old degradation will have been purged away. The purity is identified with youth, the carriers of idealism and energy. Violence is seen as regenerative, curing: It cuts off the old gangrene to permit the healthy new growth.

All of these elements are found explicitly in Dubé's play. Olivier is the only one who understands clearly what is happening in the Quebec of 1965. Though he himself is morally paralyzed and drowning his tragic vision in drink, he cannot help but see vividly the corruption around him. He knows that the root of the evil that consumes him and his friends is Quebec's colonized state. Using medical images to describe Quebec's radical sickness, he celebrates revolution—and the young who have begun to carry it out: "A revolution . . . is like a heart operation. The scalpel knows the path it must follow. . . . There are *les Anglais*, it's true, there is Ottawa, it's true . . . but the young—some of them—have given up sleeping on their feet, some have enough lucidity to see the problem as a whole, like a cancerous lung."[40]

Olivier knows that the gangrene has rotted away all classes of society and that it is too late for him and the forty-year-old friends with whom he wastes his Sundays. They are too dead as human beings, too corrupt to change the sick society in which they live. But he sees in the young people a clarity of vision and a purity that his generation lacks. He begins to believe that Quebec can be cured.

The root of the ill is hard to reach because all this history is obscure. . . . But that is why a handful of men arose in 1837 and died by public hanging. That is why young people today have enlisted in a terrorist movement, why they set off bombs and killed some men. It is clarity, it is light that they are after, it is their freedom which has been lost for centuries.[41]

Lévy passes a summary judgment on all those who diagnose a society as sick and who have a prescription for restoring it to health: they are incipient totalitarians.

Take to your heels each time someone tells you . . . that a society is"'sick," that it needs a "therapy" and, to apply the therapy, a "therapist" or a "healer": they say healer today, tomorrow they will say purifier; for whoever says sickness says germ; whoever says germ, says prophylaxis; and, behind the fine concern for curing one's fellows, behind the idea that men are sick and that their sickness is curable, there is, always, the eternal will for purity—with its inevitable cortege of concentration camps, police, and violence.[41]

The totalitarian temptation, Quebec style, the will to make Quebec new and whole by commands from above, by laws, by the constitution, by secession, did not end in 1965. The doctrine that Quebec was a colony of English Canada became conventional wisdom. It was taught in the universities. It was repeated in intellectual periodicals and political speeches. It needed no demonstration: everybody just knew it. The authors of a comprehensive survey of Quebec literature published by Université Laval took at face value the analysis offered by *Parti pris*.

The novels of cultural dispossession and of social alienation, for the most part published by Éditions Parti pris, innovated by the sustained use of the language of the people. "Joual," as it is called . . . that disgraced language is just one aspect, even if it is the most visible one, of a culture which cannot fulfil itself in French in a milieu dominated by the great Anglo-Saxon institutions. The impossibility of achieving a liberating speech symbolizes

A CANADIAN MYTH

more than anything else the constraint that weighs so heavily on the people.[43]

And so it was that, after a few short years of intellectual liberalism in Quebec, a new doctrine for rejecting *les Anglais* replaced an old one, and they were strikingly similar. Only the vocabulary had changed. What had happened?

It is often generally assumed that the Quiet Revolution swept away all the old obscurantist, authoritarian, and illiberal traits that were so obvious in Quebec before the Quiet Revolution. But that would be a rash assumption. The great French political philosopher Alexis de Tocqueville recalled that during the French Revolution, the French had made extreme efforts to eradicate every trace of the previous society, the *Ancien régime*. And yet, when he came to study the *Ancien régime,* he discovered there so much of what he had assumed was the product of revolutionary France.

The deeper I got into my study, the more astonished I was to discover time and again in the France of that time so many traits that are striking in the France of today. I found there a host of sentiments that I had thought were born in the Revolution, a host of ideas that, till then, I had thought came from nowhere else, and a thousand habits which we are supposed to have received from it. Everywhere I encountered the roots of the present society, deeply planted in that old soil.[44]

And so it was with Quebec. A Quiet Revolution was not enough to sweep away the accumulated attitudes, the rooted mythology that was developed over 120 years and inculcated in the schools, the churches, and every nook and cranny of intellectual life. Anglophobia had been the single most continuous theme of French-Canadian literature, along with its twin, the defensive attachment to a besieged French language. It returned in the 1960s in a more threatening form, because now it came with the power of a modern state.

Notes

1. For those who want an ample demonstration rather than the brief survey offered in this chapter, I recommend my book, published in French only, *Anglophobie made in Québec* (Montreal: Stanké, 1991).

2. Newspapers had been publishing for decades, and a few books had also been published, including Michel Bibaud's collection of writings in 1830, and the first volume of his *Histoire du Canada* in 1837.

3. François-Xavier Garneau, *Histoire du Canada depuis sa découverte jusqu'à nos jours,* vol. 1 (Quebec City: Aubin, 1845).

4. Étienne Parent in *Le Canadien,* 15 mai 1839, reprinted in Guy Bouthillier et Jean Meynaud, *Le choc des langues au Québec 1760-1970* (Montreal: Les presses de l'Université du Québec, 1972), p. 148.

5. Garneau, *Histoire,* vol. 1, p. 21.

6. Ibid., p. 22.

7. Ibid., pp. 22-3.

8. François-Xavier Garneau, *Histoire du Canada depuis sa découverte jusqu'à nos jours* (Quebec: John Lovell, 1852), p. 316.

9.Ibid., p. 317.

10.Étienne Parent, "L'industrie considérée comme moyen de conserver notre nationalité," speech given 22 January 1846, in *Discours prononcés par M. É. Parent devant l'Institut canadien de Montréal* (Montreal: John Lovell, 1850), p. 48.

11.Ibid., p. 9.

12.Ibid., p. 19.

13.Patrice Lacombe, *La terre paternelle* (Montreal: Hurtubise HMH, 1972).

14.Pierre-Joseph-Olivier Chauveau, *Charles Guérin* (Montreal: John Lovell, 1952). The novel was first published as a serial between February 1846 and March 1847 in *L'album littéraire et musical de la Revue canadienne*.

15.For a discussion of these themes in detail, see Johnson, *Anglophobie*, especially chapters five and six.

16.*Lettre pastorale du cardinal Bégin, archevêque de Québec, et des évêques de la province ecclésiastique de Québec contre la désertion du sol natal, 25 mai 1923*, reprinted in Georges-Marie Bilodeau, *Pour rester au pays. Étude sur l'émigration des Canadiens français aux États-Unis. Causes. Remèdes* (Quebec City: L'Action sociale, 1926), p.152.

17.Ibid., pp. 152–53.

18.Napoléon Bourassa, *Jacques et Marie*, vol. 1, *Le départ de Grand-Pré* (Montreal: Librairie générale canadienne, 1944), p. 141.

19.Octave Crémazie, "Le vieux soldat canadien" (1855), in *Oeuvres complètes* (Montreal: Beauchemin, 1896) p. 110.

20.Quoted in Mason Wade, *The French Canadians 1760-1945* (Toronto: Macmillan, 1956), p. 581.

21.This was the theme of literature. In real life, however, people speaking French and English associated in amity and intermarriage was very common.

22.Lionel Groulx, *L'appel de la race* (Montreal: Fides, 1980). The first edition was in 1922.

23.Lionel Groulx, "Notre doctrine," in *L'Action française*, 5 (Jan. 1921): 25–26.

24.Félix-Antoine Savard, *Menaud, maître-draveur* (Quebec City: Librairie Garneau, 1937). The theme of the revolt against modernity represented by *les Anglais* is developed in Johnson, *Anglophobie*, ch. 8, "La rage," pp. 123–53.

25.Louis-Adolphe Pâquet, sermon of 23 June 1902, reprinted in René Dionne, *Anthologie de la littérature québécoise*, vol. 2, *La patrie littéraire 1760-1895* (Montreal: Éditions La Presse, 1978), p. 500.

26.Savard, *Menaud*, pp. 156–57.

27.Roger Lemelin, *Au pied de la pente douce* (Paris: Flammarion, 1944); Gabrielle Roy, *Bonheur d'occasion* (Montréal: Éditions Pascal, 1945).

28.Lionel Groulx, *Chez nos ancêtres* (Montreal: Action française, 1920), p. 14.

29.Maurice Séguin, "La Conquête et la vie économique des Canadiens," *Action nationale*, 28 (Dec. 1946): 309.

30.Michel Brunet, *La présence anglaise et les Canadiens. Études sur l'histoire et la pensée des deux Canada* (Montreal: Beauchemin, 1958), p. 227.

31.Pierre Elliott Trudeau, *Le fédéralisme et la société canadienne-française* (Montreal: Éditions HMH, 1967), p. vii.

32.The RIN's manifesto is published in André d'Allemagne, *Le Rassemblement pour l'Indépendance nationale* (Montreal: Éditions l'Étincelle, 1974), pp. 139–40.

33. Louis Fournier, *F.L.Q. Histoire d'un mouvement clandestin* (Montreal: Québec/Amérique, 1982), pp. 13–14.

34.Quoted in Malcolm Reid, *The Shouting Signpainters. A Literary and Political Account of Quebec Revolutionary Nationalism* (Toronto: McClelland and Stewart, 1972), pp. 295–96.

35."Présentation," *Parti pris*, no. 1 (Oct. 1963): 3.

36.Ibid.

37.Marcel Dubé, *Les Beaux Dimanches* (Montreal: Leméac, 1968).

38.In a production by Théâtre du Nouveau Monde, directed by Lorraine Pintal, featuring Louise Marleau and Marie Tifo.

39.Dubé, *Les Beaux Dimanches*, p. 98.

40.Ibid., p. 94.

41.Ibid., p. 99.

42.Bernard-Henri Lévy, *Les aventures de la liberté: Une histoire subjective des intellectuels* (Paris: Grasset, 1991), p. 370.

43."Introduction," *Dictionnaire des oeuvres littéraires du Québec,* vol. 4, *1960–1969* (Montreal: Fides, 1984), p. xxi.

44.Alexis de Tocqueville, *L'ancien régime et la révolution* (Paris: Michel Lévy Frères, 1857), p. 5.

CHAPTER THREE

Vive le Québec libre

Nineteen sixty-seven was the year of the centennial. For a whole year, Canada celebrated the hundredth anniversary of Confederation with great pomp. The centrepiece of many outpourings of pride was the Montreal world's fair, Expo 67. But it was also the time when Quebec nationalism crested. Many—including the author of this book—worried that Canada would not survive.

In the Quebec election the previous year, the Union Nationale and its leader, Daniel Johnson, had upset the Liberals, to the astonishment of Jean Lesage and the consternation of those who espoused the Quiet Revolution.[1] Johnson seemed to represent a throwback to the Duplessis era, when he had been a minister in the government and had been implicated in a scandal involving a conflict of interest. His victory was based almost entirely on the rural areas, which had felt left behind by the Quiet Revolution. He headed a delegation of undistinguished small-town notables—a great come-down from the *équipe du tonnerre* they were replacing. It looked like a return to the obscurantism of the past.

On election night, 5 June 1966, practically the first words spoken by Johnson boded ill for the future. Radio-Canada television journalist Pierre Nadeau pointed out to Johnson that he had a weak mandate: "Mr. Johnson, your party only received 40 per cent of the vote. You don't have a majority." Johnson countered, "If you subtract the anglophone vote in Montreal, if you take away all that is English, Jewish, I am certain that the Union Nationale has a strong majority of the francophone vote."

Johnson had run on a platform of *égalité ou indépendance*—equality or independence—for the French-Canadian nation. Though his father had been an English-speaking Quebecer of Irish origin, Daniel Johnson identified with the language and the collectivity of his French-Canadian mother. He spoke English passably, but with an accent. The "nation" that he sought to govern did not include "all that is English, Jewish."

When Johnson first ran for Quebec's Legislative Assembly, in a 1946 by-election, someone at a meeting shouted out in French, "We don't want a *maudit Anglais* in Bagot!" Johnson replied, in his unaccented Quebec French, "I am a French Canadian. In 1837, there was a Nelson at the side of Papineau; there will now be a Johnson at the side of Duplessis!"[2]

Johnson was, indeed, a militant nationalist. He supported Duplessis's stance in favour of provincial autonomy against federal intrusion until Duplessis's death in 1959. When the Quiet Revolution brought the new idea of marrying the ethnic nation and the state, Johnson picked it up and pushed it to a logical conclusion, first in a book he published in 1965 as leader of the opposition, then as premier of Quebec from 1966 until his death in 1968.

Johnson's appearance and style were in sharp contrast to Lesage's. Where Lesage was Olympian, Johnson was unassuming. Lesage was patrician, while Johnson was a man of the people: slender in build, he wore heavy horn-rimmed glasses and a thin mustache. He was gregarious, loved to joke, was personally considerate of other people. For him, politics was about people, more than about ideas.

When he first came to power, Johnson was considered a lightweight. He was despised by intellectuals and by most commentators in the news media, and was often referred to by the nickname "Danny boy." Cartoonists portrayed him as a gunslinging cowboy. But, in time, as he imposed his nationalist ideas, he outgrew his raffish image and acquired the reputation of a statesman.

Under Duplessis, the Union Nationale had been the party of nationalism—a defensive nationalism centred on "provincial autonomy." Since the state did relatively little then, provincial autonomy meant especially excluding the federal government from contributing money for Quebec's technical schools, colleges, universities, and hospitals. Ottawa was also excluded when Quebec reinstituted its provincial income tax, taken over from the provinces by Ottawa during the Second World War.

But after 1960, the UN was outflanked on the nationalist front by the Liberals. At its 1961 convention, a resolution presented by a UN member of the Legislature, Antonio Flamand, proposed the recognition of Quebec's right to self-determination. That resolution was defeated.[3]

After he became leader of the UN, in 1961, Daniel Johnson resolved to regain the party's position at the forefront of nationalism which had made its fortune. His assistant and speechwriter, Paul Gros d'Aillon, has described the evolution of Johnson's constitutional ideas during the period of the Quiet Revolution: "From just special status, which was one of the initial themes of his constitutional theory, Daniel Johnson had moved to the concept of equality within a binational Canada, and this proposal was now backed up by an ultimatum."[4]

Johnson had intended to publish a collection of his speeches. Gros d'Aillon suggested that, instead, he should publish a book setting out his constitutional vision, and Gros d'Aillon wrote the first draft. Others also helped put the text into shape. As Johnson worked on the last chapter, he found his vision of Quebec radicalizing once more, as Gros d'Aillon relates: "We needed a conclusion for this little book, one that would launch a virulent attack against the present federal system. As we worked on the text during the day and dreamed of it at night, we were almost carried away by enthusiasm. One morning, Johnson told me, 'I woke up a separatist this morning. I have to hold myself back.'"[5]

Indeed, in Johnson's book, *Égalité ou indépendance,*[6] the nationalism is fervid. Johnson posited a single entity that has existed through time, which he called the "French-Canadian nation." Its history, he wrote, is "the history of a people in search of a country [*patrie*]."[7] For Johnson, a nation in the sociological sense is a community with a common culture, such as the French-Canadian nation. His conclusion is that it "is a normal outcome . . . that when the cultural community has reached a certain stage of its development, especially if it has unquestionable historic rights, it seeks to identity itself with a state. For, to fulfil itself in accordance with its own specific genius, this cultural community needs the frameworks, the institutions, the commanding levers that can come only with a state of which it is the master."[8]

Johnson shared Lionel Groulx's vision, according to which each "race" and "nation" has its own specific character, which suffers adulteration when it is subjected to powerful influences from another race or nation, and therefore should have its own state to develop fully and harmoniously in accordance with its own character. This postulate led logically to an independent Quebec. Johnson, cautious and ambiguous, did not go quite that far, though he did come close. "I admit that the French-Canadian nation has not yet reached that definitive stage [of having its own state]. . . . But the French-Canadian nation tends with all its strength and with all its fibres to realize itself on the level of the state, and its aspirations are strictly normal and legitimate," he wrote.[9] He went further than Lesage in making the state the teleogical end, the "normal" terminus, of the evolution of the French-Canadian nation.

I shall show further on why and how the French Canadians seek to identify themselves with the state of Quebec, the only one where they can insist on being masters of their destiny and the only one they can use for the complete fulfilment of their community, while the English-Canadian nation tends for its part to make of Ottawa the centre of its community life.[10]

Johnson spoke boldly, but his conclusions remained tentative, expressed in questions rather than statements about what powers must accompany Quebec's right to self-determination. "Are we *maîtres chez nous* when a Bank of Canada decision can affect the credit of our enterprises, of our financial institutions, and even of the Quebec state?"[11] By such questions, he implied that Quebec should have control over radio and television, immigration, taxation of resources and corporations, succession duties, and other matters.

The book ended with a flourish:

Federation, associate states, confederation, special status, republic, or whatever, the new constitutional regime must give to the French-Canadian nation all the powers that are necessary to take charge of its own destiny.

After three centuries of labour, our nation has truly earned the right to live freely. So much the better if it can feel at home from one ocean to the other. This implies that it be granted complete equality. Otherwise, Quebec will have to become independent. Canada or Quebec, wherever the French Canadian nation finds its freedom, there will be its *patrie*.[12]

The book was received with enthusiasm in the news media, and the 1965 party convention adopted as policy its major themes, seizing back the initiative of nationalism from the Liberals. During the election campaign that led, on 5 June 1966, to Lesage's defeat and Johnson's election, the UN used as its general slogan *Québec d'abord* (Quebec first).

But it often went farther in the course of the campaign. Johnson accused the Liberals of "collaborating with the occupier." And the UN presented itself, in contrast, as *un parti libre pour un Québec libre*—a free party for a free Quebec. The implication was that Quebec was a colony and that the Quebec Liberals, a branch of the federal Liberals who governed in Ottawa, were really puppets to an imperial and alien power.[13]

Once in power, Daniel Johnson said and did much to turn Quebec into an ethnic state. He governed only two years before his death in 1968, but by then he had anticipated or developed every nationalist idea of Lesage, Robert Bourassa, or René Lévesque.

Johnson was not a sophisticated man, and certainly no intellectual. He had grown up in the Eastern Townships, and his parents were uneducated and poor; the family of nine children often survived on welfare. He received the benefit of a secondary-school education because he was marked as a bright boy headed for the priesthood, and the local parish priest sent him to school at a seminary. Eventually, he decided against the priesthood, and he studied law at the Université de Montréal.

He shared the ideas and the prejudices of his generation, and of his milieu, from which he rarely strayed. When he became leader of the opposition, in 1961, he had never been to Europe, and he had never lived outside of Quebec. His intellectual horizons were confined to what was current in a society that put a premium on ideological unanimity. But what he did have was a great capacity to absorb those ideas, push them to their logical conclusions, and sense how the common people of Quebec would react to them.

The constitution was his obsession. For him, the role of the state was to give political and legal form to the ethnic nation. Since there were, he said, two nations in Canada, the state structure must be reformed to reflect those two nations. In the month following his election, Johnson spoke to publishers of French-language weeklies and laid out his vision of constitutional change:

Instead of clinging to an obsolete constitution that has proved unable to ensure the harmonious coexistence of the two communities, either by its terms, or by its silences, or by the way it is applied, we propose without hesitation a new alliance that would allow them both to fulfil themselves freely, each according to its particular culture, and to co-operate together in full equality in the management of their common interests. No constitution can stand against the life of a nation.[14]

During the election campaign, Johnson had used as a recurrent slogan "100-100-100": Ottawa should give back to Quebec 100 per cent of personal income taxes collected in Quebec, 100 per cent of corporate taxes, and 100 per cent of succession duties. He repeated this demand at a federal-provincial conference on transfer payments, held in September of 1966, just three months after he was elected. He insisted on a rewriting of the constitution to recognize formally the French-Canadian nation, and he demanded a transfer of jurisdictions and tax revenues to ensure that Quebec had all the powers needed to promote its identity. When Prime Minister Pearson did not agree to Johnson's demands, he threatened to hold a referendum on the subject, to be followed by a constituent assembly to adopt a new constitution for Quebec. "I am certain that 80 per cent of the Québécois will endorse the thesis of the two nations."[15]

This was followed a month later by an explicit threat, made during an interview on Radio-Canada, to secede: "If the federal government does not make up its mind to give back to the provinces the money from the income taxes, Quebec will have to separate from the rest of Canada." Years later, Gros d'Aillon recalled Johnson speaking those words, and he added, "Was he just thumping his chest? Making idle threats? I don't think so."[16] Indeed, when he opened his first session with a throne speech, in December of 1966, Johnson announced that the government would bring in a bill to enable it to hold a referendum on the constitution.

By word and by deed, Johnson moved rapidly to give Quebec the structures of a modern French independent state. Speaking to an audience of English-language journalists on 6 September 1966, he announced that he planned to bring in a bill to make French the official language of Quebec. "Quebec will be as French as Ontario is English," he told his audience.[17]

Johnson planned to change the name of the Legislative Assembly to National Assembly, to reflect his view that the Quebec legislature was the instrument of the French-Canadian nation, centred in Quebec. He did not live to carry it through, but the name was changed, as he intended, by his successor, Jean-Jacques Bertrand. Johnson had removed from the official letterhead all references to the "Province of Quebec." This became, according to the circumstances, the "Government of Quebec" or the "State of Quebec."

Quebec was the only province that still had an upper house, called the Legislative Council. Johnson wanted to reform it so that it would become the Chambre de la Nation. He thought of the planned chamber as one "convening the socio-economic and cultural groups and tendencies [to debate] great national projects. He aimed, so to speak, at creating a consensus of active Quebec, a

59

Chamber for a concerted Quebec [une Chambre de la concertation québécoise]."[18] This reflected his corporatist concept of the nation: it would act through various bodies and interest groups which were to be brought together in an upper chamber to agree on what was best for the nation. However, his successor simply abolished the Legislative Council, as Jean Lesage had planned to do.

In January, 1967, Johnson proposed to strike a special committee of the Legislative Assembly to consider doing away with the parliamentary system and replacing it with a presidential system. The president would be elected directly by the people. This reflected the unity of the nation as embodied by one person, the president. The parliamentary system has no single spokesman for the nation. The prime minister is chosen to advise the Crown because he is supported by the elected members, and each member represents only the voters of his or her constituency, not the nation.

The premier did what he could to limit the role of the lieutenant-governor, symbol of the Crown. For Johnson's first throne speech, Gros d'Aillon recounted, "the first surprise was the brevity of the speech given by the lieutenant-governor, which put an end to the former pomp and ceremony. The head of state is now the premier, officially." In dealing with foreign governments, Johnson signed his letters "Président du Conseil exécutif" rather than "Premier," and Charles de Gaulle often flattered him by calling him Monsieur le Président.

Johnson was a democrat, but only up to a point. According to the rules that he had his party adopt, the supreme decision-making body would be the caucus of elected members—which he rarely convened. There was also on paper a "national council" of the party, but he made sure that it remained a dead letter. He wanted the party and the nation to speak with one voice—his. As he often said, "We are not numerous enough to be divided. To be strong, we must agree on essentials."[19] He certainly could not conceive of the nation speaking legitimately through members of the federal Parliament elected from Quebec. For him, only the Quebec legislature, led by the premier until a presidential system could be installed, could claim to speak for the nation.

He wanted to put in place all the requisites for an independent Quebec. (He asked one expert how long it would take for Quebec to turn out enough highly qualified people to be ready for independence, and was told it would take ten years.) While demanding that Ottawa turn over the French network of Radio-Canada to Quebec, Johnson proceeded to create his own public television broadcaster, Radio-Québec, which he intended to be an instrument for the development and diffusion of the full range of Quebec culture. He announced that Quebec would create its own ministry of immigration, and he changed the name of the ministry of federal-provincial affairs to ministry of intergovernmental affairs. "Quebec thus, first and alone among the Canadian provinces, set up a true ministry of external affairs, thereby confirming the will of the government to act on the international stage."[20] Acting autonomously in international affairs was the shortest route to independence, and Johnson pushed his staff to find ways to create precedents: "In all sectors, take the initiative."[21] In response to federal objections that Canada can have only one personality abroad, Johnson had the Assembly adopt a law asserting Quebec's right to negotiate and sign agreements with any foreign country with respect to any subject that came under Quebec's jurisdiction. Again over the objections of Ottawa, which protested that any official contacts with foreign representatives in Canada should be carried out through the federal department of external affairs, André Patry, the premier's adviser on foreign affairs, addressed a letter to all consular officials and other diplomats residing in Quebec informing them of the protocol they should observe in dealing with the Quebec government.

Johnson most alarmed Prime Minister Pearson and Paul Martin, the minister of external affairs, by dealing directly with France's president, Charles de Gaulle. The year that Johnson came to power, de Gaulle withdrew French forces from the NATO command and instructed that the Canadian forces stationed in France be removed to Germany. De Gaulle resented the dominant, even hegemonic, position taken in the Western alliance by the United States, with the support of other English-speaking countries. Johnson resolved to use de Gaulle as an ally in his struggle with the federal government.

He wrote a personal letter to de Gaulle—bypassing Ottawa—pressing him to come to Quebec to visit Expo 67. De Gaulle had already turned down invitations from the governor-general and from Montreal's mayor, Jean Drapeau, and at first he declined the new premier's.

Johnson went to France in May, 1967, as Expo 67 was about to open, and was treated as a head of state. He pleaded with de Gaulle to come to the aid of French Quebec, especially by investing in Quebec's industry. Nothing much came of their talks on economic projects—Michelin, for instance, built its tire plant in Nova Scotia—but the two leaders did sign an agreement and de Gaulle increased considerably the budget for cultural exchanges.

The two had a tête-à-tête, and it seems that Johnson opened his heart to de Gaulle, telling him that he needed help in his struggle with the Anglo-Saxons for *égalité ou indépendance*. It was a plea to touch the heart of the ageing French nationalist, who had seen his country's prestige as a world power decline precipitously during his lifetime, in favour of the United States. De Gaulle's resentment of Anglo-Saxons was equal to his injured national pride. And so he agreed to go to Expo 67, which would give him an opportunity to pursue his own vision of a France reunited with its former colony of New France.

Protocol required that de Gaulle touch down first in Ottawa before going on to Montreal. But a way around this was found: if he came by ship instead of by plane, he had a justification for landing first in Quebec City. Pearson reluctantly gave his assent. It was felt in Ottawa that de Gaulle was not coming to Quebec on a French cruiser just to tour the Expo pavilions. But Johnson, back in Quebec, spared no expense to orchestrate a great media event.

During an earlier visit by de Gaulle to Canada, in 1960, the people of Quebec had shown less interest in him than had the people of Ontario. But in 1967, tides had changed, and during the three days that he spent on Quebec's soil, he touched a chord with carefully prepared statements delivered in Quebec City and during the stops of his motorcade travelling from Quebec City to Montreal, along the old highway, the Chemin du Roy.

De Gaulle stepped off a warship, the cruiser *Colbert*, which defied maritime convention by continuing to fly only the flag of France rather than that of Canada while in Canadian waters. The president of France wore the full uniform of a general of the French army—highly unusual for a head of state visiting another country in peacetime. The rhetoric that he delivered that day and the next was more appropriate to a general liberating a country from an oppressor than to a friendly foreign visitor. In fact, de Gaulle did not consider himself to be on foreign soil. His nationalism was based on a kinship of blood as well as of language and culture. For him, the French Canadians he addressed were the *Français canadiens*—French substantively, and only adjectivally Canadian.

"What we are witnessing here, as in many parts of the world, is the accession of a people which, in all sectors, wants to make its own decisions with respect to itself and take its destiny into its own hands," he said in Quebec City. "France salutes this accession with all its soul."[22] The words were not without a shade of ambiguity, but the intent could not have been clearer. De Gaulle was urging the people of Quebec to claim their independence.

The following day, 24 July, addressing an outdoor crowd in Donnaconna, he returned to the constant theme of his journey: French Quebec's emancipation.

I see the present, the present of French Canada—that is to say, a country living to the limit of its possibilities, a country that is in the process of becoming master of itself, a country that is taking its destiny into its own hands. You are a piece of the French people. Your French-Canadian people, Canadian-French people, must not depend on any but itself. And that is what is happening. I can see it and I can sense it.

The diplomatic justification for his words, if there was one, could have been that *Maîtres chez nous* had already been used by a legitimate government of Quebec. But the phrase had been contentious when it was used by the Quebec Liberals in 1962. For a foreign visitor to use it, and to emphasize and augment it by the admonition that "your people must not depend on any but itself," and that on top of a statement of supposed fact that was really another way of urging French Canadians to take their destiny into their own hands—this was of such breathtaking audacity that de Gaulle, a man of great sensitivity, would never have done so unless he knew that this was exactly what Daniel Johnson wanted him to do.

At Cap-de-la-Madeleine, he coupled his urging for his audience to become a French people that was master of itself with a promise that France would provide all its support to the process. "You will be what you want to be, that is, masters of yourselves. And I am certain that your future will be beautiful, as it must be for a French future. For my part, I bring you the salute of France, of the old country, which loves you and does not forget you."

The general who had embodied the liberation of France had now returned, in his uniform, to give a military salute to an underground that was surfacing for the coming liberation. And de Gaulle, a man who always chose his words carefully, and most fastidiously on solemn occasions, made an explicit juxtaposition between his triumphal progression that day and his journey through liberated France in 1944. "I will tell you a secret which you must not repeat. This evening, here and all along my route, I found myself in an atmosphere no different from that of *la libération*."[23] He capped his mission into occupied territory that night with the cry that has echoed ever since: "*Vive Montréal! Vive le Québec! Vive le Québec L-I-I-I-I-BRE!*"

There was consternation in English-speaking Canada, and Pearson recorded the event in his diary: "I was sitting in the small drawing-room upstairs at Sussex Drive watching him on television when he began his balcony speech. I could hardly believe my ears when I heard the words he uttered: '*Vive le Québec libre.*'"[24] What most galled Pearson, though, were the words spoken earlier in the day. "I was not as distressed about that remark as I was about the analogy he made comparing his procession on that day to his march into Paris during the liberation of 1944. That I found infuriating."[25]

Pearson immediately began to scribble the response that he would deliver the next day, on television, and that he would convey to the ambassador of France. The French president's remarks were "unacceptable": "The people of Canada are free. Every province of Canada is free. Canadians do not need to be liberated. Indeed, many thousands of Canadians gave their lives in two world wars in the liberation of France and other European countries."[26]

Jean Lesage decried de Gaulle's words. Daniel Johnson did not. Two days after the fracas, Johnson did issue a statement condemning not de Gaulle, but the federal government, which, he said, "under the passion of extremist elements," had insulted de Gaulle. For the French president, Johnson had only unstinting praise, and he associated himself with the words repudiated by Ottawa. His statement had the ring of a manifesto.

Courageous and lucid, President de Gaulle went with us right to the essence of things. Quebec was not offended. General de Gaulle was able to observe the enormous progress that modern Quebec is accomplishing. Perceiving as few have done before him the spirit that inspires this renewal, he spoke of emancipation, of Quebec taking its destiny into its own hands, of a *Québec libre*. He was repeating in his own words the ideas so often

expressed by the recent governments of Quebec. He saluted the very
conviction that is, increasingly, that of the Québécois people that it is free
to choose its destiny and that, like all the peoples of the world, it holds the
unquestionable right to make its own decisions with respect to itself by
determining freely its political status and by taking responsibility freely for
its economic, social, and cultural development. He noted the undeniable
fact that Quebec is henceforth involved in an evolution thanks to which,
democratically, it becomes each day more fully itself.[27]

Just as de Gaulle must in all likelihood have expressed what he judged to be
Johnson's sentiments, now Johnson was repeating and affirming those sentiments
in the form of a gloss on de Gaulle. Johnson's words that day are inexplicable
unless his true goal was independence—or unless he was willing to bluff recklessly
to achieve something short of independence by stimulating separatist sentiments
in Quebec.

On his return to France, de Gaulle remained preoccupied with fostering the
liberation of the Canadian French. On 1 August 1967, he promised "to the French
Canadians and their government the backing of France to help them achieve the
goals of liberation that they have set themselves."[28] On 8 September, while on
a visit to Poland, he wrote a personal letter to Daniel Johnson to be delivered to
him by hand by his minister, Alain Peyrefitte. The letter urged Johnson along,
saying that the time was ripe for "the great national operation of the accession
of Quebec, which you are pursuing." He spoke of France and Quebec as a single
entity: "For our French community, it is, don't you think, the time to accentuate
what has already been undertaken." And he ended his letter with the exhortation,
"It is time for solutions."

The general wanted to move too fast for Johnson, who had reservations about
the single national French community that seemed to be de Gaulle's design. "We
are in agreement about some reintegration of French Canada within the francophone universe," he responded with caution. "But, monsieur le Président, I must
be realistic. We have very important economic problems, and my first duty is to
act responsibly."[29]

Toward the end of that September, Johnson suffered a heart attack and was
sent by his doctors to rest in Hawaii. Meanwhile, in Quebec, the political
turbulence of the past months was making investors and the business community
jittery. Charles Neapole, president of the Montreal Stock Exchange, and Eric
Kierans, former president of the Exchange, sounded the alarm about a "flight of
capital" from Quebec. Paul Desmarais, one of Quebec's most important financiers—he owned, among other interests, the newspaper La Presse—joined
Johnson at his retreat in Hawaii and urged him to act to reassure the investors.
Johnson agreed. The statement that he made from Hawaii to a La Presse reporter
stunned many people in Quebec:

In June 1966, the Union Nationale did not receive a mandate to build a Chinese Wall around Quebec. We promised the people to exercise the rights recognized in the British North America Act and to make every effort to obtain a new Canadian constitution, made in Canada by Canadians and for Canadians, whereby every citizen, be he French-speaking or English-speaking, and whatever his ethnic origin, will feel at home everywhere in Canada.[30]

This was the language of a moderate reformer, not a radical engaged in a process of *libération*. There was consternation among the nationalist members of the Cabinet, including Marcel Masse, who had been described as "radiant" right after de Gaulle cried *Vive le Québec libre*. Johnson now spoke of "the country" as Canada, rather than only Quebec. The nationalists were outraged, feeling that he had sold out or lost his nerve. The most likely explanation is that he was himself ambivalent. He had set Quebec at the same time on two incompatible courses: *égalité* and *indépendance*. He seemed to be attracted to both and unable to resolve the dilemma.

Nearly eight years later, Jacques Parizeau, by then a pillar of the separatist Parti Québécois, commented on these incidents in a supplement devoted to Quebec of the French publication *Le Monde diplomatique:*

General de Gaulle tried to give a push to the situation. His *"Vive le Québec libre!"* was in no way a passing fancy. It came at just the right time. On the other hand, the business sector, the financial sector, then intervened powerfully. The creation in 1967 of a panic flight of short-term funds had no impact on credit, given the concentration of the Canadian banks and of their many branches. But it caused Quebec politicians to lose their heads. They had been catapulted in a few years from communal affairs into major dealings between states. The government of Quebec collapsed as an autonomist government.[31]

After his return, rested, from Hawaii, Johnson was back on the nationalist course. He prepared carefully for the Confederation of Tomorrow Conference, to be convened on 27 November 1967 in Toronto by Ontario premier John Robarts. Robarts was angry at Ottawa, shared Johnson's insistence on more revenue for the provinces, was concerned about the escalation of separatism in Quebec and worried about the future of the federation. He decided to bypass the federal government, the usual convenor of conferences on national issues, and issued an invitation to all the other premiers and to the federal government. Ottawa, however, only sent an observer.

From 23 to 26 November, just before the conference opened, about 2,400 French Canadians from across the country gathered in Montreal to deliberate on the future of French Canada as a nation. The conference, sponsored by the nationalist Sociétés Saint-Jean-Baptiste, was held under the portentous title *Les États-Généraux du Canada français*—evocative of the French Revolution.

65

The convention gave Johnson strong backing for his constitutional demands, overwhelmingly adopting a resolution that stated, in part:

1. French Canadians constitute a nation.

2. Quebec constitutes the national territory and the fundamental political milieu of this nation.

3. The French-Canadian nation has the right to make its own decisions and to choose freely the political regime under which it intends to live.[32]

The implication of the resolution was that the premier of Quebec was the head of the French-Canadian nation, and it was as head of that nation that Johnson went to Toronto. There, the premiers held their own intensely televised summit, no doubt delighted that there was no federal government to preside, dominate the proceedings, and steal the limelight. They were like the leaders of a confederacy of ten states rather than provincial premiers within a federation.

Johnson made his pitch to the other premiers, to Quebecers, and to the country. His case rested on the assumption that a cultural community with a common language constituted a nation, and the nation must have its corresponding political structure.

No matter what the term used, we can't ignore the fundamental fact that there are in Canada not only two languages, but two ways of being and of reacting, two societies, one of which has been rooted for three centuries and a half in the land of America. . . . The present constitution does still have valid elements with respect to the organization of a Canada with ten members *[le Canada à dix]*, but one has to admit that this other Canada, the Canada with two members *[le Canada à deux]*, still has for the most part to be invented. That is probably why our country has remained until now the Canada of the two solitudes.[33]

Johnson brought up the perennial argument that French Canadians are weak and isolated in North America: "It happens that, of the two Canadian cultures, it is obviously the French culture that is the most threatened in the context of North America." And he enunciated the only principle that could make possible, he said, the Confederation of tomorrow: a restructuring of Canada as two nations. Otherwise, Canada could not survive. In practice, this meant that Quebec's provincial government must be given all the powers of a national government, because it "is the only one which can speak in the name of a French majority."

He thereupon formulated the concept, so central to the Quiet Revolution, that Quebec must reconstitute itself as an ethnic state, in which French Canadians have control and exercise it on their own behalf: "For it is only in Quebec that French Canadians have the political power that comes from being in a majority. It is there only that they can give themselves the institutions, a setting for living, a milieu that has the precise dimensions of their needs and of their personality."

Quebec is the only real country of French Canadians: that was Johnson's message at the end of 1967. In an interview with Radio Luxembourg on 9

December, shortly after the conference, Johnson contrasted himself with his Quebec "compatriots" who were ready, he said, "to sacrifice the French-Canadian nation." He was not. "On the contrary, I say that we absolutely must work not only for the survival but also the expansion of the French Canadian nation—even at the price of Confederation."[34]

The Confederation of Tomorrow Conference endorsed a series of conferences with the object of rewriting the constitution. This was the opening Johnson wanted.

Meanwhile, the Quebec Liberals, in opposition, were divided about what position to take on the constitution, especially after de Gaulle's *Vive le Québec libre*. At first, Lesage and the caucus were critical of the general, but a CROP public-opinion poll, published on 12 August 1967 in *Le Devoir, Le Soleil,* and *The Montreal Star,* showed that a majority of Quebecers were happy with what de Gaulle had done about two weeks earlier. A majority agreed with the statement that "de Gaulle was right to come and to shout '*Vive le Québec libre.*'"[35]

On the day the poll was published, Johnson surprised the Liberals by proposing a motion in the Assembly to "thank General de Gaulle for coming to Quebec at our invitation, and to reprimand the federal government, which so acted that he was unable to complete his trip to Canada even though he was, at that moment, our guest."

Lesage, after a moment's hesitation, accepted the motion, saying, "I wish to add my voice to that of the premier to express my gratitude to General de Gaulle for coming to visit us. We are deeply grateful to him. . . . We are very happy with the way the population received the general. He was worthy of that reception and he deserved it because of all that he did and said for the Québécois."[36]

The next day, the member for Dorion, François Aquin, gave the first separatist speech ever heard in Quebec's Legislative Assembly. Though he had been elected as a Liberal, Aquin had broken with his party and decided to sit as an independent when Lesage criticized de Gaulle with the backing of the Liberal caucus. He thus became the first elected member publicly committed to Quebec's independence. Aquin ended his speech with the cry *Vive le Québec libre.* While the Liberals sat stony-faced, Johnson applauded.

The following month, René Lévesque's separatist manifesto was published. Lévesque had been impressed with Johnson's vision of Quebec. It was, in fact, Johnson who got Lévesque thinking along the line that would lead him eventually to choose sovereignty. In his memoirs, Lévesque quoted Johnson's words at the 1966 federal-provincial conference:

What, precisely, does Quebec want? As the fulcrum of a nation, it wants to be master of its decisions with respect to the human growth of its citizens (that is, education, social security, and health in all their forms); to their economic affirmation; to their cultural fulfillment (that is, not only arts and

67

letters, but also the French language); and to the projection of the Quebec community (that is, with certain international countries and agencies).[37]

For Lévesque, what Johnson said in 1966 sounded a lot like what he himself had said in 1963 and 1964, though more precise and complete. And, as he recalls, Johnson had upped the ante on the Quebec Liberals: "The party had no alternative, unless it wanted simply to parrot him, but to be left behind or to charge further forward. To go back was out of the question. So it was forward. But how, and how far? The more we discussed it among ourselves, the more we went around in circles."[38]

When Lévesque thought the matter through, he realized what Johnson apparently did not: his concept of two nations was incompatible with federalism. One evening, Lévesque explained the conclusion he had reached to the discussion group meeting in Robert Bourassa's basement, which included Paul Gérin-Lajoie and Pierre Laporte:

Johnson was talking about recognizing a nation, and he demanded for that nation a wide range of exclusive powers. We, who saw ourselves as preceding him and not following him on the road to emancipation, why wouldn't we go all the way to full sovereignty, rather than this half measure that would give us, at best, a broader range of autonomy, but one exposed to all the traps that were being set for it in Ottawa and elsewhere?[39]

Sovereignty meant independence. There was no substantial difference between the two. There was a practical problem, though, for Lévesque. The word *indépendance* had become associated with Pierre Bourgault's radical party, the Rassemblement pour l'Indépendance Nationale, and the RIN was associated with street demonstrations, strong actions, and violence. "Independence had travelled so much in the street with the RIN, taking on from demonstration to demonstration an absolute and hardened character, as though it were an end in itself, that its name had become, unfortunately, an invitation to be hit by a billy club."[40]

And so, for strategic reasons, Lévesque chose sovereignty-association as his identifying slogan. However, he retained much the same terminology as Johnson, such as the prospect of negotiating with the other nation of Canada "*d'égal à égal*"—between equals.[41]

When Lévesque approached Lesage with his idea of sovereignty along with an economic association with Canada, the Liberal leader wouldn't hear of it. When they continued to disagree, Lesage suggested a way out: "I said to René—I'm referring to Mr. Lévesque—Well, if you want we will simply submit the two options to a full convention of the party. And that's what we did. And René, not satisfied with the party decision, quit."[42]

The convention was to be in October, 1967. Lévesque's proposal was *Option-Québec*; the other proposal, for "special status" rather than sovereignty with an economic association, was developed by Paul Gérin-Lajoie. Both were to be presented to the Liberal delegates, each was to be moved and seconded, and the convention would vote on them.

On 18 September 1967, *Option-Québec* was published in *Le Devoir*. Lévesque wanted a full discussion of it before the convention, and it did attract considerable comment, most of it adverse. At the convention, Lesage spoke in favour of the proposal for special status, which was moved by Gérin-Lajoie and seconded by Pierre Laporte:

It is possible to build, on this corner of the earth that is ours, Quebec, a state that is master at home *[maître chez lui]* in all the areas of its exclusive jurisdictions, that is at the same time the fulcrum of all francophones in Canada and in North America. This Quebec is not a province like the others. I see it endowed with the powers that are essential to its economic, cultural, and social fulfilment, in a renewed Canadian constitutional framework that reserves for Quebec a special status because it is not a province like the others.[43]

Was "special status" workable? Was it a concept precise and stable enough to be truly a policy and not just a slogan? Lesage himself never developed a definition specific enough that it could be called a policy. It was more a distinction—Quebec was not like the other provinces and should therefore have more powers.

The concept's volatile character was manifest on 28 July, four days after de Gaulle uttered his *Vive le Québec libre*. At a press conference, Lesage said that his party favoured "a special status within Canada," and added, "Quebec must enjoy the greatest degree of autonomy that is compatible with its existence and the existence of Canada."[44] This suggested that there was no limit, no logical stopping point, no point of equilibrium, where a Quebec government would say, No more, enough. The only constraint was the point at which the existence of Quebec and of Canada would be threatened. As a constitutional doctrine, "special status" was a formula for permanent strife, with the endemic risk that someone would miscalculate and actually put the existence of Quebec or Canada in jeopardy. The only practical way to establish the limits of Quebec's autonomy was to see the results after going too far.

Lesage backed the description of special status prepared by Gérin-Lajoie.[45] The starting point of his report to the Liberal convention was similar to Daniel Johnson's. Just as Johnson had postulated a single entity that had existed through time from 1608 to 1965 in constant search of a state, so Gérin-Lajoie postulated a "collective personality" of "the state of Quebec." He laid down the "minimum needs" for the security and development of that collective personality. In principle, as he recognized, the collective personality really needed all the powers of a modern state—that is, full sovereignty and independence. However, he was willing to make some concessions to practicality, to the tendency in the contemporary world for states to create relations with other states.

It could be said that, in a sense, all of the actions, and, consequently, all of the powers of a state have a direct or indirect influence on the development of the collective personality of a people. But in a period when the interdependence of nations is inscribed in daily reality to the point of motivating all states to look for formulas of rapprochement and co-ordination, one must attempt to define what are the minimal powers that cannot be left to an external authority without putting in danger one's collective personality.[46]

He never asked what might be the minimal requirements for the federal government to function effectively for the benefit of all Canadians, including Quebecers. No, the federal government became a residual concept: it could receive whatever powers did not seem to be required at any given moment by the State of Quebec's collective personality. That didn't leave much for the Canadian federation.

The report described a range of powers that, at a minimum, had to be held by the Quebec state: jurisdiction over educational institutions, the arts, cinema, radio, and television; power to select immigrants to Quebec; exclusive jurisdiction over social security, health and welfare, manpower and occupational training; a shared jurisdiction, or at least a "role," in matters dealing with economic development, including monetary policy, interest rates, and tariffs. "This list is neither complete, nor definitive, far from it. We could add, for example, ocean-bed rights, maritime fisheries, some categories of transportation, etc."[47] The report even stated that Quebec would have the right to change its constitution at any time, "without any restriction."[48] This suggested that the collective personality of Quebec might from time to time require new rights and could simply change its constitution unilaterally, without regard to how this might affect Canada.

This was the moderate proposal offered as an alternative to Lévesque's sovereignty-association. Gérin-Lajoie characterized it as one that would make the Canadian federation unique and Quebec distinct. "This new federalism, original and specific to Canada, would provide that one of its member-states enjoys a regime that is distinct and different from the others. This distinct regime would give to Quebec full legislative and administrative powers in a great number of areas which the other provinces or states could leave to be exercised by the federal authority."

The Liberals had come a long way from "*Il faut que ça change*" in 1960, and even from "*la libération économique*" of 1962. And yet, there was a kind of inner consistency to the evolution. Those who chose special status, like Gérin-Lajoie and Lesage, and those who chose sovereignty-association, like Lévesque, started from the same political postulate, that of a "collective personality"—which was really just another name for an ethnic state. From that premise, it would follow that powers would be granted only grudgingly, if at all, to a federal state:

any concession of powers would be deemed a weakening of the collective personality rather than a strengthening of the political, social, cultural, and economic fabric of the lives of all citizens. The ethnic state as the starting point of a constitutional vision has an inherent tendency to totalitarianism, incompatible with the divided and shared sovereignty of a federation.

Was there really a fundamental difference between the visions of Gérin-Lajoie and René Lévesque? *Option-Québec* begins with a chapter entitled "Nous autres"—us. Who are *we*? *We* does not include all French Canadians. Those from outside Quebec are not considered part of *nous autres*; nor are English-speaking Quebecers. French-speaking Quebecers are *nous*—and not even all of them; only those who feel that they are part of a "collective personality" that began with the settlement of New France, that includes all the historic nationalist heroes, and includes today all those who share in the "collective obstinacy" to maintain Quebec as French. That is *nous*. All others don't belong. "All that [the heroes, the collective obstinacy, etc.] is found deep in this personality that is ours. Whoever does not feel it, at least on occasion, is not or is no longer one of us."[49]

What Lévesque described was a tribal identity. He used repeatedly the word "personality" to describe this identity, which had existed for three and a half centuries. Somehow, the same collective being had existed from the time of little fur-trading colony of New France in the early seventeenth century to the time of the urban, industrialized Quebec of the second half of the twentieth century. And no matter what variety of people exists today, they are all part of the same collective personality. In fact, "to be ourselves is essentially to maintain and develop a personality that has existed for three and a half centuries."[50]

This personality separates French-speaking Quebecers from all others in North America. It is a constraining factor that is almost impossible to escape, except for those who are "uprooted." For *nous,* though, the collective personality "goes beyond the mere level of intellectual certitudes. It is something physical. To be unable to live as we are, properly, in our language, in our own way, would be the same as having a limb severed or our heart wrenched out."[51]

In recapitulating the biography of this "personality," Lévesque mentions the heroic early period when it was all French. "Then came the conquest. We were the vanquished who struggled to survive meagrely on a continent that had become Anglo-Saxon."[52] His description of the current world of French Canada was mostly mournful. "Economically, we are colonized people whose three meals a day depend too often on the initiative and the pleasure of foreign bosses."[53] By "foreign," he does not seem to mean non-Canadian. He means foreign to *nous*—that is, non-francophone.

But there was hope. Lévesque recalled the Quiet Revolution, which showed the Québécois that they could accomplish things, they could even precede the rest of the country for the first time. They could take their fate in hand.

However, there was an obstacle keeping the Québécois from fulfilment: the straitjacket of the federal system. It had to be radically reformed, or cast off. But truly deep reform would never be accepted by the rest of Canada, so sovereignty was the only alternative.

Oddly, Lévesque never tried to demonstrate that federalism had not worked in the past for Quebecers. He simply affirmed it for the future: it can't work. But his demonstration was purely *a priori*. It can't work because it has an old constitution that was framed a century ago, when most of modern society was not anticipated by the Fathers of Confederation. Logically, this would suggest that every country that has a century-old constitution cannot work today.[54] To establish that the constitution could not work in the future, Lévesque invoked the authority of three union federations that had submitted a joint brief on the constitution. Their argument was that a federation, which has two levels of government, cannot attend efficiently to the economy.

The fact that some instruments for acting on the economy belong to the federal government, while other powers that have an impact on the economy belong to the provinces, creates a difficult problem for the rational direction of economic activity in general. From the vantage point of a greater socialization than what we have today, this situation, as well as the capacity of one government to cancel the action of the other, could engender conflicts and are apt to foster, at both levels of government, a tendency toward impotence in attacking resolutely and effectively the country's economic problems.[55]

This is an odd argument to espouse. How could one say that federations cannot work in principle, when federations were, at the time, the most prosperous countries in the world: the United States, Switzerland, Canada.

If Quebec remained part of Canada, Lévesque postulated—without offering evidence to back up his statement—a terrible deadlock would overtake both nations of Canada. The deadlock would lead to resentment, perhaps even to violence. Both French Quebec and English Canada would be threatened with disappearance.

Having evoked the spectre, Lévesque then offered the happy alternative: Quebec became sovereign, and then both Quebec and English Canada—eventually—would be happy and fulfilled. He postulated that the idea of becoming sovereign would unify the people of French Quebec and give them the enthusiasm and great energy needed to enter on a period of continuous development, a kind of permanent Quiet Revolution. "In a word, [sovereignty] is not just the only logical solution to the present Canadian impasse, it is also the only common objective which is so exalted that it can bring us together united and strong enough to face all possible futures—that supreme undertaking that is the continuous progress of a society which takes in its own hands the management of its affairs."[56]

But, at the same time, Lévesque wanted an economic association between Quebec and Canada, similar to that of the European Economic Community, Benelux, or the Scandinavian Union. This way, Quebec's economic security would be maintained. The association would include a common currency (at least for a trial period of five years), a common market, and co-ordinated fiscal policies.

The new union, as Lévesque envisaged it, would at last make Quebec the equal of Canada. He hoped "to succeed in making a place for ourselves in [this era] that is appropriate to our size, in our language, so that we might feel that we are equals and not inferiors."[57] Lévesque never doubted that Quebec, much smaller than the rest of Canada, could still expect to be treated as an equal. It could do so, he argued, because it said so in international law. "The fact that, from the point of view of numbers, we are in the minority changes nothing; just as a civilized society will never force a smaller man to feel inferior before one who is bigger, so civilized relations between nations require that they should see and treat each other as equals in law and in fact."[58] This argument was strangely utopian. Are the United States and Haiti treated as equals by the world because both are "nations"? Was a change of legal status a magic wand that levelled all inequalities and made the small the equal of the big?

Lévesque's grand project was suprisingly introverted. He argued that sovereignty and association were what French Quebec needed, but he never seriously attempted to demonstrate that Quebec could not achieve its objectives within Confederation, and even within the present constitution. Nor did he demonstrate that his objective of sovereignty with an economic association was attainable, or that it would be workable if attained, or that French-speaking Quebecers would be better off under that arrangement. His argument was conducted in a vacuum, *a priori*, like that of a man talking to himself.

Lévesque was building castles on paper. In appealing to a mystical tribal identity—the collective personality that persists as a single entity through time and contains all French-speaking Quebecers past, present, and future—he played the familiar themes of the heroic past, the conquest, the sense of a humiliating present, the glorious redemption that lies ahead if only we all wish it so. To those who accept the "collective personality" as the significant reality of French Quebec, Lévesque's proposal can seem persuasive. After all, how can a collective personality be shared with those who do not belong to it? The starting-point of a collective personality essentially rules out ethnic diversity, the non-ethnic state, and pluralism.

But for those committed to liberalism, pluralism, individualism, the central role he attributed to the "collective personality" was disquieting. The state is not the expression of a collective will—that way lies a form of totalitarianism and encompassing nationalism. For a liberal, the commitment to a state will always be accompanied by reservations and distrust. The state is the mechanism of concentrated power. The experience of the past two centuries with the nation-state, and in this century with the ideological state, have confirmed the testimony of all recorded history that the state is prone to war, inclines to extravagant expenditures on behalf of the privileged few through spoliation of the many, and tends to persecute minorities unless it is restrained. True liberals do not look to the state for secular salvation, as nationalists do.

In the event, Lévesque failed to rally the Liberal convention behind his proposal, and he stormed out with a number of his followers. He then founded a movement to disseminate his ideas. A year later, the Mouvement Souveraineté-Association became a full-fledged political party, the Parti Québécois. The concept of the ethnic state that had been sketchily elaborated by the Quebec Liberals was given full expression in the new party.

Interestingly, after Lévesque's manifesto was published, a group of the more nationalist members of the Union Nationale responded indignantly that Lévesque's proposal was a steal from a document that they had prepared for the 1966 Quebec elections, but that had never been officially adopted. As it was now leaked to the press, the UN document proposed as its first article "political sovereignty with economic association and integration." This was precisely the same as Lévesque's sovereignty-association. The UN minister of culture, Jean-Noel Tremblay, even charged, "Mr. Lévesque is a shop-lifter."[59]

It was, with variations, fundamentally the same vision that inspired the Quebec Liberals, the Union Nationale, and then the Parti Québécois. It was shared by most of the politicians and pundits who were widely admired by the intellectual and political classes in Quebec. It was in direct continuity with Quebec's long tradition of introverted resistance to the surrounding world. It had one crucial new element: the concept of the state. The shared vision was that of the ethnic state, defender of francophones and rampart against all others.

Notes

1. The Union Nationale took 56 seats, against 50 for the Liberals, though it had actually only received slightly more than 40 per cent of the vote, to the Liberals' 47 per cent. The two separatist parties divided about 9 per cent of the vote: the left-wing Ralliement pour l'Indépendance Nationale took 5.6 per cent, the right-wing Ralliement national 3.2 per cent.

2. The anecdote is related by Pierre Godin in *Daniel Johnson*, vol. 1, *1946-1964: la passion du pouvoir* (Montreal: Éditions de l'Homme, 1980), pp. 7, 9.

3. Paul Gros d'Aillon, *Daniel Johnson: l'égalité avant l'indépendance* (Montréal: Stanké, 1979), p. 90.

4. Ibid., p. 89.

5. Ibid., pp. 89–90.

6. Daniel Johnson, *Égalité ou indépendance* (Montréal: Éditions Renaissance, 1965).

7. Ibid., p. 11.

8. Ibid., p. 23.

9. Ibid., p. 23.

10. Ibid., pp. 23–24.

11. Ibid., pp. 120–21.

12.Ibid., p. 123.
13.Louis Fournier, *F.L.Q. Histoire d'un mouvement clandestin* (Montreal: Québec/Amérique, 1982), p. 130.
14.Quoted in Gros d'Aillon, *Daniel Johnson:*, pp. 135-36.
15.Quoted in Godin, *Daniel Johnson*, p. 303.
16.Gros d'Aillon, *Daniel Johnson*, p. 136.
17.Ibid., p. 137. In fact, Johnson died before carrying out his intention. But Robert Bourassa fulfilled his wishes in 1974, when he passed Bill 22, making French the official language of Quebec. Camille Laurin, the father of Bill 101, repeated in 1977, when the Charter of the French Language was adopted, "Quebec must be as French as Ontario is English."
18.Ibid., pp. 141-42.
19.Ibid.,. p. 142.
20.Ibid., pp. 144-45.
21.Ibid., p. 206.
22.Quotations from de Gaulle's speeches are taken from Godin, *Daniel Johnson*, vol. 2, pp. 219-23.
23.Ibid., vol. 2, p. 172.
24.John A. Munro and Alex I. Inglis, eds., *Mike. The Memoirs of the Right Honourable Lester B. Pearson*, vol. 3 (Toronto: University of Toronto Press, 1975), p. 267.
25.Ibid., p. 268.
26.Ibid.
27.Quoted with slight differences in Gros d'Aillon, *Daniel Johnson*, pp. 169-70, and Godin, *Daniel Johnson*, vol. 2, pp. 242-44. Robert Bourassa uttered almost the identical words on 22 June 1990, when the failure of the Meech Lake accord became irrevocable.
28.Godin, *Daniel Johnson*, vol. 2, p. 256.
29.Ibid., p. 259.
30.Ibid., pp. 270-71.
31.Jacques Parizeau, "La marche vers l'indépendance est inévitable," *Le Monde diplomatique*, Jan. 1975, p. 25.
32.Reprinted in Guy Bouthillier and Jean Meynaud, *Le choc des langues au Québec 1760-1970* (Montreal: Presses de l'Université du Québec, 1972), p. 715.
33.Johnson's statement to the conference is quoted at length in Gros d'Aillon, *Daniel Johnson*, pp. 186-90.
34.Quoted in Martin Sullivan, *Mandate '68* (Toronto: Doubleday, 1968), p. 264.
35.Godin, *Daniel Johnson*, vol. 2, p. 246.
36.Ibid., pp. 249-50.
37.Quoted in René Lévesque, *Attendez que je me rappelle. . .* (Montreal: Québec/Amérique, 1986), p. 285.
38.Ibid.
39.Ibid., p. 287.
40.Ibid., p. 288.
41.The prospect of at last achieving equality with English Canada was so central to Lévesque's sensibility and political thinking that the words *d'égal à égal*, were to be found later, in 1980, in the question that he would put to the people in a referendum: they would be asked to vote *yes* to "the proposition of the Government of Quebec for an agreement *d'égal à égal*" with the rest of Canada.
42.Lesage's version of events was given in an interview with Radio-Canada in January, 1980. Quoted in Richard Daignault, *Lesage* (Montréal: Libre expression, 1981), p. 250.
43.Ibid., p. 251.
44.Ibid., p. 249.
45.Most of Gérin-Lajoie's report is reproduced in René Lévesque, *Option Québec* (Montreal: les éditions de l'Homme, 1968), pp.86-90.
46.Ibid., p. 87.
47.Ibid., p. 89.

48.Ibid., p. 89.

49.Ibid., p. 20.

50Ibid., p. 19.

51.Ibid., p. 21.

52. *"Nous fûmes des vaincus qui s'acharnaient à survivre petitement sur un continent devenu anglo-saxon."* Ibid., p. 19.

53.Ibid., p. 23.

54.In 1977, speaking before American businessmen, Lévesque used a striking expression that he borrowed from Winston Churchill: "Canada and Quebec cannot continue to live like two scorpions in the same bottle." Lévesque, *La Passion du Québec* (Montreal: Québec/Amérique, 1978), p. 111.

55.Ibid., p. 32.

56.Ibid., p. 39.

57.Ibid., p. 24.

58.Ibid., p. 29.

59.Godin, *Daniel Johnson*, p. 265.

CHAPTER FOUR

Enter Pierre Trudeau

A t last, Daniel Johnson got his long-sought federal-provincial conference on the constitution. It was held in Ottawa on 5–7 February 1968. But it was not what he had hoped.

Ever since his election, nearly two years before, Johnson had clamoured for a totally recast constitution. He had insisted, at the federal-provincial conference in September of 1966, that Canada must be reformed as two nations, and he had brought that message to the Confederation of Tomorrow Conference in Toronto in November of 1967. But now that the first ministers were actually to meet to reform the constitution, the federal government was proposing a vision of the country that was entirely opposite to his.

On 1 February, four days before the conference was to open, federal justice minister Pierre Trudeau tabled a white paper titled *A Canadian Charter of Human Rights*.[1] It was clearly calculated to put forward an alternative to the Quebec premier's vision of two nations rather than to begin, as he had hoped, the process of implementing it. In his introduction to the document, Prime Minister Pearson proposed that reallocation of powers between federal and provincial governments be put off to a later stage—after the Charter of Rights had been dealt with: "A constitutional Charter of Human Rights will form a first stage in the continuing process of redefinition of the Canadian constitution."

Pearson had been won over to the view of Trudeau, who had argued all along that the priority should be to defuse ethnic tensions in Canada by recognizing French-language rights all across the country. When that was done, it would be simpler to resolve the question of appropriate jurisdictions; French-speaking Quebecers would no longer be motivated by atavistic distrust.

"Mr. Trudeau is apparently putting the cart before the horse," Premier Johnson commented in Quebec City when he received a copy of the white paper.[2] Central to Johnson's demands had been the claim that a new distribution of powers must enable Quebec to act as "the heartland *[foyer]* of the French-Canadian nation." Instead, Trudeau offered a recognition of human, political, juridical, and language rights, all to be vested in one constitution of Canada that would bind uniformly the federal government and all ten provinces. This went counter to what Johnson had in mind, which was to disengage and differentiate Quebec from the rest of Canada.

Trudeau's white paper quoted Cicero, St. Thomas of Aquinas, Locke, and Rousseau, and placed his proposed charter in the grand liberal tradition of human rights based on natural law and the social contract. He evoked the Declaration of Independence of the United States, the 1789 Declaration of the Rights of Man in France, the United Nations' Universal Declaration of Human Rights, and the International Covenant on Economic, Social, and Cultural Rights. Language rights for Canada were put in the context of protecting the rights of individual people.

Johnson, in contrast, spoke the language of nineteenth-century nationalism, with its postulate that the nation must be the measure of the state. While not repudiating individual rights, the premier was after collective rights—or, more accurately, collective powers—that would make Quebec a specifically franco-phone and quasi-sovereign state.

Johnson protested against the two-stage proposal for constitutional reform and took offence at Ottawa's presuming to dictate a standard of rights to the provinces. He did not want anyone "taking for granted that only the federal government can protect human rights. Within our areas of jurisdiction, we are quite able to protect all the fundamental rights of our citizens, including those of our minorities. . . . It would be a serious political error"[3] to vest in the constitution a homogeneous concept of individual and collective rights.

Johnson was really attacking the concept of a federation with essential rights defined and held in common for all. He would have rights originate in each of the two nations, according to supposed fundamental differences of culture between each nation. Above all, he feared that the Canadian Charter of Human Rights would postpone what truly mattered to him: Quebec's acquiring the powers of a nation-state. Trudeau's initiative put him in a bind. How could he come out against a charter of rights? How could he oppose freedom of expression, of conscience and religion, of assembly and association? Could he reject recognizing in the constitution the right to "life, liberty, and security of the person and enjoyment of property, and the right not to be deprived thereof except by due process of law"?

The proposed language rights were even harder for Johnson to reject. They corresponded, in fact, to what French Canadians everywhere had always pleaded for. The great nationalist politician Henri Bourassa, founder of the newspaper *Le Devoir,* would have considered it the fulfilment of his career had he lived to see what the government of Canada now proposed for a new constitution:

> The [linguistic] rights fall into two categories: (a) Communication with governmental institutions—guaranteeing the right of the individual to deal with agencies of Government in either official language. It would be necessary to decide whether this should apply to all agencies—legislative, executive, and judicial—and to all Governments—federal, provincial and municipal. (b) Education—guaranteeing the right of the individual to

78

education in institutions using as a medium of instruction the official language of his choice.[4]

"Quebec challenges the agenda of the constitutional conference," *La Presse* announced in a front-page headline on 2 February 1968. But, his point made, Johnson agreed to attend the conference, while always insisting that defining rights was the wrong way to start; until the new powers of each government were decided, a charter was premature. Johnson secured the concurrence of Ontario's premier, John Robarts: both would insist that the charter be considered only as part of a package deal, which had to include the redistribution of powers.

The conference was expected to be a major event, reminiscent of the Charlottetown Conference of 1864, which had set the course for Confederation. After the great surge of Quebec nationalism in 1967, there was a sense in the country that the moment of truth was about to arrive, and that it might take Canada in a radically new direction. Now, Daniel Johnson's demand for *égalité ou indépendance* must be answered by the prime minister and all the premiers.

Claude Ryan, publisher of *Le Devoir,* evoked the expectations for the conference on the Saturday before it opened. "Is it possible to conceive of establishing a truly bi-national state which, at the same time, is able to compete dynamically and efficiently with other countries?" He warned that the conference must deal with the aspirations of Quebec for "a measure of sovereignty that often astonishes the other provinces." Otherwise, "this country will be exposed to the gravest perils."[5]

Many wondered what role Pierre Trudeau would play. Since Pearson had announced, on 14 December, that he would step down the following April, the outrageous thought had occurred that Trudeau might be his successor. As justice minister, he had proved daring, modern, and innovative. He had scandalized John Diefenbaker by entering the Commons in sandals, and was seen around Ottawa driving a sporty Mercedes-Benz, wearing an ascot tie, a brown leather greatcoat, a wide-brimmed floppy hat.

Slender, lean, and not tall, Trudeau walked with the lithe step of an athlete. His face was pockmarked. The nose, slightly bent, recalled a boxer. The prominent cheekbones gave a hint of aboriginal ancestry. The eyes, pale blue, focused intently on the person he was addressing. He spoke French and English fluently—French with an elegant vocabulary and patrician accent, English with an abundance of slang.

Trudeau had modernized the law on divorce, previously granted only on the grounds of adultery. In Bill C-187, the grounds were broadened to include "physical and mental cruelty of such a kind as to render intolerable the continued cohabitation of the spouses." The bill even allowed divorce on the liberal grounds of "marriage breakdown." This seemed a particularly daring departure for Quebec, where, since Confederation, each divorce required a bill passed by the Senate.

Trudeau's reputation as a reformer had been enhanced in December of 1967, when he introduced an omnibus bill to overhaul the Criminal Code. It touched on sensitive issues: homosexual acts carried out in private between consenting adults were decriminalized, as were therapeutic abortions approved by a hospital committee of doctors. So he had the image of someone who did not fear to cut a Gordian knot, and who would do it with flair. But could Trudeau win acceptance in Quebec? That seemed unlikely. His repudiation of Quebec nationalism, expressed in scornful language, had offended almost every politician and pundit in the province. His insolence was breathtaking. Jean Lesage, still premier in 1965 when Pearson was about to call the elections that would bring Trudeau and journalist Gérard Pelletier into federal politics, had tried to veto the nomination of both, but labour leader Jean Marchand insisted on bringing them with him to Ottawa as a condition of his own candidacy.

"You don't take people like that and put them in politics," Lesage told Pearson. "You need professionals. Not dilettantes. Not 'deep thinkers.'" Lesage proposed several alternatives, including his deputy minister of federal-provincial affairs, Claude Morin—who was later to be a minister in the Parti Québécois government.[6]

At Marchand's insistence, Trudeau was accepted as a Liberal candidate—over the objections of Pearson's Quebec lieutenant, Guy Favreau. However, he was considered too exotic for francophone voters. He dressed like a dandy and spoke French with a Parisian accent, which made him seem snobbish and aloof. He was rich, and he had dabbled in socialist politics and trade-union work during the 1950s, when Maurice Duplessis did not like unions. He had been involved with Marchand in the violent 1949 Asbestos strike, and seven years later edited a provocative book on the subject, *La grève de l'amiante*.[7] His introduction, a sociological dissection of Quebec at the time of the strike, caused a scandal: it was seen as a contemptuous, anti-clerical put-down of all that was sacred in Quebec's still theocratic society and established him as a radical trying to subvert Quebec's religious and political foundations. Now that the Quiet Revolution had swept the province, Trudeau mocked the new sacred doctrines of special status, associate states, and sovereignty-association.

For Pearson, Trudeau posed a problem. Quebec was the power base of the Liberals, and Pearson led a minority government. Since he had become prime minister, in 1963, his government seemed to lurch from crisis to crisis, usually involving the Quebec caucus. In the winter of 1964–65, scandal or the suspicion of scandal had caused the resignations of Cabinet ministers René Tremblay, Maurice Lamontagne, Yvon Dupuis, and Guy Favreau. Other Quebec MPs were also tainted, and John Diefenbaker, glorying in his role as Torquemada, daily pointed a prosecutorial finger at some hapless Liberal from Quebec, the victim *du jour* of his blazing scorn.

The contrast between Quebec City, where modern politicians were transforming a society, and Ottawa, where Quebec politicians were regularly humiliated
and broken, had become subversive. At a time of cresting Quebec nationalism,
it suggested that provincial politics represented the future, federal politics the
unsavoury past. So Pearson needed Marchand, even at the price of taking
Trudeau.

The Liberal veterans grudgingly decided to run their hot potato in Mount
Royal, an anglophone riding whose member of Parliament, Alan Macnaughton,
was retiring. Ironically, it was against Macnaughton that Trudeau had campaigned two years earlier in support of New Democrat Charles Taylor. Trudeau
was elected in the 8 November 1965 general election. Two months later, he was
appointed Pearson's parliamentary secretary. Then, on 4 April 1967, when his
entire political career had spanned not nineteen months, he was named to the
Cabinet as minister of justice.

Pearson was taking a chance. Increasingly disenchanted with both Quebec
premiers he had dealt with, whose demands could never be satisfied, he asked
Trudeau to prepare the federal position for the federal-provincial conference that
was to launch negotiations to reform the constitution. That set the cat among the
pigeons: Trudeau was already denounced regularly as a traitor to Quebec.

Trudeau travelled to each provincial capital to consult the premiers, and
prepared the white paper that set out Ottawa's intentions. It came at a time
of exceptional tension. At the instigation of Charles de Gaulle, Premier
Johnson had been invited to participate in an international conference of
francophone ministers of education, starting on 5 February 1968 in
Libreville, Gabon. Canada was not invited. Without a word to the federal
government, Johnson announced on 17 January that Quebec would attend
as a participating state. Pearson wrote Johnson to urge that Canada should
have but one voice in international relations. He suggested that Quebec
ministers go to Gabon as part of a Canadian delegation. Johnson did not
even reply.

Also in January, de Gaulle had upgraded the French consulate in Quebec City,
making it an embassy in all but the name. The number of diplomats assigned to
Quebec was raised from ten to sixty, and de Gaulle ordered that all communications regarding Quebec should move directly between Paris and Quebec City,
without passing through the embassy in Ottawa.

Pearson, a career diplomat, understood that international recognition was the
route to independence; Canada had taken that route to separate from the United
Kingdom. Of all his conflicts and confrontations with Quebec governments, the
international issue was "the greatest single source of contention between Ottawa
and Quebec":

Both the Lesage and Johnson governments had asserted the right of the
provincial government to make direct arrangements with foreign countries

and to attend meetings with foreign representatives. I was convinced that the federal government could not abandon its sole right to conduct relations with other states on behalf of the whole country. If we did abandon this right, there would be the end of our Confederation.[8]

The Gabon incident was taken very seriously as confirming the separatist ambitions of Johnson and the interventionist intentions of de Gaulle. Pearson sent a francophone minister to Paris to request that Canada be invited to Libreville, but de Gaulle refused, to Pearson's disquiet.

We were quite content to have Quebec make cultural arrangements with France under a general overriding treaty between Canada and France. Within the authority of the Canadian government over all international agreements, Quebec or any other province could make arrangements with foreign countries; but to make independent arrangements for international cultural and other agreements went beyond the bounds of acceptabilitity.[9]

In the event, Canada broke off diplomatic relations with Gabon. But, as Pearson recognized, "we were more angry with France than with Gabon, which would never have attempted this ploy on its own initiative." And the real culprit was the premier of Quebec.

The federal-provincial conference to launch constitutional reform opened in Ottawa on the same day—5 February—as the Gabon conference. The confrontation between the governments of Canada and Quebec provided the backdrop and suggested the stakes. In the days leading up to the conference, a deadlock over the constitution became increasingly likely. In a 23 January interview with Norman DePoe and Ron Collister for CBC's *Newsmagazine*, Trudeau did not conceal his disagreement with Premier Johnson.

I think the accommodation we are looking for is not in the entrenchment of two nations, as it were, one of them to be represented by the Quebec government and the other by the other governments—this is a conception that we completely repudiate. We feel that there are two languages in Canada and that they should be entrenched in the constitution, that they should be considered as the official vehicles of communication. That's all. I don't think this leads to the existence of two nations, and we certainly deny any one government in Canada . . . the right to say it speaks for one nation.[10]

The campaign against *deux nations* accelerated when the Quebec wing of the Liberal Party of Canada met in Montreal on 27–28 January. The important business was a panel on federalism. Trudeau, the star panelist, used the occasion to put forward his vision of federalism and of language rights. He rejected *deux nations* and special status for Quebec—and, remarkably, the delegates gave him a standing ovation. He seemed to have rallied the federal Liberal caucus to his vision, which repudiated the concept of Quebec as an ethnic state.

82

The following week, the provincial Liberal caucus, under Jean Lesage, adopted a totally opposite vision in the form of Paul Gérin-Lajoie's 1967 report, slightly revised, which demanded special status for Quebec's "personality." Political Quebec was now polarized between two visions, one represented by the leaders of the Quebec federal Liberal caucus, the other by almost all of Quebec's provincial politicians.

In the days before the conference, Trudeau kept up his attack on *deux nations* and his defence of expanding French-language rights as the key to solving the conflicts of Quebec within Confederation. He did not seem to be disturbed by Daniel Johnson's threat at the Confederation of Tomorrow Conference that Quebec's independence must come within three or four years unless its demands were met. Asked whether the proposal for a phased series of constitutional amendments would not achieve the redivision of powers too late, Trudeau scoffed.

That kind of ultimatum always makes me smile a little. It took us—how long?—almost one hundred years to give ourselves a ministry of education, almost one hundred years as French Canadians to realize that the state could be a useful lever for the French-Canadian community. Because we have just discovered it, we show the zeal of neophytes and we think that we have discovered Peru and that everyone must do so at the same time as ourselves—even though we have just discovered what everyone knew for the past one hundred years.[11]

He also dismissed the vagueness and instability of Quebec's demands, first under Lesage, now under Johnson. Pearson had tried repeatedly to accommodate Quebec's wishes, Trudeau said, only to discover that the Quebec government did not really know what it wanted and that there was no end to its demands. Constitutional reform was a serious business, and all the governments should have clear and precise objectives. Then they should stick to whatever they declared to be their policy.

He had felt in 1967 that the country was not ripe for constitutional change, and now he repeated that he wasn't certain the country was much readier. He cited Quebec's flip-flop on the Fulton-Favreau formula for amending the constitution.[12] Lesage had endorsed it because it would mean that Quebec's powers could never be changed without Quebec's consent. Like the other premiers, Lesage agreed to put the enabling resolution before his legislature. Two years later, however, he changed his mind. To give each province a veto made Quebec's acquiring new jurisdictions subject to the veto of other provinces. Nationalist opinion swung against the Fulton-Favreau formula as a "straitjacket" and opposed patriation until Quebec could lock in the new powers it demanded. Quebec had come full circle between 1960 and 1966.

The Johnson government seemed no clearer about what it wanted, Trudeau argued.

For a year, or two, or three, the federal government tried to give in to the fancies of the day, but eventually we came to realize that this wasn't serious, that people were not negotiating as adults, that they were negotiating a little like ill-tempered adolescents. We have to grow up. We have to know what we want. In the Johnson government, as previously in the Lesage government, you have ministers who talk of independence, others who swear by federalism, others who stand somewhere between the two according to the mood of the day or the last Gallup poll.[13]

On the morning the conference opened, *La Presse's* lead editorial expressed the portentous expectations as the political leaders gathered to attempt constitutional reform: "How can one think of any subject other than that which brings together today in Ottawa the representatives of the ten provincial governments and the federal government? It is scarcely an exaggeration to call this exceptional conference what some, indeed, have called it: the last-chance conference for Canada."[14]

For Daniel Johnson, the first day of the conference went rather well. The prime minister was smiling and congenial, concealing his anger over the Gabon confrontation. That very day, while Johnson was in Ottawa, his education minister, Jean-Guy Cardinal, was showing the Quebec flag in Libreville. But Pearson was ever the diplomat, retaining the bow-tie, lisp, and self-deprecating charm of the small-town boy who made it on the international scene without losing his roots or taking himself too seriously.

Ontario premier John Robarts, mustachioed, portly, and raspy-voiced, enjoyed playing the role of senior statesman trying to rescue the federation from the folly of the federal government. In his opening statement, he backed Quebec's demand that the full package of reforms, including the revision of powers, should be passed at once rather than sequentially. And he sounded the note of impending calamity that Johnson himself liked to strike: "We are in the midst of a very serious crisis and it would be foolish to have illusions about that. It is a crisis of the utmost gravity for our country because . . . it is a crisis with respect to our national will to survive."[15]

Johnson followed with his own warning that Canada was not only a country with ten provinces, or, as he called it, *"le Canada à dix,"* but also a country with two nations, *"le Canada à deux."* The problem with the present constitution was that it recognized only a Canada made up of ten partners. The objective of the negotiations was to create a Canada that recognized two partners. "It is not at all necessary to destroy le Canada à dix to create le Canada à deux," he reassured the assembled first ministers. "But it has become absolutely essential and urgent to create le Canada à deux if we are to maintain le Canada à dix."[16] And he added an invitation that sounded like an ultimatum: "Let us sit down together and write a new constitution. . . . We must remember that time does not work in favour of the Canada we have today."[17]

Pearson expressed concern about Johnson's Canada of ten partners and two partners, but he passed it off with the quip that he had not studied the "new math." Several premiers voiced alarm at Quebec's proposal to rewrite the constitution. Saskatchewan's Ross Thatcher said that if it was implemented, it would be the end of Canada. Alberta's Ernest Manning and British Columbia's W.A.C. Bennett were against the Canadian Charter of Human Rights, and above all against the entrenchment of language rights. Premier Manning warned of a "constitutional Munich" if the federal government and the other provinces gave in to Quebec's demands. Premier Joey Smallwood, of Newfoundland, wondered whether the Quebec premier, in talking of two nations, was claiming jurisdiction over all French Canadians in Canada, and whether Quebec's representatives in the federal Parliament would be reduced to the role of "dummies if Quebec acquired the powers of a nation-state."

The next morning, Johnson was at his urbane best as he commented on what had been said the day before. He expressed his appreciation to the seven premiers who had accepted French-language rights, and recognized that this was an impressive breakthrough. He had a semi-thorny floral metaphor for Manning and Bennett, who had resisted the consensus: "As to British Columbia and Alberta, let us say we understand that biculturalism is not a flower that grows wild on the slopes of the Rockies. It will take time to develop a strain that can survive the climate of the Rockies on either slope."

While Johnson spoke, Trudeau, seated to the right of Pearson, listened, slightly slouched, an arm carelessly hanging over the back of his chair. He waited.

To counter Manning's warning of a Munich, Johnson said that he agreed that the federal government should have jurisdiction over some areas, such as banking. But he pointed out that the French-Canadian nation could not accept another government's control of French-language radio and television. It could happen, for instance, that all the Quebec members of Parliament were in opposition, with none in the Cabinet. In that case, an entirely English-speaking Cabinet would make decisions on French culture. This was intolerable, and on this there was unanimity of all parties in Quebec.

Trudeau scribbled a few notes on the pad in front of him.

To Smallwood, Johnson gave his assurance that he had no extra-territorial ambition to tax French Canadians in Newfoundland. About the monarchy, which Smallwood had said he wanted retained, Johnson replied that Smallwood should address his concern to Pierre Trudeau and Jean Marchand, since it was the federal Liberal Party in Quebec that had wanted to abolish the monarchy at its meeting preceding the conference.

When Johnson finished speaking, Trudeau leaned forward. He joked that he did not know if he could be permitted to intervene in "a fight between two Irishmen, Mr. Johnson and Mr. Smallwood." It was not a comment calculated to please Johnson, since it subtly cast a doubt over the latter's claim to speak specifically for "the French Canadian nation."

Then, in a series of exchanges with the premier that lasted ninety minutes, Trudeau tore apart Johnson's argument for constitutional revision based on two nations, speaking coolly, in a slightly nasal voice that conveyed a hint of condescension.[18] He disputed Johnson's claim to being the only authorized spokesman for the French-Canadian nation, and thus for all French Canadians. He offered an alternative to the vision of Quebec as an ethnic state: a vision that recognized the equal legitimacy of the federal government to speak for all French Canadians, including those in Quebec.

Johnson dropped his smile. His voice tight, his face deadly serious, he countered, "I am discovering that I will have more trouble with the spokesman for the federal government than with several provinces."

Trudeau struck back: "I wouldn't want us to leave this room and have you say that Ottawa wasn't co-operative, that the other provinces accepted our proposals but the central government rejected them. Your problems, Mr. Johnson, are not with the federal government. They are with federalism." Trudeau attacked Johnson's claim, made so often, that he articulated the fundamental yearnings of the French-Canadian nation, and offered his own, quite opposite, analysis of what those yearnings really were. "What French Canadians want," Trudeau said, "is a guarantee for their linguistic rights. That is the meaning of the equality of two nations in the sociological sense. The equality of the two linguistic communities will be achieved when it will be guaranteed in constitutional documents."

It was an "affront" to French Canadians, he said, to suggest that they needed special powers. If the equality of their language rights were guaranteed, they would have no need of special powers. "After all, they certainly don't want to be equal in all the other provinces and superior in the province of Quebec."

Trudeau then pointed out the impracticality of building a constitution around the concept of two nations in Canada. Once embarked on that line of argument, where did one stop? "If you speak of two nations in Canada, there are also two nations in Quebec. Must we also grant guarantees for the rights of anglophones in Quebec? This kind of constitutional confusion, which has been rampant in Canada for several years, must not be perpetuated."

Johnson, increasingly angry, called the justice minister "the member for Mount Royal" (the discourtesy was calculated, as had been Trudeau's jest about the "fight between two Irishmen"), insinuating that Trudeau did not even represent a French-Canadian riding, so by what right did he presume to say what French-speaking Quebecers wanted? "I am in Ottawa," Johnson pointed out, "not as the member for Mount Royal or a member of a divided Cabinet, but as the premier of Quebec and the leader of a political party that is taking a chance on Canada."

Trudeau replied that he was perhaps only the representative of the voters of Mount Royal, but he challenged Johnson's claim that he spoke for the vision of Canada held by all francophones. And he questioned whether Johnson's proposal was even workable: "The constitutional position of the Quebec government does not offer the clarifications that Canadians, such as Premier Manning of Alberta, have a right to expect. How far will the demands of Quebec go? As far as the destruction of federalism?"

Trudeau launched into a defence of the legitimacy of the members of Parliament elected from Quebec to speak authoritatively on behalf of their constituents in all matters involving federal jurisdiction. Johnson's proposal to restructure Canada as two nations would subvert this authority and turn the Quebec MPs into "dummies," just as Smallwood had suggested.

Trudeau seized on the one example Johnson had offered to argue that Quebec must have more powers: radio and television were too important to be left to exclusive federal regulation. "If that is the example that we are given in support of increased powers, why would you not extend the same logic to banking, tariffs, international law? It is certain that an English-speaking majority that wanted to oppress the French-speaking collectivity could do so with respect to every one of the areas covered by Section 91"—all the federal powers enumerated in the British North America Act.

It was a telling argument. From the beginning, the case for the ethnic state was that many matters were too important to francophones to be left to an alien government. But that argument, Trudeau pointed out, led logically to the dissolution of the federation, since few powers would be considered so unimportant to the francophone collectivity that they could be surrendered to the alien government in Ottawa.

To Johnson's argument that only the Quebec government could be trusted with power over the rights of francophones, Trudeau countered that it was the elected members of Parliament from Quebec who had the responsibility to protect Quebecers within the area of federal jurisdiction. If the Quebec government took over powers in all areas important to Quebecers, no French Canadian of substance would want to go to Ottawa, and the end result would be the separation of Quebec. "We are all politicians and we all know the importance of a power base when pleading a cause or seeking justice. . . . If you believe in federalism, you can't destroy the justification for French Canadians being in Ottawa."

This powerful argument cut to the quick of Daniel Johnson's political career. If Trudeau was right, everything Johnson had stood for over the past several years was destroyed. The Quebec premier launched into an emotional plea: "I appeal to my colleagues, to those who still believe in federalism, I ask them to trust us, not to prejudge our attitudes, not to leave the impression that the Quebec delegation came here to be subjected to trial by question. We came here to discuss between equals."

Trudeau's argument was obviously registering with the other participants, who had ceased their chatting and scribbling to listen intently to the exchange between the two Quebec politicians. They had never before seen a premier of Quebec contradicted in public so directly, almost brutally. And it was a Quebecer who was dismissing his most cherished propositions almost disdainfully, as though they were unworthy of serious consideration.

Johnson fought for his credibility under Trudeau's relentless assault:

It is the whole federal regime that must be renegotiated around a table. That is why we unveiled our basic positions in Toronto and here. People are fooling themselves if they think for a moment that Quebec will be satisfied simply because people can speak French somewhere else. The problem is much deeper. If it is ignored, we are putting Canada in more serious danger than if we face it. It is not enough just to administer aspirin.

Johnson, in his turn, was dismissing as trivial the reform proposed by Trudeau to give French-language rights to French Canadians everywhere in Canada, which would require the premiers to have the conviction and courage to pass laws in their legislatures giving French a special status. Johnson was telling his fellow premiers that such a politically risky reform would have little impact on Quebec.

As his vision came under devastating assault, Johnson resorted to threats:

If the French Canadian nation does not feel at home inside Confederation, we will soon be talking not of the French Canadian nation, but of the *nation Québécoise*. In 1966 we received the mandate to pursue equality. Ottawa has a role to play in that respect. The other provinces also have a role to play, and most of them have started. But the principal role will always be played by Quebec, whether one likes it or not. That is of the very nature of the facts.

Partway through the two-man debate as the exchange got heated, Pearson tried to intervene to bring it to an end. But Trudeau calmly overrode him and kept talking. He said that it was his role in the debate with the Quebec premier to force him to define, as the federal government had done, his conception of the Canadian federal state. And he threatened to confront the premier's views in an appeal to the French-Canadian people to establish who spoke for them. "When our respective positions are clear, we will submit these two positions, if necessary, to the French Canadians themselves."

At last, Pearson broke through the tension by calling for a coffee break. The debate between Johnson and Trudeau was over. But it had been a historic turning point, even if people did not fully realize it at the time. Constitutional discussions about the role of Quebec would never be the same again.

Johnson had the most to lose. His claim to speak for the entire French-Canadian nation had gone unchallenged until then, and when he threatened the end of Canada, the whole country was shaken. But the anger Johnson displayed at the conference was a blunder. By getting nasty, he enhanced the stature of the justice minister. A premier who claims to lead a nation does not squabble publicly with a subordinate minister of another government: that puts them at best on the same plane. As well, his loss of control betrayed a vulnerability: his sweeping claims for himself and for the ethnic state of Quebec were subject to a sudden deflation when publicly challenged.

For Quebec nationalists, 6 February 1968 was not a happy day. Johnson came out of the altercation diminished. He reflected a long tradition that stressed ideological unanimity, in which dissidence was apt to be condemned as heresy or treason. Trudeau spoke for a philsophical liberalism according to which no one can claim exclusive possession of the truth or pretend to speak for everybody. Johnson sought to transform the state to make it embody a single "nation." Trudeau sought to restrain the state to ensure that it protected important rights, including language rights.

By pointing out that Johnson's vision should logically exclude the federal government not just from radio and television, but from every federal power, Trudeau brought out the essential contradiction in his position: it was really incompatible with federalism, which implies a transferring of vital jurisdictions to another level of government even though one's "collectivity" will not be in sole control. Johnson's vision logically led to a confederacy of sovereign states, not to federalism. His *Canada à deux* and *Canada à dix* were, in fact, mutually exclusive. He wanted to taste the cake of sovereignty and still feed in the federal pantry. In other words, he did not want to choose between *égalité* and *indépendance;* he wanted both.

That day, a new star rose over political Canada. For Canadians who had been puzzled by the escalating demands of Quebec governments for the previous seven years, who were angered by the repeated ultimatums and threats of secession, to see Trudeau handle Johnson with self-assurance, to see his reasoned arguments opposed to Johnson's emotional bluster, was to feel a long-awaited sense of relief. Suddenly, Trudeau became a credible candidate to succeed Pearson.

It remained to be seen who spoke more authoritatively for Quebec and for French Canadians. Or could it be that both spoke equally for an ambivalent Quebec?

A collection of Trudeau's writings had been published the year before, and he had written a revealing introduction, which was not apt to endear him to the opinion leaders and power brokers in Quebec. He had gone to Ottawa, he explained, after having long defended provincial autonomy, because he was concerned by the drift of events in Quebec. The province had long been committed to minimal government, leaving full room for the Catholic church. During the 1950s, he pointed out, he had called for a greatly increased role for the state. But, in the 1960s, Quebecers had at last discovered the state, and they immediately plunged into statism at the provincial level. Trudeau had then shifted course. "My political action and my thought, to the extent that I embrace one, can be summarized in two words: build counterweights. And it was because the federal government was weak that I agreed to be catapulted there."[19]

He followed this with a biting commentary on the propensity of French-Canadian intellectuals to build ideological constructions and regularly to save the nation. If he had thought that French Canada was bereft of people to sing its praises, he said, he would have rushed forward to defend collective pride. "But, good God, we've had nothing else but preachers of pride and prophets of a providential mission. We are awash in vast syntheses, we build elaborate superstructures, we go gaga over constitutional or legal reforms for which the chief recommendation is that they are so far removed from reality."[20]

Trudeau went on to demolish the current sacred cow, special status for Quebec. He recognized that almost everyone was for special status, but only because it had as many meanings as there were proponents: "We are terribly lacking in consequence. Rather than concentrate our efforts to change fundamentally our intellectual, social, and economic condition, we get carried away by enthusiasm for a legal superstructure without ever asking ourselves whether it can work."[21]

Then Trudeau came to the nub of the problem for French Canadians. From time immemorial, their chief grievance had arisen from Ottawa's refusal to treat the French and English languages equally and the rejection by other provinces of minority French rights. If Quebecers achieved special status, Trudeau said, they could forget about French in the rest of Canada. "How can you turn Quebec into the national state of French-Canadians, with *really* special powers, without abandoning at the same time the request for French to be treated on the basis of equality with English in Ottawa and in the rest of the country?"[22]

He could have pushed his logic another step. If Quebec really obtained powers that other provinces didn't have, and so their representatives in the federal government could not participate on an equal basis in decisions that affected the other provinces but no longer Quebec, how could there ever be a prime minister elected from Quebec? In fact, how could there ever be a single Cabinet minister from Quebec? The Cabinet deliberates as a whole on all matters for all provinces. Would members of Parliament from Quebec be restricted to voting only on matters that affected uniquely Quebec, or that affected Quebec and all the other provinces equally, while having to abstain on matters the responsibility for which had been taken over by the Quebec government?

Trudeau made his candidacy for the Liberal leadership official on 16 February, just nine days after the close of the constitutional conference. That conference and the role he had played in it meant that his candidacy carried a specific meaning: it embodied a vision of the country.

The candidate who hoped to speak for Quebec caused a flurry of indignation when, in Hamilton, he said that separatists spoke "lousy French." The media portrayed him as saying that the Québécois, not the separatists, spoke "lousy

French." Moreover, the French press translated the slang expression literally, as *un français pouilleux*, "verminous French"—of course, a terrible insult.

Daniel Johnson, who detested Trudeau since the Ottawa confrontation, canvassed his caucus to see how they thought Trudeau would fare in the leadership race. He was told not to worry, Trudeau would be last on the ballot. Johnson put out the word among the Liberals that the premier could live with any Liberal leadership candidate but one: Pierre Trudeau.[23]

When Trudeau actually won the Liberal leadership and became prime minister, in April of 1968, Johnson threw all his support behind Progressive Conservative leader Robert Stanfield for the federal election announced for 25 June. Johnson had not backed Stanfield for the Tory leadership the previous fall, preferring the bilingual Manitoban, Premier Duff Roblin. But now, anything to stop Trudeau.

The ascension of Robert Stanfield to leadership of the Progressive Conservative Party marked a sharp break with that party's traditions: it had historically been viewed as pro-empire, pro-monarchy, pro-British, pro-Protestant. Since Wilfrid Laurier had won the 1896 elections as Liberal leader, the two parties had become differentiated chiefly on the basis of language and religion—with the French and Catholics supporting the Liberals, the Protestants and English-speaking supporting the Tories.

In the year preceding the 1968 federal election, the Conservative Party had gone to great lengths to restore good relations with Quebec. Diefenbaker had alienated Quebecers by filibustering against the adoption of the Maple Leaf flag to replace the Red Enseign, with its prominent Union Jack. When the vote came, seven of the ten Quebec Tory MPs broke ranks with their party and voted for the new flag. Diefenbaker's own "Cartier," Léon Balcer, announced that he was leaving politics because "there is no place for a French Canadian in the party of Mr. Diefenbaker."

In 1967, about to pick a new leader, the Tories were determined to build bridges to Quebec and to its premier, who, though he presided over the Union Nationale, was at heart an old *Bleu*, a Conservative—at least to the extent that he hated Liberals.

The Conservatives held a "thinkers'" policy conference shortly before the leadership convention at Maison Montmorency, near Quebec City. It was chaired by William Davis, then Ontario's minister of education. The debate on the constitution was polarized by Marcel Faribault, a long-time Conservative and president of General Trust of Canada. Faribault convinced the conference that recognition of two nations in Canada had become imperative. He himself, he told the delegates, had previously rejected special status for Quebec, but he could no longer do so: "I have not changed my mind; however the people have changed their minds."[24]

Faribault made a passionate plea, positing that recognition of *deux nations* had become a condition for the continued existence of Canada.

The question of two nations is no longer debatable in the Province of Quebec. Admit that you will put, you must put, at the preamble of a new Constitution, something which will be the recognition that there are in this country two founding peoples. You put that down, we might translate it in French *"deux nations."* You will translate it "two founding races or people" if you want. We cannot say "people" because "people" in our case doesn't mean nation, the same way as nation in English does not mean *nation.*[25]

The conference endorsed a concept that had all the ambiguity that Faribault gave it, all its possibilities for misunderstanding and for demagogy, for advancing an ultra-nationalist policy in French while putting forward an apparently innocuous policy in English. The conference resolved:

That Canada is composed of two founding peoples *(deux nations),* with historic rights who have been joined by people from many lands.

That the constitution should be such as to permit and encourage their full and harmonious growth and development in equality throughout Canada.[26]

In the context of Quebec at that time, and of the well-known positions taken by Daniel Johnson, *deux nations* would certainly be taken to refer to collective rights and different governmental structures for each nation. In practice, that would mean a powerfully reinforced Quebec government.

Eddie Goodman, who, with Tory MP Roger Régimbal, had proposed the policy conference, made his own assessment of it in his memoirs written two decades later. He called it *"almost a resounding success"*; the one "blot" was the controversy generated by *deux nations*.

The conference accepted the concept of *deux nations* not in the sense of two political states, but as a recognition of the country's two founding peoples: an English community and a French community with distinct cultural and linguistic backgrounds. It was an effort to show Quebec that the Progressive Conservative Party was sympathetic to its legitimate aspirations to maintain the existence of Canada's French culture.[27]

This interpretation was either naïve or disingenuous. The party could not adopt the political slogan of the premier of Quebec, and still maintain that it did not mean what he meant by it.

During the leadership campaign, both before and after Montmorency, the candidates tried to stake out a position that would win them support in Quebec without alienating Conservatives in the nine other provinces. This meant, generally, cultivating a degree of ambiguity on the issue of *deux nations*. Some, such as Duff Roblin and Davie Fulton, went farther than others in endorsing the concept.

The position carved out by Nova Scotia premier Robert Stanfield encouraged Quebec nationalists to understand that he was sympathetic to their cause, without his ever explicitly committing himself to *deux nations*. Stanfield's chief strategist, Dalton Camp, was far too wily ever to let Stanfield put his foot in the trap.

On 19 August, *Le Devoir* published an article submitted by Stanfield, in which he said, "The Quebec situation presents certain distinctive aspects. Quebecers feel that, in order to achieve their aims and ambitions, they must be given more authority over economic and social affairs in their province. I don't think any solutions that we will find for the problems of our federation will be able to ignore this feeling in Quebec."[28]

On 31 August, just a week before the leadership convention opened, Stanfield dealt with "special status" in such a way that he seemed to be endorsing the reality, while saying that the words were unfortunate. Special status, he said, seemed to imply special privileges. But he thought that what the people of Quebec really wanted was a "measure of authority in respect to social and economic affairs which will enable them to fulfil themselves as French Canadians."[29] And, understood that way, Stanfield said that special status constituted no threat to the federation.

Claude Ryan, a strong defender of *deux nations*, endorsed Stanfield editorially in *Le Devoir*. This made him acceptable to the Quebec nationalists, for whom Ryan was a guru.

When Stanfield gave his speech to the convention on the night before the leadership vote, he side-stepped the *deux nations* issue by proposing that it be thrashed out at a policy convention to be held by the party at some future date—such as fifteen months later.[30] He thereby acknowledged the seriousness of the demands voiced in Quebec without having to take an immediate stand on them.

In the event, the Montmorency resolution was adopted by the policy committee of the party, but it never came to a vote before the full convention. Diefenbaker threatened to storm out if it was adopted, so a compromise was worked out: it was tabled. When some delegates, including Ottawa's mayor, Charlotte Whitton, tried to debate *deux nations*, the conference chairman, Eddie Goodman, declared the tabled report non-debatable, and he cut off all the floor microphones in the vast hall so that the dissenters could not be heard. However, the resolution did find its way into the party's campaign policy handbook in 1968.

So it was that the Conservatives made a 180-degree turn in their policy toward Quebec in 1967. For the next twenty-six years, they would try unremittingly to win support in Quebec by outflanking the Liberals in an appeal to Quebec nationalism, using the nationalists' own language. It would take seventeen years before the turnaround brought the party the reward it coveted: a majority Tory government.

The Trudeau Liberals and the Stanfield Conservatives offered clear alternatives on the issue of Quebec in the 1968 elections. The Tories from the rest of Canada had formed an alliance with the Quebec nationalists, and Premier Johnson backed them with all the means at his command. He was as anxious as Stanfield to defeat Pierre Trudeau.

Johnson prevailed on Marcel Faribault to give the Tories a reasonably prominent French face by running for them. Faribault accepted, on condition that he be named Stanfield's Quebec lieutenant. After his performance at the Montmorency conference, Faribault had been named by Johnson to the Legislative Council, Quebec's upper House, and taken into the Cabinet as an adviser on economic and constitutional affairs. But Johnson sacrificed him to the cause of defeating Trudeau, and used his own influence to urge other prominent people to run as Conservative candidates.

Johnson instructed the Union Nationale to go all out to back the Conservatives against the Trudeau Liberals. He put a prominent unionist, Jean Bruneau, in charge of the UN machine for the campaign. The UN spent $100,000 just in the riding of Langelier in an attempt to prevent the election of Jean Marchand. Johnson explained to Bruneau, "You don't know Trudeau as I do. If he takes power, it will be terrible for Quebec."[31]

Johnson supervised the Tory campaign in Quebec on a daily basis. He sent emissaries to New Democratic Party leader Robert Cliche, to persuade him to turn all his fire against Trudeau; in return, the Tories did not run a candidate against Cliche. Not since the 1958 election, when Duplessis took up the cause of John Diefenbaker, had a Quebec premier been so involved in a federal election. Partway through the campaign, though, Eddie Goodman, now the Tories' national campaign director, flew to Montreal to ask the Quebec organizers to keep Faribault from travelling outside of Quebec with his message of *deux nations*. "He demanded that Faribault tone down his refrain about *les deux nations* which, everywhere in English Canada, is doing the party considerable harm. 'Trudeau, a francophone, speaks the language of the anglophones while we play up to the separatists,' Goodman complained."[32]

Throughout the campaign, Trudeau put forward his position on the constitution. "The fundamental question of the campaign is our future as a united country," he repeated over and over. His slogan was "One Canada with two official languages," or "One Canada, one nation with two languages, no special privileges to any province, no special status." He always offered French Canadians an alternative to falling back on Quebec. "Our home, *chez nous,* is not just the Province of Quebec. It's the whole of Canada," he said, echoing Wilfrid Laurier.

By the weekend before the election, it was obvious to most observers that Bob Stanfield, "the man with the winning ways," was not going to win on 25 June 1968. Whatever hopes he might have had were given the *coup de grâce* on the night before the vote, when Pierre Trudeau attended the annual parade celebrating Saint-Jean-Baptiste, the patron saint of French Canadians. He had been invited to attend by the parade's organizers, sharing the reviewing stand with Premier

Johnson, Montreal mayor Jean Drapeau, and the Archbishop of Montreal. Goodman had tried to get Trudeau's invitation rescinded, but he did not succeed[33].

The reviewing stand was set up against the façade of the Montreal Public Library, on Sherbrooke Street East. Across the street was the observers' stand for journalists and television cameras; behind it loomed the darkness of Lafontaine Park, where about a thousand noisy demonstrators had gathered, intent on showing their disapproval of Trudeau and of federalism. *"Le Québec aux Québécois!"* they shouted. They tossed leaflets playing on Trudeau's comment about speaking "lousy French": *"Pouilleux, débarrassez-vous de vos poux!"* Verminous people, get rid of your lice. And they shouted a refrain: *"Trudeau au poteau!"* Trudeau to the gallows. One youth tossed a rusty piece of pipe into the street and was immediately arrested by Mounties in plain clothes. Martin Luther King had been assassinated in April, just before Trudeau had been chosen Liberal leader, and Robert Kennedy had been assassinated since the start of the Canadian election campaign. So the separatists' threats against Trudeau were taken very seriously. The day before the parade, on 23 June, the weekly *Dimanche Dernière-Heure* had reported that an attempt would be made on Trudeau's life if he attended.

Pop bottles were thrown onto the street from the crowd at the edge of Lafontaine Park. The police began to beat up demonstrators. When the dignitaries, including Trudeau, appeared on the stand, the hail of bottles and the police repression intensified. Demonstrators were about fifty feet away from the reviewing stand. The riot squad, in full gear, took up position on the street.

The area in front of the VIP platform and the prime minister became a relief zone where wounded were patched up before being loaded into ambulances or paddy-wagons. The situation was now a full-scale riot. Police ambulances, flashers twirling and sirens moaning, pitched and backed and roared away down the street with fresh loads of wounded policemen. Wounded demonstrators got a quick field dressing, if they were lucky, and were pushed roughly into the wagons. More often they were just allowed to bleed.[34]

After the dignitaries had been in place for about an hour, a group of demonstrators broke through the police lines onto the street, and one threw a Coke bottle that arched six feet over Trudeau's head and smashed against the façade of the library. The dignitaries scrambled back toward the exit. Trudeau was bodily covered momentarily by his RCMP guard. As the stand was deserted except for Trudeau and two Mounties, the prime minister stood up, brushed away the raincoat offered him by one Mountie, sat down with his arms on the railing of the reviewing stand, and, smiling and shielding his eyes against the lights, continued to watch the parade. Drapeau, now without his wife, and Johnson eventually returned to their seats. Across the street, the journalists in the reviewing stand, carried away by the prime minister's display of bravado, stood up and cheered and clapped. Trudeau waved back.

A second bottle smashed on the street just below the reviewing stand, and the police attacked the demonstrators in a frenzy. Eventually, the parade ended and everyone left.

Whatever the appropriateness of the police action that night, what came across on television was Trudeau's bravery. When everyone else ran, he shrugged off his guards and remained. The scenario was the worst possible for Johnson and for Stanfield's Conservatives. It laid bare the political passions that were loose in Quebec and that could lead it, and possibly the whole country, to violence. Trudeau seemed to be the man equipped to face down that turmoil, even physically. The tentative and mild-mannered Stanfield seemed weak by comparison.

The confrontation also pitted Trudeau against the radicals of the RIN rather than against Johnson or the proponents of special status. It was ironic that Trudeau's bitterest enemies gave him his biggest boost of the entire campaign. He himself could not have written a more favourable end to his campaign against Stanfield and against *deux nations*.

The next day, Trudeau's Liberals carried fifty-six of Quebec's seventy-four seats, with 53.6 per cent of the popular vote. Stanfield's Conservatives, so heavily backed by the UN, received only 21.4 per cent of the vote and won only four seats. Réal Caouette's Ralliement des Créditistes took fourteen seats—ten more than Stanfield—but with only 16.4 per cent of the vote. The NDP, with 7.5 per cent, won no seats at all.

Trudeau was triumphantly vindicated, and the election results proved to be a turning-point in Quebec's history, at least for almost a quarter of a century. Until that night, it had been conventional wisdom that nothing less than special status—if that—could satisfy the wishes of Quebecers. Trudeau proved that conventional wisdom was really mythology. He demonstrated that, when a prominent Quebecer defended classical federalism as being in the interests of the Quebec people themselves, the people of Quebec believed and supported him. The decisive element was trust. As long as it was there, Quebecers could tolerate simultaneously radically divergent constitutional options among their leaders in Quebec and Ottawa. The constitutional option itself was not the critical factor—no option, in fact, had yet won the exclusive commitment of Quebecers—but strong leadership to defend the federalist option was critical.

After the election, Daniel Johnson went into a funk. He knew that the dramatic game he had played for two years was over. He had been cut down to size, and there was no prospect of his recovering his earlier stature. Just as de Gaulle had been brought down from his Olympian heights by the massive opposition in the streets of Paris that May, so Johnson now retained only the shadow of his former image. And, three months later, he was dead. Trudeau reigned as Quebec's most prestigious son.

Notes

1.Pierre Elliott Trudeau, Minister of Justice, *A Canadian Charter of Human Rights* (Ottawa: Queen's Printer, 1968).
2.*La Presse,* 2 Feb. 1968, p. 1.
3.Ibid.
4.Trudeau, *Canadian Charter,* p. 27
5. Claude Ryan, "Les défis de la conférence d'Ottawa," *Le Devoir,* 3 Feb. 1968.
6.Martin Sullivan, *Mandate '68* (Toronto: Doubleday Canada, 1968), p. 105. The course of Canadian history would have been very different had Pearson taken Lesage's advice.
7.Pierre Elliott Trudeau, *La Grève de l'amiante* (Montreal: Cité libre, 1956).
8.John A. Munro and Alex I. Inglis, eds., *Mike. The Memoirs of the Right Honourable Lester B. Pearson,* vol. 3, *1957–1968* (Toronto: University of Toronto Press, 1975), p. 259.
9.Ibid., p. 263.
10.Sullivan, *Mandate '68,* p. 293.
11.Quoted in Pierre Olivier, *La Presse,* 3 Feb. 1968.
12.It was Lesage who had demanded in the 1960 Quebec Liberal platform that the constitution be patriated. This required finding a formula for future amendments after Canada had assumed responsibility for its constitution. Both Diefenbaker and Pearson had tried to accede to Quebec's wish. Finally, at the 1964 Charlottetown conference, the prime minister and the premiers agreed on patriation of the constitution and on an amending formula. In matters dealing with the central institutions of the federation and with the distribution of powers between the federal and provincial governments, an amendment would require the consent of all the governments. The formula was named after Diefenbaker's justice minister, E. Davie Fulton, and Pearson's justice minister, Guy Favreau, both of whom had worked on it.
13.*La Presse,* 2 Feb. 1968.
14.Cyrille Felteau, "Un espoir se lève," *La Presse,* 5 Feb. 1968.
15. Robarts's statement was reprinted in *Le Devoir* on 6 Feb. 1968.
16.Quoted in Paul Gros d'Aillon, *Daniel Johnson. L'égalité avant l'indépendance* (Montreal: Stanké, 1979), p. 202. A significant point about *Canada à dix* and *Canada à deux* is that neither included the federal government, which governed the country as one whole.
17.Ibid., p. 203.
18.The account of the conference, including the Trudeau-Johnson clash, is based on newspaper reports at the time, as well as the author's own memory from watching the conference on television.
19.Pierre Elliott Trudeau, *Le fédéralisme et la société canadienne-française* (Montreal: Éditions HMH, 1967), p. ix.
20.Ibid.
21.Ibid., p. x.
22.Ibid., p. xi.
23.Related by Pierre Godin in *Daniel Johnson: 1964-1968 la difficile recherche de l'égalité* (Montreal: Éditions de l'Homme, 1980), p. 327.
24.Sullivan, *Mandate '68,* p. 171.
25.Ibid.
26.Quoted in ibid., p. 169.
27.Edwin A. Goodman, *Life of the Party: The Memoirs of Eddie Goodman* (Toronto: Key Porter, 1988), p. 136.
28.Quoted in Sullivan, *Mandate,* p. 177.
29.Quoted in ibid., p. 181.
30.Ibid.

31.Ibid., p. 201.
32.Godin, *Daniel Johnson*, pp. 341-3. This anecdote about Goodman was related to Pierre Godin by journalist Guy Larmarche, who, at the request of Daniel Johnson, had taken on the position of director of communications for the Tories' Quebec campaign. Godin, *Daniel Johnson*, p. 344.
33.Sullivan, *Mandate '68*, p. 2. I follow Sullivan's account of the events of *la Saint-Jean-Baptiste*. A reporter for *Time* magazine, he spent twelve years in Montreal and covered Trudeau that night as a reporter. His account is a careful reconstruction of what happened.
34.Ibid., p. 10.

CHAPTER FIVE

Portrait of Robert Bourassa as a Young Premier

When Robert Bourassa became leader of the Quebec Liberal Party, in 1970, few would have predicted that, except for Maurice Duplessis, he would prove Quebec's most successful provincial politician in the twentieth century. At a time of ideological turbulence, he managed to lead his party in five provincial elections, four of which he won. Defeated just once, in 1976, his career then seemed finished. He was called by George Springate, a member of his own caucus, "the most hated man in Quebec." And yet this chameleon carried off the near-impossible: he recaptured the leadership of his party and, in 1985, was again premier, to remain so for the next eight years.

Bourassa's personality, style, ideology, tactical manoeuvres, and strategic position as the leader of a Quebec party apparently committed to federalism enabled him to play a crucial role in shaping the evolution of Quebec from 1970 to the end of 1993. Part of his strength as a provincial politician was the fact that he was largely misunderstood: people thought of him as a committed federalist or, at worst, as indifferent to ideology and interested only in power. In fact, beyond his guise of a bloodless technocrat, Bourassa always held a vision of Quebec and of Canada that was close to René Lévesque's. With varying commitment, he held to that vision and tried to implement it throughout the twenty-seven years of his political career.

Unlike Lévesque, however, Bourassa pressed toward his goal gradually, pliantly, rather than in one grand leap, and was given to discreet words spoken in someone's ear rather than to memorable speeches. Most of the time, he kept people uncertain about his true intentions, and he convinced those embracing quite opposite ideologies that really, deep down, he was on their side. By temporizing and dissembling, he was able to hold united a party that was a coalition of nationalists and anti-nationalists, and to move it steadily in the direction of his own vision: that of an ethnic state of Quebec in which the apparatus of government was designed to serve the French-speaking population, within a Canadian common market governed by an elected body with taxation powers.

99

Claude Morin, who served as Bourassa's deputy minister, pinpointed his characteristic *modus operandi*. "One of his constant practices was to position himself halfway between orthodox federalists and autonomists tempted by sovereignty."[1] As long as Trudeau remained in a position to counter his nationalism, Bourassa's search for the middle kept him—and Quebec—from major incidents. The situation changed after Brian Mulroney came to power and espoused the nationalists' interpretation of recent Canadian history; then, Bourassa lurched toward a more nationalistic posture.

When Bourassa first won a seat in the 1966 provincial election, before his thirty-third birthday, the Liberal Party was uncertain of its ideological direction after its defeat by the Union Nationale; its thrust for special status had been overtaken by Johnson's *égalité ou indépendance*. Would it continue to up the nationalist ante? Or would it rediscover virtues in Canadian federalism? Weakened by the departure of René Lévesque and his more nationalist followers, the party commissioned a public-opinion poll to discover what Quebecers wanted in a leader. The answer came back: someone who would attend to the economy rather than the constitution, someone who would use his leadership to put bread and butter on every table, rather than pursuing greatness in foreign adventures.

Of all the candidates at the Liberal leadership convention of January, 1970, Robert Bourassa best fit the profile. Though he had never served in the Cabinet, was only thirty-six, and had not yet become a familiar presence across the province, he had solid academic credentials, especially in the areas that counted. He held a law degree from the Université de Montréal, a degree in economics from Oxford University, and had studied public finances at Harvard. Bourassa seemed like the kind of safe and solid technocratic manager that Quebec wanted after the radical changes of recent years.

Once chosen leader, Bourassa waged the 1970 election campaign according to the scenario indicated by the poll. His message centred on a promise to create one hundred thousand jobs in Quebec within a year. He drove home the message of jobs, jobs, jobs, so insistently that he acquired the nickname "Bob la job."

René Lévesque, meanwhile, ran his first campaign as leader of the Parti Québécois. His approach was not unlike that of the 1962 Liberal campaign: he appealed to nationalism by once again proposing *la libération,* though now *libération* was to be political as well as economic. The campaign ignited immense nationalist hopes and passions. At the PQ's mass meetings, people waved blue-and-white Quebec flags, and thousands shouted rhythmically *OUI! OUI! OUI!* or *le Québec aux Québécois*. In that atmosphere, miracles seemed possible, and a great many believed that independence was at hand.

The PQ's campaign turned not on which party would form the government, but on the birth of a nation, the accession to sovereignty, the achievement of freedom, the end to impotence and humiliation within the encumbering coils of Canada. This powerful message was projected for the first time by a credible leader who was also a master of television. The huge crowds he drew conveyed the sense that an entire people was on the march.

Bourassa went on his stolid way, speaking to much smaller and calmer crowds. He was not a spell-binder, and his message of "One hundred thousand jobs" hardly matched the passion of Lévesque's message of sovereignty. Tall, thin, and angular, his head perched at the end of a long neck that protruded from sagging shoulders, he had the air of a librarian bemused to find himself unexpectedly addressing a crowd. Heavy black-rimmed glasses accentuated his myopic look. His nose, like his neck, was long and uncertain of its direction. His voice was strong but colourless. He spoke to the fears for the future of vulnerable wage earners—in contrast to Lévesque, whose discourse of hope projected a vision of collective emancipation.

Bourassa warned that Quebec would suffer economic catastrophe if the PQ was elected: the United States would impose a blockade against the importation of Bombardier snowmobiles, and thousands of jobs would be lost. Pierre Laporte distributed the "Lévesque buck," a mock dollar bill with René Lévesque's head where the Queen's should be. One third of the bill was missing, to suggest that the dollar in an independent Quebec would lose a third of its value.

Meanwhile, Réal Caouette, leader of the federal Social Credit Party and a powerful populist orator from way back, stumped the province for the Ralliement des Créditistes, thundering, "Do you want revolution within a year? If not, don't vote for the PQ. Don't vote for socialism, communism, revolution, for blood running in the streets of Quebec."[2]

Private interests also took up the campaign against the PQ. A couple of days before the election, Royal Trust sent a caravan of Brinks armoured trucks to Ontario, supposedly carrying to safety the securities of their customers. The press was notified in advance of this photo opportunity.

When the results were in, on the night of 29 April 1970, the Union Nationale was defeated and the Liberals formed the government. Bourassa, at thirty-six, was the youngest premier in the history of Quebec. For many Quebecers, however, Bourassa's victory was illegitimate, his tenure tainted. The PQ had come second in the popular vote, with 23.1 per cent, compared to 45.4 per cent for the Liberals, 19.7 per cent for the UN, and less than 12 per cent for the Créditistes. But the Liberals captured seventy-two seats, the UN seventeen, the Créditistes twelve. Despite its splendid performance, the PQ got only seven seats. This was taken as a spectacular demonstration that the system was corrupt—that democracy, as it was practised in Quebec, was a fraud.

Bourassa emerged from the 1970 campaign with a reputation as an anti-separatist. However, his defence of federalism was based on opportunism and tactical considerations, rather than on conviction. Just as Henri de Navarre, a Huguenot, had converted to Catholicism to become King of France ("Paris is worth attending a mass for"), so Bourassa set aside his nationalism to become leader of the

101

Liberals and premier. Pierre Trudeau's decisive victory in the 1968 elections signalled a swing away from the nationalist momentum of the Quiet Revolution. Bourassa, always flexible, adjusted himself accordingly. In fact, Bourassa had already declared his nationalist convictions before it became politically dangerous to do so, in *Maintenant,* an intellectual journal published by the Dominican fathers in Montreal, which, in 1967, declared itself for the sovereignty of Quebec. In the September issue, Bourassa, then a Liberal member of the Legislature elected just the year before but already chair of the party's policy committee, wrote an article with a significant title, "Instruments de libération": "Since our collectivity lacks a solid structure of initiative, tradition, management, and economic power, it must use the state as the only lever capable of providing it with the means of taking its activity and its progress in hand."[3] This was the very definition of the ethnic state. Bourassa was clearly not referring to all inhabitants of Quebec, but only to those who were French-speaking. And, like Lévesque, he was led logically to demand that the ethnic state be reinforced to do the job. Co-operation and co-ordination of policies between the Quebec government and the federal government were not enough:

We are likely to be disappointed if we fool ourselves into thinking that we can dialogue with the representatives of the federal government and big business to compare our forecasts, co-ordinate our efforts, and make decisions in accordance with our comprehensive planning—*until such time as we have succeeded in repatriating to Quebec more economic powers and the principal centres of decision making.*[4]

Also in 1967, Bourassa put forward a constitutional proposal, "sovereign associate states," as the formula for the future relations between Quebec and Canada. In his *Option-Québec* manifesto, Lévesque credited Bourassa for suggesting the right wording for what he himself was now proposing: "To describe it, the formula that is most striking and accurate came from the pen of the member for Mercier, Mr. Robert Bourassa, in a speech he gave to the Kiwanis Club of Montreal, 'États souverains associés.'"[5]

Lévesque had hoped to the last that Bourassa would join him in his radical course, since the two had such similar ideas for the future of Quebec and had worked together on Lévesque's manifesto. However, Bourassa found a technical reason to dissociate himself from Lévesque, which he articulated in a speech in late September, 1967.[6] The first notable feature of the speech is that nowhere did he repudiate sovereignty, with or without association, even though that was the issue to be decided at the Quebec Liberal convention barely two weeks later. Bourassa's argument was about something else entirely: he claimed that setting up Quebec's own currency would entail major transitional costs, including a flight of capital, the devaluation of the Quebec currency, higher interest rates to stabilize investment, and higher repayment costs on international debts. It was an argument for retaining the Canadian dollar, not an argument for federalism or against sovereignty. Moreover, he talked only of the costs of transition; he did not suggest that these penalties would continue after the transition. So, as a public break with Lévesque, the impact of the speech was political, rather than substantive.

At the time, Bourassa was so close to Lévesque ideologically, and so hesitant and qualified in his rejection of Lévesque's proposal, that *La Presse* speculated on what his future political course might be:

Mr. Bourassa, who, last week, finally came out in favour of the option put forward by the constitutional committee of the party [as opposed to Lévesque's option] following pressure exerted on him by Mr. Kierans, did so with so many nuances and restrictions of all kinds that he will certainly encounter hostility within the Liberal caucus. And so it is quite possible that he, too, will be faced with a crisis of conscience that will lead him to leave the party.[7]

Lévesque, abandoned by Bourassa, then abandoned the *formule lapidaire* that Bourassa had suggested and named his new group Mouvement Souveraineté-Association. His patented proposal would be called "sovereignty-association," not the more cumbersome "associated sovereign states," but the difference would be semantic rather than substantive.

Thus, Bourassa, in 1967, was clearly a nationalist in the mould of the Quiet Revolutionaries. He also favoured an ethnic state for Quebec—an almost completely sovereign state of and for French-speaking Quebecers. Was this merely a passing fancy of his youth? Quite the contrary. At different times in his career, Bourassa has exposed his vision of the country, which has remained remarkably faithful to the "sovereign associated states" formula with which he began his political career.

In January, 1975, Premier Bourassa visited France for the second time. For the occasion, the French publication *Le Monde Diplomatique* ran a special supplement devoted to the politics and economy of Quebec. Bourassa contributed a guest column, a lengthy article titled "*Un État français au sein du marché commun canadien.*" That was a good summary of what the article went on to say. "Quebec has set itself the ambition of being and of remaining a French state within the Canadian common market," Bourassa wrote.[8] "France and Quebec are the two most important countries which are French by language and culture. . . . They are also two developed countries, highly urbanized and industrialized."[9] When he spoke of Canada, Bourassa never used the word "country," or even the word "federation." He suggested, rather, that Canada was a convenient economic arrangement: "The Québécois want to continue to live to the full the Canadian experience. It brings them undeniable economic and social advantages from which they could not cut themselves off without inflicting on themselves irreparable economic and social wounds which would seriously compromise the development of the whole Quebec collectivity."[10]

Bourassa's Canada, then, is an "experience" rather than a country. It is a "common market" rather than a federation. Without Canada, Quebec's development would be seriously set back. Cold words of endorsement from the premier who was the only "federalist" alternative to the overtly separatist Parti Québécois. There was only one word in the article that signalled a difference with the PQ: Bourassa spoke once of Canadians as *concitoyens,* "fellow citizens."

The premier's sentiments did not sit well with Prime Minister Trudeau. On 21 January 1975, Trudeau delivered a blast that was reminiscent of his attacks against special status and *deux nations.* He was speaking at a fund-raising dinner in Montreal, with most of his Cabinet ministers and Quebec caucus members sitting behind him on the stage.[11]

"Nowadays, we hear words in Quebec," Trudeau began. "Formerly, it was special status, and so forth, but fortunately that's been buried. But now we hear talk of the Canadian common market, a French state in the Canadian common market." Every country is a common market in the sense that it has no internal customs duties, he went on, "but let us take care, dear fellow Liberals, not to get caught in a word trap. Canada is more than a common market, because if it were merely a common market there would never have been that redistribution of $1.3 billion from the rest of the country to Quebec." He was referring to the oil subsidy that had cushioned the price of oil in Quebec since September, 1973, when international oil prices shot up as a result of a concerted action by the Organization of Petroleum Exporting Countries. Quebec received $650 million a year from Western oil revenues to subsidize its purchases of imported oil, he said, and another $650 million, net, in equalization payments from the richer provinces. The oil subsidy sustained the provinces east of the Ottawa Valley and enabled Canadians to pay one price for oil across the country. That was possible only in a strong country, not in a common market:

When we build, as we are doing, a pipeline from Sarnia to Montreal so that Montreal can have a secure supply of Western oil rather than being at the mercy of the Arab countries, there is no common market that would guarantee that. Canada is a country of fraternity where we want to share with each other. It is a country of mutual help. It is a country where we have no artificial frontiers. That is the country that we want to build.

He repeatedly used the French word *pays,* country, in referring to Canada, just as Bourassa had used the word *pays* to designate Quebec: "Would it make any sense for us to abandon our political unity to turn back to a common market, while awaiting the break-up of the country? It is not in that direction that we're going to govern the country in the coming years, and I know that it is not in that direction, either, that you want us to march."

Did Bourassa really mean what he had written? Did he really think of Canada as essentially just a common market? Was Quebec alone the country of Quebecers? Bourassa gave another strong indication of his vision in 1979, three years

104

after he had been driven from office, and while he was teaching at Université Laval. Not long before Quebec's 1980 referendum, Bourassa was interviewed by a student who asked for his constitutional view. Bourassa replied by saying what question he thought should be asked of the people of Quebec in a referendum: "Do you want to replace the existing constitutional order by two sovereign states associated in an economic union, which union would be responsible to a parliament elected by universal suffrage?" He added, "So you have a normal sovereignty which you negotiate, and you keep the federal bond for economic questions, rather like the Common Market in ten years."[12]

In 1967, Bourassa had spoken of "sovereign associated states." In 1979, he proposed "sovereign states associated in an economic union." There was not a shade of difference between the two visions, one formulated when he was a young backbencher, the other after he had been premier of Quebec for six years.

In fact, in either case, there was not very much difference between Bourassa's vision and René Lévesque's. Bourassa said as much in a 1977 interview. He expressed his regret that Lévesque had left the Liberals, because "there was not that much difference between what the Liberal Party could do within the federal regime and what [Lévesque] himself wanted to do."[13] And he stated,

One of the objectives of my government was cultural sovereignty within economic federalism. That retained part of the thesis of the Mouvement Souveraineté-Association. How can you apply cultural sovereignty in the areas of immigration and communications without having decision-making power in these areas? But, at the same time, I always maintained that an economic federalism was needed in Canada. For the Québécois, that is very advantageous.[14]

Bourassa was a federalist only after a fashion. And this was the leader of the Liberal Party and the premier of Quebec for some fifteen years while organized separatism challenged Canada's federation.

Notes

1. Claude Morin, *Mes Premiers Ministres* (Montreal: Boréal, 1991), p. 422.

2. Carole de Vault, with William Johnson, *The Informer. Confessions of an Ex-Terrorist* (Toronto: Fleet Books, 1982), p. 77.

3. Quoted in Don Murray and Vera Murray, *De Bourassa à Lévesque* (Montreal: Quinze, 1978), p. 38.

4. Ibid., p. 39. Emphasis added.

5. René Lévesque, *Option Québec* (Montreal: Éditions de l'Homme, 1968), p. 45.

6. Robert Bourassa, "Il faudrait rester associé au système monétaire canadien," speech given 27 Sept. 1967 to the Club St-Laurent-Kiwanis. Published in *Le Devoir*, 3, 4, and 5 Oct. 1967.

7. *La Presse*, 15 Oct. 1967, quoted in Don Murray and Vera Murray, *De Bourassa*, p. 57.

8. Robert Bourassa, "Un État français au sein du marché commun canadien," *Le Monde Diplomatique*, Jan. 1975, p. 24.

9. Ibid., p. 23.

10. Ibid., p. 24.

11. Trudeau's speeches during the time he was prime minister are contained on microfilm at the library of the Parliament of Canada.

12. The account of the interview was published for the first time in the Sept. 1990 issue of L'Actualité.

13. Raymond Saint-Pierre, Les années Bourassa (Montreal: Héritage, 1977), p. 52.

14. Quoted in Ibid., p. 51.

CHAPTER SIX

Bourassa and Trudeau: Two Visions in Conflict at Victoria

Pierre Trudeau and Robert Bourassa had very different political visions, and from Bourassa's election as premier in 1970 until his defeat in 1976, each tried unsuccessfully to impose his vision on the other. The result was a constitutional stalemate.

Trudeau had promised to make French Canadians at home everywhere in Canada through recognition of their language rights in the federal government and in the provinces. What he could do in Ottawa he did, with the passage of the Official Languages Act in 1969, by giving vast sums of money to the provinces to encourage the teaching of French as a first or second language, and by providing grants to francophone social and cultural groups outside Quebec.

The Official Languages Act gave English and French formal equality of status within the federal government. The ponderous machinery of the public service began to adjust so that francophones could, as much as possible, work in French. That meant that their supervisors had to be able to communicate in French as well as English, at least in the capital and in regions with a substantial French-speaking population. Senior civil servants went back to school to learn French, sometimes for months at a time. The process was slow and expensive, the objective far from achieved. But the signal was sent out across Canada, and French became increasingly recognized as important for those with the ambition to act on the national scene. Immersion French classes for English-speaking children began its phenomenal growth, making Canada a pioneer in the effective teaching of a second language through the public schools.

Though some provinces responded, notably New Brunswick and Ontario, many did not, particularly the four Western provinces. A general and permanent change required vesting language rights in the constitution, and this Trudeau promised in 1968. He set about holding a series of constitutional conferences with the premiers, but he encountered much resistance, especially from the premiers of Quebec.

Three different people in as many years represented Quebec in the negotiations. Daniel Johnson, who began it all, died in September, 1968. His successor, Jean-Jacques Bertrand, though much less nationalistic, also espoused his predecessor's *deux nations* policy, which made him look to a Quebec-based solution rather than a Canadian solution for the malaise in Quebec. At a federal-provincial conference in February, 1969, Bertrand had voiced the familiar vision: "If there is a crisis in Canada, it is not because our country is made up of individuals who speak different languages; it is because Canada is the home of two communities, two peoples, two nations."[1]

Bourassa was reluctant to take a clear position. On the one hand, he was insistent that "on the cultural level, it is absolutely obvious that Quebec is not a province like the others. We will have to reach an agreement that deals with cultural matters and social matters."[2] And he added what sounded like a threat: "There must be additional powers granted to Quebec. If they don't understand this legitimate concern of the Québécois, there will be a brutal awakening."

But, at the same time, Bourassa proved accommodating to the extent that federalism was profitable to Quebec:

> But I must admit that we are ready to show considerable flexibility because it pays financially. Even if we became an independent country, there would have to be a common policy. There are several powers that it is to our advantage to leave to the federal government because it is profitable. In fact, federalism is a technique of administration that can make it possible for us to garner important sums of money.

The negotiations came to a head when Trudeau and the ten premiers met in Victoria for a constitutional conference on 14–16 June 1971. On the agenda were the final details of the package that was to be the culmination of the process begun on 5 February 1968, when Trudeau and Daniel Johnson had confronted each other, following which there had been a total of seven formal first ministers' conferences, along with a countless number of meetings of officials and individual ministers. Now, three years into his mandate, it was time for Trudeau to deliver on his promises of 1968.

At Victoria, the first ministers agreed on a formula for amending the constitution once it became a Canadian rather than a British law, breaking the deadlock that had prevented patriation at constitutional conferences in 1927, 1935, 1950, 1960, 1961, and 1964. The formula provided that the assent of each of the four regions of the country—Ontario, Quebec, the Atlantic provinces, and the Western provinces—would be required for constitutional change. They agreed on fundamental rights, and on entrenching the Supreme Court of Canada, including Quebec's three justices. They even agreed on some important language rights, with seven provinces agreeing to make English and French the languages of their legislatures. Only the three westernmost provinces did not consent to make their legislatures bilingual.

But they did not agree on the all-important right to schooling in English or French. Bourassa was opposed, saying that the question of language rights was still under study in Quebec. Without Bourassa's support for French-language education in the other provinces, Trudeau could not get the premiers to agree to entrench these rights. After all, the purpose of the exercise was to satisfy Quebec; if Quebec's premier did not want French schools protected in the constitution, why should the premiers of the English-speaking provinces commit themselves to a politically hazardous reform?

At Victoria, Bourassa's and Trudeau's different visions were both on display. On the opening day, 14 June, Bourassa put forward Quebec's position: Quebec was different because of its French-speaking majority, and so its needs were different from those of other provinces. "In addition to sharing the problems common to any modern government—problems of economic growth and of social progress—the Quebec government has as an additional responsibility to ensure the security and the blossoming of a culture that is different and is that of a small minority on the North American continent."[3]

Bourassa defined Quebec as the "principal base for the expression of French culture" in Canada. This, he proposed, meant that the Quebec government must take responsibility for all aspects of the lives of Quebecers: "To the extent that the new constitution of Canada might affect its future and therefore its identity, Quebec is determined that there should be recognized clearly the right and the means to translate into reality the responsibility that it has toward the culture of the immense majority of its population."

Bourassa's words expressed his essentially confederal vision. Quebec spoke at the conference as an essentially sovereign state with a single spokesman: himself. And the Quebec government had to take responsibility for almost all important spheres of the lives of Quebecers: "The cultural fact cannot be reduced to its linguistic dimension alone. It extends to human activities as a whole: to work, leisure, family, and to political, economic, and social institutions." Thus, "the government of Quebec has always had a double objective with respect to constitutional reform: decentralized federalism, and the promotion of the distinct personality of Quebec." In particular, as a down payment on more comprehensive powers to be obtained later, Bourassa demanded that Quebec have primary jurisdiction over the entire field of social policy.

Trudeau tried to point out that the proposal put forward by Quebec would ultimately mean an end to federal transfers of money for such programs as unemployment insurance and the Canada Assistance Plan. If provinces could simply demand the money and set up their own programs, all of the provinces would likely do so, or certainly the richest provinces would. The federal government would then have little reason for introducing programs that had the effect of redistributing money to the poorer regions and people of the country, and its function of income redistribution would gradually be reduced to insignificance.

The constitutional change proposed [by Quebec] would bring about over the years an erosion of federal programs of income security, programs which would be replaced by purely provincial programs. In that case, old people and the poor in the richer provinces might not lose out, but in the other provinces, including Quebec, the tax base would not make possible income-security payments that were as advantageous as those that are voted by the federal Parliament.[4]

On this incompatibility of vision, the Victoria Charter foundered. Bourassa hesitated, but eventually he rejected it. In 1977, he explained why he had not accepted patriation in 1971: "I think that, once the constitution was patriated, as soon as the federal government had achieved its objective . . . in the normal course of events Ottawa would have had no interest in getting rid of powers that it already held."[5] It had been a telling choice. He knew that separatism was gaining strength in Quebec and that the unresolved conflict between Quebec and Ottawa over the constitution exacerbated the situation. He could have accepted patriation at Victoria and then lobbied afterward for redistribution of powers, a point on which several other premiers agreed with him. But he preferred to put the federation at risk rather than jeopardize his dream of Quebec as an ethnic state, with all the powers deemed necessary for it to act as the defender of francophones.

Bourassa also pointed out that if he had signed the constitutional package at Victoria, it would have made it more difficult in future for Quebec to separate.

It would have meant that Quebec put its signature to a situation that could have lasted a long time. That even applies to the separation of Quebec. Let's suppose as a hypothesis that a referendum is held, since there is a lot of talk of that now [in 1977]. And let's suppose that the result is positive. The government could accept it, in theory, and ask the British government to adopt a bill in accordance with the referendum. But if we had patriated the constitution with its amending formula, it would be necessary to get—since it would involve a radical change to the constitution—the assent of several provinces. If one of the provinces, according to the amending formula, opposed accepting the referendum, it could mean that the federal government would be constitutionally obliged to take every means to have the integrity of the territory respected.[6]

And so Pierre Trudeau's attempt to correct the fundamental flaw of the 1867 British North America Act—lack of protection of French-language rights in the provinces—ended in failure. Constitutional negotiations were deadlocked. Quebec's most highly placed politician, the prime minister, and its premier had incompatible visions of where its future lay. There was no obvious way to resolve the stalemete.

This took place just a few months after the FLQ's kidnapping of James Cross and Pierre Laporte had provoked the October Crisis, with the intervention of the Canadian army, the War Measures Act, the assassination of Laporte, and the detention of nearly five hundred people. In the aftermath of the crisis, a sense of depondency settled over Quebec which I tried to describe in an article that appeared on the first anniversary of the kidnapping of James Cross. I offer it here, slightly abridged, because I think it caught the mood of the times.

Euphoria plus FLQ equals disenchantment.

Political, industrial apathy grows in Quebec

MONTREAL—The leaves are changing color on Mount Royal amid the mansions on Redpath Crescent where British Trade Commissioner James Cross once lived, and on the west slope in Côte-des-Neiges Cemetery where Pierre Laporte is buried.

Little but memories remain of one of the great upheavals in Canadian history, begun a year ago today when Mr. Cross was taken at gunpoint from his home by the Front de Libération du Québec.

Children toss fallen chestnuts in front of the house of their former neighbor, oblivious to the armed men in unmarked cars sitting parked here and there along the street.

The house in North Montreal where Mr. Cross was held captive for 60 days has been occupied by an Italian family since May 1, normal moving day in Montreal.

In St. Hubert, southeast of Montreal, the house where the Labor Minister spent the last week of his life before being murdered by the FLQ has also changed hands.

A family with one child bought the place for $5,000 in February—the price was lowered by about a third because of that house's macabre past—and now petunias grow in a front garden and a lawn has been planted. The name of the street was changed by the town in March from Armstrong Street to Bachand Avenue, and the street number no longer appears on the door.

The present occupant, a care-worn woman with glasses in her mid-30s, says she has no feelings about her home's past.

"He died here and that is all there is to it," she said.

The fevered memories of last fall have a hallucinatory quality, as though they belonged to a different dimension of time and space from the everyday world of Montreal that remains.

But enough remains—much of it ambiguous, uncertain in its import and significance—to suggest that last fall's FLQ crisis can fairly be said to mark the end of the 1960s, the end of the decade of the Quiet Revolution.

Outbreak of hope

The Quiet Revolution that came in with the 1960s was an outbreak of hope. Suddenly, everything seemed possible. The State, from being an alien institution, distrusted, good only for dispensing patronage to a few favorites, became in the words of Minister of Hydraulic Resources René Lévesque "the first—and the best—amongst us."

A revitalized state was provided with a reformed civil service and the technocrats came to power. Reform of the police, reform of education and the creation of a Ministry of Education, nationalization of electrical power, constitutional reform and the promise of rehabilitation of the French language in Canada through the Royal Commission on Bilingualism and Biculturalism—Quebec seemed in the process of rebirth, in the midst of an economic, political and cultural renaissance of which Expo 67 was the ultimate symbol.

Everything seemed possible and for many Quebecers in the universities and the professions the natural culmination of an upward cycle of growth would be Quebec's independence, when it burst the hampering bonds of a sluggish, constricting Canada.

The cycle of euphoria was followed by a cycle of accelerating pessimism of which last fall's FLQ crisis was a symbol as well as a contributing factor.

"Industrial Quebec is declining and Montreal has lost its position as the Metropolis (of Canada)," said an editorial in yesterday's *Le Devoir*.

Today, Cabinet ministers go about accompanied by armed bodyguards. The National Assembly is entered by a single door and with presentation of identification.

A pervasive disenchantment with government seems to have succeeded the euphoria of the 1960's.

Premier Robert Bourassa came to power in April, 1970, promising to create 100,000 new jobs; his promise, after the unemployment of the past year, is now a gallows joke.

Economic, constitutional, linguistic problems seem beyond the solution of government. The demand for social justice is exacerbated, growing immeasurably beyond the effort of governments to respond.

The FLQ manifesto read on Oct. 8 1970 over Radio-Canada television found a resonant chord in so much of the population precisely because it proclaimed in everyday language, with its idioms of hostility, that social injustice is so profound and intolerable that no government tolerating the existing state can be legitimate. Much of Quebec society agrees, whether it be by the strident denunciations for every occasion of the Confederation of National Trade Unions, the fastidious contempt for government and the present society of the intellectuals, or the sullen withdrawal of much of the population.

112

The mood of disenchantment with the state was expressed in the FLQ crisis and seems to have become more pervasive, though more apathetic, in the intervening year.

Great hope was placed in the economic intervention of the state, during the early years of the Quiet Revolution. The partly state-financed General Investment Corp. was to be a tool to give French-speaking Quebecers a proportionate share in Quebec's industry and compensate the Quebecers' lack of capital with the investing power of the State.

Jobs destroyed

The experience of the GIC has been disheartening. In particular, the invasion of the forest industry by an affiliate of the GIC called Sogefor, Ltée, was catastrophic. Millions were engulfed in a venture that consisted of buying existing wood-processing companies and establishing new ones. Whatever the reason, Sogefor recently closed its last plant. The millions invested had resulted in closing down thriving plants and destroying jobs rather than creating them.

The reform of education was to be the centrepiece of the Quiet Revolution, assuring that everything good in the modern world was absorbed by a new generation of Quebec society. University students, at the same time, saw themselves as the force for transformation of society (in alliance with the workers), for the experiment that would see a just, socialist and independent Quebec established.

The reform of education, real enough, replaced familiar problems with new ones, such as a rigidly bureaucratized, centralized educational system, a chronically discontented teaching profession, a realization that more education is not enough to change a world.

The junior colleges were to be the single most important contribution to educational reform. By 1968 its students were occupying their colleges in discontent.

Discontent in the junior colleges continued last year with new occupations, and the report of a Government-appointed investigator concluded this summer that the roots of discontent lay in the very structure of the colleges as established by law.

College and university students found recently that higher education is not the guarantee of a fulfilling and well-paying job. Even college graduates were unemployed.

The student movement that was to reform Quebec society broke apart a couple of years ago in internal dissension, and the student federations at provincial and university levels voluntarily disbanded.

Last fall, the FLQ crisis caused a crisis of conscience among students. A number of faculties of the University of Montreal and the Montreal

113

campus of the University of Quebec went on strike in support of the FLQ demands.

But, with the proclaiming of the War Measures Act and its extraordinary rights of arrest and detention the student opposition dwindled almost to nothing.

The brutal action of the FLQ in murdering Mr. Laporte and the Government's step in assuming emergency powers backed by the presence of the army made much of the student rhetoric seem like posturing.

The FLQ changed its image, losing much of its gentleman-thief appeal of a Robin Hood or an Arsène Lupin. After two kidnappings and an execution, the logic of guerrilla theatre had changed. The bomb threats, or even the occasional bomb explosions, ususally following a warning, now had little theatrical value. The chiefly symbolic terrorism—with several drastic exceptions—which had preceded last October had to be abandoned (under pain of anti-climax) for a renunciation of terrorism or the embracing of a new terrorism without quarter.

Terror costs support

A frankly terrorist FLQ will not have the quasi-support enjoyed by the FLQ of former years which expressed in an ambiguous way the latent ancestral resentments of many French Canadians.

"Things have started changing since the bombs started going off," was a sentiment often heard expressed in 1964, and referring, for example, to the setting up of the Royal Commission on Bilingualism and Biculturalism. Now the FLQ support is much narrowed and hardened.

The invoking of the War Measures Act by Prime Minister Pierre Trudeau and the mass arrests and detentions without trial of last October earned the almost unanimous condemnation of Quebec's French-language intellectual community, as Secretary of State Gérard Pelletier acknowledged in his book, *La Crise d'Octobre*.

The intellectuals may have been opposed, but they found themselves powerless when it came to finding an alternative to the Trudeau Government. The attempt to form a Bloc Québécois in August by people such as *Le Devoir* publisher Claude Ryan, and Quebec's ranking intellectual Fernand Dumont came to grief. Premature publicity was blamed for the termination of the exploratory discussion. But publiclity would have made little difference if the participants had discovered any strong support for an anti-Trudeau Bloc Québécois.

The police have been a more prominent sector of society since the Quiet Revolution spawned a militantly dissident separatist movement. Since the Montreal police strike of October, 1969, with its accompanying riot, killing and looting, the police seem much more formidable.

114

The tensions within Quebec society are such that a police strike in Montreal would almost certainly be accompanied by much more serious disorders than two years ago. The population fears its criminals, it also fears the FLQ, especially in October.

The police have, since last October, a much enhanced bargaining position which they demonstrated during the Quebec Provincial Police strike last week and the settlement a couple of days later of the Montreal police contract which gave them salary parity with Metro Toronto police.

The reform of the police was an integral part of the Quiet Revolution, and one of its first steps. The new police forces are more professional in the sense of competence, but they have few scruples about using their unique bargaining position to their best advantage.

The two-day strike of the provincial police was again largely a legacy of last October's crisis. The police struck to get paid entirely in money—and not partly in time off—for working on days off during the crisis last fall. The stability of Government in Quebec was affected: Premier Bourassa came within an ace of having to call in the army. It would have been the third time in two years. Precedent was established—the police got by force what was refused them in negotiations.

The private and cultural life of Quebec remains as stimulating as ever. The public life has acquired a new grimness.

Old spectre revives

The birth rate in the province continues its decline, giving new life to the old spectre of French Canadians as an assimilated, powerless minority.

Language conflicts show no sign of resolution as two frightened minorities face each other, an English-speaking minority in Quebec and a French-speaking minority in Canada.

The FLQ held out the promise of cutting through all problems by a single cataclysmic social upheaval followed by social justice. But the population which had a close look at Paul Rose and Francis Simard was given every reason to doubt that the FLQ of Rose and Simard could carry out its promises any better than other politicians have.

The Parti Québécois of René Lévesque is perhaps as strong as ever, but since its founding in 1968 its most potent appeal has shifted from hope for a brilliant future to protection against a threatening future. The PQ, like other parties—though perhaps to a lesser extent—suffers from a general disenchantment with parties, a sense that they cannot or will not change the way of the world.[7]

In 1970–71, Quebec entered a period in which all authority was largely discredited, strikes were rampant, a new ideology of class warfare had replaced traditional Catholicism among intellectuals and in the labour movement, governments were despised as collaborators with the ruling class in its exploitation of the workers, and the federal government was attacked in addition as an instrument of colonial domination. The Quiet Revolution, begun with so much hope, had led to much bitter disenchantment.

Notes

1.Quoted in Richard Gwyn, *The Northern Magus*, PaperJacks edition (Toronto: McClelland and Stewart, 1981), p. 265.
2."Robert Bourassa, ou les mots qui parlent d'eux-mêmes," *Point de Mire*, 2, no. 7 (5 Mar. 1971): 8. The following two quotations are also drawn from this same transcript of an interview with Bourassa.
3.Bourassa's statement was reprinted in *Le Devoir*, 15 June 1971.
4.Trudeau's statement was reprinted in *Le Devoir*, 15 June 1971.
5.Raymond Saint-Pierre, *Les années Bourassa* (Montreal: Héritage, 1977), p. 56.
6.Ibid.
7.*Globe and Mail*, 10 Oct. 1971.

CHAPTER SEVEN

Cultural Sovereignty: Communication

With the constitutional avenue toward confirming Quebec as an ethnic state closed off by Pierre Trudeau, Premier Bourassa acted by other means to realize his concept of "cultural sovereignty." In 1971, the Quebec government passed three bills that claimed jurisdiction over the entire area of communications. Then, in 1974, the government passed Bill 22, which was to make French the only official language of Quebec. Both were bold pieces of legislation, promising a sharp break with the past and a great leap forward into the new era of Quebec as a French state.

The Quebec government's attempt to take over the field of communications began with a policy statement, published in May, 1971, by communications minister Jean-Paul L'Allier.[1] The policy paper was not lacking in ambition: "It is important that Quebec assume as soon as possible its jurisdiction over all the communications existing on its territory," it stated.

The federal government already occupied almost the entire field of regulation over communications, including radio and television, telegraph, telephone, and telecommunications. A decision of the Privy Council dating back to 1932 confirmed federal jurisdiction over broadcasting. But the Quebec government would have none of it; the only federal jurisdiction it recognized was in the matter of granting broadcast frequencies to avoid overlapping transmissions on the same wavelength. Otherwise, the Quebec government claimed everything. One of the three bills passed at that time was so comprehensive in its wording that it probably gave the Quebec government jurisdiction to regulate semaphore signals. The legislation was intended to set the stage for a confrontation with the federal government.

On 14 May 1971, the same day that L'Allier had made public his policy paper, the federal minister responsible for communications, Gérard Pelletier, outlined a position that maintained federal predominance over the field of communications, but suggested that there was room for the provinces to act in concert with the federal government in formulating federal policy. The condition he required, however, was that the integrity and coherence of the Canadian communications

A CANADIAN MYTH

system be maintained. "To balkanize communications is to threaten the community itself," he said in a speech at Sainte-Adèle. "The present government could not, without denying itself, accept measures apt to destroy the very cohesion of the Canadian system of broadcasting."

Curious to understand what the Quebec government was up to, I interviewed L'Allier. He was courteous and voluble. Unlike Bourassa, who was given to laconic and enigmatic pronouncements, L'Allier spoke in long, intricate sentences, weaving a broad ideological canvas. He made clear, as Bourassa usually did not, the vision that underlay Quebec's move into communications. At thirty-three, he was the youngest member of the Bourassa Cabinet, and his political career had begun just the year before. At the time he was elected, he still carried a current membership card in the Parti Québécois.

The three bills introduced in the National Assembly were, L'Allier told me, a first step toward implementing the Quebec government's philosophy of communications. Quebec would begin by regulating cable television, which it claimed as being under provincial jurisdiction, then it would expand its influence to other areas of communications.

I pointed out that the conflicting claims of jurisdiction between Quebec and Ottawa would likely end up before the Supreme Court of Canada. L'Allier made clear that he did not accept the validity of any constitutional claims, by a court or any other body, in the matter of communications. The Fathers of Confederation, he argued, had had no thought on the subjects of television, the telephone, or communications satellites. Nor would he accept as valid the provision of the British North America Act that residual power not specifically granted to the provinces reverted to the central government. He appealed to a higher court than the constitution: the rights of the French-Canadian nation of Quebec. "What the population of Quebec asks of us—as the Government of Quebec and so the government of the majority in Quebec and issuing from the majority of Quebec— the population asks us to take every means to ensure that Quebec develops as Quebec and that all its elements are protected," he told me. "Once again, this is not a political choice that we are making here. It is a mandate which has been given over a hundred years to all the successive governments." He added that Quebec's vital interests were involved in this matter. "It is essential that Quebec, as a government and as a collectivity, take every means to ensure that its character is protected, that it develops according to its priorities. Now, communications, just like social policy, just like manpower, just like a cultural and education policy, is an essential element in the protection and development of Quebec." His message was the recurring one of Quebec provincial politicians since the Quiet Revolution: the concept of the ethnic state as a sacred duty.

"It is not a question of administrative principles," L'Allier told me. "It is a question of development and survival. There are questions that any cultural group, any ethnic group already organized with institutions, with a history—and that is

118

the case of the francophone group in Canada here—with a government, institutions, schools—well, there are a certain number of things, a certain number of sectors that this group, just as any other group of the same kind, that this group must entrust to the government. But it must entrust it to its own majority government, because they are things that are too bound up with the very existence of the group to be entrusted to a majority that will always be *other.*"

The language he was using, the logic he developed, was the same as Daniel Johnson's, Paul Gérin-Lajoie's, or René Lévesque's. It was the familiar *deux nations* vision. And for L'Allier, this vision of Quebec was so critical that only its acceptance could justify the existence of Canada. "If that principle were to be rejected, Canada has no more reason to exist. So there are three levels of government, but there is one government that is the orchestra leader, if you will." Quebec had to be that orchestra leader.

In September, 1972, the Bourassa government passed regulations to which all cable companies within the province were ordered to conform, thus subjecting them to the competing claims of two governments for exclusive jurisdiction. There ensued some comic-opera episodes in which the RCMP seized the antennas of cable companies operating without a federal licence.

With Bourassa's support, L'Allier also began courting the other provincial ministers responsible for communications. To convince them that the federal government was really a usurper, L'Allier expounded the doctrine that had been generally accepted in Quebec since the Quiet Revolution: the government in Ottawa was not the national government of Canada at all, it was only the federal government. The national government was actually made up of two equal orders of government acting together, the federal and provincial governments—or even of the provinces acting on their own. Separately, the provincial governments had as valid a claim to be considered national representatives of Canada as did the federal government.

L'Allier convened a series of three interprovincial meetings at which the provincial ministers drew up a common strategy in anticipation of a federal-provincial conference on communications that Pelletier had called for November, 1973, in advance of bringing in new federal legislation to regulate the field of communications. In a policy paper published in March of that year, he had recognized the need for "consultation and collaboration on matters of policy and planning between the federal and provincial governments."

With L'Allier leading them, however, the provincial ministers were determined to wrest jurisdictions from the federal government. They did not all have the same objectives or ambitions, but they agreed that each would support the others, and that they would not contradict each other or let themselves be drawn by Pelletier into bilateral negotiations. They would negotiate as a unit.

Pelletier had opened the conference with a plea for collaboration between provincial and federal governments, and for maintaining the integrity of communications in Canada as a single system: "We cannot ignore local, provincial or regional interests, but at the same time we cannot let ourselves think in terms of two or five or ten totally distinct communications systems in a country like Canada."

The responses from the provinces were not encouraging. L'Allier said that Quebec, as a distinct French-speaking society, saw control over communications within its territory as "an absolute priority." Robert Strachan, British Columbia's minister of transport and communications, put forward the new logic that now inspired the provinces. They no longer accepted that the federal government should regulate communications. Instead, they wanted the federal Canadian Radio-Television Commission replaced by a national commission made up of representatives of the ten provinces and the federal government. Strachan made clear, at the same time, his intention that each province would be basically responsible for regulating communications within its territory, with only the functions of research and co-ordination being delegated to the national commission.

Pelletier replied that the federal government was willing to discuss anything, but there were limits to how far it could go. "The scope asked for by Quebec and British Columbia, unless I'm mistaken, is to say get out of there completely so I can take your place. No, we are not ready to consider that, because we believe that there absolutely must be a federal presence if we wish this country to keep together."

Ontario was also becoming converted to the confederacy vision. Ontario's minister of transportation, Gordon Carton, had said that his objective for the conference was to convince all concerned that there was no longer justification for exclusive federal regulation of Bell Canada, CN-CP Telecommunications, radio and television broadcasting, or cable distribution within Ontario's borders. "Technology has simply overtaken the British North America Act and subsequent court decisions," he said, and he argued that almost the entire field of communications should now be considered a joint federal and provincial area of jurisdiction. With respect to cable television, he asserted paramount Ontario jurisdiction. "The fact is that communications, as an industry, is so important a part of the social and economic fabric of our province that the government must be involved."

The following day, Pelletier tried in vain for more than an hour to get the provincial ministers to discuss the items on the agenda, including such matters as decentralization, common objectives of a communications policy, mechanisms of consultation, and competition between communications carriers. But the ministers refused to budge.

The first to speak was L'Allier. He asked the federal government for a simple yes or no answer: Was the federal government willing to consider the entire field of communications as negotiable? Pelletier would not answer categorically yes or no, and the ministers refused to go on to any other topic. "We would welcome an assurance that you are willing to negotiate," Strachan kept telling Pelletier. The conference ended abruptly, after the minister from Saskatchewan responsible for telephones, John Brockelbank, suggested that no discussions should take place until the provinces received detailed responses from Ottawa on each of the positions they had taken in their position paper.

After the federal-provincial conference broke up in disarray, L'Allier continued his work, and other interprovincial conferences were convened. By May of 1975, when Pelletier again invited the provincial ministers for a federal-provincial conference, they had agreed among themselves on three "consensus proposals."

A condition set by Pelletier in advance of the conference was that the agenda not include any item involving a transfer of jurisdiction from the federal government to the provinces. He said that such transfers would require a change to the constitution, and could not be discussed at the level of the ministers responsible for communications, but only at the level of first ministers.

The ministers' consensus proposals all involved transfers of jurisdiction to the provinces. They proposed that all broadcasting be turned over to the provinces except for the CBC, which would continue under federal control, but subject to input by the provinces; that cable be turned over to the provinces, with the federal government retaining a say only over the retransmission of CBC programs; and that each province have jurisdiction over all telecommunications carriers, such as telephone companies, which had most of their installations within the boundaries of one province.

After Pelletier responded that he had no authority to discuss such matters, the provincial ministers again refused to discuss the items on the federal agenda. Ontario's communications minister, John Rhodes, proposed that the agenda be modified to put aside Pelletier's proposals and discuss instead the respective role and responsibilities of the two levels of government—the question of jurisdiction. Pelletier called on other provinces to express their views on the issues before the conference, but none would speak until Pelletier agreed to change the agenda. So the second federal-provincial conference was also a failure.

Quebec was having extraordinary success in persuading the other provinces to consider the federal government as the common enemy. The provincial ministers, attracted by the prospect of more power for themselves, did not seem to understand how incompatible with federalism was the vision put forward by the Quebec government.

A third federal-provincial conference on communications was held in July, 1975. Premier Bourassa, in a radio interview the day before the conference was to open, said that Quebec's basic positions on communications were "non-negotiable."

This time, Pelletier succeeded in breaking up the common front and getting the provinces to co-operate with the federal government, isolating Quebec. He did so, in part, by flatly rejecting the three consensus proposals because they involved transfers of jurisdiction and maintaining that the Parliament of Canada must retain control over broadcasting as a whole.

He did promise to recommend that provincial governments be authorized to operate general television-broadcasting stations in addition to educational-television stations, and that they should share in the regulation of cable-transmission companies. As well, he accepted the provincial proposal to establish a Council of Communications Ministers, which would meet alternately in Ottawa and in a provincial capital and would be co-chaired by the federal minister and a provincial minister of communications. This structure, in which the federal minister and the provincial representatives would sit as equals, corresponded to the confederal philosophy that the other provinces, inspired by Quebec, had begun to espouse.

L'Allier said, though, that he would remain outside the new council. He stayed at the conference as an "observer," but not a participant. However, he was philosophical about being abandoned by the allies whom he had cultivated and led for more than two years. "I can understand the positions of the other provinces who say that they don't necessarily need transfers of jurisdiction. But as far as we're concerned, at the level of the communications ministers, it's all over. Delegation is insufficient. A government that delegates can later withdraw those powers at any time. What Quebec needs is the political authority to protect the instruments that are the tools for developing its culture, its personality."

So ended a major thrust on the part of the Bourassa government to achieve "cultural sovereignty." The federal government did not give in to demands that would have balkanized one of Canada's greatest assets, its integrated system of communications. The Supreme Court of Canada, in three judgments, eventually upheld federal jurisdiction over the entire spectrum of communications; the provincial government's claims were found to be unconstitutional.

The episode demonstrated just how anti-federalist was Bourassa's political vision, and showed the need for the federal government to be firm in resisting the attempts to fragment federal authority. Also instructive was the willingness of the provincial ministers to join in an assault on federal jurisdiction over an essential bond of unity for the whole country. The allure of more power and more money proved stronger for them than the need to keep the country whole.

Note

1.The quotations in this chapter are all drawn from my own work as a reporter covering these events at the time for the *Globe and Mail*. Mr. L'Allier is now the mayor of Quebec City.

CHAPTER EIGHT

Bill 22: Le français est la langue officielle du Québec

When Premier Bourassa passed Bill 22 in 1974, establishing French as the only official language of Quebec, he realized in a text of law one of the fond ambitions of the Quiet Revolution: to tranform the state in Quebec into an instrument of and for francophones.

The point of the law was not that it made French an official language of Quebec. French already was an official language, and had been at least since 1867, and it had been recognized as such in the British North America Act. The point of the law was to disestablish English, severing more than two centuries of history during which English had always unquestionably been a core language of government and society. Over that time, the two major ethnic groups in Quebec had created parallel institutions in French and English which encompassed all of life, from birth through play and schooling, worshiping, earning a living, marrying, to receiving treatment when ill, dying, and being buried.

The institutional duality of Quebec did not mean that people lived in only one or the other of two solitudes. Some people lived in an entirely French or English network, but many also moved frequently from one to the other, or lived simultaneously in both. It was an important part of what distinguished Quebec and made it attractive to many. The dual networks were not equal, however. Until the Quiet Revolution, the English networks were more modern and pluralistic, and they fostered social mobility and the creation of wealth to a much greater extent than did the French networks. In turn, they benefited from the greater wealth of the anglophone population.

With the Quiet Revolution, the French institutional sector rapidly modernized and the old inequalities diminished, were even on a curve where they would soon have disappeared. With individual equality, the disproportionate influence of English would inevitably have waned in a province where more than 80 per cent of the population was francophone. Even without any political action, Quebec was destined to become increasingly French.

Meanwhile, the idea that bilingualism was pernicious was expressed over and over again after 1960 by many of the leading writers of Quebec, including poets Gaston Miron and Fernand Ouellette, and novelists Hubert Aquin, Yves

Beauchemin, Jacques Godbout, Alain Pontaut, and Michel Tremblay.[1] Marcel Chaput, who wrote an early plea for Quebec's independence, expressed the view that exposure to two languages must trouble the brain because they convey incompatible systems of thought. "A man can have only one single system of thought. . . . Our own bilingualism is nothing but the poisonous union of two branches deprived of a trunk, a union which must have as a consequence the sickly and misshapen knowledge of our mother tongue."[2]

Bilingualism is the source of insanity. That was what playwright Michel Tremblay implied in his libretto for the opera *Nelligan*, based on the life of the poet Émile Nelligan, who wrote brilliantly until the age of nineteen, when he went mad, and he spent the rest of his days in an asylum. Nelligan's father, David, was born in Ireland; his mother, Émilie, was French Canadian. Tremblay explained Nelligan's madness by his mixed parentage, in this scene where the father wonders why things are going so wrong with his son.

David:What's wrong with our family?

Émilie:An English father. A French mother. Children forced to choose between their father and their mother. A family cut in two from the start, condemned to failure.[3]

The belief that the French language was doomed by the presence of English was taken to an absurd conclusion by a respectable orgnization. In 1971, the Quebec Association of Teachers of French published what it called a Black Paper, in which it argued that teaching French in Quebec was impossible because of the omnipresence of English: "The Quebec Association of Teachers of French wonders with anguish whether a French Quebec is still possible." The 111-page tract demanded that French be made the only official language in Quebec, because the vigour and very existence of the language was threatened. "What can there remain of French life when one speaks English at work, when one reads in English on one's return from work, when one listens to English-language radio or television at night at home? A language that is not a language of communication is fated to disappear"—although they did not offer evidence that French was disappearing as a language of communication in Quebec. They particularly attacked bilingualism: "Bilingualism, in the end, always produces a bastard people."[4]

In 1965, Jean Lesage's minister of cultural affairs, Pierre Laporte, had prepared a white paper analyzing the linguistic situation in Quebec. It repeated the fondly held conviction of the period: the presence of two public languages in Quebec involved "the risk, under current conditions, of being for French Canadians in Quebec, a synonym for cultural exile within their own borders." Translation, the white paper stated, was having dire effects, not only on the people's vocabulary, but on their very thought, and it raised the spectre that, if strong corrective action was not taken, "French will continue its course of degradation to, sooner or later, disappear."[5]

There was something impressive about this victory of faith over facts. Writers, politicians, and teachers repeated to each other that francophone Quebecers worked in English, and no one challenged the statement. Among those who affirmed it in the Quebec legislature was Liberal member Jérôme Choquette, the future justice minister, who expressed the familiar view: "There is no reason that a nation organized like French Canada should be systematically obliged, to earn its bread and its existence, to succeed in life, in business . . . to submit to the imposition of English from nine to five o'clock or even every day at all times."[6]

Liberal Yves Michaud called the Québécois "a people of translators. Our own mental universe, for each one of us, is a universe of transposing, of translating from one language to the other."[7] He even went so far as to suggest that, if things were to go on as they were, it might be better to give francophone children and grandchildren a coherent mental universe at last—by abandoning French and adopting English.

In 1968, the conviction that French was threatened inspired a school board in the Montreal suburb of St. Leonard to abolish bilingual classes for the children of Italian immigrants: they were all to be forced to attend French schools. There were riots in the streets as francophones clashed with people whose first language was Italian. Finally, in 1969, to find a province-wide solution to the disturbance, Premier Bertrand adopted Bill 63, which gave parents the choice of French or English as the language of instruction for their children. At the same time, he set up a commission of inquiry into the state of the French language, chaired by a linguist, Jean-Denis Gendron.

During its public hearings, the Gendron commission heard a submission from the Montreal Catholic School Commission, by far the largest school board in Quebec, which said, in part, "The Québécois feels no motivation to speak a quality French because he is aware that, on the one hand, the bastard language which he speaks will still get his message across and that, on the other hand, this proper language that teachers try to impose on him is of little use in a work world where the influence of English is predominant."[8]

A public-opinion poll confirmed that the people of Quebec believed what they were told by intellectuals and teachers: the Québécois worked in English, and their own language was more or less restricted to family life. Indeed, more than two thirds agreed with the proposition that the majority of French Canadians "must work in English."[9]

What was the reality? The Gendron commission hired sociologists to give a detailed account of the language in which people worked, in which they spoke to superiors, to subordinates, and to their peers, and in which they communicated in writing and orally. Careful research was to replace the exchange of mythologies that had been characteristic of debate on the language question.

Surprise. The researchers found that, on average, francophones in Montreal worked 19.1 days out of 20 in French. In English, the language in which they were all supposedly working, they actually worked less than one day out of twenty. Outside of Montreal, francophones worked in French 19.6 days out of 20. These averages meant that some francophones worked wholly or mostly in English, but that the great bulk of them worked only in French.

In commenting on these astonishing findings, so utterly opposite to what intellectuals and politicians had been claiming for a decade, the commission's research director, Pierre-Étienne Laporte,[10] used measured language:

We are in a position to assert that the use of French among francophone workers is greater than we had anticipated. We know that there exists in French Quebec a climate of opinion to the effect that the majority of French Canadians are in the sad situation of "living in French and working in English." . . . Our research has made it possible to recognize how much better is the linguistic situation of francophones at work than the general public believes.[11]

This was putting it mildly. It would have been more accurate to say that Quebec's intelligentsia had demonstrated that it had no understanding of the real situation in its own society. It had substituted old anglophobic myths for reality, grievously misled the entire population, and betrayed its function of impartially telling the people the truth.

In its report, the Gendron commission found no cause for panic, and did not recommend coercive measures against English. In fact, it recommended that the government leave Bill 63 untouched for three to five years. But even though careful research had now established that the situation of the French language was utterly different from what everyone had thought, rather than face a critical self-analysis, the intellectual class preferred simply to dismiss the research of the Gendron commission; too many had invested too much in the struggle against English and the Canadian federation to let themselves be deterred by mere truth.

It was against this background that Premier Bourassa adopted Bill 22 in 1974. Had Bourassa truly wanted to make pragmatic arrangements to ensure that the majority of Quebec's people had as few linguistic obstacles as possible in its way, it would have been possible to bring in a law that effected limited interventions in the economy and society. The bill could have included measures for affirmative action where it was shown to be needed.

But pragmatic considerations were not the issue. Redefining a society was the object. This was a matter of ideology, of symbols, of pride, of long-established mythology. The objective was to bring into being the ethnic state of Quebec, one that would be identified with the French language and with the French-speaking majority. The state would use its power to restrain and inhibit all other languages, especially English. Thus, the law was as sweeping as Bourassa dared make it. Only French was to be recognized as the language of Quebec; English would be the language of exception, the language that was sometimes tolerated and sometimes prohibited.

"Le français est la langue officielle du Québec," as affirmed by Bill 22, was not an accurate statement of fact; section 133 of the British North America Act conferred an official character on both French and English in Quebec that Bill 22 was unable to erase. But that sentence was a programmatic statement: it established that the state would henceforth be authorized to penetrate where it previously had feared to tread. To achieve the pre-eminence of French, the state could now remove long-held rights, limit freedoms, intrude into contractual relations, and establish a vast program of state supervision of most areas of life outside the family and religion.

Bill 22 was a milestone. As the most statist law ever passed in Canada, it changed the relationship between the individual and the state in pursuit of the ideological commitment to transform Quebec into a French society. *Dirigisme,* the trusteeship of the state over the individual, was established in principle. Individuals could not be trusted to make enlightened choices: if left to themselves, they would continue to use English as well as French. The state must now stand guard over the whole society to ensure the preeminence of French.

The Official Language Act lasted for less than three years. It had only just begun to show its effects, especially in the world of work, when it was replaced, in 1977, by a somewhat more stringent law, the Charter of the French Language. But the two bills were different in degree, not in kind. Both expressed the same vision of Quebec as the ethnic state of francophones. Both asserted the determination of the government of Quebec to restrain English as the way of promoting French. English-speaking Quebecers, no matter how long their ancestors had enjoyed the freedom of Quebec, now held restricted rights, many of them revocable at the pleasure of the majority.

René Lévesque, in his memoirs, praised Bourassa for showing "definite courage, for once." Lévesque did not find Bill 22 very different from what the Parti Québécois itself was demanding: "His proposal did not differ that much from our own point of view."[12]

Most English-speaking Quebecers and many who had grown up with another mother tongue were deeply disturbed by this law, which, at one stroke, removed the freedom and institutional equality that they had previously enjoyed. There followed a revolt against the Liberal Party in the English-speaking community; the anger and withdrawal would contribute to the defeat of the Liberals two years later.

Notes

1.See William Johnson, *Anglophobie made in Québec* (Montreal: Stanké, 1991), chapters 7 and 12.

2.Marcel Chaput, *Pourquoi je suis séparatiste* (Montréal: Les Éditions du Jour, 1961). Quoted in Guy Bouthillier and Jean Meynaud, *Le choc des langues au Québec 1760–1970* (Montreal: Les presses de l'Université du Québec, 1972), p. 656.

3.Michel Tremblay, *Nelligan. Livret d'opéra* (Montreal: Leméac, 1990), pp. 43–44.

4.*Le livre noir. De l'impossibilité (presqu'absolue) d'enseigner le français au Québec*, 1991.

5.Pierre Laporte, *Livre blanc sur la politique culturelle*, reprinted in Bouthillier and Meynaud, *Le choc*, pp. 689–93.

6.Ibid., p. 731.

7.Ibid., p. 736.

8.Reprinted in Bouthillier and Maynaud, *Le choc*, pp. 719–25.

9.Pierre-É. Laporte, *L'usage des langues dans la vie économique au Québec: situation actuelle et possibilités de changement*. Study conducted on behalf of the Commission d'enquête sur la situation de la langue française et sur les droits linguistiques au Québec, table I.6.

10.Now chair of the Conseil de la langue française, the Quebec government's official advisory body on language.

11.Laporte, *L'usage*, p. 42.

12.René Lévesque, *Attendez que je me rappelle* . . . (Montreal: Québec/Amérique, 1986), pp. 357–8.

CHAPTER NINE

Meet Brian Mulroney

I first met Brian Mulroney in December, 1972. I had heard that he was Robert Stanfield's trusted eyes and ears in Quebec, and arranged to interview him.

Two months earlier, Stanfield had taken his Progressive Conservatives to the very brink of victory over Pierre Trudeau's Liberals. In that election of 29 October 1972, the Conservatives took 107 seats, the Liberals just 109. It was agonizingly close. If Stanfield had taken just one more seat from the Liberals, he could have formed the government. And it was Quebec, only Quebec, that deprived him of the victory. In Quebec, the Conservatives won just two seats to the Liberals' fifty-six. Now, with a minority government in Ottawa, it looked as though the rematch might come at any time. And, next time, the big Tory effort would surely be made in Quebec. A breakthrough there, or even a small victory, seemed all that was needed for the accession of Prime Minister Robert Stanfield.

Brian Mulroney, of course, had much to gain by improving Conservative fortunes in Quebec. Stanfield was counting on him more than on anyone else to make the difference. If the Tories won, Mulroney could count on the gratitude of the party and its leader.

When we met, Mulroney made a strong impression on me. After the interview, I produced a two-part profile to introduce him to readers of the *Globe and Mail*. It was unusual to devote so much attention to a so far unsuccessful backroom operator. But there was something about him that left you thinking, This is an unusual man.

As a matter of interest, here are, somewhat abbreviated, the two articles that I wrote at the time, long before anyone knew he would someday be prime minister. The first was published on 29 December 1972.

Political ghosts haunt work of Quebec PC organizer.
Mulroney hopes to beat historical handicaps.

MONTREAL—The ghost of Louis Riel haunts the nights of Brian Mulroney, the Progressive Conservative Party's chief organizer in Quebec.

"Why did John A. Macdonald ever hang that son of a bitch Riel?"

Mr. Mulroney's rueful musing is only half serious. But he is deadly earnest about the crushing handicap that history has placed on the hopes of the Conservatives in Quebec. . . .

In fighting the Liberals, Mr. Mulroney feels he has more than living men to contend with. Behind them are memories of historical figures such as Sir Wilfrid Laurier, who became Liberal Prime Minister of Canada in 1896 (the Conservatives have never had a French-Canadian leader), and Louis Riel, the half-French Métis leader of western rebellion that Quebec espoused as one of its own after he was hanged in 1885 by a Conservative Prime Minister.

Mr. Mulroney, 33, was picked by PC Leader Robert Stanfield earlier this month to head a committee of six responsible for party organization in the province of Quebec in preparation for the next federal election. . . .

A Montreal labor lawyer, Mr. Mulroney is one of the few authentic Quebecers to have Mr. Stanfield's confidence from long acquaintance. He was born and brought up in the Lower St. Lawrence town of Baie Comeau, an almost entirely French-speaking company town where he learned fluent and accentless French. Though he went away to high school in Chatham, N.B., and to college at St. Francis Xavier in Antigonish, N.S., he returned in the summers to work as a laborer or longshoreman and so kept up his French.

He first met Mr. Stanfield, then provincial opposition leader in Nova Scotia, in 1955 when Mr. Stanfield visited the University's Conservative association. Mr. Mulroney became its president, then executive vice-president of the national Young Progressive Conservatives. Meanwhile Mr. Stanfield had become Premier of Nova Scotia in 1956, and Mr. Mulroney stayed on after graduation in political science to work in Mr. Stanfield's 1960 provincial campaign.

Mr. Mulroney came to know Conservatives who would later become prominent in the party, such as Dalton Camp, who became national president of the party; Flora Macdonald, now MP for Kingston; Finlay MacDonald, who was national campaign chairman for the party for the 1972 election, and Norman Atkins, a chief organizer for Ontario Premier William Davis.

"I was doing a lot of the radio work for Stanfield," says Mr. Mulroney, who speaks in a baritone. "Dalton would write the copy and I would read it and record it at Finlay's radio station."

Mr. Mulroney then went on to study law at Laval University in Quebec where he was president of the Law Society and secretary of the university's student union. He took six months off from his studies in 1962 to be executive assistant to Alvin Hamilton, then minister of agriculture. Active in the party without running for office, he supported Davie Fulton in the PC leadership campaign of 1967, then passed to Mr. Stanfield's camp with most of the Fulton supporters after their candidate finally withdrew from the balloting.

130

He was active in the election of 1968. "I was looking for candidates, looking for money, helping with organization. I spoke at rallies, I was doing the same thing as I always did."

In 1971 Mr. Stanfield set up a three-man organizing committee in Quebec under the chairmanship of Claude Dupras, and Mr. Mulroney was one of the three members.

This year, when negotiations were carried on to entice Mr. Wagner off the bench and bring him into the party as a federal candidate, Mr. Mulroney was the man who represented Mr. Stanfield in the delicate discussions.

Tall, muscular in build, square-jawed, green-eyed, with modishly long hair parted at one side, he has at the same time the hearty style of the politician and a frankness in analyzing his party's problems in Quebec that are unexpected in the man who is now chiefly responsible for raising the party's fortunes.

He made it clear in an interview yesterday that in future the Quebec wing of the Conservative Party will be closely integrated into the national party instead of going off on a course of its own as it did in 1968 under its then Quebec leader, Marcel Faribault, and again in 1971 under its Quebec president, Fernand Alie, who resigned when his demand for recognition of the two-nation thesis was denied.

In the recent election, the national Conservative Party was almost ignored in the party's publicity in favor of a campaign centered on the personality of Mr. Wagner or purely local issues.

"I think it was a legitimate criticism made of our efforts last time that we strayed away from the national trend," he says.

"I don't want the Quebec party to be operating as a flying wing. To the extent that it's possible I want our organization to be fully integrated into the national camapaign effort, and I want us to take full advantage of the expertise that's been developed in the national campaign."

He said there had been too much duplication and frittering away of resources. The Quebec Conservatives must operate as part of a national party, while maintaining distinctive interests which they would press for acceptance upon the national leadership.

"But if 70 per cent of the Canadian people are concerned about unemployment, we're not going to be talking about the constitution."

So ended the first of the two articles. The second appeared on 30 December 1972.

Mulroney's cure for PC ills in Quebec—early organizing
"We have *du vent dans les voiles*"

MONTREAL—Brian Mulroney, chief Progressive Conservative Party organizer in Quebec, doesn't know whether to wax confident or to cry when you question him about the party's prospects in this province.

131

The Tories won only two of the 74 Quebec seats on Oct. 30, and Mr. Mulroney is the man picked by Leader Robert Stanfield to whip the party into shape to pick up the extra seats that would mean the difference between being in opposition and being in power. . . .

"I think there's been a big change," Mr. Mulroney says. "Politics is really in many ways a question of psychology."

During the 1972 election campaign few people thought Mr. Stanfield could defeat Prime Minister Pierre Trudeau, in either English or French Canada. But now Mr. Stanfield has become credible as a likely Prime Minister.

"In Quebec as in the rest of Canada we have what is known as *du vent dans les voiles*—the wind in our sails," Mr. Mulroney says.

"It will be much easier for us in the upcoming campaign when you have Stanfield sitting in the House with 107 seats and Trudeau there with 109. The guy whose feet of clay are showing is Trudeau."

Mr. Mulroney plans to have the party in Quebec on a war footing by March 1—when his mandate as chairman of a six-man provincial organizing committee expires.

Next week he is scheduled to begin a provincial tour, meeting defeated candidates, gathering their suggestions and looking for new candidates. The party will begin nominating candidates in earnest about the middle of January.

"If we have learned one thing, it's that a Conservative, however great his reputation, can win in Quebec only if he begins organizing very early," he says in French. In the course of the interview he switches back and forth between English and flawless French.

Five weeks before the last election only about a dozen Conservative candidates had been nominated. The newly nominated candidates had to begin building their organizations from scratch. Next time, with an early start, it will be different, Mr. Mulroney says. "Then, we want to use Stanfield to a much greater extent in Quebec."

The PC leader will be making frequent personal visits, television appearances and meeting with candidates in the coming months. A $50-a-plate fund-raising dinner will be held on February 18, with Mr. Stanfield as the star speaker.

Mr. Mulroney hopes to sell at least 2,000 tickets. Last year, acording to Yvon Sirois, the party's executive director, about 1,400 tickets were sold for a similar dinner.

There are also plans for a policy conference for the provincial wing, though the date has not yet been set.

But the sanguine tone changes when Mr. Mulroney is asked to explain why the party did so poorly on October 30. He lists a number of factors,

132

but almost all of them could be expected to operate again to the Conservatives' disadvantage when a new election is called.

"For 75 years this province has belonged to the Liberals. In this election campaign you had the third French-Canadian leader of the Liberal Party going into an election with 10 French Cabinet ministers and 56 members of Parliament."

Next in importance he cites the Social Credit Party, led by another French Canadian, Real Caouette, with 13 members of Parliament and 12 members of the National Assembly, each with a strong personal organization in his constituency. The party took 15 seats on October 30.

He mentions the provincial Liberal Government, with 24 Cabinet ministers and 72 members of the National Assembly, each with a strong constituency organization.

The Liberals, federal and provincial, "have material resources at their disposal that they've never been shy to use."

Against this Liberal power and Social Credit entrenchment stood Mr. Stanfield and a single Conservative candidate who had been elected as a Conservative in 1968.

"I think that had Bob Stanfield been running against anyone other than Pierre Trudeau in the province of Quebec the results would have been quite different." . . .

"Blood is thicker than water," Mr. Mulroney concludes in analyzing the past election.

What about next time? Can the Conservatives hope to borrow some muscle from their closest provincial counterparts, the Unité-Québec, the most recent name of the Union Nationale? The Union Nationale, then in power, gave strong organizational and financial support to the federal Conservatives in 1958 when they carried off 50 seats in Quebec. There was no Social Credit Party at the time, however, to divide Quebec's anti-Liberal vote.

Mr. Mulroney replies that he has had no discussions with UQ Leader Gabriel Loubier or any other party representative.

"But it seems to me that if I were Loubier I'd be looking over my shoulder pretty quickly at the Créditistes."

The recently formed provincial wing of the Social Credit Party won 12 seats in the election of 1970, its first attempt on the provincial scene. Most observers think its strength has increased.

"I think that in these constituencies where a small c conservative has a chance it would be in Loubier's interests to make sure that our people get support."

Mr. Mulroney says that the two parties will probably be talking together in the next couple of months. . . .

The October 30 results left the Conservatives strongest in the ridings of the Montreal area where Social Credit is weak, but where the Liberals have huge majorities. Elsewhere, Social Credit strength has reduced the small Conservative vote.

Where, in these circumstances, can Mr. Mulroney see the Conservatives taking even 10 of Quebec's 74 seats in the next election?

"Do you see why I go home at night and have a scotch and cry?" he replies.

Looking back, much that would be significant for the future was revealed by Mulroney in that interview. There was the brilliant personality, the striking turn of phrase ("Why did John A. Macdonald ever hang that son of a bitch Riel?"), the taking of his interlocutor into his confidence, establishing immediate rapport. Mulroney spoke to a reporter he had never met before almost as though he were talking to a friend, blowing hot and cold, confident and discouraged ("Do you see why I go home at night and have a scotch and cry?").

He spoke with surprising candour, but this served a personal purpose: to reveal how difficult his job was. If the Conservatives had done badly in two elections, 1968 and 1972, in both of which he played a major role in Quebec, it was simply because his task was impossible. The other message, one that would come to fruition a few years later, was that the Conservatives could not defeat history. Riel was history; Laurier, Saint-Laurent, and Trudeau were history. The Conservatives could change their history by picking a leader from Quebec, as the Liberals had done three times now.

This would be Mulroney's message when he ran for Conservative leadership in 1976, at the convention that elected Joe Clark. It almost worked. Above all, that message made him a highly credible candidate, even though he had never been elected to Parliament or to any office in the party since he left college, and it would enable him to win the leadership in 1983.

Meanwhile, however, he was struggling against impossible odds: not only were there Trudeau and his fifty-six Liberal members of Parliament, including ten Cabinet ministers from Quebec, but the provincial Liberal government, under Robert Bourassa, had seventy-two members of the National Assembly, including twenty-four Cabinet ministers. With all that firepower arrayed against the Progressive Conservatives, the only solution was to try to isolate the federal Liberals, which meant making strategic alliances with anybody willing to join the fight against them, for whatever reason.

After Pierre Trudeau confronted Daniel Johnson and stonewalled all those who yearned for special status, associate states, sovereignty-association, or just plain independence, the great bulk of those who wanted to fight the Trudeau Liberals were the Quebec nationalists. They, and they alone, had the passion, the hatred, the fire in the belly. So Mulroney tried to win elections not by building a Progressive Conservative party, but by creating an ad hoc, eclectic, anti-Liberal coalition drawn from many parties. Most of them had a single common denominator: they were Quebec nationalists.

The federal election of 1968 was the first in which Robert Stanfield ran against Pierre Trudeau. Stanfield knew Mulroney well from the campaign in Nova Scotia, and he was probably the only person in Quebec whom Stanfield trusted. Stanfield phoned the law firm where he was employed and asked if they would give him six weeks of paid leave to work on the Tory campaign. It was granted, and Mulroney's title was assistant to the chairman of the party's Quebec election campaign committee.

It was almost certainly Mulroney who made the approach to Premier Johnson to win Union Nationale support for the Tories. Mulroney knew Johnson well from the days when he was a student at Université Laval, in Quebec City, in 1960; he had made it his business, while studying in Quebec, to get to know all the major politicians and members of the press corps of the Quebec legislature. It was easy to do. Political Quebec City was like a village, with everything happening within just a few blocks.

"Sometimes leaving the Aquarium [restaurant] after midnight, Mulroney might head up the street and around the corner to the Château Frontenac, where he would slip into the bar and manoeuvre himself over to Daniel Johnson," John Sawatsky relates in his biography of Mulroney. "Johnson and Mulroney each had a roguish charm that appealed to the other. When Johnson looked at Mulroney he saw an image of himself as a younger man, someone who had risen from a humble background by massaging egos, building networks, remembering names, and keeping track of where all the dead bodies lay."[1]

It was Mulroney who had negotiated Marcel Faribault's candidacy as a Conservative.[2] Faribault did not come easily; he was, after all, a member of the Legislative Council and president of Trust Général: he would have to resign both positions to run for the Tories. "Mr. Johnson had to be very insistent and Mr. Stanfield had to designate him as his first lieutenant, had to accept a kind of two-headed leadership of the Conservative party, for Mr. Faribault at last to agree," recalls Paul Gros d'Aillon, who was close to the negotiations.[3] Faribault was a firm believer in the *deux nations* theory, and this was that theory applied: Stanfield in the rest of Canada, Faribault in Quebec. In the Quebec campaign, Faribault gave many speeches on reorganizing Canada as two nations.

In the end, it probably did not make a great deal of difference to the outcome that Faribault preached *deux nations* with Stanfield's approval. Faribault was defeated in his own riding. Only four Tories were elected in Quebec, and Stanfield lost. But what if the strategy promoted by Brian Mulroney had worked and the Tories had won? Daniel Johnson, instead of being the caged ultra-nationalist, would have been the king-maker. His vision of *Canada à deux* would have been endorsed by the Quebec electorate. His man Faribault would have been the spokesman for the party in Quebec, where he would have won the election for the Tories. Faribault would have been the one to answer the question, What does Quebec want?

The 1968 *deux nations* campaign did have one long-term effect. The party that had previously been known for hanging Riel and imposing conscription in the First World War was now known in Quebec as the party of *les deux nations,* the party that fought Trudeau's vision of "One Canada with two official languages." For most Quebecers, this had little impact. But for the nationalists in the political class, the image of the Progressive Conservative Party had changed, and it was now seen as the best vehicle for the fight for their ideas. *Deux nations* would return.

The results were not long in coming. People who had agreed to be candidates in 1968 took very seriously the commitment to two nations that had been the core of the party's Quebec message. When they did not see Stanfield move after the election to act on the two nations concept—it would have been suicidal for the party after Trudeau's successful campaign—some of them became restless.

On 20 April 1971, the president of the Quebec wing of the Progressive Conservative Party, Fernand Alie, erupted. He came out publicly for a form of separation of Quebec by small steps—exactly what Daniel Johnson had been practising before his death. Addressing a citizens' group in Montreal, Alie said that he and René Lévesque "agree on fundamental, basic long-term objectives. In the final analysis, what we both want is the greater well-being of the people of Quebec, the reconquest, let us say, of the greatest possible number of sovereignties." The difference between himself and the separatist leader, Alie said, was that "Mr. Lévesque proposes that we obtain [sovereignties] by means of a separation that I call traumatizing and perhaps even rather violent—I don't know, we will only know when it is done—but I say that if we do it by a progressive decentralization, very gradual and well thought through, it can be done in a digestible way." Thus, the difference between them was purely one of procedure, not substance. "So we do not contradict each other, but I think that we simply arrive progressively in the one case, in the other case he wants to get there massively—it is total and global decentralization in a single operation." [4]

Alie had another interesting thought for his audience. He said that he had been considering for some time the desirability of grouping together all the federal parliamentarians from Quebec. He could not accept, he said, that Quebec's voice in Ottawa should contradict Quebec's voice at the provincial level, which he called the most natural and spontaneous voice of the Quebec people.

How did it come about that the president of the Quebec Tory wing was advocating separation by stages? A week earlier, on 14 April, Alie had published a letter in *Le Devoir* in which he asked Stanfield to implement the conception of Canada as a country composed of two nations and to recognize that the Quebec government was the real voice of the Quebec people. This would mean creating parallel English and French structures at all levels of the party. He also demanded a transfer of jurisdictions from Ottawa to Quebec City.

A few days after his speech, Alie asked for a vote of confidence from the provincial council of the party. No doubt, he knew its members well enough to be sure that many shared his ultra-nationalist ideas. But the provincial council refused to take a stand; it neither supported nor condemned him, so Alie decided to resign.

This episode was not simply an unaccountable aberration. Alie knew that his ideas were popular among the leading members of the party in Quebec, or he would not have acted as he did. He had been a municipal politician for eleven years, and he knew his constituency in the party. It is significant, too, that the party's provincial council did not censure its president for publishing separatist views in a newspaper and developing them in his speeches; it merely said that he was speaking for himself, not for the party, and should make this clear. It did not dare denounce his views: too many of its members must have shared them, and they clearly feared the desertion of the nationalists if they rejected them.

The seeds of Alie's 1971 defection were planted in the 1968 campaign, when the Conservatives decided to court the nationalists. "You dance with the one that brung ya," as Mulroney was later to say. In 1968, the party danced with Daniel Johnson, Marcel Faribault, Fernand Alie, and others with an ideological commitment to *deux nations*. These people did not simply fold their tents and vanish once they were defeated in 1968. They and their commitments remained lodged in the party.

Alie's resignation was followed by that of Roch LaSalle, one of the four Conservative members of Parliament from Quebec elected in 1968. LaSalle left the Tory caucus to sit as an independent, citing the same reasoning as had Alie.

There was a postscript to Alie's resignation. Three months later, he resurfaced in the news as a promoter of a "Bloc Québécois" (that is exactly what he called it in 1971). Ideas have consequences. The following account appeared under my byline in the *Globe and Mail* on 2 September 1971:

MONTREAL—A decision on whether to form a Quebec nationalist party that would run candidates in the next federal election may be reached tonight when a group committed to Quebec autonomy meets to plan its future.

The group first met secretly on August 17 to explore the possibility of a Quebec bloc in federal politics. A subcommittee was appointed to draw up a manifesto and present it to the full group for action tonight.

Among the 15 people who met are Fernand Alie, who resigned in May as president of the Quebec wing of the Progressive Conservative Party; Claude Ryan, publisher of *Le Devoir*; General J. V. Allard, former chief of staff of the Canadian Armed Forces, and Camille Laurin, parliamentary leader of the separatist Parti Québécois.

The group includes one member of Parliament, Roch LaSalle, who was PC member of Joliette until he resigned in May to sit as an independent. There was also a representative of the Confederation of National Trade Unions and of the French Catholic teachers' union, the Corporation des Enseignants du Québec. Louis Laberge, president of the Quebec Federation of Labor, had been expected at the meeting but he did not show up.

Several of the group are active in nationalist organizations, including Gilles Noiseux, past president of the Fédération des Sociétés Saint-Jean-Baptiste, François-Albert Angers, president of the Montreal branch of the Société Saint-Jean-Baptiste, and Rosaire Morin, a businessman who was vice-president of the nationalist Estates-General of French Canada.

The group includes intellectuals such as Fernand Dumont, a sociologist, Rev. Louis O'Neill, whose book on corrupt political morality in Quebec following the 1956 provincial election is considered to have helped launch the Quiet Revolution, and Pierre-Louis Guertin, a young scholar who returned in July from political science studies in France after writing a book on President Charles de Gaulle's visit to Quebec in 1967.

Some of the members, including Guy Bertrand, a defeated Parti Québécois candidate in the last Quebec election, and Mr. Guertin, favor all-out political action. Mr. Bertrand said yesterday that he was confident a Quebec bloc could take 25 to 30 seats in the federal election.

He has been a chief mover of the group, calling on the Parti Québécois to invade the federal scene since shortly after the last provincial election.

"The 600,000 people who voted for us in the last election should not have to prostitute themselves by voting for an anti-separatist party in federal elections."

The PQ rejected any commitment at the federal level, though the matter is to be reopened at the next meeting of its national council, an informant said.

Mr. Bertrand originally favored a separatist federal party, but he has shifted his position because of the general opposition he has found among both separatists and non-separatists. Now he favors a party that would not be explicitly separatist, but would be committed to "take sides in favor of Quebec even if that displeases Canada."

He and Mr. Alie convened the August 17 meeting.

Mr. Guertin advanced his conception of the new political movement in a pair of articles published last week in *Le Devoir*. He wants a bloc in Ottawa committed to the sovereignty of Quebec and supported by the Parti Québécois.

"The real electoral success of the bloc will be the fall of the Trudeau Government, the last great federalist thrust to come out of Quebec, the last illusion which brakes the collective awakening of the Québécois. The

138

destruction of his regime can be brought about if the bloc takes 20 or 25 seats from him."

He also argues that the bloc could weaken the central government to the benefit of separatism by bringing about minority governments.

In any case, he argues, separation of Quebec can hardly be brought about without a strong expression of separatist support in a federal election.

"The seed of liberty for Quebec must be sowed like a poison in the very heart of the central power, the federal Parliament."

Mr. Alie chiefly opposes federal parties. Party discipline often brings members of Parliament to vote against the interests of Quebec, he said. He would like to see regional parties that represent the interests of their regions. Better still, he would like to see Parliament reorganized so that provincial legislatures would delegate their own elected representatives to Ottawa.

For André L'Heureux, a representative of the CNTU and member of its political action committee, the important objective is to "destroy the Liberal monolith in Quebec." At its last meeting, the provincial council of the CNTU reversed a decision of its executive no longer to support the former drivers of G. Lapalme Inc., who lost their jobs in a switch of postal contracts, and ordered the executive instead to declare war on the Trudeau government. The presence of Mr. L'Heureux in this group is consistent with his union's policy.

Mr. Alie said yesterday he thought the movement would first try out its efficacy as a pressure group and, only if that did not work in changing the policies of the present federal government, become a political party as a last resort.

Mr. Ryan, who has recently been questioning himself about his own political commitments in the editorial columns of his paper, said recently that summer is a time for reappraisals. He is travelling through the province on a holiday, meeting people and presumably thinking out his future political course.

He told a radio reporter this week that he backed the Quebec bloc as an ideological pressure group and that, if it should become a political party, he would have to consider whether to leave his position in journalism for a political career.

This initiative, even down to the name, was prophetic. The central arguments put forward then were exactly the arguments put forward two decades later by Lucien Bouchard, founder of the 1990 Bloc Québécois. In both cases, Brian Mulroney's ambitions had paved the way.

But, back in 1971, the attempt was premature. The publicity turned on the secret discussions embarrassed some and scared others away. At the last minute, the meeting that was to have been held on 2 September 1971 was cancelled. The attempt to mount a federal Bloc Québécois would succeed only years later, after Mulroney had done much more to strengthen nationalism in Quebec.

For the 1972 federal election, Brian Mulroney continued his tactic of looking anywhere for anti-Liberal support in Quebec. This time, he chose a man with a populist image, a former Cabinet minister in Jean Lesage's government, Claude Wagner. When Lesage resigned as party leader, Wagner, known as a firm defender of law and order, had been by far the most popular candidate to succeed him. But at the Liberal convention, the *ex officio* delegates from the party establishment rallied behind Robert Bourassa and made him the leader of the opposition. A bitter Wagner was named to the bench, where he made sensational statements about organized crime reaching into the highest ranks of society. His pronouncements kept him in the public eye as a kind of crime-fighting judge and sustained his popularity.

Mulroney was interested. A public-opinion poll suggested that the Tories, led in Quebec by Claude Wagner, could defeat the Liberals. Mulroney sold Stanfield on the idea of centring the next Conservative campaign in Quebec on Wagner. But Wagner required assurances of financial security before undertaking such a perilous mission, so Mulroney arranged to set up a secret trust fund of $325,000 for him if he would leave the bench and run as a Tory. He did, and the 1972 Quebec campaign was entirely focused on the name and personality of Wagner, to the almost total exclusion of Stanfield and the Progressive Conservative Party.

As in 1968 with Faribault, the 1972 results were crushingly disappointing. People had loved Wagner as a Liberal minister and as a judge. When he ran as a Tory, they were not interested. He was in danger even in his own riding, which had been hand-picked for him. And while the Conservatives in the rest of the country beat the Liberals handily, in Quebec they took only two of the seventy-four seats—half of what they won in 1968. In fact, if they had won the same four seats as they had in the last election, Stanfield could have formed a minority government. Instead, Trudeau held on with a minority.

Mulroney returned to the tactics of 1968: he went after the support of the nationalists. It was not as easy as it had been the previous time around; Mulroney's friend, Daniel Johnson, was dead and the Union Nationale had been driven from power by the Liberals under Robert Bourassa in the 1970 Quebec election. The man who won the Union Nationale leadership at the convention in 1971, Gabriel Loubier, had changed the name of the party to Unité Québec. The UN, or UQ, still had the second-highest number of seats in the National Assembly because its vote had been concentrated in rural areas. In popular vote, however, it was far behind the party founded by René Lévesque, the Parti Québécois.

Since the eclipse of the UN, the PQ was where the bulk of the nationalist vote was to be found. There, too, burned the passion to fight the Liberals of Pierre Trudeau, who was seen as the great roadblock on their journey to sovereignty. But how could Mulroney approach them? It would entail considerable risks. Any overt collaboration between the Péquistes and the Tories could cause a backlash in the rest of Canada, and it would reveal the Stanfield Conservatives as opportunistic and reckless.

So what did Mulroney do? Let me describe what I found when, as a reporter, I covered the two-day convention of the Quebec wing of the Progressive Conservative Party, held at a hotel in Trois-Rivières on 28 and 29 April 1974.

In the hall, the highlight of the event was a two-hour bear-pit session during which Robert Stanfield sat alone on a bare stage while members of the audience went to the microphones on the floor and asked him questions. Wandering the hotel corridors, I obtained a backstage look at the preparations for that public event. The people who were to ask Stanfield questions at the bear-pit session were all picked in advance. They were coached on their questions in a room on the fourth floor of the hotel by Richard LeHir, a rising star in the party. Meanwhile, in his third-floor suite, Stanfield was being fed the answers in French by his special assistant for Quebec, Richard Lelay. Most of the questions and answers had been prepared by a policy adviser to Stanfield, sociologist André Robert, with input from others.

Stanfield then performed impressively on the stage, turning this way and that in his swivel chair to face his questioners, displaying the command of policy and language and the leadership qualities that would, it was hoped, bring him victory in the elections that were expected momentarily. The bear-pit session was treated as a performance to provide footage for the campaign publicity that would shortly be needed. Seven banks of floodlights illuminated the scene, and delegates had sweat running down their faces. Three television crews and a photographer circulated through the hall, recording the question-and-answer session for future use.

While people were making speeches, glad-handing, asking questions, and electing a slate of officers for the association, the real action was taking place in the hotel rooms upstairs, where people who held no elected office were conducting the truly important business of the party. One of them was René Daviault, who had, for the past year, been setting up the riding associations, the basis of local grass roots support for every party. His role was especially crucial in that period of minority government when, any day, the Liberals might lose a vote in the House and be forced to call an election.

Daviault was not a Conservative, but a Péquiste. In fact, he had been campaign manager in the 1970 Quebec election for one of the most prominent Parti Québécois candidates, Jacques-Yvan Morin. Morin, a constitutional-law professor at the Université de Montréal, had chaired the 1967 Estates-General of French Canada when it rejected federalism and opted for Quebec sovereignty and was later to be minister of education in the Parti Québécois government. I asked Daviault why he was setting up constituency associations for the Tories. "I'm a man who likes to take up a challenge," he told me. "I had always dreamed of building a party up from the grass roots. I jumped at the chance."[5]

Organize at the grass roots, he did. Claude Dupras, the party president, told the convention that before the 1972 elections, there had been barely a dozen PC riding associations in Quebec. He went on to congratulate Daviault publicly for having brought into being another fifty-eight PC associations, to bring the total up to sixty-eight.

Daviault, a businessman who owned a cleaning-supplies business, devoted himself in effect full time to the work of organizing for the Tories during the year preceding the 1974 policy convention, when he toured all parts of the province twice. When he went into a new area of the province to organize, Daviault told me, he did not search out the local Conservatives. He asked who were the politically keen people—regardless of what party they supported. "If I find a good man who is called Joe Blow, I don't care if he is Péquiste, Liberal or Créditiste, as long as he tells me, René, I'm going to build you an organization."

Daviault had been recommended for his position as chief organizer by Florian Toutant, a lawyer with his political roots in the Union Nationale. Toutant had been a key organizer for Marcel Masse when the latter ran unsuccessfully for the UN leadership in 1971. Now, Toutant was the éminence grise of the Tory campaign in charge of selecting Tory candidates in Quebec for the looming election. In his hotel room, he was so busy interviewing a constant stream of prospective Tory candidates and experienced political organizers that he scarcely had time to grab a bite to eat.

He was the quintessential backroom man, short, balding, with a poker face. He spoke quietly, lucidly, dispassionately about politics, and he stressed the need to bring together people from all parties in an anti-Liberal coalition. "The party is open to people of different parties, and we welcome people of all political hues, because to win, we have to increase our vote, and we won't succeed by frowning on those of other political persuasion," he told me.

Toutant was one of six men appointed by Stanfield to head the party's "organization" in Quebec, as opposed to the PC association. They formed what was called "the strategy committee," and met every Friday to direct the effort to win Quebec for the Stanfield Conservatives.

Another of the six was Richard LeHir, a lawyer who had been appointed the party's director of operations in Quebec for the coming elections. LeHir was not a Conservative.[6] He was twenty-seven, and had done graduate work in linguistics in Europe before studying law. He told me that he was a Quebec nationalist. "But I feel that, as long as Quebec remains within Confederation, we must be concerned about federal politics." And, he added, "The only party which is able to recognize the role the provinces must play in Confederation is the Conservative Party."

Richard Lelay recruited LeHir for the Conservative campaign, and he had also recruited sociologist André Robert. He had known Robert at the University of

Ottawa, when Robert was president of the social-sciences student body and Lelay was vice-president. Robert was known as a separatist, although "I prefer to define myself as a sovereignist," he told me. He had agreed to work for the party because he wanted Stanfield to be exposed to the views and concerns of Quebecers. "I consider that it is an extraordinary privilege to be able to participate in the process by which Quebec can make itself heard by the leader of a national party."

The other three members of the strategy committee were Jean Bazin, a Conservative and chairman of the legal committee; Guy Charbonneau, then chairman of the Conservatives' Quebec finance committee and a long-time Tory bagman; and a Montreal lawyer, Michel Cogger, a former Université Laval classmate of Mulroney's and his long-time friend. Cogger had been executive assistant to former justice minister Davie Fulton—for whom Mulroney also worked for six months.

From the convention, I wrote my report on Daviault and the members of the strategy committee who were nationalists rather than Conservatives. The information was seized upon by Prime Minister Trudeau, who used it to denounce the Tories in a speech in the House, accusing them of welcoming separatists into their ranks. The Conservatives ran for cover, at a time when elections were about to be called. LeHir was fired from his post as director of operations of the Quebec campaign. Daviault, who had worked so hard for the party setting up riding associations, was now told that he could not run as a Conservative candidate. "The party told me that they didn't want any Péquiste candidates," he told me. "I was told clearly that, even if I contested a convention and won the nomination, I would not be allowed to run as a Conservative."He would not say who had ordered his candidacy blocked, but it came from "high up," he said, and it did not come from the Quebec campaign management committee, which wanted him to run. "Before the article, everyone accepted that I should be a candidate and they were anxious for me to announce it because that was going to attract an enormous number of nationalist votes," Daviault told me.

So ended another episode in the life of the Conservative Party in Quebec during the time when Brian Mulroney was its most influential member as Stanfield's personal representative. Mulroney's flirtation with ultra-nationalists and separatists did not work in 1974. When the election came, Stanfield went down to a worse defeat in Quebec than he had experienced even in 1972. As Trudeau's support got stronger with each election, Stanfield's weakened.

But Brian Mulroney would keep on trying to attract the nationalist vote, and his day would come.

Notes

1.John Sawatsky, *Mulroney: The Politics of Ambition* (Toronto: Macfarlane, Walter & Ross, 1991), pp. 113, 114.
2. Ibid., pp. 193–4.

3.Paul Gros d'Aillon, *Daniel Johnson: l'égalité avant l'indépendance* (Montreal: Stanké, 1979), p. 208.
4.Report by William Johnson, *The Globe and Mail*, 21 Apr. 1971.
5.This and the remaining quotations in this chapter are from personal interviews that I conducted in 1974.
6.He ran as a Parti Québécois candidate in the 1994 election campaign.

CHAPTER TEN

"Je n'ai jamais été aussi fier d'être Québécois"

The victory of the Parti Québécois, on 15 November 1976, led to an extraordinary outbreak of euphoria. In the streets around the Paul Sauvé Arena, where the triumphant Péquistes were gathering, caravans of cars paraded through the streets with people leaning out the windows waving Parti Québécois campaign placards and Quebec flags. Many sounded their horns rhythmically to the beat of *Ce n'est qu'un début, continuons le combat!*[1] A whiff of revolution stirred in the air. People waved at each other, raising two fingers in a sign of victory, or a fist to signal a more serious intent.

At the arena itself, so many people had crowded in that the doors were closed and guarded and people were being turned away. Only my press pass got me in. I pushed through the wildly excited throngs. Strangers hugged and kissed each other, people screamed and chanted *Le Québec aux Québécois!* The loudspeaker played the PQ's campaign theme song, which suddenly seemed full of prophecy and portent: *"À partir d'aujourd'hui, demain nous appartient."* From today on, tomorrow belongs to us. On the stage, Claude Charron, the curly-haired thirty-one-year-old who had been a member of the National Assembly since 1970, was wracked with sobs, the tears streaming down his face. One arm was around the shoulders of fatherly psychiatrist Camille Laurin, who had just been re-elected after his defeat in 1973.

René Lévesque stood once more in the same hall where, in 1973, forlorn, he had dared speak of hope to his shattered followers. Now he seemed overwhelmed by the gravity of what had happened that evening and what lay ahead. Quebecers had elected seventy-one members from the Parti Québécois, twenty-six Liberals, eleven members of the Union Nationale, and two independents in the 110-member House.

Lévesque stood there as the chants from the triumphant throng washed over him. Finally, he summed up his pride and his conviction that Quebec's sovereignty was going to be achieved: *"Je n'ai jamais, je n'ai jamais pensé que je pouvais être aussi fier d'être Québécois!"*[2] What did it all mean? Was Quebec marching on to sovereignty, as many believed that night? It seemed that the dream

145

of the ethnic state, a Quebec of and for French-speaking Quebecers, *le Québec aux Québécois,* was now about to be realized.

The great troubadour of Quebec song, Félix Leclerc, was travelling in Europe when he heard the news of the Parti Québécois's victory. He took up his pen and wrote a prose-poem with the portentous title: *"Le 16 novembre 1976 l'an I du Québec."* Year One of Quebec: Leclerc was appropriating the analogy of the Christian era from which most of the world enumerates its history. "For too much time, for too long, the land belonged to the cowards, to the lazy, to the cheaters. May he take it, he, my son, it is his turn. . . . Good luck to you and to your descendants."[3] And Lise Payette, the television personality who was elected on 15 November and became minister of consumer affairs, called the PQ's coming to power a "peaceful coup d'état."[4]

There was much illusion in the euphoria. During the election campaign, the Parti Québécois had put the issue of sovereignty almost out of sight. Lévesque did not bring it up unless he was asked about it, at which point he would state that the party's platform was to begin negotiations with the federal government for separation soon after the PQ was elected. But he made it clear that those preliminary talks, if they were held at all, would be a formality: "It would be a miracle if Ottawa accepted to negotiate, because we would be asking for a return to us of full powers. That is where the referendum on independence comes in. We have made a solemn commitment that we would never push people into independence against their will."

La Presse noted the silence about separatism in a front-page story on 10 November, five days before the election: "The Parti Québécois is well on the way to achieving the unthinkable feat of campaigning for 28 days without talking—except in passing, and gingerly—about the key article of its program: the independence of Quebec."

Instead, PQ radio commercials complained about high taxes. Newspaper ads denounced the Liberals' billion-dollar deficit and vaunted the PQ's *"la caisse propre"*—a play on words meaning their clean campaign fund, but sounding like *"la caisse pop,"* the familiar neighbourhood credit union. The most common message was *"On a besoin d'un vrai gouvernement"*—we need a real government.

As any other opposition leader would, Lévesque had denounced the patronage and the suspicion of scandal that had undermined the reputation of the Liberals. Statesmanlike, he had put forward, day by day, his proposals for improving medical services and dental services, and for relieving the pressure on municipal governments—anything but sovereignty, everything but separation or independence.

The constantly repeated message paid off: this was not an election to deal with the question of sovereignty, it was an election to choose "a good government." Polls showed that a good half of the people who would vote PQ were not in favour of Quebec's independence.

But, once in power, would the PQ respect its limited mandate? And even if it did, would it not use all the resources at the disposal of the government to promote the idea of sovereignty among the people? Right after the election, the polls showed a sharp surge in the popularity of the PQ. Could that popularity not lead to a strong increase in support for sovereignty?

A long period of uncertainty and suspense settled over the country; a question mark hung over Quebec that would not be removed until Lévesque held his referendum. Many wondered whether Pierre Trudeau had been wrong to oppose special status for Quebec over the previous eight years, and in Ottawa, the leaders of the three opposition parties blamed Trudeau for the Parti Québécois's victory.

"You can't govern a country like Canada as though there is only one government which counts," Joe Clark remarked.[5] He had become leader of the Progressive Conservatives just a few months before and was already developing a vision of Canada as what he was to call a "community of communities." In a speech in Montreal a few days earlier, Clark had pledged, "We of the Progressive Conservative Party propose to replace the policy of extreme centralization by another policy of decentralization."

Pierre Trudeau, however, rejected the decentralization solution: "I say it is a grave illusion to believe that those who seek the breakup of Canada would suddenly cease to pursue their objective simply because the provincial governments have increased their powers in some areas, say, immigration or communications or taxing powers or cultural matters."

He indicated that he was ready to negotiate some constitutional changes that would give the provinces additional power, but he maintained that the answer to separatism was to make French-speaking Canadians at home everywhere in Canada—in Vancouver and Toronto as well as Montreal. A transfer of powers from Ottawa to the provinces would not achieve that end. He signalled at the same time that he would not use force to try to keep Quebec within Confederation. "I am one of those who believe that Canada cannot, that Canada must not, survive by force. The country will only remain united if its citizens want to live together in one civil society."

Trudeau's vision of federalism was now on the defensive. It had always been opposed by most of Quebec's political class, but he had demonstrated in three election campaigns that he had the support of the Quebec people. Now, the PQ victory and the nationalist euphoria that followed cast doubt on his approach to solving the discontents in Quebec. Was it obsolete, and was he yesterday's man, as many now believed?

Claude Castonguay, the former minister who, more than anyone, had convinced Robert Bourassa to reject the Victoria Charter, had retired from politics in 1974 for a career as a financier. Castonguay now suggested, in the *Globe and Mail*, that Trudeau was contributing to separatism by his rejection of decentralization. "Although the Canadian problem primarily exists at the collective level, a choice was made in favor of an institutional bilingualism, which consequently is largely artificial," he wrote. He warned that Trudeauism, based on a strong central government with two official languages, might lead Quebecers to choose separation in the referendum. "When the question is put, one can anticipate that many Quebecers, in the absence of an option based on a true federal system which recognizes the existence of two distinct societies, will choose the sovereignist option in preference to the maintenance of the status quo."

And what did René Lévesque himself consider his mandate to be? That was my first question when I interviewed him just before Christmas of 1976, when he had been selected as Man of the Year by the *Report on Business* of the *Globe and Mail*.

He sat in his office—until recently Bourassa's office—behind the desk that had been Maurice Duplessis's, with its curved maple leaves carved on the side and a royal crown carved centre front. Three ashtrays on the desk caught the gathering mound of cigarette butts as we spoke. He was wearing the expensive, conservative blue suit that had been bought for him for the election campaign to give him a reassuring image; he now wore it daily. He exuded a sense of serenity: power became him; he showed none of the irritation or bitterness that he had been unable to conceal after the defeats of 1970 and 1973. There was now less brooding in the blue-grey eyes over the pouches.

"What mandate do you feel that your government received on November 15?" I asked him.

"Well," he answered, "I think a very clear-cut mandate as a provincial government. One of its rather unprecedented aspects is that it is clearly a mandate which came nearly exclusively from the French-speaking majority in Quebec. In that sense it's a sort of national mandate from our point of view." In spite of the fact that he had been elected with only 42 per cent of the vote, he used the expression "national mandate" four times in the course of the interview.

But there is a sort of national—in our sense—a sort of national dimension to that mandate. . . . That added dimension of a sort of national mandate by the French majority in Quebec, which is unmistakable—there is a deep need for change, in many ways there is a very rapid evolution of Quebec society . . . and the cumulative effect of that evolution is in a sense embodied—and that makes it quite a bit different from, let us say, a traditional provincial government—is embodied in the fact that we are committed to a referendum on the basic question of independence.[6]

Lévesque had always made a distinction between two classes of people in Quebec. There were the French-speaking Quebecers, who formed a nation and thus could confer a "national mandate" on the Parti Québécois. And there were the anglophones, who were somehow not quite full participants in Quebec. He had expressed this view more clearly after his electoral defeat in 1973, when, in a bitter post-mortem of the election campaign, he called the victorious Liberals

148

"le parti des autres, " the party of the *others*—of Ottawa, of big business, and of the anglophones.[7]

The first bill introduced by the PQ asserted that Quebec was an ethnic state, and that the power of the state was to be used to enforce its character of and for francophones. Bill 22 had not gone far enough; there were too many compromises in the 1974 Official Language Act. The PQ would bring in a far more revolutionary bill, one intended to kill forever the vision of Quebec as a territory with two official languages.

The father of Bill 101, the Charter of the French Language, was Camille Laurin, a psychiatrist with hair dyed a funereal black and a cigarette dangling almost perpetually from his fingers. His mild, maternal manner concealed the temperament of a revolutionary. He was a Jacobin, ready, like Robespierre, to enforce *la République de la vertu.* What Laurin sought to enforce was a French linguistic and cultural integrity; in pursuing that goal, he had none of Lévesque's ambivalence.

Before he entered politics, Laurin published a series of articles in a medical journal in which he expounded on his vision of society. The articles were then collected in a book,[8] in which he presented French Canada as a child traumatically wrenched away from its natural parent, France, and taken over by a brutal foster parent, *les Anglais.* Laurin saw French Quebec as a neurotic child in need of psychotherapy; he used the language of psychiatry to explain his political vision: "In this country which is, after all, our own, the rupture of 1760 taught us to repress our most authentic emotions. They can only find their way confusedly, through a thousand external dangers, divisions, alienations, anguishes, and collective character formations."[9]

In his view, the French community was "humiliated, impoverished, and wounded" by the "English masters." The seat of government, Ottawa, was a unilingual capital, where the colonizers treated French Canadians with the utmost contempt. "The few francophones that they tolerated there have always been *rois-nègres* who, in English ('Speak white!'), always played the role of sacred hostages, lieutenants, or lackeys."[10] Quebec was now an adolescent, ready to break away from the master that had kept it subservient.

Laurin was a true disciple of Lionel Groulx, and he proposed the same remedy. "Our doctrine can be contained in this brief formula: we wish to reconstitute the fullness of our French life," Groulx had said. "We wish to prune this [ethnic] type of foreign growth in order to foster in it intensively the original culture, and to graft onto it the new virtues which it acquired since the Conquest."[11] Laurin would put that program into action.

On 1 April 1977, Laurin published a white paper on the French language. It is the best summary, the most complete expression, the logical conclusion of the assumptions shared by Jean Lesage, Daniel Johnson, René Lévesque, Robert Bourassa, and a host of Quebec intellectuals, artists, and politicians since 1962.

Although *La politique québécoise de la langue française*[12] was presented as a summary of all previous research, it in fact repeated all the myths that had circulated among the intelligentsia in the 1960s and 1970s and that the empirical research for the Gendron commission had revealed as unfounded.[13] Francophones, according to Laurin, had incomes as low as aboriginal Canadians'. They all had to speak English at work. The French language was in constant deterioration and in danger of disappearing. English-speaking Canadians all agreed that English was the only language of Canada.

If there was one egregiously false statement that stood out, it was the following sentence, which the white paper claimed was based on the research of the Gendron commission: "English predominates clearly in general communications at work: 82 per cent of all communications are carried out in English in Quebec as a whole; 84 per cent in Montreal, and 70 per cent in the province outside Montreal. English is also preponderant in more specific modes of communication."

This affirmation that almost all Quebecers worked in English was so contrary to what I knew of the Gendron commission's findings that I phoned Laurin's office to find the source of his statement. I was not given a reply. I searched through the Gendron commission's research and found at last the pertinent passage. Here is what it had found for the work situation of *anglophones*: "The predominance [of English] is found, as with francophones, in their general evaluation of the use of languages at work: over all, they use English 82 per cent of the time at work; in Montreal, 84 per cent, and 70 per cent in the province outside of Montreal." These were the very figures, applicable only to anglophones, that Laurin's white paper applied to all Quebecers.

Having established the mythical justification for drastic action, the white paper went on to describe the French ethnic state that the PQ proposed to erect. The Charter of the French Language was to be the new decalogue. To underline its solemnity, it was to be called Bill 1.[14] The white paper made clear that the chief purpose of the law would be to attack the power of English-speaking Quebecers and to use the state to establish the hegemony of French in all sectors of life in Quebec.

"The Quebec that we want to build will be essentially French," the white paper proposed. "The fact that the majority of its population is French will at last be clearly visible, at work, in communications, in the scenery. It is also a country where the traditional balance of power will be changed, particularly as regards the economy: the use of French will not merely be generalized to mask the predominance of powers other than that of francophones.

"In a word, the Quebec whose portrait as a whole is already sketched out in the Charter is a French-language society. There will no longer be any question of a bilingual Quebec," the white paper promised. "This use [of French] will symbolize and favour a reconquest by the French-speaking majority of Quebec of the control which it should have over the levers of the economy."

The spirit of the new legislation was expressed by the preamble of Bill 1, which swept away two hundred years of dualism: "The National Assembly acknowledges that the French language is, and always has been, the language of the people of Quebec and that it is this language which enables them to express their identity."[15]

While the debate over the Charter of the French Language was under way, Laurin gave a remarkable speech, on 30 May 1977, to the Montreal Personnel Association. He was explicit in naming anglophones as the scapegoats to be blamed for poverty among francophones. "There exists in the enterprises run by anglophones a system whereby francophones are exluded from the head offices and the administrative hierarchies," he said. "This facilitates the preservation of the power of the anglophones over certain key sectors of the economy of Quebec. . . . The problem, then, is how to break the system of exclusion."

Laurin went on to explain why anglophones systematically shut out francophones: it was because the anglophones were really foreigners, *étrangers*. There had been little improvement in the lot of the francophones, Laurin maintained, because "the economic life and the labour market of Quebec are dominated by interests which are foreign to the majority and by an economic elite that does not speak our language."

Laurin stated his conviction that the situation could not be corrected without the "firm intervention of the Quebec state." And he was ready to intervene firmly: "A government that has taken on the responsibility to give back to Quebecers their collective identity does not have the right to refuse this task even if it seems an enormous challenge." If the state did not intervene, he argued, the forces that created and maintained the existing order would continue to operate, and francophones would continue to be excluded from good jobs. "We cannot help francophones to fulfil themselves in all areas of activity in Quebec without opening up to them the doors of the management of the large companies and large establishments in Quebec."

Laurin assured his audience that his intention was not to disrupt life in Quebec: "It is social peace that we wish to assure. But social peace and harmony cannot be achieved if we tolerate striking injustices and visible and recognized inequalities."

An abundance of information was available to disprove Laurin's slander against the English-speaking population. A few years before, economist Pierre Harvey, a noted Péquiste and a professor at the Université de Montréal's business school, the Hautes Études Commerciales, had considered a thesis almost identical to that which Laurin put forward as fact, and had rejected it.[16] In 1977, three different analyses of data from the 1971 Census of Canada all established that French Canadians had made rapid economic progress between 1960 and 1970— the years of the reforms of the Quiet Revolution. For instance, François Vaillancourt, an economist at the Université de Montréal, showed that in 1960, people of British origin earned 55.1 per cent more than people of French origin. Ten years later, they earned 31.6 per cent more. In ten years, almost half of the 150-year-old gap in income between the two groups had been closed. Laurin asked Vaillancourt to summarize the available information on income according to language and ethnicity. Vaillancourt cited findings from another study: "The difference in salary between English-Scottish and French Canadians decreased strongly, from 50 per cent to 30 per cent from 1961 to 1971, and simultaneously the salary gap between the French and the labour market as a whole also decreased, from 9 per cent to 6 per cent."[17] How, then, could Laurin have maintained in his speech that little had changed or could change?

Moreover, the change accelerated between 1971 and 1977, as later research was to show. In 1979, Université de Montréal sociologists Paul Bernard and Jean Renaud published a study that they had carried out for the watchdog on language, the Office de la Langue Française, titled *The Evolution of the Socio-Economic Situation of Francophones and Non-Francophones in Quebec, 1971–1978*. They found that, from 1971 to the year after the Charter of the French Language went into effect, the number of francophones in positions of management increased by twenty thousand, while the number of non-francophones in management positions decreased by eight thousand. In the job category of natural sciences, engineering, and mathematics, according to Bernard and Renaud, the number of francophones increased by 26,000, the number of non-francophones by 271.

A study by Jac-André Boulet, published in February of 1979, found that among male workers in Montreal, the income gap of 51 per cent in favour of anglophones in 1961 had decreased to 30 per cent by 1971 and to 15 per cent by 1977. At this rate, Boulet predicted, the income gap would disappear altogether by 1982. Boulet also reported that francophones represented only 44 per cent of earners in the top-15 percentile salary bracket in 1960; by 1977 they made up 70 per cent of those in this bracket.

But the mythology in Quebec at that time blinded the great majority of people who took part in the language debate. Many continued to see things the way Lévesque did when he said, in 1967, "The situation in Quebec is the same as in Rhodesia. A privileged minority governing a backward majority."

The Charter of the French Language was a law geared precisely to overthrow the supposed colonial situation of the privileged governing minority. English-speaking Quebecers got the unmistakable message conveyed, first, by the Liberals' Official Language Act of 1974, and then, more strongly, by the Parti Québécois's Charter of the French Language of 1977: the government of Quebec, whichever party governed, considered them a dangerous minority to be contained and restricted. Between 1976 and 1986, 202,113 English-speaking Quebecers left Quebec for other provinces. This was a massive exodus, unprecedented in Canadian history: it amounted to 25.4 per cent of the anglophones who were in Quebec in 1976, the year before Bill 101 was adopted.

Bill 101 was also not without cost for the great bulk of French-speaking Quebecers who were not the new managers, directors, or owners of businesses backed by the Caisse de dépôt or the Société de développement industriel. In June, 1977, while debate over the language bill continued, Société d'Études et de Changement Organisationnels Inc. (SECOR),[18] a management-consulting firm, produced a study on the costs of implementing the language policy at the request of the Quebec Chamber of Commerce, and it became part of the Chamber's brief to the parliamentary committee studying the language legislation. The study showed that the bill, if passed as it stood, would mean the flight of 22,900 jobs from Quebec and an annual loss of $405.9 million in salaries.[19] In addition, SECOR estimated, implementation of the law in Quebec's private sector would cost between $260 million and $460 million. According to the study, the legislation would hurt French-owned and -operated companies, especially the smaller ones, because they would have to compete with large companies suddenly undergoing francisation and demanding francophone executives. "Francophone managerial resources are not very elastic in the short term. Too rapid an action would only redistribute a limited number of cadres, and the indigenous enterprises and the francophone small and medium enterprises in particular could be the big losers in this game of musical chairs."

The SECOR study predicted that the law would have the effect of discouraging future investment by firms that produced for markets outside Quebec:

Bill [101] will have its greatest effects on investors and on firms looking for investment opportunities. The language legislation will not hinder them from investing in Quebec in the natural resources sectors and in goods and services aimed specifically at the Quebec market. But it is hard to see how, in such an environment, a Canadian or international firm oriented to the whole Canadian market would establish its administrative head office in Quebec.

Finally, the study warned that companies would transfer many of their operations elsewhere. Seven months later, a striking instance of SECOR's prediction was made public: the management of Sun Life Assurance Co. of Canada, the largest Canadian-owned life insurer in terms of world-wide premium income and assets, announced that it intended to move its head office from Montreal to Toronto and would be asking permission of its shareholders the following month. The announcement, made on 7 January 1978 by Sun Life president Thomas Galt, pointed to Bill 101 as its reason for leaving:

Our policy holders reside in all parts of Canada and in several other countries, and English is the language of the majority of them. . . . We don't anticipate as probable the separation of Quebec from the rest of Canada. Nevertheless, as it now seems evident that the language of the Province of Quebec will become, by law, largely French, we can no longer believe that it will be possible for us to recruit or to keep in Montreal, or to bring there from outside of Quebec, a sufficient number of English-speaking people with the qualities and the competence required for the day-to-day operations of the company."[20]

Finance minister Jacques Parizeau was furious. He threatened retaliation against Sun Life if the company did not return to Quebec some $400 million which, he said, was the difference between the $1 billion that the company received from Quebec in premiums and what it invested there. He intended to get back the money "by moral suasion and moral blackmail, or by legislation." He claimed that the real reason for Sun Life's departure was not Bill 101 at all, but that the company knew that it had been caught cheating on its Quebec investments. "The game was up. They use Bill 101 as an excuse, which is charming on their part, but not very convincing." Parizeau called Sun Life "one of the worst corporate citizens that Quebec has known," and vowed that the company would not get away with "exploiting" the people of Quebec. "I don't intend to lose one million dollars," he said grimly.

To show that he meant business, Parizeau recalled that Sun Life held the insurance policies for Hydro-Québec employees, then between 17,000 and 22,000 people, depending on the time of year. He clearly was not going to let Sun Life keep those policies. He called on all Quebecers to boycott Sun Life, "one of the worst exploiters of the Quebec economy that decides that, the historical game being over, it is time to leave the ship." He even recommended that employees of Sun Life resign, since they had no future with a company that was going to lose its business in Quebec. The great display of rage did not prevent Sun Life from moving. It did serve, though, to attenuate some of the political fall-out of the company's departure. Quebec citizens might have begun worrying about the adverse effect of the language law on their pocketbooks had not Parizeau reassured them that the Charter of the French Language had nothing to do with Sun Life's departure. His threats also would induce other companies to go quietly, if they were leaving Quebec, and at least to leave a shell of a head office to avoid the concerted wrath of the Quebec government and of the unions, which immediately joined the call for a boycott.

So the Charter of the French Language became law. It provided for a twelve-member advisory body to the government on language questions, called the Conseil de la langue française. When its members were appointed, there was no English-speaking Quebecer, though one was of Italian origin and another of aboriginal origin. When questioned in the National Assembly about the absence of a representative for hundreds of thousands of English-speaking Quebecers, Camille Laurin could see no problem. "I would simply like to say that there are several minorities in Quebec," Laurin replied. "There is provision [in Bill 101] for two ethnic representatives. The law doesn't enshrine the right of any particular minorities to fill these two positions." Premier Lévesque also defended the absence of any anglophone representation. He argued that there was no need for a representative, when the premier himself spoke fluent English. At a press conference, he maintained that anglophones would have been "insulted" to be appointed as representatives of an ethnic group, since they did not consider themselves to be one.

The attitude of Lévesque and Laurin was not altogether surprising. They had passed a law with the object of attacking English presence and power. They did not want someone on the council, especially in the first years, to be a critic of that operation. Besides, the systematic exclusion of Anglo-Quebecers was a vested attitude. The government party had not a single Anglo member in its caucus. When, in 1977, Lévesque appointed someone to serve as his liaison with the English-speaking community, he chose Beverly Smith, an attractive young translator from Sault Ste. Marie with no obvious qualification for the job; she had been in Montreal for less than a year and had no roots or background in English-speaking Quebec. Laurin hired as his liaison to the English-speaking community David Payne, a British ex-priest immigrant who had studied in Rome.

Laurin showed his profound contempt for the rights of anglophones when, in December 1979, the Supreme Court of Canada found unconstitutional the chapter of Bill 101 dealing with the language of the Legislature and the courts. Altogether, seventeen judges had sat in judgment at different times and places on that part of Bill 101. All of them, including nine francophone judges, unanimously found Bill 101 unconstitutional. Instead of apologizing to the English-speaking community for violating its constitutional rights, Laurin gave a most demagogic speech in the National Assembly:

By the judgment of the Supreme Court, the federal power obtains what it was seeking. It reimposes on Quebec the century-old yoke, the straitjacket that Quebec had freed itself from, by asserting by legislative vote its own linguistic and cultural identity. The federal power thus reasserts its sole and sovereign authority, that Quebec remains an internal colony, that it can't escape political subordination to the central state, it cannot recognize and inscribe in laws its fundamental reality. . . . The Supreme Court, true to its established bent, preferred to perpetuate the power relations of 1867, consecrating the injustice and the domination to which Quebec was then subject.

Laurin spoke as though the federal government, not the courts, had struck down parts of his law, or as though the court had acted politically rather than interpreting the constitution. A true revolutionary, he placed his own vision above the law and the courts. It was a performance that was true to the man, and true to the anti-English prejudice that was central to the mythology of the Parti Québécois.

When Quebec rejected the previous language tolerance and adopted the Charter of the French Language, English-speaking Quebecers left Quebec in droves. Nationalists rejoiced that "Quebec will now be as French as Ontario is

155

English," as Camille Laurin often said. But Quebec and, especially, Montreal would suffer as a result an economic decline from which they have not yet recovered.

Notes

1.The cry of the demonstrators in France of 1968: This is just the beginning, keep up the fight.
2.I never thought I could be so proud to be a Québécois.
3.Félix Leclerc, *Le petit livre bleu de Félix* (Montreal: Nouvelles éditions de l'arc, 1978), pp. 126–27.
4.Lise Payette, *Le pouvoir? Connais pas!* (Montreal: Québec/Amérique, 1982), p. 29.
5.Report by William Johnson, *Globe and Mail*, 25 Nov. 1976.
6.Report by William Johnson in *Report on Business* of the *Globe and Mail*, 1 Jan. 1977.
7.Report by William Johnson, *Globe and Mail*, 6 Nov. 1973.
8.Camille Laurin, *Ma traversée du Québec* (Montreal: Éditions du Jour, 1970).
9.Ibid., p. 94.
10.Ibid., p. 95.
11.Lionel Groulx, "Notre doctrine," in *L'Action française*, 5 (Jan. 1921): 25.
12. Gouvernement du Québec, Ministère du développement culturel, *La politique de la langue française* (Quebec City: Éditeur officiel, 1977).
13.Pierre-É. Laporte, *L'usage des langues dans la vie économique au Québec: situation actuelle et possibilités de changement*. Study conducted on behalf of the Commission d'enquête sur la situation de la langue française et sur les droits linguistiques au Québec, table I.6. See above, chapter eight.
14.Because of a procedural fumble, Bill 1 was eventually adopted as Bill 101.
15.After outcries in the French press that this preamble went too far, Laurin changed it, when Bill 1 was reintroduced as Bill 101, to the following: "The French language, the distinctive language of a people that is in the majority French-speaking, is the instrument by which that people has articulated its identity."
16.Pierre Harvey, "Pourquoi le Québec et les Canadiens français occupent-ils une place inférieure sur le plan économique?" *Le Devoir*, 13 and 14 Mar. 1969.
17.As well, a study by Jac-André Boulet, an economist with the Economic Council of Canada, studied the income of males in Montreal. He found that the income of the average French male had increased by 70.6 per cent over ten years, while the income of men of English and Scottish origin had increased by only 47.2 per cent. And Calvin Veltman, a State University of New York sociologist, compared incomes of males in the Montreal area. He found that the median income of unilingual anglophones had increased by $1,100 over ten years, while that of unilingual francophones had increased by $1,900, or almost twice as much.
18.The findings cited are from Boulet's study (see note 13A).
19.SECOR had been retained by the former Liberal government to devise the regulations for partial francisation of industry proposed, but never implemented, under Bill 22, and was also the adviser to the Régie de la Language Française, the watchdog agency set up under the bill.
21.Report by William Johnson, *Globe and Mail*, 8 Jan. 1978.

CHAPTER ELEVEN

The 1980 Referendum

The Parti Québécois came to power with a sense that its mission was to fulfil French Quebec's destiny in history: to become a sovereign state. To achieve that, the Parti Québécois government had to win the referendum it had promised.

René Lévesque gave his first major speech as premier on 25 January 1977, when he addressed the prestigious Economic Club of New York. The PQ victory had made investors nervous and brought a slight drop in the value of Quebec bonds. However, most American financiers did not take Lévesque's separatism seriously. They thought of him as a decentralizer who raised the spectre of separatism to wrest concessions from the government of Canada—a French-speaking Jimmy Carter in a hurry.

But the premier soon gave them an insight into Quebec nationalism. "Independence for Quebec now appears as normal, I might say almost as inevitable, as it was for the American states of two hundred years ago," he told the financiers. "It would be senseless, like King Canute trying to stop the tide, to waste efforts in order to delay the final outcome of something as natural and irreversible as growth itself." He promised, however, that the independence of Quebec would come about with little disruption—in fact, with nothing but co-operation between a newly independent Quebec and what used to be Canada. "Once again, if you consider how delicate such matters can be, the evolution is going on in an atmosphere of remarkable serenity. Initially there were a few tense moments, but now there is nothing but patient democratic work, so that after the Quiet Revolution, we are entitled to expect Quiet Independence in the near future."[1]

A university professor, appointed to ask the first question after Lévesque finished his speech, sent a laugh rippling through the ballroom, where sixteen hundred people had gathered to hear Lévesque. He prefaced his question, "I would like to commend Premier Lévesque for a very informative and reassuring speech." In fact, few were reassured. They could see, at last, that Lévesque was serious about wanting sovereignty for Quebec. But they also saw a premier who looked at the future through rose-coloured glasses. Lévesque's speech probably enhanced his stature as a leader with great ambitions, but it did no good for Quebec's credit rating.

As Lévesque left New York, his speech had the immediate effect of further driving down the value of Quebec bonds and lowering the value of the Canadian dollar. For the next couple of years, there was little private investment in Quebec. What new employment there was came almost exclusively from the public sector, and especially from Hydro-Quebec and its huge project in the James Bay region.

A few days after Lévesque's New York speech, Pierre Trudeau travelled to Quebec City to offer a very different vision in a forty-six-minute speech to the Quebec Chamber of Commerce that was carefully crafted and delivered without notes in a low-key, almost conversational tone of voice. His theme was that after twenty years of soul-searching about its national identity, Quebec must soon come to a clear decision. "The choice must be definitive and final. If the referendum is lost, it should not be reopened for 15 years," Trudeau said.

He challenged Lévesque to prove that Quebec would be better off as an independent state than as a part of Canada. Almost every objective that the premier had proposed for an independent Quebec could be achieved within the federation, he asserted. He recalled that he had entered politics in 1965 because at that time, in the universities, the only question on people's minds was separatism. There was no possibility of interesting people in law or in anthropology or in "the real problems," including the economy, equality of opportunity, career possibilities for young people, and quality of life.

He had opposed opening up the constitutional question. "I said that, if we got off on that, we'll lose another twenty years. Meanwhile, while we remain in indecision, others are making choices. They are making them for us. Others are determining the conditions of our existence." However, he was now ready to open up negotiations on the constitution without preconditions other than respect for men and women and for certain basic rights. His only commitment was to "functional policies"—that is, to settling questions of jurisdiction on the basis of what is better for the people and for good government. "Everything else is just quarrels among politicians. We all think that we can do a better job than other levels of government."

He welcomed, he said, the fact that the election of the Parti Québécois now required Quebecers to make a choice, to "put an end at last to agonizing over our political identity. Let's get it over with so that we can talk about the real problems. If it is not we Quebecers and we Canadians who build the country, it is others who will do it for us."

He received a standing ovation, and the crowd of fifteen hundred business people burst out singing of *O Canada*. "I found it dazzling," one Chamber of Commerce member said as he left the hall. "I think it is *the* speech of Mr. Trudeau's career."[2]

Over the next three years, the people of Quebec were constantly solicited by the opposing visions of their two most celebrated leaders. Lévesque appealed to the atavistic sense of *nous*, us, the French-speaking ethnic group, defensive and distrustful, surrounded by enemies, which must form a state of its own. Trudeau

158

appealed for commitment to a broader, inclusive political community that would make choices based on what was better for the people rather than on ethnicity. The two visions were not totally mutually exclusive. Lévesque did not exclude anglophones from Quebec—insofar as they were kept to a small minority and restricted in where they could use their language. As long as the hegemony of French and francophones was ensured by coercive law—the Charter of the French Language—Lévesque welcomed a limited number of anglophones and immigrants. But the immigrants, whatever their mother tongue, must be forced to attend French schools and integrate into a French institutional structure.

Trudeau was not indifferent to the cultural security of French Canadians, but he believed that the security of French Canadians in every sphere—language, social, economic, and political development—was better assured by extending their dynamism to all of Canada than by falling back on Quebec. He pointed out that French-speaking Quebecers would not be freed from having to learn English in a separate Quebec. On the contrary, they would be forced to use more English, not less, than within a Canada that gave national recognition to French.

In 1977, Lévesque tried to deprive Trudeau of his best issue in Quebec by making a proposal to the other premiers. Quebec's Charter of the French Language would exclude from English schools future migrants from other provinces. However, Lévesque would allow English-speaking children from other provinces into Quebec's English schools if the province of origin signed an "agreement of reciprocity" with Quebec, under which francophone children from Quebec moving to those provinces would also be guaranteed access to French schools.

Lévesque was trying to achieve by interprovincial action what Trudeau kept trying to achieve by the constitution: the guarantee of French-school rights in the other provinces. If he had succeeded, he would have undercut Trudeau's appeal to Quebecers and provided a demonstration that sovereignty-association could work: there was no need for a federal government to protect French Canadians when the Quebec government could negotiate as an equal with other provincial governments.

When the premiers met in St. Andrews, New Brunswick, for their annual conference, the other nine rejected Lévesque's proposal for reciprocal agreements, but they did sign a joint statement committing themselves to provide schooling in French wherever numbers warranted. Then, at a follow-up meeting in Montreal in February, 1978, all ten premiers signed a statement that accepted the principle of schooling in the minority language, but left its application to the discretion of each province:

Each child of the French-speaking or English-speaking minority is entitled to an education in his or her language in the primary or the secondary schools in each province, wherever numbers warrant. It is understood, due to exclusive jurisdiction of provincial governments in the field of education, and due also to wide cultural and demographic differences, that the implementation of the foregoing principle would be as defined by each province.[3]

For Lévesque, this was a coup. His own Bill 101 prevented English-speaking children from other provinces from attending English schools in Quebec, and he would not change the law. But he had persuaded the other premiers to declare themselves publicly for a principle that they had always refused to Trudeau: that French-speaking children were entitled to an education in French.

Trudeau, meanwhile, continued his quest for constitutional reform and the protection of French rights. He had failed at Victoria because of Robert Bourassa's veto. He had tried again after he won a second majority government in 1974, determined to patriate the constitution unilaterally if necessary. But Bourassa foiled him a second time, by putting together a common front of the provinces and calling a snap election in 1976 precisely to stop patriation without the consent of the provinces.

After the PQ victory, Trudeau tried again. He toured the provincial capitals, looking for a consensus that would make patriation possible—including language rights—before Lévesque held his referendum. This would provide the best argument for Canada, he believed. But he found little support among the premiers.

He kept trying. He introduced a bill in June, 1978, that proposed a reform of the constitution in two stages, over three years. Patriation would be carried through, along with a first set of amendments dealing with matters under purely federal jurisdiction, by 1 July 1979. The second phase, to be completed by 1991, would deal with constitutional changes that required the agreement of the provinces. This latest proposal resembled the earlier ones in putting a statement of rights, including language rights, at the heart of the constitution. Trudeau also proposed that the Senate be transformed into a House of the Federation, with half the members named by the federal government, half by the provinces. As for redistribution of powers, Trudeau suggested that it should work both ways. "The Canadian federation is already characterized by its very great decentralization and so a massive transfer of powers from the federal government to the provinces would not solve our problems," according to a federal statement. "The government anticipates rather a judicious combination of changes, in either direction."

But this latest attempt to secure a Canadian constitution was no more successful than the earlier ones. Premier Lévesque immediately denounced the proposal and followed the same course as had Bourassa: he rallied the provincial premiers to oppose the plan, and the premiers chose to align themselves with the separatist premier of Quebec rather than with the federalist prime minister.

When the premiers met in Regina in August, 1978, their attitude was expressed by Ontario's premier, William Davis. They had opposed just about every part of the federal proposal, including the timetable. At a press conference, Davis maintained that much more time was needed for discussions across the country.

"You know, you just don't rewrite a constitution of a country, certainly not a country like ours, in a matter of two or three months," Davis said. A CBC reporter: "Seven years?" Mr. Davis: "Well, seven years, even. I mean, it's not just quite as simple as that." Another reporter: "Fifty years?" Davis: "I don't know. I haven't been around for fifty years."

As in 1976, the premiers were against patriation unless all their individual demands could be met at the same time. The idea of Canada as a confederacy of sovereign provinces was gaining ground among the premiers, for it gave each of them a far more splendid role. At two constitutional conferences, one in October, 1978, and the other in February, 1979, the deadlock between the prime minister and the premiers continued. The premiers didn't care much for patriation and language rights, which were Trudeau's concern, but they did want extensive new powers, which Trudeau refused.

The constitutional proposals became a dead letter when a federal election was called for 22 May 1979, and Trudeau and the Liberals lost. Trudeau's dream of a charter of rights and of French Canadians being able to exercise language rights in every part of the country seemed gone forever. He announced his retirement from politics, and the Liberals prepared to hold a leadership convention.

For the PQ government, Trudeau's defeat by Joe Clark's Conservatives was a gift from heaven. Clark, it was true, had won only a minority government. Though the Tories took more seats, the Liberals had actually received more votes. Quebec, in fact, elected sixty-seven Liberals, six Social Credit members, and only two Progressive Conservatives; Trudeau's Quebec vote had actually gone up, while the Liberals were rejected in the rest of the country. Late that election night, a PQ minister, Jacques-Yvan Morin, gave me his impression of what Trudeau's fall would mean in Quebec. "Quebecers have been schizophrenic," he said. "They voted for René Lévesque and they voted for Pierre Trudeau, though the two men represent incompatible concepts of the future of Quebec. But now Quebecers will cease to be schizophrenic."[4]

It was a dream scenario for Lévesque, and he made the most of it the next day in the National Assembly. "In two societies, visceral reflexes opposed each other. . . . Each people made a choice based on its own identity." He mocked the election slogan of the Quebec Liberals, "Speak Loudly, Quebec": "You could say that [the two societies] spoke loudly. Probably more loudly than ever before." From the political polarization of the country along language lines, Lévesque drew the conclusion that underlay the very foundation and existence of the Parti Québécois. "Every attempt, no matter how sincere, no matter how brilliant, to try to build a Québécois power outside of Quebec has always been ephemeral and, in the last analysis, condemned to failure. . . . There is only one power and one government that can belong to us Québécois and be at our service permanently, and it is here in this House that you will find it."[5]

But then the preposterous intervened. Prime Minister Clark presented a tough budget, then forgot to count heads in the House, where his minority government held a precarious sway. Clark was defeated in December, 1979, and the following February Trudeau was again prime minister, just three months before the referendum. The Péquiste rejoicing of the previous May gave way to gloom. This was their worst-case scenario, improbable almost beyond belief. Politically dead and almost buried, Trudeau had returned to life, and he was haunting the Parti Québécois.

Lysiane Gagnon expressed in *La Presse* the dismay that overtook the PQ members of the National Assembly when faced with the Clark government's defeat:

That vote in Ottawa completely upset the strategy so carefully laid down for the referendum. The Péquiste government had banked heavily on the fact that the federal government would henceforth be embodied by a prime minister and a Cabinet both essentially English-speaking and non-Quebec. Indeed, it was for this reason—to bring down the "French Power" that, the PQ believed, was confusing matters by making francophone Quebecers think that they were at home in Canada—that the Lévesque government went so far as to back openly the Créditistes of Fabien Roy: all means were fair when it came to beating the Liberals.

Not only was Trudeau back, he was more popular with Quebecers than ever before. In a public-opinion poll taken by the Institut Québécois d'Opinion Publique between 5 and 12 December, 1979, as the parties were about to begin their election campaigns, only 26.9 per cent of Quebecers had a favourable opinion of Joe Clark, but an incredible 83 per cent had a favourable opinion of Pierre Trudeau.

The Quebec government, meanwhile, had set about putting in place the legislative framework for conducting the referendum. By judicious leaks, then by public statements, Robert Burns, the minister responsible, led the press to believe that Quebec would adopt the model that the United Kingdom had used in 1975, when it held a referendum on Britain's continuing membership in the European Community. In fact, Quebec's referendum bill was utterly different. The British law was democratic; the Quebec law violated freedom of speech, freedom of association, and elementary rules of fairness.

In Britain, the government entrusted preparation of the referendum to a committee of civil servants headed by the deputy minister of education; elected members of Parliament, including the Cabinet, were kept at arm's length from the process. In Quebec, Burns maintained that he, too, was remaining at arm's length from the preparation process. In fact, the referendum policy was piloted by three men, of whom two, Louis Bernard and André Larocque, were long-time committed full-time employees of the PQ; the third, François Renaud, had been hired specifically to work on the referendum policy.

These three produced something very different from the British model. Britain had presented a referendum bill that dealt specifically and exclusively with the referendum on the European Community. It included the date of the referendum and the question to be asked. In Quebec, a white paper was published in August, 1977, which announced for later a bill on referenda in general—umbrella legislation. A parliamentary committee held hearings on the white paper, rather than on the bill, so that witnesses before it were forbidden from discussing the coming referendum on sovereignty-association, on the grounds that the white paper was about referenda in general. One expert witness, sociologist Maurice Pinard, was called to order when he began to discuss the effects that different referendum questions about sovereignty could have. Pinard apologized sarcastically for not having prepared his material on the subject of chastity belts.

The British white paper had bound the government in advance to consider the results of the referendum as final: "The Government has agreed to be bound by the verdict of the British people, as expressed in the referendum result." Contrast this clear-cut commitment with the evasive statement contained in the Quebec white paper: "A government can always commit itself explicitly to accept the result of a referendum." But of course, the Quebec government made no such commitment with respect to the referendum on sovereignty-association.

The real sleight-of-hand in the Quebec bill was to turn two voluntary associations from the British referendum policy into compulsory "umbrella committees." In the former case, the two associations, one for each side, each received a grant of 125,000 pounds to help them fight the referendum, but no one was forced to campaign under their aegis, and they were not forced to spend exactly the same amount of money. In fact, the association favouring Britain's remaining in the European Community spent about ten times as much as the association opposed, because it was the much more popular option.

In Quebec, on the other hand, no one was to be allowed to campaign except under the two umbrella committees, set up entirely by the politicians of the National Assembly, who were to divide into a Yes committee and a No committee, and were therefore given the legal mandate to control totally the public debate during the referendum. Freedom of association was suspended. People could not band together to conduct their own campaign on the themes and with the leaders they chose: the leader of each side was picked by the politicians, and the only alternative available outside of the committees was an individual expenditure of up to three hundred dollars to rent a hall. Six million people, in their thousands of communities, were regimented into just two committees, which had to approve all the campaign expenditures for every street, neighbourhood, village, town, or city, to make sure that the sum total of all the expenditures was within the limit set by the National Assembly. This effectively discouraged most people from participating, especially citizens at large who were not already committed to a political party.

To justify transforming the permissive British system into the coercive Quebec machine, Burns claimed over and over, before the press, the parliamentary committee, and the National Assembly, that in Britain all parties regretted not having done it the Quebec way in 1975. When he went to Britain in 1977, he said, everyone, whether for or against Britain's staying in the European Community, expressed the regret that they had not imposed a control on total expenses. (In fact, the UK's next referendum, on devolution of powers to Scotland and Wales, like the previous one, had no ceiling on total expenditures.) He also told the parliamentary committee that Australia controlled total expenditures in referendums as Quebec was about to do, and allowed a maximum expenditure of one dollar per voter, while Quebec would allow fifty cents. In fact, this was untrue. A bill had been introduced, but never passed, in Australia that would have controlled the total expenditures of the political parties, but not of the citizens.

The government had good reason to throw up a smokescreen around its radical legislation. It was tailored to give the Parti Québécois every advantage, and to make it as difficult as possible for the federalists to campaign. Under a semblance of concern for equity, the PQ was really serving its own sacred cause. René Lévesque was the unquestioned leader of the separatists in Quebec, except for fringe groups, and he had at his command an integrated party. His ascendency over all the nationalist organizations, such as the Société Saint-Jean-Baptiste, was unquestioned. A referendum in which the Yes side was put entirely under the control of the Parti Québécois was exactly what Lévesque wanted. It even allowed the PQ to silence the extremist fringe groups on the separatist side.

The federalists, on the other hand, were divided, with clashing visions and conflicting interests. When they met to form what was called the Pre-Referendum Committee (later called the Pro-Canada Committee), in December of 1977, there were seven political parties represented: the Liberal Party of Quebec, the federal Liberals, the Union Nationale, the Ralliement Créditiste, the Progressive Conservatives, the New Democratic Party, and the Parti National Populaire. The federal Liberals and the Quebec Liberals had very different ideas about Canada and Quebec, and about referendum strategy; the Quebec Liberals and the Union Nationale not only had different visions, they also had competing interests as parties that fought each other in elections; and so it went with the other political parties. The committee kept announcing that it was about to launch a great publicity campaign, but the dissension within always kept it stalemated. The referendum campaign would involve mobilizing many thousands of people who had never been actively involved in politics before, and the issue of who would reap the benefits of this massive mobilization was of utmost significance. No party could accept its leader being out of the limelight.

Finally, in February of 1979, the months of wrangling came to an end. The pretense of a common front was removed, and the Pro-Canada Committee was disbanded. Instead, Claude Ryan's Liberals took control and ran the No campaign as an extension of the Liberal Party, just as the Parti Québécois ran the Yes campaign as an extension of itself. (After the referendum, the Union Nationale, which had elected eleven members to the National Assembly in 1976, effectively ceased to exist as a political party, as did the Ralliement Créditiste and the Parti National Populaire. All three were steam-rollered under a law that was supposedly meant to give voice to the free expression of the people.)

Meanwhile, Lévesque kept up his "us versus them" rhetoric. When he gave his inaugural message for the session of the Assembly that was to include the referendum, he launched into an attack on federalism on the grounds that Quebecers had to pay taxes to an alien government. What are *they* doing with *our* money? "Half of the taxes of Quebecers still feed the coffers of Ottawa. And this part of our taxes is that which most directly affects our economy. It gives to another government, which is at the service of another majority, the strategic margin of manoeuvre and the great levers for intervention that are terribly lacking to Quebec."

As the referendum approached, government spokespeople spoke less and less about sovereignty under any form. Instead, what they sold was an appeal to a strategic vote: vote Yes to get negotiations—any negotiations—under way. A strong Yes vote would show English Canada that Quebec is serious—about something. "A positive referendum would have an immense political weight and would bestow at last on Quebecers the power, sought for so long, to unblock the impasse," said Claude Morin in a speech in March, 1979. "Outside Quebec they presently reject everything: separation, sovereignty, association, special status, renewed federalism. The system is blocked. Only the referendum can open up new perspectives."[6]

The message: the referendum is only nominally about sovereignty-association. It is really about constitutional change, any constitutional change. This strategy meant that a majority Yes vote, if it was obtained, would have no precise significance or objective: it would only be an instrument of pressure for bargaining. As the date approached at which the party had to keep its promise and call a referendum, the objective became less to win support for sovereignty than to avoid its manifest repudiation. A Yes, just about any Yes, however meaningless, became the object of the exercise.

With its referendum machinery in place, in March, 1980, the PQ government held its thirty-five-hour debate in the National Assembly on the wording of the question to be put to the public on 20 May. Rather than ask the people of Quebec whether they favoured sovereignty, the PQ proposed to ask for "a mandate to negotiate" a new Quebec-Canada agreement. The wording of the question also promised that no constitutional change would take place in Quebec without a second referendum to approve whatever changes the PQ had negotiated.

During the parliamentary debate, equality of the two sides, supposedly such a concern for the Parti Québécois, simply did not exist, since there more than twice as many Péquiste members of the National Assembly as there were in the opposition parties combined and each got the same amount of time to speak. The Péquistes avoided the supposed subject of the debate—the wording of the referendum question—and used all their time in front of the National Assembly cameras to urge the population to vote Yes. It was a very uneven contest, with the plodding Liberals debating the question, while the Péquistes soared to great heights of oratory, denouncing Confederation and all the disloyal citizens—like Claude Ryan—who supported it.

Camille Laurin, as usual, found the words to stigmatize Ottawa and English-speaking Canadians. "The essence of federalism is the domination over the provinces, and especially over Quebec, by a strong central power which has kept to itself all the important powers . . . and which is manipulated to its advantage by the Anglo-Saxon economic power." For Claude Ryan, who had published in January a proposal for renewed federalism, Laurin had nothing but contempt. "The Ryan proposal seems to me to put Quebec in mortal danger; to accept it would be to consent to suicide." Laurin then dismissed it as "demeaning" and "abasement."

Another theme put forward by the Péquistes was that a Yes in the referendum was the logical continuity of what Quebec premiers had wanted from the time of Honoré Mercier in the last century, through Louis-Alexandre Taschereau, Maurice Duplessis, Jean Lesage, Daniel Johnson, and even Robert Bourassa. The PQ was the heir of Quebec nationalism, and a Yes vote in the referendum would be its latest manifestation. This grand invitation to all nationalists, whatever their constitutional convictions, had been symbolized in 1977 when the government dusted off a statue of Maurice Duplessis that had been completed but never displayed. Lévesque, who had despised Duplessis, had the statue proudly ensconced by the south entrance of the Assembly. The sacred unity of all nationalists was thereby proclaimed.

Rodrigue Biron, who had defected to the PQ from the leadership of the Union Nationale, symbolized this rallying of the nationalists, invoking the names of all previous UN leaders to suggest that they, too, were they still alive, would be voting Yes:

I take up and continue the fight of Duplessis, [Paul] Sauvé, Johnson, and Bertrand, a fight for autonomy, a fight for equality. To say Yes at this time of our history is to ensure an authentic survival to all that was truest, most solidary, most beautiful, greatest, during the administrations of Jean Lesage and Robert Bourassa. From now on, I accept completely the history and heritage of my predecessors by committing myself irreversibly to the Yes, a Yes to the desire to achieve, with the rest of Canada, negotiations on a new political agreement based, this time, on the juridical equality of the two founding peoples of Canada.

As the debate went on in the National Assembly, a poll showed the Yes side pulling ahead of the No side. Ryan and the Liberals put on a performance that was totally negative, criticizing the wording of the question and suggesting that the Péquistes were liars and hypocrites. The Péquistes, on the other hand, were positive as well as negative, playing to the pride of Quebecers, speaking of a "new agreement" as though they were proposing to build Confederation instead of dismantle it.

Claude Charron, the PQ's House leader and its most eloquent orator, even evoked the memory of Joliette and Marquette, who explored the Mississippi, and LaVérendrye, who, Charron said, discovered the Rockies. But then came the Rebellion of 1837 and the Union government, created to assimilate French Canadians. The same policy had applied ever since.

Our people, who were told they were fully Canadians, who were offered that mirage to entice them into Confederation, soon understood that once they crossed the Ottawa River or the Baie des Chaleurs, they put themselves in danger. When I say our people, I mean those of Manitoba, the francophones, who, as soon as they became a minority in 1890, were refused the right to speak their language in their parliament, unconstitutionally, as we discovered ninety years later. Some of our people who worked for us, who thought it was their country, were hanged in Saskatchewan, despite the insult that was to the Québécois.

Tribalist grudges going back centuries were exhumed. According to Charron's history lesson, the French Canadians, the Québécois, were ever reviled, oppressed, swindled. Economically, Confederation was all for Ontario. "Why must the Québécois always have the last share of economic development?" And always, the Québécois were fed the illusion, never realized, of a renewed federalism. "One is born a renewed federalist, one dies a renewed federalist."

In comparison, the riposte of the Liberals seemed querulous, weak. Solange Chaput-Rolland, a columnist and broadcaster before she became a Liberal member, protested against the treatment meted out to the proponents of the No side, who were being called traitors. She warned that the government's strategy was turning Quebecers against Quebecers. Paraphrasing a psalm, she said, "It is not the enemy who treated me outrageously . . . but you, my like, my brother. . . . I say no to an intolerant society, which our debates have allowed us to glimpse as a possibility."

Meanwhile, the real issue of the referendum became increasingly lost under all the talk of a "new agreement." Girerd, the deft cartoonist of *La Presse*, caught the PQ's strategy perfectly in a front-page cartoon. He portrayed René Lévesque smoking, shrugging, and saying: "Look, the *OUI* is so small a *oui* that it's practically a *non*. So why vote *non?*"

167

Justice minister Marc-André Bédard expressed the thrust of the PQ's case, which was to suggest that, instead of doing something negative, instead of proposing separation from Canada, the PQ was really proposing something positive for both Quebec and Canada: "This new agreement is an act of faith and of hope in Quebec and in the rest of Canada, an act of faith in the ability of our two democratic societies to agree while negotiating on the basis of equality. That is the agreement that we are proposing. I am convinced that not only the future of Quebec, but also the future of Canada, lies in a mandate which is firm, solid, massive for the Government of Quebec to negotiate this new Quebec-Canada agreement."

The government also did everything to reassure Quebecers that there was utterly no risk in voting Yes, for it was asking for no more than a moral mandate to help it in its negotiations with Ottawa. As Claude Charron put it, "If the government of Quebec gets this mandate, what will be different the next day? Nothing. We continue to work the day after the referendum, we continue to pay taxes to Ottawa, we continue to receive unemployment insurance or old-age pensions the day after the referendum. Nothing is changed, but in another respect everything is changed, because the Government of Quebec can now negotiate with the backing of the population."

Oh, wondrous referendum. It changed nothing and everything. The Yes campaign became an exercise in consciousness-raising and swelling pride for the Québécois. People would get together, make public confessions, discuss the oppressions of the old regime, acquire strength from each other, overcome old fears and doubts, link hands, sing, let joy course through them, contemplate the bright new collective identity that became possible after their consciousness had been raised to the level of liberation, rub shoulders with political and entertainment stars who shared their consciousness, shout with joy the word that would make everything possible: *OUI!*

Non, in comparison, lacked a certain *élan*, a *joie de vivre*. Claude Ryan, craggy and severe, hardly emanated good feeling as he warned constantly that the PQ was misleading the population with a trick question, and that a Yes would really lead to independence. He played upon fears and insecurities. But his message did not seem as effective in reaching the population as did the message of future joy sung by the PQ.

The turning point for the Non side did not come from a development on the constitutional front. Instead, a slip by Lise Payette, the minister responsible for the status of women, changed the momentum of both campaigns. Speaking to a meeting of the Parti Québécois in Montreal, Payette read from a primer that contained a stereotypical little boy and little girl named Guy and Yvette.

Guy plays sports, swimming, gymnastics, tennis, boxing, diving. His ambition is to become a champion and to win many cups. Yvette, his little sister, is joyous and nice . . . she always finds a way to please her parents.

Yesterday, at dinnertime, she sliced the bread, poured hot water over the tea in the teapot, she carried the sugar bowl, the butter dish, the jug of milk, she also helped serve the roast chicken. After breakfast, she was happy to dry the dishes and sweep the rug. Yvette is a helpful little girl.[7]

Payette then suggested that the stereotype of Yvette was exactly what the No side in the referendum had in mind. She complained that more women than men were intending to vote No, "like the anglophones." She went on to say that Claude Ryan was the kind of man she "hated." He wanted to keep Quebec women passive and subservient, like the Yvette of the reader. Carried away, she went further. Ryan, she said, "is married to an Yvette."

A single reporter was among the 750 people in the audience. Renée Rowan of *Le Devoir* reported Payette's words about the newspaper's former publisher and his spouse, Madeleine. A few days later, Lise Bissonnette published a zinger of an editorial, in which she took Payette to task for turning women against each other for political purposes. She accused Payette of old-fashioned sexism: "To think that she 'hates' [Ryan] to the point of denigrating his wife, and links a woman to the personality of her husband in a way that just isn't done and hasn't been since the first utterances of feminism!"[8]

"Yvette" became the rallying cry for women committed to voting No. Rather than repudiate the contemptuous title that Payette had given them, they wore it as a badge of honour and protest. On 30 March 1980, at a time when the federalist camp was full of disquiet, with a sense that the Yes side had stolen ahead, women organized a brunch at the Chateau Frontenac in Quebec, to which seventeen hundred turned out. It was a low-key but warm affair. Senator Thérèse Casgrain, the pioneer feminist who had won the vote for women in Quebec in the 1940s and had stormed Mackenzie King's office to make sure that the mother's name was on family-allowance cheques, spoke before the "Yvettes" of her love of Canada, from St. John's to Vancouver. Other speakers were Madeleine Ryan; Monique Bégin, who had been research director for the Royal Commission on the Status of Women and was now federal minister of health and welfare; and Solange Chaput-Rolland. They then rented the Montreal Forum and had an even bigger success, with women from many walks of life giving their testimony in favour of Canada.

That such a revolt, as much against the superciliousness of the PQ as it was for federalism, should have sparked the No campaign tells much about the state of ideology in Quebec. So much tribal historiography had been inculcated that it was difficult to mobilize people around the defence of federalism, which had brought Quebecers such a high level of prosperity and freedom. It was easier to mobilize in reaction to the relentless avant-gardism of the PQ and its monopolistic claim to represent patriotism and progress.

On 20 April, a poll published by the Institut Québécois d'Opinion Publique showed that the Yvette phenomenon had had a major impact. Among women,

169

43.5 per cent said that they would vote Yes in the referendum in March; by April, this proportion dropped to 34.3 per cent. The Yes vote among men was 13.8 percentage points higher than among women. As a result, the sample as a whole showed a dead heat: 41.1 per cent of Quebecers said they would vote Yes; 40.9 per cent said they would vote No.

The Yes and the No campaigns contrasted sharply in style. A typical No meeting in Beauport, a suburb of Quebec City, on 22 April, was held in a church basement. The hall was decorated with posters carrying the slogan of the No campaign: *MON NON EST QUÉBÉCOIS.*[9] The hall was full to overflowing. The master of ceremonies established his credentials as *pure laine*—a Québécois through and through. "My ancestors arrived here in 1634," he said. "I think that we can say, like the separatists, that our *non* is *Québécois.*"

On the stage, about two dozen dignitaries sat on hard-backed yellow chairs: they were mostly members of the county's No Committee. All were introduced, several were applauded. And fifteen of them gave speeches, one after the other, in relentless succession. They were local mayors, doctors, school trustees, a high-school principal, a psychiatrist, a few businessmen. Only the visiting politicians were widely known outside their home community. They had been instructed to speak for no more than ten minutes, but for quite a few, their fervour to keep Quebec in Canada inspired many more words than could be packed into that short a time.

For journalists covering the event, only Claude Ryan's speech was likely to deserve reporting. But he was kept till the last, and the deadlines for reporting came and went. Ryan, from his seat at centre stage, smiled and applauded through it all. He did not care about deadlines. When his turn came, at 10:12 p.m., he spoke for fifty minutes. He said that he had been advised not to hold evening meetings, that it was better to hold meetings in time for the television news. But, he said, he did not intend to tailor his campaign to the needs of the news media: "If they don't talk about it, then people will transmit the message by word of mouth across the province." This was an old-fashioned town meeting from the days before radio and television.

The Parti Québécois, on the other hand, ran a razzle-dazzle campaign made for television, but also designed to get local people involved. Lévesque flew around the province, and everywhere he went he received petitions from small groups of people who brought him a testimony of their support for the Yes side. The premier ceremoniously accepted the testimonies, and in return presented a parchment commemorating the event.

A medical doctor would come forward with his petition and announce that fourteen doctors of the Lower North Shore were on the Yes side. Or it was 475 employees of Wabush Mines, or employees of the supermarket chain Provigo, or artists, or senior citizens. The premier presented each group with a personally signed certificate, bearing a fleur-de-lys and a big *OUI.* On it was the name of the group, followed by the words ". . . entrusts to the Government of Quebec the mandate to negotiate, with the rest of Canada, a new agreement based on the equality of peoples." The time and the place of the commitment were noted. Lévesque's acceptance of the particular group was also noted on the parchment: "Upon this commitment, I give notice that this group becomes a section of the *Regroupement National pour le OUI.*"

This was what PQ strategists had spoken of as their "secret weapon." Reminiscent of such public commitments as the First Communion, it resounded shrewdly with Quebec's old religious rituals. The technique used peer pressure to bring people from all walks of life to declare themselves publicly for the *oui*. They then became models for others of the same estate. People were solicited individually by a friend or a respected member of the same profession, the same club, the same old-folks home. And, once someone had let his or her name go forward as a supporter of the Yes side, that person's commitment was not likely to waver.

The PQ transformed every meeting into a love fest, a joyous gathering, an affirmation of solidarity, an utterance of pride in *nous*, a rejection of past indignities and persecutions, a kind of closing of the ranks to win constitutional concessions from English-speaking Canada. As Lévesque campaigned in public meetings, he never used the word "sovereignty." He spoke of the pride of Quebecers in the great hydro projects such as James Bay, which attracted experts from all over the world. He said that the same people who had said in 1962 that the power companies would never negotiate were now saying that Ottawa and the other provinces wouldn't negotiate. But 1962 was there to prove that it wasn't so. He also spoke of Quebec's no-fault automobile insurance for personal injuries, adopted in 1977, which was the marvel of the world. And, in every speech, he said that a No vote would put an end to all hope for change, while a Yes vote would lead to a *déblocage*.

In its last mailing to the voters, about a week before the referendum, the OUI committee ignored completely any suggestion that the referendum was about sovereignty-association. Neither word was mentioned once:

OUI, to negotiate for real. To negotiate seriously, a clear mandate is needed. For too long we've been going round in circles, from conference to conference, from commission to commission, from promise to promise. For the rest of Canada to decide at last to negotiate seriously, the weight of a *OUI* is needed in the scales. Without a *OUI*, the discussion will not bear on a Québécois proposal. With a *OUI* by the people of Quebec, we can be sure that Quebec will be at the centre of negotiations.

The pamphlet went on about what a trustworthy negotiator René Lévesque had proven himself to be. But not a word was said about the substance of the eventual negotiations. The PQ was asking the people of Quebec to say Yes to Oui.

The two sides seemed about evenly balanced before the intervention of Pierre Trudeau. In a series of speeches responding to the PQ's campaign, he flatly countered that he would not negotiate if a majority voted Yes in the referendum. Speaking in Quebec City on 7 May, he tried to impose his own interpretation of the significance of the referendum. It was not about a "new agreement"—there would be none. It was not about a *déblocage*—it would lead to the opposite, to a stalemate.

There is a question, and it is: Do you want to stop being Canadian? No! That is our answer, and that is what Canada is going to hear on May 20: No, we do not want to separate from this country. We want to build it, we want to make it better, we want to go on making it even more free. That is what will be at stake on May 20. Do you want to separate from Canada? No.[10]

Lévesque challenged Trudeau to a debate. Trudeau refused in the form of a press release that rebuked Lévesque for trying to get around his own referendum act. "Contrary to the spirit and letter of his own referendum law, he is asking me to short-circuit the No Committee and its leader, Claude Ryan, by debating the referendum question directly with him. My answer to him is an unequivocal Non merci."

Trudeau's campaign reached its climax on 14 May 1980, when he gave a speech at a mass meeting in Paul Sauvé Arena. He addressed his words not to those who had already chosen independence or federalism, but to all the others, to those who were still undecided.

If the answer to the referendum question is No, we have all said that this No will be interpreted as a mandate to change the constitution, to renew federalism. I am not the only person saying this. Nor is Mr. Clark. Nor is Mr. Broadbent. It is not only the nine premiers of the other provinces saying this. It is also the seventy-five MPs elected by Quebecers to represent them in Ottawa who are saying that a No means change.

He then made the pledge that would be repeated and distorted by many, including one of his successors.

And because I spoke to these MPs this morning, I know that I can make a most solemn commitment that following a No vote, we will immediately take action to renew the constitution and we will not stop until we have done that. And I make a solemn declaration to all Canadians in the other provinces, we, the Quebec MPs, are laying ourselves on the line, because we are telling Quebecers to vote No and telling you in the other provinces that we will not agree to your interpreting a No vote as an indication that everything is fine and can remain as it was before. We want change and we are willing to lay our seats in the House on the line to have change. This would be our attitude in the case of a No vote.

172

With the referendum less than a week away, Trudeau attacked directly the foundations of the whole PQ's campaign.

Mr. Lévesque has asked me what my attitude would be if the majority of Quebecers voted Yes. I have already answered this question. . . . Mr. Lévesque will be welcome to come to Ottawa, where I will receive him politely, as he has always received me in Quebec City, and I will tell him that there are two doors. If you knock on the sovereignty-association door, there is no negotiation possible.

The other provinces, Trudeau said, had already turned down any suggestion of association to go with Quebec's sovereignty. So Lévesque would have no one to associate with. And what about Lévesque's argument that "democracy" would require that the rest of Canada accept the will of Quebecers?

It is like saying to Mr. Lévesque, "The people of Newfoundland have just voted 100 per cent in favor of renegotiating the electricity contract with Quebec. You are obliged, in the name of democracy, to respect the will of Newfoundland, are you not?" It is obvious that this sort of logic does not work. The wishes of Quebecers may be expressed through a democratic process, but that cannot bind others—those in other provinces who did not vote—to act as Quebec decides.

Finally, Trudeau took up a snide comment that Lévesque had made shortly before, in which he had said (he said it often) that Trudeau took the position that he did because he was more Elliott than Trudeau. He pounced on the implicit exclusivism of that remark, which allowed him to contrast his own inclusive and pluralist vision with the restrictive vision advanced by the PQ.

That, my dear friends, is what contempt is. It means saying that there are different kinds of Quebecers. It means saying that the Quebecers on the No side are not as good Quebecers as the others, and perhaps they have a drop or two of foreign blood, while the people on the Yes side have pure blood in their veins. . . . Of course my name is Pierre Elliott Trudeau. Yes, Elliott was my mother's name. It was the name borne by the Elliotts who came to Canada more than 200 years ago. It is the name of the Elliotts who, more than one hundred years ago, settled in Saint-Gabriel-de-Brandon, where you can still see their graves in the cemetry. That is what the Elliotts are. My name is a Quebec name, but my name is a Canadian name also, and that's the story of my name.

Trudeau then evoked other names which were, he said, Québécois: Pierre-Marc Johnson, Louis O'Neill, Robert Burns, Daniel Johnson. He mentioned the chief negotiator for the Inuit, Charlie Watt, who had announced that he and his people would vote No. "Is Charlie Watt not a Quebecer? These people have lived in Quebec since the Stone Age; they have been here since time immemorial. And Mr. Watt is not a Quebecer?"

173

It was a masterful final performance, perhaps the most effective in Trudeau's career. It illustrated, simply and powerfully, the contrast between the acceptance of differences that characterized federalism and the ethnic supremacy that motivated the drive for a separate state.

Trudeau's speeches complemented the gruelling campaign that Claude Ryan was conducting. And on referendum night, the people voted No by a margin of 60 per cent to 40 per cent. Not just most Quebecers, but more than half of francophone Quebecers voted No.

The Parti Québécois had tried, by hook or by crook, to win a Yes to a procedure rather than to sovereignty. It failed to obtain even that. The Parti Québécois had lost its gamble to gain legitimacy as a separatist party that spoke for Quebec. The presumption that Quebecers were colonized or a captive people was now destroyed.

Notes

1.Report by William Johnson, *Globe and Mail*, 26 Jan. 1977.
2.Report by William Johnson, *Globe and Mail*, 29 Jan. 1977.
3.Report by William Johnson, *Globe and Mail*, 24 Feb. 1978.
4.From a personal conversation of Mr. Morin with the author.
5.Lévesque's statement can be found in the National Assembly's *Journal des Débats*, 23 May 1979.
6.The quotations reproduced in this chapter without reference are drawn from my work at the time as a journalist reporting on the events.
7.Lise Payette, *Le pouvoir? Connais pas!* (Montreal: Québec/Amérique, 1982), p. 183.
8.Ibid., p. 81.
9.The slogan was a play on words based on the French title of a popular spaghetti Western, *Mon nom est personne. . .* My name is nobody.
10.The texts of Trudeau's speeches of 7 May and 14 May 1980 are available in the Library of Parliament in Ottawa.

CHAPTER TWELVE

Patriation at last

Pierre Trudeau did patriate the constitution at last. It was to be his crowning achievement. At last he would keep the promise made to French Canadians in 1968 to protect their language rights across the country and make all of Canada their home.

But the manner and significance of the patriation would become immensely controversial a few years later, when Prime Minister Mulroney maintained that Trudeau had broken his solemn promise made to Quebecers during the 1980 referendum campaign. For the sake of history and the future, it is important to know what really happened between May of 1980 and April of 1982, when Canada became independent and fully sovereign and a charter of rights was created to define the fundamental rights of all citizens.

The very day after the victory of the No side in the referendum, Trudeau sent justice minister Jean Chrétien on a tour of nine provincial capitals—the exception was Quebec. And, in a speech in the Commons, Trudeau declared that he would patriate the constitution. The only terms he considered non-negotiable were that Canada must remain a true federation and it must have a vested charter of rights.

On 9 June 1980, Trudeau convened the premiers at 24 Sussex Drive for a day's discussions on the constitution. He proposed two series of reforms that should be negotiated separately: a "people's package," which would include patriation and a charter of rights, and a "governments' package" dealing with division of powers. A week later, he announced that if there was no agreement on the constitution among the first ministers by September, he might act unilaterally.

In July and August, a cortege of ministers and officials negotiated their way from Montreal, through Toronto and Vancouver, to Ottawa, trying to reach agreement on a twelve-item agenda. By the time the first ministers met again in Ottawa in September, they had agreed on practically nothing. That four-day meeting was full of animosity. The premiers resented the fact that Trudeau was preparing a resolution to put before Parliament and send on to Westminster in case they could not agree.

The Quebec government had prepared a plan to set up a common front of the provinces. On the third day of the meeting, the Quebec delegation circulated among the provincial delegations a discussion paper titled "Proposal for a

175

Common Stand of the Provinces." It was a shrewd gambit, because it suggested that the Parti Québécois government was willing to help renew federalism. The document put forward a list of all the fondly held objectives of each province so as to garner maximum support; it even included Alberta's cherished formula for future amendments to the constitution: unanimity.

The Quebec proposal was not separatist, but it was thoroughly provincialist, and could never be acceptable to Trudeau. It proposed, for instance, that the charter of rights be shorn of language rights; minority language rights in the provinces would be protected, instead, by multilateral agreements among the provinces. It also suggested curtailing many of the federal government's powers and giving the provinces responsibility for such matters as communications and social affairs. If the first ministers agreed on such a program, Quebec suggested, then Ottawa could go ahead with its patriation resolution, but the new constitution would come into effect only when it had been adopted in all ten provinces. In other words, any province could veto it.

The attempt to derail the patriation train was transparent. And yet it worked. The next morning, 12 September, over breakfast at the Chateau Laurier, the premiers discussed the Quebec proposal for ninety minutes and decided to use it as a counter-proposal to Trudeau's. When they presented Trudeau with the "Chateau Consensus," he dismissed it out of hand.

The conference broke up, a failure, the next day. Newfoundland's premier, Brian Peckford, stated at the final press conference that he preferred René Lévesque's vision of Canada to Trudeau's.

So, according to plan, on 2 October 1980, Trudeau went on television to announce the package that he was going to present unilaterally for passage by the United Kingdom, after the appropriate resolution had been passed by the two houses of Parliament. It included patriation, a charter of rights with minority language rights, and provision for a referendum on an amending formula if, after two years, the federal government and the provinces still had not been able to agree.

Twelve days later, the premiers met in Toronto to consider their course. Ontario's Bill Davis had immediately endorsed Trudeau's action, and called on members of Parliament to support it. But the other premiers discussed legal action to stop the patriation. On 23 October, the attorneys-general of six province— Manitoba, Quebec, Alberta, British Columbia, Prince Edward Island, and Newfoundland—met in Winnipeg and decided to test the legality of patriation in the courts of Manitoba, Quebec, and Newfoundland.

At the suggestion of Quebec, the premiers also began lobbying the members of Parliament at Westminster to get them to oppose passing a patriation bill to which the Canadian provinces objected. Gilles Loiselle, Quebec's agent general in London (and later Kim Campbell's minister of finance in Ottawa), persuaded Sir Anthony Kershaw, chairman of a select committee on foreign affairs, to prepare a report on the question. In January, 1981, he recommended that the British Parliament not pass the required bill unless it had a proper degree of provincial support.

The first of the three court decisions came down, also in January of 1981. The Manitoba Court of Appeal ruled, four to one, that Ottawa could legally proceed unilaterally.

Some of the premiers, notably Sterling Lyon of Manitoba and William Bennett of British Columbia, were of the opinion that the six provinces opposing patriation should come up with a counter-proposal. In the ongoing battle for public opinion, the Chateau Consensus was tainted because it had come from a separatist Quebec government. Bennett sent a minister to all the provincial capitals to canvass the premiers, and a common position began to take form. The premiers moved toward accepting patriation, but without a charter of rights, and without an amending formula until one could be agreed upon by negotiations that would take place after patriation.

At a meeting in Montreal in late January, 1981, Quebec's intergovernmental affairs minister, Claude Morin, convinced the five other delegations that Quebec was sincerely interested in reforming federalism, but that mere patriation was too little for Quebec to accept, when for years it had opposed patriation unless it came with a new division of powers. Quebec could accept patriation, he said, only if it were accompanied by an amending formula. "Our purpose was to drop the Trudeau plan, start with the one we had signed, and have three years of discussions," Morin said later. "Maybe Trudeau would go away by then. He was one of the problems."[1]

Morin also urged that Allen Blakeney of Saskatchewan and John Buchanan of Nova Scotia be urged to join the dissident premiers, because eight premiers would have a much better chance than six of persuading Westminster not to pass the patriation resolution. By 26 February, the two new recruits had joined the group that now met frequently to work out a common position.

In early March, Lévesque called an election for 13 April. The common front's negotiations for an accord continued during the campaign, and the Quebec government participated through conference calls and through Morin's deputy minister, Robert Normand.

The amending formula on which the dissidents were coming to agreement was a reworking of a proposal Alberta had made in 1976, when the premiers met in Edmonton to create a common front against Trudeau's intention to patriate. At that time, Alberta had insisted that any constitutional amendment should require unanimity of the provinces. Now, Alberta accepted a modified formula that was to be called the Vancouver formula: an amendment would pass if it received the assent of the Parliament of Canada and of two-thirds of the provinces, with a majority of the population of Canada. But Alberta also insisted that no constitutional amendment that diminished a province's rights should apply to that province without its consent. This meant that a province would have the right to opt out of any such amendment.

Reluctantly, the other premiers had bowed to Premier Lougheed's unbending insistence. But British Columbia demanded that the right to opt out should not be exercised easily: it should require a vote by two-thirds of the concerned province's legislators. Quebec then added a new demand: a province that opted out should receive full fiscal compensation. The other provinces did not particularly like this idea, because it would make it all but impossible to enact such a constitutional amendment unless both the big provinces and the rich provinces agreed to take part. But, to safeguard the common front, all agreed to the Quebec proposal.

During the election campaign, Lévesque kept secret what he had agreed to with seven other premiers, and for good reason. The political class of Quebec would have been astonished to know that their premier endorsed an accord that proclaimed in its preamble that all the provinces were equal. What about distinct status? Quebec premiers had never before agreed that New Brunswick or Prince Edward Island was the constitutional equal of Quebec. Moreover, the amending formula meant that Quebec no longer had a veto on constitutional change, since such change could proceed with the assent of any seven provinces, as long as they included half the population of Canada, and Quebec, with 25 per cent of the population, could not act by itself.

The signing ceremony for the Group of Eight was slated for 16 April 1981. Lévesque arrived in Ottawa the night before, but he then refused to sign unless the accord was changed to remove the requirement that opting out of constitutional change require a two-thirds vote. After hours of argument, the other premiers finally gave in.

Meanwhile, Joe Clark and the Conservative members of Parliament had used procedural tactics to filibuster against the patriation resolution. In the midst of these manoeuvres, on 31 March, the Newfoundland court brought down its judgment: it found unanimously in favour of the provinces and against unilateral patriation. This meant that the federal government would have to clarify the legality of its procedure by applying to the Supreme Court of Canada. A judgment by the Quebec Court of Appeal on 15 April found, four to one, in favour of the federal government, but by then the judgment had become irrelevant. The Supreme Court would decide. Meanwhile, the patriation resolution would not come to a vote.

When the decision of the highest court came down at last, on 28 September 1981, it was a Pyrrhic victory for both the federal government and the provinces. The court ruled, by a split decision, that no law prevented the federal government from presenting a resolution to Westminster which would enable the British Parliament to do in Canada what Ottawa itself could not do. To that extent, Ottawa won. But the court also ruled that a convention existed which required a "substantial measure of provincial consent" for a constitutional amendment that would diminish the rights of the provinces. Therefore, to proceed unilaterally with patriation would be "unconstitutional in the conventional sense."

The judgment led Trudeau to make a last attempt to reach an agreement with the provinces. He could not be certain, now, that Westminster would pass a unilateral federal resolution. But the premiers also had a new reason to search for a negotiated solution. The court had ruled that unilateral patriation would be, in effect, illegitimate, but not illegal. So it was possible that the British members of Parliament would "hold their noses" and pass the resolution.

The prime minister invited the premiers to Ottawa for a conference to begin on 2 November 1981. He indicated in the opening session that he was ready to compromise.

For three hours, on the first day, the first ministers presented their opening statements. Some things had changed since they all had met fourteen months earlier. For one, there seemed more genuine readiness to achieve a negotiated settlement. For another, the rules of the game had changed because the Supreme Court had defined more clearly than before what was required for constitutional change within the conventions: "a substantial measure of provincial consent." How substantial, the Supreme Court did not say; but clearly, unanimity was no longer required.

In fact, all of the first ministers expressed a readiness to be flexible, except for Lyon of Manitoba, Lougheed of Alberta, and Lévesque of Quebec. And Lévesque was the only one who positively excluded any negotiations on Trudeau's proposed charter of rights. He took the position that the provinces had already compromised on 16 April when they had agreed to patriation and to an amending formula. "It's Ottawa's turn to walk the rest of the way," Lévesque said. "The compromise we are looking for is already on the table." Lévesque was disturbed that other premiers, notably Blakeney and Bennett, seemed to be searching for a compromise with Ottawa. He was determined not to budge an inch.

On the second day of the conference, Premier Davis made a proposal for a compromise: he would accept the amending formula proposed by the Group of Eight, if they would accept vesting in the constitution a national charter of rights.

The charter of rights had become the make-or-break issue of the conference. Trudeau was absolutely resolved to vest in the constitution the protection of French-language rights. Paradoxically, his most inflexible opponent was the premier of Quebec, who preferred sacrificing the rights of francophones in other provinces to making concessions to English in Quebec.

The other premiers were being forced to choose between Trudeau and Lévesque, both of whom were intransigent on this issue. They looked for a compromise. Bennett, whose year it was to be official spokesman for the premiers, sent emissaries to Louis Bernard, the most senior civil servant in the

Quebec government and Lévesque's former executive assistant. They encountered total inflexibility:

Bill Bennett's senior officials meet Quebec's top-ranked civil servant, Louis Bernard, Lévesque's cool and competent Clerk of the Cabinet. They had one question: can the Gang of Eight make any compromise on language rights? There is one answer: No. For about 90 minutes the group explores every conceivable possibility, even that of making the minority language guarantees totally salutatory, without meaning. The answer is the same. We've gone too far already, Bernard says.[2]

This account is confirmed by Claude Morin, who attended the conference as Quebec's minister of intergovernmental affairs. "Would Quebec accept a concession from the Group of Eight on [language rights]? The answer: no. All our concessions have already been made and Lévesque had repeated often that Quebec would never consent to a reduction of its powers over language."[3]

The impasse seemed absolute. The Group of Eight, which met every morning over breakfast, had agreed that none of them would change his position without first consulting the others. But the solidarity of the group was destroyed on the third day of the conference, 4 November, when René Lévesque leaped at a suggestion made by Trudeau that if no agreement was reached within two years on the charter of rights, the question should be settled by a referendum.

Later, politicians and journalists would shroud in legend the events of 4 and 5 November 1981. René Lévesque, Claude Morin, Lucien Bouchard, and Brian Mulroney, among a host of others, would portray Lévesque as having been betrayed by his allies, and Quebec as isolated at the constitutional conference. The real story is contained in the news accounts which appeared at the time. *La Presse* reported:

After two days of fruitless negotiations and an emergency meeting of his Cabinet Tuesday evening, Mr. Trudeau finally made that astonishing proposal yesterday noon. Emerging from a morning session of intense discussion, Mr. Trudeau had explained that there was "big news." "There is a Quebec-Canada alliance which is developing. We will try for two years to improve the charter. If we cannot agree, we will consult the population by asking the question: "Do you want a charter, yes or no?"[4]

Lévesque followed Trudeau to the microphone and said nothing to contradict Trudeau's claim; quite the contrary. "Speaking in his turn to the journalists, Mr. Lévesque said that he found Mr. Trudeau's suggestion in accordance with democratic principles and it put an end to unilateralism. 'We find it a respectable and extraordinarily interesting way of getting out of this impasse.'"[5]

By making this unilateral move toward Trudeau, Lévesque alienated his partners in the Group of Eight in several different ways. First, he broke ranks with them, contrary to their agreement that none would move without informing the others. Second, because Trudeau's proposed referendum would be run according to the Victoria formula—to carry, it would have to garner a majority vote in each of four regions of the country—Lévesque was repudiating the position on equality of the provinces that he had signed; he was accepting that Quebec and Ontario would each have a veto that no other province had.

"This Canada-wide referendum does not run the risk of plunging Quebec again in the same kind of conflict which it experienced during the conscription crisis," explained Minister Claude Charron. Indeed, Quebec would keep its right to a veto, since the referendum would require a "regional majority," that is to say that it must be ratified in Quebec, in Ontario, in the Maritimes and in the West. If it fails to obtain an agreement in one of these regions, the charter can't come into effect.[6]

So, who isolated Lévesque? Was he betrayed by the other members of the Group of Eight, as legend has it? The headline in Le Devoir on the same day said it all: "Coup de théâtre de Trudeau—le Front des Huit s'effondre." Spectacular move by Trudeau, the common front of the Eight collapses. Le Devoir's reporter, Jean-Claude Picard, had gone to Ottawa from Quebec City, where he normally covered the National Assembly. His comment on what happened that day is illuminating.

At that moment the Quebec delegation was jubilant and, even at the risk of offending its partners in the common front, did not hesitate for an instant to climb aboard the train proposed by Ottawa. . . . "It's the ideal solution for us. We put off the threat for two years and we are certain of winning the referendum," said the government's parliamentary leader, Claude Charron.

Le Devoir's Michel Vastel caught better than anyone else what Lévesque's move meant for the Group of Eight.

The anglophone provinces waged a pitched battle yesterday against Prime Minister Trudeau's proposal for a referendum. By evening there were bitter feelings between René Lévesque and his former allies in the common front of the Eight, while New Brunswick's Richard Hatfield, the former black sheep, now threatens to join the camp of the adversaries of Mr. Trudeau. The other members of the Group of Eight set about to organize a new common front to block the proposed referendum:

The Western premiers, especially Allan Blakeney of Saskatchewan and Peter Lougheed of Alberta, tried all afternoon to put together a common front of the anglophone provinces against the Trudeau-Lévesque proposal. The objective of the operation, as several provincial delegations indicated, was to rally enough opposition to the Trudeau-Lévesque project to block it by making it unconstitutional.

Vastel returned to the subject in Le Devoir the next day, 6 November, after the other premiers had reached an agreement during the night among themselves,

181

without Lévesque. In retracing why the Group of Eight had broken up, he put the blame on Lévesque's move of 4 November.

Since the previous day, and Mr. Lévesque's dramatic outburst in favour of Mr. Trudeau's proposal for a referendum, Quebec had lost its last allies. During the night of Wednesday to Thursday, while everyone suspected that deals were being made, a senior Quebec civil servant, when asked why he did not make a last attempt to keep the provinces together as he had done in September 1980, replied in a disenchanted tone, "We no longer have any credibility after what happened at noon."

The story that later gained currency—that poor René Lévesque was asleep in Hull, innocently unaware that his allies were betraying him—simply does not square with the events as they unfolded. Here are the comments of columnist Richard Daignault, the day after all the first ministers but Lévesque had reached an agreement.

What completely changed the situation? The threat of a national referendum on the charter of rights. It was a gun put to the heads of the English provinces, who didn't want to hear of it. . . . Just imagine what the Ontario Tories would look like campaigning for Trudeau's project. . . . While Premier René Lévesque accepted the challenge of a national referendum conducted according to the rules of the Victoria formula, which gave Quebec an absolute right to a veto, the other provinces panicked at this improbable and incredible Quebec-Canada front that had emerged.[7]

Even Claude Morin seems to concede that the anglophone leaders believed that Lévesque had destroyed the common front when he accepted the referendum proposal. He recalls that Roy Romanow, then Saskatchewan's minister responsible for the constitution, had come to see him on the fatal Wednesday: "Romanow, upset, had returned to see me just when the session was ending. I had the feeling that, for him, a catastrophe had just fallen on Canada. He was certain that in his province, Trudeau would win the referendum and that, in any case, the country would come out of it torn. Why had we agreed to such a destructive procedure?"[8]

Lévesque had abandoned the common front. The other premiers had the choice of searching for a compromise with Trudeau or with Lévesque, who had already made plain that, with him, no compromise was possible. Trudeau, on the other hand, did compromise. He surrendered his proposal to put into the constitution a recourse to a referendum when there was an impasse between the federal government and the provinces. He accepted the "notwithstanding" clause, which allowed governments to suspend fundamental freedoms. He gave up his proposal for vesting mobility rights between provinces. And he was unable to win back Quebec's veto over constitutional change, which Lévesque had bargained away as a ploy to set up the common front against him.

Morin was contemptuous of Trudeau for making these concessions: "Compared to his previous positions, the text under study contained clauses which, normally, must have been exceedingly objectionable to the federal prime minister. . . . Would Trudeau agree to such a compromise of his deep convictions? Or, to put the question another way, how much honour did he have left?"[9]

In return for his compromise, however, Trudeau got the constitution patriated at last, he won a guarantee for French school rights, and he revolutionized the constitution by vesting in it a charter of rights that would make all Canadians increasingly sensitive to the importance of freedom. Lévesque was angry, but he had only himself to blame. This is what I wrote on 5 November, 1981, when the prime minister and the premiers made public the agreement that ten of them had reached overnight. The analysis still applies, despite what revisionists would say later.

Stunning! High statesmanship! A high point in Canada's political history.

At last, after a generation of trying and failing, after countless conferences, innumerable meetings of first ministers that brought nothing but frustration, after years of negotiations, of search for unanimity, of compromise, of striking bargains, of giving quid pro quo, of pressuring, pleading, threatening, warning, praying, cajoling to no avail, after the long, long search for a way out of the fundamental Canadian deadlock, an agreement is found.

The dark shadow over it all is the dissent of the Government of Quebec. Premier René Lévesque is not only in disagreement with the other 10 first ministers; he is sad, bitter, angry, threatening.

"The consequences could be incalculable," he said ominously to a press conference after the constitutional conference ended.

He felt that Quebec had been abandoned by the other premiers, isolated as it had been traditionally in the history of Confederation. He spoke of "the kind of habit, when the moment of truth comes, of leaving Quebec in its corner." He called the abandonment of Quebec "the Canadian way"— bitterly ironic with the words used so often by the other premiers in self-congratulation.

And he threatened. "Never will the Government of Quebec or I accept capitulating on this. We will take very means remaining to us to keep it from happening."

What now? The premier was clearly hinting at dramatic means of fighting the agreement reached by all the other first ministers. He could be thinking of elections, or a referendum, or even considering civil disobedience on those parts of the proposed Canadian constitution that he rejects.

Despite the angry words, Mr. Lévesque is in a difficult position. To some extent he is an architect of his own woes.

The agreement reached yesterday is clearly constitutional, as spelled out by the Supreme Court of Canada. But it was Mr. Lévesque who decided to appeal the patriation to the Supreme Court, Mr. Lévesque who went around quoting with approval sentence after sentence of its decision. The court found that unanimity is not required for amendments to the constitution. Quebec thereby lost its traditional veto. Can Mr. Lévesque now say that he no longer accepts the court's decision that he used to praise?

Will he say that yesterday's agreement, though constitutional, is illegitimate? Will he claim that the rest of Canada is forcing it on Quebec? It won't wash. The chief architect of the constitutional reform is Pierre Trudeau, backed by his 72 loyal Liberals from Quebec. Quebec was massively represented at the bargaining table this week by its federal representatives. An agreement backed by every other Canadian province and by the Quebec federal Liberals is a legitimate agreement, one that will be seen as legitimate by the citizens of Quebec, regardless of what the premier says or does. Mr. Lévesque is isolated, not Quebec.

True, a minority of Quebecers will be outraged. But that is a just reflection of the divisions within Quebec. Mr. Lévesque, on language policy as on the question of sovereignty, leads an important minority that will be outraged by any political act that strengthens the national cohesion of Canada. Their opposition is predictable, but it cannot invalidate an expression of the national will.

On each of the major points of contention, Mr. Lévesque's position is weak. He was outraged yesterday because Quebec loses its veto under the new arrangement. But it was he who signed an accord in April agreeing to give up the traditional veto in favor of the Vancouver amending formula. Now he can't claim that the loss of the veto is unacceptable in principle.

On language policy, the new accord seems to mean that every English-speaking province will guarantee French school rights if Quebec guarantees English school rights. That is exactly what Mr. Lévesque proposed in substance to the premiers at St. Andrews in 1977, and it actually is written into Bill 101. How can Mr. Lévesque claim to be against it in principle when it is guaranteed by the constitution rather than merely by the reciprocity agreements that he proposed in the past?

The agreement reached yesterday conforms closely with the aspirations of Quebec leaders going back beyond Confederation. Quebec, more than any other province, was its architect. It is an achievement for which Quebec, more than any province, can be proud.[10]

Patriation of the constitution was essentially an all-Quebec operation. The process began in 1960, when Jean Lesage's Liberals demanded patriation in their election platform. It continued with the acceptance of the Fulton-Favreau amending formula in 1964, followed by Jean Lesage reneging on his signature.

The issue of the constitution was reopened by Daniel Johnson. Then all the other governments, including the federal government, were drawn into the process. Quebec had many different views of what the new constitutional order should be, with many different formulas being put forward, including special status (Lesage and Paul Gérin-Lajoie), two nations (Daniel Johnson and Claude Ryan), sovereign associated states (Robert Bourassa), and sovereignty-association (René Lévesque).

There was no consensus on any of these formulas. Trudeau, having promised Quebecers to settle the issue of the constitution, now was determined to impose his own solution, which he had already put before the people of Quebec in five election campaigns: one Canada with two official languages, and rights (including minority language rights) vested in a charter. In Ottawa in November of 1981, the other premiers were forced to choose between two Quebecers, one of whom would not compromise, and the other who did.

On previous occasions, the other premiers had all or almost all lined up with the Quebec premier—with Bourassa in 1976, Lévesque in 1978–79 and in 1980 and most of 1981. Now, at the last, they negotiated a compromise with Trudeau. But they were not the moving force behind the agreement of November, 1981: Quebec leaders, for reasons which had everything to do with Quebec politics, had driven the process from start to finish.

The people of Quebec recognized that this was above all an issue between Quebecers, and they did not display a sense of outrage as they would have had they believed that the rest of Canada had imposed something on them. This was totally different, for instance, from the conscription crisis of 1942, when a plebiscite across the country overruled the anti-conscription votes of Quebecers. On the contrary, in 1981–82, though Quebecers were divided, they remained quiescent—to the dismay of the nationalists.[11]

In the National Assembly, the PQ government moved a resolution condemning the patriation because it did not recognize Quebec as a "distinct society." The PQ had taken over the phrasing of a Liberal policy in order to secure Liberal support, and most Liberals voted with the government on the resolution.

But, just as significantly, Lévesque did not do what he had threatened to do—that is, take "every means remaining to us" to stop the patriation. He did not call an election on the issue, or hold a referendum, or even mobilize mass demonstrations. There had been talk of inviting Quebecers to fill the Olympic stadium in protest, but the plan was soon shelved because the PQ feared too few would turn out.

The apathy of the people was a source of anguish to the nationalists:

This situation contained all the elements apt to provoke huge demonstrations of Quebec nationalism: Quebec was isolated, scorned, reduced to silence. Yet nothing happened. That majority of Quebecers which had always been favourable to "renewed federalism" remained strangely silent and resigned. No mass meeting, no concerted opposition; only a few letters to newspapers and that was it. People were glum or just not interested in the constitutional question.[12]

But if there was so little reaction, the obvious reason is that Quebecers did not feel "isolated, scorned, reduced to silence." Patriation had been brought about by the most respected Quebecer, Pierre Trudeau, and even those who disagreed with the action did not, for the most part, have strong feelings on the subject.

The rejection of sovereignty-association in the 1980 referendum had deprived Quebec nationalism of most of its legitimacy. For a generation, nationalist premiers had presumed to speak in the name of Quebec. A generation of poets, songwriters, novelists, playwrights, and filmmakers had presented the Québécois as colonized and yearning for liberation from the grip of Canada. When the people of Quebec spoke at last, it was to reject the assumptions of a generation of writers and provincialist politicians.

After the patriation, nationalist sentiment in Quebec did not get stronger, as it would have had Quebecers felt that they had been the victims of a gang-up by English-speaking Canada. In fact, it got weaker. In March, 1982, CROP carried out an opinion poll for *La Presse* and found that 41 per cent favoured either sovereignty-association or independence. A year later, in March–April 1983, CROP again did a poll, this time for the Council on Canadian Unity, and found that those who favoured sovereignty-association or independence had dropped by 8 percentage points, to 33 per cent.

Support for Quebec sovereignty was still considerable. But separatism had been discredited by the referendum and neutralized by the successful patriation. Sovereignty ceased to be an issue discussed in public forums. Polling companies stopped asking Quebecers about their constitutional preferences. As an issue, it seemed passé.

It could, of course, be revived again by a demagogue or a sorcerer's apprentice rash enough to set loose once again the nationalist demons that had tormented Quebec for two decades.

Notes

1.Robert Sheppard and Michael Valpy, *The National Deal: The Fight for a Canadian Constitution* (Toronto: Fleet, 1982), p. 190.
2.Ibid., p. 277.
3.Claude Morin, *Lendemains piégés. Du référendum à la nuit des longs couteaux* (Montréal: Boréal, 1988),p. 294.
4.Gilles Paquin, Gilbert Lavoie, and Louis Falardeau, *La Presse,* 5 Nov. 1981.
5.Ibid.
6.Ibid.
7.Richard Daigneault, *Le Soleil,* 6 Nov. 1981.
8.Claude Morin, *Lendemains piégés, p. 301.*
9.Ibid., p. 309.
10.*Globe and Mail,* 6 Nov. 1981, p. 8.

11.A CROP public-opinion poll carried out 9–11 November, 1981 asked Quebecers whether they thought Lévesque should have signed it. For 42 per cent, the answer was yes; for 40 per cent it was no; and 18 per cent said they did not know. Four months later, just a month before the new constitution was proclaimed, support for Lévesque's stand had dropped, and support for the agreement had risen. Between 2 and 10 March, 1982, CROP asked whether Quebecers agreed with "the position of the government of Quebec, which refused to sign the agreement." Only 32 per cent agreed, while 48 per cent disagreed, and 20 per cent had no opinion. At the same time, when the respondents were asked whether they agreed with "the decision of the government of Canada to proceed with patriation of the constitution without the approval of the Quebec government," only 25 per cent said they agreed, while 55 per cent disagreed. Two months after the constitution was proclaimed, a Gallup asked whether, in the long run, it would be "a good thing for Canada, yes or no?" Among the Quebec respondents, 49 per cent said it would be a good thing, only 16 per cent said it would not be a good thing, and 35 per cent did not know.

12.Louis Balthazar, *Bilan du nationalisme au Québec* (Montreal: L'Hexagone, 1986), p. 185.

CHAPTER THIRTEEN

From Joe Clark
to Brian Mulroney

Quebec was never kind to Joe Clark, even though the man from High River, Alberta, always did his best to woo Quebec. He learned French. He denounced Pierre Trudeau's concept of a "centralized" federation. He spoke of Canada as a "community of communities." He invested enormous time and money in Quebec. And yet the Conservative vote there declined in the two elections with him as leader.

Quebec, faithful to Trudeau, prevented Clark from winning a majority government in 1979, when he carried the rest of Canada. The Quebec members of Parliament, Liberals and Créditistes, then brought him down after he had been prime minister for only nine months. Three years later, a Quebec-based cabal led by Brian Mulroney deprived Clark of the resounding vote of confidence he expected from the Winnipeg convention of his party. Clark called a leadership race, and he lost to Mulroney, whose strength was his Quebec base. Quebec reduced Clark's place in history to a few ironic paragraphs.

From the time he won the Conservative leadership in 1976, Clark had a Quebec problem. He defeated Quebec's favourite son, Claude Wagner, on the last ballot. Also defeated was Quebec's other favourite candidate, Brian Mulroney. Clark soon had to pay for his effrontery in winning without substantial Quebec support.

When the Quebec wing of the party met for the first time under his leadership, in November of 1976, a power struggle between Clark and Wagner erupted: each tried to impose his own candidate for the presidency of the party. Clark's candidate, MP Roch LaSalle, defeated Wagner's candidate, Jean-Yves Lortie, who had set up most of the PC riding associations after the party's rout in the 1974 elections. The contest left two of Clark's four Quebec MPs in open rebellion,[1] and all the top party organizers, who had backed Lortie, were bitter. "The unity of the party has been compromised by the dictatorial action of the leader himself," Wagner told me in an interview right after the vote.[2] The people Clark alienated then—notably Lortie—would provide the nucleus for Mulroney's challenge a few years later.

Conservative leaders had never developed a clear policy with respect to the place of Quebec in Confederation. Since the disastrous *deux nations* adventure with Marcel Faribault in 1968, the Tories under Robert Stanfield had cultivated Quebec nationalists, but without taking an identifiable policy position. They had, rather, a stance: they criticized Pierre Trudeau as a centralizer.

Clark, faulted before the 1979 elections for lacking a vision of Canada, responded with a speech in which he spoke of Canada as a "community of communities." Some pundits, notably the *Globe and Mail*'s Tory-minded columnist Geoffrey Stevens, proclaimed that Clark now had a vision. What it meant would be harder to define. "The whole is strong when the local communities are strong," Clark said. It was a vision tailored to appeal both to Quebec nationalists and to alienated Western Canadians. The most definitive assessment of it was etched by *Globe* reporter Jeffrey Simpson in his study of the short-lived Clark government: "Clark's oft-repeated phrase 'community of communities' resonated with harmony and brotherhood. It was pleasing to the ear, soothing to the mind, and even inspirational for the soul. As long as no one asked what the phrase meant, or how it should be applied, it stood the test of political rhetoric by offering no offence and inviting a wide range of interpretations."[3]

In the clashes between Trudeau and the provincial premiers, Clark laid the full blame on Trudeau, whose arrogance and excessive centralization would not be imitated by a Clark government, he averred. On the contrary, he would resolve some outstanding quarrels by withdrawing the federal government from jurisdictions that provinces coveted—such as control over off-shore resources—and he would bring a new spirit of co-operation to federal-provincial relations.

"We have the capacity, uniquely, to draw together the premiers of six of the provinces—premiers of our party—and to find common cause with other premiers who want to make the kind of changes that will make the system work," Clark said. "We can establish the trust that Mr. Trudeau has wasted."[4]

Clark's attitude meant little to most Quebecers, but it won the attention of the nationalists, who saw him as their best hope of dislodging Trudeau. A public opinion poll by the Institut Québécois d'Opinion Publique in September of 1978 showed that 55 per cent of those planning to vote Conservative said that they would vote Yes in the referendum. Among those planning to vote Liberal, only 31 per cent said they would vote Yes. As well, 40 per cent of the Conservatives said they favoured sovereignty-association, as compared to only 22 per cent of the Liberals.

In the 1979 federal elections that were to bring Clark to power, a separatist party ran in Quebec. The Union populaire was headed by Camille Laurin's former executive assistant, Henri Laberge, and backed by the Société Saint-Jean-Baptiste. Laberge later complained that René Lévesque had favoured the Tories.

Barely a year ago, the leadership of the Parti Québécois tried to have its rank and file adopt a discreet directive to back the Conservative Party. Ministers and members of the National Assembly encouraged their friends to run in the ranks of this federal party or to work at the level of organization. When the grass roots showed little enthusiasm for this incredible directive, the professional strategists of the PQ fell back on another formula. The grass roots are to back in each riding the candidate, Conservative or Créditiste, who has the best chance of beating the Liberal candidate.[5]

Clark was elected nationally, though the high-level PQ support did him no good in Quebec. The Tories took only two of Quebec's seventy-five seats in 1979, only one seat in 1980.

Once in power, Clark found that he had at least as many problems as Trudeau had had in dealing with Conservative premiers, notably Alberta's Peter Lougheed and Ontario's Bill Davis. Both met the young prime minister with bare knuckles, Davis because Clark proposed to raise the domestic price of oil rapidly toward the world price, and Lougheed because Clark proposed to put some of the windfall gains from the higher prices into a stabilization fund to help cushion the shock in the consuming provinces.

The Clark government needed a policy toward Quebec. When it was elected, in May, 1979, the Quebec referendum on sovereignty was less than a year away, and the Conservatives did not know where they stood beyond favouring a "community of communities."

As his chief constitutional adviser and expert on Quebec, Clark chose Arthur Tremblay, a former Quebec civil servant who, along with Claude Morin and Jacques Parizeau, had been one of the principal architects of the Quiet Revolution. Clark appointed Tremblay to the Senate, where his main task would be to guide the Conservative caucus and government toward a policy for Quebec.

Tremblay's vision was very different from that of the Fathers of Confederation, who intended provinces to deal with what they called "local" matters, and the federal government to deal with national issues. "There are two Canadas; federal Canada and interprovincial Canada," Tremblay had said. "That is a very important basic principle, in my opinion."[6] In his vision, the federal government had no more claim to be a national government than did the provinces.

Tremblay had been deputy minister of education under Paul Gérin-Lajoie at the time of the great reforms that were a cornerstone of the Quiet Revolution. He had impressed Bill Davis in the late 1960s, when Davis was Ontario's minister of education, and he recommended Tremblay to Clark. Tremblay had studied at the Sorbonne and Harvard, spoke English well, and was very bright.

But Tremblay had pursued another career in the upper ranks of the public service. From 1971 to 1977, he replaced Claude Morin as Quebec's deputy minister of intergovernmental affairs. During the years of Robert Bourassa's first two mandates, he was the strategist for Quebec's attempt to wrest control over communications from the federal government, and for setting up the common front of the premiers in 1976 to stop Trudeau from patriating the constitution unless he turned over a long list of powers to the provinces.

This man, whose job had been to devise schemes to frustrate patriation, whose only experience in the rest of Canada was in meetings to rally the other provinces against Ottawa, was now named by Clark to be the federal governmment's chief adviser on the constitution and chief expert on dealings with Quebec. It was a spectacular reversal.

The Clark government did not last long enough to develop a constitutional policy. But Clark and his ministers proved receptive to Quebec nationalists, as Clark showed in a Radio-Québec interview on 10 September 1979:

Interviewer: Mr. Prime Minister, if the majority of Quebecers vote Yes in the referendum, yes to sovereignty-association, you will be obliged to negotiate with the Quebec government?

Clark: I am obliged to negotiate with Quebec today. Federalism is negotiation. I have negotiated with Quebec and with Ontario. It is a constant task of a prime minister.

Interviewer: So you will not refuse to negotiate with the government of Quebec if the Parti Québécois obtains a massive Yes in the referendum?

Clark: Whether it's Yes or No, I will be there to negotiate.

This exchange was later quoted in the Lévesque government's white paper on the referendum as proof that a Yes vote would lead to a breakthrough in negotiations with the federal government.[7]

After losing power, Clark had remarkably little to say during Quebec's referendum campaign. To preside over his caucus committee on the constitution, Clark chose Jake Epp, a high-school teacher from Manitoba who knew little about Quebec and its complex aspirations.

In August, Clark met with his caucus and came out publicly with the proposal that a new constitution be drawn up by a constituent assembly, possibly to be ratified afterwards by a referendum. The proposal met with coolness or indifference. Clark was simply not taken seriously during the constitutional manoeuvres between Trudeau and the provinces.

When Trudeau went on television, on 2 October 1980, to announce his plan for patriating the constitution unilaterally, Clark took a strong stand against the proposal. He accused Trudeau of betraying his promise that he would renew federalism and maintained that the proposal violated the rights of the provinces. He promised to use every means to oppose Trudeau:

There are times when a government proposes to act against the essential interests of the nation. At such a time, the role of the opposition leader is not to submit to the government but to fight for the larger interests of Canada. The Trudeau government has a majority in Parliament. It will not be stopped unless the people of Canada can be aroused to the abuse—to the potential damage to our country—that the government now proposes.[8]

Clark was as good as his word. The Conservative caucus filibustered in March and April of 1981, slowing down passage of the patriation resolution long enough for the Newfoundland Court of Appeal to render its decision against the federal government.

On the charter of rights, Clark's Conservatives took a compromise position. They said that it should not be part of the package passed by Westminster, which should only include patriation and an amending formula. After Canada was in charge of its own constitution, Parliament should pass the charter and recommend that it be adopted by the provinces in accordance with the "Vancouver formula" for constitutional amendment—that is, it would be passed if seven provinces with at least half the population of Canada adopted it.

When the Group of Eight premiers endorsed a common position on patriation in April of 1981, Clark took up the cause that had been proposed by René Lévesque, and that the other premiers accepted only reluctantly: a province that opts out of a constitutional amendment should receive financial compensation equivalent to what it would have received had it taken part. As Trudeau had pointed out, that would encourage the provinces, especially the richer and bigger provinces, to opt out of amendments and would lead to a "checkerboard Canada."

Clark championed the proposal even after the nine other premiers had dropped it, during the final parliamentary debate on the patriation package. Thus, "the Tories, wishing to be champions of Quebec, turn[ed] financial compensation into a steamy issue."[9] Throughout the entire 1980–82 federal-provincial struggle over the constitution, Clark bolstered the reputation of the Conservative Party among nationalists in Quebec. As a *Globe* columnist observed, "Mr. Trudeau faces an opposition leader, Joe Clark, who believes his Conservative Party's route to political strength in Quebec lies in appealing to Quebec's nationalist vote."[10]

Brian Mulroney, when he occasionally expressed himself, took the opposite tack. He established his credentials within the party as a defender of the federal government against the provincialist, Clark. At a private meeting in 1980 attended by just a few people, including Clark, Mulroney, and Montreal lawyer Peter Blaikie, then national president of the Progressive Conservative Party, Mulroney said to Clark, "Joe, you've got to back Trudeau all the way."[11]

Mulroney took the same position on the constitution as did Premier Davis—that it was time to patriate, and that the Conservatives should join the Liberals in bringing the constitution home. Both backed Trudeau in carrying out the operation even over the objections of eight premiers. In conversations with a number of journalists, Mulroney denounced Clark for opposing patriation and expressed his support for what Trudeau was doing.

When, at last, Mulroney had succeeded in engineering such opposition to Clark that the latter, in 1983, declared a leadership convention, Mulroney ran as a hardliner on the question of Quebec separatism, in implicit contrast to Clark, who was deemed soft. At meetings with delegates to the convention, Mulroney often used the line, "Before I give away a plugged nickel of Canada's money to René Lévesque, I want to know what he's going to do for Canada."

But the strongest argument that Mulroney made for his own candidacy, over and over, was that the Conservatives had almost constantly been shut out of power in the twentieth century because they had never had a leader with whom French Canadians could identify. There were 102 ridings in the country, Mulroney repeated, where francophones made up 10 per cent or more of the population, and in 1980 Trudeau had taken 100 of them: "You give Pierre Trudeau a head start of 100 seats and he'll beat you ten times out of ten." It was a telling argument. In Canadian politics, the fundamental political realignments have come as the result of a national party being taken over by a regional chieftain. Two striking examples were the accession of Wilfrid Laurier to the leadership of the Liberals, and that of John Diefenbaker to head the Conservatives.

The weakness of the Conservatives in Quebec has often been attributed to the fact that John A. Macdonald had Louis Riel hanged in 1885. But in fact, in the election that followed, in 1887, Quebec returned thirty-six Conservative members of Parliament and only twenty-nine Liberals. Then Wilfrid Laurier was chosen Liberal leader in 1887. In the elections four years later, even though John A. still led the Conservatives, Quebec returned only twenty-nine Conservatives, along with thirty-four Liberals. The great shift had taken place, and it would last almost a century.

Before Diefenbaker became Tory leader, in 1956, the prairies voted mostly Liberal in federal elections. In 1953, the Liberals won eight seats in Manitoba to the Conservatives' three, five seats in Saskatchewan to one for the Conservatives, and in Alberta, three to one. In the first campaign under Diefenbaker, in 1957, Manitoba had shifted to eight Tories and one Grit, Saskatchewan to three Tories and four Grits, Alberta to three Tories and one Grit. By the next election, in 1958, the reversal was complete: the Liberals were entirely shut out of the prairies.

Including Joe Clark, the Conservatives had had fourteen national leaders: four from Ontario, four from the Maritimes, five from the prairies, and one from Quebec. But the one from Quebec, Sir John Abbott, was a caretaker leader; at the age of seventy, he was asked to take over when Macdonald died in 1891. Abbott had retired four years earlier from the Commons to the peace of the Senate. Ill health forced him to step down as the prime minister after seventeen months, without facing an election.

At any rate, Abbott represented the *other* Quebec, that of English-speaking merchants and the railroad.[12] In 1849, he had been so incensed at a bill to provide compensation for the victims (mostly francophones) of the 1837–38 rebellion that he had signed a manifesto for annexation to the United States.

Quebec had become increasingly alienated from the Conservative Party, especially after the conscription issue in the election of 1917. That alienation was manifested in the eight elections that preceded Mulroney's emergence as leader: the Conservative share of the vote in Quebec dropped from 30 per cent, in 1962, to hover around 20 per cent from 1963 to 1974. In the two elections with Joe Clark as leader, the Tories won only 13.6 per cent and 12.7 per cent of the Quebec vote. In the latter election, in 1980, Clark simply turned over the campaign in Quebec to the Union Nationale; the Quebec Conservative Party was nothing but a shell.

In choosing Mulroney to lead the Tories, the party was preparing another realignment of party support in Canada, starting with the reconciliation between the party of Macdonald and the province of Laurier:

As in 1967, history now sets off in a new direction. . . . The party, by choosing this able Quebecer, renews with its own distant past. It brings Quebec again into the mainstream of the party and the country. It will take time, but Quebec will loosen its panicky grasp on a single federal party. The regional polarization of the country will ease.

In contrast with Mr. Trudeau, the prophetic leader, Mr. Mulroney brings the talent of a conciliator. Quebec will become important in the thinking of the Tories, but Quebec will cease to be a main issue dividing the country.

. . . I warrant that a new era of regional healing and reconciliation has begun. Canada, it seems, is in for sunnier days.[13]

I wrote that column under the assumption that Mulroney would continue, as Tory leader, to espouse the same policy on national unity as had Pierre Trudeau. Many Quebecers made the same assumption, including the three hundred members of the Parti Québécois's national council, who met the day after Mulroney's victory. It seemed to whip them into a fighting mood, and they adopted in principle a resolution to create a separatist party to contest the next federal elections. "*On y va! On y va!*"—Let's go!—they chanted after receiving a report favourable to such an action from the PQ's chief organizer, Marcel Léger.

As *La Presse*'s astute columnist Lysiane Gagnon observed, for those who favoured the independence of Quebec, "Brian Mulroney was the man to stop, because he is too Québécois, he is too close by basic culture to the francophones, he has too much of a gut involvement in everything concerning Quebec, he would inevitably tend to oppose every sovereignist tendency with a violent passion. In other words, he would be another Pierre Elliott Trudeau!"

This prediction seemed borne out when, shortly after the new leader gained a seat in the Commons, the governing Liberals introduced a resolution that invited the Manitoba government and legislature "to take action as expeditiously as possible in order to fulfil their constitutional obligation and protect effectively the rights of the French-speaking minority of the province." Mulroney was faced with his first national-unity crisis—and he passed it with flying colours. He managed to keep his party united on the question that had always been most sensitive in Quebec that, historically, had constantly divided the Conservatives: the treatment of French-Canadian minorities in other provinces.

He made it clear that any member of his caucus who voted against the resolution would be out the door. And, on 6 October 1983, he made, in the Commons, one of the great speeches of his career. "The purpose of this resolution is one which has touched the soul of Canada for decades," he began. "A francophone minority, which had enjoyed an historical protection of its language in Manitoba, was suddenly cut off—amputated—from this guarantee which was so vital. . . . This resolution is about fairness. It is about decency. It is an invitation for co-operation and understanding. It speaks to the finest qualities in this nation."[14]

That speech established Mulroney as a courageous defender of French rights—a role that had been played until then by the Liberal Party of Canada. The Liberal claim to this title was soon thrown away by the man who succeeded Trudeau as Liberal leader: John Turner.

A handsome, hyperkinetic man with striking blue eyes, Turner had become a legend as Trudeau's heir presumptive. But, when he returned to politics after a few years' absence, Turner proved inept, lacking in judgment and in understanding of the country he hoped to govern and the traditions of the party that he hoped to lead. At his first press conference as a leadership candidate in 1984, he tried to duck the issue of language rights in Manitoba. He was asked by a reporter, "Mr. Turner, could you elaborate on the language question in Manitoba . . . an issue that is going to be ongoing and quite important to the fabric of Canadian society?"

"On the Manitoba question," Turner began slowly, "I support the spirit of the parliamentary resolution, but I think we have to recognize that what is at issue here is a provincial initiative, and that the solution will have to be provincial."[15]

A firestorm followed that answer. Defending the two official languages of Canada had been the single greatest priority of the federal Liberals at least since 1968. And now, the man assumed to be the next leader of the Liberal Party was announcing that defending French minority rights was a provincial matter. Turner had just surrendered the chief raison d'être of the federal Liberals, in the eyes of Quebecers. He unheedingly threw away the heritage of Pierre Trudeau, to have it picked up by Brian Mulroney.

Thus, Mulroney entered the 1984 election, his first as party leader, with a strong claim to the loyalty of Quebec. If he could win Quebec's commitment, while retaining the traditional support for Conservatives in the rest of Canada, he would restore the Conservatives as a truly national party—and the only national party, since the Liberals under Trudeau had atrophied in the four provinces west of Ontario. In 1980, for instance, the Liberals had elected only two members of Parliament west of the Ontario border, both in Manitoba.

During the campaign, though, Mulroney suddenly changed course. In a speech on 6 August in Sept-Îles, he broke sharply with the policies of Trudeau and moved toward the separatists' reading of recent history. He followed the example of Joe

Clark in making Trudeau and the federal Liberals responsible for federal-provincial strife, but he went beyond Clark's rhetoric in denouncing Trudeau's policies toward Quebec.

After the referendum, the men and women of [Quebec] underwent a collective trauma. . . . One thing is certain: not one person in Quebec authorized the federal Liberals to take advantage of the confusion that prevailed in Quebec following the referendum in order to ostracize the province constitutionally. My party takes no pleasure in the politically weak position in which these deplorable events have placed Quebec.

Mulroney, who had supported the patriation undertaken by Trudeau, who had even argued against the position taken by his own leader, Joe Clark, was now calling that patriation a "collective trauma." How could such a staggering reversal have come about?

Lucien Bouchard, who worked as a Mulroney speechwriter during the 1984 campaign, explained the mystery in his 1992 political memoirs. Mulroney, he said, had decided that his speech in Sept-Îles would be on his economic policies. He asked Bouchard to write the draft, and gave him the name of two or three economists to consult for ideas. But when Bouchard called them up, they couldn't help him: they were working for the Liberals. So, Bouchard said, he phoned Mulroney and suggested that he give a speech on federal-provincial relations instead. Mulroney agreed. "I wrote the speech as though I would be giving it myself, giving free reign to the indignation that I felt over Quebec's being pushed aside," Bouchard explained.[16]

The only person whom Bouchard consulted for the speech was Senator Arthur Tremblay. Bouchard noted the paradox that Mulroney was now to be inspired by the vision that he had rejected when it was articulated by Clark following Tremblay's advice. "The ideas of Joe Clark's adviser, thrown into the garbage during the leadership campaign in order to win the West for Brian Mulroney, were now resurfacing during the election campaign to mobilize Quebec."[17]

Mulroney, Bouchard said, gave the speech exactly as he had written it. And the speech suggested that, under the Liberals, Ottawa had acted as a bully, had pitted province against province, invaded provincial areas of jurisdiction, and sown dissension across the country. It was an utter denunciation of the Liberals, but it was so sweeping that it amounted to a repudiation of federalism itself as practised in Canada for at least half a century.

Those who view Canadian federalism as a power struggle naturally seek to usurp provincial jurisdiction. That was the Liberals' favourite sport. Nothing could be more contrary to the spirit of our constitution, and nothing could more surely provoke provincial distrust. In the performance of its federal responsibilities, a Progressive Conservative government will be guided by the principle of respect for provincial authority.

The limits of federal jurisdiction had been a subject of contention at least since the time of Maurice Duplessis, who had a fundamentalist and comprehensive view of provincial jurisdiction. The Sept-Îles speech now placed Mulroney on the side of those with a restrictive view of the scope of Ottawa's responsibility.
You will not see us using subterfuge, as the Liberals did, to allow the federal government to interfere with provincial policies. . . . The Liberals invented a scheme to usurp provincial jurisdiction under the pretext of standardizing Canadian policies throughout the country. They have managed to accomplish this by linking federal government funding to conditions governing the management and orientation of policies—conditions which were tantamount to federal legislation.
This put Mulroney in the position of attacking the basic health and social programs—medicare, aid to post-secondary education, the Canada Assistance Plan—that most Canadians saw as a glory of their country. Did Mulroney realize what he was saying as he read Bouchard's words?
The speech would be remembered mostly for its promise of reconciliation between Quebec and the federal government. The parts quoted in the newspaper accounts, and remembered by most people during that election campaign, were lofty and ringing. They showed the Conservatives as wanting, above all, to heal the wounds caused by patriation between 1980 and 1982.
I know that many men and women in Quebec will not be satisfied with mere words. We will have to make commitments and take concrete steps to reach the objective that I have set for myself and that I repeat here: to convince the Quebec National Assembly to give its consent to the new Canadian constitution with honour and enthusiasm.
But, at the same time, Mulroney espoused the vision of the nationalists: that a deep wrong had been inflicted on Quebec, and that it was up to the rest of Canada to make amends for the profound injustice inflicted on Quebec by the outgoing federal government. That vision was to have serious consequences.
But, on that election night of 4 September 1984, Mulroney had achieved his life's goal. He had won Quebec for the Progressive Conservative Party, taking fifty-eight of his home province's seventy-five seats. He had also swept the country. He had become prime minister, with a historic majority. It was like a storybook ending: the electrician's son from the boondocks went to the big city, made a name for himself, got rich, went into politics, and did what no one before him had been able to do.
His triumph also boded well for the country, which was united from coast to coast. After the turbulent years of federal-provincial strife, the prospect seemed to be for a few years of healing and strengthening. All signs pointed to a bright future. Even the economy, battered during the 1980–82 recession, was now in full recovery and into a seven-year period of continuous growth. Canada seemed,

for a while, like an enchanted kingdom led by a prime minister out of a fairy tale. But Mulroney himself was soon to give a different turn to that story.

Notes

1.Jean-Yves Lortie was nominated by Hochelaga MP Jacques Lavoie, who called on the delegates not to allow the Quebec association to be run from "Ottawa"—a patent reference to Clark. Lavoie soon defected to the Liberals. Wagner himself defected in April 1978 by accepting a seat in the Senate.

2.Report by William Johnson, *Globe and Mail*, 22 Nov. 1976.

3.Jeffrey Simpson, *Discipline of Power. The Conservative Interlude and the Liberal Restoration* (Toronto: Personal Library, 1980), p. 175.

4.Ibid., p. 177.

5.Report by William Johnson, *Globe and Mail*, 19 Apr. 1979.

6.Richard Daignault, *Lesage* (Montreal: Libre expression, 1981), p. 193.

7.Gouvernement du Québec, conseil exécutif, *La nouvelle entente Québec-Canada. Position du gouvernement du Québec pour une entente d'égal à égal: la souveraineté-association* (Éditeur officiel du Québec, 1979), p. 80. After his answer provoked an outcry, Clark backed away and said that he would not negotiate sovereignty-association.

8.Quoted in Robert Sheppard and Michael Valpy, *The National Deal. The Fight for a Canadian Constitution* (Toronto: Fleet, 1982), p. 99.

9.Ibid., pp. 96–7.

10.Michael Valpy, *Globe and Mail*, 6 Nov. 1981, page 6.

11.Peter Blaikie, interview with the author.

12.Abbott was heavily involved in the Pacific Scandal as legal adviser to Sir Hugh Allan, head of the group building the Canadian Pacific Railway, who contributed $400,000 to the Conservatives for the election of 1871.

13.William Johnson, *Globe and Mail*, 13 June 1983, page. 8.

14. *Hansard*, 6 October 1983.

15.Greg Weston, *Reign of Error. The Inside Story of John Turner's Troubled Leadership* (Toronto: McGraw-Hill-Ryerson, 1988), p. 47.

16.Lucien Bouchard, *À visage découvert* (Montreal: Boréal, 1992), p. 143.

17. Ibid.

CHAPTER FOURTEEN

Meech Lake

When Brian Mulroney became prime minister, in September of 1984, Canada was more at peace than at any time since 1962. The great surge to turn Quebec into the ethnic state of and for francophones had crested, and nationalism no longer seemed to be the dynamic force driving Quebec's political or intellectual life. For a while, it seemed that the nationalist frenzy of two decades belonged safely in the past.

The previous April, veteran Liberal minister Marc Lalonde had declared that separatism in Quebec was obsolete: "It has become literature. . . . It will continue to be there, it will still be talked about in the next election, but as a political force that carries away the new generation, in my opinion, it is dead."[1] René Lévesque himself was not far from the same opinion. Veteran Quebec journalist Dominique Clift wrote a series of articles in which he maintained that nationalism was already in decline at the time of the 1980 referendum and would necessarily continue to decline thereafter.[2] Laval University political scientist Louis Balthazar, himself a nationalist, wrote a book on Quebec nationalism that was published in 1986, the year before the Meech Lake Accord. "Since the beginning of the 1980s, nationalism has ceased to inspire the bulk of activities of the society. The spirit of the Quiet Revolution . . . has certainly disappeared. The state of Quebec is no longer glorified. The *nation Québécoise* is no longer the privileged point of reference. So we must acknowledge the end of a period of Québécois nationalism."[3] As late as 29 April 1988, Keith Spicer and I interviewed Lucien Bouchard for the *Télémédia* television program, *Sur la colline*. Bouchard had announced that day that he would be running for Parliament for the Tories in Lac St-Jean in a 20 June by-election. As I wrote in my column in *The Gazette* the next day, "We asked him, of course, about his past as a Péquiste, as someone who gave speeches for sovereignty-association during the 1980 Quebec referendum campaign. He said he no longer believes that Quebec ever will be independent, and that he is working sincerely within the framework of the Canadian federation."

So how did it come about that nationalism would rage more virulently than ever just two or three years later? It strains credulity to suggest that the manner of patriating the constitution from 1980 to 1982 caused the nationalist fevers of 1989 to 1991. No, it was the prime minister of Canada who, more than anyone, reactivated nationalism, undermined the federalist forces in Quebec, discredited the 1982 constitution's vision of Canada as one country with two official languages, and rehabilitated the Quiet Revolution vision of Quebec as the ethnic state of French speakers.

Mulroney did not do it alone. He worked closely with premier Robert Bourassa, who returned to power in December, 1985. He was aided and abetted by the nine other provincial premiers, by Liberal leader John Turner and NDP leader Ed Broadbent, by compliant elected representatives in Ottawa and Quebec City, by a complacent press, by a largely consenting academic community, by a complicit business class, and even by the labour elites outside of Quebec.

With good will, but a nearly fatal lack of understanding, the elites across the country acquiesced to the Quebec political class's atavistic infatuation with the ethnic state. Various code words had been used in the past to demand the transformation of Quebec into an ethnic state, and they had been stonewalled by Pierre Trudeau when he was prime minister. But now the right-thinking people of Canada embraced the same principle, smuggled in under the formula of "distinct society." The attempt to appease Quebec nationalism revived it powerfully, stirred resentment in the rest of the country, precipitated a fundamental though one-sided debate over the vision of society to be vested in the constitution, pitted the elites against the common people, and discredited the country's leadership, ultimately leading to the rise of the populist Reform Party and the emergence of the Bloc Québécois as Canada's official opposition party.

Initially, though, Mulroney's offensive to win the Quebec government's retroactive acquiescence to the 1982 constitution had the effect of dividing the Parti Québécois. Many of the Quebec Conservative candidates in the 1984 elections were nationalists who had campaigned for the Yes side during the 1980 referendum. For Premier Lévesque personally, Mulroney offered a chance to redeem himself by the 6 August promise in his Sept-Îles speech to "convince the Quebec National Assembly to give its consent to the new Canadian constitution with honour and enthusiasm." That put the onus on the federal government to find the means to win Lévesque's consent.

At a press conference three days later, Lévesque called Mulroney's speech "a very remarkable opening." Honour and enthusiasm were precisely what Lévesque lacked most in 1984. In June, a public-opinion poll in *Le Soleil* showed the PQ with only 23 per cent support, while the Liberals were flying astronomically high, at 68 per cent.[4]

After the exalted beginnings of his regime in 1976, Lévesque had fallen on hard times. Quebecers had rejected even a feeble "mandate to negotiate" sovereignty-association. He had won the election of April, 1981, only to govern Quebec during the worst recession since the 1930s. His government, hard pressed by shrinking revenues and ballooning welfare costs, had passed special legislation to claw back the rich salary increases granted public-sector employees just before the referendum. This led to massive, bitter confrontations with the unions, the teachers, the health and welfare workers, the civil servants—the very core constituency that had carried the PQ to power.

What most humiliated Lévesque was that he and Claude Morin had botched the constitutional negotiations, failing to prevent patriation and forfeiting Quebec's traditional veto. Despite the smoke screen of "betrayal" which was thrown up around the endgame of November, 1981, the fact was that they had been outmanoeuvred by their arch-enemy, Trudeau.

Lévesque was attracted by Mulroney's promise. The problem was that the PQ, at its convention of June 1984, had committed itself to fight the next election on sovereignty, straight sovereignty, without benefit of association, and without the promise of a referendum. "A vote for a Parti Québécois candidate will mean a vote for Quebec sovereignty," the resolution stated. That was hard and clear, but suicidal. There simply was no market for nationalism in Quebec at that time. And, with such a policy, the PQ government could not hope to strike a deal with Mulroney to repair the humiliation of 1981–82.

So Lévesque began backing away from the commitment to sovereignty. He did not repudiate it, but he put it off into an indefinite future. At a meeting of the PQ's national council within three weeks of Mulroney's remarkable victory of 4 September 1984, Lévesque responded to the Sept-Îles invitation. The Quebec government, he said, had the obligation to negotiate in good faith the renewal of federalism. It must act as a government with an exclusively federalist mandate. Lévesque recognized that such a commitment would make selling sovereignty problematic, but he was willing to run that risk: "So, if federalism should function less badly, and even really improve, doesn't that risk smothering our fundamental option, and sending sovereignty to never-never land? Obviously, there is an element of risk. But it is a *beau risque*, and we don't have the luxury of not taking it."[5]

Those words were followed up on 16 October, when Lévesque opened a new session of the National Assembly with an inaugural address that, for the first time, made absolutely no reference to sovereignty, but proposed that constitutional negotiations be reopened for "the correction of an injustice." His government, Lévesque said, was ready to co-operate with the federal government to that purpose. This was incompatible with the party's commitment to hold the next election on sovereignty. Therefore, Lévesque, urged on by his heir-apparent, Pierre-Marc Johnson, began to retreat from that commitment.

By then, the PQ was split into two camps, with Lévesque on the side of the revisionists, and Jacques Parizeau and Camille Laurin the most prominent of the "orthodox." On 19 November, Lévesque issued a statement that took sovereignty off the PQ's agenda and repudiated a proposal by some dissidents to pursue sovereignty bit by bit, sector by sector. "We must surely resign ourselves, in my humble opinion, to the fact that sovereignty must not be at stake."[6]

In his study of the PQ in power, Graham Fraser underlines how remote the prospect of sovereignty seemed to Lévesque on that day, less than two months after Mulroney came to power. "Sovereignty would remain an ideal, and Lévesque called on party members to keep the faith. But it seemed clear that he no longer believed that Quebec independence was on the public agenda for the foreseeable future. Sovereignty was, he said, an insurance policy."[7]

When the PQ held its convention, in January of 1985 to endorse the postponement of the commitment to sovereignty, an opinion poll published in *La Presse* showed that support for sovereignty had declined to 23 per cent, of which 19 points were for sovereignty-association, and only 4 for independence.[8] Lévesque told the convention, "We are still, as we have been from the beginning, sovereignists," but he recognized that "realism" demanded a compromise. The hardliners were decisively beaten, by a vote of 869 to 469. A quarter of Lévesque's Cabinet resigned on the issue, and the "orthodox" ministers who insisted on sovereignty included some of the pillars of the party, such as Parizeau, Laurin, and Jacques Leonard.

The negotiations to get the PQ government's signature on the constitution did not get far. The PQ put forward twenty-one conditions, many of which were unacceptable to a federalist regime. Lévesque soon stepped down, to be replaced by Pierre-Marc Johnson. Four months later, in December of 1985, the PQ was defeated and the Liberals of Robert Bourassa were back in power. It looked as though the final curtain had fallen on nationalism.

Bourassa had won the election on a platform that included concessions to the English-speaking minority. He had committed a Liberal government to rescind Bill 101's prohibition of languages other than French on commercial signs. It was an issue of intense significance: for anglophones, the ban on English symbolized the utter rejection of the English language and so of English-speaking people. For most nationalists, the ban was the ultimate proof that Quebec would be coercively and integrally French.

With the Liberals back in government, nationalist agitation began against any change to weaken the character of Quebec as a solely French state. The Charter of the French Language had required setting up three distinct agencies, including an official advisory body on language, the Conseil de la langue française, and a watchdog body, the Commission de protection de la langue française, mandated to prosecute people who violated the law—for instance, by having any English on a commercial sign. The heads of both agencies, ardent defenders of French unilingualism, tried to arouse the population to a new threat to French: the Liberal government. One of them announced that uncertainty about the future language policies of the government was encouraging people to display English signs. His agency prepared a totally biased "study," soon leaked to the press, which suggested that the use of French on public signs was declining, replaced by English. Three French newspapers gave enormous and uncritical publicity to the effort. It was an egregiously successful propaganda campaign, which became more strident after publicity was given to a "poll" by a former PQ minister which suggested that the use of French was declining in commerce in favour of English.[9] It reached its peak in December, 1986, as the Quebec Court of Appeal was expected momentarily to render its judgment on Bill 101's prohibition of other languages than French on signs. *"Ne touchez pas à la loi 101!"* Don't touch Bill 101: the slogan was pasted on walls all over Montreal. The big labour-union federations and the usual patriotic associations pressured the government not to reintroduce bilingualism on signs.

It was at this critical moment that the Mulroney government entered the debate—on the side of those opposed to permitting English on signs. Conservative MPs, including the prime minister himself, picked up and appropriated the anti-bilingualism slogans of the nationalists. The PQ was warning against any *"recul,"* or retreat, on "the French face of Montreal." This was the code for prohibiting all other languages but French on signs. The federal minister in charge of Quebec, the ultra-nationalist Marcel Masse, travelled to Montreal on 6 December to showcase the position on language taken by the Quebec Conservative caucus. Here, in part, is the account of his speech published in *La Presse,* under the headline "The Mulroney Government Opposes Any Retreat of French in Quebec."

Minister Marcel Masse took a stand yesterday in the name of the Mulroney government against any retreat of the French language in Quebec.

"We agree with the Québécois who demand that French be the usual language in Quebec, the language used normally and everywhere," Mr. Masse declared at a meeting of the presidents of the Quebec Conservative riding associations. The riding association presidents applauded warmly the position taken by Mr. Masse.

This statement represents tacit support for the Parti Québécois and the various groups that have arisen over the past few months in order to defeat the amendments to Bill 101 that the Liberal government of Premier Robert Bourassa wants to bring in.

During the federal election campaign of 1984, the Parti Québécois, which was then in power, had implicitly backed the Conservative Party of Mr. Mulroney and had put at his disposal part of its infrastructure.[10]

This was an astonishing development, absolutely contrary to the constant tradition, since 1867, of the federal government acting as the defender of minority language rights against provincial governments repressing them. Now, the federal government was openly campaigning for the continued repression of English.

On that same day, coincidentally, Premier Bourassa spoke on a Montreal radio station to try to reassure the population that his first priority was to protect French, but he suggested that he would allow some English on signs. "I have said it many

203

times, Quebec is and will remain French," Bourassa told his radio audience. "But, that being achieved, it also intends to remain open toward its minorities, which contribute every day to enriching its economic, social, and cultural heritage." Bourassa called on the people of Quebec to keep the debate over language "at an acceptable level."

Did Marcel Masse have Mulroney's support for intervening at a crucial moment in an emotional debate? The answer was not long in coming. The prime minister made a two-day visit to Montreal to shore up his party's sagging support in Quebec. On the second day, he took part in an open-line program on Montreal's radio station CKAC. Here, in part, is the story *Le Devoir* ran on the event at the top of its front page.

Prime Minister Mulroney intervened yesterday in the language debate and gave a strong helping hand to the defenders of Bill 101 when he pleaded resolutely in favour of the French face of Quebec. "There must be no retreat." . . .

Later, questioned by journalists, he gave his unequivocal support to the protest movement that is aimed at countering the intentions of the government to liberalize Bill 101.

Asked, "Do you favour keeping Bill 101 unchanged?" the prime minister first said that he didn't want to intervene in a debate taking place in the National Assembly. Then he added immediately, "I think it essential that Quebec maintain its French face and that the use of French not be set back. We have seen important progress over the past few years in Quebec in the use of French. And there must be no falling back."

When he was invited to give his opinion on the intention of the Bourassa government to introduce the principle of bilingual signs, the prime minister began by recalling that the question was now before the Court of Appeal. Nevertheless, he gave his opinion. "The French face of Quebec and of Montreal must be maintained."[11]

It was extraordinary: the prime minister of Canada, himself an English-speaking Quebecer, pleaded for maintaining a repressive law against English, one of the official languages of Canada. He went on to maintain that coercive French unilingualism did not violate the rights of the English-speaking minority. And he repeated: "French must be strengthened and we must not retreat."

Not suprisingly, Quebec's cultural affairs minister, Lise Bacon, who was responsible for language policy, told Mulroney the next day to mind his own business. "Mr. Mulroney has enough problems of his own without meddling in our affairs," she said. "He should leave us to deal with this."[12] On the other hand, Parti Québécois leader Pierre-Marc Johnson, delighted, said that the prime minister had gone to the heart of the debate in saying there should be "no retreat"—the PQ's own phrase.

The English-speaking community of Quebec reacted limply to this powerful attack on its rights. *The Gazette*'s news story on Mulroney's extraordinary intervention was perfunctory and brief. Readers would have had to turn to *Le Devoir* or *La Presse* to get the full story. The editorial that appeared in *The Gazette* reacting to the event did little more than say tut-tut and tap Mulroney on the fingers. Under the headline "Mulroney on thin ice," the editorial began, "Prime Minister Mulroney's intervention in the Quebec language debate this week was insensitive and inopportune. Wittingly or not, the prime minister played into the hands of extremists with his off-the-cuff bluster about 'no retreat' on Quebec's French fact and French face."

Thin ice? Insensitive? Off the cuff? The editorial writer clearly had no understanding of the scope and implications of what Mulroney had done. He had not come into Quebec without knowing in advance that he would be questioned first and foremost about the most sensitive and controversial issue in Quebec politics at that time. His reply had to be carefully considered in advance and deliberate, as Masse's statement two days earlier in the name of the Conservative government had made clear. Both were enunciating the policy of the Conservative caucus, not just tossing off casual remarks.

The lesson of Mulroney's intervention and *The Gazette*'s editorial was not lost on the Bourassa government. The prime minister had flagrantly and publicly betrayed his responsibility to the vision of Canada as a country with two official languages. He had thrown English-speaking Quebecers to the wolves, and the *Gazette* had responded merely with the equivalent of "watch your language." This marshmallow response suggested that English-speaking Quebecers had come to accept *de facto* the repressive features of Bill 101.

In the event, Bourassa never did bring in his promised legislation to permit English on signs, even after the five judges of the Quebec Court of Appeal ruled unanimously, later that month, that Bill 101 violated the Canadian and Quebec charters of rights. Why should the premier infuriate the nationalists when Quebec's leading English-speaking politician, the prime minister of Canada, demanded that unilingualism be maintained and when the chief voice of English-speaking Quebec, *The Gazétte,* barely bleated like a lamb at such a betrayal? And so it happened that the principle of Quebec as a coercively French ethnic state was maintained at the insistence of the prime minister. That episode set the framework for the Meech Lake accord, not five months later.

Bourassa's Liberal platform for the 1985 election had responded to Mulroney's invitation to reopen negotiations on the constitution. It proposed a list of five conditions, the most significant of which was that Quebec be recognized as a "distinct society" in the preamble of the constitution.[13] This approach broke with the past, in recognition of the drastically weakened bargaining position for any nationalist demands. The constitution had been patriated, and so Bourassa's old ploy of holding up patriation as a pressure tactic was no longer available. And because the constitution had been reformed in depth only three years before, it was difficult to argue the need to make sweeping new demands so soon. The threat of encouraging separatism as the alternative, which Bourassa had used so skilfully in the past, was no longer credible in the becalmed atmosphere of 1985, when the PQ itself had put off sovereignty to a wistful future.

The principle was, in substance, the same that had been espoused by the last five Quebec premiers, including Bourassa himself. But now Bourassa used terminology better adapted to the circumstances and his cautious, ambiguous, flexible, but tenacious approach to politics. It was an expression, a code word, that seemed innocuous and incontrovertible but at the same time contained the nucleus of recognition of the ethnic state: Quebec as a *distinct society*.

Mulroney had no problem with "distinct society." And John Turner did not share Trudeau's reservations about such formulas. Like Mulroney, Turner had no political vision, and his only goal was to win seats in Quebec, where he had lost disastrously in the 1984 elections.

Turner's most prestigious recruit from Quebec, Raymond Garneau, an economist by training, had been executive assistant to Jean Lesage, and had also been on the staff of the Liberal Party of Quebec. Then, elected to the National Assembly, Garneau had served as Bourassa's minister of finance. After Bourassa's defeat in 1976, Garneau ran to succeed him; the party chose Claude Ryan instead, and Garneau left politics. In 1984, invited by Turner to run federally, he had been elected to Parliament, one of the few to resist Mulroney's sweep of Quebec. Although now a Liberal MP, Garneau still had the vision of the Quiet Revolution and of the provincial Liberal Party in which he had spent most of his adult life. His urgent advice was that Turner should endorse Bourassa's concept of the "distinct society," even though it went against what the federal Liberals had stood for since 1968.

Turner gave an interview to the editorial board of *Le Devoir*, which was published on 13 June 1986. Without consulting his caucus, he announced, "I have no difficulty inserting in the preamble to the constitution a recognition of Quebec as a unique and distinct society in our Confederation." As he had done two years earlier, Turner had just recklessly thrown away a Liberal family jewel and overturned a policy that had brought peace to the country after two decades of turmoil. Before leaving for that fateful interview, Turner had explained to his executive assistant, Stewart Langford, "I'm just trying to do a few things there and get the Quebec people happy and see if we can get a position out ahead of Mulroney."[14]

Then it was the turn of the premiers. At their annual meeting in Edmonton in August, 1986, they agreed to reopen constitutional negotiations, as Mulroney proposed, with the purpose of getting Quebec's agreement to the 1982 patriation. The English-speaking premiers saw little problem with Bourassa's five conditions. They did not grasp that "distinct society" was a code word which would have consequences far beyond their anticipation. Pragmatic men of limited vision, they had no understanding of the arcane dialectics current in Quebec. They agreed that a first constitutional round should be devoted *exclusively to meeting Bourassa's terms; demands by other provinces would be put off to a second round.

So it was that the "Quebec round" was negotiated at Meech Lake and in Ottawa during two marathon sessions in April and June of 1987. The atmosphere was very different than it had been when Pierre Trudeau was prime minister. Under Mulroney, there was no polarization between the prime minister and the premiers, and especially not between the prime minister and the premier of Quebec. Mulroney acted at the negotiating table as the chief sponsor and advocate for Bourassa's positions.

This prime minister, unemcumbered by a vision, looked only for a deal, and he got it by giving Bourassa what he wanted, and much more. The 1985 Quebec Liberal program, *Maîtriser l'avenir*, had asked for special recognition of Quebec: "It is high time that the constitution recognize Quebec explicitly as the heartland of a society that is distinct by its language, its culture, its history, its institutions and the mode of life wanted by its population. . . . Such a statement, we think, must be found in the preamble to the new constitution." At Meech Lake, Bourassa obtained that recognition as a clause in the body of the constitution, one in the light of which the entire constitution was to be interpreted. It would thereby sanction, at last, the ethnic state that Quebec premiers had been striving for since 1962.

It was the words of the Charter of the French Language that the Meech Lake accord now echoed. The Charter began:

Whereas the French language, the distinctive language of a people that is in the majority French-speaking, is the instrument by which that people has articulated its identity;

Whereas the National Assembly of Quebec recognizes that Quebecers wish to see the quality and influence of the French language assured, and is resolved therefore to make of French the language of government and the law, as well as the normal and everyday language of work, instruction, communication, commerce, and business . . .

The first "whereas" of Bill 101 is echoed in Meech in the concepts of "distinct society" and "distinct identity." And, without using the word "French," Meech Lake echoed the second "whereas" by affirming the role of the Quebec legislature and government in promoting the distinct identity of Quebec, without qualification. The parallelism was not fortuitous: Bill 101 and Meech Lake projected exactly the same vision.

In the National Assembly, Bourassa and intergovernmental affairs minister Gil Rémillard outlined the significance of the distinct society clause in Meech Lake, which prepared the way for later very broad jurisdictional claims to promote Quebec's distinct identity. Bourassa, in particular, indicated the scope of his concept of the distinct society: "The French language constitutes one fundamental characteristic of this specificity, but it also involves other aspects, such as culture, political, economic, and juridical institutions." He mentioned English rights, but not as part of Quebec's history and identity; he viewed them only in the light of "the only limitations on our power" in matters of language. "The only road that we are taking," he declared, "is that of strengthening and consolidating the French language."

Rémillard concurred: "We all know that this distinct society is fundamentally, essentially founded on the French language and culture." And now, the Quebec state was to be given the specific role of "promoting" that society so conceived: it was to be an ethnic state.

The normal guardians of civil liberties, the guardians of minority rights, the guardians of English rights, those concerned with maintaining a workable federation that recognized two national languages, could have been expected to set off alarm bells over Meech Lake. Bourassa was at that very time insisting on maintaining clauses of Bill 101 which the courts of Quebec had judged unanimously to be a violation of fundamental rights and incompatible with the values of a free and democratic society. To accept Meech Lake while Bourassa maintained those violations of freedom was to accept tacitly the violations, to say that they were unimportant or even acceptable. It was to condone the spirit and the letter of Bill 101, including all its anti-English provisions. And this is the message that political leaders sent to Bourassa and to the entire country by endorsing Meech Lake without demanding first that the oppressive law be rescinded. In the National Assembly and the federal Parliament, the abdication of principle was flagrant.

The same abdication was also displayed elsewhere. On 28 May 1987, not for the first time, *The Gazette* gave its consent to the distinct society clause and the Meech Lake package without even demanding as a minimal precondition that the prohibition against English on signs be rescinded. "But Quebec *is* a distinct society within Canada," an editorial stated. "Is it so bad for the basic law of the land to recognize reality?"

Alliance Quebec, a federally funded association with the mandate of protecting the rights of English-speaking Quebecers, went before the parliamentary committee that held public hearings on the Meech Lake accord. Did Alliance Quebec demand a restoration of English rights in Quebec before there could be any question of countenancing in the constitution the Quebec government's mandate to promote Quebec's distinct identity? On the contrary. Having learned nothing from Bill 101 or Bourassa's opposition to bilingual signs, or from Mulroney's support for French unilingualism, or from the increasingly hostile climate in Quebec toward English, Alliance Quebec proclaimed with blind fatuity:

No one can say for certain what the recognition of Quebec as a distinct society within Canada will mean or what effect it will have on the

French-speaking and English-speaking communities in Quebec. However, the hallmark of Alliance Quebec has been its conviction that we can and must have trust in our fellow citizens and in our democratic institutions. We are prepared, therefore, to make the leap of faith into the uncharted waters into which this new clause may take us because we have confidence in Quebec and the fairness of Quebec society.

But the waters were not, in fact uncharted: their treacherous shoals had been amply marked by the constant growth of nationalism since 1962 and the constantly reinforced assertion of the ethnic state. The political compliance and tactical ineptness of the opinion leaders of English Quebec in 1987 invited the suppression of English on signs by Bourassa the following year. Bourassa must have concluded that, no matter how their rights were violated, English-speaking Quebecers would never stand up for themselves or for liberal principles.

What would the distinct society clause mean in practice? The Conseil de la langue française submitted a ninety-page opinion in which it urged the government to legislate "quickly, systematically, and visibly" to establish Quebec's "specificity," and to show that the government was constantly inspired in its actions by that specificity.[15] The Conseil insisted that, before being a legal concept to be defined by the courts, the "distinct society" clause was "a vision of society." And, indeed, it was.

A few leading figures did understand what Meech Lake implied. In May, 1987, Pierre Trudeau published in *La Presse* and the *Toronto Star* a diatribe against the accord. "Those Canadians who fought for a single Canada, bilingual and multicultural, can say goodbye to their dream. We are henceforth to have two Canadas, each defined in terms of its language." But still most opinion leaders did not understand. Both *The Gazette* and the *Globe and Mail* denounced Trudeau patronizingly in their editorials.

A group organized by constitutional lawyer Deborah Coyne, then teaching law at the University of Toronto, set out to fight Meech Lake in the courts and in public opinion. Calling itself the Canadian Coalition on the Constitution, the group argued that the accord would weaken the charter and undermine the central government. At first, their struggle, in the face of the unanimity of the federal parties and the provincial premiers, seemed hopeless. But, defending the vision that Pierre Trudeau had bequeathed the country, they provided a beachhead for a counterattack against the weakening of the federation implicit in Meech Lake.

They could not, though, prevent the House of Commons from adopting the Meech Lake resolution. When Mulroney spoke in favour of it in the House on 22 October 1987, he was at his most tricky, oily, and false. He spoke as though the resolution, which actually condoned the suppression of English-language rights in Quebec, did the opposite by protecting them.

In voting for this accord, members are upholding the rights of our language minorities, English-speaking in Quebec and French-speaking outside Quebec. . . . If I, for one moment, thought that anyone's rights were being overridden by this accord, I would not have recommended it to my colleagues in government, and the Government of Canada would never have brought it forward for consideration in Parliament today.

From the start, ambiguity surrounded the Meech Lake agreement. For the other nine premiers, it represented the "Quebec Round," which was to be followed by a "Canada round." The premiers saw it as the final act in satisfying the demands made by premiers of Quebec since the 1960s. What Bourassa was asking seemed modest enough compared to what his predecessors had claimed. Once the accord was passed, they thought, the patriation of 1981–82 would have been completed, with the premier of Quebec joining the other premiers in a an all-Canadian consensus. That done, the other premiers could serve themselves, as Quebec had been served at Meech.

This assumption led the premiers to postpone their own demands, notably for reform of the Senate, which was so important to Alberta. They did not understand that the "Quebec Round" was merely, for Bourassa, the prelude to a far more important Quebec round, during which recognition of the principle of the distinct society would be followed by claims for the substance: the broad powers required to protect and promote Quebec's distinct identity.

On 14 May 1990, Rémillard, who was Quebec's chief negotiator on the constitution, gave a speech in France in which he shed light on the intentions of the Quebec government. Through Meech Lake, he said, "the Quebec government wanted to establish on a solid basis the foundations of a comprehensive constitutional reform to come in a second stage of negotiations."

But, of course, no one spelled out the scope or the nature of this comprehensive transformation, for this would have shaken the other premiers and the public out of their illusions that Quebec's appetites would be satisfied by Meech Lake. It can be safely surmised that Bourassa's objective was still "sovereign associate states," his aim since 1967, when he wrote of the need to repatriate to Quebec "the principal centres of decision-making."

Yet, even before or beyond any future amendments, the government of Robert Bourassa—and, presumably, any other Quebec government—would use the distinct society clause to exercise more powers. This was confirmed at a press conference held on 8 November 1989 by Bourassa and Rémillard. When asked whether Quebec intended—as a distinct society—to demand "new powers" from Ottawa, Rémillard responded, "We will use this criterion, and all the other criteria of the constitution. A constitution is there to be used."[16]

Still, no one publicly admitted all the implications of Meech Lake. Mulroney, who had defended French rights in Manitoba in 1983, could hardly announce publicly that he wanted the constitution to encourage the Quebec government to repress English. Nor would he acknowledge that Meech Lake would set up a constant tug-of-war in which Quebec would be trying to wrest ever more powers from the federal government under the guise of promoting its distinct identity. In fact, however, it was an open invitation to the Quebec government to demand more powers in the second round of negotiations, and meanwhile to pass laws whereby Quebec exercised such powers *de facto*. Meech would encourage any future Quebec government, federalist or separatist, to go the limit in exercising more jurisdictions. It would make it more difficult for the Supreme Court to rule such laws invalid. And it would make it politically difficult and damaging to overturn such laws.

Jacques Parizeau, interviewed by Barbara Frum on *The Journal* on 25 October 1989, hinted at the use he could put the "distinct society" clause to if the Parti Québécois came to power.

If we come to power, there is no doubt that I'm going to use—if the Meech Lake clause of a distinct society that hasn't been watered down is still there, I'm going to use that for everything it's worth. It's remarkable how much one could get through that clause if the courts say, Well, yes, in some circumstances, it can override certain dispositions of the Charter of Rights. If the courts ever say that, my God, what a weapon it could be for people who have the sort of—shall we say, political project that I have.

But most federal politicians, business leaders, and editorial writers spoke as though nothing more was involved than recognizing the obvious reality that Quebec was different from Ontario, as though the "distinct society" clause did no more than put an appropriate constitutional label on a province that was, indeed, rather different. Mulroney himself said as much in a Toronto speech on 10 May 1990:

Perhaps the most discussed feature of the accord is the "distinct society" clause. This is the clause that affirms that Quebec is a distinct society, "within Canada." But there is nothing very new about that. It simply reflects reality. This doesn't mean that Quebec is privileged or gains any special powers. It simply confirms the obvious: that Quebec is different and that that difference is very much worth conserving in the interest of Quebecers and of all Canadians.

So, the distinct society clause added nothing new. One was left to wonder why Bourassa and others made such a fuss over it.

Along with the proposition that the distinct society meant little, Mulroney and his ministers constantly drove home their version of the 1982 patriation: Trudeau had broken his referendum promise to renew federalism. Instead, he had inflicted a trauma on Quebec by patriating the constitution, leaving Quebecers in a piteous state of isolation and humiliation. The patriation became, in the epic incantations of the prime minister, a drama of perfidy and betrayal, the tragedy of an entire people rejected and scorned. It was a dangerous interpretation to give to recent history, especially when directed at a community that already had been conditioned by a tribalist literature in which it was depicted as under constant attack.

There were two risks in repeatedly plunging the knife in the wound: the portrayal of the federation as having betrayed and rejected Quebec in the recent past might have effects persisting long after Meech had passed, sowing permanent distrust in the minds of many Quebecers. Or, worse still, Meech might not pass at all, and then Quebecers would feel doubly betrayed. Mulroney never seemed to grasp how reckless and destructive was his course of misrepresenting history.

Although he had supported patriation in 1982, this did not prevent Mulroney later from denouncing the patriation time and again as a terrible affront to Quebecers. In a speech given in Montreal at a fund-raising dinner on 3 December 1989, he repeated his thesis that Trudeau had broken his promise to Quebecers and, worse, had trampled on their feelings:

"We want change," he said, "We are putting our seats on the line for change." A few days later, Quebec responded to the prime minister of Canada's solemn promise by voting for change. And there was change, just as Mr. Trudeau had promised: the following year, Quebec was excluded from the constitution. . . .

We have seen a federal prime minister erect a stage on Parliament Hill and with great pomp, surrounded by his ministers, sign a constitution that isolated and humiliated Quebec. That Canadian prime minister was not Brian Mulroney! Because, for Brian Mulroney, a constitution without Quebec is absolutely inconceivable—it would be a major error written in capital letters in the history of our country.

Mulroney's words were partisan and hypocritical. But, far worse, the prime minister was telling Quebecers that a previous prime minister had lied to them. They were no longer in the constitution of Canada. The constitution of Canada itself was illegitimate. Mulroney had adopted the rhetoric and the vision of the Parti Québécois. Coming from an English-speaking prime minister from Quebec, the words were infinitely more subversive and inflammatory.

In his year-end interviews for television in December of 1989, Mulroney again evoked Trudeau's promise, again depicted Quebec as betrayed, left out of the constitution, isolated and humiliated. Appearing with Madeleine Poulin on the 21 December Radio-Canada television program *Le Point,* he evoked the "party" thrown by the Liberals, with the Queen invited to Ottawa to celebrate the "illegitimate" constitution from which Quebec had been excluded. He then contrasted this flagrant and grievous injury with the modest demands made by Bourassa for Quebec to be readmitted to the constitution. And now, as a new injury, these modest demands were under threat of being refused. If Meech Lake were not accepted by all, Mulroney hated to even think of what the consequences would be.

By repeatedly asserting that Quebec was outside the constitution, outside the Canadian family, and even outside the country, Mulroney was flirting with danger. If Quebec were not already part of Canada, it would not likely join the federation. The strongest reason for remaining in Canada was the heavy cost of separation. But Mulroney drove home the message that Canada had already separated from Quebec, and that Meech Lake was a means to allow Quebec back into Canada. This raised a natural question: if Meech failed, why should Quebec make efforts to get back into Canada? Having been thrust out ignominiously, it would be free to rejoin or not, as it chose.

In addition to misleading Quebec, Mulroney also seriously misled the country by insisting that the Meech Lake agreement was, at last, the answer to the old question, What does Quebec want? He implied that if Meech Lake were adopted, Quebec's vexatious constitutional demands would cease. In fact, the Meech Lake agreement was anything but the answer to the full list of Quebec's demands. Nor was it what "Quebec" wanted. It was no more than a controversial proposal of the Liberal government. When that Liberal government passed from the scene, its successor would want something more. The Parti Québécois would consider Meech only as a foot in the door in advance of the real thing—sovereignty—much as Bourassa's Bill 22 had prepared the way for Bill 101.

The Bourassa government held parliamentary hearings on the Meech Lake accord in May and June of 1987. Of all the briefs submitted, 19 per cent were in favour, and 81 per cent were opposed. The three favourable briefs were submitted by Alliance Quebec, representing English-speaking Quebecers and the chambers of commerce of Montreal and Quebec. This was the answer to what Quebec wants?[17]

Nor did public-opinion polls reveal any enthusiasm in Quebec for Meech Lake. Except at the very first, most of the polls throughout the three years of the debate over Meech showed half or less of Quebec's population in favour. A very large proportion said they didn't know what to think about Meech.[18] Even after the week-long conference of the first ministers in June, 1990, when it was thought that the accord was going to be adopted by the last hold-out provinces, an Angus Reid poll published on 12 June in the Ottawa *Citizen* showed support in Quebec at 49 per cent, opposition at 33 per cent, and 17 per cent without an opinion. That was not too different from opinion in the rest of Canada: 44 per cent approved, 41 per cent disapproved, and 15 per cent had no opinion. In fact, by 1990, there was more support in Quebec for sovereignty—better than 60 per cent in most polls—than there was for Meech Lake. Must we conclude that sovereignty was the real answer to "What does Quebec want?" For Meech Lake was, at best, an unstable amendment, a temporary and transitional arrangement before much more serious demands were made for further change. Meech would simply have confirmed Quebec on the track of the ethnic state. The rest was to follow.

Having reopened the constitution, one of the great wounds in the country, which had just recently been closed, Mulroney now rushed to reopen another old point of division: the status of the official languages. In June, 1987, just after the eleven first ministers endorsed Meech Lake in its final form, Mulroney introduced

Bill C-72, comprising major revisions to the 1969 Official Languages Act. The earlier law, passed by Trudeau, had dealt almost exclusively with giving English and French equality of status within the federal government. In reality, Ottawa had gone far beyond that, offering hundreds of millions of dollars to the provinces to induce them to provide schooling in French and English as minority languages. The federal money also funded immersion French classes and gave core funding to associations defending minority official-language rights, as well as to various cultural enterprises such as theatre groups.

Bill C-72 now made explicit what had not been spelled out in the Official Languages Act: the federal government would promote French and English not only within the federal government so as to serve Canadian citizens in their choice of English or French, but throughout Canadian society. Ottawa would foster the use of English and French in schools, in the business community, in labour unions, at meetings of professional associations, and in voluntary, non-government organizations.

As with the constitution, so with official languages: there was no pressing demand to reopen the recent settlement. In fact, to raise again formally, insistently, the rights of French and English was to plunge the country again into controversy, at a time when it was important to let wounds heal. The 1982 constitution required each province to offer instruction to French and English minority children wherever numbers warranted. This was controversial in the three westernmost provinces, where there was great resistance to compelling their governments to recognize special status for French. And in Quebec, the new constitution overrode Bill 101's exclusion from English schools of practically all children unless their parents had studied in English in the province itself. It forced Quebec to admit all children whose parents had studied in English anywhere in Canada. This was an imposition that the Lévesque government fought all the way to the Supreme Court of Canada, where it lost.

Into the highly sensitive issue of language charged the Mulroney government, with the enthusiastic backing of John Turner's Liberals and Ed Broadbent's New Democrats. The bill was likely to arouse opposition from two different quarters: the Quebec government and the West. It is interesting to contrast the way in which Mulroney dealt with each.

In its wording, Bill C-72 committed the federal secretary of state impartially to promote French and English—French in nine provinces and the territories, English in Quebec. The Quebec government was delighted to have French promoted elsewhere, but did not appreciate the promotion of English in Quebec. An explosive indication of official Quebec's sensitivities on the matter appeared after the commissioner of official languages, D'Iberville Fortier, tabled his annual report on 22 March 1988 and had the temerity to suggest that Quebec was not doing the right thing by its restrictions on the English language. Fortier's words were allusive rather than directly critical—"The salvation of French, in Quebec or elsewhere, must surely lie in positively asserting its own demographic weight, cultural vigour, and innate attractiveness, and not in humbling the competition"— but that did not save him from a torrent of abuse.

Bourassa called Fortier's statement "irresponsible, imprudent and unacceptable." The National Assembly held an emergency debate and censured Fortier unanimously; even the English-speaking members joined in the vote. And Brian Mulroney, the prime minister and bold defender of French rights in Manitoba, hung the besieged Fortier out to dry. Mulroney said that he "did not feel humiliated anywhere in Canada, whether it be in Manitoba, in British Columbia, or in Quebec." In other words, how could Fortier talk about Quebec's English-speaking community being "humiliated," when Mulroney, himself an Anglo-Quececer, denied that he was humiliated in Quebec?

That very weekend, by coincidence, the Quebec wing of the Progressive Conservative Party held its annual meeting in Montreal. The Quebec Tories voted to censure Fortier. The governing federal party had joined the howling mob.

At that meeting, Mulroney said not a word in defence of the rights of English-speaking Quebec; he whispered not a word on behalf of the beleaguered commissioner who was defending the official languages. On the contrary, he finessed the sensitive topic by dealing with it only indirectly, denying that there was a problem with rights in Quebec. He recalled that weekend what he had said about Meech Lake in the House the previous October: "If I, for one moment, thought anyone's rights were being overridden by this accord, I would not have recommended it to my colleagues in the government." So did Mulroney continue to sell out English Quebec and one of the official languages to win the support of the Quebec nationalists.

The prime minister then carried off another coup. On 31 March 1988, he appointed Lucien Bouchard to the federal Cabinet as secretary of state. He also named him immediately to the powerful inner cabinet. And, to complete the triple crown, within two years he would name Bouchard his Quebec lieutenant, replacing Marcel Masse. Bouchard had never run for office; Mulroney had appointed him Canada's ambassador to France. (This was one of many appointments of high-profile separatists to senior positions in the federal public service.) But the appointment to the Cabinet was particularly sensitive. As ambassador, Bouchard had carried out the policies made by others. In the Cabinet, he would be making policy, and as secretary of state he would be the minister in charge of official languages. In this position, "He [would] also hold immense power over the prime minister. He [could] always threaten resignation, which would disrupt the party in Quebec."[19]

The appointment of Bouchard to handle official languages sent a signal to Quebec about the Tories' intentions with respect to Bill C-72. Quebec need not worry about the promotion of English in Quebec: Bouchard would see to it that Ottawa did nothing to offend nationalists.

On 21 April, the Conseil de la langue française told the Quebec government that it should oppose Bill C-72. While the Conseil found it fine that Ottawa should be promoting French in the other provinces, it could not abide that English be promoted in Quebec, for this would put the federal government in violation of the intent of Bill 101. According to the Conseil's president, Pierre Martel, Quebec should tell Ottawa that it opposes "a bill that provides that the two official languages should be treated the same everywhere in the country." His justification for this position was revealing. "This symmetry is quite simply the denial of the recognition in 1987 [in the Meech Lake accord] of the distinct character of Quebec society." For Martel, the distinct character of Quebec was to be French, only French. English would detract from that distinctiveness.

On 7 June, Gil Rémillard sent a letter to Bouchard in which he warned the federal government that it would be "unacceptable" for Ottawa to promote English in Quebec as a language of educational institutions, trade, the workplace, communications, voluntary organizations, or health organizations. "You know the importance that we attach to a complete and harmonious application of the Charter of the French Language. In this perspective, we are concerned about certain incompatibilities between the requirements of the Bill [C-72] and those of our Charter."

Rémillard then invoked Meech Lake to justify his objections to the promotion of English in Quebec:

We consider that our position is in complete conformity with the constitutional accord that we just concluded. On the one hand, the French language constitutes one of the two poles of the Canadian linguistic duality, and when we protect this language in Quebec, we are obviously protecting the linguistic duality in its very essence. On the other hand, the French language represents a fundamental element of the distinct character of Quebec.

But Rémillard suggested a way out which would allow Ottawa to promote French in nine provinces and not promote English in Quebec. The federal secretary of state should promote English only to the extent that the Quebec government agreed to have it promoted:

Obviously, future federal interventions under the bill that affect Quebec institutions or bodies under provincial jurisdiction and are carried out under the mandate given the secretary of state to favour the progression toward equality of status and of use of French and English, could not be countenanced without previous formal agreements between our two governments.

We are convinced that this way of proceeding, which would no doubt not be easy, as we admit, would be such as to protect the full powers of the National Assembly in matters of language.

Clearly, the fix was in. It was no coincidence at all that Bouchard happened to be in Quebec City the day that Rémillard made his letter public; he rushed over to the Quebec legislature to say that, of course, he would take up Rémillard's suggestion. And he gave many other assurances, such as the promise that Bill C-72 held no threat to the Charter of the French Language.

At their joint press conference, Rémillard used the words that had been pasted on posts and buildings everywhere in 1986, as a warning to the Bourassa government not to keep its promise to allow bilingual signs: *Ne touchez pas à la loi 101!* Bouchard agreed with Rémillard that French, not English, needed protection in Quebec: "Never will the federal government, at least as long as we are there, never will the government headed by Mr. Mulroney . . . want to or try to intervene in the language of work, the language of communications, and so forth."

In the rest of Canada, Bill C-72 set off a new wave of opposition to the expansion of French. One beneficiary was the Association for the Protection of the English Language in Canada (APEC), the anti-French association run from Thornhill, Ontario, which gathered members and momentum as a result of the bill. In January, 1988, APEC's newsletter warned, "The new act is a racist document which, in time, will lead to the francisation of Canada." It pointed to the contrast between federal efforts to promote French and Quebec's law to repress English. "Every attempt is made by the [federal] government to indicate to all concerned throughout the entire world that the language of this country is French. Within the Province of Quebec, however, an attempt is made to eliminate every vestige of the English language." APEC began successfully to agitate to have municipal councils pass resolutions declaring themselves unilingually English.

Bill C-72 caused a revolt within the Tory caucus, which, since the days of John Diefenbaker, had been bitterly divided on the place to be given French in the country.[20] As the bill came up for debate, the opposition of eighteen Tories did not include only what used to be called "rednecks." Alex Kindy, for instance, the psychiatrist representing Calgary East, had studied medicine at Université Laval in French, and practised in Montreal and Sherbrooke before moving west. He felt that Bill C-72 should not be passed as long as Quebec was repudiating the basic social contract on language. The dissidents, who soon adopted their opponents' name for them, the "dinosaurs," proposed fifteen amendments that, in fact, would have gutted the bill. "The new language bill should reaffirm the right of Canadians to remain unilingual without prejudice, and to commit the government to servicing the unilingual public to the best of its ability," they said in a position paper.

Meanwhile, the party leaders abdicated their responsibility for demanding even-handed linguistic justice. Liberal Leader John Turner did not mention Quebec when he spoke on the bill. The Liberal critic for official languages, Jean-Robert Gauthier of Vanier, waxed eloquent about the new spirit of linguistic understanding in Canada. "There is a willingness to accept and appreciate *la différence*. . . . There has developed in Canada over the last twenty years a new era of understanding." Understanding in Quebec?

Marion Dewar, the NDP's chief speaker on the bill, burbled about the marvelous change in Quebec. "As a native Quebecer I saw a lot of discrimination happening to the majority of the community there when I was growing up. Today, I see the progress which has been made." Dewar could recognize discrimination against French, but not against English. In the Quebec public service, fewer than 1 per cent of employees had English as a first language. And Premier Bourassa was speaking of introducing a bill in the National Assembly to extend coercive francisation to companies with from ten to fifty employees; the Parti Québécois in its 1977 law had required this only from companies with more than fifty employees.

What the right-thinking elite did not understand was that Bill C-72, like Meech itself, would undermine the support for two official languages across the country. When Pierre Trudeau spoke before the Senate on 30 March 1988, his words about the distinct society clause of Meech applied also to the Conservatives' entire policy of support to the suppression of English in Quebec.

I think Canadians would discover, to their surprise, that the accord has empowered one provincial government to subordinate the rights of every individual Canadian living within its borders to the rights of a chosen community, presumably the French-speaking majority. I know what that would do to French-speaking Canadians in other provinces, and I think they know.

You cannot go around saying that the Anglos will not have a right to put English even on the French signs in Quebec, but in the rest of Canada, we are asking you to be good, and bilingualism is the way of the future. So we will have what? The possibility of building one Canada will be lost forever.

Bill C-72 continued to raise the tensions over language in the country. The "dinosaurs" packed the parliamentary committee holding public hearings on the bill, and waged guerrilla warfare against it by inviting as witnesses all of the suddenly abundant anti-bilingualism groups and individuals. In Alberta, *Western Report* published on its front page a paragraph in French, with the false statement that people who couldn't read it would be excluded from jobs in the public service. All the old resentments from the 1960s and 1970s resurfaced, this time legitimated by Quebec's repression of English and the federal government's complicity.

The three political parties in the Commons united finally to gag opponents, and the bill was passed on 7 July 1988. In the end, only nine diehard "dinosaurs" resisted all the blandishments and threats from Mulroney and voted against it.

The divisive effect of the bill was not restricted to Western Canada. In Quebec, editorial writers took it as an insult to all French-speaking Canadians that a few MPs had opposed the bill. Claude Masson, then editorial-page editor of *La Presse*, was vehement: "English-speaking Conservative MPs have just insulted the French Canadians of this country by trying to limit the thrust of the language law at last adopted yesterday in Ottawa." Masson held Mulroney partly responsible for having allowed the dissidents to sound off for so long unchecked. And he predicted that the damage done would last. "Even if only nine MPs, all of them Conservatives, four of whom will not be running in the next general elections, voted against Bill C-72, the whole country knows from now on that *bonne entente* between the two peoples has not yet been achieved." *Le Soleil* and *Le Devoir* also expressed their outrage at this insult to French.

Canadians were given a better sense of what promoting Quebec's distinct identity would mean after the Supreme Court of Canada, on 15 December 1988, struck down the prohibition in Quebec of languages other than French on signs. The court found, unanimously, that the prohibition was unjustifiable in a free and democratic society. Premier Bourassa almost immediately brought in a law, Bill 178, that used the "notwithstanding" clause of the Charter to suspend freedom of expression in Quebec by reimposing a ban on other languages than French on signs. The law was not exactly the same as before: it allowed some English on signs inside small commercial establishments. But it banned bilingual signs outside, even in small enterprises of no more than four employees, which previously had been exempted. So the law was at least as repressive as before.

Mulroney's reaction was instructive. He who had argued eloquently for French rights in Manitoba now appeared in the Commons only to hem and haw. He used obscure phrasing to avoid plainly condoning or condemning Bill 178. He acted as though it was unclear what Bourassa would do—after Bourassa had clearly announced his intentions. And Mulroney burst into a rhapsody of praise—in French, to make it less likely that English television would pick up his words—for Quebec's treatment of its English-speaking minority.

The long and noble tradition of justice in Quebec toward the English-speaking minority is well known. In many respects, I consider that the anglophones of Quebec generally live a reality that the other provinces might advantageously take as an inspiration in the treatment of their francophone minorities. . . . It is important to underline that Quebec has no lessons to learn from anyone whatever, in respect of the way that it treats its language minorities.

That entire week, while in Quebec City a law was being passed that struck a blow to the heart of Canadian unity, in Ottawa the parliamentarians played their usual games, oblivious to the fact that Bill 178 constituted the most serious danger to the country since the conscription crisis of 1942 because it invalidated the terms of the settlement that the country had come to accept under Lester Pearson and especially Pierre Trudeau: one Canada with two official languages and no special status. The bill proclaimed that English was illegitimate in Quebec. This was the action not of a separatist party intent on breaking up the country, as Bill 101 had been, but of the supposedly federalist Liberal Party. Quebec, through its two political parties, through the mass demonstrations in the streets, through the consensus of its intelligentsia, was rejecting English in the most potently symbolic way: banishing it from sight.

How could the rest of the country be asked to pay the heavy price of accommodating French, which meant revising traditions and overcoming ethnic jealousies, when Quebec was so flagrantly, so insolently rejecting English—and doing so in the face of the unanimous judgment of three levels of the judiciary that such an exclusion violated fundamental freedoms and was incompatible with the values of a democratic society? By explicitly invoking the "notwithstanding" clause to suspend the rights guaranteed by the Charter, it admitted that it was a tyrannical law. It was, in addition, one that spat in the face of English-speaking Canada.

Did Bourassa realize the implications of what he had done? Almost certainly not. Bourassa had no feeling for the attitudes of ordinary Canadians outside Quebec; all his dealings were with the elites. And the elites of English Canada had sent him the message that he could banish English, no problem. Brian Mulroney had urged him on: "no retreat" on the "French face of Quebec." John Turner and Ed Broadbent and the nine other premiers had all approved of Meech's "promoting Quebec's distinct identity" at a time when Bourassa's own actions made it clear that promoting that identity meant maintaining and strengthening Bill 101. Again, no problem.

So why would there be a fuss now about banning English from signs, when English had been banned from signs for eleven years and Bourassa had openly insisted before the Supreme Court that it must continue to be banned? The elites, including *The Gazette*, had taken the Meech Lake accord to their bosom, even though its single most obvious purpose was to continue banning English. Meech Lake was Canada's own Yalta: the political elites from every part of the country, including English Quebec, had told Bourassa that he could do what he liked in Quebec, they would pretend they didn't notice.

Bourassa—and the elites—had not reckoned on the sense of justice of the ordinary people of Canada. *They* knew what Bill 178 meant. It was an official, unequivocal, arrogant, dictatorial rejection of English. It was a rejection of the settlement whereby the whole country would honour two official languages, English and French. If Quebec rejected English, why should the rest of the country go to great lengths, at great cost, to make room for French?

The *Globe and Mail*, in an editorial on 20 December 1988, expressed perfectly the true significance of Bill 178.

> The signs issue carries heavy symbolic freight, and this thumping decision sends a clear message to the anglophone minority in Quebec. . .
> The message says; you are intruders here, you don't belong and never

220

did, you are illegitimate, your language pollutes the atmosphere and even to see it on a sign is an insult; pack up and go. Sadly, many of them will.

The consequences outside Quebec are equally grave. As of yesterday, Meech Lake was dead in the water, perhaps simply dead. Worse, the generous vision of Canada that has transformed public policy in the last quarter century will come under renewed attack.

But the politicians in Quebec and in Ottawa did not, apparently, appreciate the stark import of Bill 178. The Commons had held an emergency debate when the European Community banned the importation of Canadian furs, but when one of the official languages of Canada was banned from the streets of Quebec, not one member of Parliament stood up to express the conviction of Parliament that Quebec's action was a blow to the unity of Canada. The Commons could have taken a ringing stand in favour of minority language rights, as it had done twice, in 1983 and 1984, to urge Manitoba to restore the rights of its French-speaking community. Mulroney could have given again his splendid speech of 6 October 1983, substituting Quebec for Manitoba, and English for French: "The purpose of this resolution is one which has touched the soul of Canada for decades. . . . An *anglophone* minority, which had enjoyed an historical protection of its language in *Quebec*, was suddenly cut off—amputated—from this guarantee which was so vital." But Mulroney preferred, instead, to tiptoe around the destruction of rights in Quebec, and so did the other members.

On 20 December, Clifford Lincoln, Herbert Marx, and Richard French resigned in protest from the Quebec Cabinet. "Rights are rights are rights," Lincoln said in his resignation speech. But in Ottawa, the MPs chose to look politely the other way until the victim being mugged on the corner stopped screaming.

During the Commons question period, Liberal MP Jean-Robert Gauthier asked Mulroney, "Can we know what is [the prime minister's] position today?"

"My position today is the same as yesterday," Mulroney replied. The day before, he had given his gushing praise of Quebec's treatment of its English-speaking minority.

Instead of forcing Mulroney to take a stand for or against the Quebec legislation, Gauthier asked him about the different position that he and Lucien Bouchard were taking on the "notwithstanding" clause: Bouchard had said he was for it, Mulroney said he was against it. So the debate went off on the tangent of the pros and cons of the "notwithstanding" clause in the abstract. But, about the very concrete violation of the rights of a very concrete community being debated that very moment in Quebec, neither man said a word.

Instead, Mulroney restated a hypothetical position that ignored Bourassa's clearly declared intentions, and Bill 178, and the resignation of the three ministers. "The position of the federal government is very simple. We hoped that the Quebec government would be able to work up a bill that would respect the two important aspects raised by the Supreme Court, in its decision. That's our position."

On 24 December, I tried to bring out in a column the gravity of what had happened in Canada that week—the gravity of Bill 178, and the seriousness of the Commons' failure to respond.

If even a few small words in English on commercial signs are unacceptable, are a threat to Quebec's French identity, then how much more unacceptable, more threatening, is a federal government in which French-speaking Quebecers are a minority? The Commons this week chose the road of cowardice, of expediency, of a false peace in our times, an unreal national reconciliation. The Commons chose not to remind Quebec that Canada represents something, and that what Quebec did this week violated the identity of Canada.

Once free trade is in place, there will no longer be an economic imperative for Quebec's remaining part of Canada. If Canada represents nothing noble and enriching, nothing inspiring and elevating, if it remains as merely an obstacle to Quebec's fully French identity, then Quebec will soon remove itself from Canada.

By its silence, Parliament loudly proclaimed this week that Canada stands for nothing.

In different ways, other should-be defenders of the rights of English-speaking Quebecers proved equally inept. Royal Orr, the president of Alliance Quebec, declared that Bill 178 was only "a temporary political setback." Mulroney, during his dodging and weaving in the Commons, had produced a letter from Orr to prove what a protector of minority rights he was. The letter congratulated Mulroney for having passed the Official Languages Act.

The Gazette displayed an equivocal vision. On the one hand, in an editorial of 21 December, it congratulated the three ministers who had resigned on principle. "To stay in a government which had abandoned solemn promises to restore minority language rights would have been to tell the world they had no convictions, that they would sit still for any government act, even the wiping out of basic rights. So they left the Cabinet, and this was the right thing to do." But after that strong, clear stand, *The Gazette* took up the case of the English-speaking minister who chose not to resign but to vote with the Quebec government to suppress English rights: "This is not to condemn the fourth anglophone minister, John Ciaccia, for choosing a different path." How was it possible for Ciaccia's staying in the Cabinet to mean something different than it would have meant for the other three to stay? With sublime disregard for logic or consistency, never mind principle, *The Gazette* found that it was all right for Ciaccia to keep his job as minister and vote to suppress the rights of his fellow English-speaking Quebecers. The editorial noted that Ciaccia thought he could serve his community better from within Cabinet. "That is an important consideration. It is, of course, vital to have strong anglophone representation in the Quebec Cabinet." This absence of discrimination between upholding rights and violating them, between the heroism of those who resign on principle and the heroism of those who keep their prestigious job and chauffeured limousine by voting to violate rights, had been characteristic of the leaders of English-speaking Quebec as a whole over the previous decade. The confusion and moral ambiguity simply came out more clearly in times of crisis, such as that of December, 1988.

Earlier that year, the Saskatchewan legislature had passed a law abolishing French as an official language. The Supreme Court of Canada had found on 25 February that an old law of the Northwest Territories, though never applied, still existed in Saskatchewan because it had never been rescinded. The prime minister wrote a letter of disapproval to the premier, Grant Devine. On 10 April, he sent three of his ministers to visit Devine and expostulate in favour of French rights. Now that Quebec had acted against English, Mulroney's advisers told him that he could do no less than send a similar letter to Bourassa. He could not be seen to have a double standard.

The letter was drafted. Lucien Bouchard protested; he did not want Bourassa's action criticized. The letter was softened, as Bouchard relates in his memoirs; he still protested, and more drafts were submitted, always softer. Bouchard recounts that Mulroney called him in, read the last draft aloud, and pointed out that the criticism was pretty muted. "But I told him that, muted or not, a formal letter blaming [Bourassa] was unacceptable to me and that, as a result, I would be unable to endorse it by remaining in his government."[21] The threat to resign worked. The letter was never sent.

Mulroney revealed that day, as he had the previous December in Montreal, that he had sold his soul to Marcel Masse, Lucien Bouchard, and all the other nationalists. He was unable to defend freedom of expression and the rights of official-language minorities. Instead, he grovelled. His Faustian bargain with the nationalists had won him power, but Canada would pay a heavy price.

A revolt against Mulroney and the accommodating elites began at the grass roots. In Montreal, the sense of outrage of English-speaking Quebecers was given form by Steven Nowell, a small-time bookseller. He called a protest meeting in Westmount's Victoria Hall, and at least twelve hundred people showed up to vent their indignation; the meeting had to be held in two shifts. The revolt continued with the foundation of the Equality Party by a twenty-eight-year-old architect with no political experience and no reputation, Robert Libman. His party was committed to fight for civil rights and freedoms. In the Quebec election that followed later in 1989, the Equality Party took four seats and a majority of the anglophone vote in every riding in which it ran candidates.

The discussions on the constitution gradually annulled the effects of the 1980 referendum and the 1982 patriation. Nationalist ambitions that had been driven off Quebec's political agenda now returned in force. There had been divisive debates in the National Assembly in 1987 leading up to the adoption of the Meech Lake resolution in June. The Parti Québécois, led by Pierre-Marc Johnson, opposed Meech on the grounds that it gave Quebec too little.

Meech Lake was then debated before a joint committee of the Commons and the Senate in August and September of 1987. It was debated in October in the House and adopted. It was debated again before the Senate in March–April, 1988, and the Senate demanded amendments. The resolution then went back once more to the House, to be again debated and adopted. The constitution was put front and centre on the national agenda.

Quebec's existential fate was kept a live issue by developments in each of the provinces, which were immediately echoed in the Quebec news media. In September, 1987, New Brunswick premier Richard Hatfield was defeated by Liberal leader Frank McKenna; McKenna had run on a platform of opposition to Meech Lake, which the province's legislature had not yet adopted. McKenna's election raised doubts over whether the accord would be passed by Parliament and the eleven provincial legislatures within the three-year deadline.

And so it went. Since Meech Lake was defined as the "Quebec round," and had first been adopted in Quebec, all opposition in other provinces, no matter how principled and legitimate, was played in the Quebec media as a rejection of Quebec itself—even though opposition in Quebec itself to Meech Lake had been very broad. Only Quebecers, apparently, had the right to question or oppose any part of the accord.

Sharon Carstairs, the Liberal leader in Manitoba and a disciple of Pierre Trudeau, fought the 1988 provincial election campaign above all on rejecting Meech, and the people of Manitoba reacted. "I gave a speech in Dauphin with 420 people, and when I talked about my opposition to Meech Lake, they all stood up and applauded," Carstairs told me in an interview two days before the 26 April election.

From sole Liberal member of the provincial legislature, she now vaulted with her party into second place, and became leader of the opposition facing a minority Conservative government. She made it clear that she would defeat the government if it tried to pass Meech Lake unchanged. "I am particularly opposed to the lack of prominence of the Charter of Rights and Freedoms," she told me, "and that would be a fundamental change that I would require before I would recommend it to a Manitoba legislature."

After the election of Clyde Wells as premier of Newfoundland in April, 1989, it seemed certain that Meech Lake was doomed to defeat. Wells was a principled and determined opponent of the accord. On 22 March 1990, he introduced a motion in the House of Assembly of Newfoundland and Labrador to rescind the resolution in favour of Meech Lake that had been adopted on 7 July 1988 by the government of Brian Peckford. Meech Lake, for all practical purposes, was dead.

Mulroney could have done what Lester Pearson did in 1966 when Jean Lesage reneged on patriation and on the Fulton-Favreau formula, or what Pierre Trudeau did in 1971 when Bourassa rejected the Victoria Charter: back away and change the subject. But instead, Mulroney decided to get Meech Lake passed at whatever cost to the country.

When the first ministers met on 9 November 1989, supposedly to discuss the economy, Mulroney delivered a tirade, using his position as chairman to harangue Wells long and hard on the subject of Meech Lake. He trotted out his usual argument that it was unconscionable to patriate the constitution over the objections of Quebec and that Trudeau would never have patriated over the objections of Ontario. Wells replied that no one province should be allowed to hold up the constitutional evolution of Canada. Mulroney made it clear, though, that he was determined to get Meech Lake adopted by hook or by crook, even over the objections of Newfoundland.

Meanwhile, one victim in Quebec of the revived separatist sentiments was Pierre-Marc Johnson, who had initiated the move in 1984 to remove sovereignty as the Parti Québécois's main plank for the following elections. Johnson's program of "national affirmation"—occupying each area of jurisdiction to the fullest extent possible—now seemed too moderate. Rather than face prolonged internal opposition, Johnson resigned, to be replaced by the more radical Jacques Parizeau.

In January, 1990, as the deadline for Meech approached—it would fail if not adopted by all provinces by 23 June—the pro-Meech forces gathered and began a public pressure campaign. On 5 January, the "Friends of Meech Lake" held a press conference in Ottawa. Some one hundred personalities had endorsed Meech Lake, and three attended: Robert Stanfield, Stephen Lewis, and Solange Chaput-Rolland.

Stanfield could be remembered for the 1968 *deux nations* Conservative campaign in Quebec and for his continuing flirtation with the nationalists. Lewis, the former NDP Ontario leader, had been appointed Mulroney's ambassador to the United Nations. Solange Chaput-Rolland was a writer and broadcaster known for her emotional prose. A Liberal member of the National Assembly at the time of the 1980 referendum, she had opposed sovereignty-association, but she was for the reconstitution of Quebec as an ethnic state, like Bourassa and Claude Ryan. Mulroney had appointed her to the Senate in September, 1988.

Chaput-Rolland had expressed her political views in 1988:

I know today in a definitive fashion that, in the current circumstances of our national life, my country is not and will never be Canada. . . .

Since national bilingualism turns out to be a vast joke, let us stop believing in it and let us put our energy to obtain the creation, not of privileges for one province out of ten, but for equality for a French state alongside an English state.[22]

225

And she took *deux nations* to its likely conclusion: "I have learned with difficulty, painfully and definitively, that to remain faithful to the deepest direction of my past, of my present and of everything which makes up my being, French by language and culture, I must live in Quebec in a country which, some day, will perhaps become my country." Carried away by her prose, she saw the dream of the Quiet Revolution realized:

After [the creation of Quebec as a French state], if, within this French state we prove ourselves capable of conducting ourselves as a free people . . . we will easily obtain our independence. . . .

An independent nation, one which has the courage to fight to become such, engenders individuals who carry their independence in their fists and their pride in their heart.

Chaput-Rolland wasn't carrying her independence in her fist at the press conference. She was fighting for a revision of the constitution of Canada rather than for the constitution of an independent Quebec. But she provided a good illustration of the instability of Quebec nationalism based on a tribal sense of identity, and of the built-in escalation of its demands when inspired by the vision of the ethnic state.

That same month, a leading voice opposing Meech Lake appeared on the political scene. Jean Chrétien, who was expected momentarily to announce that he would be a candidate to succeed John Turner as Liberal leader, gave a lecture at the University of Ottawa's faculty of law on 16 January 1990 in which he criticized the accord from the perspective of individual rights, and of the century-old Liberal conception of Canada.

Chrétien quoted Wilfrid Laurier: "We are French Canadians, but our country is not limited to the territory stretching below the Citadel of Quebec. Our country is Canada." Meech Lake, he said, rejected that vision of Canada. "By proposing that the distinct character of Quebec society be affirmed in an interpretative clause of the constitution, for practical purposes it cuts the country in two: Quebec on one side, the nine other provinces on the other."

He rejected the implicit territorial dualism of Brian Mulroney, Robert Bourassa, and Meech Lake in favour of the Canada-wide linguistic dualism of Laurier, Henri Bourassa, and Trudeau. "The Meech Lake accord contains no obligation or commitment on the part of the federal government or of any other government to support the French fact across the country, he said. "The accord would isolate Quebec linguistically. It's a losing strategy for French-speaking Canadians, and so a losing strategy and a cultural impoverishment for all of Canada."

Chrétien dismissed the apocalyptic prophecies that Meech Lake must be adopted or it would be the end of the federation. "The earth will keep turning and French Canadians will continue to speak French," he said ironically. While he rejected Meech Lake, he did not reject the five conditions that Bourassa had formulated in 1985 for accepting the 1982 constitution, notably putting the recognition of Quebec in the preamble rather than the body of the constitution. He did reject Meech's requirement of unanimous provincial consent for reform of the Senate and of national institutions, but he did not reject Bourassa's demand for Quebec having a veto, as it would have had in the Victoria Charter.

The re-emergence of Chrétien and his rejection of Meech were badly received by the news media in Quebec. Many portrayed him as a hatchetman for Pierre Trudeau, who was himself described by phone-in host Gilles Proulx of Montreal's CJMS radio station as having made a career of "keeping Quebec in its place." Marcel Masse said that Chrétien was "giving a flicker of hope to all the *mange-Canayens* in this country"—he used an old expression meaning bigots who hate French Canadians.

The Liberals were offered a choice of positions on Meech Lake. Sheila Copps, who kicked off her run for the leadership on 15 January, and Paul Martin, who declared his candidacy on 17 January, both announced their commitment to it. "I unconditionally back the Meech Lake accord, with or without a parallel accord," Martin told a press conference; he had earlier proposed that the first ministers might negotiate a parallel agreement to complement Meech Lake and so soften some of the objections to it.

Across the country, linguistic and regional tensions were rising. On 29 January, the council of Sault Ste. Marie passed a resolution: "The Council of the Corporation of the City of Sault Ste. Marie declares English to be the official language of the said Corporation." The vote was accompanied by a petition signed by twenty-five thousand people out of a population of eighty-five thousand. Since Quebec had passed Bill 178, a backlash against French had set in across the country, especially in rural areas and small cities left outside the mainstream. At the instigation of APEC, some 40 small municipalities of Ontario's 839 had passed resolutions similar to that of Sault Ste. Marie. It was part of a growing revolt of the masses against their elites, a loss of trust in the leaders.

Elite opinion condemned the Sault resolution—even the *Sault Star* was against it. Ontario premier David Peterson expressed his disapproval, while recognizing that Bill 178 had poisoned the atmosphere. The *Globe and Mail* wrote, "This is gratuitous foolishness with a nasty edge, fashioned out of a sad misconception of what Canada is all about." In Quebec, the Sault resolution caused a storm of outrage. Lucien Bouchard, now minister of the environment, saw in the incident the beginning of the end of Canada. "It wouldn't take many Sault Ste. Maries for the rope to snap," he said in St. Bruno. He called the council's vote "the summit of a reaction of intolerance which will destroy this country." This was the same Bouchard who had approved of Bourassa's suspending Charter freedoms in order to ban English from signs and who had threatened to resign if the prime minister sent a letter of disapproval.

An editorial in *Le Devoir* rejected Peterson's explanation about the effect of Bill 178. "On the contrary, what we find here is an old current which expressed itself long before the Quebec laws and which today adds the excuse of 'persecution' of English in Quebec to try to impose its dream on the rest of Canada."

In the Commons, John Turner proposed that the House pass a resolution in favour of minority language rights across the country. He who had remained silent when English was banished from Quebec signs fourteen months earlier now proposed to come to the defence of French and, incidentally, of English: "Resolved, that this House reaffirm its commitment to support, protect and promote linguistic duality in Canada." NDP Leader Audrey McLaughlin immediately endorsed the resolution. But Mulroney dodged and weaved. Promote linguistic duality? That would mean promoting English in Quebec. What would Bourassa say?

Mulroney insisted that he could support the resolution in favour of bilingualism only if it was accompanied by a qualification: "as reflected in [the Meech Lake accord] and the 1988 Official Languages Act." In other words, the House was in favour of linguistic duality, subject to the Quebec government's right to promote Quebec's distinct identity. Not only did this undercut the sense of the resolution, it also associated linguistic duality with the unpopular Meech Lake accord. Moreover, Mulroney knew that both the Liberals and the New Democrats were divided over Meech Lake. His ploy of inserting it in the resolution was seen by all commentators as a partisan move to embarrass the two opposition parties.

Meech Lake had become Mulroney's insistent theme. A by-election was to be held in the Quebec riding of Chambly on 12 February 1990. Mulroney tried to turn it into a referendum on the accord. The riding was plastered with signs saying, "Meech: Chambly speaks for all Quebec." Mulroney sent Bouchard on the stump there, and even went there twice himself to campaign on behalf of his Conservative candidate. On 15 December 1989 he gave a speech to the Richelieu Valley Chamber of Commerce in the Chambly riding. The theme was Meech Lake: "It is vital that the Québécois, in the face of all those who could cast doubt on this obvious solidarity [of Quebec around the Meech Lake agreement], should proclaim loud and clear: Yes, we want the Meech Lake accord. Yes, we want Quebec to rejoin the Canadian constitutional family with honour and enthusiasm."

He soon got his answer. The Conservative candidate, Serge Bégin, was drubbed, getting only 9.8 per cent of the vote. The people of Chambly elected Philip Edmonston of the New Democratic Party—a vote for the man, a well-known consumer advocate, rather than for the party.

Chambly did speak for Quebec, and it demonstrated how false and dishonest was the pretension that Meech Lake was the answer to the question, What does Quebec want. The Liberal candidate, Clifford Lincoln, the former Quebec minister of the environment who had resigned over Bill 178, received only 17 per cent of the vote, though he and his party both supported Meech, like the

Conservative candidate. The NDP, on the other hand, at its convention in Winnipeg two months earlier, had refused to endorse Meech Lake.

Turner's resolution affirming duality came up for debate on 15 February, three days after the Chambly by-election. Mulroney was true to himself. He gave a long discourse on the affronts to French in Canadian history: an 1890 Manitoba law struck French from the provincial legislature and from the Catholic schools; Regulation 17 restricted the teaching of French in Ontario in 1912; in 1905, when Saskatchewan and Alberta were created as provinces, French was not vested in their constituent law. He did refer to Bill 178 briefly, but he spoke about it in English only, making it unlikely that his words would be broadcast on French television. He equated it with Saskatchewan and Alberta's rescinding a Northwest Territories law that had never been applied in either province. "In all three cases the provincial legislatures used existing powers to limit rights that had been confirmed by the Supreme Court of Canada. In each case the government and, I suppose, most if not all members of the House of Commons and I personally deeply deplore the actions taken."

The claim that all three provinces "overrode" the judgment of the Supreme Court was fantasy. The court had found that the dormant Northwest Territories law had never been rescinded, and hence it was still in effect unless and until it was rescinded. But the court clearly pointed out that rescinding the law was an option open to the two provinces. That was different from the court's utter condemnation of Quebec's prohibition of other languages on French signs as contrary to the Charter and a violation of fundamental freedom.

By equating the actions of Alberta, Saskatchewan, and Quebec, Mulroney gave an alibi to Quebec: it was only doing what Saskatchewan and Alberta were doing. In fact, Alberta and Saskatchewan, while legislating to remove the official status of French, actually gave new practical rights to their francophone citizens which they had not previously enjoyed. By lumping the three together, Mulroney avoided addressing Quebec's flagrant violation of historic and fundamental rights.

He even described Bill 178 in such a way as to lay the blame for it on the "notwithstanding" clause rather than on the Quebec government. "Because of that clause, it was open to Quebec, in enacting Bill C-178 respecting external, commercial signs in 1988, to override freedom of expression provisions of the Canadian Charter."

As a result of Mulroney's manoeuvres, the resolution on minority languages was passed by the Commons almost furtively, with only one speaker from each party taking the floor. The impact that a ringing declaration by a united Parliament in favour of minority languages could have had was utterly lost.

As the mood in the country soured, the prime minister and the Quebec premier both ratcheted up the tension by adopting apocalyptic rhetoric that threatened the very dismemberment of Canada unless Meech were passed. Bourassa, in particular, as he saw nationalism rising in Quebec, became increasingly bold in articulating an overtly nationalist stance. While on a business trip to Germany in January, 1990, he suggested that if Meech Lake failed to be adopted, the Canadian federation might be replaced by a "political superstructure." He assured investors at the same time that the economic space of Canada would be maintained. He even suggested that Canada might follow the example of the European Community. Other members of his Cabinet also radicalized their rhetoric. "If Meech is rejected, we will have to question our adherence to Canada," said municipal affairs minister Yvon Picotte.[23]

Bourassa added to the provocation by suggesting that Quebec would be profoundly humiliated if Meech Lake did not pass. "I don't have a mandate to negotiate on my knees," he said. The message played big in the media. "Quebec will not get on its knees," headlined the Ottawa daily Le Droit. Le Devoir bannered at the top of its front page, "Bourassa says no to any 'federalism on our knees.'" But who or what had suggested that Quebec should be on its knees?

And representatives of the Quebec Liberal Party were quite explicit about threatening the separation of Quebec if the Meech Lake agreement did not pass. A delegation, including the president and vice-president of the party, appeared before the New Brunswick legislature's parliamentary committee studying Meech Lake. According to Robert Benoît, then president of the Liberal Party, "The isolation of Quebec cannot continue much longer without putting in question the very foundations of our federal regime. The Legislative Assemby of New Brunswick bears a heavy responsibility toward the rest of Canada."[24]

Why the heavy-footed threats to break up the country if Bourassa did not get his way? It was uncharacteristic of Bourassa publicly to take hard-edged stands from which it would later be difficult to back away. His usual modus operandi was to lull public opinion rather than arouse it. Part of the answer lay in the opinion polls.[25] The foundations of federalism were fast crumbling in Quebec. A Gallup poll published on 3 May 1990 showed that an all-time high 42 per cent of Quebecers were in favour of independence. Under the influence of the debates over Meech, Quebec was moving strongly toward secession.

The new rhetoric of threatening secession was taken up by Bourassa's former minister of social affairs, Claude Castonguay, the man who had persuaded Bourassa to reject the Victoria Charter. "We are like the couple, so immersed in recrimination and pettiness, they they are getting to the point where the only way out is divorce," Castonguay said in February, 1990. "Divorce while living under the same roof, perhaps, because of the children and other considerations, but divorce all the same."

At a 23 February press conference, Mulroney called Castonguay's words "very moderate." The alternative to Meech Lake, indeed, was likely to be "divorce." "The alternative to Meech Lake is no Meech Lake, and no Meech Lake sets in motion some consequences that, for example, Mr. Castonguay, a very thoughtful person, invited Canadians to reflect upon the other day."

Pierre Trudeau's reaction to Castonguay's words was quite different. When he re-emerged in the public eye, on 20 March, for the launching of a book on the Trudeau years, he was asked by a journalist, "Are you worried if Meech Lake fails?"

"I'm not worried," Trudeau replied. "Are you worried? Because Mr. Castonguay told you that Quebec will separate? Or because Mr. [Joe] Clark told you that you would have terrorism? You take that seriously?" He dismissed as "blackmail" the warnings that Quebecers would see a rejection of Meech Lake as a rejection of Quebec. That's always been Quebec's way, he said. "I think we always have a tendency in our constitutional negotiations to engage in a little blackmail. 'If you don't sign the agreement, it means that you won't want us, and we are going to go away.'" He also commented ironically on the absence of any federalist critique of Meech Lake. No major figure in business or in politics in Quebec dared stand up against the agreement. "Silence. Not a word. Because people would look askance."[26]

At a time when opposition to Meech in the country was strong and growing, when Quebec was divided about it, and when two or three other provinces had profound objections to it, Mulroney was raising the stakes. His all-or-nothing approach raised the pressure on the recalcitrant provinces. It ensured that if Meech Lake failed, as seemed most likely, the fall-out in Quebec would be terrible. Even if the agreement passed, there was no guarantee that Quebec nationalism would return to its earlier quiescence.

The pressure brought Premier Frank McKenna of New Brunswick to search for a way to pass Meech Lake, thus satisfying Bourassa and "Quebec," while keeping in the constitution the principles in which he believed. On 21 March, he proposed a "parallel accord" or a "companion resolution" that would complement Meech Lake. For example, where Meech spoke of the federal government's responsibility only to *preserve* the existence of French-speaking and English-speaking Canadians, McKenna proposed that the Parliament and Government of Canada be bound by a companion resolution to *promote* that fundamental characteristic of Canada. The resolution, however, would have placed no such obligation on the provinces.

It was obvious that McKenna was acting in concert with Mulroney and with his minister responsible for constitutional negotiations, Lowell Murray. The very day that McKenna's proposal was made public, Mulroney announced that he would address the nation the next evening. When he appeared before the television cameras, Mulroney announced a change of heart. For almost three years, the federal position had been that not a syllable could be changed in the Meech Lake accord. Now he seemed to open the way to changes. "I believe that Canadians want to participate, themselves, in the resolution of this great national issue," he told the country. He intended to put McKenna's proposals in the hands of a special committee—headed by Jean Charest—which would hold hearings across the country and then make recommendations. "Once the resolution has been given a full hearing, it will be brought to Parliament for a vote—with whatever suggestions for further improvements that emerge from the hearings."

The response of the Quebec government was hardly encouraging. On the same evening, Bourassa went on television to dismiss any negotiations until Meech had passed. "We have no objection to people chatting or discussing. But it's out of the question for Quebec to undertake negotiations on the content before Quebec has returned to within the constitution."[27]

The day after the McKenna resolution was made public, Rémillard rejected the proposal that the federal government should "promote" linguistic duality. "This New Brunswick proposal is obviously what worries the Bourassa government, which has stated through Rémillard, 'Quebec will not accept to modify by one iota the criterion of the distinct society and that of Canadian dualism, which create an equilibrium between the rights of the minorities.'"[28] Rémillard also suggested that if the right of Parliament to promote minority official languages were to be put in the constitution, Quebec would exercise the right to withdraw from that program.

Another person who was upset at the prospect of "promoting" Canada's linguistic duality was Lucien Bouchard. He relates in his political memoirs that when he read the wording of the companion resolution he was above all upset by the linguistic duality clause: "While, in the accord, [the federal government] was bound only to protect it, the companion resolution gave it in addition the obligation to promote it. Without question, the fragile balance of June 1987 would thereby be destroyed."[29]

The view that Quebec could not allow the promotion of the English-speaking minority, that it requires the unfettered right to repress English, was also expressed by newspaper editorials. "Mr. McKenna ignores the Canada of the communities, he rejects the Canada of the regions, he throws out the Canada of the two nations," a *Le Soleil* editorial argued on 22 March. "And he chooses the Canada that levels every kind of disparity. The very essence of the recognition of the distinct society requires a disparity of powers between Quebec, Canada and the other provinces."

Mulroney tried to manoeuvre cautiously, on the one hand suggesting that he was open to changes to Meech to win over the public in English-speaking Canada, while on the other hand trying not to alienate Bourassa or the nationalist members of his own caucus. "Let us not lose sight of the most crucial issue: the Meech Lake accord must be proclaimed by June 23 or it will die," he told the Commons on 27 March, when the resolution to explore New Brunswick's companion resolution was introduced in the Commons. "Simply put, the New Brunswick resolution is intended to complete Round One so that we can get on with Round Two."

But any hope of achieving some acceptable compromise vanished on 5 April when the Quebec Liberals and the Parti Québécois united to vote for a resolution that excluded any change to Meech.

The Government of Quebec rejects officially, in the name of all Quebecers, all constitutional proposals, including those of New Brunswick, which were put before the House of Commons by the prime minister of Canada, which could constitute an amendment or a change to the Meech Lake accord for the purpose of allowing the ratification of said Accord, and this, in accordance with the commitment repeated many times before this Assembly.

The two major political parties of Quebec were issuing an ultimatum to the rest of Canada. To the government of New Brunswick, to the prime minister of Canada, both seeking a way to get Meech to pass by hook or by crook, they issued a final word: pass Meech, nothing but Meech. And there was an implicit threat in this repudiation of any attempt at some sort of compromise: the country would be polarized, with Quebec standing united against the all the other governments.

Did Bourassa still want Meech to pass? It hardly seems likely, since the resolution cut off any flexibility and undercut the legitimacy of the Charest committee before it had held a single public hearing. It is much more likely that Bourassa was now only waiting for Meech to fail to go after a bigger, more comprehensive agreement, using a referendum in Quebec as a gun put to the head of the rest of Canada in order to get his way.

Mulroney had gambled on Quebec nationalism and won in two elections. There was poetic justice in the Gallup poll published on 19 April, which showed Mulroney running twenty-seven points behind the Liberals in Quebec. And the more nationalistic members of his Quebec caucus were beginning to show their colours. François Gérin, the Tory MP for Mégantic-Compton told *La Presse* in an interview published on 6 April that the next step could well be to elect to the federal Parliament MPs committed to Quebec's sovereignty. Gérin did not spell out exactly what he had in mind, but it seemed very close to what would soon emerge as the Bloc Québécois. According to *La Presse*, "While insisting that he had no precise plan in mind, Mr. Gérin judges that one must think of MPs in Ottawa who will commit themselves to defending exclusively the interests of Quebec, MPs clearly identified as '*Option-Québec.*'" That, of course, was the title of René Lévesque's separatist manifesto.

Another whose thinking ran along the same lines was Louis Plamondon, the MP for Richelieu. In an interview with Presse canadienne, he said that he had voted for sovereignty-association in 1980; now he began to see its time coming. He said he intended to run again in the next elections and to remain in the Tory caucus—unless a group of MPs split off to form a *bloc québécois*.

Obviously, if Quebec were to accede to the status of a sovereign state, that would not happen overnight. It will take several years. And, more than ever, [Plamondon] believes, it will be important for Quebec to be able to count on MPs from Quebec in Ottawa who are fully devoted to the defence of the interests of Quebec. . . . He even dreams of the impact that a solid Québécois bloc of some 40 or 45 MPs, he says, could have in Ottawa if it held the balance of power.

If Mulroney was worried about the impatient separatists in his caucus, he didn't show it. He was questioned in the House by Liberal Herb Gray on 11 April about a controversial statement made by Lucien Bouchard. After Premier Wells had rescinded Newfoundland's resolution adopting the Meech Lake package, Bouchard had said that Canada would have to choose between Newfoundland and Quebec. "I ask the prime minister to take this opportunity to explain the controversial statement made by his environment minister last Friday to the effect that Canada will have to choose between Newfoundland and Quebec."

Mulroney responded that Bouchard "had indeed said that, but that he also said something else which, taken in context, could only lead a reasonable person to conclude that the minister of the environment favours national unity and the inclusion in this country of all provinces, be it Quebec or Newfoundland and Labrador." To suggest the contrary was outrageous. "Surely the leader of the opposition is not suggesting that he has the slightest doubt in his mind as to whether I and all my colleagues stand for a united Canada. Surely there can be no doubt in his mind about that." The following month, Bouchard stormed out of the party and launched his crusade for Quebec's sovereignty.

The debate over Meech Lake had become something else entirely, as Clyde Wells pointed out when he appeared before the Charest committee. He noted that the terms and merits of the package itself had been lost. Instead, people were being told that they must sign on to Meech or the country would fall part, they must sign or be stigmatized as anti-Quebec, they must sign to avoid a period of turbulence and disruption in Canada's national life.

The Tory ministers, meanwhile, went about the country spreading half-truths and blackmailing the country, in the process further fostering Quebec nationalism. Joe Clark played Cassandra: "No one should underestimate the reaction in Quebec to a rejection of Meech Lake," he told the Manitoba Chamber of Commerce on 1 May. He maintained that federalism had won in the 1980 referendum in part "because Pierre Trudeau promised, invoking my name and those of others, that there would be real constitutional change, to take account of the legitimate concerns of Quebecers who believe in Canada. The constitutional agreement of 1982 broke that promise, and caused many of those Quebec federalists to reasess their commitment to Canada."

Clark was peddling the nationalists' own view of events. In addition to being subversive, his comments were contrary to reality. Trudeau had delivered real constitutional change when he protected minority language rights in the constitution and revolutionized the Canadian legal system with the Charter of Rights. It was real change, but not the change that the nationalists wanted. Why would Trudeau have delivered a change that he did not believe in, and one that would have done little or nothing for the great majority of French Canadians? The nationalists had lost the referendum. Should they get from the prime minister of Canada in their defeat what he had stood against for his entire political career? Clark's proposition was absurd. But he was repeating Mulroney's revisionist account of recent history, just as Mulroney repeated the account of Lucien Bouchard and the separatists. "If Meech Lake is rejected . . . many reasonable Quebecers will inevitably conclude that Canada does not want Quebec," Joe Clark continued. He thus raised the stakes, increased tension, endorsed the false assumption that a rejection of Meech Lake was a rejection of Quebec, and ensured that, if Meech failed, there would be a hard landing.

Some of the ministers added muscle to their inflammatory words. Newfoundland's social services minister, John Efford, told the *Toronto Star* on 3 May that Barbara McDougall, then the minister responsible for immigration, had told him that "it would be easier to get federal help for Newfoundland's immigration and fisheries problems if the province changed its position on the constitutional accord."

And Brian Mulroney still went about misinforming the public. Speaking in Toronto on 10 May to a group backing Meech Lake, he repeated once again: "In the sixties and seventies, English Canadians grappled with the question of what Quebec wanted. The Meech Lake accord is the answer." He also held out a false hope to Canadians suffering from constitutional fatigue that passing Meech Lake would be the end, instead of the beginning, of constitutional struggles. "It can give the rest of Canada the security of knowing that Quebec is, once and for all, a fully engaged and fully committed partner in the Confederation." Did Mulroney really believe that Bourassa would rest content with Meech Lake, or that the separatists, now apparently the majority of Quebecers, would be content once it was passed?

Gilles Rocheleau, the Liberal MP for Hull, gave an interview in the *Journal de Montréal* on 13 May in which he maintained that Quebec would separate, whether Meech Lake passed or not. "If Meech passes, it's still my feeling that important consequences will remain. And, contrary to the referendum of 1980, where we fought between Québécois, it is Quebec as a whole that is caught facing a Canada that rejects us." Rocheleau concluded that Meech meant nothing in any case. "Quebec wins nothing with Meech. All it does is re-establish a *de facto* situation. At our next demand, *les Anglais* will continue to tell us, Get out! And we will have a decision to make within ten years."

It should have been obvious to anyone that public opinion in Quebec had entered a period of extreme volatility, which would make any ambiguous constitutional arrangement such as Meech unstable. The separatists were preparing for the post-Meech era. And the Quebec Liberals? On 14 May, Gil Rémillard gave a speech in France that spoke of second-stage "comprehensive constitutional reform" and expressed the vision on which it would rest. "It seems evident that the Québécois now form a nation and that they wish to live together on their territory in the light of the common good as formulated by their provincial government in a federative context." Rémillard also had a prediction for the prospects if Meech failed: "The consequences of a non-ratification of this agreement could be serious for the future of the country, and Quebec would then be bound to achieve—taking into account its history as a distinct society—a substantial refashioning of the association which binds it to the Canadian federation to adapt it to this new situation."

In other words, if Meech Lake passed, we would get a "comprehensive constitutional reform" based on Quebec being a nation. If Meech did not pass, we would get "a substantial refashioning of the association." In either case, the objective was the same: the remodeling of Canada on the basis of Quebec being a distinct nation. Twenty-three years after formulating his concept of sovereign associated states, Bourassa seemed within striking distance of achieving it— whether Meech Lake passed or failed.

Meanwhile, Jean Charest's parliamentary committee on the "companion resolution" toured the country, trying desperately to reach a unanimous position. It was helped in its task by Jean Chrétien, who had abandoned his strong position of 16 January that the Charter must not be weakened. Chrétien latched on to a proposal by a former deputy minister of justice, Roger Tassé, to add a clarification to Meech Lake to the effect that the distinct society clause was merely an interpretive clause, that it would work with the Charter, not override it. This seemed to provide an assurance that the distinct society clause would not be used to infringe rights protected by the Charter.

In fact, in the opinion of Deborah Coyne, who served as adviser to Clyde Wells through the last nine months of the Meech drama, Tassé's proposal would only have reinforced the effectiveness of the distinct society clause as a justification for infringing on Charter rights: "The Tassé recommendation or any variation of it would have done nothing to eliminate, and indeed would have reinforced, Quebec's powers to limit our rights and freedoms in a way that other Governments could not. Effectively, it would have created different classes of Canadians and a hierarchy of rights."[30]

When the Charest committee made its report public, on 17 May, it had done its best to come up with a companion resolution that would allow Meech to pass unaltered and still extend hope to those who had misgivings that their concerns would be assuaged. It had a little something for everybody: The Tassé soother for those concerned about the Charter being weakened; a hope and a prayer for those, like Clyde Wells and Don Getty, who believed passionately in a Tripe-E Senate.

Two developments ensured that the Charest committee report would be dead almost on arrival. Lucien Bouchard condemned it, and used it as his justification for breaking with the Mulroney government and coming out openly for sovereignty. And the Quebec press and politicians raised a "humiliation" chorus: Quebec had been grievously insulted by these various proposals to try to save Meech Lake.

Lysiane Gagnon, the influential columnist for *La Presse*, provided a striking example. She had shown many reservations about Meech Lake from the start; on 28 April 1990, three weeks before the Charest report was published, she began her column, "What do you prefer? That Meech passes or not? Do you prefer the flu or hay fever?" But she was furious when Parliament proposed what were chiefly cosmetic additions to try to get it passed:

The insult is not in the recommendations taken singly. Nor is the insult in the Charest report, but in the process that led to it: in the tone, the manner, in this new grocery list, in this package of demands that is thrown in our face to put us in our place. The insult is in the irresponsible obstinacy of the three recalcitrant provinces to "readmit" Quebec into the "family" on their own conditions. It is this obstinacy, this caricature of democracy, that the Charest report conveys by taking up in turn each of their demands.

Gagnon did not even think it necessary to examine the report and bring out in what respect the recommendations were unacceptable. It was enough to rend the skies with cries of "insult" and "humiliation."

How far will Quebec have to contort itself to slide through the fissure that now replaces the doorway into the country that its ancestors were the first among Westerners to till and name? It is always possible, if need be, to become a tenant after having been the owner and chief occupant, but there is a limit. First the back room, then the basement, then the shed . . . And after that? Will the poodle have to crouch on the last step of the staircase?

This remarkable column summed up an entire intellectual tradition in Quebec. Eleven first ministers had signed an agreement at Meech Lake to please only Quebec. For some of them, the agreement threatened their own interests—for instance, making a Triple-E Senate most unlikely. But they signed anyway. Three of them then were defeated in elections, and the others did all they possibly could do to get the three newcomers to accept the agreement signed by their predecessors. That was the significance of the Charest report: it was meant to give the three dissidents a fig leaf to cover their surrender before the Meech steamroller. But Gagnon could see nothing but *lèse-Québec*.

Whether or not [Bourassa] goes to this first ministers' conference, whether the others give in on some point or other, and dig out from

237

mothballs some morsel to make the humiliated province sit up and beg, what does it matter? The damage is done. The legal texts are not what matters. That's not where the humiliation resides. It's in the head.[31]

The surge of tribalism in Quebec, the sense of *us* versus *them* that had taken over political attitudes, evoked wild speculation about the future. Just before the Charest report was made public, Radio-Canada radio reported that a member of the Parti Québécois met Bourassa at a social event and begged him to lead Quebec to sovereignty. "That would require a coalition," Bourassa is said to have replied. "Would you be prepared to enter my government?" According to the report, the PQ took Bourassa seriously enough to discuss the matter in their caucus.

It was in this charged atmosphere that, on 18 May, Tory MP François Gérin announced that he was bolting the Conservative Party and would be sitting as an independent member of Parliament, committed to the separation of Quebec. There were rumours that others would soon follow, notably Tory MP Gibert Chartrand and Liberal MP Jean Lapierre.

Thereupon, environment minister Lucien Bouchard sent a telegram to the national council of the Parti Québécois, which was meeting that weekend in Alma, Bouchard's own riding. He was travelling in Europe at the time, and the occasion was the tenth anniversary of the 1980 referendum on Quebec's sovereignty. In his telegram, Bouchard did not merely recall a ten-year-old historic event, he explicitly associated himself with the separatist side. He did not impartially recall all Quebecers who took part in that referendum, including the 60 per cent of Quebecers who voted for federalism. He recalled only the pride of voting for separation, and suggested its continuing timeliness.

Your meeting will underline the tenth anniversary of an important event in the history of Quebec. The referendum concerns us all very directly as Québécois. Its commemoration is yet another occasion to recall loudly the sincerity, pride, and generosity of the Yes that we then defended, at the side of René Lévesque and his team.

The memory of René Lévesque will unite us all on the weekend. For he made the Québécois discover their inalienable right themselves to decide their own destiny.[32]

As the country focused increasingly on the dangerous disaffection growing in Quebec, Bouchard's telegram caused a shock wave of indignation across the country. This was a message from a minister of the Crown and the chief representative from Quebec in the federal Cabinet? Bouchard received a call from Paul Tellier, the clerk of the privy council. Solemnly, Tellier told him that the telegram had caused a very bad reaction in Canada. Bouchard burst out angrily, "I don't give a damn about the telegram!"

Bouchard himself saw nothing wrong. What did the prime minister or the country expect when the Conservative caucus was made up of so many people like himself, who had favoured sovereignty-association in 1980? Did they expect them to renounce their past or abandon their convictions? Mulroney had built his party in Quebec by appealing to the nationalists. But now the pigeons were coming home to roost—or, rather, they were flying the coop. Bouchard's telegram was only the first step of his departure from the Cabinet, from the Conservative government, from the caucus. He was breaking with his old friend Brian, and with federalism.

The stated reason for the breach was the Charest report. Bouchard had been deeply disturbed when Mulroney endorsed Premier McKenna's proposal for a "companion resolution" and had set up the Charest committee. Now, he claimed, his worst fears had been realized.

I was first used, then faced with a fait accompli. The prime minister knew that I would abhor the Charest report: and here he had struck a deal behind my back with Jean Chrétien. He had bet on thirty years of friendship and of reciprocal services, on the weakness that I had shown when I agreed to go along with the McKenna resolution, on my attachment to the ministry of the environment, on the $5 billion that he had promised me for the Green Plan, on my reluctance to break my bonds with a party and a group of friends. He had been mistaken, that was the long and the short of it. A gambler doesn't come up with a win every time, nor with everybody.[33]

Mulroney tried everything to dissuade Bouchard from breaking away. He sent a special assistant, Luc Lavoie, to speak to him as soon as he arrived back in Ottawa from Europe. Bouchard was inflexible. Mulroney sent Paul Tellier to plead with him, and then Bernard Roy, another old mutual friend from university days, who had been Mulroney's first principal secretary when he became prime minister. Bouchard admitted afterwards that this was the hardest appeal to resist, because he was very fond of Roy and had a high opinion of his integrity. Roy brought the message that Mulroney wanted to see Bouchard.

Surprisingly, considering the long friendship between them, considering how much Mulroney had helped Bouchard's career, Bouchard had intended to walk out without so much as a word, face to face, with him.

The atmosphere got tense when [Roy] asked me if I would see the prime minister. I replied that I didn't think that was necessary. Had he not ignored me for the past ten days, merely sending me messengers? Bernard took it badly. "You mean to say that you would leave without meeting him?" he cried. "I will not refuse to see him if he wishes," I replied, "but I would not advise him to see me if he thinks he can talk me out of it. I will not change my mind."[34]

The two men who had shared so much met for the last time. Bouchard insisted that he could not accept the Charest report, and he handed over his letter of resignation. Mulroney read it and asked him to strike out a passage that he found particularly offensive. "I mentioned in it," Bouchard recalled, "that Pierre Elliott Trudeau himself, when he was shaping the constitution at will in 1981, had not dared to include a clause for promoting bilingualism, which he was about to do, following the Charest report."[35] Bouchard agreed, they parted, and they never spoke to each other again.

His letter of resignation was not a traditional one, but it was pure Bouchard. It was more a manifesto for the future than a withdrawal from the past, summarizing recent history from the point of view of a committed separatist and, above all, laying the groundwork for future political action to achieve the independence of Quebec. He saw the Meech Lake accord as a recognition by all the first ministers that they owed Quebec "reparations" for the harm done in 1982. "All then understood that this road [to national reconciliation] led first and foremost to a gesture of reparation which the country as a whole had to make toward Quebec, ostracized by the coup of Pierre Elliott Trudeau."[36] Meech Lake had set the conditions for Quebec's "adhering to the constitution." These conditions were, all Quebecers thought, "quite paltry." In fact, many held that "Quebec would be erasing at too much of a discount the base act of 1982." Bourassa had "cut to the bone the price for Quebec's forgiveness and its return to the constitutional family."

But instead of forgiveness, the rest of the country turned nasty, trampling on the Quebec flag and accusing those who had been for sovereignty of racism and treason. Instead of showing generosity and respect toward Quebec, the rest of the country was turning Meech Lake into an opportunity to bring out "the fault line" of the country. "And so, what was supposed to be an exercise to obtain Quebec's forgiveness, instead put Quebec on the hot seat."

Bouchard then proceeded to analyze the Charest report. It proposed new clauses to be put into the constitution which, he said, would have changed the "essential conditions" of Meech Lake. In particular, it would have "trivialized the distinct character of Quebec society by including in the same section the equality of the anglophone and francophone communities of New Brunswick." It was an unacceptable dilution of the "distinct society" clause to say that the clause was to be interpreted together with the Charter of Rights. And he worried that the unanimity requirement for change to the Senate would be weakened—even though Quebec's own veto was presumably to be retained.

These were important concerns. But one proposal in the Charest report was especially offensive: "Above all, I consider it totally unacceptable to attribute to the federal Parliament and government, not just a role in protecting the linguistic duality, as the Meech Lake accord proposes, but also a role of promoting it."[37] This part of the "companion accord" had been put forward to dilute the character of Quebec as an ethnic state which was implied in Meech. But the ethnic state, undiluted, was precisely what Bouchard demanded as a minimum for recognizing the constitution. "The government of Quebec cannot subscribe to these proposals. Of that I am certain, and that I hope. Quebec will find itself once again isolated, which is exactly what was to be avoided at all costs. The role of victim imposed on Quebec in 1982 is already odious; so why force Quebec into the role of culprit in 1990?" He projected the image—as he would do again and again in the following years—of Quebec being "on its knees": "He who begins negotiations on his knees is most likely to end them flat on his stomach."[38]

The Charest report, Bouchard anticipated, would be presented to a meeting of the first ministers, at which Quebec would be either forced to submit or be designated as the inflexible partner that undermined agreement. "In the last resort, better honour in the midst of disagreement than agreement in dishonour. And worst of all would be dishonour in the midst of disagreement, which is what awaits those who would try in vain, as I believe, to convince Quebec to attend a conference which is a trap, in order to extort final concessions which cannot be other than humiliating."[39]

Bouchard claimed to be leaving the government because of the Charest report, but he was, in effect, outlining the rationale for a future political party.

The Québécois, in particular, must redefine the degree, the structures, and the conditions of their participation in the Canadian composite. For me, this participation, whether it is called associational, confederal, or something else, will require another negotiation: the true one, this time, that will deal with the fundamental issues. . . . Only a Quebec state that has democratically armed itself with a clear mandate, one based on recovering its full attributes, will have the political authority necessary to negotiate the Canadian association of tomorrow.[40]

It might seem like a strange leap from the Charest report to evoking a referendum in which the Quebec state would ask for a mandate to "recover its full attributes." But it was consistent with the changed climate in Quebec, one in which it seemed most likely that a referendum on sovereignty would now carry, reversing the judgment of the 1980 referendum. Bouchard had earlier abandoned the dream of a sovereign Quebec because it seemed impossible to achieve, perhaps ever. Like René Lévesque, he had committed himself to the *beau risque* of federalism as defined by Mulroney. But now, sovereignty seemed possible, even probable. The climate was ripe; every poll showed Quebecers increasingly ready to take the plunge that they had refused a decade earlier. All that was required, it seemed, was decisive political leadership to guide the people toward the promised land of sovereignty toward which they were, in any case, already speeding. There was already the Parti Québécois. But a powerful second front could be opened up in Ottawa itself. The federal regime could be undermined from within, in its very sanctum of the House of Commons.

Had Bouchard's letter of resignation ended with the rejection of the Charest report and the insistence that Meech Lake must be passed as is, without later additions, his cover story that he was leaving because of the Charest report would have been credible. But Bouchard's letter led to a quite different position: it led to the "real negotiation," which was not Meech Lake at all. It led to what would soon be officially founded as the Bloc Québécois.

This was implicit in the letter of resignation, but quite explicit when Bouchard met journalists on 22 May, minutes after announcing his resignation in the Commons. "This country doesn't work," he said. "I think that the solution is sovereignty-association." He said that he wanted Meech Lake, and yet he insisted that it wasn't nearly enough. "I still insist that Meech must be passed as it is," he said. And yet he soon added that the "distinct society" clause was merely "a statement of fact." And it was the federal system itself that was at fault, not merely the absence of Meech Lake. What would the accord change? The system is "out of date. . . . It is a formula that condemns us to sterile discussions, and especially to low level discussions on petty questions."

And again, rather than offer Meech Lake insistently, he told reporters that the country had to be remade. "For me, it is more than repatriating areas of jurisdiction. For me, it's a matter of reconstituting the sovereignty of Quebec. And then, a Quebec which has recovered the full measure of its powers and its attributions can discuss as between equals with the rest of Canada."

Bouchard's break with Mulroney placed the separatist leader in a strong position and the Conservative leader in a difficult one. Having abandoned the prestige and perks of a ministerial office, Bouchard immediately acquired an enhanced credibility with the public, which had become cynical about politicians. The fact that he was Mulroney's close friend and his alter ego in Quebec gave a Corneillian elevation to the break: he had chosen the path of principle and honour rather than that of friendship and power. On a dismal political scene, he emerged as a shining knight and a powerful opponent of federalism. He could speak as one who had been inside, but who had found the system hostile to the interests of Quebec. Federalism was not reformable, he testified. The only way Quebec could achieve a better deal with the rest of Canada was to turn inward, concentrate all its political forces in a sovereignist party, and make a break, as he had done, with the all-Canadian solidarities. Only then should Quebec reopen negotiations with Canada.

Bouchard's defection and immediate, total repudiation of the Charest report heightened the stakes of the Meech Lake accord to ever more dizzying levels. Tensions were increased, issues were polarized, and it was now almost impossible to offer a compromise solution to the three dissident provinces of Newfoundland, Manitoba, and New Brunswick. They would have to take Meech Lake as is, with no assurance that their concerns for the constitution would ever be met. As for Bourassa, he had already dug in to a Meech-or-nothing position by approving the April resolution repudiating the McKenna companion resolution. Bouchard's dramatic action removed the last possibility that he would compromise.

In the Commons, on 23 May, Mulroney again put forward his version of events, according to which a rejection of Meech Lake or the demand for improvements was an insult to Quebec. Again, he gave a mythical evocation of what Meech would mean: "Three years ago, the government of Quebec concluded with all the other provinces and the federal government a document of adhesion to Canada, to the Canadian constitution—an adhesion freely consented, which would make of the country a state that was united. . . . At last, we had a document that permitted us all to say that we have a Canada that is strong and united."

Strong and united? With separatism at the flood tide? With a new separatist prophet spawned by Mulroney's own manoeuvres? That was gross misrepresentation. But Mulroney did not hesitate to hold the three dissident premiers responsible for jeopardizing the idyllic future that lay ahead if only Meech Lake passed. "Three provinces since [1987] have repudiated the signatures of the premiers given earlier, which creates a serious problem for Canada."

Mulroney's tactic of increasing the pressure was abetted by *Globe and Mail* columnist Jeffrey Simpson, who penned a vitriolic attack against all the major politicians opposing Meech: Clyde Wells, Sharon Carstairs, Frank McKenna, Premier Gary Filmon of Manitoba, and Manitoba NDP leader Gary Dewar: "Atta boy, Clyde. Way to go, Sharon. Nice reasoning, Frank. Well done, Gary and Gary. You're now reaping what you sowed, a whirlwind in Quebec." Simpson lectured them for daring to oppose Meech Lake even after enlightened people such as Mulroney and himself had warned them that people in Quebec wouldn't like it. "They were told, by English Canadians of good faith and superior understanding of Quebec and by French-speaking Quebecers what would likely happen. But they did not listen." Of course, in Simpson's judgment, leaders from Quebec—including Mulroney and Bourassa—had nothing to do with the crisis gripping the country. It was all the fault of the bad Anglos. "The tragedy of our current discontents, especially of Quebec's retreat into tribalism, is that English-Canadian reaction has been the root cause."[41]

But Mulroney pressed on. He invited the premiers to meet him privately in Ottawa on the weekend of 26 May. Whatever was said in private, the public statements before the television cameras continued to raise the tension. On 28 May, Bourassa yet again suggested that the country was likely to break apart unless he got Meech as is. "The reason we have a problem now with Meech Lake is that one province had imposed on it a reduction of its powers with the patriation of the constitution in 1982. That is the cause of the problem that we are going through and that calls into question the future of the country."

His was a highly coloured interpretation of recent reality. In 1982, with the Charter of Rights, a gift of freedom was bestowed on all citizens, by placing limits on all governments. Bourassa's quarrel was with the Charter of Rights. And it was to have the power to overcome the limits on the Quebec government imposed by the Charter that Bourassa wanted so badly Meech's mandate to promote Quebec's "distinct identity." But rather than quarrel explicitly with the Charter of Rights, Bourassa preferred to trumpet the version that had Quebec

243

isolated, plundered, and humiliated—the version that had been repeated again and again by Mulroney over the years.

Mulroney still had in reserve his most ambitious psychodrama for imposing Meech. On 31 May, he announced that the first ministers would be meeting the following Sunday. And, in advance, he laid out the scenario under which this last-chance meeting would be held. The issue was saving the country, and those who threatened the country were the three hold-out premiers. "What is in dispute is modest, extremely modest, when compared with what is really at stake," Mulroney told the Commons. "What is really at stake is Canada."

And he went on to suggest what a good country it was that Wells, McKenna, and Filmon were preparing to sacrifice on the altar of constitutional quibbles. "People across the world are genuinely troubled why anyone would fail to understand the magnificence of this great country, Canada. Elsewhere, political repression and poverty, famine, and natural disasters, not arcane constitutional debates, are the stuff of national turmoil."

All the pressure for concession and surrender was placed upon the unspeakable three. But what about Bourassa? Only he explicitly, repeatedly, continually threatened the destruction of Canada unless the other premiers overcame their objections, their doubts, their concerns, their defence of the interests of their constituents. He alone threatened to destroy the country, so he alone had to be satisfied at all costs. And, to complete the blackmail scenario, Mulroney promised that the country would achieve peace at last if only it gave in to Bourassa and himself. "Quebec's voluntary endorsement of the existing constitution will make it a vibrant document of unity and hope for Canada and the future."

That same day, Bourassa played his part in confirming the doomsday scenario for the coming meeting. *"Je pense qu'il faut tenter la dernière chance,"* he said publicly. I think we have to try one last time.

When Bourassa arrived for the first ministers' meeting on 3 June, he confirmed his inflexibility, and again put all the onus for compromise on the dissidents. "Every change is unacceptable. I don't just say this myself, I say it with the support of almost seven million Québécois." He would not even countenance an addition to the Meech Lake canon that would clarify what was meant by some of its clauses. "I always said," he commented, "that if you bring a clarification in a political statement, in most cases that is the equivalent to a constitutional amendment."

The doomsday scenario provided the theme for the week the first ministers spent in Hull-Ottawa, agonizing behind closed doors over Meech Lake while the television cameras stood on guard outside day and night. The whole country was drawn into a moment-by-moment death watch. Would Canada survive? It all seemed to hinge on whether those eleven first ministers could come to an agreement—and that meant that three would have to surrender unconditionally.

On the second evening, in an obviously choreographed move, Frank McKenna abandoned his last shred of opposition to Meech Lake and declared that it had to pass. Never mind, now, his previous concerns. All that mattered was saving the country—and that meant adopting Meech Lake now and hoping for something better later. All questions of principle were trampled in a panicky rout, a *sauve qui peut.*

The pressure from the prime minister and the other eight premiers now concentrated on Clyde Wells and Gary Filmon. There was only the barest pretense of arguing the case for Meech Lake on its merits. The hold-outs were told that if they didn't sign, Gil Rémillard would go the way of Lucien Bouchard. If the accord did not pass, Bourassa's Cabinet would split apart, as would the Quebec Liberal caucus. Bourassa would be forced to call elections, which the Parti Québécois would win.

Bourassa stood back and let Ontario's premier, David Peterson, and others argue his cause for him, as though it were the very cause of Canada. On the Thursday, Bourassa even announced that he would no longer take part in any discussions on the distinct society clause. And Quebec turned down a harmless "Canada clause" that would have recognized as a fundamental characteristic of Canada the country's aboriginal people and the cultural contribution of people from many countries. The best Quebec would offer was to talk about it some other day. "You will not see a Canada clause for this conference," Rémillard told reporters. "But you will see, probably, a commitment concerning discussion for a Canada clause in a second round." Oh, wonderful.

The moment-by-moment, day-by-day suspense generated by the "last chance" conference polarized the country. A solid majority of Canadians were against Meech Lake. They resented the high-pressure tactics to try to wrest consent from Wells and the Manitoba leaders. And they wondered if their leaders would cave in. In Quebec, the suspense was cast into a senario in which the rest of the country was resisting Quebec's modest, legitimate wishes and saying no to Quebec. Bourassa made an unconsciously ironic comment on the Thursday, when he thought there would be a deal: "It's not completely done, but it could be a great day for Canada." Indeed.

At last there was a deal, more or less. Nine premiers accepted Meech in its 1987 version, with a few accompanying words of reassurance. One premier, Clyde Wells, agreed only to put the matter to his legislature. To the public, waiting anxiously outside the Ottawa Conference Centre or in homes across Canada, it looked as though Meech Lake was now a sure thing, and destined to become part of the constitution of the country.

The companion agreement offered no real remedies, however, for those who had found Meech Lake unacceptable as originally adopted. There was no Canada clause, though that had been the chief concern of Manitoba. Instead, a commission was to travel the country after 23 June to gather the views of Canadians on their country's fundamental characteristics. What it would lead to, if anything, was anybody's guess. The "distinct society-distinct identity" clause remained as it was, though this had been a chief concern for Clyde Wells. A legal opinion, appended to the agreement, changed nothing in the clause but gave vague reassurances to those easily reassured. It was not signed by any of the first ministers, but only by a few constitutional lawyers—whose views were denounced by other constitutional lawyers.

The only new element of substance wrung out during the week of intense meetings was that Ontario agreed to surrender some of its Senate seats to the four western provinces and Newfoundland if a period of negotiations over the Senate proved fruitless, as expected. It was a long way from Triple-E, but it offered a consolation prize.

The first ministers sang *O Canada.* Mulroney preened, certain that he had won his desperate wager. But vanity overcame him when he gave an interview to the *Globe and Mail,* which was published on 12 June. He boasted that he had decided a month earlier to hold the first ministers' conference at the eleventh hour, when the premiers would be presented with an all-or-nothing ultimatum. "That's the day we're going to roll all the dice," said the man who gambled with the country.

He seemed to have his victory, but it came at a price. Wells had promised Newfoundlanders that, if he disapproved of the final agreement, he would put it to the people of Newfoundland and Labrador in the form of a referendum. Mulroney's timing produced the final product too late to hold a referendum before the 23 June deadline for passing Meech Lake. If Wells held his referendum later than that date, the first two provinces to have passed the agreement, Quebec and Nova Scotia, would have had to pass it again so that all approvals fell within the required three years from the time of the first approval. But Quebec and Nova Scotia refused to consider passing the agreement a second time.

Wells arrived back in St. John's shaken and humiliated by the ordeal he had been subjected to day and night for the previous week. When he landed at the airport on 10 June, there were tears on his cheeks as he greeted the people who had come to meet him. He then spoke resentfully of the extreme pressure that had been exerted on him in Ottawa. At a press conference the next day, he was sad and disenchanted. "I don't consider there's been a complete capitulation, but our achievement is very modest indeed." Although he had signed in Ottawa, he remained unconvinced; the concerns he had enumerated had all remained unaddressed by the agreement reached in a pressure-cooker atmosphere. His anguish was unmistakable: "I'm very apprehensive about the position of New-foundland in fifty years as a province of Canada."

Premier McKenna passed the Meech resolution, but he made clear when he spoke in his legislature on 13 June that he had surrendered to threats of the disaster that would supposedly follow the failure of Meech rather than to approval of its content: "We accepted the arguments that the failure of Meech Lake would result in rising interest rates, in a falling Canadian dollar, economic instability, the very real prospect of increased unemployment and the very real prospect of a major economic recession. We also accepted that, should Meech Lake fail . . . the separatist forces in Quebec would be beyond our control . . . and we would be facing the potential disintegration of Canada."

Gary Filmon made a similar admission in the Manitoba legislature on 20 June: "I would rather that, if Quebec is to separate, it will be because they make that choice on their own, not because it is seen that one province or two provinces or one area of the country does something that forces them out."

Sharon Carstairs, who had made it to leadership of the Manitoba Opposition on the strength of her opposition to Meech, explained her surrender in Ottawa by a similar concern for the country. "Trust is a difficult thing. But I want [Manitobans] to realize that this is not a French-English issue. This is not a Quebec-Manitoba issue. This is a Canada issue. And I'll say yes to Canada."

The last hold-outs seemed to have given up the fight. But the gods were not entirely crazy. From Red Sucker Lake, they sent their prophet, Elijah Harper, to humble the vainglorious pharaoh Mulroney and the satrap Bourassa. In the same week that Mulroney boasted of his coup, the quiet-spoken Harper brought all his proud schemes to nothing. He refused the unanimous permission required to suspend the rules of the legislature which required that, before Meech could be approved, there had to be public hearings. Mulroney's timing made public hearings before 23 June impossible.

Mulroney had been too cute by half. And, with Harper and the native leaders who stood behind him, Mulroney's intimidation tactics did not work. Harper was not terrorized at the thought that Canada might break up. He raised his eagle feather and said "No" each time permission was asked to debate Meech without public hearings. Nor did Bourassa's tactic of claiming the status of victim work. When Bourassa said that Quebec had been "left out," Harper was not impressed. "If you look at our relationship with the country, we have been left out for many years," Harper said on 15 June. "I don't think a few [more] years would matter. I think what needs to be done is for the aboriginal people to be taken seriously and also to be accorded a rightful place at the constitutional table. And we want to be recognized as founders of this country."

The "Quebec round" had left the aboriginals out. Now Harper set out to prove that there could be no constitutional change without the aboriginals. And the chiefs of Manitoba sent a letter that same day to Bourassa, turning against him the same kind of language that he regularly invoked to make other Canadians feel guilty. "We, the original people of this country, have inherited through the original traditions of our forefathers fifty-five distinct original languages. Fifty-two of these original languages of Canada are now on the brink of extinction.

Unlike you, we cannot retrieve these languages from our mother country. Our mother country is Canada."

Phil Fontaine, head of the Assembly of Manitoba Chiefs, ran a variation on the concept of distinct society. "I want to say that we have never opposed Quebec's recognition as a distinct society. We recognize that and support that. But if Quebec is distinct, we are even more distinct. That's the recognition we want, and we'll settle for nothing else."

Bourassa, who had announced in 1971 that he would flood the homelands of the James Bay Cree without giving them the courtesy of even a phone call, now found the native people of Manitoba, Quebec, and the rest of Canada rising to frustrate his designs. Aboriginals from Quebec met on June 15 in Quebec City and gave their full support to what was happening in Manitoba. "Elijah Harper is holding the fort on our behalf. Elijah is doing what he needs to be doing," said Konrad Sioui, who represented Quebec natives at the Assembly of First Nations.

Gil Rémillard responded with threats. He said that Quebec had supported self-government for aboriginals, but might reconsider if the passage of Meech Lake continued to be delayed in Manitoba. He urged the aboriginals of Quebec to put pressure on Harper if they wanted Quebec's support. Bourassa, for his part, demanded that they wait until another round to press for their constitutional demands. Phil Fontaine was not impressed. "We've trusted before, and we've been sold out every time. And we're not prepared to be sold out this time."

Mulroney, getting desperate, put a resolution before the Commons on 20 June: "The House urges the Manitoba and Newfoundland legislative assemblies to exert efforts to bring about the full ratification of the Constitution Amendment 1987 by June 23 1990." When he spoke on the resolution, Mulroney tried to evoke the brave future that awaited the country if only Meech would pass. "Ten days hence, on July 1, I believe that we can all celebrate together a new beginning of our future as a more united and more confident Canada, the kind of Canada that will engender greater social justice, greater equality of opportunity, greater prosperity for our children, greater dignity for all of its citizens, and a citizenship, a Canadian citizenship, that will be a source of pride for all the world."

Then, in an attempt to influence the Newfoundland House of Assembly, he spoke there on 21 June, the day before Newfoundland was expected to vote on Meech Lake. His argument was simple. On the one side was Robert Bourassa, who "loves Canada." On the other side was the Parti Québécois leader, Jacques Parizeau, who would get to hold a referendum on separation if Meech was not passed. But pass Meech, and all will be well. "We get to keep Canada, awkward, ungainly, magnificent Canada. We get to keep it, and to pass it on to our children in the certain knowledge that they perhaps will do a better job than we did, and improve it in their own way, in their own time, so that it can then be passed on to their children."

Part of Mulroney's argument for passing Meech could as easily have been invoked against it. He recalled that, in 1980, almost half of French-speaking Quebecers voted Yes to sovereignty-association. He then quoted figures from a poll in that day's *La Presse* which showed 57 per cent of all Quebecers now favourable to sovereignty. Among French-speaking Quebecers, the proportion rose to 63 per cent. His implication was that, if Meech Lake was passed, separatism would recede. But the poll had been taken shortly after the first ministers' conference, when it was in fact assumed that Meech Lake would pass. Separatism was clearly surging, whether the accord passed or not. Was Meech Lake the solution, or was it part of the problem?

In the event, Mulroney's last efforts were wasted. Elijah Harper had no intention of allowing Meech Lake to pass. And Wells, to spare his province the odium of voting down the agreement, decided it was futile to call a vote in the House of Assembly. Meech Lake died amid a chorus of whimpers.

In Quebec's National Assembly, on 22 June, a solemn mood prevailed. The Meech Lake episode was now history. Jacques Parizeau extended his hand to his premier and called for the union of all French-speaking Quebecers, to the exclusion of *les autres*. "Since, tonight, we find ourselves *entre nous* [within the family], let's simply accept to be able to meet each other *entre nous*, to discuss *entre nous*—not with all kinds of other people—*entre nous*, about our future and about what must happen to us."

And Bourassa evoked in his fashion General de Gaulle's call from the balcony of Montreal's city hall to announce that Quebec was henceforth *libre*: "English Canada must clearly understand that, no matter what anyone else says or does, Quebec is today and forever a distinct society, free and able to undertake its destiny and its development."

Notes

1.Quoted in Graham Fraser, *PQ. René Lévesque and the Parti Québécois in Power* (Toronto: Macmillan, 1985), p. 353.
2.Dominique Clift, *Le déclin du nationalisme au Québec* (Montréal: Libre expression, 1981), p. 167.
3.Louis Balthazar, *Bilan du nationalisme au Québec* (Montréal: L'Hexagone, 1986), p. 187.
4.Fraser, *PQ*, p. 347.
5.Ibid., p. 359.
6.Ibid., p. 364.
7.Ibid.
8.Ibid., p. 371.
9.Marcel Adam, "Ceux qui font déraper le débat linguistique," *La Presse*, 4 décembre 1986, p. B-2.
10.Report by Guy Taillefer in *La Presse*, 7 Dec. 1986.
11.Pierre O'Neill, "Mulroney enfourche le cheval de la loi 101," *Le Devoir*, 9 Dec. 1986, p. 1.
12.*The Gazette*, 10 Dec. 1986.
13.The other conditions were that Quebec have a veto over constitutional amendments affecting its powers; that it have the right to opt out of joint federal-provincial programs and receive financial

compensation for the advantages forgone; that the minimum of three judges from Quebec on the Supreme Court of Canada be protected in the constitution, along with the Quebec government's role in naming them; and that Quebec have a recognized role in immigration policy.

14.Greg Weston, *Reign of Error. The Inside Story of John Turner's Troubled Leadership* (Toronto: McGraw-Hill Ryerson, 1988), p. 237.

15.*La Presse*, 15 June 1988, p. 1.

16.Report by Denis Lessard in *La Presse*, 9 Nov. 1989.

17.According to political scientist Max Nemni, among those who rejected the accord, many of them quite virulently, were the three major union federations, the Confederation of National Trade Unions, the Quebec Federation of Labour, and the Centrale des Enseignants du Québec; the Alliance des Professeurs de Montréal; all nationalist political parties and associations; the Writers' Union; the Union des Artistes; the Union des Producteurs Agricoles; and even the Quebec branch of the NDP.

18.In a Gallup poll published on 28 April 1988 by *La Presse*, 63 per cent of Quebecers said that they were "not informed" about the accord. Asked whether it would be "a good thing for Canada," 32 per cent said it would be, 18 per cent said it would not be, and 50 per cent didn't know. In November, 1989, another Gallup poll found 38 per cent of Quebecers saying it was a good thing, 17 per cent said it was not a good thing, and 45 per cent didn't know. In March, 1990, 40 per cent said it would be good for Canada, 20 per cent said the opposite, and 40 per cent didn't know.

A Toronto Star-CTV poll published in the *Toronto Star* on 6 February 1990 asked a somewhat different question: "Are you in favour of the Meech Accord?" In Quebec, 48 per cent said yes, 25 per cent said no and 28 per cent didn't know. Thus, more than half were either opposed or uncertain.

19.William Johnson in *The Gazette*, 1 Apr. 1988.

20.In 1969, when the Official Languages Act was passed, Tory Leader Robert Stanfield had been unable to prevent seventeen members of his caucus from voting against it. Again, in 1973, when the Trudeau Liberals introduced a resolution backing the use of English and French in the federal public service, sixteen Tory MPs voted in opposition.

21.Bouchard, *À visage*, p. 272.

22.Doris Lussier, *Vérités et sourires de la politique* (Montreal: Stanké, 1988), p. 48.

23.*Globe and Mail*, 23 Feb. 1990.

24.Mario Fontaine, "Le Parti libéral brandit la menace du séparatisme," *Le Devoir*, 9 Feb. 1989, p. 1.

25.On 22 March 1990, an IQOP poll published in *La Presse* put to a sample of Quebecers the same question that was asked in the 1980 referendum. In 1980, the vote was 60 to 40 against a mandate to negotiate sovereignty-association. Almost ten years later, two thirds of the interviewees said they would vote Yes. Setting aside those who did not answer or said they were uncertain, 76.7 per cent said they would vote Yes. Among francophones the Yes vote was 83.1 per cent.

On March 26, a CROP poll, also published in *La Presse*, showed that 56 per cent of those surveyed declared themselves favourable to sovereignty; only 37 per cent said they were unfavourable. The pollsters asked the hardest question of all: "Personally, are you very favourable, rather favourable, hardly favourable or not favourable at all to the separation of Quebec from Canada?" In answer, 43 per cent said they were favourable to separation, with 53 per cent unfavourable. Among francophones, 49 per cent said they were favourable to separation, with only 46 per cent opposed.

26.Column by William Johnson, *The Gazette*, 21 Mar. 1990.

27.*La Presse*, 23 Mar. 1990, p. 2.

28.*Le Devoir*, 22 Mar. 1990.

29.Bouchard, *À visage*, p. 302.

30.Deborah Coyne, *Roll of the Dice. Working with Clyde Wells during the Meech Lake Negotiations* (Toronto: Lorimer, 1992), p. 86.

31.Lysiane Gagnon, "Screech Lake," *La Presse*, 19 May 1990, p. B3.

32.The telegram is quoted in Bouchard, *À visage*, p. 313.

33.Ibid., p. 315.

34.Ibid., p. 318.

35.Ibid., p. 319.

36.Ibid., p. 320.
37.Ibid., p. 322.
38.Ibid., p. 324.
39.Ibid., p. 325.
40.Ibid., p. 324.
41.*Globe and Mail*, 23 May 1990.

CHAPTER FIFTEEN

The Aftermath of Meech: A Season of Hyper-Nationalism

When Meech Lake failed, on Friday, 22 June 1990, all the clocks in Quebec seemed suddenly to have turned back to 1967. Nationalism swept back into fashion and into passion and became again what it had for a few brief years ceased to be: the most dynamic political force in Quebec.

Vive le Québec libre echoed again, as though the twelve-year interval since Charles de Gaulle's cry had vanished into a black hole. The counter-revolution of Pierre Trudeau seemed itself overthrown. The failed Parti Québécois referendum on sovereignty of 1980 was cancelled. Nationalism emerged triumphant once again, regaining the initiative and the presumption of moral superiority. Federalism was stigmatized as having failed.

The mood in Montreal on the weekend following the failure of Meech Lake had its paradoxes, even its contradictions. Quebec had supposedly wanted Meech Lake and now felt rejected by the rest of Canada. That was the message sounded everywhere by Premier Bourassa. But the crowds celebrating Saint-Jean-Baptiste hardly displayed disappointment. What came across in public was a great surge of joy and defiance.

The Saint-Jean-Baptiste parade wended its way through the streets of Montreal heralded by ranks of Quebec flags and separatist placards. The old cries were shouted again: *"Le Québec aux Québécois!"* and *"On veut notre pays!"* [We want our country] and *"In-dé-pen-dance!"* There was a sense that night and in the following months that Quebec was now breaking radically with its past. Out with the endless, tedious, inconclusive constitutional negotiations of the past thirty years. It was time for decisive action.

After Meech failed, Bourassa announced that he would no longer attend the first ministers' conferences; he would deal only with the federal government one on one. This suggested a radical, even revolutionary, break with the Canadian constitution. Bourassa had declared his emancipation.[1]

This meant a return to the nation-to-nation vision (*"d'égal à égal"*) of Quebec's relation to Canada which Daniel Johnson had tried unsuccessfully to impose from 1966 to 1968 and which René Lévesque had asked the people of Quebec to endorse in the 1980 referendum. Bourassa was following up on his declaration on the night Meech failed that Quebec was free to choose its destiny "no matter what anyone else says or does." Quebec's freedom to choose its future was the guiding motto for Bourassa's political action over the following year. And Quebec seemed more radicalized than at any time since since 1837–39.

Bourassa projected defiance toward the rest of Canada when he was interviewed three days after Meech's failure on the current-affairs show *Le Point*. Despite repeated prompting, he refused to say whether or not he was a federalist, but he insisted that federalism was on trial and would be sentenced. "What I can tell you on that score is that the federal system as it now operates cannot be acceptable to Quebec, to the extent that Quebec's reasonable proposals are refused. So we must do some thinking to replace the constitutional program of my government or my party, which was backed by a majority of the Québécois. And I don't want to prejudge in advance what the conclusion the Québécois will draw."

With Meech Lake dead, Bourassa implied, anything was possible. He announced, in a press conference on 3 July, that a commission would be appointed to hold hearings and recommend the future choice that Quebec should make; he and Jacques Parizeau, leader of the opposition, would work together to choose the commission's members so as to put it above partisanship.

The commission began to take on the stature and portentousness of estates-general convened to lay the new foundations of a future society, of a future country. The premier signalled his intentions when he appointed its first member: none other than the separatist star, Lucien Bouchard. The symbolism was powerful. Bouchard was a member of Parliament, and so hardly an obvious candidate for a commission under the authority of the National Assembly. By choosing Bouchard first and holding a joint press conference with him, Bourassa appropriated the message that Bouchard had been preaching since he had broken with the Tories not two months earlier: all Quebecers must form a sacred union to create a *"rapport de force"* with English-speaking Canada. Their will and determination must be demonstrated in a referendum in which they voted massively for sovereignty. Then, and only then, could they exert the leverage to wrest new arrangements from English-speaking Canada.[2] According to Bouchard, the Québécois had been naive to believe that English-speaking Canadians would adopt Meech Lake to expiate the affront of having left Quebec out of the constitutional agreement in 1981–82. "It was only late in the day that our eyes were opened. We thus discovered that the patriation of 1982, far from being a matter for repentance, counts as among the noblest moments of Canadian history for our anglophone fellow citizens."

At the joint press conference with Bourassa, Bouchard said that he saw as the mission of the new commission precisely to prepare the way for such a referendum. "We will make a tabulation [of constitutional policies], we will look at reality, and we will define the needs of Quebec without the constraints of the straitjacket of the present constitution. And then, at the end, we will try to travel as far as we can together, and we hope we can come together to the same finish line. I hope it will result in a proposal for sovereignty."

Bourassa did not contradict his prize nominee; he simply injected a note of caution: "If we hold a referendum, we have to be certain that we will win. Because you can imagine the situation if there were a defeat in a referendum, and what the consequences would be for the future of Quebec." Bourassa had often faulted the Parti Québécois for holding and losing the 1980 referendum. It had weakened Quebec and opened the way for Trudeau to patriate the constitution. It had bound Quebec by a charter of rights—including the ultra-sensitive language rights—without the consent of the Quebec government. That was a mistake that he himself would never make, Bourassa implied.

And so what was to be called the Commission on the Political and Constitutional Future of Quebec began to take form. Its final report, issued eight months later, would follow exactly the logic proposed by Lucien Bouchard at that July press conference. Bourassa knew what he was doing when he named Bouchard as his first choice.

Meanwhile, Brian Mulroney was a prime minister bereft of moral authority. He had lost the support of the public in every province, as shown by public-opinion polls, and the provincial premiers outside of Quebec were wavering in their faith in the federation. Several conveyed an attitude of each province for itself. British Columbia premier William Vander Zalm said that he didn't know what sovereignty-association meant, but he probably wanted it. "[British Columbia] will certainly seek a different type of Confederation, perhaps similar to Quebec-style association within Canada," he said on 25 June 1990. And premier Grant Devine of Saskatchewan speculated, "We will be forced, I believe, to be more independent as a province." The bonds of the federation were loosening, perhaps unravelling.

That fateful Saturday, 23 June, when Meech expired, was, coincidentally, the day that Jean Chrétien won the leadership of the Liberal Party of Canada. At the convention in Calgary, Chrétien was caught on camera embracing Clyde Wells and saying, "Thank you, Clyde, for all that you've done." This was widely taken in Quebec to mean, "Thank you for helping defeat Meech Lake." Quebec nationalists saw it as another betrayal by the man who had done the most, under Trudeau, to patriate the constitution by circumventing René Lévesque and the National Assembly.

Two Liberal MPs, Jean Lapierre and Gilles Rocheleau, held a news conference a few days later to say that they were leaving the Liberal Party because they could not serve under Chrétien. Rocheleau in particular, a former mayor of Hull and a former minister in the Bourassa government, displayed the sectarian face of nationalism, saying, "Jean Chrétien is a traitor to Quebec. He is a hypocrite and a liar." He soon added the title of "Judas" to his collection of names for the new Liberal leader.

On 26 June, three members of Parliament from Quebec announced that they were leaving the Tory caucus to join a "bloc Québécois." That brought to six the number of Tory defections over Meech Lake.

One of the defectors, Louis Plamondon, a backbencher, had been recognized chiefly as the brother of Luc Plamondon, Quebec's premier lyricist, author of the words to such hits as the rock opera *Starmania*. Louis Plamondon had first entered politics in 1984 as a nationalist rather than a Conservative, because he wanted to fight the Liberals of Pierre Trudeau. In that respect, his political profile resembled that of many others in Mulroney's Quebec caucus. His speech on 26 June to explain why he was crossing the floor was a cry of pure tribalism, an anthem of angry ethnicity: "The ambiguity that is imposed on us as a people is not a recent development. From our earliest cohabitation with the English-speaking element, they treated us as the vanquished while making a point of our belonging to this great country." Plamondon then drew a thumbnail sketch of more than two centuries of history. In his lament, the collective experience of French Canadians could be summed up in a word: humiliation. "The first English governor, James Murray, said about our ancestors of 1763 that if they had left the country, it would have been a great loss for the British Empire. But what have they done since to invite us to share fully in this great empire?" His *cri du coeur* recounted unflagging Anglo hypocrisy, bad faith and oppression: "From the Royal Proclamation of 1763, the avowed objective of our new conquerors was to assimilate us." And the Quebec Act of 1774, which recognized the laws of New France and so implicitly accepted the French language? Mere opportunism. "For fear of the Americans, and to get around us, they did recognize us as a distinct society in the Quebec Act." Even when *les Anglais* did the right thing, it was for the wrong reason. So it was, too, with the elected assembly which Lower Canada received from the British Crown in 1791: "When we finally achieved at the turn of the century, after so many pleas, our own legislative assembly, it was not given at the same time the powers normally bestowed on a legislature. What a parody of democracy and of magnanimity!" The best of what *les Anglais* did to French Canadians was bad. But what about the rest? "We built this country with our blood and sweat. The thanks we received was to be humiliated and to be treated as a people without a history or a literature":

Never, as the founding people of this country, will we forget the many humiliations that were inflicted on us within this great country that we thought was ours: the humiliation of the Conquest, the humiliation of the Patriotes, the humiliation of the Act of Union, the humiliation of Louis

Riel, the humiliation of conscription in the two world wars, the humiliation of the War Measures Act, the humiliation of 1982 by the patriation of the constitution without Quebec, the humiliation of the Meech Lake accord.

That summer, after the defeat of Meech Lake, Prime Minister Mulroney almost disappeared from public view. Where was he? There were rumours, unfounded, that he had fallen into a deep depression, or that he had been hitting the bottle and was being treated in a detoxication centre. He reappeared briefly in La Malbaie on 29 July, just as Bourassa and Parizeau were setting up the commission on the constitutional future of Quebec. "You can take it for granted that I will not be waiting for a grocery list coming from Quebec," he announced. "I won't be waiting for some Quebec parliamentary committee to finish its inquiries across the province, and that they are presenting their requests saying, 'Here is a list, or a new approach for federalism.' This is a country we have here. We will be involved in this. All of Canada will be involved in this." In fact, as events seemed to be spinning out of his control in Quebec, Mulroney insisted somewhat optimistically that he was really in charge—or going to be: "The federal government and the federal Parliament will be leading the national debate and dialogue."

If Ottawa was the leader, the Quebec political class seemed not to have noticed. In the National Assembly, Bourassa introduced Bill 90 to give full legislative authority to the commission. The preamble to the bill seemed, in fact, to thumb its nose at Parliament and all other provincial governments. "Quebecers are free to choose their own destiny, to determine their political status and to ensure their economic, social, and cultural development," it proclaimed.

Rather than defend federalism, Bourassa continued to attack its legitimacy. "The constitution was modified substantially in 1982 without the consent of Quebec," he told *Time* magazine, as reported in its 9 July 1990 issue. "The constitution is applicable to Quebec, and we have to respect it. But we are not part of the constitution. We are not part of the Canadian family." The interview with *Time* was revealing because, once again, Bourassa held up the example of the European Community as his ideal model for Canada.

Time: Will your constitutional program leave Quebec inside Canada or outside?

Bourassa: Well, there are many ideas. But one thing is sure: in no way can we accept the present constitutional process. There is no way any Quebec premier could go to Ottawa and say, "I will agree to have eleven governments involved, as we have had in the past three years." This is no longer acceptable.

Time: Where are your new ideas going to come from?

Bourassa: Look at Europe. When I was defeated in 1976, I went to Brussels and studied the Common Market. For me, it is one of the greatest achievements of human history. My political idol is Jean Monnet, who worked to bring together people who had just been fighting a war among themselves. Now they are talking about political union and a common currency.

Time: But the European countries are giving up sovereignty and specific powers, not gaining them back.

Bourassa: Yes, but you know what's going on there now. They're discussing a common foreign policy more and more. You have a French-German military brigade. Many Quebecers say we want sovereignty in association with Canada, but they would prefer to have members in the Canadian Parliament. How could that work? Let's say that [the EC] is an interesting and probably appropriate reference.

And the premier blamed English Canada, not just Elijah Harper or Clyde Wells, for the failure of Meech. The accusation that English Canada collectively violated a social contract with Quebec became Bourassa's oft-repeated justification for considering Quebec freed of its previous obligations under the constitution.

Lucien Bouchard's new Bloc Québécois, meanwhile, began to define itself more precisely. Its seven members—six ex-Conservatives and ex-Liberal Jean Lapierre—published a statement on 25 July outlining the Bloc's "mission":

Our national allegiance is to Quebec. The territory to which we belong is Quebec, heartland of a people French by culture and language, and whose sovereignty we intend to promote. We consider the National Assembly of Quebec as being, in right and in fact, the supreme democratic institution of the Quebec people. That is where its sovereign authority must be exercised.

While the Bloc prospered, the Liberals in Quebec seemed carried away on the nationalist wave. On 5 July, six of the ten members of the executive of the Quebec section of the federal Young Liberals, all of them Francophone, including the president and vice-president, resigned in protest against the failure of Meech Lake and Jean Chrétien's accession to the Liberal leadership. Of the four executive members who did not resign, one was an anglophone and the other three had neither French nor English as a first language . Three of the departing executive members also announced that they would be working for Bloc Québécois candidate Gilles Duceppe in the Laurier-Ste-Marie by-election that was to be held the following month.

As the nationalist resolve became stronger and moved toward a showdown, Mulroney showed that he had learnt nothing from his flirtation with separatists. His own candidate in the Laurier-Ste-Marie by-election was an avowed separatist. According to La Presse, "Christian Fortin was for the Yes in the 1980 referendum, and he hasn't changed his views. And Brian Mulroney knows it, he says."

In an interview with La Presse, Fortin said that it didn't matter to the prime minister what his candidate in the by-election thought of Canada. All that mattered

257

was that he hated Jean Chrétien. "I met Mr. Mulroney on Thursday [21 June 1990]. We spoke, the two of us alone, for 25 minutes," Fortin told *La Presse*. "I spoke about my deep disgust with Jean Chrétien, and he told me that, together, we would make a terrific team to get Jean Chrétien out of Quebec."

After losing six of his members to the Bloc Québécois, Mulroney was apparently not content with the depth of separatist talent remaining in his caucus. He proposed to replenish the ranks.

The NDP's candidate in the by-election was also a prospect for Bouchard's growing anti-Canada caucus. "Louise O'Neill, NDP candidate for the federal by-election in Laurier-Ste-Marie, voted Yes in the [1980] referendum and admits she's in favour of a sovereign Quebec," according to a Canadian Press story carried in *La Presse* on 29 June.

The NDP leader, Audrey McLaughlin, showed a forbearance for separatism equal to that of the prime minister. According to a Canadian Press story of 27 June, "Federal NDP leader Audrey McLaughlin says she doesn't have a problem with Quebec's inevitable evolution toward sovereignty-association."

It seemed as though the surge toward sovereignty had become irresistible. On 5 July, *Le Journal de Montréal* published a Léger & Léger poll that showed 70 per cent of Quebecers saying they were "very favourable" or "rather favourable" to the proposition "Are you in favour of Quebec becoming a distinct country?"

The evolution of opinion in Quebec on the question of sovereignty was evidenced by various Gallup polls. Since 1968, Gallup had asked the same question: "There has been quite a bit of talk recently about the possibility of the province of Quebec separating from the rest of Canada, and becoming an independent country. Would you, yourself, be in favour of separation or opposed to it?" In 1979, the year before the Lévesque referendum, 18 per cent of Quebecers polled had been in favour of separation, but 70 per cent were opposed. In July, 1989, almost a year before Meech failed, the proportion in favour of separation had zoomed up to 34 per cent, with 55 per cent opposed. In July, 1990, 41 per cent said they favoured separation, with 46 per cent opposed.

On 2 August, Gallup published a poll taken 11–14 July in which it asked another perennial question: "Some people say that the differences among the various parts of Canada are now so great that they will never be solved, and that Confederation will break up. Do you agree with this, or do you think that these differences will be solved?" In Quebec, 51 per cent thought that Canada would break up; only 37 per cent thought that the differences would be solved.

"This [51 per cent] is the highest this statistic has registered in the 45 years since Gallup first posed this question," the polling firm said in an analysis that accompanied the poll. In 1980, when Quebec had been about to hold a referendum on sovereignty, only 31 per cent thought that the country would break up. The highest response previous to that of 1990 had been in 1969, when 47 per cent of Quebecers thought that the country would break up.

On the weekend of 11–12 August, the provincial Young Liberals held their annual meeting and adopted a resolution to declare "full political autonomy for Quebec" and then delegate certain powers to a "Quebec-Canada economic community." Some commentators said that they were really asking for "sovereignty-association," but in fact their resolution followed reasonably closely Robert Bourassa's perennial proposal of a Canada modelled on the European Community as Bourassa supposed it would soon become after further integration.

The logic put forward by the Young Liberals to demand political autonomy was identical to that invoked by Lucien Bouchard to demand sovereignty: the fact that French-speaking Quebecers were supposedly "different."

By its history, its culture and its institutions, Quebec constitutes a society that is different from those which surround it. The Québécois share aspirations and values which are theirs alone, and they want to give themselves the means to assert their specificity. It appears fundamental in the elaboration of a political structure to guarantee to the Québécois that the decisions which affect them fully respect their reality.[3]

The Young Liberals' proposal included a common parliament with limited power to raise taxes, a common currency, a common central bank, and a customs union with free circulation of people, goods, and capital within the Quebec-Canada economic space. But, aside from shared economic institutions, "Quebec would hold all powers over its territory, to make decisions according to the aspirations of the Québécois." The premier attended the last day of the Young Liberals' meeting, on 12 August, and in his speech he praised their proposal fulsomely as "innovative, realistic, lucid, and applicable."

There were some divergences. Michel Bissonnette, the president of the Young Liberals, maintained that the Young Liberals were the first group within the Liberal party ever to come out for "sovereignty." Bourassa said he preferred to consider the proposal one for "renewed federalism." In fact, much depended on what the Young Liberals meant by saying that Quebec should hold "all powers" over its territory. If it meant merely delegating powers to the common "supranational" parliament without losing the right to reclaim them, the Young Liberals were indeed proposing full sovereignty. If the delegation of powers was irrevocable, the proposed system could be called federal.

The day after the Young Liberals' meeting, the Bloc Québécois elected its first member under the Bloc banner. Gilles Duceppe, the son of actor Jean Duceppe, was returned in Laurier-Ste-Marie with an overwhelming majority. The riding had voted Liberal in 1988, but now the rebellious mood in Quebec swept aside the three traditional parties in favour of the sovereignist newcomer. Duceppe had received the support of the labour unions and of a constellation of performers, as well as of disaffected Liberals and the Parti Québécois. In Laurier-Ste-Marie, Lucien Bouchard's ambition of uniting all the population in a sacred union behind the quest for sovereignty seemed for the first time to be realized.

As Quebec nationalism was triumphantly on the march, in Ottawa the federal parties seemed impotent and divided. The Liberals, under Jean Chrétien, saw their public support in Quebec drop sharply. Chrétien was reviled by the Quebec news media and much of the population as the man of too many unpleasant yesterdays. The NDP, with its long-standing fondness for movements of national liberation, did not know whether to cheer or jeer the developments in Quebec. The lone NDP member of Parliament from Quebec, Phil Edmonston, told *Le Devoir* in September that he was in favour of sovereignty-association as the "strict minimum" to define the future relation between Quebec and Canada. If Canada could not accept that, he said, Quebec should hold a referendum on "pure and simple political independence." Edmonston had been appointed by Audrey McLaughlin as the NDP's associate caucus critic on the constitution and the critic on Quebec.

The focal point of Quebec's progression toward a new relationship with Canada in the fall of 1990 was its constitutional commission. The very terms of the bill setting up the commission implied that Quebecers were no longer bound by the constitution of Canada but could adopt unhindered whatever political and constitutional configuration they chose. The consent of other Canadians was not a consideration.

Bourassa himself, in his 4 September speech on the bill in the National Assembly, played on ambiguity. He spoke only about what he thought would be put in common between Quebec and Canada: a customs union, a common market, a monetary union, perhaps even a common environmental policy; and, of course, a parliament which could be given some powers to tax. The federal deficit made such taxing power imperative: "We can't resolve the problem of the federal deficit, which is considerable, which is enormous, just by saying that it can come under the powers of a parliament which is Canadian, community or supra-national, unless we give that parliament taxation powers to finance it."

Tortuous language for tortuous reasoning. Bourassa ignored the crucial questions of legitimacy to discuss process and arrangements. He spoke as the European negotiators for the Treaty of Rome might have spoken when they first planned a coal-and-steel community, and then an increasingly encompassing economic union. But, in fact, Bourassa was doing the direct opposite of what they had done. Under the pretense of supposedly giving powers to the "community or supra-national" parliament, Bourassa was really proposing to dismember the existing Parliament. Lise Bissonnette caught Bourassa's perverse reasoning in an editorial in *Le Devoir:* "Mr. Bourassa is not a Jean Monnet proposing to the warlike nations of Europe to unite. He is, rather, involved in a process of deconstructing Canada as we know it."

Why the double talk? No doubt to make his proposal for a European-style union seem positive rather than negative, constructive rather than destructive, and moderate rather than radical. The people of Quebec, generally moderate, might have taken alarm if they thought that their premier were about to reduce the government of Canada to a "superstructure."

But the substance of what Bourassa was proposing in September, 1990, was the same weakened federation or quasi-federation that he had recurrently proposed for years. The September, 1990, issue of the newsmagazine *L'Actualité* published for the first time the report of an interview which a student at Laval University had obtained from Bourassa when the then ex-premier was teaching there in 1979. In that interview, Bourassa had defined his vision of Quebec's constitutional future. He put it in the form of the question which, he said, the Parti Québécois government should ask Quebecers in the upcoming referendum: "Do you want to replace the existing constitutional order by two sovereign states associated in an economic union, which union would be responsible to a parliament elected by universal suffrage?" He added, "So you have a normal sovereignty which you negotiate, and you keep the federal bond for economic questions, rather like the Common Market in ten years."

The Commission on the Political and Constitutional Future of Quebec was launched, under two co-chairs: Marcel Bélanger, a banker and one-time adviser to René Lévesque for planning the take-over of the electric power companies in 1962, and Jean Campeau, a long-time provincial civil servant and former head of the Caisse de dépôt et placement. Bélanger was thought to be a federalist, though he himself would call that assumption into question during the commission's hearings. Campeau was known to be a sovereignist (he was to be a candidate for the Parti Québécois in the 1994 Quebec election).

The commission was given six months to make its recommendations. This was fast by the standard of other important commissions: the Tremblay Commission on the constitution was created by Maurice Duplessis in 1953 and submitted its report in 1956; the Parent Commission, which led to the reform of education was created in 1961, and its final report was produced in 1966. But the Bélanger-Campeau commission, with a much more ambitious mandate than these, was given a fraction of the time. There was a sense of urgency. Great decisions would have to be made soon.

In its make-up, the commission was divided almost equally between "federalists" and "separatists." But the political atmosphere in Quebec ensured that federalists were on the defensive, while separatists were on the attack. Separatists knew what they wanted: a referendum on Quebec's sovereignty to justify secession. Federalists also assumed that the "status quo"—the existing federation—was excluded as an option from the start. All the members seemed to accept the fundamental premise that the constitution of Canada was discredited, that Quebec had been badly treated, and that a radical proposal was expected of them.

One of the supposed federalists on the commission was Gil Rémillard, the minister of intergovernmental affairs, the man responsible for constitutional negotiations. Rémillard gave a long interview to *Le Devoir*, published on 24 September, in which he exposed his views of the future association between Quebec and Canada.[4]

According to Rémillard, using the amending formula established by the 1982 constitution was out of the question. It would require negotiations between Quebec and ten other governments, and that had not worked for the past thirty years. Instead, Quebec would negotiate with Ottawa on a basis of "nation to nation." But this did not mean that the federal government would hold a veto over Quebec's choices. On that question, Rémillard swept aside the constitution and put forward exactly the same view as Lucien Bouchard: "We need to have the political power to go and get what we need to go and get. And that political power is based on one and one only factor, that is the will of the people that has been clearly expressed. That is the basis of legitimacy."

For Rémillard, the failure of Meech Lake discredited the constitution of Canada and freed Quebec to make decisions on its future based solely on the will of the people of Quebec. On that, he said, the Liberal government found a consensus among the people of Quebec: "The Québécois tell us that that's it, we can no longer continue in the system which led to the failure of Meech Lake." In particular, the amending formula, requiring the consent of eleven governments, was now discredited. It had become "unacceptable," and Quebec would no longer consider itself bound by it. "Quebec can't continue as it has been doing since the beginning of the 1960s, asking constantly for constitutional reforms at the risk of being told no."

Rémillard even asserted that he was no longer interested in convincing English Canada to accept Quebec's proposals. "My point of reference is the Québécois people. The contract that we will propose to Ottawa is what the Québécois will have decided. We are not at the mercy of the rest of Canada, we are here as a nation, as a society able to assume its own responsibilities and to assert what we are." The association that he envisaged might or might not include a monetary union, Rémillard said. It might or might not involve a common army. And, he stated, there was no longer any notable difference between the positions of the Quebec Liberal Party and the Parti Québécois.

Meanwhile, with the Bélanger-Campeau commission soon to start its public hearings, Bourassa sent out ambigious and contradictory signals. At one moment he sounded like a federalist, then moments later he seemed intent on destroying the Canadian federation. Federalists and separatists could both believe that, deep down, he was one of them.

The premier was interviewed on Montreal radio station CKAC on 21 October. He told the radio audience that he was open to what he described as "very, very major changes," as long as they didn't affect the province's economy.[5] "I don't want to make any compromises whatsoever in that respect," Bourassa said. "I'm not prepared to take any risks." Recalling the ravages caused in Quebec by the 1982 recession, when tens of thousands of young Quebecers left the province to find jobs in Toronto, he said that he had then resolved that he would never do anything that could jeopardize the stability of Quebecers. He said that Quebecers should decide what they wanted their constitutional future to be before they approached the rest of the country to work out a deal. "Let's find the formula first and then we'll sell our point of view."

Prime Minister Mulroney's Conservative caucus was in a precarious state. Many of his Quebec MPs were ideological soulmates of Lucien Bouchard. The election of Gilles Duceppe confirmed what the members from Quebec could experience at first hand whenever they returned to their ridings: the people had swung away from the Conservatives and were backing the Bloc. Mulroney's freedom of manoeuvre was sharply curtailed: if he came out strongly with a federalist policy, he could lose dozens of his Quebec members to the Bloc. If he continued sounding the same Quebec nationalist line as he had previously, he could face a revolt of his other MPs. His Meech Lake policy had already cost him the defection of one veteran Tory MP, Pat Nowlan, who had held his seat in Nova Scotia since 1965. In 1990, Nowlan crossed the floor in disgust to sit as an independent.

The nationalist mood of the Quebec caucus was on public display as its members prepared to hold their annual meeting at Mont-Ste-Anne in early November. They had written several resolutions that were likely to embarrass the prime minister, including one affirming Quebec's right to self-determination.

Pierrette Venne—who was to defect to the Bloc the following year—and a number of other MPs had drawn up a constitutional proposal that would redraw the political configuration of Canada with a free hand: the country would have five largely autonomous regions instead of ten provinces and two territories. One of these regions, unsurprisingly, would be Quebec. And, lo and behold, Quebec would also include Labrador, which belongs to Newfoundland, but which Quebec has long claimed. The Atlantic provinces would be replaced by an Atlantic region, minus Labrador. Ontario would remain the same. The three Prairie provinces and the Northwest Territories would be amalgamated into a region. Finally, there would be one region made up of British Columbia and the Yukon.

Another set of constitutional alternatives had been prepared by Charles de Blois, a former television journalist and the MP for Montmorency. The alternatives ranged from the status quo to outright independence; but apparently most of the MPs working with de Blois preferred turning Canada into "the union of autonomous states which decide to put in common some of their jurisdictions. It's the Canada of the regions," as de Blois explained to Le Devoir. "There is a strong nationalist current running, the Bloc Québécois is breathing down our necks, our political future is at stake."

Mulroney chose to make public a proposal for action on national unity just a day before the Quebec caucus was to begin its two-day meeting, and five days before the Bélanger-Campeau commission was to begin its public hearings. In case anyone doubted that the prime minister was in charge, on 1 November, he announced the creation of the Citizens' Forum on Canada's Future, to be headed by Keith Spicer, chairman of the CRTC and former commissioner of official languages.

The Citizen's Forum turned out to be a national disunity debating society, a travelling open-line radio talk show, a coast-to-coast toll-free number that anyone could call, anytime, to sound off. "Every Canadian who wants to will be able to have a say," Mulroney promised as he unveiled this first riposte to the Bélanger-Campeau commission. After talking constitution, constitution, constitution for the past three years, Canadians were now invited to talk more constitution.

There were important differences between what had been announced in Ottawa and what was about to take place in Quebec. The public hearings in Quebec were to be an emanation of both major parties in the National Assembly aimed at a decisive plan of action for the future, while Mulroney was sending a flying wedge of sages to stimulate discussion. But what would the talk accomplish other than a national ventilation on a scale worthy of the *Guinness Book of Records*?

At the heart of Mulroney's initiative was a giant, yawning vacuum. No clamour of words, no illusion of decisive action, could conceal the fact that the Citizens' Forum was largely a giant suggestion box. Any Canadian could send in her or his suggestion to refashion the country. But even if the suggestions filled up the Peace Tower to the clock, to the bells, to the flagstaff, the sum of the suggestions could never amount to a policy. Fragmentation of the country had not occurred because grass-roots voices were not heard, nor would twenty-six million voices shouting together change the fundamentals. Only a political party in government could do that. And the prime minister's party and caucus were too divided to project a coherent vision to the country.

The prime minister played for time and for a cooling of passions. The Citizens' Forum gave the impression that he was doing something and directed public attention away from the fractured vision of the Tory MPs. It also gave him the opportunity to make yet again his speech denouncing Pierre Trudeau and the Liberals for patriating the constitution in 1981–82 over Quebec's objections. That was the source of all the country's unity problems. It was the right speech to hold his restive Quebec caucus together, though it hardly promoted the legitimacy of the federation in Quebec.

The Bélanger-Campeau commission began its public hearings on 6 November on a grave, even portentous note. Its members conveyed that they approached their task with immense seriousness: they saw themselves as laying the foundations for a different country. "Following the failure of the Meech Lake accord," said co-chairman Michel Bélanger, "the political and constitutional status of Quebec will be determined by Quebecers. Quebec will decide its own future."

Premier Bourassa made the same presumption. "For me, the failure of Meech had the effect of discrediting the process for constitutional change which existed in Canada. Henceforth we can no longer rely on the mechanism for constitutional negotiation and change which involves eleven governments."

For Jacques Parizeau, the only way to sweep away the constraints of the constitution of Canada was to begin by having Quebec officially declare itself a sovereign country:

Sovereignty is the only act with deep, fundamental political implications which the Québécois can execute without being subjected to the constitutional acceptance of the rest of Canada. . . . It is the only act that the Québécois can carry out themselves without asking for permission elsewhere.

All of those who spoke on that first day ruled out any alternative but an increase of powers for the Quebec government. The two co-chairmen said that the work of their commission "takes its place in the long historical process of Quebec's self-affirmation." They evidently saw historical continuity only in the "affirmation" of "Quebec." The remarkable affirmation of Quebecers in Ottawa, the restructuring of the entire federation to give more space to French, seemed to play no part in their understanding of "self-affirmation." Theirs was a perspective focused on the Quebec government, limited to the vision of the nationalist ideology that had prevailed in most of Quebec's political class on the provincial scene since 1962.

Two assumptions, both unfounded, were evident in the opening speeches of Bourassa, Rémillard, Parizeau, and Parizeau's chief whip, Jacques Brassard: all implied that "English Canada" had refused to recognize Quebec as a distinct society. And all suggested that the rest of Canada had rejected Quebec's "minimal," "modest" conditions for endorsing the 1982 constitution. These assumptions overlooked the fact that the leaders of English Canada had given Meech Lake overwhelming support, and that even its major opponents, notably Clyde Wells and Elijah Harper, also recognized Quebec as a distinct society. In fact, native leaders had objected to a restructuring of the constitution that left them out, and Wells had opposed Meech because it attacked his cherished principle of the equality of the provinces, and it would make exceedingly unlikely any future Senate that could be "elected, equal, and effective." There were many other good reasons for opposing Meech Lake, such as Trudeau's objection that the ambiguity of its distinct identity clause was likely to weaken the Charter of Rights and lead to a violation of freedom of expression in Quebec.

The most fundamental ambiguity voiced that day was to present Meech Lake as the sum of Quebec's constitutional demands, when it was merely the springboard to the "comprehensive reform" of the constitution that Rémillard had spoken of.

But none of these distinctions or realities were heard from the thirty-six members of the Bélanger-Campeau commission on that first day. They projected a scenario of Quebec's victimization as the starting point of their deliberations. It was convenient to portray an inflexible, unreasonable English Canada that denied the very reality of Quebec, because this justified declaring Quebec free of its constitutional obligations.

Rémillard made this very clear in his opening speech. "After thirty years of fruitless discussions, the Québécois now tell us very clearly: That's enough, let's make our decisions." And Rémillard evoked some of the major themes of the demands by different Quebec premiers over the years: "After *égalité ou indépendance, souveraineté culturelle, souveraineté-association* and the Meech Lake accord, we have, in a sense, come full circle, but enriched by the experience of the past thirty years."

It was true that there had been a tug-of-war over the powers of the Quebec government over the years. But what Rémillard chose not to recognize was that the tug-of-war had taken place primarily *within* Quebec, not between Quebec and English Canada. It was Trudeau, backed by a solid Liberal caucus, who had opposed and defeated Daniel Johnson's *égalité ou indépendance*. It was Trudeau who defeated Robert Bourassa's *souveraineté culturelle* and René Lévesque's *souveraineté-association*. And Trudeau defeated the ambitions of the Quebec premiers by appealing to the people of Quebec over the heads of the political class and gaining the support of the people.

Had the demands for *égalité ou indépendance* and all the other demands cited by Rémillard been truly supported by the people of Quebec, there would have been no impasse. But the ambitious constitutional postures of the provincial leaders were not supported by the people. When the Parti Québécois ran on its sovereignist platform in the elections of 1970 and 1973, it was roundly defeated by "Bob la Job" Bourassa, who in those years did not run as a nationalist. The PQ won in 1976, but only on a platform of *un bon gouvernement*. It was Bourassa who ran that year on a nationalist platform: he called a snap election to stop Trudeau from patriating the constitution and lost. On the single occasion when a Quebec premier put to the people of Quebec an explicitly nationalist question, that dealing with sovereignty-association, in the 1980 referendum, the people voted the proposal down.

In fact, the premiers of the other provinces had most often sided with Bourassa and Lévesque against Trudeau. The one crucial exception was in November, 1981, when the other premiers rallied at last to Trudeau, after long supporting Lévesque. Even then, they did so because Lévesque had broken ranks with them and they were forced to choose at last between the two, when Lévesque had indicated that he would make no compromise, while Trudeau agreed to meet many of their objections.

Even the case of the Meech Lake accord did not bear out the thesis of Quebec stymied by a rigid and closed-minded English Canada. Quebecers themselves were deeply divided over Meech Lake, as every poll showed. If Meech had been put to a referendum in Quebec, it well might have been voted down. And the Quebec government itself had an unacknowledged but heavy responsibility in the failure of Meech Lake. By invoking the "notwithstanding" clause to suspend freedom of speech and to ban English from signs, Bourassa had shot a torpedo into his own project.

But these considerations were far from the minds of the members of the Bélanger-Campeau commission on 6 November 1990, when, during a heavy snowstorm, the chief representatives of Quebec's political class began their public deliberations. They preferred to articulate solemnly the tribalist myth of Quebec's victimization. Reality must not spoil the poignant story, as they prepared to launch out on a brave new future.

Rémillard invoked the principle of legitimacy which he and other members of the commission thought could now replace that of the constitution: the self-determination of peoples. "The present world context places us as a people, as a nation, as a society, in the international movement of the simultaneous emergence of nationalisms and of essential links of association."

So did the Bélanger-Campeau commission set off on its epic mission. Now, it seemed almost certain that nothing could stop Quebec's political class from achieving at last the objective that it had pursued—with a few notable exceptions, such as Trudeau, Gérard Pelletier and Jean Marchand—since 1962: recognition for Quebec as a nation-state, an ethnic state, the real country of and for francophone Quebecers.

How could that mission possibly fail?

Notes

1.The *Gazette*, in a 24 June editorial, approved. "This is a thoroughly justifiable position for Quebec to take." *The Gazette* also echoed Bourassa's contention that Quebec had been outside the constitution of Canada since 1982. The editorial spoke of Meech as "an accord that would have brought Quebec willingly into the Canadian constitution."

2.In 1993, Bouchard would maintain that Premier Bourassa had encouraged him to form the separatist Bloc Québécois, and had shown him private polls that indicated the support he would receive from Quebecers.

3.Extracts from the document of the Liberal Youth Commission were published in *Le Devoir*, 7 Aug. 1990, p. 11.

4.Pierre O'Neill, "Le pas de plus de Gil Rémillard. L'autonomie politique dans un fédéralisme d'association," *Le Devoir*, 24 Sept. 1990, pp. B-1, B-2.

5.See Claude Arpin, "Sovereignty doesn't mean separation: Bourassa," *The Gazette*, Oct. 22, 1990, p. A 4.

CHAPTER SIXTEEN

A Passage to a New Country: The Allaire and Bélanger-Campeau Reports

In the first half of 1991, Quebec's political class reached at last the logical conclusion implicit in the main thrust of the Quiet Revolution, centred on a Quebec state, and Quebec nationalism reached its zenith. After three decades of building model countries on paper and in speeches, of building up the size and power of the Quebec government and its public sector, of waging ideological and political warfare against the English language and the federal government, after a century and a half of holding *les Anglais* responsible for the economic, social, and cultural problems of French Canadians, now, at last, in twin reports on Quebec's constitutional future, the Allaire report and the Bélanger-Campeau report,[1] the political class made the same recommendation: that the Quebec government should hold a referendum before the winter of 1992 on either a vastly decentralized federation or on outright sovereignty.

The Allaire and the Bélanger-Campeau reports both reached their key recommendation based on exactly the same assumption: that Quebecers could choose at will whatever constitutional future they fancied because the rest of Canada had failed to accede to the claims for more powers of Quebec governments since the Quiet Revolution. The supposed "impasse" in the federation gave Quebecers just cause to consider their obligations to the federation at an end, both reports implied. And both made much of Premier Bourassa's statement on the night Meech Lake failed: "Quebec is now, and always will be, a distinct society, free and able to assume its destiny and its development." They treated Bourassa's statement in the National Assembly as the equivalent of a formal and ratified declaration of independence from the constitution of Canada.

Both reports also maintained a characteristic ambivalence evident from the beginning of the Quiet Revolution: the political class wanted Quebec to be almost free from Canada, but without a decisive break. It wanted autonomy, but it also wanted to maintain such links with Canada that the transition would be painless and Quebec would keep the advantages of the federation, such as a free-trade zone, the Canadian dollar, and equalization payments, while enjoying full decision-making powers over Quebec's cultural, social, and economic life.

And both reports shared the assumption that, once Quebecers had expressed a certain choice by a referendum, the rest of Canada would fall obligingly into line, and either the semi-dismantlement of Canada or Quebec's independence could be achieved smoothly, without major inconvenience to anybody. It would be business as usual, with the only major difference being that Quebec would have achieved the long-sought dream of its political class: autonomy.

The Allaire report—named after the chairman of the Quebec Liberal Party's constitutional committee, lawyer Jean Allaire—was particularly interesting, because it was the proposal of the governing Liberals, supposedly the federalist alternative to the separatist Parti Québécois. And yet, the political vision advanced in the report, and adopted with minor changes at the Liberal Party's 1991 general convention, was essentially the same as the vision that had been formulated over the years by the Péquistes. As Lise Bissonnette observed when the report was first made public, "it espouses the fundamental and constant analysis of the Parti Québécois."[2]

The "federalist" alternative proposed in the Allaire report involved a truly radical restructuring of the federation. Almost all powers would be vested in the Quebec government, though a few would also be shared. The only exclusive powers that would remain with the central government would be those dealing with defence and territorial security, customs and tariffs, currency and the national debt, and equalization payments to the poorer provinces, including Quebec. Even if Canada accepted this drastic dismantling of the federal state, the arrangement would not necessarily last. Quebec would reserve the right to withdraw from the federation at any time; the only requirement would be that it give notice.

The Allaire report produced a shock in the rest of Canada. Jeffrey Simpson, columnist for the *Globe and Mail,* drew a dismal conclusion after reading it:

The separation of Quebec from Canada is just a matter of time, following the release of new constitutional proposals from the supposedly federalist Liberal Party of Quebec.

The proposals are dead on arrival outside Quebec. They would so emasculate the federal government, so radically dismember Canada that Canadians would be suckers or idiots even to contemplate a deal. Better separation, with all the anguish and bitterness it would bring, than the laughing stock of a country contemplated in this report.

Within Quebec, as well, commentators found the Allaire report disquieting, a strange basis on which to propose a new, scaled down central government.

269

"Nothing in the report explains why this complex structure, which would force change on the rest of Canada as well as Quebec, is justified," Lise Bissonnette wrote in *Le Devoir*.

And yet, the Allaire report was consistent with the thinking that had been developed within the Quebec Liberal Party over the years, as the premier argued in an interview with *La Presse* on 2 February 1991, under Denis Lessard's byline.

Mr. Bourassa insisted on the fact that the report of the Allaire committee is in direct continuity with the constitutional positions that he had advanced over more than twenty years. Moreover, some of the conclusions of the committee can be found in Claude Ryan's Beige Paper, and in the report of Paul Gérin-Lajoie who, as far back as 1966, also proposed a complete reform of the constitution.

All that was missing at that time was the proposal for a deadline, the ultimatum of the referendum. . . . "If we do not set a compelling time limit, the status quo will continue. If it weren't for the referendum that it put forward, no one today would be talking about the Allaire report. People would say, 'Another report . . .' and they would turn to CNN," Mr. Bourassa stated.

The premier himself certainly could have no complaint with the general thrust of the Allaire report. He had voted in favour of Gérin-Lajoie's proposals when the Liberal caucus adopted them in 1968 as party policy. But Bourassa himself, unlike Gérin-Lajoie, had never before been so imprudent as to spell out the shopping list of powers that he demanded for Quebec, or to set a specific timetable, or to threaten separation explicitly if his demands were not met by the deadline.

Did Bourassa really believe, now, in the full list put forward by the Allaire report, which he had signed? "What we are asking for corresponds to the interests of Quebec," Bourassa told Lessard. And, while he seemed open to some compromises, he stood by the general outline of powers as proposed by Allaire. "The essence of what we will have decided will have to be accepted" by the rest of Canada for there to be an agreement. And he offered as the justification for such an ultimatum the fact that Quebec governments had not got what they wanted by way of constitutional change since the Quiet Revolution:

"After twenty-five years of sterile discussion, Quebec has no other choice but to propose a new pact to the rest of the country," and the process will lead either to a more efficient central government, or to a Quebec that is "sovereign in a confederal structure," that is, associated politically and economically with the rest of Canada.

Gil Rémillard also defended the Allaire proposals in a speech in Quebec City on 14 February. He suggested that Allaire's proposal to settle Quebec's consti- tutional status was brought on by the failure of previous negotiations: "It is not a threat or an ultimatum, but the acknowledgment that thirty years of talks have failed."[3]

Rémillard also seemed to suggest that Quebec was proceeding with a referendum as an alternative to the "humiliation" encountered in negotiations with English speaking Canada. "It takes two to tango . . . but you don't dance the tango on your knees and, as Premier Bourassa has said, Quebec will not go down on its knees to accept federalism. We are not beggars."

In early March, over the objections of Claude Ryan and Clifford Lincoln, the convention of the Quebec Liberal Party adopted the Allaire report, slightly amended. A very weak federation or Quebec's sovereignty thus became the only official policy alternatives put forward by the Quebec government.

Though it was to be remembered chiefly through the name of the chairman of the committee that produced it, the Allaire report was not a one-man effort, nor was it a rogue report that betrayed the thinking of the party that had produced and adopted it. On the contrary, the report came out after a year of the most thorough consultation in the history of the Liberal Party. Included on the committee that produced it were some of the party's most seasoned and respected members, such as former ministers Fernand Lalonde and Thérèse Lavoie-Roux; the then president of the party, Jean-Pierre Roy; its director-general, Pierre Anctil; Gil Rémillard's own executive assistant, Suzanne Lévesque; and, not least, Robert Bourassa himself.[4]

The fundamental recommendation, coming after a minute description of all the new powers that Quebec demanded, left no ambiguity about the decisiveness of the alternatives that were to be put to the people of Quebec. There was no room for anything that resembled the existing Canadian federation: "Should the rest of Canada accept the platform proposed above, the Quebec Liberal Party proposes that the referendum deal with the ratification of the new Quebec-Canada pact. Should the rest of Canada reject the platform, the people of Quebec will be asked to decide whether or not Quebec should become a sovereign state."[5]

It was a gauntlet thrown in the face of the rest of Canada. As arresting as the drastic restructuring, which would have left Canada a skeletal state, was the hostile, truculent tone and style of the report. "Canada in its present form has become scarcely governable," pronounced the report, which described a country supposedly in a chronic state of "crisis" and conflict. "The least disagreement turns into a crisis. . . . It becomes clearer and clearer that the Canadian federation rests more on a dynamic of conflict than consensus, on controversy rather than harmony."

This sounded like the prelude to a petition for divorce rather than the foreword to a proposal for a new form of national marriage.

The relationship between Quebec and the rest of Canada within the present political and constitutional regime is at a dead end. The opposition of political visions, of perceptions, and of national identities has become such that the accommodation of the differences within the framework of the present arrangements could henceforth be impossible.

Quebecers had become free of their legal, moral, and political obligations to Canada, the country which they had helped found. And why? Because federalism had failed. Allaire gave the nationalist version of the 1980 referendum: "This state of affairs culminated in the promise made by the federal government at the time of the referendum for a federalism renewed according to the aspirations of Quebec. That commitment was not kept."[6]

Allaire repeated the familiar charge that Pierre Trudeau's promise of change meant change as the nationalists defined it rather than as he had always defined it. In this light, the 1982 patriation of the constitution was illegitimate, and, "in a way, the Meech Lake accord recognized the illegitimacy of a constitution that failed to include Quebec." But the rest of Canada turned Meech Lake down. "By refusing to allow the Province of Quebec to be different, [Canada] refused in fact to the people of Quebec the right to be different."

And yet, from 1867, Canada was created as a federation rather than a unitary state precisely in recognition of Quebec's difference, which was to be protected by the constitution. It was given concrete form by the right to have a provincial government, to pass different laws, to have a different system of education and property rights. That difference was central to the course of Canadian history after 1867. And Quebec's recognized right to be different was expanded rather than contracted by "co-operative federalism" after 1960. Within the structures of the federation, Quebec's right and ability to be different was very, very evident. Why did Quebec require new confessions in the constitution of its right to be different? That was the real question, and it never received an answer. For Quebec's political class, the "difference" was apparently such a matter of consensus that to demonstrate a further need for it was redundant.

Moreover, the charge that Canada had refused to the people of Quebec the right to be different, presented as so gross an enormity that it cancelled the legitimacy of the federation, overlooked one incongruous fact. "Canada," insofar as it rejected the distinct society clause of Meech Lake, was merely being consistent with the position of Pierre Trudeau, a position that the people of Quebec had endorsed in five federal elections. How could the constitutional posture most explicitly endorsed by the people of Quebec from 1968 to 1980 suddenly become, in 1990 or 1991, an affront to Quebec so terrible that it relieved Quebecers from their constitution obligation to the federation? It was, after all, Quebecers, not the majority of other Canadians, who had ensured that Trudeau would govern Canada for most of those years. Was the legitimacy of the country so volatile that it changed its sign and its direction with a change of prime minister?

In the fundamentalist view projected by the Allaire report, everything that Ottawa did over the years to co-ordinate social and cultural policies, to act like a national government, was an unwarranted intrusion into Quebec's jurisdiction.

The report simply brushed aside a whole series of court decisions that confirmed the constitutionality of the federal actions impugned by Allaire. When the Bélanger-Campeau commission published its own report in March of 1991, it offered fundamentally the same analysis of Quebec's situation as had the Allaire report, even if it went about it somewhat differently. The latter had described the terrible history of Confederation, then followed up with a glowing description of Quebec since the Quiet Revolution. The former began with the glowing description of Quebec since the Quiet Revolution, then moved on to find that the federation had failed Quebec. The secretary of the commission, who directed its work under the instructions of the two co-presidents, was Henri-Paul Rousseau, a committed separatist who had been president of the *Économistes pour le Oui* during the 1980 referendum campaign.

From the 1960s, the report stated, "Quebec made the adjustments necessary for the emergence of a modern, complete society, one that was open to the world."[7] The Bélanger-Campeau commission's version of history, like Allaire's, was decidedly selective. The fact is that Quebec already enjoyed well before 1960 the advantages of a modern society, including a high standard of living. The transformation that was pushed through after 1960 had as its primary objective to modernize the institutions of French Quebec, the most central of which had resisted or stood outside the modernization of the economy and of the education system achieved mostly by English-speaking people. By pretending that Quebec's modernization had begun in 1960, the Bélanger-Campeau commission was able to cancel the debt that all Quebecers owed to Canada, and it equated modernization with all the nationalistic manifestations which developed after 1960, including the restrictions placed on English. By definition, these were all steps into the future. The commission's entire review of the previous thirty years, in fact, was entirely biased, self-congratulatory, and uncritical. But it was concordant with the tribalist perspective which had come to dominate political analysis in Quebec.

The chapter of the Bélanger-Campeau report dealing with the "impasse" in the federation was similarly uncritical. It stated as a fact that the federation served Quebec badly, when that was at best a postulate of Quebec's political class. By begging the question, the commission spared itself having to demonstrate that which, precisely, needed demonstrating if the case was to be made for a fatal "impasse": that Quebec fared badly within the federation. It was enough to say that "Quebec" needed more powers, QED.

The major reforms undertaken in Quebec during the 1960s demonstrated how essential it was to reallocate the federal and provincial governments' jurisdictions, which had been made problematic as the result of the evolution of the federal regime, and their respective financial resources. Quebec wanted to preserve and reestablish its autonomy in its exclusive spheres of jurisdiction, and in some sectors obtain a larger measure of autonomy to ensure the full development of Quebec society. In this way it asserted itself as a distinct society and claimed the recognition of a special status, special aspirations, and special needs.[8]

The glowing description of Quebec's "modernization" during the 1960s was presumed to have "demonstrated" the need for more powers. Logically, the Bélanger-Campeau commission's description of the Quiet Revolution could more persuasively have led to the opposite conclusion: that Quebec had been able to carry out far-reaching changes within the existing constitution, and so the need to refashion the constitution was not evident. But, without even the slightest attempt to show why new powers were required, the report asserted the need by a circular reasoning. Quebec had become increasingly different from what it had been, and so it needed special constitutional status, different powers. With that postulate in place, the Bélanger-Campeau commission then followed the familiar nationalist paths to demonstrate that constitutional conferences from 1968 on "did not produce any results that corresponded to the requests of Quebec."[9]

Bélanger-Campeau, like Allaire, recalled Trudeau's promise in the 1980 referendum campaign, a promise supposedly broken. And then followed the familiar argument that the 1982 patriation had illegitimately diminished Quebec's control over the language of education, and had left Quebec without a veto over further constitutional change.

Bélanger-Campeau's nationalist version of history also included a less frequently formulated complaint: that the 1982 constitution recognized the "multicultural heritage" of Canadians. The commission saw in this another betrayal. Quebec was thereby subjected to "a constitutional vision that did not necessarily reflect its reality within the Canadian whole: Canada was defined as a multicultural society, without constitutional recognition of the principle of 'Canadian duality' and the specificity of Quebec."[10]

This argument was manifestly absurd: it was simply untrue that the recognition of the "multicultural heritage" of Canadians placed the French language on the same footing as any other language, as the report claimed: "In the eyes of several people, the French language and French cultural origins are among the many languages and cultures of origin which form the multicultural heritage of Canada and are their equal: the French language and French cultural origins should not, therefore, require special recognition or guarantees in the constitution of Canada."[11]

To make this argument showed either rank demagogy or abysmal ignorance. The French language is given constitutional protection in the 1982 constitution that is equal to that of English, and given a national status that only these two languages hold. To compare the status of French in the constitution with that of Italian or German or Urdu is simply to ignore the iron-clad protection contained for French in the Charter of Rights as an official language. Even the right to instruction in English in Quebec is not as broad in the 1982 constitution as the right to instruction in French in the rest of Canada.[12]

Bélanger-Campeau also served up the nationalist version of history in maintaining that the 1982 constitution was "adopted despite the opposition of the province that contains nearly 90 per cent of Canadian francophones, and that represents more than a quarter of the population." In its perspective, the opposition of the National Assembly to the 1982 constitution meant that "the province" was opposed, even though almost all its federal MPs assented, and there was no evidence that the people of Quebec were opposed. And so, "although, as a matter of law, the 1982 act still applies to Quebec, it has remained bereft of political legitimacy, because it never received the full and free acceptance of Quebec."[13]

The presentation of the constitutional "impasse" between Quebec and the rest of Canada as argued by the Bélanger-Campeau commission did not stand up to serious scrutiny. It repeated widely held nationalist myths, but made no attempt at genuine analysis or critical scrutiny. It maintained, for instance, that there was widespread opposition to the Meech Lake accord in the rest of Canada—but not in Quebec. And so it was the rest of Canada that frustrated *Quebec*'s desires. But that assumption flies in the face of the considerable opposition to Meech Lake that had been expressed within Quebec as well, for instance by the Parti Québécois, the New Democratic Party, the labour and farmers' federations, the patriotic societies, and most of those who came as witnesses before the National Assembly in the spring of 1987 (see chapter fourteen).

From its analysis, Bélanger-Campeau drew two conclusions: that a consensus within Quebec held the status quo as unacceptable and untenable; and that two options and only two options remained: radical decentralization or sovereignty. To break out of the status quo and achieve one or the other of the two options, the commission proposed that a referendum be held on sovereignty. It did not recommend a referendum on radical decentralization, but implied, if one read between the lines, that the referendum could be held on a proposal for radical decentralization if a sufficiently interesting and binding "offer" come from the rest of Canada. A committee of the National Assembly was to be set up to receive and evaluate such "offers." Presumably, if these offers were close enough to the Quebec government's demands, they could be submitted to the people as a last chance given to federalism for its renewal.

The recommendations of both Allaire and Bélanger-Campeau invited Quebec and all of Canada to set off on an ambitious, almost reckless adventure to design the structures of a new country—or two new countries—in just a few months, then carry out the design within a year or two. They served an ultimatum to the rest of Canada: Give us what we demand, or we are gone. The adventure was of doubtful legality, economically risky, politically unpredictable. Would the people of Quebec go along with so daring an enterprise, one that broke sharply with a

150-year tradition of gradualism and moderation? Would Quebecers repudiate the Canada that their ancestors had so largely contributed to create and define? The recommendations of the two committees would have seemed absurd only five years earlier. But nationalism was ascendant in Quebec in early 1991, as it had been increasingly over the previous two years. A CROP public-opinion poll published in the January, 1991, issue of *L'Actualité* showed 64 per cent of the sample of Quebecers saying they were "very favourable" or "rather favourable" to Quebec's sovereignty; among French-speaking Quebecers, 67 per cent said they were in favour of sovereignty, with only 26 per cent not in favour. The support in public opinion for a radical alternative to federalism was the new factor that had not existed during the earlier years when Robert Bourassa, from 1970 to 1976, was demanding more powers, or when René Lévesque was proposing sovereignty-association in 1980. But now, with a population radicalized during Brian Mulroney's tenure as prime minister, anything seemed possible.

The *L'Actualité* poll also showed that Quebecers were now ready to act unilaterally on their recently acquired sovereignist inclinations. The respondents were asked, "Do you think it is possible to reach an agreement with the rest of Canada, or will Quebec have to decide its political future unilaterally?" Only 39 per cent thought an agreement with the rest of Canada was possible; an astounding 54 per cent agreed that Quebec would have to act unilaterally.

Some Quebecers wanted a radically decentralized federation. Others wanted an independent Quebec. But what seemed to unite the political class and much of the population following the failure of Meech Lake was the conviction that the ordinary arts of negotiation could not achieve either objective. Only a forceful fait accompli could bring about either, as *L'Actualité* observed. "All the parties— the Parti Québécois, obviously, and the Bloc Québécois, but also the leaders of the Liberal Party—have reached the conclusion that, to force the achievement of a new confederal pact, they will have to go first by way of sovereignty."

So what the political class proposed, led by both Bourassa and Parizeau, was a referendum that would ensure that Canada would no longer be the country of Quebecers. Only Quebec would be their country, possibly joined to Canada by a weak "superstructure," as Bourassa had earlier called it. At the very least, it seemed that the outcome must be the realization of Bourassa's 1975 dream of Quebec as "a French state in a Canadian common market." What counterforce, either within Quebec society in the rest of Canada, could now stand against the resolve of Quebec's political class to achieve the objective of the Quiet Revolution?

And yet, from the perspective of the rest of Canada, the proposal of either Allaire or Bélanger-Campeau for a radically renewed federalism was absurd. Both demanded that Canada practically dismantle itself, in the hope that the Liberal government would find the "offer" sufficiently attractive to call off its referendum on sovereignty. But what would be the point of trying to comply with such an ultimatum? The Liberal government could lose power two years later to the Parti Québécois, which would find no offer short of sovereignty acceptable. And even a later Liberal government might decide to invoke the clause giving Quebec the right to secede after giving notice. So, after dismantling itself to a skeleton, the federation might find just a few years later that its self-sacrifice had not been enough, it would have to start all over again. Mature countries do not undertake to dismantle themselves on the basis of such frivolous arguments or in the fragile hope of being granted a speculative stay of execution.

On 26 March, the day after the Bélanger-Campeau commission adopted the proposal for a referendum on sovereignty, Prime Minister Mulroney reacted in the Commons by going on the attack. He dismissed the importance of the commission that had been set up with such solemnity to chart Quebec's future course. He clutched at the words of Gil Rémillard, who had noted that, if a sufficiently attractive offer came from the rest of Canada, the referendum on sovereignty might be postponed. Then, Mulroney recalled, as he did so often, that he had negotiated the Meech Lake accord. All would have been well had Meech Lake passed, for it "was intended to reintegrate Quebec in the constitutional fold." And he shouted an attack on Jean Chrétien, who was absent from the Commons recuperating from surgery: "The leader of the Liberal Party turned his back on Canada."

A public-opinion poll taken in late January 1991 also showed little readiness in the rest of Canada to accommodate the kinds of changes proposed by Allaire and Bélanger-Campeau. CROP put the following question to Canadians outside Quebec: "Imagine that Quebec demands additional powers and a reform of the federation, otherwise it will become independent in two years' time. Should Canada negotiate to satisfy Quebec's demands?" In reply, 26 per cent were in favour of such negotiations to satisfy Quebec, while 10 per cent did not give an opinion; a massive 65 per cent said they were opposed.[14] In reply to other questions, the respondents gave the same refusal to the kind of constitutional status that Quebec's political class was demanding. A total of 71 per cent said they were against decentralization, 75 per cent were against additional powers for Quebec, and only 34 per cent agreed that Quebec's demands should be negotiated bilaterally between Quebec and the federal government; 55 per cent insisted that all first ministers should be involved.

So the prospects of an accommodation to resolve the gathering confrontation seemed slight. All the strong leadership was on the nationalist side. The federalists were weak and divided; they seemed to have lost all conviction, all vision. A referendum in Quebec on sovereignty seemed inevitable. This time, a referendum would be quite unlike that of 1980, when Quebecers fought Quebecers over sovereignty-association. This time, both major Quebec parties and all but a few figures from the past were determined to push through a decisive change. There seemed to be no way out of the mousetrap carefully contrived by official Quebec.

Many Canadians began to think what had seemed impossible: that they would have to envisage a future without Quebec. And, in Quebec, it seemed as though Menaud's dream of driving out *les Anglais* was about to be realized.

In May, 1991, Premier Bourassa introduced Bill 150 in the National Assembly to implement the recommendations of the Bélanger-Campeau commission. One would expect such a momentous bill to spell out in legal terms every aspect of the referendum which, supposedly, could lead to Quebec's secession from Canada. But the bill said almost nothing about the referendum on sovereignty, devoting just two short sentences to the heart of the matter: "The government of Quebec will hold a referendum on Quebec's sovereignty between 8 June and 22 June 1992, or between 12 October and 26 October 1992. The results of the referendum will have the effect, if it is favourable to sovereignty, to propose that Quebec acquire the status of a sovereign state exactly one year from the date that it is held."

Both sentences dealt only with timing. But what about substance? Under what rules would the referendum be held? What question would be put? How would the results be interpreted? Would a 50 per cent plus one vote be deemed a mandate for sovereignty, or would a higher standard be required for so portentous a decision? And what would be the consequence of the vote in legal terms?

There was no answer to these fundamental questions, no real explanation as to what the referendum would mean. To explain would have meant to make plain that the referendum had no legal consequence. If it had claimed otherwise, the bill could have been tested in court and declared *ultra vires*.

And so the pretense of an explanation was contorted, suggestive, imprecise. It did not say that Quebec would acquire the status of a sovereign state. It did not say that the National Assembly would declare Quebec a sovereign state. Those would have been statements of real legal repercussions. Instead, it said that the *result* of the referendum would *propose* that Quebec acquire sovereignty. How can results propose? Do they speak? Do they rise in an assembly and make a motion?

While the two sentences on the referendum occupied just six lines, they were preceded by a preamble that took up fifty-six lines. The preamble was really political rhetoric with two objectives. The first was to affirm the assumption that the failure of Meech Lake was such a cataclysmic event that it relieved Quebec of its obligations under the constitution of Canada. The other objective was to soothe various constituencies and assure them that they had nothing to worry about, no matter what the future. To nationalists, the preamble offered another incantation—altogether irrelevant to the referendum bill—that Quebecers wanted to make French "the language of the state and of the law, as well as the normal and habitual language of work, education, communications, trade and business." But, in case non-francophones took fright at the assertion of French hegemony in all areas of life, the preamble also made a bow to English-speaking Quebecers, to natives and "cultural communities," as well as to francophones outside Quebec. None of them need worry; their rights would be assured.

The body of the bill mostly was taken up with describing two committees of the National Assembly that would be struck: one to explore all facets of Quebec's accession to sovereignty, the other to study offers from the government of Canada for "a new partnership of a constitutional nature." Just to describe the membership of the committees took up thirty-five lines—six times as much space as the section on the referendum. Now, the bill was getting down to real politics.

And that was the problem with the bill: it was fundamentally dishonest. It pretended to give a power to a referendum that such a referendum could not have. And it pretended to justify extreme measures by invoking a state of illegitimacy and unconstitutionality which simply did not exist. It was a collective masquerade directed equally at the rest of Canada and at Quebecers themselves. But it could have serious consequences because most Quebecers didn't know that their political leaders were bluffing. Many were apt to take these political games seriously, with unpredictable effects.

The bill was passed in June, almost on the first anniversary of the death of Meech lake. It was passed, again, amid ambiguity. The Liberals voted for a referendum on sovereignty, which they presumably really opposed. The Parti Québécois voted against a referendum on sovereignty, which they presumably really favoured, invoking the fact that the bill made possible a referendum on a new partnership with Canada as a justification to oppose it.[15]

On 24 June, St-Jean-Baptiste Day, there was not quite the same outpouring of anti-federal sentiment that had characterized the celebration a year earlier. In 1991, the theme of the parade through the streets of Montreal and of the evening concert was, "We are giants, giants, giants. We must stand tall, tall, tall."

Notes

1. The Allaire report was titled *A Quebec Free to Choose*. The page that followed the title page was entirely taken up with one quotation, attributed to Robert Bourassa: "Quebec is now, and always will be, a distinct society, free and able to assume its destiny and its development." The Bélanger-Campeau report, published in March, 1991, was titled *Rapport de la commission sur l'avenir politique et constitutionnel du Québec*. It quoted the 1990 bill that had set it up: "Whereas Quebecers are free to undertake their own destiny, to determine their political status and to ensure their economic, social, and cultural development . . . Whereas it is necessary to redefine the political and constitutional status of Quebec . . ."
2. *Le Devoir*, 1 Feb. 1991.
3. Rhéal Séguin, "Quebec will talk, minister asserts," *Globe and Mail*, 15 Feb. 1991, p. 1.
4. The committee also included William Cosgrove, the hapless Liberal candidate in Westmount in the 1989 election, who was defeated by the Equality Party's Richard Holden.
5. *A Quebec Free To Choose. Report of the Constitutional Committee of the Quebec Liberal Party for Submission to the 25th Convention*. January 28, 1991, p. 46.
6. Ibid., p. 12.
7. Commission sur l'avenir politique et constitutionnel du Québec, *Rapport*, March 1991, p. 18.
8. Ibid., p. 31.

9.Ibid., p. 32.
10.Ibid., p. 33.
11.Ibid., p. 39.
12.Parents who have received their schooling in French anywhere in the world can claim French schooling for their children anywhere in Canada. But, in Quebec, only those who have received schooling in English somewhere in Canada can claim access to English schooling.
13.Commission, *Rapport*, p. 35.
14.*L'Actualité*, 15 Mar. 1991, p. 24.
15.Journalist Jean-François Lisée has written a book that takes Robert Bourassa to task for fooling the people of Quebec by pretending to back the decentralization-or-sovereignty alternatives, when in fact at the same time he was assuring Prime Minister Mulroney and various premiers that he would never hold a referendum on sovereignty. In fact, Bourassa misled just about everyone throughout his career. He would not, in fact, hold a referendum on sovereignty in 1992. But no one can be certain that he would not have done so if the public-opinion polls had shown the same enthusiasm for sovereignty in August of 1992 that they had shown in 1990 and the first half of 1991. See Jean-François Lisée, *Le tricheur. Robert Bourassa et les Québécois 1990-1991* (Montreal: Boréal, 1994).

CHAPTER SEVENTEEN

The Great Showdown: Preparing by Marking Time

When Keith Spicer's Citizens' Forum on Canada's Future reported, in June of 1991, its most pointed finding was that the country was furious at Brian Mulroney. In effect, Spicer invited the prime minister to help the country recover by resigning. Mulroney chose not to take that advice, which had cost almost $25 million.

The report as a whole found a widespread opposition to any special concessions for Quebec. However, the commissioners, having decided that there was great deal of ignorance in the country about constitutional realities, proceeded to ignore the expressed wishes of the vast number of people whom they had heard, directly or through a toll-free number. They recommended exactly what the many citizens consulted had opposed: special status for Quebec.

The Spicer commission soon sank with scarcely a trace. A month later, who could remember what it had had to say?

On 2 December 1990, Mulroney announced a second initiative in his attempt to regain control of the national agenda. At a fund-raising dinner in Montreal, before a partisan audience who had paid $500 a plate for the privilege of hearing him, Mulroney unveiled his plan for "a special joint committee of the House of Commons and the Senate to examine in detail various alternatives to the current process for amending the constitution."

Premier Bourassa and Gil Rémillard had blamed the amending formula in part for the failure of Meech Lake. So now Mulroney proposed to find a better amending formula. A joint all-party committee of the House and Senate, which would be chaired by a constitutional expert, Senator Gérald Beaudoin, and Alberta MP Jim Edwards, would hold hearings and propose a new formula for amending the constitution.

In the existing circumstances of danger to the unity of the country, it was important to get the support of all the political parties and of the population. But Mulroney not only made his announcement before a partisan gathering, he seized the occasion to revile the federal Liberals and Jean Chrétien. "We know that those who lulled Quebecers in 1980 by promising them a renewed federalism, only to exclude them from the constitution, will not persuade us now that they

281

genuinely want to modernize federalism," he told his followers. "We remember only too well Mr. Chrétien congratulating Clyde Wells—'Thanks, Clyde, for all your good work'—to believe for a moment that the party leader who rejected five modest conditions can bring about the important constitutional changes that are needed. Through their duplicity, they have lost all moral authority to speak to Quebecers about renewing federalism. Jean Chrétien's Liberals are reaping what they sowed in Quebec and Quebecers will never forgive them their double-dealing."

The next day, in the Commons, Mulroney claimed that Chrétien was responsible for everything happening in Quebec because he opposed the Meech Lake accord. That was why Mulroney now had to appoint the Spicer commission and the Beaudoin-Edwards committee.

The question is, why are they required? On the ninth of June, when we signed the Meech Lake accord in the conference centre, Premier Bourassa said that, in 1981, with the 1981 constitution, Quebecers felt that they were part of a legal constitution, but with the conclusion of the Meech Lake accord, Quebecers for the first time felt they were part of a real constitution and a real country. . . . This was dashed a few days later because some people believed the statement by Mr. Chrétien that Meech Lake could be rejected without consequences, and the fact that his short-sighted partisanship prevented him from endorsing Meech Lake then means that we as Canadians have to work hard now to maintain the unity of Canada that he placed in jeopardy.

In fact, the constitutional amending formula, adopted when the constitution was patriated in 1982, had worked very well in its first big test. A constitutional amendment, unlike ordinary law, is intended to be difficult to pass and to require a large consensus in the land. Such a consensus did not exist around Meech Lake.

Rather than deal with the substance of the constitution and a vision of the country, Mulroney focused all attention on process. And he continued his habit of denouncing the legitimacy of the constitution in Quebec. In the Commons, he said, in French, "Many Quebecers find it hard to understand that the constitution, patriated ten years ago, the very document that should have expressed their will to fulfil themselves within Canada, consecrates, instead, their absence from the Canadian constitutional family."

A fate similar to that of the Spicer commission awaited this second initiative taken by Mulroney to ward off the threatened break-up of the federation. Soon after it presented its report, on 20 June 1991, Alberta shot down the committee's main proposal, which would have given a veto to each of four regions of Canada.[1] In the name of equality of the provinces, Alberta rejected a formula that would give a veto to Quebec and Ontario but to none of the other provinces individually. And, to change the amending formula, all the provinces would have to be unanimous.

When the Quebec Liberal Party's Allaire report was made public at the end of January, 1991, it seemed to confirm Premier Bourassa's radical intentions. Mulroney set off on a speaking tour to try to counter the surge toward secession and evoke the outline of a federalist alternative.

Before the Canadian and Empire clubs in Toronto, on 12 February, Mulroney made a hand-on-the-heart profession of federalist faith. "My country is Canada. I intend to strengthen it and I intend to keep it." And he warned the utopian thinkers in Quebec, "Let me be clear: Canada is not up for grabs. Either you have a country, or you don't. You can't have it both ways."

He enunciated "six basic principles" that he said constituted his "bottom lines" in the coming negotiations aimed at "restructuring Canada."[2] The Toronto speech, while short on specifics, did send a warning shot across the country: Brian Mulroney would defend the federal system. The Allaire report, which would have left a skeletal federal government, was a non-starter. Still, Mulroney was open to negotiations to decentralize the federation and remove overlapping jurisdictions.

It was in Quebec City the next day that Mulroney gave his real tub-thumping speech. "Today I say frankly to Quebecers: beware the merchants of illusion, those who tell you that they can destroy a great country and then rebuild it easily, who say that they are able, alone, to control the course of history." He did not mention the Allaire report, but obviously he had Allaire very much on his mind, as well as the sovereignists like those in the Bloc Québécois who thought they could romp their way to secession. "My country is Canada. I intend to strengthen it and I intend to keep it."

He showed that day that he could plead eloquently and powerfully in favour of a good cause. It was, at last, the prime minister of Canada who was pleading the cause of Canada in Quebec rather than running Canada down as he had made a practice of doing. Without getting into specifics, he signalled that he was open to significant change: "I intend to propose to Canadians a concept of a country that could lead to a Canada that has been reconstituted, proud of its diversity and strong in its unity."

He told Quebecers what a privilege it was to be part of Canada. And what did he talk about to defend the federation? French power, just as Trudeau used to. He pointed out how central Quebec has been to the federation: "Since the creation of the Canadian federation 123 years ago, Quebecers occupied the post of prime minister of Canada for 47 years. Since Canadians have held the position of governor-general, namely since 1952, Quebecers were named to be head of state for more than half the period."

During the 1972 federal election campaign, a Liberal commercial had showed Pierre Trudeau seated at a table with some of his ministers from Quebec, talking about the power being exercised by French-speaking Quebecers in the federal government. Mulroney, in Quebec City, sounded exactly the same theme.

Starting with the Supreme Court of Canada, where the chief justice is a Quebecer, we find Quebecers, for instance, as clerk of the Privy Council, which is the most important responsibility in the Canadian public service, and among the most influential deputy ministers, as president of the CBC, and among the highest positions in the Canadian diplomatic corps, including our representative to the United Nations.

It sounded as though Mulroney had changed speechwriters, from Lucien Bouchard to Jean Lemoine, who used to write speeches for Trudeau. He now spoke to Quebecers' pride rather than their resentments and their humiliations. "What would Quebecers gain if Canada lost its privileged and coveted place at the table of the Seven, with the government leaders of France, Britain, Italy, Germany, Japan, and the United States?"

The pirouette of his Quebec speech, in which he attacked the nationalists for the first time, earned him the rebuke of Lucien Bouchard, who accused him of ingratitude. In his column in the *Journal de Montréal*, Bouchard noted that the Conservative candidates had been elected in 1984 and 1988 with the support of the nationalists:

They even used the campaign workers of the Parti Québécois. For there is no Conservative electoral machine in Quebec. There is not even a grass-roots base of Conservative partisans. Most of the speeches given in Quebec, including those of Mr. Mulroney, could just as well have been given by Péquistes. They repeatedly invoked the name of René Lévesque to praise him. Many of the Conservative candidates boasted of having voted Yes in the 1980 referendum.[3]

But the chasm between the political attitudes of Quebecers and those of other Canadians was demonstrated in an Angus Reid-Southam News poll published on 1 March. The sample of Canadians was asked whether they "support the transfer of powers to Quebec from the federal Government as recommended by the Allaire commission." While 81 per cent of Quebecers said that they supported the transfer of powers, 79 per cent of Canadians outside Quebec said that they were opposed. The respondents were asked whether they supported the transfer of the same powers to all provinces, not just Quebec. In Quebec, 83 per cent said they supported this massive decentralization. Outside Quebec, 51 per cent approved. Finally, a key question: "Would you support or oppose an economic union between a sovereign Quebec and the rest of Canada?" Among Quebecers, 71 per cent said that they supported it, but only 25 per cent of other Canadians did. Fully 70 per cent said they were opposed.

How does one govern a country with such opposite tendencies between one major constituent part and the rest of the country? So far, Mulroney's main strategy had been to play for time, to avoid the fundamental issue while seeming to do something about it. So far, he had engendered a lot of talk.

The first substantial federal move was to take Joe Clark away from his external-affairs portfolio and put him in charge of a much more demanding diplomatic mission: Canadian constitutional affairs. The announcement was made with a Cabinet shuffle on April 21. Ironically, Mulroney turned to his old rival and the man he had schemed to unseat from the Conservative leadership. And Clark accepted to take up the difficult task of picking up the constitutional pieces.

The first formal statement of the federal government's intentions for dealing with the constitutional crisis came on 13 May 1991 in the Throne speech, which spoke of comprehension and consensus. "My government will work to create a climate in which Canadians can deepen their understanding of their history and traditions and their appreciation of their country's rich diversity." The speech outlined a constitutional process in four stages. First, within the next few months, the federal government would "formulate new proposals to focus public discussion on the goal of a more united and prosperous Canada." Second, in September, a travelling parliamentary committee would tour the country with those proposals "to consult with Canadians." It would meet publicly with provincial legislators and aboriginal groups in each province, as well as with members of the public. The parliamentary committee was to submit its report to Parliament by February, 1992. Then, in a third stage, the government would reflect on the committee's report and formulate its definitive proposals. Finally, in a fourth stage that was not spelled out, the people of Canada would be asked to ratify the plan for a renewed federalism.

The final proposals, the Throne speech said, would entail changes in federal and provincial powers and responsibilities and in national institutions. And a test was established for determining whether or not the proposals were accepted: they would have to gain the cumulative support of each part of the country, rather than be aimed primarily at gaining the assent of Quebec, as the Meech Lake package had been.

But the recognition of Quebec as a distinct society was a starting point about which there could be no question. "Quebec's unique character must be affirmed and the particular interests of the West, the Atlantic provinces, Ontario, the North, and aboriginal Canadians must be recognized as well."

At last, the federal government had finished marking time, waiting for Quebec to strike its colours, waiting for the sovereignist sentiment in Quebec to subside. Now, it was Ottawa's turn to go on the offensive.

The following night, Bloc Québécois leader Lucien Bouchard gave a speech to the nationalist Société nationale des Québécois in a church basement in Hull, in sight of the Peace Tower. In the year since he had broken with Mulroney, Bouchard had emerged as the most popular politician in Quebec. He and his separatist message were now uppermost in the minds of Quebecers.

Bouchard attacked the federal proposals in the Throne speech, and put on display his own stuff. He gave a good, old-fashioned, firebrand speech, the kind

Maurice Duplessis would have appreciated. Bouchard spoke fast, he spoke passionately—and half of his appeal was to paranoia. Quebecers, he warned, beware. There is a plot against you. A terrible assault is being prepared against you, the like of which has never been seen.

He was not content to break with his former leader and colleagues, to say that his vision of Quebec's future was different from theirs. No, he invoked a plot, in which Mulroney was conspiring against Quebec with Jean Chrétien and Audrey McLaughlin. "We are faced with mortal perils that threaten us," he warned. Even the betrayal of Quebec by Pierre Trudeau and the nine premiers in 1981 was nothing compared to what lay ahead. "This government is preparing a *coup de force* without precedent": it would hold a national referendum on the constitution. "The danger is devious and very real. I tell you that the danger of a national referendum is very real. We must be vigilant." A referendum. Was that the unprecedented *coup de force* against Quebec? Bouchard did not say that the federal government would hold a referendum in which the votes of Quebec would be overwhelmed by the votes of other parts of Canada. That would have been manifest nonsense. Neither Mulroney nor Chrétien would consider a referendum binding unless Quebecers had also voted Yes.

Was Bouchard's real fear that Quebecers would vote Yes in a federal referendum? Was that the greatest threat ever to befall Quebec? If so, it might explain why Bouchard called on Robert Bourassa in apocalyptic terms to say no to a federal referendum—which he called "walking over the body of democracy in Quebec," for "There will be no legitimate referendum on sovereignty other than the one that will be called by the government of Quebec."

Could it be that Bouchard did not trust Quebecers? Did he fear that Quebecers might vote Yes to sovereignty in a Quebec referendum, then vote Yes to renewed federalism in a federal referendum? Was that the unparalleled peril against which all must be vigilant?

The proof of the federal perfidy, according to Bouchard, was that Mulroney proposed in the Throne speech a federal-provincial conference to set goals for education in Canada—"an invasion of Quebec's jurisdiction, and there is not one Conservative member to raise his voice."

Ultimately, Bouchard's argument rested on one postulate: *we* are *we*, *they* are *they*, and never the twain can meet. There cannot be a common vision between French- and English-speaking Canadians, and so no offers for renewing federalism would ever come from English Canada, because none could. His whole speech was an appeal to tribalism.

Two weeks earlier, at the end of April, Jean Chrétien had given a speech in Montreal that was well received by his supporters. After nearly a year of fumbles from the time he won the Liberal leadership, Chrétien was beginning to recover some of the old-style that had made him so popular in the Liberal Party. "Ladies and gentlemen, as everyone knows, I am a francophone first. I am proud to be a Québécois and I am proud to be a Canadian. Vive le Canada!" It might have been corny, but it was effective.

And he was even more effective as he went after Lucien Bouchard. "Mr. Bouchard, the humiliated man," Chrétien called him. "He is right, it is humiliating when you leave Chicoutimi and go directly to Paris, and when you have a house on Faubourg St. Honoré and you have a big car with the flag of Canada on the hood. That's humiliating." Chrétien warmed to his theme, to the delight of the Liberals: "And then, when you come back to be named minister before even being elected, that's humiliating. Simple mortals like us, André [Ouellet], [Francis] Fox, [Donald] Johnston, and all the others, we were obliged to get elected before becoming a minister. It is humiliating to be named minister before you're a member of Parliament."

Mulroney could never turn on his old friend Bouchard, Chrétien continued sarcastically, because that might remind the audience of the prime minister's egregious bad judgment in making a national figure of the man who now led the separatists in the federal Parliament. "I expected to read speeches about the beauty, the greatness, the generosity of Canada, pronounced by Mr. Bouchard when he was secretary of state of Canada, and then senior minister. It's humiliating, he wasn't able to get his work done so he resigned."

Chrétien ended on a triumphant affirmation. "As for me, I am not a humiliated gentleman. And I know that the Québécois are not humiliated people."

In August, 1991, the Progressive Conservative Party held a policy convention in Toronto, at which it overwhelmingly adopted a resolution that stated, "Be it resolved that the recognition of the right of Quebec men and women to self-determination be confirmed." The party governing the country was declaring, as words were used at the time, that the people of one province had a right to secede, at a moment when separatism in Quebec was running dangerously high. What other meaning could the resolution impart? No conditions or qualifications were attached to the statement. It was a blank cheque.

Why did Mulroney do it? He was a prisoner of the nationalistic militancy of his own Quebec caucus, which had adopted precisely such a resolution on Quebec's right to self-determination at its meeting the previous fall at Mont-Sainte-Anne. This was the price the prime minister had to pay to keep many of his Quebec members from bolting to the Bloc Québécois. The bargain with the nationalists made in 1984 had not come without a price.

Notes

1.This was a return to the 1971 Victoria formula. It would have replaced the amending formula adopted in 1982, which required the assent of at least seven provinces with at least 50 per cent of the population.
2.Change must lead to a more efficient and competitive country, and it must be approached without dogma or ideology. He wanted a country of diversity, but also equality. He would maintain certain

national standards. He would consider any arrangment that would have the effect of moving decision-making closer to the people. He would safeguard the rights of all Canadians.

   3.Bouchard's comments about the absence of a Conservative organization without the nationalists would prove true in the general elections that followed in 1993, when nationalist voters deserted the Conservative Party for the Bloc Québécois.

CHAPTER EIGHTEEN

Mission Impossible

The gulf that separated the political vision of the rest of Canada and the appetites of official Quebec became obvious when the federal government finally presented its "offers" on 24 September 1991, in a paper titled *Shaping Canada's Future*. It included twenty-eight separate proposals for change, some for the benefit of Quebec, some for the benefit of a few provinces, some for the benefit of aboriginals, and even one or two for the benefit of all Canadians. But the menu for Quebec was thin, after all the sound and fury of the previous fifteen months. If anything, the proposals bore out what Lucien Bouchard had always said: Quebec and the rest of the country had different visions, and Quebec's leaders would not get what they wanted by traditional negotiations. An open question remained: could they get what they wanted by other, more forceful means? Could a referendum cut the Gordian knot?

The unveiling of the federal proposals set off an eleven-month national roller-coaster ride of committees, conferences, forums, negotiations behind closed doors, public posturings, informal approaches, whispers in the ear, rumours, trial balloons, horse-trading, searches for a deal, all carried out under the guillotine of Quebec's impending referendum, while the clock ticked down toward the fatal day of 26 October 1992. The whole country became involved in an immense, almost convulsive effort to reconcile the irreconcilable, to square the circle, to find the elusive formula that would establish a consensus among interests and visions of the country which were more than diverse and divergent: they were actually incompatible.

What Ottawa was offering Quebec was again a "distinct society" clause, somewhat similar to what had seemed so all-important in the Meech Lake package. For official-language minorities, there was a clause with weaker language than even Meech had contained.[1]

But the all-important issue for Quebec governments since the Quiet Revolution had been the division of powers. What Ottawa now offered was, in the first place, to curtail or eliminate the extraordinary levers given to the federal government by the original BNA Act: the "peace, order, and good government" clause, which gave the federal government general residual powers over matters not specifically covered in the constitution, and the federal declaratory power, which allowed

289

Ottawa to take over any "work" within a province simply by declaring it to be to the general advantage of Canada.

Ottawa also offered to withdraw from some areas that arguably were already under provincial jurisdiction, but in which the federal government was active: tourism, forestry, housing, mines, recreation, municipal affairs. Labour-market training was to come under exclusive provincial jurisdiction as an extension of the education system. The proposals also envisaged special arrangements with respect to immigration, culture, and broadcasting. But this did not mean that Ottawa would withdraw entirely from these fields: communications minister Perrin Beatty soon promised that, under any circumstances, the major national cultural institutions, such as the CBC, the National Film Board, and the Canada Council, would remain under federal control. Thus, the most important cultural levers, next to the systems of education, would continue to elude Quebec's grasp.

So, from the perspective of official Quebec, what Ottawa put on the table as a counter-offer was little compared to the demands and the expectations traced out by the Allaire and Bélanger-Campeau commissions. Moreover, the package did not contain Quebec's prime requirement of a security guarantee in the form of a veto against any constitutional change that affected the equilibrium of the federation. The veto was left out deliberately, to avoid the loss of the whole package, as had happened with Meech. All of the proposals required only the assent of seven provincial governments representing 50 per cent of the population. The veto—a change in the amending formula— would have required unanimity.

Since this was the "Canada round" rather than the "Quebec round," the offers included the promise of an elected and reformed Senate—but not the Triple-E Senate demanded by Alberta and Newfoundland. For aboriginals, the package promised self-government within ten years and guaranteed seats in the Senate— but not recognition of the "inherent right" to self-government that aboriginal leaders demanded.

The first significant rejection of the package came from Ovide Mercredi, grand chief of the Assembly of First Nations. "Consistent with our continued sovereignty and aboriginal title is our right, aboriginal right, to govern ourselves. Since this right comes from our being aboriginal to this land, and from the duties and responsibilities given to us by the Creator when we were put on this land, it is an inherent right." Mercredi refused to take part in the consultation process on the federal proposals. The natives, he insisted, must have their own separate consultation process. Joe Clark quickly agreed and provided a budget. But the federal "offers" were off to a bad start.

In Quebec, the news media focused immediately on a section of the proposals that aimed at creating a genuine economic union, with free circulation within Canada of people, capital, goods, and services. To this end, Ottawa had suggested a Council of the Federation, with representation from the federal, provincial, and territorial governments.[2] It was envisaged as a genuine decision-making body, with authority to impose common economic policies on the various governments or to strike down protectionist provincial legislation, provided the council had the support of at least seven provinces representing 50 per cent of the population.

When, the next day, Premier Bourasssa gave his first response to Ottawa's offers before the news media, he came across as his cautious, ambiguous, noncommittal self. He resisted the temptation to shoot down the package on sight. A joint parliamentary committee was to tour the country, hearing submissions, and it would make a report, including additional proposals for change, by 28 February. So the federal proposals were not offered on a take-it-or-leave-it basis; they could be expanded over the following months. Bourassa spoke encouragingly of "positive aspects." He cautioned that the proposals on the economic union needed clarification, but he defended the concept of an economic union and held back from a negative judgment until he had better information.

Bourassa's moderate response was the exception. From most of the articulate sectors of Quebec society came a common and vehement response: *Non*. The rejections were peremptory, while what few endorsements did emerge sounded timid, partial, or defensive.

The Parti Québécois was in full throat, especially its leader, Jacques Parizeau. "In the section on the economy . . . we see proposals presented which aim at centralizing economic powers in Ottawa to an extent never seen before except in wartime," he said on 25 September. "They used the excuse [of an economic union] not to recognize that the economic space exists and must be maintained, but to centralize economic policies, which will be made to reflect a centralized economic policy."

He argued that the proposals, had they been in force, would have made impossible Quebec Inc.—the made-in-Quebec collaboration between the provincial government, business, and labour to favour Quebec-based business enterprises, francophone managers and entrepreneurs, and Quebec-based workers, at the expense of people from other provinces.

Parizeau was almost certainly right. The intent of the proposals was to remove protectionist policies that treated non-residents of a province in a discriminatory fashion. These protectionist policies fragmented the Canadian economic market and made the economy less efficient. But Parizeau wanted to maintain the protectionism that bound Quebec entrepreneurs and labour unions to the government of Quebec. It would have been illegal under the Free Trade Agreement with the United States, had Quebec been a country instead of a province of Canada— and it would have been illegal had Quebec been a member of the European Community.

In fact, Parizeau made an extraordinary admission to journalist Jean-Francois Lisée. He recognized that, with respect to the economy, Canada was already less centralized than was the European Community: "There are many who say that if we asked for an economic association on the European model, a sovereign

291

Quebec would have fewer economic powers than it has today. I agree, but that is not what we're asking for."[3]

The dim prospects of reaching an agreement were confirmed on 15 October, when a public-opinion poll by Environics Research Group, published in *La Presse* and the *Toronto Star,* illustrated the cleavage in the country: 76 per cent of respondents in the rest of Canada would oppose any attempt to give Quebec more powers, while in Quebec 66 per cent supported more powers for the provincial government. Moreover, the poll showed that, in Quebec, 70 per cent supported constitutional recognition of Quebec as a distinct society, while in the rest of Canada 57 per cent opposed it. The poll offered only one sign of hope for a future settlement: support for sovereignty-association had dropped from 66 per cent, in November, 1990, to 52 per cent in October, 1991. Support for outright independence had declined from 58 per cent to 41 per cent over the same period.

Canadians were frustrated; they resented how the politicians were running the country, and they displayed their anger whenever the opportunity presented. On 17 October 1991, the people of British Columbia threw the Social Credit government out of office and reduced the party to a rump, behind the NDP and the Liberals. Four days later, the people of Saskatchewan tossed out their Conservative government in favour of the NDP.

The only good politician, it seemed, was an opposition politician, or, better still, a non-politician politician. The two parties that were surging in popular support were both regional protest parties: the Reform Party on the prairies, and the Bloc Québécois in Quebec. Both were headed by unconventional leaders: Preston Manning, who had never been elected to office, and Lucien Bouchard, who, barely two years after he was first elected, had broken with his party and with the federal system and given up his position in the Cabinet.

Above all, public resentment was directed at the ruling Conservatives. The Gallup poll published 17 October showed them with a vestigial 13 per cent country-wide support, just one point ahead of the Reform Party. They were unpopular everywhere, even in their former fortress in the prairies, where they now had the support of only 8 per cent, and in Quebec, solid bastion of the two Conservative majority governments, where their support had fallen to 15 per cent.

The prime minister went on the road in the last week of October to sell his new constitutional proposals, but his speeches illustrated why he was unlikely to be more successful than he had been with Meech Lake. On 23 October, in his address to the Montreal Chamber of Commerce, his speech was pointed to the specific interests of Quebecers. He defended his proposals for an economic union, which had come under heavy attack, and reassured his audience that the new proposals would not threaten Quebec's unique financial institutions.

The next day, in his speech to the Empire and Canadian clubs in Toronto, his subject matter was similar: "Canadians today face the choice we have faced repeatedly throughout our history: in 1774, 1791, in 1840, in 1867, and 1980. That choice is simple: Quebec will either be a distinct society within Canada, or it will develop as a distinct society outside Canada." To the people of Toronto, the prime minister continued to speak almost wholly of his constant obsession, Quebec. "The French language and culture, in such a minority position in North America, must continue to find in Canada the freedom and oxygen that will enable them to flourish and endure." He had nothing specific to say to the people of Ontario, to link them to the process of changing the constitution of their country. He spoke the words "Quebec" or "Quebecer" thirteen times, the words "Ontario" or "Ontarian" only four times—and then only in passing, in relation to Quebec.[4]

The day before Mulroney set off on his speaking tour, Premier Wells made a speech that he should have heeded. "Western Canada has been concerned that the present constitutional structure does not permit them to have an effective say in the exercise of federal legislative power and the development and implementation of national economic policy," Wells told the Newfoundland and Labrador Committee on the Constitution. "The concerns of Atlantic Canada are somewhat similar in that Atlantic Canadians feel the present constitutional structure has not permitted them to have an effective say in the exercise of national legislative power and the development and implementation of national economic policy."

The sense of alienation of the Western and Atlantic provinces was real, and justified by the very constitutional proposals put forward by the federal government to meet the demands for change of the whole country. On the issues of most concern to Quebec, such as the distinct society, the federal language was precise, firm, and probably immutable. But on the issue of most concern to several other provinces, reform of the Senate, the language was tentative and open to every change, any suggestion, any future play of pressure and negotiations.

That was the typical disparity. What concerned Quebec was close to Mulroney's heart, and he took a strong personal stand, as the champion of Quebec's interests. But toward the concerns of other provinces, he had no strong personal commitment. He would entertain any possibility. Let them go ahead and prove a case, he would listen.

While in Montreal, the prime minister had called on federalists in Quebec to come forward. It wasn't enough just to wait for offers, he said. That would never work. It was true that, on the federalist side, almost no one wanted to raise a head that could become a target. Everyone was waiting for someone else. But what about Mulroney's own Quebec lieutenant, Benoît Bouchard? Surely he, the number one federal politician in Quebec next to Mulroney, would defend with utmost vigour the "offers" being made to Quebec to head off a referendum on sovereignty.

Bouchard was his engaging, ambivalent, uncommitted self on 26 October when he was interviewed by Denise Bombardier on her Radio-Canada television

293

program, *L'envers de la médaille*, the other side of the coin. Bouchard told Bombardier that he would not make up his mind on whether to choose federalism or sovereignty for Quebec until probably the following year.

Bouchard:I began a process in 1984. It will perhaps end in the fall of '92, and I will have choices to make. But I don't want to reach that point while there are still debates under way and while Quebecers haven't yet chosen.

Bombardier: Some people will accuse you of refusing to take a stand.

Bouchard:Absolutely. That's the risk we run. . . . There are eras and moments when people must go to extremes. I'm unable to. I've always hated intolerance. I've always hated to take the stand that all is bad on one side or the other. Sovereignty is not all bad. Federalism is not all bad.

Bombardier: But Mr. Bouchard, you will finally have to make a choice.

Bouchard:Absolutely. Just so long as I'm not forced to make a choice before other Quebecers. Why should I absolutely have to make a choice today when it's said that Quebec will maybe make a choice in the fall of '92? Then, when the time has come for me as a Quebecer to make a choice, without hesitation, Madam, I'll make it.

Benoît Bouchard sounded like a benevolent and open-minded spectator of the political scene rather than a member of Parliament and the prime minister's Quebec lieutenant. The silence of Marcel Masse, Pierre Blais, Jean Corbeil, and all the other members of that huge delegation from Quebec to Ottawa was thundering. This was the new federalism that Brian Mulroney had created in Quebec: a great void.

Meanwhile, the Special Joint Committee on a Renewed Canada had quickly set out to tour the country with the twenty-eight federal proposals that had been put forward for national debate. "The committee is going to listen, it is going to absorb, it's going to be responsive and it's going to try to talk to as many people as it possibly can," co-chair Dorothy Dobbie promised when interviewed on Newsworld on the day the proposals were unveiled.

The choice of the co-chairs—Claude Castonguay from the Senate, and Dorothy Dobbie from the Commons—was decidedly weighted on the provincialist side. Castonguay, a dignified and ponderous man, had been involved with Quebec's Quiet Revolution since the Lesage era, when he had advised on how to set up the Quebec pension plan so as to pre-empt a Canada-wide pension plan. He had helped design Quebec's health and welfare system, then implemented it as minister of social affairs. In 1971, he had argued at Victoria that Bourassa should not accept the Victoria Charter because it did not give Quebec enough powers. He had retired from politics in 1973 with his prestige undiminished, for a career in banking. Naming him to head the committee signalled that the committee's report was pre-ordained to satisfy Bourassa's demands.

294

Dorothy Dobbie, in contrast, seemed to have been chosen to give as little weight as possible to the federalist viewpoint. A businesswoman from Winnipeg, she was unknown on the national scene and a novice in politics. She had been elected to Parliament not three years earlier. She had never served in a Cabinet, nor did she have a strong constituency of her own to back her up politically. She did not speak French. And she would quickly prove unequal to her challenging assignment.

The committee set out on a populist mission to hold hearings in a multitude of settings, and its members split up in small sub-committees to take in more meetings. But while the committee was willing, the people held back; the expected throngs simply did not materialize. There had been so many committees. Now, the proposals under discussion were specific, the issues complex, and there was little time to prepare a response.

The committee moved about like a helter-skelter, disorganized caravan in its first, critical weeks. Was its role to go out and hear people and reflect on what they said? Or was it to sell the government's constitutional package to the public? In fact, the committee sold those parts of the package that were held as untouchable. On peripheral parts, the committee was prepared to listen.

Its first witness at hearings in Toronto was law professor Katherine Swinton of the University of Toronto, who promptly admitted that she had had a hand in drawing up the proposals. The committee showed its colours when it heard lawyer Sheldon Godfrey, who appeared on behalf of the Ontario region of the Canadian Council of Christians and Jews. Godfrey gave one of the most erudite and thoughtful presentations that the committee was to hear. He said that he favoured recognition of Quebec as a distinct society. However, he also expressed concern about the long-term effect of the clause as it was written, because it "raises the questions of whether there is now to be a state culture and whether those of other cultures can participate equally in society." Since 1851, he said, there had been no official state religion or culture in Canada. "Canada has evolved as a new kind of country in the world, a country where there is no cultural majority, but where a number of different cultures live in mutual respect. Canada is, in a way, a model for the world to come." But the distinct society clause as written, he said, identified that distinct society with the French-speaking majority and a "unique culture." Godfrey questioned the implications. "The recognition of Quebec as a distinct society in the proposed Constitutional Act amendment would mark the first official recognition since the nation was formed in 1867 that Canadian society no longer has equal cultures."

The members of the committee showed their displeasure: they repeatedly interrupted Godfrey's presentation, saying they wanted to question him. Instead, when the time came for questions, they chose to rebut what he had said. Liberal MP Warren Allmand went on the attack with a reasoning that entirely missed the point. "I am a lawyer from Quebec; I am an anglophone. I don't consider that I

295

am a second-class citizen because I have to practise civil law." Two Tory members of Parliament from Quebec conspicuously walked out during Godfrey's presentation. Lynn Hunter of the NDP and Alberta Tory Kenneth Hughes joined in the rebuttal. Afterwards, Liberal André Ouellet said to the press, "I think it's regrettable that the gentleman who is supposed to speak on behalf of a national organization that promotes good will and understanding would come and present the view he did." The message seemed to be that anyone who disagreed with the proposals on Quebec should stay away. The ideological view that Quebec must be recognized as an ethnic state had become accepted wisdom. To question its appropriateness was shocking.

Finally, in early November, the committee reached a moment of truth when it convened a meeting in Manitoba and no one showed up. Discontent within the committee exploded. Amid rumours of resignations, the committee then cancelled hearings scheduled to be held in Manitoba, northern Ontario, and Alberta. Jean Chrétien called for the resignation of Dorothy Dobbie.

During this time of federal disarray, on 9 November, Bourassa and Parizeau held a two-hour debate in the National Assembly on Ottawa's proposals. Four days earlier, Gil Rémillard had rejected the constitutional package utterly. "I think the federal government is realizing now that these proposals are unacceptable," Rémillard told reporters. "It's obvious that the federal government should go back to the drawing board and write something else. The way it is now, it's obvious that it's not acceptable."

The debate between Bourassa and Parizeau proved more significant for what both left unsaid. Bourassa maintained his usual ambiguous stance by saying that the constitutional proposals were not acceptable, and yet were a basis for further discussion: "The government of Quebec will have to act on its responsibilities when the final offers are made. We have been very clear on the fact that what was offered Quebec made it possible to maintain a dialogue, but only just. Still, there are interesting principles there with respect to [Quebec's] traditional requests."

Parizeau tried to smoke the premier out of his hole. Rather than advancing a program or an analysis of the needs of Quebec society as a basis on which to attack the federal proposals, he tried to get Bourassa to contradict himself. Did the proposals amount to Meech Lake, to Meech Lake plus, or to Meech Lake minus? They were clearly less than Meech, Parizeau maintained. So how could Bourassa consider them a basis for discussion when he had said many times—and Parizeau quoted chapter and verse—that the Quebec government could never accept less than Meech Lake?

Bourassa counter-attacked. Why did Parizeau make a fuss now about Meech Lake, when in the past he had said that Meech Lake was nothing? He also reminded Parizeau that his party, in 1981, had fumbled away Quebec's traditional veto, after losing the 1980 referendum. "The Parti Québécois held a referendum.

It held it without being sure of winning. . . . The defeat in the referendum resulted in the unilateral patriation of the constitution, leaving Quebec in a weak position. "

For the benefit of Ottawa, Bourassa gave an inkling of some of his requirements. He expected complete control over manpower policy and training, and this should be spelled out in the constitution. He expected a transfer of resources from the federal government to ensure Quebec's "cultural security." And he would accept no terms of an economic union that would diminish the powers of the Quebec government. He described the proposals for an economic union as "authoritarian federalism," since it would allow the federal government, with the support of seven provinces, to strike down laws or practices in Quebec that restricted the mobility of capital, labour, goods, or services. The country, he said, could no longer afford the "competitive federalism" of the past decades, and he demanded a new division of powers that "furthers the effectiveness of the political system." He left the impression that the difference was mostly a matter of pacing between himself and Parizeau. "It is normal for the opposition to go too fast, too far. Before history, it is not good to be late. But it is not good to be too soon."

Although both leaders demanded more powers for the Quebec government, neither showed that such powers were needed for the better functioning of Quebec as a society, or for the greater good of Quebecers as individuals. Did the average citizen really care whether the federal proposals were Meech Lake plus or Meech Lake minus? Surely the concern was whether the citizens would be better served under these proposals, or under the more sweeping demands being made by the two leaders, than under the status quo. Neither Bourassa nor Parizeau attempted to make that demonstration of the superiority of their respective proposals; more powers for the Quebec government had become axiomatic.

At this time of federal fumbling and Quebec's leaders demanding, Joe Clark put an end to the circus of the Castonguay-Dobbie committee. In effect, he put the two co-chairs in trusteeship; the committee was to be administered by a senior civil servant who was to take his direction from a steering committee, rather than from them. The committee would no longer split into panels to hear small groups in the hinterland.

It was a new beginning after a false start. Claude Castonguay, humiliated, soon resigned, on the grounds of his poor health. In interviews with Quebec reporters, he made it plain that the government—that is, Joe Clark—had given the committee an impossible mandate, and he reproached himself for accepting a nebulous mission. Clark replaced Castonguay with Senator Gérald Beaudoin, a rotund, exuberant, constantly smiling constitutional expert whose bubbling personality was in marked contrast to the dour Castonguay's. The loss of Castonguay was a setback for Mulroney. Beaudoin was highly reputed in his field, but without the political stature of Castonguay, or his closeness to Bourassa. And there were other setbacks.

Toward the end of November, Clark announced that he would be introducing before Christmas a bill to allow Ottawa to hold a national referendum on the constitutional proposals, as announced in the Throne speech. However, the Quebec Conservative caucus raised such an outcry, with its members threatening to vote against the bill, that Clark publicly backed down. The Quebec MPs showed no enthusiasm for any part of the federal approach. A reporter canvassed all the Cabinet ministers from Quebec, but he was unable to find one who could produce the text of a speech he or she had given in Quebec to sell the federal proposals.[5]

In Quebec, Mulroney's great ally showed displeasure. The National Assembly passed a resolution on 27 November calling on the federal government to "respect the process established by Bill 150" whereby Quebec was to hold its referendum on sovereignty. The resolution insisted that Ottawa should not "initiate a Canada-wide referendum touching on the political and constitutional future of Quebec." Instead, by refraining from a referendum, the federal government would recognize the right of Quebecers "to choose freely their own destiny and to determine alone their political and constitutional status."

Benoît Bouchard was browbeaten in Quebec City by Gil Rémillard for suggesting that the federal government had as much right as the Quebec government to hold a referendum in Quebec. This happened when Bouchard was in Quebec on 28 November, to announce that the federal government was investing $160 million in Quebec for economic development. Rémillard did not bother to maintain even a veneer of politeness. "It's no use their saying that the federal referendum could have a majority in Quebec or in other provinces," he said. "That's beside the point. But the mechanism, the question, the regulatory process [of a referendum] must be accepted and overseen by the National Assembly of Quebec."

Mulroney and his ministers could be bullied because they needed Bourassa to achieve any semblance of a constitutional settlement. On 23 November, the Young Liberals of Quebec met and rejected the federal proposals as being nowhere near the transfer of powers outlined in the Allaire report. Bourassa was in a position to say yes, no, or maybe to Ottawa—or all three, on successive days. He held the fate of the Mulroney government in his hands.

Mulroney's response was to roar against the separatists in a speech delivered on 1 December to a PC fund-raising brunch in Montreal. "The separatists, in their haste to break up the country, are hoping Quebecers will take up bungee-jumping *en masse*! 'Dive off the platform—head first,' they say. 'It's OK, you'll be safe, your left foot is still attached to Canada.' But it will not be. When you leave Canada, you leave its strength, security, and all of the benefits behind."

Take that, you separatists. Ah, but wait. The prime minister got tough in those parts of his speech where he spoke in English, as Radio-Canada reporter Julie Miville-Deschênes observed. "Even though the vast majority of his audience was made up of francophones, he made his worst threats in English. Perhaps it was a way of demonstrating to the rest of Canada his firmness toward Quebec." Or perhaps it was more convenient to denounce the separatists in English than his problematic partner, Bourassa, in French.

As 1991 ended, on the eve of a new year that would bring a Quebec referendum, the federal government, as well as much of the press and the public in English-speaking Canada, acted as though a satisfactory outcome to the crisis were possible only if people outside Quebec were generous, understanding, and willing to compromise. They had to get down to constitutional reflection expeditiously. "The clock is ticking," Joe Clark warned from Manitoba.

Brian Mulroney had always intended that Ottawa would keep control of the process of constitutional change, within the terms set by Robert Bourassa. Accordingly, the prime minister wrote the premiers in January of 1992 to promise that Ottawa would consult them before coming up with the final proposals: "After the joint parliamentary committee report is tabled, we will consult with all provinces, territories, and the national aboriginal leaders on the format and the substance of any government response to be put before Parliament."

Consultations, yes, but not negotiations, and certainly not co-authorship. Ontario premier Bob Rae upset Mulroney's plan when he appeared before the Beaudoin-Dobbie committee on 13 January 1992. "Don't expect Ontario to go along with a deal that we haven't been involved in fashioning," he said flatly and emphatically. Ontario, he pointed out, had not been consulted by the federal government before Ottawa unveiled its twenty-eight proposals for constitutional renewal on 24 September. Ontario was also without a voice on the Beaudoin-Dobbie committee studying the twenty-eight proposals, which was to report by 28 February. And what would happen after 28 February? Ray had absolutely no idea.

He feared that secret talks or negotiations were under way between Ottawa and Quebec, from which Ontario was excluded. And he also feared that, at the last minute, Ontario would be faced with a take-it-or-leave-it proposition, negotiated between the federal government and Quebec. That scenario would not fly, he warned. This was a federation, and premiers were essential partners in any process aimed at changing it. In that sense, the proposals currently under study could not in any way be considered the offers that would be made to Quebec and the rest of Canada.

"The real negotiations in this country have yet to begin," Rae said. The federal government was going to have to deal with Ontario, the sooner the better, and certainly before Ottawa announced its own definitive "offers" in April, after receiving the Beaudoin-Dobbie committee's report. Rae laid out some parameters of what he would be defending for Ontario. And he warned at the same time that Ontario now had such problems of its own that it would not, as in the past, simply act as the magnanimous "have" province that stood aside while other provinces asserted their own interests.

Above all, Rae would not be a party to the radical weakening of the federal government. "There is no market in my province for a wholesale devolution of federal powers. None." He did favour some devolution in the name of efficiency—for example, manpower training would best be vested in the provinces, but only if the money to carry out the job came along with the responsibility—and it should not be just a one-way street. Why didn't the federal government, for instance, obtain responsibility for regulating securities right across the country, as was done in the United States?

He had a limited tolerance, Rae said, for Quebec's achieving powers and responsibilities—special status—different from those exercised by other provinces. "If you pull it apart too much, the centre will not hold, and other Canadians will not see that it makes sense." He was suspicious of bilateral deals between Ottawa and Quebec, because those who were not at the table ended up short-changed, as had happened in the deal on immigration signed a year earlier between Ottawa and Quebec, whereby Quebec got 30 per cent of all federal funds dedicated to help immigrants get settled, even though Quebec received only 18 per cent of immigrants. He defended his proposal for a social charter to be vested in the constitution, so that the right to medicare, education, housing, and basic social services would be permanently protected.

Finally, Rae had a message for Donald Getty, Clyde Wells, and others: Ontario had serious reservations about a new Senate with equal representation from each province. "Triple-E, stated baldly, is not acceptable to Ontario."

That strong statement, coming from the leader of Canada's largest and richest province, changed the course of the constitutional negotiations, by limiting how far Mulroney could go to accommodate the Quebec government. Bourassa had intended to deal only with the federal government. He counted on the prime minister to use the power and prestige of his office to pressure the other premiers into line, as he had done at Meech Lake in 1987 and again in Ottawa in 1990. That had been the logic behind his systematic boycott of federal-provincial and interprovincial meetings since Meech Lake had failed.

But now, Rae had given public notice that he would not go along with federal leadership. He intended to help shape whatever offers were to be made to Quebec. His strong stand made unlikely any massive transfer of powers from the federal government to all the provinces, or from the federal government just to Quebec. From the moment he spoke, the Allaire scenario of an autonomous Quebec in a residual federal state became a pipe dream. Quebec would have to choose between sovereignty and a streamlined version of the existing federation.

But would any "offers" to Quebec emerge at all? It would obviously not be easy for the "rest of Canada" to agree on a constitutional settlement that would prove acceptable not just to Quebec, but to all the other provinces as well.

The day after Rae spoke, Newfoundland's Clyde Wells took his turn before the Beaudoin-Dobbie committee, and delivered a stern message that was in collision with that of the Ontario premier, insisting that the Triple-E Senate, and only the Triple-E Senate, was the essential solution to Newfoundland's chronic poverty.

Rae had warned against curtailing constitutional reforms in the current round to a short list. In fact, he wanted to expand an existing section of the constitution dealing with regional inequalities—section 36—to turn it into a "social charter."[6] Wells argued that section 36 already constituted a social charter. It spelled out a principle of social rights for individuals and equalization for provinces. That is what the constitution was for, said Wells: to state principles. It should not go into detailed enumerations such as were proposed by Rae.

To ensure that the intent of section 36 was achieved, Wells insisted, a Triple-E Senate was essential. All federal programs conceived for economic development of the poorer regions eventually failed, and always would fail, because Ontario and Quebec used their majority of MPs to obtain equivalent programs in their provinces. Since the larger provinces were better able to take advantage of the programs, they drained away the federal development funds.

On another important issue, though, Wells agreed with Rae: there should be no large-scale devolution of powers toward all the provinces and there should be no special status for Quebec achieved through bilateral negotiations between Ottawa and Quebec City.

A relief from the hard-edged premiers was provided by the Nova Scotia delegation when premier Donald Cameron appeared before the Beaudoin-Dobbie committee flanked by Liberal leader Vincent MacLean and New Democratic Party leader Alexa McDonough. The three spoke with one voice, each taking a turn to read from a single text. The unusual non-partisan unanimity was matched by a determination to come to terms with the other partners in Confederation. "Our focus should be on issues which affect all Canadians. We cannot afford—no one in this country can afford—to hold the unity of Canada to ransom until their particular concerns are met."

Even on the one issue on which Cameron expressed the strongest feelings, his statement was more a cry from the heart than a call to some barricade. "Quebec feels very strongly about its culture and language. I want to assure you that Nova Scotians feel very strongly about our economic circumstances, and we will not accept a have-not status for the next hundred years as we did in the past."

The concern for maintaining the federal role in redistributing wealth and opportunity between richer and poorer provinces ran through the presentation. Nova Scotia wanted the federal government to be made constitutionally responsible for providing a communications infrastructure—roads, railways, airports, and harbours—of equal quality right across the country. It wanted a guarantee in the constitution that transfer payments from the federal government would not be reduced unilaterally, as had happened in recent years. It opposed a general devolution of powers that would weaken Ottawa, but it was ready to entertain special arrangements for Quebec—in effect, special status. "We are ready to recognize that Quebec has distinct needs and acquires certain powers to protect and promote its distinct society. [But] that does not mean that Nova Scotians are prepared to accept a major decentralization of the powers of the federal government to the extent that Ottawa can no longer meet the needs of all provinces."

The Nova Scotians' spirit of accommodation no doubt reflected their acute awareness of the blight that would lie ahead for the province if Quebec separated. "We need not tell you that the separation of Quebec would be an economic disaster for Nova Scotia and Atlantic Canada," Cameron said. "Our concerns about the economy now would be nothing compared to our concerns about an economy destabilized by Quebec's separation from Canada."

The openness of the Nova Scotians provided a refreshing respite. But, as the premiers unveiled their opening positions, the country seemed headed for an impasse. There was too little common ground evident between the federal government and nine premiers, or between them all and Premier Bourassa.

The dynamics of the constitutional process took another turn in mid-winter, when a group of some two hundred people met in Halifax on 17–19 January for the "Renewal of Canada Conference." For almost three days, participants from all over the country came to the World Trade and Conference Centre to share close quarters, exchange views about the country, and reason together. It soon became evident that a chemistry was operating.

They were in many ways a disparate group. Some were politicians and ex-politicians from all levels of government. Some were community leaders, union leaders, business managers, academics, heads of lobbies such as the National Action Committee on the Status of Women. And there were a few dozen people who were drawn by lot from among those who had submitted their names. Altogether, they represented a fair cross-section of Canada's elites. The partici- pants set to work, divided into thirteen workshops, and promptly proceeded to stand Ottawa's program for constitutional change on its head. The government had proposed to meet the demands of Quebec by vacating certain fields in which it had been engaged. The thrust of the Halifax conference was to reject a general withdrawal of the federal government, while accepting that Ottawa could withdraw from spending in those and other fields in Quebec. The participants opposed weakening the federal government in the rest of Canada, while accepting that a special accommodation would have to be made for Quebec. The words differed, but the most common expression used was "asymmetrical federalism": there would be one federal regime for the rest of Canada, another for Quebec. In other words, what was being proposed was what had generally been called "special status" for Quebec. The conference rejected the approach of Meech Lake, which consisted of weakening the federal government in favour of all provincial governments, while conferring on Quebec no more than an undefined mandate to promote its distinct identity. The participants seemed ready to accept special status for Quebec up front, and a very special status at that.

What would be the implications? Would Quebec MPs still be allowed to vote on laws which bound the rest of the country and not Quebec? If not, how could any Quebec MP become a Cabinet minister, let alone prime minister? How could a government be formed thanks to MPs from Quebec, when these Quebec MPs would be passing laws that bound the rest of the country but not Quebec? These ramifications were left unconsidered in the euphoria of apparently having cut a Gordian knot or two. The conference espoused without a qualm exactly what Pierre Trudeau and René Lévesque had rejected as unworkable.

There were to be five such conferences in all. Unexpectedly, they had quite an electrifying effect. By seizing the initiative and drawing public attention away from governments and from the plodding and often disorganized parliamentary constitutional committee, the five conferences brought constitutional discussion to the level of private citizens, circumventing the generalized distrust and dislike of Canadians for the Mulroney government.

The debate at the second conference, in Calgary on 24–26 January, also had a strong element of drama and passion. The Tripe-E Senate had become the very symbol of what could save "outer Canada" from decades of alienation, by solving the second of the two fundamental problems of Confederation: the preponderant demographic and political power of Ontario and Quebec. The participants had to deal with a dilemma: the future Senate seemed bound to leave Quebec and Ontario unhappy if Triple-E was endorsed, and several other provinces bitter if Triple-E was rejected.

The debate opposed people from different regions of the country. It also divided those who wanted the Senate to represent the provinces and those who wanted it to represent categories of people, such as women, aborignals and official-language minorities.

The outcome, a victory for a Senate that was elected, effective, and equitable—less than equal in provincial representation, but with a representation based on provinces rather than regions—seemed like a nation-building compromise, especially when it was endorsed by Mr. Alberta himself, Peter Lougheed. The former premier seemed to accept pragmatically that two of the three E's were enough. "The question of equality would probably be the last one," Lougheed said in an interview on Newsworld. "But my experience in this constitution business ten years ago is that people shouldn't draw up too inflexible positions, because you might not win here, but you can win there, and it's a process of working it together, because Canadians so much want us to resolve it and to keep the country together."

The Senate, as projected by the Calgary conference, was to increase the representation of the eight smaller provinces and have a mandate to protect Quebec or French Canada in matters of language and culture through the requirement in these matters of a double majority. Many agreed with Joe Clark's estimate that equal provincial representation would be as as likely as a "second virgin birth."

The conference did examine one other proposal at length, the creation of a Council of the Federation,[7] but rejected it decisively. Participants judged that it would only create another layer of bureaucracy, make governments less accountable, and perhaps duplicate the functions intended for a reformed Senate.

In a concession to Quebec, the participants seemed disposed to let a province choose the mode of sending its representatives to the Senate—they could be elected by the people, or "elected" by the members of a provincial legislature. But one important issue remained unresolved: who should hold a veto within the federation? Participants from Quebec stressed that it was important Quebec hold a veto over change to the central institutions of the federation. Others were divided over the issue.

Lougheed saw the double majority as giving Quebec the equivalent of what it lost: a veto over constitutional change.

They can't get their veto because there's no way that they can get the veto without changing the amending formula. You're not going to change the amending formula. Certainly Alberta's not because it got what it wants, and [a change to the amending formula] has to be unanimous. But maybe there's another way of doing it. For example, what about a Senate that requires the majority of all Quebec senators on any matter that relates to the distinct-society clause? What does veto mean? It means that I can stop something. Should I be able to stop something that involves the fishery business in Newfoundland and British Columbia by a veto in Quebec? That's really not what they want. They want to protect their particular distinct society, and maybe we can find a different way of doing that.[8]

At the third conference, in Montreal from 31 January to 2 February, the participants rejected constitutionalizing the federal proposals for a more perfect economic union. They chose the untidiness of the political process for the future pursuit of interprovincial and federal-provincial harmonization and integration, rather than entrenching a degree of integration for which the country was not yet ready. Donald McDonald, former head of a royal commission on Canada's economic prospects, pointed to the heart of the issue in a keynote speech: "The federal system is not one for tidy minds."

The fourth conference, in Toronto on 7–9 February, repudiated a mere maintenance regime for official-language minorities, which was what the federal government had proposed the previous September. Though the treatment of French minorities had been the root historic cause of Quebec separatism, though the violation of the freedom of expression of Quebec's English-speaking minority had contributed powerfully to the defeat of Meech Lake, the federal government had not seen fit to hold a conference on the fate of the official languages in Canada.

A federal publication that explained the government's proposals on Canadian identity had chapters on "the aspirations of Quebec," "the aspirations of the aboriginal peoples," and several other topics—but no chapter on the official languages of Canada, which were at the heart of the social contract of Confederation. By indirection, by silence about fundamentals, the federal government projected its vision of Canada as one made up of a distinct Quebec and a distinct rest of Canada—two distinct nations.

The Toronto conference repudiated that narrow vision. It gave strong support for a constitutional guarantee that would entrench not merely the "preservation of the existence" of official language minorities, but a commitment to their development and vitality. And so the distinct society clause was to be balanced by a clause that protected the minority official languages and thereby corrected the historic mistake of 1867: leaving French unprotected outside of Quebec, Parliament, and the federal courts.

The chief opposition to supporting the minorities came, ironically, not from supposed "rednecks" but from Québécois participants, who, like the Quebec government, preferred to sacrifice the francophone diaspora rather than forgo any power to repress English in Quebec.

By the fifth conference, in Vancouver on 14–16 February, the inherent right to self-government of aboriginal people had been recognized. Contrary to the atmosphere of confusion and disintegration two or three months earlier, the conferences had created a sense of momentum, of accommodation, of renewed hope. But they did so by espousing principles that were abhorrent to some provincial governments. For instance, they rejected the equality of the provinces by favouring "asymmetrical federalism" and unequal provincial representation in the Senate. Even in the best of circumstances, the constitutional road ahead promised to be long, tortuous, bumpy, and even perilous.

Joe Clark injected a note of fatuous naïveté when he addressed this last conference. "The tensions in this country are real, and complex and urgent," he said. "Facing them now can solve them for a long time. . . . If the Canada round collapses, the country is in serious trouble. But if the Canada round succeeds, there will be no need to have another one, in 1993, 1994, or 1996. Success in the Canada round will free us all for other Canadian priorities."

Quebec separatism had stimulated an equal and symmetrical separatism among aboriginal leaders. What Quebec had, what Quebec wanted, the aboriginal leaders wanted. Quebec was a distinct society? The aboriginal nations were more distinct. Quebecers were a founding people? The aboriginals had been there long before the first European stepped ashore.

On the Monday before the Vancouver conference opened, 13 February, Ovide Mercredi appeared before the Beaudoin-Dobbie committee and spelled out his principles and some of their implications. "First nations have always been sovereign," he said. "It is clear that first nations have never surrendered their sovereignty. It continues to this day. It has merely been suppressed."

He did promise that first nations would not assert their sovereignty to become independent states, if Canada accepted their view of things. Otherwise? Mercredi did not disguise a threat. "Canada will not become one big Swiss cheese. However, this can be avoided only by the recognition and acceptance of our rights as first-nations citizens. Continued denial of our rights will only endanger the integrity of this country." To make the threat more explicit still, Mercredi warned that Canada must settle soon. "The longer Canada denies our rights, the longer Canada will be subject to our right to international status."

Mercredi was not talking about just any recognition of the rights of first-nations citizens, but only recognition of the inherent rights to self-government and to self-rule in almost all areas of life. He also meant the right to a standard comparable to that of other Canadians.

The federal proposals made public in September had outlined a number of principles with respect to aboriginals. They were to participate in the current constitutional deliberations, and they would receive in the constitution "a general justiciable right to aboriginal self-government within the Canadian federation and subject to the Canadian charter of rights and Freedoms." This meant a real right to self-government, enforceable by the courts. The right to go to court, though, would be suspended for up to ten years, to allow all the governments and the aboriginal people to "come to a common understanding of the content of this right."

The Assembly of First Nations had rejected participation in a common constitutional process—until they saw how effective the joint conferences in Halifax, Calgary, and Montreal were in reaching public opinion. Then Mercredi appeared at the Toronto conference in a magnificent feathered headdress to claim self-government for aboriginal peoples, and an Algonquin elder performed the sweetgrass ceremony to purify the minds of the participants. Now, the aboriginal leaders insisted on a televised constitutional conference of their own.

As Mercredi explained to the Beaudoin-Dobbie committee, the main problem with the federal proposals for aboriginals was that they did not take as their starting point the fact that the first nations were already sovereign. The proposals would confer self-government upon them through the constitution of Canada. That was unacceptable. "Since this right [to aboriginal self-government] comes from our being aboriginal to this land, and from the duties and responsibilities given to us by the Creator when we were put on this land, it is an inherent right." Mercredi would not even accept a statement from the constitutional committee saying that first nations enjoyed an inherent right to self-government, if that right was qualified by words such as "within Canada" or "under the constitution of Canada." So, Canada was to have governments that derived their legitimacy from the constitution, and would-be governments of first nations that derived their legitimacy from God and a long line of ancestors.

On 1 March 1992, the Beaudoin-Dobbie committee issued its report, so eagerly awaited, in which it put forward its blueprint for refashioning Canada, while making "offers" to Quebec. This was to be the second response to the Allaire and Bélanger-Campeau reports, following the preliminary federal proposals of the previous September.

After stormy negotiations between the federal Conservatives, Liberals, and New Democrats, the committee had come up with a set of propositions on which all three parties agreed. But, for Robert Bourassa, the report showed clearly that the federal parliamentarians were unwilling to undertake the general dismantling of the federal government for the benefit of Quebec that the two Quebec constitutional reports had called for. The ultimatum delivered by Allaire, by Bélanger-Campeau, by Bill 150, by Bourassa's own rhetoric, all of which brandished the threat of secession if Quebec did not get its way, had failed

Beaudoin-Dobbie did propose that Quebec be recognized as a distinct society, and that the Charter of Rights be interpreted so as to allow for the preservation and promotion of Quebec as a distinct society. But that long-sought recognition was limited and weakened, from Bourassa's perspective, by the addition that the Charter was also to be interpreted in a manner consistent with "the vitality and development of the language and culture of French-speaking and English-speaking minority communities throughout Canada." Quebec could not operate fully as an ethnic state if it was to be forced to recognize the right to a full existence of its English-speaking minority.

Quebec would also gain guarantees against the tyranny of the Canadian majority: a restored veto on fundamental changes to the 1867 pact, and a double majority system in the Senate, so that "measures affecting the language or culture of French-speaking communities should require the approval of a majority of Senators voting and a majority of francophone Senators voting." The three Supreme Court of Canada justices from Quebec were also to be constitutionalized. And Quebec's jurisdiction over culture was to be explicitly affirmed, with a concomitant restriction on Ottawa's use of the spending power in the field of culture, which was to be conditional on the approval of the province.

But the Quebec government's demand was, above all, for more powers. On that score, the chief means offered to satisfy Quebec's demands was what Beaudoin-Dobbie called "flexible federalism," which involved creating two new powers in the constitution. One was a power of "legislative delegation," whereby "the Parliament of Canada or the legislature of a province may delegate to the other any of its authority to make laws." The second, similar in effect, was to create a new power whereby the federal government and a province could enter into binding agreements on such topics, for instance, as the conditions under which the federal government would be allowed to spend money in support of culture in the province.

This was the very heart of Beaudoin-Dobbie. It was meant to reconcile the demands of Quebec for more power and security with the attachment of the rest of Canada to a strong central government. It avoided creating an obvious special status for Quebec because the agreements could, in principle, be entered into between the federal government and any other province that wanted them.

And, though the agreements were not explicitly to be entrenched in the constitution as amendments, they were to have some of the security and permanent character of constitutional amendments through the wording of the umbrella clause under which they were to be made: "An agreement, contract, or other arrangement approved under this section may not be amended or removed except in accordance with its terms or by a further agreement, contract, or arrangement approved as provided in this section." In other words, an airtight and long-range agreement between Ottawa and Quebec could be drawn up to guarantee Quebec's interests, worded so that it would exist in perpetuity unless Quebec agreed to its revocation.

These proposals were ingenious; they could give Quebec great additional latitude, while tampering with the constitution itself as little as possible. They postponed fundamental changes in the equilibrium of the federation to a later stage, when the actual delegations and intergovernmental agreements between Ottawa and Quebec were to be negotiated.

But this approach did not change the formal distribution of powers between Ottawa and Quebec, and Premier Bourassa expressed his disappointment in terms that, for him, were unusually clear. "On the key question of the sharing of powers," he told a news conference in Quebec City on 3 March, "There is not much on the table. There are formulas proposed, but . . . it's very vague and it's difficult to conclude that this is implying a real transfer of powers to Quebec."

Bourassa said no in strong terms that practically excluded this approach to satisfying Quebec by constitutional change. He spoke of the Beaudoin-Dobbie report as projecting a "dominating federalism." No more damaging words could have been imagined in Quebec's political lexicon. "They think that they must be present in all sectors, and that, to all intents and purposes, they could have the last word. And this is not an approach, in our view, that respects the constitution of Canada." He called for a clearer demarcation. "It must be clear what is of Quebec's or provincial jurisdiction, and what is federal jurisdiction."

So it was that the whole approach proposed by Beaudoin-Dobbie to allow Quebec to achieve special status without manifestly weakening the federal government across the country came to naught. And time was getting short.

The dynamics of arriving at "offers" had to be revised when Joe Clark convened the representatives of the provinces for consultation on 12 March 1992. Bob Rae arrived in Ottawa with a full-blown plan to achieve constitutional proposals. He swept aside both the original federal proposals of the previous September and the proposals of the Beaudoin-Dobbie committee, which had been made public not two weeks earlier. Rae's plan involved negotiations that were to be held over the following two months. They would include the federal government, the provinces, the two territorial governments, and—most significantly—the representatives of the aboriginals as full and equal participants.

Rae's plan, quickly backed by other premiers, put Clark in a quandary. To start negotiations all over again in this new forum would mean giving up federal control over the process. Clark would chair the meetings, but he would be outnumbered fifteen to one in what soon came to be called the Multilateral Ministerial Conference on the Constitution. Each participant, a power wielder with a defined constituency, would come with his or her own agenda; each would be trying to pull public opinion in a different direction. And to admit four aboriginal representatives as full participants, as Rae insisted, would strengthen immeasurably their negotiating power in a way that was not likely to please Bourassa. Aboriginals had prevented the adoption of Meech Lake; they had turned a local confrontation at Oka into an international *cause célèbre* that had tarnished Quebec's reputation; and they were leading an effective public-opinion battle in the United States against Quebec's hydro-electric development plans at James Bay and Hudson Bay. What would they do in this new constitutional round? The whole process would be headed in an unknown direction, driven by complex new dynamics.

Nevertheless, Clark capitulated. Perhaps he had no choice. Rae was premier of Canada's largest province; his backing was essential for a constitutional deal. And Rae, together with fellow New Democrats Michael Harcourt and Roy Romanow, the premiers of British Columbia and Saskatchewan, represented provinces with more than half the population of Canada. No constitutional deal could be passed over their objections, even if every other premier went along. Then, too, the native cause had caught the imagination of the Canadian public ever since Ovide Mercredi had taken the Toronto Renewal of Canada conference by storm the previous month. To exclude aboriginals was now bad politics. So the number of hands rewriting the constitution increased by six, even though the amending formula recognized only the federal Parliament and the provincial legislatures.

For Bourassa, the new vehicle for reaching constitutional change was hardly what he had planned. He had repudiated constitutional negotiations *à onze* as discredited by the failure of Meech Lake. He had insisted that he would only take part in negotiations *à deux*. And now Clark had raised the number to seventeen.[9]

Bourassa thus reaped the consequence of his decision to boycott constitutional negotiations. By being absent from the table on 12 March, he was unable to veto the expanded roster of players. He had sent along two Quebec civil servants as observers, but they were not authorized to speak officially on behalf of the Quebec government. Bourassa's strategy of conspicuous absence would bring more unpleasant surprises.

So began the saga of the travelling negotiators, trailing politicians, civil servants, public relations advisers, and journalists in a cortege through Halifax, Ottawa, Edmonton, Saint John, Vancouver, Montreal, Toronto, and again Ottawa. As we will see, always without Quebec, the perambulatory constituent assembly chaired by Clark would eventually, on 7 July, reach the "historic" package that would stun Quebec because it proposed to reduce Quebec's representation in the upper House to eight senators from twenty-four. That, at last, would persuade Bourassa that it was time for him to declare a victory of sorts and re-enter the process of constitutional negotiations.

Notes

1.While Meech had included a commitment to "protect" the "existence" of English-speaking Canadians in Quebec and of French-speaking Canadians in the rest of Canada, what was now proposed involved merely "the *preservation* of the existence of French-speaking Canadians, primarily located in Quebec, but also present throughout Canada, and English-speaking Canadians, primarily located outside Quebec but also present in Quebec." To move from *protection* to *preservation* of the existence of the minorities was hardly reassuring. The clause would presumably be invoked in the unlikely event that some government attempted genocide or mass deportation of its official-language minority.

2.Other proposals included defining the mandate of the Bank of Canada as being to maintain price stability, and reforming the procedures of the House of Commons to diminish partisanship and allow more free votes.

3.Interview by Jean-Francois Lisée, *L'Actualité*, 1 Nov. 1991.

4.Half of his references to Ontario were in this one sentence: "Quebec's single largest customer by far is Ontario, which buys 29 per cent of all Quebec exports; and, as you know, Quebec is Ontario's most important Canadian customer."

5.Paul Gesell in the Ottawa *Citizen*, 25 Nov. 1991.

6.Section 36 says, in part, "Parliament and the legislatures, together with the Government of Canada and the provincial governments, are committed to (a) promoting equal opportunities for the well-being of Canadians; (b) furthering economic development to reduce disparity in opportunities; and (c) providing essential public services of reasonable quality to all Canadians. Parliament and the Government of Canda are committed to the principle of making equalization payments to ensure that provincial governments have sufficient revenues to provide reasonably comparable levels of public services at reasonably comparable levels of taxation."

7"The Government of Canada proposes the establishment of a Council of the Federation composed of federal, provincial and territorial governments that would meet to decide on issues of intergovernmental coordination and collaboration."

8.Peter Lougheed, interviewed on Newsworld.

9.Bourassa explained to CBC's *The Journal*, "It was already quite difficult to reach an agreement with eleven and I thought that at seventeen it will be more difficult." Quoted in Susan Delacourt, *United We Fall. The Crisis of Democracy in Canada* (Toronto: Penguin Books, 1993), p. 140.

CHAPTER NINETEEN

The 1992 Referendum: Defeat

W as it a sign of a spring thaw? In his speech at the opening of a new session of the National Assembly on 19 March 1992, premier Robert Bourassa had kind words for the Canadian federation. And he repeated them the following weekend at the Quebec Liberal Party's general council meeting. There was joy in Ottawa at the sudden profession of federalist faith.

Bourassa stated that a renewed federalism was Quebec's first choice. "Canada, as no one can deny, is a country of rare privilege in the world in terms of peace, freedom, justice, and standard of living." And he also pointed out the costs and the risks involved in breaking up a federation that had existed for 125 years, particularly when foreigners held some $260 billion in Canadian debt.

But at the same time, he made clear that federalism, renewed on his terms, would be weak: "In this federalism, Quebec aims at getting all the powers to manage its social, cultural, and economic development." As a federalist credo, that was rather noncommittal. If Quebec obtained "all the powers" to control its "social, cultural, and economic development," what did that leave for Ottawa? It was exactly the same vision that he had put forward in 1967. [1]

And, in the same breath, Bourassa stated that his renewed federalism meant that Quebec could become independent at any time it chose. "[Quebec] also recognizes that, in this federalism, it keeps its right to self-determination or its right to sovereignty which was recognized *de facto* in 1980. I remember clearly a speech which I gave on 18 June 1987, when I proposed the ratification of the Meech Lake accord; I mentioned on that occasion, very clearly, that with the Meech Lake accord, we kept that right to self-determination."

In spite of the egregious qualifications, Brian Mulroney was impressed. He happened to be in New York the day after Bourassa's speech, and he brought it up when he spoke to the editorial board of the *New York Times*. As he related to Canadian journalists afterwards, he told the Americans that he was confident Quebec would remain part of the Canadian federation, citing the speech by Bourassa as evidence to back up his optimism. Mulroney's Quebec lieutenant, Benoît Bouchard, also expressed delight at Bourassa's speech.

The following weekend, at the meeting of the Liberal Party, the premier told reporters that it would be irresponsible to hold a referendum in Quebec that he could not win. Indeed, in recent months a referendum on sovereignty had turned into an unattractive prospect for Bourassa, whatever his deeper convictions. Public-opinion polls now showed that support for sovereignty had stabilized at a level considerably below where it had stood from late 1989 until early 1991. In fact, evidence indicated that opinion in Quebec was about evenly divided for and against sovereignty. Whatever slight advantage for sovereignty the polls might suggest was counterbalanced by the well-established fact that, since at least 1970, public-opinion polls had systematically underestimated the federalist vote.[2]

As a realist, Bourassa knew that the worst possible outcome was a referendum on sovereignty in which the result of the vote was within the range of 45 to 55 per cent: this would be a formula for deadlock, for intensified conflict, and perhaps even for a return of terrorism. It would not show enough support to legitimate a declaration of sovereignty, but would effectively undercut the legitimacy and stability of federalism, leaving Quebec with the worst of both options, causing a flight of capital, discouraging investment, and weakening the bargaining position of the Quebec government vis-à-vis the rest of Canada. By the spring of 1992, that was precisely the most likely result of any referendum. In such a dead heat, the presumption would be in favour of the existing constitution rather than the extra-legal course of independence.

So Bourassa, in March, 1992, was proclaiming a preference for federalism. But his federalist commitment was far from boundless. Within the ten days before the opening of a new session, Bourassa had twice thrown his party's support behind a slightly amended Parti Québécois resolution to express disapproval of the Beaudoin-Dobbie constitutional proposals and to confirm that Quebec would stay away from the multilateral constitutional negotiations. Bourassa even withdrew the two senior officials who had been present as observers at Joe Clark's negotiating table.

The same day as Bourassa made his "federalist" speech, his communications minister, Lawrence Cannon, made public a letter he had written to federal communications minister Perrin Beatty, in which he denounced as an "unacceptable *coup de force*" (meaning a political assault) the recently introduced federal legislation to regulate telecommunications, which simply asserted the federal jurisdiction over telecommunications that had been confirmed by the Supreme Court of Canada in 1989. The bill had originally been announced by then federal minister of communications Marcel Masse, a certified Quebec nationalist. Under vehement denunciation from Quebec, Masse had backed down and postponed introducing the bill.

Cannon told reporters that section 7 of the bill was "a serious threat to the cultural identity of Quebecers." And what did that ominous section 7 say? It proposed that telecommunications in Canada should "contribute to safeguard, enrich, and strengthen the cultural, political, social, and economic fabric of Canada." For the Bourassa government, even at the time of its "federalist" confession, the cultural identity of Canada was considered incompatible with the cultural identity of Quebec.

Also on the day of Bourassa's speech, Quebec's environment minister, Pierre Paradis, denounced in virulent terms a bill requiring the federal government to carry out environmental assessments in all large-scale projects that involved federal financial contributions or federal jurisdiction. Like the telecommunications bill, the environmental legislation had originally been introduced in a slightly different form by a recognized Quebec nationalist, Lucien Bouchard, when he was minister of the environment. In a letter to his federal counterpart, Jean Charest, that hardly reflected a strong commitment to federalism, Paradis wrote that the federal bill "contains all the elements that make it a perfect example of the dominating and totalitarian process that is current in the relations between the federal government and Quebec."

Meanwhile, Bourassa set about to give credibility to his threat to make Quebec either a semi-independent country in a loose federation or a fully sovereign country linked to Canada only by economic arrangements. He assigned to a few top figures in the Quebec Liberal Party the task of secretly working up a strategy for a referendum on sovereignty.[3]

Their report, titled *Trame et scénario d'un discours référendaire*, was ready by June, 1992.[4] It detailed how a referendum on "shared sovereignty," or on complete sovereignty along with a proposal for an economic union, could be sold to the people of Quebec. It assumed that no acceptable offer was possible from the rest of Canada because Quebec and the rest of Canada had incompatible political visions. "These two opposed visions of Canada neutralize each other in a zero sum game which helps to make the country less and less governable, while paralyzing every serious attempt at reform," the report stated. Because "Canada is unable to grant to Quebec even a fraction of the powers that Quebec needs," the report proposed as a solution for Quebec "to proclaim its sovereignty while proposing a far-reaching economic agreement with the rest of Canada."

The timetable proposed in the report followed the spirit, though not the letter, of Bill 150, the legislation setting up the referendum on sovereignty. Assuming that Quebecers backed the proposal in a referendum, the report recommended that the Quebec government immediately proclaim the sovereignty of Quebec, and then propose a "new deal" to the rest of Canada. A year would be allowed for setting up the new, supranational structure. The new "Government of the Union" that was to replace the federal government would be elected by the citizens of both countries, Quebec and Canada, with representation according to population, giving Quebec about one quarter of the seats. The new government, while exercising far narrower jurisdictions than the federal Parliament, would have responsibility for the monetary system, defence, a free internal market, mail, criminal law, and setting environmental standards. It would have the power to raise taxes to carry out its responsibilities.

The "new deal" followed closely what Bourassa had envisaged since the 1960s as the ideal solution for Quebec. The only truly different element was the mechanism for achieving that goal: a referendum, followed by a declaration of sovereignty. The writers of the proposal anticipated no great upheaval as a result of putting the plan into action; they estimated that Quebec's gross domestic product would decline by a mere 1.5 per cent in the first year, but that this would soon be compensated for by the savings achieved by the elimination of existing duplications between the federal and Quebec governments.

The fact that planning on so radical a proposal had gone so far indicated that Bourassa was not bluffing when, after the failure of Meech, he set in motion such vast machinery for radical constitutional change. In the event, though, he never implemented the plan prepared by his advisers. Why not? Surely not because he would obtain what he wanted through the process of negotiating with the other first ministers. Perhaps it was because, deep down, he did not believe in sovereignty. But the most obvious explanation is that he recognized, as his party did not, that the "declaration of sovereignty" route was highly perilous and would require overwhelming support from the people of Quebec to succeed. To proclaim Quebec's sovereignty and to act on it would be to repudiate the constitution of Canada, which is also the constitution of Quebec. It would be to have the National Assembly take a step that clearly was not within its competence under the law. Without overwhelming support to justify it politically and to carry it through, a declaration of sovereignty would be to plunge into an adventure and risk a flight of capital on a scale never before seen in Quebec.

Would the people of Quebec support such an adventure? Bourassa seemed to think so at the time of the Allaire report. More than a year later, support had softened. To run such a risk was not in Bourassa's style. He preferred to set the stage for a great confrontation, an epic adventure, then, at the last minute, settle for the best deal he could get without putting his threat to the test. He was not the stuff of a national hero who founds a new country.

The same polls that diminished the threat of a referendum on sovereignty encouraged a new aggressiveness in the prime minister. At the end of March, during a visit to his riding, Mulroney ridiculed the nationalists as "fine intellects, those who dream today of imaginary countries." He contrasted them with those who would bear the brunt of the costs if Quebec separated, "those who go to work with a lunch pail, as our parents did—not those who discuss macro-economics at the Club St-Denis."

And now Mulroney made increasingly explicit the threat that he would go to the people in a referendum if agreement with the provinces could not be reached at the negotiating table. "If the very, very challenging efforts of the minister responsible for constitutional affairs [Joe Clark] should prove to be unsuccessful over the next five or six weeks, then, at the appropriate time, we would come to the House with some suggestions as to how we might be able to convey to the people of Canada the options that are there," Mulroney told the Commons on 1 April. "One thing is for absolutely certain, that should we encounter a wall that would paralyze the activity, and with the clock ticking elsewhere, we will not sit idly by and allow damage to be done to Canada without allowing Canadians themselves to make determinations about their well-being, the future of this great country and how they they want to keep it together." He spoke increasingly about the true alternatives facing Quebecers as being separation or federalism: federalism, renewed if possible, but federalism. "If you ask Quebecers whether you want independence or a united Canada, they will say a united Canada ten times out of ten," he said.

And he took to ridiculing Jacques Parizeau in a comedy routine that delighted his followers: "Mr. Parizeau wants a sovereign Quebec with Canadian money, Canadian citizenship, the benefits of the Canada-U.S. free trade agreement, the Canadian passport, flag, and the Queen." Then came the punch line. "You know, in hockey, it would be quite a game. Mr. Parizeau wants to play for a separate Quebec, but wearing the federalist Canadian sweater." In this way, he shifted the presumption away from Bourassa's message that Canada must face radical decentralization or accept Quebec's sovereignty. It was to be separatism—represented by Parizeau—or Canada.

The changed circumstances were also reflected in the different attitudes of the Conservative caucus of Quebec MPs. Also on 1 April, most of them withdrew their previous objections to a federal referendum bill. The previous fall, they had forced Clark to back away from introducing the referendum legislation the Throne speech had announced, viewing the federal bill as an attempt to counter a referendum called by Quebec. But now it had become the best way of getting Bourassa off the hook. A referendum on federal "offers" would no longer be a club against Quebec nationalism, but against the reluctant premiers of the other provinces, such as Clyde Wells and Don Getty.

At the perambulatory Multilateral Ministerial Conference, Joe Clark had run into difficulties. The deal-breaking issue was no longer Quebec's mandate as a distinct society, but the form and powers of the Senate. In Halifax, on 8 and 9 April, the negotiators rather quickly agreed to a distinct society clause. Even Wells, who had held out so stubbornly against Meech Lake's distinct society clause, now withdrew his objections to giving Quebec a mandate to curtail the rights of Quebec citizens. As long as only Quebecers were affected, he would no longer object.

But the Senate issue had become intractable. Getty, taking a very different tone from that of the conciliatory Peter Lougheed, insisted that he would not sign a deal that did not include a Senate with equal representation. And Alberta's constitutional affairs minister, Jim Horsman, warned Clark that he would lose his riding of Yellowhead at the next election if he did not get behind a Senate with the third E—equality of representation.

So Clark moved away from his position that equality was as likely as another virgin birth. "I think the possibility of an equal Senate would be greater if its powers were reduced," he told journalists on 14 April.

It was not easy to find common ground among the premiers. The Select Committee on Ontario in Confederation frowned on equality of representation and recognized that it was not likely to be acceptable to Quebec. "It is not realistic to expect that Quebec, with its enormous proportion of the French-speaking population of the country, could accept a reduction to 10 per cent of the second chamber's membership." But Ontario did keep the door of equality open a crack—if the powers of the future Senate were reduced so as to give the Commons "ultimate supremacy" over it.

Faced with conflicting pressures and complicated calculations, Clark said regretfully, "It would obviously be easier for all of us, on this topic which has not been discussed extensively in federal-provincial conferences before, if all provinces were at the table. Particularly on an issue like the Senate, because it would give us a greater sense as to where durable agreement that could reach across the entire country might lie."

Clark did not name the single province that was not at the table, but Quebec was always on everyone's mind. Quebec, absent, dominated the discussions or, at least, was a constant point of reference in every discussion. What would Quebec think of whatever item was on the agenda at a given moment? The negotiators contacted Quebec officials or Gil Rémillard, or even Bourassa, and received impressionistic answers. It was all rather like the children's game in which one child tries to guess what the others have chosen as the designated object in the room; as the child moves about, the others cry, "Cold, cold, colder, warm, you're getting warm . . ."

By the end of the multilateral conference which met in Edmonton at the end of April, the negotiators had delivered expeditiously on four of the five conditions that the Bourassa Liberals had put forward before the Meech Lake negotiations: the distinct society, Quebec's right to three justices on the Supreme Court of Canada, the right for Quebec (and other desirous provinces) to control immigration to Canada via the province, and limitations on the federal government's spending power within provincial sectors of jurisdiction. That left the all-important question of a veto for Quebec over future constitutional change, with which the core of Meech Lake would have been reconstituted.

To encourage the process, Bourassa and Rémillard journeyed to British Columbia on 3 May and met with Premier Harcourt, then the chairman of the premiers' conference. From there, they visited in turn premiers Don Getty of Alberta, Roy Romanow of Saskatchewan, and Gary Filmon of Manitoba. They would not participate in formal negotiations, but they found it useful to have earnest chats with the premiers one by one. Time was running short; Joe Clark was supposed to conclude his negotiations by the end of the month, and the negotiators still seemed far away from what Bourassa could consider a success. They still had not dealt with the most pressing issue in the post-Meech Lake era: Quebec's demands for vast new jurisdictions.

Mulroney was also preparing for the likely failure of Clark's itinerant conference. On 15 May, the federal government introduced Bill 81, to authorize holding a referendum across the country. Mulroney now had the support of his caucus, including the Quebec members. However, the bill provoked a storm of indignation and vituperation from Quebec nationalists because it did not enforce equal spending limits on the Yes and No sides in a referendum. In other words, it did not resemble Quebec's authoritarian and coercive legislation.

To apply the Quebec rules across Canada would not only have been a violation of freedom of speech and of association, it would have been physically impossible. How could one umbrella committee for the Yes and another for the No approve in advance all the spending for the referendum campaign from coast to coast to coast, in every city, town, hamlet, block, and reserve of Canada? Just to draw up the budget for expenditures would take more time than would be available in any referendum campaign. The elitist control it implied would have defeated the very idea of a referendum, which is to allow the considered voice of the people to be heard, beyond the usual power brokers and appointed spokespersons.

Jean Lapierre, then House leader for the Bloc Québécois, put the Quebec nationalists' case in stark form:

This referendum bill is the most illegitimate and anti-democratic legislation ever seen in the Parliament of a British regime. . . . The democratic values that have been so precious to Quebecers, for instance in 1980, are going to be violated by this legislation. . . . This referendum bill has only one enemy: Quebec. . . . No Quebecer will feel bound by your illegitimate legislation. You can show whatever results you want. You can spend all the millions that you want, but none of us will feel bound by the results of a defective, unworthy, and implausible piece of legislation.

Lapierre's Bloc Québécois colleague, Louis Plamondon, was if possible, even more virulent;

This is a hold-up of democracy, in which Conservatives are accomplices. . . . The Conservatives have become collaborators, just like the Nazis were, or like we saw in France during World War Two. . . . This is terrible. Here is a repugnant, immoral bill, without spending limits, something intolerable in a western democratic society. Something never seen before! You do not want a referendum, you want to be able to buy the conscience of citizens and block Quebec's aspirations."

The federal legislation was adopted, and the 26 October referendum was to be held everywhere outside Quebec under its rules. The result was to show why the obsession of Quebec leaders with controlling total spending by both sides was unnecessary. Though the Yes side outspent the No side by more than ten to one, the No side won.

Joe Clark, meanwhile, was trying to reach an agreement on the aboriginal package with the provincial and territorial ministers and the representatives of four aboriginal organizations: the Assembly of First Nations, representing status Indians; the Inuit Tapirisat of Canada, representing the Inuit; the Métis National Council, representing Métis; and the Native Council of Canada, representing mostly urban aboriginals. In Toronto, at the end of May, as time was running out, the negotiatiors reached a compromise that allowed them to move forward. They accepted a proposal from the Métis National Council that the right to self-government would be, in principle, recognized from the start and enforceable in court. But all parties would, at the same time, undertake not to appeal to the courts for at least three years while negotiations on the definition and terms of self-government continued. So the crunch was put off into the future: the negotiators decided to constitutionalize aboriginal self-government immediately and find out what it meant later.

The issue not so easily postponed, though, was that of Senate reform. By 27 May, Clark and Bob Rae, still opposed to a Triple-E Senate, proposed instead a lower-grade Triple-E: elected, (moderately) effective, and with equal representation from each region rather than each province. British Columbia delivered what seemed like the *coup de grâce* to Triple-E by changing its earlier position in favour of equal provinces to equal representation from each region—as long as there were five regions, rather than the existing four. The proposal was that British Columbia, the Yukon and the Northwest Territories would form a fifth new region, and each region—including Quebec, Ontario, Atlantic Canada and the Prairies, would hold 20 per cent of the Senate seats.

But still Alberta held out, and, without a resolution, the constitutional negotiations went into overtime, after a ten-day respite for all to reconsider their positions. When the negotiators resumed, in Ottawa on 9 June, five provinces, two territories, and the Métis National Council put forward a document called a "Comprehensive Proposal for Equal Senate." It offered a Senate with eight senators elected from each province and two from each territory, for a total of eighty-four senators. The document, backed by Newfoundland, Manitoba, Saskatchewan, Nova Scotia, and Alberta, left no room for compromise on an equal Senate, which, it said, represented the very principle of federalism.

The deadlock on the Senate seemed insoluble. Clark hinted that the federal government would "assume its responsibilities" and put forward a package with, he hoped, the support of the other federalist parties in the Commons. The federal government seemed prepared to act unilaterally. The next day, 10 June, Benoît Bouchard left the talks for good. He had been present to watch over the interests of absent Quebec, but he had come to the conclusion that there was no hope for a settlement on the Senate, and he said he had other things to do.

That same evening, Romanow had thrown the negotiations into a ferment by arriving unexpectedly from New York and putting forward a new plan, involving an equal number of senators elected from each province, with the senators casting votes of different weightings on different issues. On some issues, the votes would be of equal weight. On most, the weighting would vary according to the population of the province. His proposal was a variation of one made earlier by Quebec's Claude Beauchamp, which had been rejected immediately by Horsman. But Romanow added a sweetener for Alberta: on issues dealing with natural resources, the senators would vote with an equal weight and would have an absolute veto over bills coming from the Commons. But still, Alberta remained opposed.

Brian Mulroney intervened to break the deadlock. He convened the nine premiers to a lunch at 24 Sussex on 29 June, and he told them that a solution to the problem of the Senate was up to them. Could the premiers, by themselves, come to an agreement?

So the premiers met in Toronto the following Friday, with Clark there only as an observer. The dynamics had changed. There was no Benoît Bouchard to interpret what would or would not be acceptable to Quebec, and no federal chairperson to argue the national interest. Instead, there was Bob Rae outnumbered eight to one. Rae was stigmatized by the other premiers as the one who was standing in the way of an agreement. Ontario, the fact cat of Confederation, was preventing a new deal for the smaller and poorer provinces.

At last, Rae capitulated. Ontario would bow to Triple-E, more or less. Rae was caught by his own logic. He had said categorically all along that there would be an agreement at the end of the negotiations, as there had to be. But Getty and Horsman would agree to Triple-E and nothing but Triple-E. Unlike Rae, they were willing to run the risk of there being no agreement. So, at the end of the day, it had to be their way or no way.

What was the formula? A Senate that was elected and equal. Each senator would have the same vote. But there would be various vote levels required for blocking a bill from the Commons. For bills that fell entirely within federal jurisdiction, a vote of 75 per cent would be needed to veto the Commons' decision. For a bill that fell under shared federal and provincial jurisdiction, a 60 per cent vote would be needed. For bills dealing with topics under provincial jurisdiction, the federal spending power could be stopped with a 50 per cent vote.

At the end of that Toronto meeting, Joe Clark was optimistic. He said that he had spoken on the phone with Robert Bourassa and had outlined the new proposal to him. While not commenting on Bourassa's response, Clark left a clear impression that there was no sign of a negative reaction from the Quebec premier.

The breakthrough gave the promise for a restored Quebec veto over the central institutions—the Commons, the Senate, the Supreme Court, and the monarchy. Both Wells and Getty had said repeatedly that they could not agree to a veto unless they had the Triple-E Senate, but that day's breakthrough changed the equation. Getty confirmed that he considered the Senate proposal consistent with what he had demanded: "The principles that we have advocated are still the same, and they are in it." Getty and Wells both implied that they could accept a veto for all provinces—hence for Quebec—if that day's proposal was accepted.

When the Multilateral Ministerial Conference resumed on the following Monday, with Joe Clark once again in charge, the participants were able to deal rapidly with the remaining issues, such as the economic union, aboriginal government, equalization, and the veto. By Tuesday evening, the premiers (minus Bourassa) had joined the negotiations; at the end of the day, they announced triumphantly their agreement on the full constitutional package. Clark, visibly moved, announced that it was a "historic moment" for Canada, with the broadest package of constitutional changes seen since 1867.

Not everyone, however, was as euphoric. Brian Mulroney, abroad in Munich at the time, told a press conference the next day that he did not believe in miracles. He seemed anything but delighted at Clark's *tour de force*.

In Quebec, Bourassa waited until the second day before reacting publicly. He had asked, on the night that Meech failed, "What does English Canada want?" Now, he seemed to have an answer. It was a long way from Allaire, or from the European Community that he had held up so often as a model. In fact, under the 7 July package, Quebec saw its representation in the proposed Senate fall from twenty-four to six seats.

Bourassa reacted cautiously at his press conference. He said neither yes nor no, although he was impressed with the good will shown by his partners in Canada. He did not reject any of the proposals out of hand; he was studying them, asking for clarifications. He was waiting for definitive texts rather than the drafts he had seen so far. And he was waiting for Mulroney to take the next step: either convene a meeting of the first ministers, or announce that he was introducing a resolution in the Commons.

What Bourassa did above all was play for time. He presented as small a target as he could. He raised questions, expressed concerns. He would have to look very carefully at the equal and elected Senate, and decide whether Quebec could live with it. He had concerns about the proposals for aboriginal self-government, and he would refuse any proposal if it threatened the territorial integrity of Quebec. He was also concerned about the proposal that made the creation of a new province possible without the assent of Quebec. He expressed concern about the division of powers, and wondered whether the proposal gave Quebec overall direction of human resources, including retraining programs for the work force.

But, at this moment, after the other governments had wrestled with each other for months and had at last come to an agreement, Bourassa was careful not to burn one bridge. Even on the Senate proposal, which had caused the most shocked commentary in Quebec, his tone was conciliatory. He and his colleagues would study it carefully, he said. He recognized that, on the face of it, the proposed Senate involved an enormous loss of power for Quebec. At the same time, he was ready to concede that political reality might be quite different from what the numbers of proposed senators would suggest.

"The debate on the Senate has not taken place in Quebec," the premier said. That was true, in large part, because of his absence from the negotiating table. Political Quebec had not followed the evolution of thinking on the Senate at the Multilateral Ministerial Conference. Until the premiers' meeting in Toronto, a Triple-E Senate had seemed so out of the question that little was said about it in Quebec by politicians, academics, or journalists.

The premier was careful not to put himself out ahead of the curve of public opinion. But he did signal to his fellow premiers from the western provinces that he understood why they wanted the Senate so badly. He acknowledged publicly that some $80 billion had been transferred during the oil boom from Alberta to the rest of Canada, including Quebecers. That fact, he said, needed to be understood and respected when pondering the Senate proposal.

In fact, Bourassa's single most telling message came when he praised Canada as the "first country in the world," and he said that his party was deeply committed to developing Quebec within the Canadian federation.

That message was a far cry from what Bourassa had communicated during 1990 and early 1991, when he had seemed so confident that Quebec's sovereignist mood was there to stay, or even in March. What could explain the change in tone? The likely answer was a CROP public-opinion poll published in the June, 1992, issue of L'Actualité, in which Quebecers had shown a surprising attachment to Canada. Even the Canadian Charter of Rights, product of the oft-decried, supposedly illegitimate 1982 patriation, was endorsed by 73 per cent of the respondents. Most important, 54 per cent said they wanted Quebec to remain a province of Canada rather than become an independent country. Quebecers were obviously not ready for a revolution, for a great upheaval, for a unilateral declaration of independence, for leaping up on the high horses of humiliation and hurt feelings to charge into the unknown. This limited Bourassa's options. He had practically only one option left: to reach a settlement with the rest of Canada. But on what terms? The 7 July "historic" agreement was greeted, after an initial embarrassed silence, with an almost unanimous chorus of rejection in Quebec. Its only defenders there were Brian Mulroney and Ghislain Dufour, president of the Conseil du Patronat du Québec.

The denunciations came from everywhere: from ministers Marcel Masse, André Bourbeau, and Benoît Bouchard; from Tory backbenchers Jean-Pierre

Blackburn, Monique Tardif, and Gabriel Desjardins; from Conservative Senators Gérald Beaudoin, Roch Bolduc, and Solange Chaput-Rolland; from the Quebec civil servants' union; from Jean Allaire; from political guru Léon Dion; and from Mario Dumont, president of the Quebec Young Liberals.

Senator Claude Castonguay, who had been Mulroney's first choice to lead the country to a brave new settlement, had his strictures spread across the top of page one of *La Presse* on the Saturday following the announcement. "What we had to fear has come about," said Castonguay. "It has become a round in which the voice of the aboriginals and of the small provinces is preponderant." Castonguay found that both Quebec and Canada were losers. In particular, he deplored the reduction by two thirds of Quebec's voice in the Senate, the recognition in the constitution for the first time of the federal spending power in areas of provincial jurisdiction, the absence of major changes to the division of powers, and the granting of the power to create new provinces to the federal governmment alone. Under the proposed arrangement, he said, "Quebec will become totally vulnerable."

Claude Masson, associate publisher of the federalist *La Presse*, maintained that Quebec "was had" with the patriation of 1982 and the failure of Meech Lake in 1990. He deemed the Clark package unacceptable in its current form. "Without other compromises on the part of Ottawa and the other provinces, without changes and not just clarifications to the offer that was tabled, the Bourassa government cannot run the risk of a referendum. It would be headed for its own loss and a massive rejection by Quebecers."

In Quebec City's *Le Soleil*, Raymond Giroux argued editorially that Quebecers would not accept the proposed Triple-E Senate without more powers for the Quebec government. "As with the federal proposals of last September, as with the Beaudoin-Dobbie report of last winter, as with the interim report last month from Joe Clark [on the multilateral negotiations], there is still one major element missing in the reform: a significant division of powers. And, without new powers, as the Allaire report demanded, there will be no salvation."

According to a poll by Léger and Léger published in *Le Journal de Montréal*, those who had made up their mind were mostly against the package (43.9%), and more were undecided (28.7%) than were in favour (26.6%). Furthermore, 55.5 per cent now said they would vote for Quebec's sovereignty in a referendum. The agreement reached by the negotiators from the rest of Canada seemed to have further alienated Quebecers rather than reconciled them to the federation.

Bourassa faced a dilemma. His strategy of threatening to destroy the federation unless the rest of Canada bought him off with suitable "offers" had failed. The referendum that he had set up as a guillotine to frighten the rest of Canada now was hung over his own head. To hold the referendum on sovereignty was likely to lead to a deadlock. But what alternative did he have, after all the blustering rhetoric and threatening manoeuvres of the past two years? His only hope was that the prime minister could salvage something from the mess that their respective policies had created. Both leaders had invested immense political capital in a constitutional deal that would satisfy Quebec, and both would be equally devastated if all the time, money, stress, and confrontation with which the country had been taxed were to come to nothing.

Mulroney was also in a quandary. Clark had brought nine provinces, two territories and four aboriginal associations, against immense odds, to a formal agreement after almost four months of private negotiations and public wranglings, posturing, pressuring, and final compromise. That "historic agreement" could not now be waved away without destroying irremediably any hope of a constitutional settlement. Clark would have no recourse but to resign. The Triple-E provinces, which had wrenched at last a commitment to a Triple-E Senate of sorts, would walk away from any further negotiations that took their Senate off the table.

Mulroney himself was probably the most unpopular and distrusted prime minister in the history of Canada. Without the support of Clark and the provincial premiers, he could not now go to the country with a referendum on a constitutional package that was supported only by Ottawa.

Mulroney held one of his rare press conferences on 10 July. He was obviously speaking to all the first ministers, but above all to Bourassa, when he commented before the news media on the week's constitutional developments. He made it obvious that no one—especially Bourassa—should think of the deal reached at the eleventh hour that Tuesday as merely the starting point for new negotiations. That deal, more or less, was pretty much what had to be endorsed if there was to be negotiated constitutional reform, Mulroney said several times. And he launched a campaign-style speech to defend the two most vulnerable elements of the constitutional package: the Triple-E Senate and aboriginal self-government.

Still, he signalled—cautiously—that the 7 July agreement was not set in stone. He said that his senior officials would spend the next few days travelling to provincial capitals to examine with provincial representatives "matters requiring clarification" in the constitutional package. The mission was obviously intended as a probe, out of the public eye, to establish what elements were still negotiable, what changes could be made, what could be added, subtracted or amended.

While the federal officials were on their mission, Clark appeared on Newsworld on July 16 and talked semi-tough, putting the best face he could on the political quandary that had been created for the country under his chairmanship. "So far as I'm concerned, the basic elements of the package are intact," Clark told interviewer Don Newman. "We're so close to home, and the challenge, now, is to get there."

Again and again, he repeated like a mantra the word "intact." He recognized, though, that there was a major problem in Quebec; the solution he evoked was to add sweeteners to the deal as negotiated. Clark was confident that it could be done, especially if the first ministers—including Bourassa, at last—got together for an "informal" meeting some time in the following week. "If we can get all the governments at the table again," he said, "there may be some things that we can add to the proposal that will take into account the concerns in Quebec without reducing at all the effect of the proposal that we have now." What he was urging sounded rather like the attempts in 1990 to save the Meech Lake accord by the addition of a "companion agreement." Only now it was Quebec that wanted the add-ons, and the Triple-E provinces that wanted to keep what they had negotiated.

Clark had some suggestions for improving the package. More senators could be added to represent French-speaking Canadians from the rest of Canada. This would strengthen the French dimension of the new Senate, which Bourassa had found so lacking. Clark also speculated that, just as there was to be a double Senate majority based on language for bills that dealt with French language and culture, so there could be a requirement for the support of a minimum number of Quebec's senators.

And Clark stressed that he had been in close contact with the Quebec government throughout the negotiations. "We didn't do anything blind in the discussions. Quebec wasn't there, but we were taking extraordinary precautions, as you can imagine, to make sure that what we were looking at was something that Quebecers thought had a chance of surviving."

Behind the scenes, the negotiations continued. Quebec proposed a new "distinct society" clause, to replace the clause that had been agreed to by the multilateral negotiators. The federal government passed the Quebec draft on to the provinces, territories, and aboriginal organizations for their approval.[5] The draft spoke volumes about the thinking of Bourassa's "federalist" government: it read more like a statement to guide Quebec on its road to independence than an amendment to the constitution of Canada. What the negotiators had agreed to on 7 July was that the Charter of Rights was to be interpreted in a manner consistent with "the preservation and promotion of Quebec as a distinct society within Canada." The words "within Canada" had also been part of the Meech Lake distinct society clause. But now the Quebec government asked that the clause be changed to drop the words. Quebec was to be a distinct society, period.

At Meech Lake, the clause that most threatened liberal values and the Charter of Rights was that which stated, "The role of the legislature and government of Quebec to preserve and promote the distinct identity of Quebec . . . is affirmed." That wording gave the Quebec government a moral mandate which, given the dominant ideology since 1962, would certainly be used to create an ethnic state. The clause was a threat to the freedom of all Quebecers, but especially to non-francophones, who had already experienced the violation of freedom enacted by the Parti Québécois's Charter of the French Language, and the Liberals' Bill 178 prohibiting bilingual signs.

In the 7 July agreement, this mandate for the Quebec government had been omitted. But it was reinstated with a vengeance in the Quebec government's latest proposal. "Quebec bears a special responsibility to preserve and promote its distinct society, which includes a French-speaking majority, a unique culture, and a civil law tradition. . . . The role of the legislature and government of Quebec to preserve and promote the distinct society of Quebec is affirmed." As the clause had been formulated in the Meech Lake agreement, Quebec's "distinct identity" had not been defined. It could, arguably, have included the historic status of English, as confirmed by Section 133 of the constitution. In the formulation now put forward by Quebec, any reference to English was excluded; the distinct identity was to be characterized only by the French-speaking majority, by a supposedly "unique" culture, and by the civil law.

In other words, the mandate of the Quebec government to act as the coercive arm of an ethnic state was now to be made explicit and inescapable. The Quebec government would be compelled by the constitution to promote Quebec's "distinct" society, as defined by its French majority. The words were plain. If the legislators had meant to include the English-speaking population as part of what was to be promoted, they would have said so. The omission had the effect of an exclusion.

The intention to establish Quebec constitutionally as an ethnic state was further confirmed by another change proposed by the Quebec government. At Meech Lake, French-speaking Canadians and English-speaking Canadians, in all parts of the country, were recognized as a "fundamental characteristic" of Canada, and all governments, federal and provincial, were to "protect" that fundamental characteristic. In the 7 July agreement, that recognition of linguistic duality was considerably strengthened. It was to be spelled out in the Canada clause as one of eight "fundamental values" of Canada, and the Charter of Rights was to be interpreted in accordance with "the vitality and development of the language and culture of French-speaking and English-speaking minority communities through-out Canada."

But Quebec now proposed to water that commitment down to a bland statement: "Canadians are committed to the vitality and development of official language minority communities throughout Canada." That was the English version. In the French version, Canadians were not even *committed*, they were only *attached* to the vitality and development of minority communities. There was to be no reference to the role of legislatures regarding the minority official language communities, nor one to the Charter of Rights and Freedoms, which would have made the rights enforceable in court. Instead, all that was to be offered was a pious statement of fact, which placed no obligation on governments and conferred at best weak legal rights. Once again, in its pursuit of the French ethnic state, the Bourassa government preferred to sacrifice French-speaking communities in the rest of Canada rather than accept a limitation on the Quebec government's power to repress English in Quebec.

After all the backroom skirmishing and negotiating, at last Bourassa consented to attend a luncheon that the prime minister had convened for the premiers on 4 August at his summer residence, Harrington Lake. The first ministers were invited there to take part in "informal discussions" rather than negotiations. Bourassa told journalists that he had obtained "clarifications" of the 7 July agreement. "I got total satisfaction on the distinct society," he said, and he announced that he was ending his boycott of federal-provincial meetings.

That was partly true. He did not succeed in removing the words "within Canada" from the distinct society clause. But he did obtain that the whole constitution of Canada, including the Charter of Rights, "shall be interpreted in a manner consistent with . . . [the fundamental characteristic of Canada that] Quebec constitutes within Canada a distinct society, which includes a French-speaking majority, a unique culture, and a civil law tradition." So he had won recognition of the principle of the French ethnic state, and he had succeeded in keeping the recognition of linguistic duality to a descriptive statement.

He also succeeded in getting removed from the 7 July agreement the commitment that new provinces could be created with the consent of only the federal government. In addition, he exacted from Joe Clark a political commitment that no new province would be created without Quebec's consent. Clark wrote a letter to the territorial governments in which he confirmed that the federal government would not give its consent to the creation of a new province unless all the "regions" approved. This meant that Quebec, one of the regions, would hold an indirect veto over any new province.

When the first ministers met on 4 August, they talked for six hours, and agreed to meet again the following Monday. Bourassa had hardened his position against the Triple-E Senate since his press conference of 9 July. He told journalists, "What is important is to take all legitimate means to try and reach an agreement. No one in Quebec will underestimate the risks which could follow a failure. I don't think that I would be carrying out my responsibilities as premier if I didn't take every measure to try and reach an agreement acceptable to Quebec and acceptable to Canada, if I didn't take every measure to avoid the break-up of the Canadian federation." The real message, conveyed as usual by indirection, was that the Canadian federation would break up if Quebec's demands were not satisfied—and Bourassa presented himself as the reasonable leader who was going the extra mile in an attempt to prevent that break-up. His posture required chutzpah, given his own actions of the previous years. But it apparently was taken literally by the other premiers, who saw him as a great Canadian trying to resist the overwhelming forces of separatism.

Clark, meanwhile, confessed that he had mistakenly believed that an equal Senate would be acceptable in Quebec, that he now knew it was not, and that some other solution would have to be found if Quebec was to be drawn into the constitutional consensus.[6] It was a shattering admission for Clark to make, given the central place of the equal Senate in the 7 July bargain. Without it, that whole package would have to be renegotiated.

After they met a second time, on 10 August, the first ministers, including Bourassa, announced that they would resume formal negotiations. The Quebec premier opined, at the same time, that the federal government would have to act unilaterally if the first ministers could not reach an agreement, so as to avoid the destruction of the country.

The "destruction of the country" rhetoric was so habitual with Bourassa that Quebec journalists took it up unquestionably, as though it were a matter of established fact. On 10 August, *Le Devoir* ran on on its front page a Presse canadienne story that began, "The constitutional conference of the eleventh hour resumes today with, as its first objective, to find a compromise which would make it possible to save Canadian federalism." Jean Bédard, a reporter with Radio-Canada television news, used the same rhetoric in a report from Harrington Lake about the country being on the verge of destruction. There had been many last-chance conferences over the past three decades, and somehow, miraculously, the federation survived until the next last-chance conference.

But, at last, it happened. The first ministers gathered in Ottawa on 18 August, along with the territorial leaders and the representatives of the aboriginals, for a renewed attempt to square the constitutional circle. This time, the prime minister presided and Bourassa was a full participant. There was no more question of "clarifications" or "informal discussions." These were the make-or-break negotiations, and all were aware of the imminent deadline for Bourassa to call the referendum on sovereignty ordained by Bill 150 for 26 October, or to abort it, or to substitute a referendum on "offers" from the rest of Canada.

At first, the prospects were unpromising. The Senate was the fundamental stumbling block, as Bourassa made clear before the news media.

How can you expect the premier of Quebec to return to Quebec and say: in a new institution which will be central to the functioning of the country, a new pillar of the powers of Canada . . . one of the founding peoples will be practically marginalized. . . . They can look for all kinds of formulas to attenuate that, such as increasing the number of seats in the House of Commons. But the fact remains that, if the Senate is to have real power. . . . I think that the historic role of one of the founding peoples must be respected."

Listening to the premier, one might well have wondered why he had not said this before 7 July, during one of those frequent phone calls with Joe Clark or Bob Rae.

And Don Getty seemed equally immovable on the subject of the Triple-E Senate. For him, any suggestion that some provinces could have more senators than other provinces was profoundly insulting to the pride of Albertans. "They don't like to be told, You're not as good as some of the others," he told journalists. One was left to wonder why it was not equally insulting to the citizens of Ontario or Quebec to have less electoral power in the Senate than the smaller provinces, or why Albertans would not find it insulting to be told, You're not as good as some of the others, when they had fewer MPs in the Commons than Ontario or Quebec.

The regional tensions of the federation were such that rewriting the constitution seemed almost impossible. Yet, in just four days, the negotiators accomplished feats of compromise rare in the history of this country. On 19 August, they reached an agreement on aboriginal self-government. On 20 August, they reached agreement on a form of Triple-E Senate. And, on 21 August, they reached agreement on the division of powers. By the time they left Ottawa that week, they had all but finalized a full package of agreements that they could take to the electorate in a referendum. The deal would be formally ratified on 28 August in Charlottetown, the birthplace of Confederation.

The agreement on the Senate was especially ingenious. The smaller provinces would get their Triple-E Senate, as agreed on 7 July. And Quebec accepted that the number of its senators would fall from the current twenty-four to six. But, in return, Quebec and Ontario would gain in the Commons the eighteen seats that they lost in the Senate. And Quebec was offered a constitutional guarantee that, forever, no matter how much its population dropped as a proportion of Canada's, it would retain no less than 25 per cent of the seats in the Commons.

This was a remarkably generous gesture on the part of the nine other premiers—and one that would prove unpopular with much of the public, especially in Harcourt's British Columbia, where the call-in radio and television programs heard a torrent of reproaches to the effect that Harcourt had been taken to the cleaners in Ottawa.

If the agreement went ahead, two provinces, New Brunswick and Nova Scotia, stood to lose four representatives each in the combined Houses of Parliament. Five provinces and the two territories would see no change in their totals. British Columbia, Alberta, and Prince Edward Island would see their totals increased respectively by four, two and two representatives. In the long term, though, as the centre of gravity of the country shifted to the west, Quebec's guarantee of 25 per cent of the seats in the Commons would mean that other provinces would forfeit seats to maintain Quebec's average.

Aboriginal government was another sensitive issue, especially in Quebec. After the experience of the Oka armed stand-off in 1990 and the blockade of the Mercier bridge to Montreal, many Quebecers feared an agreement that might lead to anarchy. So three additions were made to the package on aboriginal government. First, no one was to go to court for five years, during which time the parties to the agreement would attempt to define the terms of aboriginal government by negotiation; beyond the five years, in case of failure, the courts could require the negotiators to return to the table if the judges thought that they were being asked to create constitutional law rather than interpret it. Second, any future law passed by an aboriginal government must be consistent with peace, order, and good government in the federation and in the provinces. Finally, it was to be specified that recognition of the right to self-government would not create new rights to land or threaten land tenure in Canada.

The third touchy issue for Quebec was the division of powers. Obtaining vast new powers had been a central objective since the Quiet Revolution; it had been the justification for a distinct society clause at Meech Lake, and for the Allaire and Bélanger-Campeau recommendations for a referendum. The new powers might go part of the way or all the way to full sovereignty—that had been the basis for distinguishing the Liberals from the Péquistes, at least in the past. But both parties and almost the entire political class agreed that the new powers must be sweeping.

The Quebec government's interest in the Senate and aboriginal government amendments was chiefly defensive: it wanted to lose as little power as possible to a reformed Senate or to aboriginal governments. But the increase in its own powers was itself the object of Quebec's clamour for constitutional reform; it was the very point of the whole exercise.

In the event, Bourassa did not get the fundamental restructuring of the federation that he had set out for. The other premiers wanted no part of a radically weakened federal government, or of a radically asymmetrical federation. Bourassa had to accept what he could get, such as it was, or lead Quebec into a referendum on sovereignty. The stakes had risen since he had said no to the Victoria Charter in 1971. This time, in the end, Bourassa acquiesced.

"It is less than we had hoped for, but we have made important gains," Bourassa told reporters. It was a pragmatic decision, but pragmatism was not what his own leadership over the past two years had prepared Quebecers for. When the agreement was announced, it caused shock in Quebec, especially among the members of the political class and Bourassa's own closest advisers.

He did get a commitment that the federal government would withdraw from some contested areas of jurisdiction, and he did get a commitment to hedge federal spending power with a new set of rules that would be elaborated at a future conference. Ottawa, the negotiators agreed, would withdraw at the request of any province from spending in such areas as mines, forestry, tourism, and leisure. In other areas—such as culture, regional development, immigration, telecommunications, and manpower training and development—federal action would require an agreement with the provinces, individually or severally.

But all of this fell far short of the Allaire report or of Bourassa's constant comparison, the European Community. Despite new limits to be placed on intrusion into provincial jurisdiction, Ottawa would largely retain the power to spend money on behalf of individual Canadians across the country. This meant that the federal government could continue to play a national role in support of culture despite the agreement that the provinces would have the exclusive right to legislate on culture. And on communications, the area where the Bourassa government had exerted the greatest efforts over the years to establish its own paramount role, the negotiators agreed only to come up in future with a communications policy that would "co-ordinate and harmonize" federal and provincial actions.

The chagrin of the nationalists became apparent when the Quebec media had their first opportunity to question the premier about the Ottawa agreement. Several reporters leaped on the new linguistic duality clause that had emerged from the negotiations: "Canadians *and their governments* are committed to the vitality and development of official language minority communities throughout Canada." How could the premier agree to a clause that would commit the Quebec government to the vitality of Quebec's English-speaking community?

Nevertheless, in an atmosphere of self-congratulation, the first ministers and the other negotiators solemnly confirmed on 28 August in Charlottetown the agreement in principle that had been reached in Ottawa. The symbolism of the venue was chosen deliberately: this agreement was to represent a reconfederation, a kind of rebirth of the country that the Charlottetown Conference of 1864 had begun to create. In the speeches at the end of the day, the word "historic" was spoken repeatedly. And the first ministers agreed to a referendum that was to be called on their agreement—the same package would be voted on by the people of Quebec and other Canadians.

Frank McKenna of New Brunswick struck a hopeful note when the day's arduous negotiations were over: "I predict that this campaign will be led by citizens who want to see this country finish its constitutional wrangling, make peace with its neighbours, make peace among its linguistic communities, and get on with the serious economic and social questions which confront our nation."

At first, it looked as if the referendum campaign would be a romp to victory. Carol Goar, in her *Toronto Star* column of 1 September, expressed the brief euphoria of the times. "Mulroney relishes this ordeal," she wrote. "He's putting the nation through the unity vote because he's sure he will win."

Indeed, the Yes side, outside of Quebec, had the support of almost all the beautiful people, the literati and the cognoscenti, the rich and the powerful. Almost every English-language newspaper endorsed the Yes. Every party in the Commons except the Bloc Québécois, all the provincial and territorial governments, almost every provincial opposition party, supported the Yes.

The first opinion poll of the campaign, conducted by Angus Reid for Southam News, was published on 2 September. It suggested a Yes landslide. "The poll found 61 per cent of Canadians outside Quebec would vote to accept the deal with only 20 per cent prepared to reject it and 18 per cent undecided." Even in

Quebec, according to the poll, the Yes side led by 49 per cent to 38, with 13 per cent undecided.

Columnist Geoffrey Stevens waxed enthusiastic on 6 September in *The Gazette* over the Yes side's "Dream Team"—the high-powered organizers of the Conservative, Liberal, and New Democratic parties, who had joined together to plan the Yes side's referendum campaign. It seemed that so much talent could not lose. "The Yes team does not have to defend the agreement as the best or most permanent of all possible constitutional deals," Stevens wrote. "It has simply to invite the public to compare the Dream Team in Yes colors to the ragtag bunch on the No side and to conclude that the good guys' agreement is better than anything the bad guys can offer."

Indeed, the "ragtag bunch" arguing against the Charlottetown deal outside Quebec could not compare in power and reputation with the armies of the Yes. They included Deborah Coyne, former constitutional adviser to Clyde Wells; Preston Manning, head of the Reform Party, which had only one seat in the Commons; and Judy Rebick, head of the National Action Committee on the Status of Women. At first, their fight seemed quixotic. Coyne had also been the main instigator of the resistance against the Meech Lake accord, but this time most of her former allies—including Premier Wells himself—had abandoned her. "I don't think we have a hope of winning, but what can you do? At least we've got to try," Coyne said early in September.[7] Most of the former opponents of Meech Lake had resigned themselves to supporting the Charlottetown accord, which was in many ways more threatening to liberal values, not because they believed in it, but because the alternative seemed worse. The federalist forces had so disintegrated in Quebec since Mulroney and then Bourassa came to power that an agreement supported by Bourassa, almost any agreement, seemed like the only chance to keep Confederation together long enough to maintain alive the hope of fighting for a liberal vision another day.

In Quebec, Bourassa defended the Charlottetown accord in a speech to the National Assembly on 9 September. That speech should be read carefully by anyone who wants to understand Bourassa's political vision and his legacy to Quebec during his almost fourteen years as premier.[8]

He began with what had become the official version of recent history and the *casus belli* invoked to justify condemning the constitution of Canada: the 1982 patriation, with the inclusion of minority language education rights in the Charter. That patriation was "unilateral" and "unacceptable," and consequently the Liberal government "could not ratify [it] without changes to the constitution." A beginning of the required changes were contained in the 1987 Meech Lake accord, which "included sufficient changes to the constitution to justify Quebec's return to the negotiating table." However, two provinces did not ratify the agreement, "with the consequence that the negotiation process was discredited in the eyes of the Quebec government."

331

The Charlottetown accord then was negotiated in replacement of Meech. Bourassa did not hide the fact that his enthusiasm for Charlottetown was limited. It showed "real progress," even though "I admitted readily that we had not achieved *this first time* our objectives as a whole." That is, Charlottetown was only a beginning, not a permanent constitutional settlement.

Still, he praised the Charlottetown accord for the "unprecedented gains" that he had obtained. One gain was the fact that Quebec would acquire control over the "linguistic, cultural, social, and economic integration of immigrants to its territory." The kind of dragooning of immigrants to pressure them to become French, which Quebec had been practising since the Ottawa-Quebec agreement of 1991, would now be protected in the constitution. In additon, Quebec would receive money from Ottawa to carry out the operation: according to Bourassa, it would average $80 million a year for the next eight or nine years.

Bourassa mentioned as another gain the distinct society clause, which "constituted a very important gain for the security of Quebec." He spoke of three levels of "security" in the constitution, and all three involved the power of the government to exercise coercion. In addition to the distinct society clause, a second level of security was the right to limit freedom granted by section one of the Charter of Rights when "reasonable limits prescribed by law" could be "demonstrably justified in a free and democratic society." The third level was, when such justification could not be demonstrated, the ability to override freedom by invoking the notwithstanding clause.

Yet another "gain" was the fact that Quebec had obtained that its senators in the proposed reformed Senate should be chosen by the National Assembly rather than by the people. "I often said during the debates that I would never accept that constitutional reform should affect the powers of the National Assembly." It was a "gain" that the people of Quebec would not have the power to vote for their senators.

Bourassa repeatedly returned to his old, familiar concept of Canada as a common market. "We know that geography urges us, and urges Quebec, to share its economic powers. We must be realistic. In the economic area, I can't see why we should not have this Canadian common market. . . . We know that in the other areas, in the cultural field, in the social field, in the field of education, Quebec possesses the principal powers."

Bourassa noted that the Quebec government had succeeded in establishing itself in an area that, he said, the constitution ascribed to the federal government. He himself had signed an agreement with Russia's president, Boris Yeltsin, dealing with the economy, culture, and communications. "And so, even if, in the 1867 constitution . . . foreign affairs come under the exclusive jurisdiction of the federal government, it does not prevent, with the evolution of time, events, and opportunity, the constitution from being adapted and conferring on us powers in the international sphere, such as Quebec has exercised on several occasions.

So, for the functioning of the common market, we agree to this sharing of sovereignty so as to profit from the gains of the whole."

Almost defensively, Bourassa cited the experience of Europe, including the Maastricht Treaty, to justify participating in the federation. But he did so with a purely pragmatic argument about the monetary gains that the federation could bring. "It seems logical, in accordance with common sense, opportune, not to exclude agreements with our partners."

This was Bourassa's defence of federalism; this was the measure of his commitment to Canada. The Canadian common market was useful. In a similar vein, he insisted on getting control of manpower training, because something like a billion dollars would come to Quebec from Ottawa along with the responsibility. But, by the same logic, he did not insist on getting control of unemployment insurance. "We can readily understand that unemployment insurance is exclusively federal. And I have said on several occasions that I did not see the advantage for Quebec in repatriating this exclusive area. It would result, according to the figures that have been made public, in a loss of $1.2 billion for Quebec."

At the same time, the premier reiterated his party's policy according to which Quebec had the right to self-determination. "In my speech on the Meech Lake accord, in June, 1987, I mentioned very clearly that the resolution of my party, in 1980, establishing Quebec's right to self-determination remained intact, and, during the discussion at the convention of my party on 29 August last, we repeated that resolution on Quebec's right to self-determination. So we are after an additional security, we are getting guarantees for a better functioning of the common market."

As he spoke in the National Assembly, so Bourassa remained, on the hustings, a discreet federalist. Characteristically, when he eventually launched his referendum campaign as leader of Quebec's Yes committee, he made no mention of Canada in his first major speech, and there was no Canadian flag in evidence on the platform. Later still, when he debated Jacques Parizeau before the television cameras on 12 October, he minimized the differences in vision between the Quebec Liberal Party and the Parti Québécois.

Parizeau had just charged that Bourassa had chosen the wrong word to describe Quebec constitutionally. Rather than *distinct society*, he should have chosen *distinct people*. "In legal terms, a people has meaning. A people can promote, develop, not only its language, not only its culture, but also its economy, its social relations, its international relations. A people is complete."

Bourassa had his riposte ready. "Where does the expression *distinct society*, come from? The expression *distinct society* comes from the Parti Québécois government, in a resolution that you yourself voted for on 1 December [1981]." He maintained that the difference was merely one of semantics. "If we had chosen the word *nation*, you would have said, that's how we speak of the aboriginal nations, the aboriginal peoples, and now we're talking about the Quebec people.

333

We chose an expression that you yourselves proposed. And now, suddenly, you say that we should have chosen another expression. If we had chosen the word *nation*, you would have said, Why not *distinct society?"*

Bourassa represented perfectly one face of Quebec's political elite since the Quiet Revolution: the paranoid fear of the rest of Canada; the simultaneous opportunistic desire to wring the maximum advantage out of Canada, while also trying to reduce it to a shadow by wresting from it every possible "gain"; the constant attack on the legitimacy of the federation while claiming to represent the federalist option in Quebec politics. This was the politics of the "third option," of "renewed federalism."

Together, the two options represented by Jacques Parizeau and Bourassa kept federalism under a constant crossfire, to which was added a third line of fire from Brian Mulroney, who, though himself lacking a vision, chose to pursue electoral victory and a base for government by associating himself with the visions of the other two.

But one voice from Quebec spoke out strongly against the Charlottetown agreement and the political posture which produced it. On 21 September, an essay by Pierre Trudeau appeared simultaneously in *L'Actualité* and *Maclean's*. It offered Trudeau, the writer, at his best—the polemicist, the ironist, the master of scorn with a razor wit, slicing away the masks and exposing naked truths.

Consider that, for the past 22 years, the province of Quebec has been governed by two premiers. The first is the "profitable federalism" man. We will stay in Canada if Canada gives us enough money, this premier urges. Of course, however, adds the Allaire report, which he ordered up, the rest of Canada must cede us just about all its constitutional powers, except, of course, that of giving us a lot of money.

And, to give more edge to the blackmail, no opportunity is lost to point out that the (supposed) right of Quebec to self-determination is written into the program of the party led by this premier—the same who makes a point of not practicing "federalism on a bended knee."

Take that, Robert Bourassa. And now for René Lévesque.

The other premier was the "sovereignty-association" man. He demanded for Quebec all the powers of a sovereign country, but insisted at the same time that this country not be independent. His referendum question postulated precisely that a sovereign Quebec would be associated with the other provinces, and that the Canadian dollar would continue to hold dominion. Always back to money!

Afer skewering the premiers, Trudeau took on Quebec's beautiful people, business people, and journalists for playing the same ambiguous game, backing the blackmail tactics of the politicians while holding on to the security of Canada.

The professors of political science and their students, of course, rather than coldly analyze all these fantasies, endorse them almost unanimously.

Some even propose negotiating with English Canada "with a knife to the throat" while maintaining that, under one plan of independence, Quebecers could still elect representatives to the federal Parliament (from which, as you know, comes the equalization money).

Here Trudeau was satirizing the comical corkscrew twists and turns of political scientist Léon Dion—a guru taken very seriously by the Quebec news media and by himself—who, in one of his numerous and contradictory public proposals, suggested the policy of the "knife to the throat" and flexible independence. At first, he was for renewed federalism, but a month later he discovered that he was not really a federalist.

Trudeau also brought out all the incongruity of the "distinct society" clause as a condition for continuing in the federation. Quebec was distinct, of course, as it had been for two centuries. It was Quebec that had persuaded the other provinces to accept a federal system rather than a unitary state, and Quebec's distinctness was already recognized in the constitution. "Why, then, do so many politicians, publicists and businessmen in Quebec clamour to have inscribed in the constitution a right and a reality which are already there? And why did they declare themselves humiliated when others questioned the need to do so?"

Trudeau concluded his dissection of the nationalist "blackmail" by inviting all Canadians to refuse to play the game of giving in to the nationalist threats.

For unscrupulous politicians, there's no easier appeal to sentiments than to sound "the call of the race."[9] . . . French Canadians will only be able to rid themselves of this kind of politician if blackmail ceases to be profitable, that is, if Canada refuses to be blackmailed. Objective history demonstrates that it was by just such an attitude that separatism was pushed to the edge of the grave between 1980 and 1984.

Trudeau reminded the country, if nothing else, that blackmail and mediocrity were not always the order of the day in Canada.

The day after the publication of Trudeau's diatribe against political blackmail, the Yes side for the rest of Canada officially launched its campaign in Ottawa. The National Canada Committee included an impressive roster of personalities: Yves Fortier, former ambassador to the United Nations; former premiers Peter Lougheed, Robert Stanfield, William Davis, and Gerald Regan; tycoon Laurent Beaudoin of Bombardier; Marc Garneau, astronaut; and former NDP leader Ed Broadbent.

But, at the press conference in Ottawa, one picture was worth a thousand words, and the country soon got both the picture and the thousand words. The picture was of the huge YES, in English only, that formed the backdrop to the representatives of the Canda Committee. And the same YES, in English only, decorated the French-language publicity material handed out to the news media. The journalists had a field day. The embarrassed dignitaries on display, including Fortier and Michel Bastarache, former head of the Société des Acadiens du

Nouveau-Brunswick, knew that the unilingual YES would out-thunder anything they might try to say. It was the referendum story of the week. It played big on Radio-Canada television news that evening and led all the hourly radio news broadcast on Radio-Canada the next morning. *Le Devoir* made it the top news story on the front page.

Lucien Bouchard made capital out of the gaffe in a speech to the Laval Chamber of Commerce. "I don't think it's ill will. Quite naturally, in their camp, they see the country that way. For them, it's a case of Canada's Yes against Quebec's Non," the Bloc Québécois leader told reporters.

Mulroney, meanwhile, had apparently learned nothing from Meech Lake. He scampered about Quebec warning that the sky was falling. A No vote would mean the end of Canada, he suggested in a formal speech delivered in Sherbrooke. "It is clear: a vote for the No means a direct contribution to the separation of Quebec." Having turned all those who would vote No, for whatever reason, into separatists, the prime minister then went on to campaign against separatism, just as if that were the issue in the 26 October referendum.

We have to see things as they are, because separation would have very serious consequences for all Quebecers and for all Canadians. It is not psychological terrorism to say that dismantling a country also turns its economy upside down, and often irreparably; it is the truth, but it's a truth that separatists would rather hide. But Quebecers are not blind. They know very well that when you destroy a country, you are not making it more economically powerful.

No doubt it was easier to campaign against separatism than for the Charlotte-town agreement. But the Charlottetown agreement, not separatism, was on the ballot. Mulroney was following the same script as Premier Bourassa, who also tried to turn the vote into a referendum on sovereignty. "A No vote could mean a possible breakup of the federation," the premier told reporters in St-Jérôme on his first day of referendum campaigning.

The two leaders were repeating their 1990 strategy, when they had wrapped the deeply flawed Meech Lake package in the Quebec and Canadian flags and had conditioned the public to view its rejection as the very rejection of Quebec. Now, they accredited the view in Quebec that it had to be the Charlottetown deal or separation. It was a high-risk gambit. If Charlottetown went down to defeat as Meech Lake had done, Quebecers might believe what the two leaders said: that separation was the only alternative.

Pierre Trudeau re-entered the scene on 1 October as the speaker at a dinner sponsored by *Cité libre* at a Chinese restaurant with the incongruous name, La maison egg roll. It was in St-Henri, Montreal's most fabled slum. This was to be Trudeau live, speaking on the constitution in the midst of the referendum campaign. What would he say? Would he use the rapier or the sledgehammer? Would he tease his audience, or would he come out with all guns firing? Would this be simply a last hurrah, a showing of his flag for the last time, or would it be all-out war? In the prime minister's office, they dismissed Trudeau's appearance: he was yesterday's man, and would have no discernible effect on the campaign. But, two hours before Trudeau was to speak, a mob of journalists had gathered in front of the restaurant while a couple of police patrol cars stood by. Trudeau could still bring out the news media as no one else could.

Inside, the rooom was jammed. The four hundred diners sat elbow to elbow, and sometimes elbow to rib. The tickets had sold out in a matter of hours, and hundreds were turned away. Most of the journalists were herded into a small room downstairs to listen to the former prime minister's voice over a loudspeaker. His message was also broadcast live over the Télémédia radio network of some thirty stations.

Trudeau spoke more in the style of a professor of constitutional law than in the fierce satirical tone of his onslaught against Quebec nationalism in *Maclean's*. He did occasionally lapse into sarcasm, but most of his talk dissected the Charlottetown constitutional package clause by clause. He pointed out that the Charlottetown agreement was not so much an agreement as a rought draft. It left many important questions unsettled. It included twenty-six asterisks at different clauses to signal that more discussion and a political solution would be required before that clause was settled.

So much for the form. But Trudeau's main attack was on the substance. His message was that the accord placed collective rights above individual rights, weakened the Canadian Charter of Rights and Freedoms, and created a hierarchy of six different categories of citizens. He went through the Canada clause, which would be placed right at the top of the constitution, and which was to direct the courts in interpretation of the rest of the constitution. The first class of citizens was created by the clause dealing with Quebec: Quebec was a distinct society with a French-speaking majority and a unique culture, and the Quebec legislature and the Quebec government would have the mandate to promote this distinct society, so understood. This meant, said Trudeau, that people who were not part of the French-speaking majority in Quebec had fewer rights. And the rights granted in the Charter were subordinated to Quebec's distinct society.

The aboriginal governments were the second class of citizens, with a recognized right to promote their cultures, languages, and traditions. And it was left an open question whether non-aboriginals living within their jurisdiction had a right to participate in the governments which ruled them. Trudeau called this racist.

The official-language minorities—English in Quebec, French in the rest of Canada—also had rights defined by the "commitment" (in the English text) or *"attachement"* (in the French text) of Canadians and their governments. But for racial and ethnic minorities, there was to be no commitment of governments to their equality. Only "Canadians are committted . . ." So it was to be, too, with the equality of women and the respect for individual and collective human rights: governments were not to be committed, but only "Canadians." Finally, Trudeau pointed out, the lowest category of citizens, with the least protection in the constitution, included everyone else.

It was a devastating demonstration. Trudeau brought out the vision of society that underlay and would be projected by the Charlottetown agreement. In it, individuals were not equal, rights were not equal, and individual freedoms were subordinated to governments.

Trudeau's analysis, though heard live only in Quebec, had an immediate and strong impact in the rest of Canada. In Quebec, though, the Yes campaign was already stumbling badly. A poll by Léger and Léger, published on 2 October, the day after Trudeau's speech, showed the No side 14 percentage points ahead of the Yes. As the referendum date of 26 October approached, support for Charlottetown progressively weakened.

Bourassa was now paying the price for his long flirtation with separation. He had surrounded himself with ultranationalist constitutional advisers, like Louis Bernard, who had been the right-hand man of Camille Laurin and René Lévesque, and whom Lévesque had appointed to head the Quebec civil service after the PQ came to power. Bernard was a committed, disciplined, superbly competent separatist. Bourassa also chose as his chief advisers for the post-Meech constitutional negotiations Diane Wilhelmy and André Tremblay. Wilhelmy had been a university administrator before PQ premier Pierre-Marc Johnson hired her to work on his constitutional team. Presumably, he found her views compatible with those of the PQ.

Through much of September, the hottest constitutional story in Quebec was about a phone conversation between Wilhelmy and Tremblay, which had taken place just a few days after the Charlottetown agreement was concluded. One of them used a cellular phone, and the conversation carried by the public airwaves, was recorded by someone and sent to a local radio station. Learning that the private conversation was going to be broadcast, Wilhelmy got a court order to prevent its publication in Quebec. She succeeded only in heightening interest, feeding rumours, and prolonging the life of the story as the transcript of her conversation was published in the *Globe and Mail* on 16 September and then passed on from fax to fax, and person to person, throughout Quebec.

In their conversation, Bourassa's chief advisers agreed that the premier had "caved in" so completely, so ignominiously, that it was a disgrace. Wilhelmy confided that she considered the agreement such a catastrophe that, for three days, she remained stunned and just couldn't believe it. Tremblay replied that he himself had been crawling for so long that his knees had holes in them.

Their conversation was all the more damaging because the judgment came from Bourassa's chief constitutional advisers, who were speaking with brutal frankness because they thought their private conversation would remain between the two of them. The attempts to keep the public from leaning what they had said only increased the effect of their words.

And this was not to be the only leak. Confidential briefing notes prepared by Bourassa's own officials, extremely critical of the positions that Bourassa adopted at Charlottetown, were leaked to *L'Actualité* and published about a week before the day of the referendum. It seemed clear that Bourassa could not trust his own civil servants. Some of them, at least, were betraying him and working for the other side.

But Bourassa could not claim to be an innocent victim of separatist plots. He himself had encouraged for almost three years the radicalization of his public service, his party, and the entire population of Quebec. He had presented the full sovereignty of Quebec as legitimate, as probably imminent, as the most likely alternative that should be adopted by the people of Quebec given the obduracy of the rest of Canada. After abetting separatism so spectacularly, he could not suddenly turn around within two months of the referendum, accept a moderate agreement that had no comparison to what his party and his legislature had proposed as necessary to secure Quebec's future, and still expect Quebecers to spin around with him.

So it was with Jean Allaire, who had presided over the Allaire committee, and with Mario Dumont, now president of the Young Liberals, who had been key figures in promoting the autonomist turn of the Liberal party in 1990 and 1991. When Bourassa abandoned the party's own solemnly adopted platform of near-sovereignty at a special party meeting on 29 August, many of the leading Young Liberals and other dissidents decided to work for the No side and against the Charlottetown accord. They refused to follow him in his last pirouette, and so did the public.

To try to sell the deal, Mulroney and Bourassa went around Quebec praising the "gains" that Bourassa had made in negotiating the Charlottetown accord—the "greatest gains" for Quebec of any premier since Confederation, they said. The implication was conveyed that whatever was wrenched from the federal government was a gain for Quebec. Mulroney melodamatically held up a list of the "gains" and tore it up: that is what Quebecers would be doing to those gains if they voted down the Charlottetown accord.

Their rhetoric set a high standard for the next premier to match. If these gains were the best gains that could be obtained under the circumstances—and Bourassa admitted that he had not really got what he wanted—then more gains would surely be pursued in future. So he asked Quebecers to think of Charlottetown as the second prize in a lottery. He urged them to pocket the prize "and buy more tickets."

But Quebecers were not won over. They had been promised much, much more. Bourassa and Mulroney had sowed the nationalist wind. Now they were reaping the hurricane. Nationalists would not be content, even temporarily, with the Charlottetown deal.

The rest of Canada followed the reports from Quebec and could see that the referendum was failing there. At best, a weak Yes might be eked out, but it would prove to be the prelude to instability rather than to a settlement. The strength of Quebec nationalism was now such that any agreement passed in 1992 could only last for a short time, soon to be repudiated by the next PQ government, or even by a Liberal government anxious to show it could make still more gains.

The prospect of instability undercut what had been the chief argument in favour of Charlottetown in the rest of the country: the hope for peace, for an end to constitutional squabbling, for a return to normality where citizens were not forced to confront their existential identity almost every day. If a Yes vote would, in the best of circumstances, be followed by instability, why vote Yes? Might No not offer a better alternative? The best solution might be to recognize reality and stop hitting a brick wall year after year in the vain hope of a constitutional settlement.

The attack against the accord on philosophical grounds also had an increasing effect. Canadians worried about the vision of the country and the fundamental values that were to be embedded in the constitution. They did not like what they heard from a growing chorus of experts.

Trudeau was not alone in maintaining that the accord would create a society in which different people had different levels of rights. Queen's University law professor Beverly Baines made a similar argument in the October issue of *The Network*, published by York University: "The Canada clause actually establishes a hierarchy of rights that will reduce the protection of the gender equality provisions in the Charter."

As the date for the referendum approached, twelve legal experts published a detailed anaysis of the draft text of the Charlottetown accord, which had finally been made public on 12 October, barely two weeks before the referendum. They offered a devastating evaluation.

Our conclusions are as follows:

1. The Canada clause creates a hierarchy of values which will reduce the content of Charter rights and expand the basis on which Charter guarantees can be limited.

2. The distinct society provisions have the potential to erode existing protection of Charter rights and freedoms in Quebec.

3. The aboriginal self-governments will operate free of the democratic rights guaranteed by the Charter; will exercise many powers unconstrained by Charter rights; and will have power to override Charter rights without democratic legitimacy.

The twenty-page analysis was signed by Lorraine Eisenstat Weinrib and seven others from the faculty of law of the University of Toronto; by Peter Benson and J.P. Humphrey of the faculty of law of McGill University; by R.E. Fritz of the

University of Saskatchewan; and by A.N. Store, retired senior legislative counsel of Ontario.

In dissecting the Canada clause, the authors pointed to the essential characteristic of the vision that was to be introduced into the constitution: its statist and authoritarian predilection. The new constitution would give the highest priority to the powers of government, whether federal, provincial, or aboriginal; the rights of the citizens were to be placed on a lower level of priority.

A notable feature of the Canada clause is that the eight "fundamental features" are not described in a uniform way. This variety of language creates a hierarchy of values, so that in any case where these values conflict, values higher up the hierarchy will prevail over those lower down.

What makes this especially unfortunate is that the highest values are governmental powers. Under our present constitution, the guarantee of rights constrains governmental powers. The Canada clause reverses this arrangement: it mandates the primacy of those very powers in the interpretation of the rights.

This primacy was most conspicuous in the accord's section on aboriginal governments. The legal experts left no doubt about one point: aboriginal governments would not be constrained by the Charter of Rights to hold elections, as federal and provincial governments must. Nor would the aboriginal people subject to those governments be guaranteed the right to vote or the right to run for elected office.[10]

The statist vision, whether incorporated in the special regime for the Quebec government or for aboriginal governments, was defended in the Charlottetown accord as conferring "collective rights." But the authors of the legal analysis pointed out the dangerous ambiguity of the concept of collective rights. They focused on a subsection of the proposed Canada clause which stated, "Canadians are committed to respect for individual and collective human rights and freedoms of all people."

We know what is meant by individual rights because presumably this is a reference to the Charter itself. But what is meant by collective rights? The only collective rights referred to here are better labelled as collective powers, that is, the powers of the aboriginal communities to make laws to forward their collective interests and the power of the Quebec government to make laws to forward the province's collective interests.

This intervention in the referendum debate provided the most complete, closely argued, and trenchant explication available of the vision of society that the Charlottetown accord would have lodged in the constitution of Canada. Their argument was never refuted. Pierre Trudeau had conducted such an exercise on 1 October at La maison egg roll. These experts went further, reducing the Charlottetown accord to chop suey.

In defending the accord on the hustings, Mulroney did not deign to consider what vision of the country he was attempting to have the people adopt. His debate was at another level entirely. He argued that it was up to the opponents of the accord to come forward with a common position as an alternative to Charlottetown. "To be fair, the No side—Mr. Parizeau, Mr. Trudeau, Judy Rebick, Sharon Carstairs, Lucien Bouchard, Preston Manning—they should get around the table and they should come up with their alternative," the prime minister told *The Gazette*'s editorial board.

It was a fallacy to suggest that all who reject a package must agree on the alternative. They agreed that the package should not be adopted, which meant that they agreed on the status quo for the time. That was the clear alternative, the only alternative that the referendum question made possible. Canadians were not being presented with a two-part question which asked, Are you in favour of the Charlottetown agreement, yes or no; and, if not, what is your alternative?

But the Charlottetown package was losing the battle for public opinion, and Mulroney tried every rhetorical trick to regain the initiative. The more the campaign advanced, the more people turned against it. The Yes side relied on ads that ignored the substance of the proposal. One ad showed a baseball player at bat: he waited for the perfect pitch that never came, and so he was struck out. Another commercial showed a pot on a hot stove. The message was that there was going to be an explosive mess in Canada unless people vote Yes. But, somehow, the ads failed to connect with the mood of Canadians.

The Parti Québécois had long capitalized on fears for the French language as its strongest selling point in favour of independence. Under its new guise as the No committee, the PQ played on the fear that the Charter of the French Language would be threatened under the Charlottetown accord, and that therefore the French language itself would be threatened. "*À ce prix là, c'est non,*" was the constant message. At that price—the threat to the French language and to the autonomy of Quebec—the only answer was no.

As he had done so often in the past, Mulroney now played into the hands of the Quebec nationalists by confirming the validity of their campaign based on stimulating existential fears. On 19 October, just a week before the referendum vote, Mulroney told a Toronto radio station that, without special protection for Quebec's distinct society, Quebecers would become like Louisiana's Acadians. "French-Canadians inevitably will become Cajuns, and they don't want to become dancers in Louisiana with banjos." The statement was particularly damaging because Louisiana had become the very symbol, constantly evoked, of what French Quebec would become unless strong action was taken to repress English.

It was hokum and paranoia. Less than two weeks before Mulroney uttered his scary message, Quebec's Conseil de la langue française published a report showing that French was thriving in Quebec. In Quebec as a whole, between

1971 and 1986, people with French as a first language increased from 80.7 per cent to 82.9 per cent. Even in Montreal, the most frequent venue for nationalist nightmares, the proportion of those with French as a first language increased from 66.3 per cent to 69.7 per cent. This was the road to Louisiana? In addition, the Conseil reported that the proportion of English-speaking Quebecers who could also speak French rose nineteen percentage points over those fifteen years. Among immigrants to Quebec who arrived between 1981 and 1986, and whose first language was neither French nor English, 37 per cent spoke French but not English; another 23 per cent spoke French and English; and only 23 per cent did not speak French at all. There were pages and pages of such statistics showing French getting stronger, but Mulroney's long cultivation of the nationalists' vision overrode both reality and Canada's national interest. The prime minister trumpeted the nationalists' most compelling nightmare.

On the day before the vote, the leaders of the Yes camp, knowing they were headed for an almost certain loss, displayed a resignation that contrasted markedly with their euphoria on 28 August in Charlottetown. Joe Clark looked more than two months older as he appeared on CTV's *Question Period* and recalled that happier day when the accord was signed. "You know the history of the twenty-four years before this. We've failed, and failed, and failed, and failed. And this time, on every single major constitutional issue, we have agreement. That means a Clyde Wells agreeing with Robert Bourassa, it means a Bob Rae agreeing with a Don Getty, it means a Rosemarie Kuptana and Ovide Mercredi agreeing with all the non-aboriginals."

Bourassa campaigned that Sunday on Radio-Canada's television program *Aujourd'hui Dimanche*. He seemed most appalled at the thought that a No vote would mean the victory of his old enemy, Trudeau. Bourassa, who had been so constantly checked and even ridiculed when Trudeau was prime minister, had soared in stature during Mulroney's prime-ministership. It had seemed for a while that he would obtain, with the help of the man from Baie Comeau, what Trudeau had refused him during the 1970s. But now, with Quebec preparing to vote No, Trudeau would have the last word. "If we say No, we go back to the constitution that Pierre Trudeau imposed on us. I gather Mr. Parizeau said Friday evening that he did not accept to be called Pierre Trudeau. But, in fact, he is working for the glory or the heritage of Pierre Trudeau right now by voting No."

When the people themselves spoke at last on 26 October, they buried the Charlottetown accord, they buried all Brian Mulroney's and Robert Bourassa's constitutional manoeuvrings, they repudiated almost the entire establishment of English-speaking Canada.

That night, Mulroney was stunned. After the results were known, he bowed his head to the will of the people—or so he said. But he kept repeating obsessively his lines from the referendum campaign, as though for him the campaign would never end. Like the Ancient Mariner, he seemed condemned forever to justify over and over the devastation he had imposed on the country. "The federal and provincial and territorial and aboriginal leaders achieved unanimous agreement," he said. "Agreement, as it turned out, on the most comprehensive constitutional reform in Canada in 125 years. To achieve agreement, all of us made compromises, difficult but honourable compromises."

Too late. Now, it would forever be too late for Mulroney. He remained prime minister still, but his era was effectively over, and it had ended on a great and costly failure.

Aboriginal leaders Ovide Mercredi and Ron George also spoke bitterly that night, blaming mainstream Canadians for the rejection of what they presented as aboriginal demands. But the aboriginals on the reserves who did vote in the referendum actually turned down the accord by a greater margin than other Canadians: more than 60 per cent. The aboriginal leadership had also lost touch with its members and forfeited their confidence.

The referendum brought an end to three decades of Quebec nationalists' search for a "third way" between federalism and separatism. There was no third way; it had always been an illusion, since it in fact covered a multitude of very different and shifting positions, extending from a barely modified federalism to a scarcely disguised separatism. It was really a name for a constant escalation of demands, as Bourassa himself had demonstrated by his progression from his 1985 election platform, to Meech Lake two years later, and then to the Allaire and Bélanger-Campeau reports. When he tried at the end to back down, he left the people behind.

The people's vote meant the end to one long-cultivated illusion: that Quebec could have all the advantages of the federation while repudiating its structure, legitimacy, and authority. Henceforth the people of Quebec would have to make their choice between the federalism they had or the separation the Parti Québécois proposed to them. All the utopias in between had lost their credibility.

Notes

1.In an interview with Jean-François Lisée in April 1991, Bourassa gave perhaps the most candid account of his true objective: "The best option for Quebec is not independence, which could be very theoretical because of the North American context; it is to have the greatest possible autonomy. And that is what is going to happen. Because the rejection of the Meech Lake accord forces Ottawa to put more on the table. They can't come back with the Meech Lake accord. I will work very hard to obtain the most important renovation of federalism that has been known in 123 years." Quoted in Jean François Lisée, *Le Tricheur: Robert Bourassa et les Québécois 1990–1991* (Montreal: Boréal, 1994), pp. 521–22.

2.See, for example, André Blais, "The Quebec Referendum: Quebecers Say No," in Kenneth McRoberts and Patrick Monahan, eds., *The Charlottetown Accord, the Referendum and the Future of Canada* (Toronto: University of Toronto Press, 1993), p. 202.

3.The group included the Liberal party's secretary-general, Pierre Anctil; the then chairman of its policy committee, Pierre Saulnier; the policy committee's past chairman, Jean Allaire; the man who would become the committee's next chairman, Thierry Vandal; and Michel Bissonnette, who, as chairman of the party's Youth Committee in 1990 and 1991, had piloted the radical resolution in favor of a quasi-sovereign Quebec through the Young Liberals' convention in the summer of 1990, and then fought successfully for the adoption of the radical Allaire report at the party's convention in March, 1991.

4. The report remained secret until ten months later, when *La Presse* reporter Denis Lessard broke the story: "The Liberal Party of Quebec had a detailed plan for shared sovereignties. The secret committee, clearly sovereignist, predicted only passing economic consequences." *La Presse*, 15 Apr. 1993, p. B-1. The quotations from the report are drawn from this account.

5. Ovide Mercredi held a press conference on 21 July to reveal what Quebec was proposing.

6. Moe Sihota, British Columbia's constitutional affairs minister, claimed that Bourassa and his top officials had signalled their acceptance of the Triple-E Senate before the 7 July agreement was announced, according to the *Globe and Mail*. And an Ontario official was quoted as saying, "Quebec was fully informed. . . . They never exercised what you might call a veto." As at Victoria in 1971, Bourassa made a practice of misleading his partners in constitutional negotiations.

7. Brooke Jeffrey, *Strange Bedfellows, Trying Times. October 1992 and the Defeat of the Powerbrokers* (Toronto: Key Porter, 1993), p. 137.

8. All quotations from the speech are found in the National Assembly's *Journal des Débats*, 9 Sept. 1992.

9. Trudeau was evoking the title of the famous novel by Lionel Groulx.

10. The current section 3 of the Charter, dealing with political rights, was to be modified by the Charlottetown accord so as precisely to exempt aboriginal governments from the Charter's protection of political rights. The Charter reads, "Every citizen of Canada has the right to vote in an election of members of the House of Commons or of a legislative assembly and to be qualified for membership therein." But the draft legal text of the accord modified this so as to exempt aboriginal legislative assemblies. The new text was to read: "Every citizen of Canada has the right to vote in an election of members of the House of Commons or of a legislative assembly *of a province* and to be qualified for membership therein." (Italics added.) Moreover, the legal experts pointed out that the aboriginal governments were to take over fields of jurisdiction currently exercised by the provincial and federal governments, whose legislation was subject to the Charter of Rights—but, "when laws were to be made in these fields by the new aboriginal governments, Charter rights would not attach."

CHAPTER TWENTY

The 1993 Federal Election:
The End of an Era

The loss in the referendum, coming after the loss of Meech Lake, left Brian Mulroney wounded but uncowed. An Angus Reid poll showed, ironically, that Mulroney had been second only to Pierre Trudeau in convincing people to vote No in the referendum. Twice he had struck out. He would not be given a third strike at the country: the referendum had made sure of that. But Mulroney swore, nevertheless, that he would make mincemeat of Jean Chrétien in the coming federal election.

The *Edmonton Journal* probably echoed the sentiments of the country in an editorial with the somewhat ironic headline, "Mulroney in fine form":

Fresh from his successes on the constitutional front, Prime Minister Brian Mulroney now declares he will lead his party into the next election—and he will win it. The prime minister, let us say, could use a reality check. . . .

No one expects him to rub ashes on his head or go into hiding. Still, the picture of the most unpopular prime minister in Canadian history singing a chorus of "Yes, we can do it again" at a $500-a-plate fund-raiser and boasting of economic triumphs is not one that squares with Canadians' notion of reality.[1]

A Gallup poll published on 26 November was apt to bring him down to earth. It showed that 54 per cent of Canadians wanted him to resign. Only 39 per cent wanted him to continue, while 6 per cent said they were undecided. Among Quebecers, for whose approval Mulroney had staked so much, a bare plurality, 47 per cent, preferred that he remain in office. In contrast, Gallup reported, 57 per cent of Quebecers wanted Robert Bourassa to remain on as premier, with only 33 per cent wanting him to resign.

If Mulroney really had intended to stay on, dig in, and fight the 1993 election, his prospects dimmed further when, on 7 January 1993, Robert Bourassa underwent an operation for cancer, foreshadowing that he would soon be leaving public life. Mulroney needed Bourassa, his friend and accomplice in the constitutional wars, to back him against Jean Chrétien in the electoral showdown.

346

The Tories needed every bit of support they could get. In Quebec, where the Tories had no machine of their own, Mulroney had built his power on a coalition of separatists and nationalist Liberals. The Conservative Party was largely a general staff without troops other than those seconded by the PQ and the provincial Liberals. The defection of Lucien Bouchard and the founding of the Bloc Québécois meant the Tories had lost the separatists. Without Bourassa's leadership, the provincial Liberals were likely to join with the federal Liberals to fight the coalition of their enemies: the Bloc Québécois and the Parti Québécois.

In February, another event nudged Mulroney toward the exit: Joe Clark announced that he was leaving politics. Clark was one minister whose reputation had survived the attrition of power and the disaster of Charlottetown—even though he could be considered its chief architect. Mulroney, by acting as though he would stay on as leader, had deprived Clark of his best reason for remaining in politics: the hope of again winning the leadership. Once the despised Clark had announced his departure, Mulroney could be sure that he would not succeed him, and he lost one reason for staying on.

Four days after Clark's rather forlorn announcement, on 24 February, Mulroney apprised his caucus and the country that he was about to take his place in history and make room for his successor. To hear him speak, he was leaving on a high note, despite his own and his party's low standing in the polls. "I shall hand over to my successor a government and a party in very good shape, ready to fight and to win the next election campaign," he told a press conference.

For a while it seemed as though his boast would be borne out. As soon as his imminent departure was official, public attention focused on Kim Campbell, the recently appointed minister of national defence. People actually knew little about her, but, by the time Mulroney announced his departure, she had become the sentimental favourite to succeed him. While the Tories were disliked and distrusted as no previous Canadian government, Campbell stood out from the pack. She was a recent Conservative: until she had decided to run on under the Tory banner in 1988, her political career had been chiefly with Social Credit, first as an aide to B.C. premier Bill Bennett, then as an unsuccessful Social Credit candidate in the 1983 provincial elections, and thereafter as the most unlikely candidate for the Social Credit leadership when Bennett stepped down. She came to Ottawa as an outsider to the ruling Conservatives, as a maverick, as an intellectual—and, of course, as a woman. All those characteristics of dissidence would prove assets during her pursuit of the leadership in 1993.

The most decisive factor in her ascent, though, was the decision of the nationalist leadership of the Quebec caucus to bolt to her side early, publicly, and en masse. The Quebec members held a strategic advantage over other provincial caucuses: they could act in a relatively unified way, and their support was thought to be critical for the electoral success of the party. Within days of Mulroney's announced departure, Marcel Masse and Gilles Loiselle, president of the Treasury Board, announced their support for Kim Campbell, and Masse introduced his protégée around Montreal's Conservative bastions. The two queen-makers were soon joined by Pierre Blais, the minister of justice, also co-chairman of the national Tory election campaign and the chief of the party's organization in Quebec. Blais stepped down from his positions at the top of the organizational pyramid to bring his muscle to serve Campbell's cause. This move seemed likely to deliver Quebec's votes in a block to her.

When other candidates from outside Quebec came calling, they found that they could not get commitments: people were already on Campbell's bandwagon, or were holding back for a possible favourite son from Quebec. One after the other, the ministers who had seemed sure bets to run for the leadership—Barbara McDougall, Michael Wilson, Don Mazankowski, and Perrin Beatty—abandoned hope when they discovered that they could not break into Quebec. Beatty spoke for many of them on 15 March when he announced that he did not have a chance of winning and threw his support to Campbell. "An unprecedented consensus has developed that one potential candidate, the honourable Kim Campbell, best exemplifies the qualities that are needed to lead our party and our country, and I agree with that consensus."

The next day, environment minister Jean Charest decided to become a candidate after considerable arm-twisting by the prime minister, and after hesitating to the very last minute because he was faced with such seemingly impossible odds. There had even been talk of cancelling the scheduled leadership convention altogether because of the prospect of a certain coronation. When Charest announced—he was all of thirty-four at the time—he was widely perceived as a sacrificial lamb who was going to the slaughter purely to give the party the attention to be generated by a leadership contest, and to earn political IOUs for a serious run for the leadership at a later date. No one, except perhaps himself and his wife Michèle, thought that he had a chance to win.

Charest's candidacy was opposed by the same people who gave the biggest push to the Campbell bandwagon: the nationalist ministers from Quebec. Early in March, to drain Quebec support further away from Charest, they encouraged labour minister Marcel Danis to run as an alternative favourite-son candidate from Quebec. He would sop up support that didn't go directly to Campbell, and presumably would throw his support to her at a strategic moment, thus enhancing her debt to the Quebec nationalists for ensuring that she became prime minister.

Chantal Hébert, then parliamentary correspondent for *Le Devoir* and well connected among Quebec nationalists, revealed the rejection of Charest in a story that ran on 2 March, only six days after Mulroney's announcement. "The big guns are spurning Charest," the story stated. "In the summer of '91, the young minister is considered not to have embraced with sufficient fervour the nationalist creeds of the senior ministers from Quebec." Among those Hébert mentioned were Loiselle, Masse, Danis, external relations minister Monique Vézina, and health minister Benoît Bouchard, who was also the prime minister's Quebec lieutenant. She quoted nationalist MP Jean-Pierre Blackburn, who said that these ministers "must have decided that another candidate better corresponds to the aspirations of Quebec." That was clearly the issue: the vision of Quebec's place in Canada. For the nationalists, Charest did not support a sufficiently decentralized federation in the Cabinet discussions that led to the government's constitutional proposals of September, 1991. Hébert also quoted an unnamed source who was present for the closed-door discussions: "The least you can say is that they obviously don't have the same vision of federalism."

Those same nationalist ministers found themselves in sympathy with the views of Kim Campbell. "According to the source, major Quebec figures like Marcel Masse and Gilles Loiselle then developed greater affinities with Minister Campbell."

This ideological line-up cast light on the prospective candidacy of Danis, who was utterly unknown outside Quebec, but with some following in the province. Danis had been Joe Clark's chief organizer in Quebec for the 1983 leadership contest won by Brian Mulroney. He described himself as a Quebec nationalist, and he revealed his reasons for running to Michel Auger of the *Journal de Montréal*. "These are important years ahead. There might be another referendum in Quebec. The Conservative Party must maintain its tradition of openness to Quebec nationalists." Danis told Auger that he was "in the nationalist tradition of [Daniel] Johnson." And he wanted to enter the race in order to influence the policies of the party and the new leader. "There isn't just the choice of the new leader, there will also be debates between the candidates during which it will be possible to get ideas across. If I can contribute to getting my ideas accepted by being a candidate, it is worth the effort."

In the event, Mulroney prevailed on Danis not to run. Instead, he was given a ceremonial role as co-chairman of the leadership convention, which kept him officially neutral. But the Quebec nationalists were obviously playing the key role in anointing the leader of the party that had adopted the resolution, "Be it resolved that the recognition of the right of Quebec men and women to self-determination be confirmed." Because of their plumping, Campbell seemed to have the field almost entirely to herself—even in Quebec.

An Angus Reid poll on 22 March, three days before Campbell declared her candidacy, showed her restoring the dismal prospects of the Conservatives right across the country. The results in Quebec were particularly interesting. According to the poll, a Progressive Conservative Party led by Campbell would take 47 per cent of the vote in Quebec, the Bloc Québécois would fall back to 32 per cent, the Liberals would be reduced to 14 per cent, and the NDP to 6.

For two years, the BQ had led the polls in Quebec, with between 40 and 50 per cent indicated support. Then, along came Campbell—before she had even declared—and pouf! the BQ fell back to a distant second. The poll confirmed that the Quebec electorate was volatile. It had preferred Bouchard, but still he was not an overwhelming choice. All it took was a hypothetical change of leader for a sample of Quebecers to swing away from the BQ and put the Conservatives—who had been trailing at about 14 per cent in the polls—way ahead at 47 per cent. This suggested that support for the BQ was not a decision for separating from Canada. It was a protest vote and a regional vote.

Campbell soon began to show that she was being tutored by the Quebec nationalists on her language policies. Columnist Lysiane Gagnon wrote in the *Globe and Mail* as the leadership campaign was ending, "Ms. Campbell, who knows very little about *la belle province,* actually 'subcontracted' the Quebec portion of her program to her Quebec advisers, notably Cabinet ministers Marcel Masse and Gilles Loiselle, who acted from the start as her Pygmalions on the *question nationale.* . . . Throughout the campaign she echoed her mentors' views."

When, in March, the United Nations Committee on Human Rights condemned Canada for infringing freedom of expression with Quebec's Bill 178, Campbell refused to comment on the grounds that it was a provincial matter. In fact, she had been minister of justice when her department had sent to the UN committee a defence of Quebec's bill.

Campbell's policy on language became apparent at the second of the debates between the leadership candidates, held in Montreal on 21 April, in which the two front runners at last displayed their opposite visions of Canada. Kim Campbell demonstrated that she supported bilingualism in the federal government, period. Despite two opportunities to take a stand on the rights of official-language minorities, she kept silent, and her silence spoke louder than her words.

In response to a question about her position on bilingualism, she said, "I am in favour of bilingualism in the Canadian institutions," she replied. And then, instead of talking about bilingualism outside the "Canadian" institutions—which, in the terminology used in Quebec, refers to federal institutions—she changed the subject immediately to the teaching of history: "But, to support our sense of identity, I think that we must encourage all the provinces, all the educational institutions, to take as their objective the teaching of our history, the history of all our regions."

Charest, in contrast, was quite explicit. "I think that the prime minister of Canada has the duty to encourage the government of Quebec to be more open," he said, to strong applause. "I will remind you that Brian Mulroney did this in Manitoba in 1983. Brian Mulroney had the courage to go to Manitoba to speak to Manitobans and share with them his deep convictions. And I, as prime minister, I have the duty to do the same thing here in Quebec, and elsewhere for Franco-Canadians." Again he received thunderous applause.

Campbell had a second chance to show her colours when nuisance candidate John Long launched into an attack against bilingualism as too costly, and proposed that the people of Canada should decide its fate by a referendum. Charest then spoke up again, saying that the prime minister must "defend the rights of the linguistic minorities everywhere in the country, including Quebec."

He challenged the other candidates also to take a stand. But Campbell again avoided the question of language rights for minorities. "I would just add a word with regard to bilingualism. Bilingualism reflects a deeper aspect of our country, which is biculturalism. And I'm speaking especially of the fact that, in Quebec, there is a system of law which is different from the common law which exists outside Quebec." She went on to praise the two systems of law.

That was her answer to Long's attack on the official languages, which the Conservative government had committed itself by law to "promote" in every part of Canada. It was safer to praise a vague "biculturalism" than to take a stand on the rights of linguistic minorities. By deliberate ducking, by changing the subject, by keeping silent even when Charest challenged her to declare herself, Campbell conveyed that she would not defend minority-language rights—neither the rights of English-speaking Canadians in Quebec nor the rights of French Canadians in all the other parts of Canada.

On another issue of national significance—the distribution of power between the federal government and the provinces—Campbell had avoided taking a clear position from the start. On 25 March, the day she launched her leadership campaign, she was questioned by Jean-François Lépine about her position on the constitution on the Radio-Canada program *Le Point*. Campbell avoided committing herself to constitutional change. "I think that, in Quebec and everywhere in the country, people are not ready to take up that process again. It is more important, in my opinion, to create the environment where we will be able in two years, three years, four years, to take up the process once again." As opposed to working to change the constitution, Campbell suggested that it was more important to "reinvent the government." As a British Columbian, she said, she shared many of the same concerns as Quebecers "with regard to the intrusion of the federal government in provincial fields."

During her leadership debate in Montreal, Campbell again sent out impressionistic signals. She spoke of Canada as "a country which draws its strength and its creativity from its cultural diversity and the vitality of its regions." No mention there of official languages. She spoke of "a distinct Quebec" and "the two founding peoples of the federation." This was the traditional nationalist rhetoric. And she ended with a touchstone reference to Pierre Trudeau, whom she emphatically disavowed. "Kim Campbell will never permit any bureaucracy or any lobby to revive in this country the arrogant, dominating, and centralizing federalism of the Trudeau-Chrétien years, which almost brought Canada to an end."

It was Robert Bourassa who had used the words "dominating federalism" to refer not to Trudeau, but to the Beaudoin-Dobbie report, which represented an all-party consensus of the House of Commons. By using those patented words, and repudiating "centralizing federalism," Campbell defined herself as outside the Commons consensus and on the decentralizing fringe, where, the ideological kinship with the Quebec nationalists became apparent.

As the leadership campaign advanced, Campbell increasingly distinguished herself by her slips and her errors of judgment rather than by her positions on matters of substance. Her initial attraction was largely that she seemed so different from the widely despised Mulroney and all other politicians. As the campaign wore on, however, observers watched her turn more and more into the portrait of the master. She who had won his favour by being such a gung-ho loyalist during the campaigns for free trade, Meech Lake, and Charlottetown began to sound like him, for instance when she spoke of the opposition parties as "the enemies of Canadians."

On 5 June, Campbell answered in writing questions put to her in writing by the *Financial Post*. One of the questions dealt with the official languages: "Would you eliminate, change, or maintain in their present form federal policies on bilingualism and multiculturalism?" Her answer was revealing: "I support bilingualism for Canadian federal institutions."

Since the question and the answer were both in writing, it could not be a slip of the tongue when Campbell limited her support for bilingualism to federal institutions. That position was very different from that of the Conservative government that had passed the 1988 Official Languages Act. Section 41 of the act went far beyond federal institutions: "The government of Canada is committed to (a) enhancing the vitality of the English and French linguistic minority communities in Canada and supporting and assisting their development; and (b) fostering the full recognition and use of both English and French in Canadian society." Sections 42 and 43 went on to detail the responsibility of the federal secretary of state to foster English and French in Canadian society.

During her big speech to the convention the night before the leadership vote, she again demonstrated her lack of interest in the country's two official languages. She referred to "this Canada which speaks *several languages* but will express itself in a single voice, that of justice." Of Canada's two official languages, she said not a word.

On 13 June 1993, a new, if short, era opened. A woman was chosen to be prime minister. Power was to be transmitted from one Conservative leader to another, for the first time in about a century. But Canadians had reason for concern. Campbell was following in Mulroney's footsteps in relying on nationalists to secure a power base in Quebec. Mulroney got himself and the country into trouble that way. He thought he knew Quebec and was confident that he could use the nationalists without losing control. He was proved wrong. Even with his strength of personality, his deep roots in the party, his many links with opinion leaders in all sectors of Quebec society, despite the strong personal bonds that linked him to leading nationalists, he still miscalculated. The country paid a heavy price.

Campbell had none of Mulroney's advantages. She was indebted to the nationalists, not vice-versa. Her roots in the party across the country were, to say the least, shallow, and in Quebec they were nonexistent, except as grafts on the nationalists. She had little of Mulroney's political finesse, as she had proved during her accident-prone leadership campaign. She seemed destined to become the nationalists' hostage.

Barely had she been chosen leader when the provincial Liberals in Quebec proposed a bare-faced ultimatum: if Campbell wanted their support, she had better give in to their demand to transfer the field of manpower training to Quebec. Though the Quebec government's demand was argued in terms of greater efficiency and an end to duplication, it also involved the transfer of big money and the power that goes with it. In Quebec, the federal goverment spent about $1 billion annually on manpower training, including funds recently diverted from unemployment insurance benefits into retraining.

In July, the Quebec government returned to the attack. Quebec's manpower minister, André Bourbeau, sent a public message through reporter Danny Vear, who wrote in *Le Devoir* on 8 July, "Bourbeau believes that manpower training will be the central issue of the next federal election in Quebec, and that the Conservatives' slowness in settling the matter could cost them dearly."

The day before, it was federal human resources minister Bernard Valcourt who had sent a message through *Le Devoir*. After interviewing him, the same reporter had written, "Ottawa is half opening the door to Quebec in the matter of manpower training." He quoted the federal minister as saying, "We've got to stop getting hung up over the fine print and over questions of jurisdiction. We've got to find solutions."

But that wasn't enough for Bourbeau, who said that he saw little new in Valcourt's statement, though he continued to hope. "It's possible that the Conservatives have finally understood that it is in everyone's interest to settle the matter."

In fact, after the Charlottetown agreement was voted down, Valcourt had announced that he would not turn manpower training over to Quebec, as would have happened if the Charlottetown agreement had been ratified in the referendum. But now, under Quebec Liberal pressure and with an election approaching, he changed his tune.

In the dying days of their mandate, it would have been cynical to sign an agreement with Quebec to turn over $1 billion of the taxes paid by the people of Canada. All major federal-provincial financial arrangements were to come up for reconsideration over the next few months, so rationality required renegotiating the equilibrium of the federation as a whole, not bit by bit.

Finally, on 8 September, Campbell called the long-awaited election. To judge by the speeches by the party leaders, it was to be a weird and wonderful campaign. The Tories were running as a government without a record, the Liberals were running against Brian Mulroney, the New Democrats were running against the Liberals, the Reform Party was running against parties that had a program, and the Bloc Québécois was running against Canada.

Prime Minister Campbell presented herself as someone new. She pronounced the word "new" nine times in a five-minute speech: she evoked "new leadership," "our new banner," a "new and confident course of reform, of renewal." In French, she said, "We will offer a new program."

But her most characteristic promise, to eliminate the $32 billion deficit in five years, was in the tradition of Michael Wilson. Her program implied a huge reduction in government spending, but she wouldn't tell Canadians how and where she would cut the services they received. Why? Because she must consult the provinces and the people, she said. Only after the election would she unveil her "new program."

Chrétien, whom Campbell presented as the man of the 1970s, promised an action plan to get the economy moving and create jobs, to be unveiled during the campaign. But mostly he tied Campbell to the Tory government in power since 1984. "They may try to run away from Brian Mulroney's record. It's their record. Kim Campbell wants to keep the economic policies set by Mulroney and Wilson. I want to change them."

The NDP leader also invoked Mulroney against Campbell on the first day of the campaign. "Brian Mulroney may be gone, but his economic policies live on," McLaughlin said. From Calgary, Preston Manning criticized the other leaders for launching their campaigns by announcing a program. They should have first gone out and listened to the people, Manning claimed, and then put forward a program inspired by the people.

Lucien Bouchard, in Montreal, claimed that English Canada had said no to Quebec for the past thirty years, and had refused to let Quebec have a political status corresponding to its reality. Quebecers held the poverty championship, he claimed. They would never emerge into prosperity until they had achieved sovereignty. He called on Quebecers to send MPs to Ottawa who would be committed only to the interests of Quebec.

It soon became clear that very different campaigns were being fought in different parts of the country. Kim Campbell tried to sell herself as the new leader of a new party, but it was Brian Mulroney's Canada that she had to deal with, a Canada refashioned by Mulroney's appeal to Quebec nationalism, to "distinct society," to supposed betrayal, isolation, and humiliation. There was an obvious poetic justice to what the Conservatives were now faced with in Quebec: a nose-to-nose confrontation with Bouchard's Bloc Québécois, which Mulroney had spawned. So the children of Brian Mulroney, the Conservative *Bleus* and the Bloquistes, fought each other in what was really a family feud.

Bouchard had campaigned on a separatist platform from the time he left the Tories in May, 1990, until the 25 October 1993 election, and for almost that entire period he was by far the most popular politician in Quebec. On 12 May, while the Tories were still in the midst of their leadership contest, Bouchard had proudly unveiled his separatist party's first detailed policy statement, a fifty-seven-page document titled *A New Party for the Decisive Stage*.[3] A slogan opened the chapter titled "The Role of the Bloc Québécois." It consisted of six memorable words: "One People, One History, One Territory."

The BQ slogan had notorious predecessors. The slogan of Ontario's nineteenth-century Orange Lodge, dedicated to suppressing French and Catholic schools, was "One School, One Flag, One Language." Then, there was the slogan of the Imperial Order of the Daughters of the Empire: "One Flag, one Throne, one Empire." Much more memorable was the slogan of Hitler's Nazi Party: *"Ein Reich, ein Volk, Ein Fuhrer"*—One Realm, One People, One Leader.

Militant revanchist movements that seek to unite the "Volk" invariably evoke a history of indignities and injustices to which the "people" have been subjected. The BQ document had a shade less than was usually found in Bouchard's speeches, as *La Presse* noted in its account of the BQ manifesto. "We are a long way from the great lyrical flights, the 'humiliation' that the former Conservative minister regularly evoked after he slammed the Cabinet door." Still, the whole justification offered by the BQ's manifesto for its existence was the assertion that Quebec has always been betrayed, short-changed, slighted in the federal system.

At what moment, in the course of its history, did Quebec ever find itself in a position of strength? In 1839, the Patriotes had just been crushed. In 1864–65, the French Canadians did not have the weight needed to improve to their advantage the new Canadian federation. And the promises over language were broken. In 1942, the war was used as a reason and a pretext for the fiscal surrender. In 1980–81, after its defeat in the referendum, the Quebec government was bereft of a safety belt. In 1990, it was shamefully scorned by two small provinces which made themselves the spokesmen for Canadian public opinion which was in great majority opposed to the Meech Lake accord.

According to the BQ's version of history, people who were elected from Quebec to the federal Parliament became corrupted, co-opted, or coerced into a system that invariably worked against Quebec. This was why Quebecers must elect BQ members; they, alone, would defend Quebec's interests: "More than ever, we must make sure that the interests of Quebec are defended with vigour and sheltered from the all-Canadian compromises which have so often done us harm."

For the Bloc, Canada was a country made up of two nations, two founding peoples, and the political reality of Canada had been obscured, deformed, because the Canada-wide parties did not recognize that fundamental division of Canada into two component parts. But the reality of the ethnic nations would become clear when the Bloc entered Parliament. "The Bloc Québécois MPs will have no other fidelity except toward Quebec," the manifesto stated. It defined the Bloc MPs as representing only Quebec: "The representatives of English Canada will have before them, in the House of Commons, those of Quebec. The thesis of the two founding peoples will be confirmed at last in the daily functioning of the parliamentary institution."

A federation works—unlike a confederacy, which always fails sooner or later—precisely because national parties achieve compromises in which each region sometimes benefits, sometimes loses, but with the assurance that all are better off in the long run. The BQ proposed to undermine the very practice of federalism by promising an uncompromising commitment only to Quebec's interests in every instance. "When [the BQ] is faced with a bill that affects Quebec directly, its objective will be to maximize Quebec's gains. When a bill will have no major impact on Quebec, [the BQ] will negotiate its support in exchange for further gains for Quebec." The BQ was not merely secessionist. Its plan, if successfully implemented, for instance, in a minority government situation, would have made Parliament unworkable for all.

When Lucien Bouchard launched his campaign on 8 September, he articulated that same vision of the state which must be based on "one people." Quebecers needed independence from Canada, he said, because they were a different kind of people. A classic nineteenth-century nationalist, he took ethnicity, or nationality, as the criterion by which the state and the society had to be measured. People of different nationalities were by definition different kinds of people, with different values and visions.

Bouchard said that Quebecers wanted to find and apply "their own solutions, in conformity with their own needs and their own values." This presumed that their needs and values differed from those of other Canadians. He added that, as a federal MP, he had lived "the bitter experience of the profound incompatibility of the Quebec and Canadian visions." A separatist by ideology and by sensibility, he must indeed have found his vision incompatible when he functioned as a minister in a federalist party, and in the federal Parliament. His bitterness was understandable. But he made the mistake of projecting his own values and visions on Quebecers as a whole.

L'Actualité's poll on the attitudes of Quebecers, which appeared in its July, 1992, issue, surprised many by showing the attachment of Quebecers to Canadian symbols. The cover story began, "The Québécois are deeply attached to Canada and to its symbols." The poll established that Quebecers were attached to the

Canadian Charter of Rights (73 per cent), to the Canadian flag (63 per cent) and to other symbols of Canada.

In fact, Bouchard was typical of Quebec nationalists in consistently ignoring the fact that far greater differences of vision and values were to be found within Quebec, between Quebecers, than one could find between Quebec as a whole and Ontario as a whole, or between Quebec and the rest of Canada.

A division within Quebec that Bouchard ignored was that over Quebec's constitutional future, which had kept Quebec in a state of tension for thirty years. Bouchard maintained that Quebec needed a different constitutional arrangement, but that for thirty years the rest of Canada had said no to Quebec. He was repeating the fallacy so popular after Meech failed that it was the rest of Canada, rather than a clash of visions within Quebec itself, that had kept Quebec in a state of deadlock for so many years. The circle of nationalists who built their dozen different models of castles on the St. Lawrence over the last thirty years could not recognize that the people of Quebec refused to follow them into their pipe dreams. The people of Canada must have been at fault.

Bouchard toured the province telling the Québécois that they were swindled within the federation. The members of Parliament they sent to Ottawa dared not speak out for the interests of the Québécois. Jean Chrétien was a *vendu*. He had been a leader of the assault on Quebec in 1980–82 when the constitution was patriated over the Quebec government's objections. And almost all the other MPs from Quebec participated in that same ignominy.

Quebecers were swindled every day, every year, according to Bouchard. "While Ottawa raises 23 per cent of its revenues in Quebec, a much smaller proportion—less than 19 per cent—returns to us in the form of goods and services from the federal government. Because we pay more than we get, the losses for Quebec's economy are serious. For just the year 1991, the loss to Quebec's firms and workers is estimated at $1.3 billion. Over the past 10 years, more than $10 billion have gone to enrich the other provinces at our expense."

Bouchard's message systematically deformed reality. Quebecers were robbed by the rest of Canada? According to Statistics Canada's economic accounts, the federal government raised $28.4 billion in Quebec in 1991, and spent $34.8 billion there, including Quebec's share of payment on the national debt. From 1981 to 1991, inclusive, Quebec's net gain was $73.1 billion. That is being robbed? Bouchard's constantly repeated speech was a shameless calumny against his fellow citizens in the rest of Canada. But his message of tribalist spite sold well.

In one variation of his speech, given in Quebec City on 7 October, Bouchard expressed the hope that Quebec would send to Ottawa a majority of MPs "who will stand up to the elected representatives of English Canada." As he developed that thought, Bouchard made clear the hostility and the bad faith that he presumed in English-speaking Canada. "I wonder why the fact that Quebec stands on its feet could be dangerous for Canada?" he asked ironically. "How does Canada prefer Quebec, if it doesn't like it on its feet? Quebec on its feet, is a Quebec that defends its interests, that fully carries out the role its electoral support gives it. A Quebec on its feet is a Quebec that is not sitting down, not lying down, not on its knees." The suggestion of Canada wanting Quebec on its knees was gratuitous. But it served his cherished scenario of Quebec and English Canada facing each other in a perpetual state of tribal opposition.

"We have to get out of the party lines and give ourselves a party that will defend only the interests of Quebec in Ottawa," Bouchard told a radio audience in Trois-Rivières. "We Québécois have tried everything in Ottawa. We tried to vote *rouge* [Liberal], to vote *bleu* [Conservative], to vote *bleu* and to vote *rouge*, we tried women of quality and men of quality. But we know that in those parties, they have their hands tied, they are muzzled, they can't work for us on the great issues that most concern us."

When Bouchard gave a speech in Toronto on 20 September before the Canadian and Empire clubs, he gave the more restrained version of his tribalist message. Bouchard claimed to understand Canadian nationalism, which wants Canada to be independent of the United States. "Now more than ever before, English Canadians want a real country," Bouchard informed his audience. "They know how they want to be governed and, even more, how they definitely don't want to be governed." The message was that, just as English Canadians want to be independent of the United States, so Quebecers want to be independent of Canada—but while retaining a common "Canada-Quebec economic space allowing for the free circulation of people, capital and services, as well as a common currency."

Bouchard's parallel between Canadian nationalism and Quebec nationalism omitted the critical fact that Canada is not part of the United States. Were Canadians also Americans, a secessionist movement would be unlikely, because most North Americans recognize that secession is a very difficult, costly, and uncertain adventure, to be undertaken only for the most compelling of motives. The tribalist imperative that the ethnic nationality must become a state is simply not part of the ideological baggage of the rest of Canada.

Bouchard spoke as though the people of Quebec wanted to break away from Canada. When put to the test in 1980, the people of Quebec had repudiated the separatist who presumed to speak in their name. Only a very rash person would be confident that a similar repudiation of separatism could not happen again.

Brian Mulroney's legacy was not to be found only in the Bloc. By a strange reversal, Mulroney was also the father of the Reform Party's success in 1993. His Quebec-driven constitutional obsessions, his espousal of two founding peoples and of Quebec as a distinct society, his promotion of French in other provinces while he condoned the repression of English in Quebec, all contributed to destroy the Conservative Party precisely where it had been strongest until Mulroney became leader: on the prairies.

Mulroney, along with Preston Manning, was the best promoter of Reform west of Ontario. Mulroney gave a bad name to concessions to Quebec, to the Official Languages Act, to elite accommodation, and, ultimately, to the Progressive Conservative Party. Mulroney accomplished what no one could have believed possible a few years earlier: he made Reform the number one party in Alberta and British Columbia.

Preston Manning was hardly a firebrand orator. He did not have Lucien Bouchard's ability to evoke tribal resentments or ancestral humiliations. The oratorical style he displayed was anything but demagogic. Manning laid out in his speeches, in his even voice with a touch of a twang, the program of his party. He never thundered, as John Diefenbaker used to. He rarely cracked a joke, unlike Brian Mulroney. He lacked the open-hearted sentimentality of a Jean Chrétien. In fact, his rapport with his audience was almost purely intellectual. His speeches were cerebral.

He cut, in fact, a strange figure in politics. His message was populist, but his personality was not. He wanted a smaller, leaner government at all levels. He wanted the federal government to vacate the field of language and culture—no more Official Languages Act. He called for more direct rule by the people: referendums, recall of elected officials if the people were dissatisfied. More free votes, without party discipline. Members should reflect their constituents' wishes. But the populist had no natural emotional rapport with the people. There was a reserve, a restraint, that would prevent his ever becoming a tribune of the people. He never raised his voice, never rose to that fevered pitch that comes from the chemical reaction sometimes generated between speaker and audience.

I had breakfast with Manning at his hotel in Ottawa in November 1992, just two weeks after the referendum. He was dressed in a perfectly pressed brown suit. He used his white, expressive hands to make gestures in the air before him as he spoke. But the nails on all eight fingers and both thumbs were chewed down almost to the quick. It was almost the only sign of the inner tensions of this son of a legendary Alberta premier and minister of the church who, now, was making his own great plunge into national politics. His eyes were surprisingly blue and gentle behind the silver-rimmed glasses. But, though I sat just to his right at the table, he rarely looked right at me as he put forward his ideas. This was a shy man, more at ease with ideas and policies than with people.

And yet, when Manning had spoken to a large crowd the night before, he held his audience because he articulated a disenchantment with all current traditional politicians—in fact, with all elites. The audience, equally disenchanted, had sensed for several years that the country was badly led, was on a destructive course, was being governed from the top according to principles that outraged the common sense of the people. And so the audience responded to Manning's message and to his convictions rather than to any oratorical spell.

Manning was a man with a powerful message because he expressed what the whole country had begun to suspect: that our leaders had no clothes. But he was also often portrayed as a right-wing fanatic by the news media of central Canada, by the same people who had backed the Meech and Charlottetown adventures. At a press conference the evening before our breakfast meeting, a reporter for a French-language Quebec television station asked him with a smirk, "Would you say that you are a cross between Ross Perot and Jean-Marie LePen?" By LePen, he meant the demagogic leader of France's racist Parti National. LePen was best known for demanding the expulsion of immigrants from France.

Manning wanted the number of immigrants reduced from about 250,000 to about 150,000 per year. That was hardly the proof of racism, considering that the former Liberal government had reduced the annual intake of immigrants to fewer than 100,000 in 1983–84.

Over breakfast, a soft-spoken Manning defended himself against the accusation of being an anti-immigrant racist. "If one looks at the base of the Reform Party, it originated in western Canada, which is one part of the country that was populated as the result of a federal pro-active immigration policy. So it would be highly unusual for a party with its origins in the West to be anti-immigrant." As for racism, "the more racially neutral our immigration can be, the better."

Manning was particularly reviled in Quebec. He was perceived not just as a man with a somewhat different political philosophy, but as an extremist, a racist, even a nut. *The Gazette* described him in an editorial as "peddling some poisonous snake oil" and added that "the man's callousness is stupefying." A story by *Presse Canadienne* out of Ottawa described him as "a politician used to sophistries and half-truths," without any explanation, as though it were self-evident.

Because he objected strenuously to the Charlottetown accord and to official bilingualism, because he refused the Mulroney-style concessions to Quebec, he was perceived as anti-Quebec. "No, no, we're not anti-French or anti-Quebec," Manning told me. "We want Quebec to remain in Confederation. We'd like to see a new Quebec in a new Canada. A lot of Reformers are discontented federalists who are not happy with the way the federal system is working, and in that way we think we can identify with a lot of people of Quebec that aren't happy, either, with the way that federalism is working."

But he recognized that he had, to say the least, a communication problem in Quebec. "I do find that the French-language media—and this is what Quebecers themselves tell us—distort, filter, and censure virtually any evidence of the new federalism emerging outside of Quebec."

The communication gap was part of the reason he gave for the party not yet organizing in Quebec, even though he wanted the Reform Party to be implanted in Quebec and he believed that the same message of disenchantment with "top-down" federalism could strike a responsive chord with Quebecers. But first, he would need to have the message delivered in French in Quebec by people who understood the local sensibility. "Ultimately, we've got to find Quebec federalists who represent a view similar to ours, who can say this in Quebec, in the Quebec milieu—not just in the language, but in the nuances of Quebec politics. Just like it would be very hard for someone to build the base that we have got built in western Canada if they didn't understand western politics."

Manning was also under attack in Quebec for his rejection of the Official Languages Act. "We support territorial bilingualism as distinct from the official bilingualism of the federal government," he told me. "We would say that language and culture ought to be a provincial responsibility rather than a federal responsibility, with the only role of the federal government being preventing discrimination and safeguarding freedom of speech."

One might disagree vehemently with Manning's position. But his position should hardly be offensive to Quebec separatists, who promoted a very similar position without provoking a similar scandal. "The way that our policy would work out, you'd end up having French as the working language of Quebec, with the Quebec government as the guardian and developer of that if Quebecers so chose, and English as the working language of the rest of the country."

Much of Manning's appeal during the 1993 election campaign was his rejection of the "Old Federalism" and his espousal of "New Federalism." When Manning described the "Old Federalism," he was taking aim precisely at the vision of Canada that Mulroney had promoted during his years as prime minister. "Arrayed against the separatists in Quebec are the Old Federalists of the traditional parties," Manning said during a speech shortly before the election. "As an alternative to the separatist constitutional model, they offer Quebecers the Old Federalist model of Canada as an equal partnership between two founding races, the English and the French, in which special status may be granted to groups of citizens based on race, language, and culture."

Where Manning went wrong, though, was in identifying his version of the Old Federalism with Pierre Trudeau as well as with Mulroney. In fact, Trudeau, unlike Mulroney, had emphatically rejected the model of Canada as an equal partnership between two founding races, two founding peoples, two nations, the English and the French. He had rejected special status based on race, language or culture.

"The Old Federalists' constitutional model is embodied in the 1982 Constitution Act, which they sought unsuccessfully to enhance through the Meech Lake and Charlottetown Accords," Manning continued. "The Old Federalists also see the federal government as the guardian of the French language in Canada, a concept which finds expression in the federal Official Languages Act."

Manning erred in equating the 1982 constitution with the Meech Lake and Charlottetown accords. The first was liberal in conception and based on individual rights. The second was illiberal, promoted collective rights, and enhanced the powers of government at the expense of the rights of the individual, especially in Quebec and in native communities. But distinctions tended to get lost in the 1993 campaign, when the mood in the country was toward tossing the rascals out. Not everyone discriminated between rascals. The chief beneficiary of that mood was Jean Chrétien.

The country was divided, suspicious, disenchanted, worried. If one theme linked the disparate trends of the campaign, it was that of mistrust. Kim Campbell made a fundamental mistake when she began her campaign appealing to the people with the message: trust me. She centred the Conservative campaign on herself rather than her policies—on her personality, her novelty, her "new way of doing politics," on a process that involved future consultations with provincial governments and of the people. Only when her consultations were finished—safely after election day—would she reveal how she would reduce to zero the federal deficit in five years or explain how she would reform social programs.

Campbell soon found that her campaign strategy didn't work: the people would not take her on trust. She was forced to produce a hastily cobbled plan of "for instances" for eliminating the deficit. Then, too, people didn't believe her, especially when she got lost in her own figures and journalists had to explain to her the important elements of her own plan.

Liberal leader Jean Chrétien always knew that the people wouldn't trust him. So his party put together a detailed program of government that was unveiled in the early days of the compaign. It was a risky manoeuvre. It set up a target for everyone to shoot at for five weeks. And, once the plan was unveiled, what would he talk about for the next thirty-five days?

Chrétien's strategy worked because it suited the distrustful mood of the country. The people wanted to be shown what they were getting, since they had little faith in the leaders. The Liberal program gave the equivalent of contractual guarantees at a time when a leader's word was worth little. And the problem of what Chrétien would talk about once his program was unveiled was soon solved by Campbell's campaign, so inept and gaffe-prone, which offered him up daily topics for critical commentary.

Lucien Bouchard and Preston Manning both scored regionally with their dissimilar campaigns, which had in common that they both appealed to the mistrust of the electorate. Bouchard appealed to the Québécois' tribalist mistrust of *les autres*. His entire message to the Québécois was that they must not trust anyone but themselves. Preston Manning also carried a message of mistrust: mistrust of the national parties, mistrust of the elites, mistrust of Quebec. His very persona, unlikely as it is for a successful politician, was apt to inspire trust in him as the messenger of mistrust. His plain-Joe features, cracked voice, rustic drawl, and negative charisma suggested an anti-leader leader too guileless to lead the people astray. His persona was diametrically opposed to Brian Mulroney's, mellifluous and oily. That, in itself, was a recommendation in the climate of 1993.

Audrey McLaughlin and the NDP suffered from the collapse of trust in ideology and disenchantment with the politics of virtue. Particularly after the experience with Bob Rae's NDP in Ontario, the people no longer believed in salvation through politics, be it of the left or of the right, through meditation or levitation with the Natural Law Party, or through vanity candidate Mel Hurtig of the National Party.

On 25 October 1993, the people voted their anxieties rather than their hopes. They cast their ballot for a lesser evil rather than a bright new tomorrow. And Jean Chrétien, with his long experience, his record clean of any scandal, his history of fighting the Quebec nationalists, his promise not to open up the constitution under any circumstances, seemed like the safest of the national leaders. In the end, most of English-speaking Canada voted for him and for stability, giving him a solid majority government with representation in every province. It was a vote for him, and against the constitutional eruptions of the Mulroney years.

Quebec gave almost half of its votes and 54 of its 75 seats to Lucien Bouchard, making him the leader of the official opposition. This irony was, in a sense, the last act of the Mulroney era. It expressed the anti-Canadian thrust of what Mulroney had initiated, the utopian nationalist expectations that he had unleashed in Quebec and the frustration and spite when those expectations crashed.

Quebecers expressed their alienation, but they did it safely, and within the system. There was no outbreak of terrorism, no formation of political armed gangs. And, perhaps the most conspicuous sign of Quebecers' prudence, both the prime minister and the opposition leader were from Quebec, expressing both sides of Quebecers' historic ambivalence toward their English-speaking compatriots.

Altogether, a dreadfully misguided era in Canadian history had come to an end. Canadians exacted a terrible punishment of the Progressive Conservative Party, which had built its control of the federal government on an alliance with Quebec nationalism. Only one member of Parliament who had served under Brian Mulroney survived the slaughter as a Tory: Jean Charest, whom the Quebec nationalists had ostracized because they found him too federalist. Kim Campbell, who had tried to travel Mulroney's road to power by catering to the Quebec nationalists, Quickly found herself a footnote to history.

Such was the Canada that emerged on 25 October 1993, somewhat battered from nine years of Tory government and three decades of Quebec revolutionary nationalism.

Notes

1.*Edmonton Journal*, 25 Nov. 1992.
2.*Ottawa Sun*, 4 Dec. 1992.
3.*Un nouveau parti pour l'étape décisive*. It was published in French only.

CHAPTER TWENTY-ONE

The Anglophobic Matrix
of Nationalist Politics

I n reviewing political events, it is usual to consider them as though they existed in a world by themselves, somehow separated from the culture of the people who elect the political leaders who then direct the course of history. And yet, it is often impossible to account for the flow of history without understanding the cultural matrix in which it takes place.

Although one cannot establish a direct, precise causal connection between pervasive anglophobia and a specific political event, it is important to recognize the one as the matrix within which the other occurs. In chapter two, I sketched the themes of the intellectual history of French Quebec, which prepared the ground for the nationalistic course that the Quiet Revolution took scarcely two years after Jean Lesage came to power on a platform of change. In a previous book,[1] I traced the outpouring of anglophobic novels, poems, plays, films, and essays in Quebec during the three decades which preceded its publication in 1991. In this chapter, I'll point out some of the anglophobic intellectual productions that I have observed since that book was published. This is anything but an exhaustive list.

In January, 1992, at the start of a year during which Quebec was to make a solemn decision on its future by way of a referendum, Radio-Canada made an important contribution to the debate. Its flagship public-affairs television program, *Le Point,* produced a four-part series titled *L'histoire du nationalisme québécois.*

Le Point usually brings informed commentary and analysis to current affairs. Its English-language equivalent, at the time, was CBC's *The Journal*. But, instead of dealing directly with what was expected to be the most important political event of 1992, the referendum, *Le Point* approached the topic through what it claimed to be a history of Quebec nationalism. Anyone watching the series would have been guided to only one conclusion: Quebec should separate because it has always received nothing but mistreatment from the rest of Canada.[2]

That television series was published in the form of a book,[3] which was reviewed by Michael Behiels, chairman of the department of history at the University of Ottawa. His comments apply as accurately to the television series:[4]

364

"In reality, the broadcasts and the book constitute a not very subtle form of ideological propaganda which should have been subsidized by the nationalist associations and the separatist parties, and not by a Crown corporation."

The form of the series was a succession of interviews with six historians and one political scientist, who recalled conflicts between French-speaking and English-speaking people in Canada from the Conquest down to the present. Remarkably, for a state-owned television network and a program on public affairs, Radio-Canada made no pretense of following the usual journalistic or historical canons of fairness. The seven academics who put fo ward their views were all francophones identified with Quebec nationalism. There was no attempt to balance their perspective on French-English conflicts by consulting even one English-speaking historian who has written on the subject, such as Ramsay Cook. And, as Behiels pointed out, eminent francophone historians who have criticized the nationalist interpretation of history, such as Pierre Savard, Jean Hamelin, and Fernand Ouellet, were shut out of the series.

The series was "history" to the extent that it reviewed a considerable period of time in the history of Canada; however, the treatment was ahistorical. It presented French Canadians as constantly oppressed, duped, or abandoned by the federal government and by English-speaking Canadians. In this "history," what emerged is a long, continous struggle between *us* as victims and *them* as oppressors, between *us* as good and *them* as bad.

The starting point of the account was a collection of historical events, abstracted from their context to fit a tribalist myth of constant, polarized enmity. Occasional confrontations were turned into absolute and permanent oppositions. Discrete events became part of a single grand scenario, a dramatic story of ignominy that stirred passions and evoked hostility against *les autres*. Conflict, it seemed, was the only reality and the true significance of Canadian history. And the story carried an implicit message: the logical conclusion, after reviewing such a sorry record, is to punish *them* for their unfailing arrogance and to vindicate *us* in the end, by secession, by achieving Quebec's independence.

Take the Riel affair. Some might consider it a case of injustice toward the prairie Métis. According to *Le Point*, however, it was really an attack against French Canadians. "Louis Riel . . . like most of the Métis, was a francophone and Catholic. . . . After a trial tainted by irregularities, the six jurors, all English-speaking, found him guilty, while recommending clemency." The execution of Riel, according to the on-camera historian, took on transcendental meaning: "The French Canadians of the time understood that this person and the event he represented took its place in the perennial combat between French Canadians and English Canadians. When Riel was hanged, it was one of our compatriots who was hanged."

The conscription crisis of the First World War and the attendant riots supposedly left French Canadians permanently disillusioned with Canada. "There was, at that time, a division between the two countries [Quebec and the rest of Canada]. . . . In fact, French Canadians became more aware that the Canada in which they believed was impossible. The best proof of this was the famous Francœur resolution." In the heat of the conscription debate, a Liberal member of the Quebec Legislative Assembly, Joseph-Napoléon Francœur, presented a motion to the effect that "the province of Quebec would be ready to accept the rupture of the 1867 federation if, in the other provinces, it is believed that [Quebec] is an obstacle to union, to progress, and to the development of Canada." The motion, incidentally, was withdrawn before it ever came to a vote. If that motion is the "best proof" of the impossibility of Canada, then how cogent can the rest of the case be?

At the height of the conscription crisis in 1917, a riot occurred in Quebec City in which five people were killed and seventy were wounded. This was, indeed, grievous. But, in every society, every state, there are terrible incidents of atrocities recorded. In France, during the same war, literally thousands of people were killed for desertion, or for their opposition to the war or to conscription. But, because of the French-English opposition as the nationalists' theme of history in Canada, a Quebec historian presented these five deaths as a national symbol, and they remain forever frozen in their unforgiving pose: *J'accuse le Canada!*

Thus, it was mistreatment by other Canadians which, according to *Le Point*, led French Canadians to withdraw into a reactionary mode of thought: "Being in the minority, feeling their desire for equality betrayed by the federal government, the French Canadians of Quebec withdrew inside themselves: it was a period which was called *la grande noirceur*."

In reality, nationalism in Quebec has ebbed and flowed. A true history would consider the moments of conflict, but also the long periods when conflict was resolved, when tensions eased, when reconciliation and co-operation loomed larger than polarization. But in the mythological drama presented by *Le Point*, no slight was ever forgotten, no tension ever reduced. French-speaking Quebecers simply went from one peak of conflict to the next more towering ignominy. History was a single Himalayan succession of humiliations.

No indignity was too small to be dredged up. "In 1962, the president of CN, Donald Gordon, declares that he is unable to find among his employees any French Canadian able to take up one of the twenty-eight top positions of the railroad. It is the kind of opinion that was held at the time by a good number of English Canadians about francophones." That opinion, incidentally, was also held by a good number of French Canadians, as was expressed in novels before the Quiet Revolution.

The patriation of the constitution in 1981–82 occurred as the result of the betrayal of "Quebec." As one of the experts explained, "Quebec was part of a common front with the other provinces. During the night of 5 November 1981, in what would thereafter be called 'the night of the long knives,' Quebec was to be cast off by the other provinces. Ottawa was able to patriate the constitution without the agreement of Quebec. Once again, Quebec felt isolated and betrayed." Betrayal, in the nationalist mythology, was followed by an unseemly ceremony of triumph. "On 17 April 1982, in Ottawa, in the course of a neo-imperial style ceremony, the Queen of England and Canada signed the new Canadian constitution."

When the Meech Lake agreement failed, it was because "Newfoundland and Manitoba said no to the distinct society." As for 1992, when Quebec was to make a decisive choice, nationalist political scientist Louis Balthazar explained on camera what the crisis was about: the rest of Canada would not allow Quebecers to be Quebecers first, and only then Canadians. "What is happening today, at least what we hear from a lot of English-speaking Canadians, is the following invitation: be Canadians first, and only secondly Québécois. And that, I think, they will not soon get from the Québécois."

Early in 1992, as Quebec was preparing for the approaching referendum, a book titled *Le référendum confisqué*[5] revisited the 1980 Quebec referendum on sovereignty-association. The book offered a wealth of information. Its author, Claude-V. Marsolais, a *La Presse* journalist, was assigned to the National Assembly at the time of the 1980 campaign, and he covered the leaders of the Yes and No sides, René Lévesque and Claude Ryan. For Marsolais, the referendum was about the emancipation of French-speaking Quebecers. Therefore, there was only one legitimate side to the question on the ballot: yes to the sovereignty of Quebec.

Ah, but the no side won. Even some 52 per cent of francophone Quebecers voted no. Marsolais's explanation is that the federal government confiscated the referendum by spending millions of dollars on propaganda. As well, René Lévesque and his followers were poor strategists. Francophones voted no because they were immature and misled. "The Québécois have time and again proven the immaturity of their political judgment," Marsolais wrote. "Instead of trying to take themselves in hand by going the route of sovereignty, they instinctively sought their collective security in unanimity, by a massive vote for one party or the other on the federal scene, so as to have a voice in a country that they don't dominate. It is an illusion, because all they do is gain a little time before the next crisis, which comes faster than the previous one."[6]

As for the some 95 per cent of anglophones who voted no, Marsolais had a ready explanation: they were colonizers trying to remain masters of Quebec. "The reasons that the anglophones voted as a block against political emancipation are well known to the francophones. They conquered us and behave as our masters, maintaining their rights and privileges (rights to their language, to their schools and health institutions)."[7]

That paragraph spoke volumes. It defined all English-speaking Quebecers as the enemy. *They* are the conquerors, *they* behave as masters, even in 1980, 113

367

years after English-speaking and French-speaking Canadians joined together with two other former colonies to form a federation in which all were equal before the law and had the same political rights. Even the free choice of Canada by Quebecers in the 1980 referendum changed nothing, in Marsolais's view. It didn't count because it was confiscated by Ottawa.

From Marsolais's perspective of history, he was able to say that *they* "used to say in the last century that an English people can never be vanquished by a French people."[8] He attributed this attitude to all anglophones, and used it to explain the behaviour of Quebec anglophones in 1980. In fact, the reference was to a quotation by a certain Adam Thom, published on 22 December 1835 in the *Montreal Herald,* and cited by nationalist historian Maurice Séguin. This single unknown from Lower Canada was quoted 157 years later to explain the behaviour of all anglophones—those from before the Union and before Confederation, as well as those after the Quiet Revolution and during the 1980 referendum.

A similar tribalist perspective was projected in another book published in the spring of 1992, Josée Legault's *Les Anglo-Québécois.*[9] The author, who had adapted a study originally written as a master's thesis in political science, was instantly hailed as an expert on English-speaking Quebecers. Three excerpts from her book were published in *Le Devoir*, and she was invited to participate in open-line radio programs, forums, and conferences. She became an instant celebrity.

The essence of her book is quickly summarized. English-speaking Quebecers, descendants of the conquerors of 1759, acted like conquerors for more than two centuries, until Bill 101 reduced the conquerors to minority status. But Anglo Quebecers long to return to their former status as conquerors and as the privileged caste in what Legault called a system of "apartheid," so they develop ideologically inspired rhetoric portraying themselves as victims, as a down-trodden minority, as a collectivity threatened by dwindling numbers and eventual disappearance.

Legault exposed this discourse as fraudulent and warned against any softening of the measures required to hold down the English-speaking minority. She made clear her vision of anglophones on the very first page of her book:

> History has played a nasty trick on these descendants of the British, today surrounded by six million Franco-Québécois. Deprived of their prestigious status of "conquerors," those who are now called the Anglo-Québécois are reduced to lamenting in the pages of *The New Yorker*. Their laments did not begin yesterday, though, but have returned periodically since that fatal day in 1791 when the British Crown, their Crown, divided the former New France in two and created the Province of Lower Canada, where the "conquered" could enjoy their own territory and their own government.[10]

Legault was identifying as descendants of the British "conquerors" the Jewish writer Mordecai Richler, who had written about Quebec in *The New Yorker*, and Robert Libman, then leader of the Equality Party, also Jewish. For Legault, all

Anglo-Quebecers are in the straight line of the conquerors. "This minority is the product of a historic accident, which enclosed within the frontiers of Quebec the descendants of a conquering nation."[11]

Are Anglo-Quebecers descendants of a conquering nation? According to the 1991 census, 78 per cent of Quebec's anglophones are of origins *other* than British. Of the 716,150 people in Quebec whose home language was English, only 132,315 were of English origin (single origin); 22,160 were of Scottish origin; 655 were of Welsh origin; and 215 were of some other British origin, for instance Shetland Islanders. All these together account for only 22 per cent of Anglo Quebecers.[12] If you add those who are partly of British origin, you get another 51,810 people—7 per cent. So those who are wholly or even *partly* of British origin make up no more than 29 per cent of Quebecers who speak English at home. To call all Anglo-Quebecers "the descendants of a conquering nation" is grossly wrong and a baseless provocation. Most Anglo-Quebecers are descendants of the French and the Irish, Jews, Italians, Greeks, Jamaicans, Chinese, who have come to this country to be equal citizens, not conquerors.[13]

But Legault, the instant expert on English-speaking Quebecers, saw only conquerors and their descendants, the same in 1992 as in 1791. Confederation never took place for Legault; Quebec's French majority had remained, until the passage of Bill 101 in 1977, under the heel of the conquerors. "If the anglophones say they no longer feel 'at home' in Quebec, that's mostly because some of the measures advocated by Bill 101, such as the partial francization of the workplace or of commercial signs, brought an abrupt end to a state of social, cultural and economic 'apartheid' that had lasted more than two centuries."[14]

Legault viewed the Quiet Revolution as, above all, a process whereby a subject people began to emancipate itself from its conqueror.

For francophones, the Quiet Revolution of the 1960s set off a true struggle of national liberation. For the immense majority of Quebec's French Canadians, the Liberal government of Jean Lesage represented not only their passport to modernity, but also the essential tool for *their* liberation from the economic domination exercised until then by the Anglo-Saxons. From carriers of water to chief executive officers, French Canadians made themselves more and more Québécois by taking their place in a state from which they had been, so to speak, excluded.[15]

French Canadians had been excluded from the government of Quebec? Legault, who was teaching at the Université du Québec à Montréal when her book came out, repeated faithfully the myth of Quebec as colonized which had so charmed Quebec's intelligentsia since the Quiet Revolution. It provided a convenient ideological justification for transforming the government of Quebec into the instrument of an ethnic state at the service of the French-speaking majority. The more horrible the fate of francophones, the more arrogant their conquerors, the more easily justified were stern measures to repress English.

Moreover, Legault found a clever stylistic device to drive her message home. The subject of her thesis, she said, was the *dominant* language articulated by some people and some institutions identified with English Quebec. The word *dominant*, next to the word *anglophone*, recurred repeatedly throughout the book, as often as four times on a single page. Over and over, "dominant, dominant, dominant" was driven home in juxtaposition with anglophones.

To support her argument that only Bill 101 had ended the anglophones' status as conquerors, Legault repeatedly distorted data. "In 1977," she wrote, "the gap in income between anglophones and francophones remained unchanged." In fact, economist Jac-André Boulet of the Economic Council of Canada had found that, in 1960, male anglophones in Montreal earned 51 per cent more than male francophones, but by 1970 the gap had narrowed to 32 per cent, and by 1977 to only 15 per cent.

Legault claimed that the Gendron Commission on the French language "revealed that only 64 per cent of francophone workers worked in their language." False again. The Gendron Commission had found that, in Montreal, 64 per cent of francophones worked in French *exclusively*. But, as we have seen, they also found that, in Montreal, francophones worked in French on average 19.1 days out of 20, and in the rest of Quebec, they worked in French 19.6 days out of 20.

Legault even blatantly distorted the Supreme Court of Canada's 1988 decision that total prohibition of languages other than French on commercial signs was a violation of freedom of expression. "Thereby, the English language recovered a status equal to that of the French language," she wrote. In fact, the court upheld the prohibition against English-only signs, while French-only signs were obviously not prohibited. In addition, the court upheld as within the pale of admissible restriction the requirement that French be on all signs, and even be strongly predominant on all signs. For Legault, intent on proving her thesis, this gave equal status to French and English.

Anglophobia—and concurrent anti-federalism—was also to be found in fiction during this pre-referendum period. One example was Jean-Claude Lauzon's film *Léolo*, which represented Canada at Cannes. It was an extraordinarily original film in every respect but one: the personification of evil in the movie was an English-speaking Quebecer.

Léolo, the hero, recalled as a child picking up discarded newspapers with his older brother to sell to a fishmonger, who used them to wrap fish. A local bully slapped the brothers around and told them they couldn't sell old papers any more: that was his turf. The bully, of course, was an Anglo. Léolo's older brother dreamed of making himself invulnerable to bullies and spent his time developing his physique. A few years later, he has bulging muscles and the strength of a champion weight-lifter.

Again the brothers encounter in the street the Anglo bully, who is obviously frail, now, compared to Léolo's colossus of a brother. But the Anglo comes forward and slaps the brother in the face, daring him to fight back. The colossus slumps into a weeping, quivering mound of frustration: he can't fight back. Irrational? Yes. The Anglo bully has some preternatural power that makes his evil influence irresistible. That kind of irrational fear makes official Quebec resist whatever could give more power, development or vitality to its Anglos, seen as dangerous bullies. A long tradition has conditioned Quebecers to see English-speaking Quebecers as all-powerful in their destructive influence.

That is why, like Léolo's brother, who spent all his time building up his constitution, Quebec's political class works constantly to develop an ever more powerful constitution, to give the Québécois security against the Anglos. No constitution is ever strong enough, though. Quebecers, weak and vulnerable according to an enduring myth, must have an iron-clad constitution that gives the Quebec government all the powers of an ethnic state, to ensure that French-speaking Quebecers are promoted and *les autres* are restrained: otherwise, they will harm the Québécois.

A different facet of anglophobia was exhibited in the novel by Gabrielle Gourdeau, *Maria Chapdelaine, ou le Paradis retrouvé*,[16] which in 1992 received the Robert Cliche Award for best first novel. It is a sequel to *Maria Chapdelaine,* projecting the life of Maria after she was left as a young woman by her creator, Louis Hémon, at the end of the earlier novel.

In Gourdeau's novel, Maria works as a maid for an English-speaking family, the Macdonalds, who treat her, as she says, worse than their dog. "What can you expect? They have the heavy end of the stick, the English end."[17] Maria lives to see the 1980 Quebec referendum—she is an ardent sovereignist. And she rails against "the campaign of terror" of the Anglos who "look down their noses at us." She wondered why René Lévesque treated them with kid gloves: "When you're dealing with primates, you do your talking with a club."[18]

Another instance of presenting English-speaking Canadians as conquerors was found in the novel by Michel Dallaire, *Terrains vagues*, which won the Jacques Poirier Prize for 1992. The narrator, a Franco-Ontarian woman, describes Franco-Ontarians as conquered people who are treated like slaves: "White negress of New Ontario! Dispossessed. Wolfe and Montcalm. Dominant and dominated."[19] She rails against the French-speaking middle class, "This decadent and submissive petite bourgeoisie which gives up everything and is satisfied with small comforts which suit the victor, even so many years later. A few crumbs, thrown at the feet of the slaves."[20]

Two plays of the pre-referendum period also project a similar vision. One was *Conte d'Hiver 70* by Anne Legault, which played through most of February 1992 at Montreal's *Theâtre d'aujourd'hui*.[21] The other won the 1992 Governor-General's Award for best French drama in 1991, Gilbert Dupuis's *Mon Oncle Marcel qui vague vague près du métro Berri*.[22]

Both plays present a wretched view of Quebec society. Both evoke the Front de Libération du Québec in virtuous contrast to the ambient evil. And both suggest that *les Anglais* are somehow ultimately behind the pervasive corruption or are its symbol.

Legault's play is set during December of 1970, just as the police are closing in on the kidnappers of James Cross. Two FLQ members are hiding out in a rooming house that is part of a general store *cum* post office near Montreal. The two Felquistes are idealists: they wanted to accelerate history and bring about social justice. One has assassinated the Quebec minister of labour, the other is the sister of the man who kidnapped a British diplomat.

The woman who runs the place is a poor soul who barely manages to make ends meet. Her drafty house lacks central heating. One day, someone steals a mailbag from the post-office counter she runs: $2,500 is missing. An inspector from the RCMP comes by to investigate. He had earlier questioned the Felquistes, but without knowing who they were. Still, the fascist brute threw their books on the floor and beat the young woman.

Through threats, the RCMP officer gets the landlady to sign a paper undertaking to pay back the missing $2,500 out of her meagre earnings. She is so poor that she will be forced to put her twelve-year-old daughter in an orphanage if she has to make the payments. But even that is not vile enough for this representative of the federal state. He also forces the woman to perform fellatio on him. Such is the corrupt and degraded society that has driven the FLQ to desperate measures in the search for regeneration. The woman is too downtrodden to formulate a proper analysis of the political source of her misery, but it is obvious that *les Anglais* are ultimately responsible. One of the Felquistes tries to raise the woman's consciousness. He points out to her that, when she travelled in the southern United States, she was polite to black waitresses: "*Les Anglais* are like you. They are very polite because they have a lot on their conscience. You are their nigger."[23]

The play ends after the woman has betrayed the FLQ boarders for money. But her winsome daughter, representing the future, recites a poem to Liberty. Some day, it is implied, Quebec will be free of its colonial, degrading bondage.

Dupuis's play is more sophisticated. It is set among street people, including prostitutes, drunks, a retired terrorist, and a man who went mad after he lost his job as a mechanic because he was considered "obsolete." The street becomes a metaphor of society, which is utterly evil. A thug, who is a shylock, pimp, and extortionist, with the appropriate name of Dollar, runs a bar that is the very symbol of hell. It has an English name: The Lost Paradise.

The man who went mad after losing his job had been fired, of course, by an *Anglais* boss. "He doesn't speak French like us. He lives on the mountain. You have to say to him: money, money."[24] In contrast to this utterly degraded world is the memory of an uncle, Marcel, who went out to British Columbia during the Great Depression, stood proudly on his two feet and refused to submit, but revolted against the exploitation in "Bennett's concentration camps." He was found with his throat slit.

Uncle Marcel is offered as the prototype and model of what the Québécois should be: "This is the story of my family. . . . That story is my inheritance."[25] The Québécois have had their throat slit in the federation. But they have an example to follow. Revolt against evil, including *les Anglais,* is the only way out of The Lost Paradise, the only way back to regeneration, to salvation, to paradise regained.

The most ambitious project presenting the FLQ terrorists as heroes is a film by Pierre Falardeau, *Octobre.* The film follows closely the events of the Chénier Cell, led by Paul Rose, which kidnapped and assassinated Pierre Laporte. It shows us a group of idealistic young men driven to desperate measures by the quasi-slavery to which French-speaking Quebecers are reduced by their Anglo masters.

In one key scene, the principal character, François, is working in a sweat-shop, or rather a steam shop, where he gets burned because his cruel Anglo boss always pushes him to work harder, harder, at the risk of his life. Here, according to the scenario submitted to Telefilm Canada, is how François described his living hell:

There was dust everywhere, steam—I was burned all over my arms. The boss was short and aways excited, a real rat, he was always shouting: "fucker . . . bastard" [in English in the text]. It was always push, push, push, go, go, go. We didn't have time to go for a leak. And that cur, when we were on the night shift, he would make the girls go up to his office and he would screw them. All of them. Those who refused, he fired.

Clearly, Quebec at the mercy of the Anglos was like Algeria under the French. And that frightful reality explains why these brave young men oppose exploitation even at the risk of their lives. They are willing to go all the way, even to commit the "necessary and unjustifiable" act of assassination, and to burden their consciences with a frightful deed that will never again let them be at peace. That is their tragic, heroic fate.

Interviewed by *La Presse*'s movie critic Luc Perreault in February, 1994, Falardeau explained his national-liberation perspective: "For me, nothing has changed. It has lasted ever since the Conquest. It has been going on for 233 years. There still has not been a national liberation. Quebec is still not a country." Falardeau received $1.1 million from Telefilm Canada and the equivalent of $400,000 in production facilities from the National Film Board to make a film that belongs to the long tradition of treating English-speaking Quebecers as exploiters, as conquerors, as aliens, as threats to French Quebec.

The tradition of anglophobia led naturally to political nationalism and to separatism, especially and precisely when the state assumed overwhelming importance after 1960. But, after a century and a half of anglophobic propaganda, nationalism and separatism have assumed a life of their own. There are, obviously, nationalists and separatists who are not anglophobic, and there are interpretations of reality that are biased by nationalism even though they show no sign of anglophobia.

Le mouton noir, a film by Jacques Godbout, is supposedly a National Film Board documentary on the failure of the Meech Lake accord and the political year in Quebec that followed, from June, 1990, until the St-Jean-Baptiste parade of June, 1991. It takes the form of Godbout's diary for a year in which he recalls events, interviews people, passes judgment. He is seen reflected in a mirror as, paper and pen in hand, he meditates deeply on the passing scene, trying to make sense of what is happening in Quebec during the year that included the founding of the Bloc Québécois, the highly publicized hearings and report of the Bélanger-Campeau Commission, the Quebec Liberals' Allaire report, Keith Spicer's Citizens' Forum, and the adoption of Bill 150 by the National Assembly to hold a referendum on the secession of Quebec.

From the beginning of the film, Godbout accuses the rest of Canada of having broken its promise and betrayed its word to Quebec as, he maintains, Canada did repeatedly in the past. "Before being a country, Canada remains a contract forever under negotiation," he says. "But, in June, 1990, the signatories to the Canadian contract went back on their word." In fact, Elijah Harper, who was conspicuously not a signatory to the Canadian contract, prevented the adoption of Meech in Manitoba. Standing in the room at Meech Lake where the first ministers came to an agreement on amending the constitution in 1987, Godbout says, "By going back on their signatures three years later, the Canadians will have made famous a lake in Quebec which never asked for such a fate." All the premiers who signed in 1987 later stood by the Meech Lake accord, often at great political cost. The premiers who rejected Meech were those, like Frank McKenna and Clyde Wells, who had not signed the accord, who in fact had campaigned and won election on their opposition to Meech. But Godbout was not bothered by minor scruples. He preferred a scenario of betrayal and rejection. "Canada doesn't want us any more? Too bad. We'll be the black sheep of Confederation."

The film, monumental in length (four hours), is a monument not to Quebec, as the title would imply, but to Jacques Godbout, his friends, his opinions and prejudices, his nationalist sensibilities, and, ultimately, his illusions. "Tuesday, November 27. My birthday. Robert reached the same age on July 14th. We are no longer children."

"Robert" is, of course, Robert Bourassa, the premier of Quebec. Godbout introduces him as a personal friend, "one who goes back to my childhood," and, whenever he interviews him, he uses the familiar "*tu*." And Godbout interviews at length, repeatedly, Daniel Latouche, a political scientist who had been an adviser to René Lévesque. "He is a friend," Godbout explains.

Godbout interviews Jacques Parizeau, who is also presented as a personal friend. He addresses the ultra-dignified Parizeau with the familiar *"tu."* "I got to know Jacques through his wife, Alice," he tells us, "who always made sure that she surrounded him with friends."

There are few federalist voices in this little coterie, and those who do appear are almost invariably dismissed with contempt: "The old guard is not sovereignist, including Claude Ryan, who hates adventure and risks in politics. The young cannot identify with this pontiff of another era."

The young, in fact, are the true heroes of *Le mouton noir*. Godbout follows with obsessive interest the Young Liberals who debated and adopted a resolution in favour of Quebec sovereignty in August, 1990, and then led the fight to have the Allaire report adopted as party policy at the Quebec Liberal convention of March, 1991. Godbout manifestly believed that the Young Liberals, who then took a turn toward radical nationalism, were the wave of the future. The filmmaker lavishes attention on Michel Bissonnette, president of the Liberals' Youth Commission in 1990, and on Mario Dumont, his successor, as well as on Jean-François Simard, the president of the federal Young Liberals, who resigned in protest against the election of Jean Chrétien as leader. (Simard defected to the Bloc Québécois.) Here, Godbout implies, as he follows the young politicians with his camera, is the future of Quebec, to which the people are led by a vanguard of idealistic youth. Included among the young standard-bearers of sovereignty is Joseph Facal, president of the Parti Québécois's youth wing. Godbout repeatedly interviews these young makers of history and lovingly records every twist and turn in their thinking.

But not all young politicians are so favoured; only those who are sovereignists. Thus, Denis Coderre, a Young Liberal who ran in the 1990 Laurier-Sainte-Marie by-election that was to be won by the Bloc Québécois, is dismissed contemptuously for saying that the constitution is not the major issue in that by-election. "The demagogues always use the same technique," Godbout comments. "They maintain that constitutional problems are not real, as though human suffering did not have a political dimension."

The object of Godbout's special contempt, though, is Jean Chrétien. "I will not pretend to like Jean Chrétien," he says. "His speeches and his accent make my flesh crawl. If he becomes prime minister of Canada, I'm going to emigrate." Chrétien is shown campaigning for a seat in Parliament in the Acadian riding of Beauséjour. As he is giving a political speech, the camera pans slyly on a sign outside the hall: *PEPSI*. "Pepsi" is a slang name for a dumb, doltish French Canadian.

Throughout the documentary, Godbout displays his sense of irony toward the Canadian federation. He has an actor, playing John A. Macdonald, say, "Gentlemen, we are here to create a nation." But Godbout immediately comments, "In reality, what interested those lawyers and businessmen was the financing of a railway and a plan for a common market." A federation of deal-makers on the take. In another scene, a band is playing *O Canada*. Godbout remarks, "It is useful to remember that this national anthem was composed by Calixa Lavallée to words by Basile Routhier for the celebration of Saint-Jean-Baptiste in 1880. . . . Today it is played by the firemen of Ottawa." (In Quebec, the word *pompier* [fireman] has the double meaning of "ridiculously pompous.")

But, toward Quebec nationalism, Godbout never betrays the slightest hint of irony or doubt. During a season when nationalism was in style, Godbout turned an always-admiring camera on the nationalists. In the last scene, while the credits roll, the camera pans on a wall bearing the words *QUÉBÉCOIS DEBOUT*. That is the final message: Quebecers, stand on your two feet, stand up to English Canada.

Le mouton noir is the sequel to and the mirror opposite of Denys Arcand's 1981 film on the Quebec referendum of the previous year, *Le confort et l'indifférence*. Arcand's film was bitter and cynical in tone. The people of Quebec had just refused to vote yes to sovereignty-association in a referendum. Arcand's film pursued the answer to the question, How could they have been so stupid, so cowardly, so vulgar, so materialistic, so blind, so grossly self-protective as to vote no? Arcand used the character of Niccolo Machiavelli as the amused, cynical observer and conscience of the film: Ah, Machiavelli commented, it was all so predictable. Half a millennium ago, a worldly wise Florentine sage had explained it all in advance. And the defeat of the referendum was inevitable. After all, who controlled the army?

Godbout's film, on the other hand, is triumphal. A miracle has happened in the years since 1980: the people of Quebec, in the aftermath of Meech Lake, seem at last resolutely engaged on the road to independence. In this film, it is Godbout who plays the role of Machiavelli. He, too, acts cynical and worldly wise, but only toward the manifestations of federalism.

While *Le confort et l'indifférence* contrasted the high solemnity and glittering pageantry of René Lévesque's official visit to France with the vulgar, burlesqued speeches of Camille Samson, Jean Marchand, and Jean Chrétien, *Le mouton noir* shows us streaming Quebec flags leading what appears prophetically to be a victory parade. There is just a small clutch of anti-independence antagonists to satirize, in addition to Chrétien, who is the goat of the piece. These opponents are hardly threatening: Claude Ryan, Richard Holden (then still in the Equality Party before his metamorphosis into a Péquiste), and Robert Libman are made to do as the foils and the voices of the past, who will surely be defeated by the march of the young. The old guard who form the antagonists of 1990–91 cannot compare to the Pierre Trudeau, at the height of his power and popularity, who blocked the road to independence as the chief antagonist in Arcand's film on 1980.

For Godbout to have brought out such a monument of a documentary—about the length of Abel Gance's *Napoléon*—he clearly was convinced that he was making his *Birth of a Nation*. But the future was to show how badly he had misjudged the events of 1990–91. Quebec was not, as he so confidently implied, at the start of a revolutionary ferment that would end in a declaration of independence, and the Young Liberals and Young Péquistes and Young Bloquistes and other young crusaders for sovereignty whom he so fawningly lionized were, in fact, very, very young. Their political triumphs of 1990–91 ended up hollow because they were divorced from Quebec's reality. Godbout, adulatory and uncritical, proved to be a poor journalist.

At the end of the film, Godbout asks his young heroes to prophesy the future. "It's been a year since Meech failed, and there are a bunch of polls where sovereignty has dropped, and where people are starting to say that maybe the Québécois don't want sovereignty," Michel Bissonnette responds uneasily. But then he added, "As for myself, I'm convinced that the choice has been made since June 1990, and it's just a matter of time." Two years later, Bissonnette was handling publicity for the neo-federalist Liberals, his sovereignist convictions apparently put on a back burner. The vision of Quebec's youth leading the way triumphantly to sovereignty turned out to be a fantasy. In the end, the *Black Sheep* was just another white elephant.

Notes

1. William Johnson, *Anglophobie made in Québec* (Montreal: Stanké, 1991).
2. My critique of the series was published in *The Gazette*, 29 and 31 Jan. 1992.
3. Gilles Gougeon, *Histoire du nationalisme Québécois. Entrevues avec sept spécialistes* (Montreal: VLB Éditeur and Société Radio-Canada, 1993).
4. Michael Behiels, "Quand l'histoire nationaliste devient mythe et propagande," *Bulletin* of the Association québécoise d'histoire politique, 3, no. 1 (Fall 1994).
5. Claude-V. Marsolais, *Le référendum confisqué: Histoire du référendum québécois du 20 mai 1980* (Montreal: VLB éditeur, 1992).
6. Ibid., p. 9.
7. Ibid., p. 133.
8. Ibid., p. 134.
9. Josée Legault, *L'invention d'une minorité: les Anglo-Québécois* (Montreal: Boréal, 1992).
10. Ibid., p. 17.
11. Ibid., p. 19.
12. These data were communicated to me orally by an official of Statistics Canada.
13. According to Statistics Canada, of the 82,790 Quebecers who, in the 1991 census of Canada, gave "Irish" as their single origin, 64.7 per cent spoke French at home, 1.7 per cent spoke both French and English, and only 33.5 per cent spoke English.
14. Legault, *L'invention.*, p. 88.
15. Ibid., p. 19.
16. Gabrielle Gourdeau, *Maria Chapdelaine, ou le Paradis retrouvé* (Montreal: Quinze, 1992).
17. Ibid., p. 108.
18. Ibid., p. 191.
19. Michel Dallaire, *Terrains vagues* (Montreal: VLB Éditeur, 1992), 107.

20.Ibid., 108.
21.Anne Legault, *Conte d'hiver 70* (Montréal: VLB éditeur, 1992).
22.Gilbert Dupuis, *Mon Oncle Marcel qui vague vague près du métro Berri* (Montreal: L'Hexagone, 1991).
23.Legault, *Conte d'hiver 70*, pp. 82–83.
24.Dupuis, *Mon ONcle Marcel*, p. 63.
25.Ibid., p. 152.

CHAPTER TWENTY-TWO

A Liberal Non-ethnic Nationalism?

Nationalists leaders today cloak their nationalism in a modern dress, and often their protestations are taken at face value by others. When Lucien Bouchard visited Washington, in March, 1994, he hastened to reassure the Americans, "Ours is not an ethnic nationalism—ours is a territorial nationalism." He repeated the message when interviewed for a French publication specializing in international affairs:

The notion of "nation" in Quebec has much evolved along the decades. The nationalists of the 1930s were centred on the francophone ethnic group. . . . On the contrary, the nationalism that I profess and that inspires our action is essentially territorial and economic in nature. It no longer is based on the conception of an ethnic group, but recognizes that the "nation québécoise" is constituted by the people as a whole who inhabit Quebec.[1]

Bouchard's "new-wave" nationalism conforms to columnist Lysiane Gagnon's description of the currently approved model of separatism: "In progressive circles, it doesn't do to be a passionate separatist, let alone 'anti-English.'. . . Nowadays, the 'correct' way to be a sovereigntist is to emphasize the territorial, rather than ethnic, dimension. For right-thinking sovereigntists, the rationale for sovereignty is not rooted in the French-Canadian nation, as it was in previous times, but in the fact that Quebec as a whole, including its minorities, is a distinct society with its own culture and institutions."[2]

The claim that the old, anglophobic ethnic nationalism has been transformed into a new, liberal, non-ethnic nationalism is accepted by some usually sophisticated commentators. Michael Ignatieff, in his recent book on nationalism, is inclined to absolve current Quebec nationalism of its anglophobic past: "Nationalism in Quebec has long ceased to be the nationalism of resentment. The old scores have been settled. It is now a rhetoric of self-affirmation. The basic motive driving it is no longer the memory or myth of past injustice; the motive that counts is the sense of power and accomplishment."[3]

In his review of Ignatieff's book for *The New York Times*, Francis Fukuyama, celebrated for an essay entitled "The End of History," accepted the claim that

exempted Quebec nationalism from reactionary vindictiveness: "Quebec nationalism is not the backward-looking revolt against modernity that characterizes the
clashes in parts of Eastern Europe: the Québécois yuppies whom Mr. Ignatieff
interviews in Montreal are all the products of Quebec's rapid economic modernization in the last generation. They make clear to him that their version of
nationalism is liberal, non-ethnic and non-discriminatory."[4]

Ignatieff and Fukuyama clearly have not examined Quebec nationalism
closely. On better acquaintance, they would become aware of the immense corpus
of anglophobic poems, novels, plays, films, and essays that has accumulated over
the years, and that continues to grow. The multitudinous voices presenting the
English language as a threat, or *les Anglais* as eternal enemies, speak louder than
those who insist that Quebecers no longer practise the nationalism of resentment.
The anglophobic voices are not those merely of a few marginal cranks, anachro-
nistic soreheads who have not caught up with the new "liberal, non-ethnic"
nationalism. On the contrary, the anglophobic statements continue to be articulated by some of Quebec's most prestigious writers, such as Yves Beauchemin,
author of *Le matou*, and anglophobic works continue to win prizes awarded by
prestigious juries. The anglophobic tradition, so rich and pervasive, has never
been frankly recognized and denounced by Quebec's intelligentsia. Until that
demystification has been carried out, children in school and students in colleges
and universities will still be infected with the same old malevolent virus.

Current Quebec nationalism still aims, aggressively, at imposing the hegemony of French-speaking Quebecers and their language on all other Quebecers.
The main difference between now and thirty years ago is that English-speaking
Quebecers have now been declared invisible, marginal, a mere adjunct, restricted
and controlled, to a Quebec that has been declared essentially French. Anglos
have now been stripped of the legitimacy and public recognition they enjoyed in
1960, and had for the previous two centuries. The new rhetoric merely hides the
fact that the same old ethnic nationalism has gone a step further, declaring a
victory over the formerly entrenched *Anglais*.

Nevertheless, the nationalists continue to fear that the present controls to hold
down all languages other than French might not be enough. More forceful
measures are required. To see these ethnic anxieties in action, one has only to
study the 1994 edition of the Parti Québécois's program.[5] The ethnic nationalism
of Quebec's most popular party leaps out on the very first page, where the PQ
defines Quebec by reference to a "people" that was and is French-speaking, and
French-speaking only. More than two hundred years of cohabitation with
English-speaking fellow citizens, first under the British Crown, then as an
independent democratic country, are ruled out of existence.

Canadiens of the seventeenth century, *Canadiens français* of the nineteenth century, and now *Québécois*—rarely has one seen a people search
so long for its identity. . . . From the start, it has been French in language

380

and has constantly sought to reinforce the basis of its culture and the foundation of its solidarity. Francophones of America: that is how the Québécois want today to put down their name on the list of peoples who forge the civilization of the planet.[6]

This is "territorial" nationalism? The PQ is not satisfied with describing Quebecers as a people that is French. In its 251 pages, the program describes in detail how a future Parti Québécois government will intervene with all the force of the law to ensure that Quebec is a French society, one where other languages are tolerated only to the extent that they are carefully circumscribed by law and kept marginal.

Future immigrants to Quebec will be selected so as to give preference to those who can speak French, "with the objective that they should constitute a majority of all immigrants."[7] Before these immigrants leave their native lands, and again when they arrive in Quebec, they are to receive "intensified information" on what the PQ calls "the specificities of the culture of Quebec . . . its language, its geography, the great moments of its history and its values..."[8] Immigrants must be warned from the start of the (only) language, the (only) culture, and the (only) values that they must adopt: those of French Quebec. No other is even acknowledged to exist.

To ensure that immigrants and all Quebecers know conclusively that Quebec is French, all signs, whether public or private, inside or outside establishments, are to be in French only.[9] The PQ proposes to "abolish Bill 86," which allows the limited, carefully controlled presence of languages other than French on commercial signs, provided they are on the premises of the firm.[10] When choosing between freedom and linguistic purity, the PQ rejects freedom.

All those who move to Quebec—and their descendants in perpetuity—will be required to attend French school, whatever their mother tongue. This includes English-speaking people coming to Quebec from Canada, as well as immigrants from the United States, Britain, or elsewhere. An independent Quebec, freed of the constraints of the Canadian Charter of Rights, will close Quebec's English schools to all but those who have a certificate saying they are eligible for English schooling because they have a parent who studied in English in Quebec.[11]

Until now, the restrictions on English education applied to the elementary and secondary levels, but the PQ has radicalized its determination to make Quebec French. It proposes to extend the same restrictions to the junior colleges: only students with "certificates of eligibility" will be allowed to enrol in English-language CEGEPs.[12] Since these colleges are the feeder institutions for Quebec's English-language universities, enrolments at McGill, Concordia, and Bishop's will decline.

Attendance will also be cut back in other ways. The program commits a PQ government to "encourage, by appropriate measures, the enrolment of students in French institutions of higher learning."[13] In addition, those whose mother tongue is not French will find it much more difficult to get into any university. The program states that all students will be prevented from going to university unless they have achieved "full mastery of French."[14]

A *Gazette* journalist asked the PQ's language critic in the National Assembly, Jeanne Blackburn, whether the program really meant what it said. She confirmed, "Mastery of French applies to all Quebec universities. I am comfortable with the idea of requiring anglophones to have a full mastery of French to get into university."[15] She added that anglophones should be "perfectly bilingual." As the *Gazette* article points out, 29.6 per cent of the student body of McGill University is from outside Quebec. At Bishop's University, in Lennoxville, the proportion from outside the province is 58.6 per cent. The mastery of French requirement would be an almost insuperable hurdle for a great number of students. "Many of these students come to Quebec now, hoping to learn French here. But according to the PQ's vision of an independent Quebec, these 'foreign' students would have to perfect their knowledge of French *before* coming to university here."[16]

After sovereignty has been achieved, the PQ proposes to ensure that life will be increasingly difficult in Quebec for those who do not "master" French. "The sovereignty of Quebec will, without question, strengthen the status of the French language. Mastery of it will become increasingly essential for any real and fair participation in the life of the host society.[17]

The state will intervene to reduce the number of English-language radio and television stations: "We must correct the historic imbalance that persists in the attribution of radio licences in Montreal, and we must regulate the French and Québécois content of the broadcasts of the French stations."[18] The PQ also proposes to "ensure the development of francophone television networks, which are faced with the massive presence of the anglophone networks, notably the American ones, and will give priority to the French language networks in the attribution of signals by cable and satellite."[19] Movies will also receive the government's scrutiny. The PQ proposes to "set quotas for the place of French on movie screens, as well as for film production and for subsidized film festivals."[20]

To earn a living in any language but French, will be made increasingly difficult. At present, firms with more than fifty employees must obtain a certificate that proves that they operate in French at all levels. The program commits a PQ government to extend the same obligation to all establishments with ten or more employees.[21] Moreover, the francization legislation is to be strengthened to ensure that any employee "who is wronged for linguistic reasons has access to an adequate, quick, and effective recourse."[22] In addition, "a policy of periodical inspections" of all firms is to be instituted."[23]

The teaching of English in French schools will be forbidden before grade four.[24] And learning to speak French will not be enough in the new Quebec.

People will also be pressured to adopt the right attitudes and values, as defined by the government: "It is urgent that our education system not limit itself to teaching French as a mere instrument of communication. French must also be seen and taught as a system of values and of historic references, and as a privileged instrument to develop projects which will define the future of modern Quebec.[25]

Moreover, the state will be vigilant to ensure that people speak *good* French. The program says, "The necessary measures will have to be taken to ensure that the proper quality of French is respected in all sectors, and especially in the media (television, radio, newspapers, ads). [The PQ government] will have to see to it, in particular, that the Commission de surveillance de la langue française carries out its mandate more strictly."[26]

The government will be watching, especially in Montreal, where the numerous presence of *les autres* could create a problem. The program specifies that the institutions where services are provided must not be bilingual. "These services, located at reasonable distances from those who use them, must include, in particular, quality CEGEPS, cultural institutions (libraries, cultural centres), hospitals, social services, sports facilities, and recreational services. In every case, *the concept of bilingual institutions must be excluded.*"[27]

A PQ government would insist that people in restaurants, at the hairdresser's, in stores, or in a doctor's office will be addressed first in French, without having their ears jarred by initial contact in English, or having to ask for service in French. The PQ proposes to amend the Charter of the French Language to bring in new sections "that must be made enforceable" to strengthen the Charter's sections ensuring the right to work, be informed, and be served in French. "It will provide that service in French will be automatically available, without delay and without one having to ask."[28]

These proposals, we must remember, are commitments from a party that takes its official program as seriously as a catechism, and they are commitments to use the coercive power of the state to enforce the desired state of affairs. There is probably not one area of life, other than the privacy of the home, where the purification effort will not bring the state to intervene in the lives of the citizens.

To justify such a draconian legislative agenda, the PQ invokes a siege mentality. The reason that measures so repressive are to be enforced against English is that the French language is under constant threat from English, and can be saved only by stringent means.

Our language, the French language, is the basis of our identity and the vehicle of our culture. Threatened—when it is not excluded—everywhere else on the North American continent, it is in Quebec that it finds its rootedness and the space where it can blossom. . . . Our language, which names things and delineates concepts, also constitutes—since that is its first function—a way of thinking, of reflecting, and of understanding the world.

We will not renounce this manner of being and speaking. We will not accept that our language should degenerate to the point that it only serves to translate Canada for us, before declining here to the status of a dead language.[29]

No one has ever established that the French language is under threat in Quebec, that it is declining or degenerating to the level of a dead language. But Quebec nationalism is characterized by an endemic mythology which holds that French is about to disappear, done in by English. This mythology then serves to justify a state of militant, tribalistic, opposition to English, a permanent collective paranoia. No repressive measure ever suffices to ensure the safety of French; more stringent laws against English must ever and always be called for.

There is a continuity in nationalist thinking, as becomes clear when one compares the 1994 PQ program with Lionel Groulx's already cited summary of his own ideological program in 1921: "Our doctrine can be contained in this brief formula: We wish to reconstitute the fullness of our French life. . . . We wish to prune this [ethnic] type of foreign growths in order to foster in it intensively the original culture, and to graft onto it the new virtues which it acquired since the Conquest"[30]

Groulx also had a political program. He dreamed of a French state to correspond to ethnic French Canadians. Until such a state became possible, he advocated the maximum political autonomy for Quebec. "Always, to the extent they could, our fathers never conceived of our existence under British domination otherwise than as a French group constituting an autonomous ethnic and political unity.[31] His nationalism, like that of the PQ, was clearly ethnic, rather than civic or territorial. Groulx, wanted to "shake off rapidly the Anglo-Saxon *maquillage* [cosmetics] to reconstitute the organic unity of our laws and of our language."[32]

Groulx's marching orders were clearly being followed, more than seventy years later, by the political party that was favoured in French Quebec. The obsessiveness about repressing any sign of English, past or present, indicates how shallow and unfounded is the claim to a liberal and non-ethnic nationalism. It is non-ethnic only to the extent that a strenuous suppression of all other ethnicities has been carried out, and will be carried out in future, leaving plausible that Quebec and French are one.

What about the other major political party, the Liberal Party of Quebec, the party most favoured by non-French Quebecers? It was this Liberal government that argued in 1987 before the Supreme Court of Canada that, to allow even some English on commercial signs, would threaten Quebec's French culture. An indication of that Liberal government's "liberal, non-ethnic and non-discriminatory" nationalism was shown in the instruction given to new immigrants to Quebec in the schools set up for that purpose, called COFIs,[33] in which they receive language training and an introduction to what they should know about their adopted country.

In 1991, Brian Mulroney's government concluded an agreement with the Quebec government whereby Canada would hand over to Quebec responsibility for helping immigrants to the province to adapt. Along with the responsibility, Ottawa turned over a pot of money: $332 million over four years, with a minimum of $90 million a year beginning in 1994. So how did the Liberal government carry out its responsibility? An article by linguist Monique Nemni in the March–April, 1994, issue of *Cité libre* was an eye-opener.

"Bienvenue au Québec! Le Canada, connais pas" was the title of the article. Welcome to Quebec. Canada? Never heard of it. The author, a professor at the Université du Québec à Montréal, recounts that she taught students who, as immigrants to Quebec, had attended a COFI. She asked them what they had been taught about Canada, and they burst out laughing. "There is no Canada, Madame," one student told her. Another said, "There is only Québec, Québec, Québec." A third added, "When we asked the professors to speak to us about Canada, they answered, 'You are in Québec, here, not in Canada. You must learn to get better acquainted with Québec.'"

Nemni, intrigued, studied the 150-page teachers' manual prepared by the Quebec government for instructors in the COFIs. In it, the word "Canada" appeared but once, to name the Canada Manpower Centre. The word "Quebec" or "Québécois" recurred seven times on page one and fourteen times on page two, after which Nemni stopped counting.

This manual was to initiate immigrants to their adopted country, but the country presented was Quebec; they were to become "citizens" of Quebec. "Quebec is a francophone society," it maintained. "The French language allows the Québécois people to express its identity." It also stated that "Quebec is a francophone, democratic and pluralist society." But pluralism had its limits: "The francophone collectivity is the axis for the integration of new arrivals," and this principle "is one of the guidelines within which pluralism is inscribed in our society." Nemni comments, "In other words, Quebec is pluralist only to the extent that one has integrated into the francophone collectivity. If someone has chosen the anglophone or Chinese collectivity, pluralism no longer applies."

Immigrants are taught in the COFIs that they are bound by a "moral contract" to integrate into the francophone community. They must not only abide by the laws of the society, but also be guided by the "values of the host society." General values of Western culture, such as liberty, equality, and respect for others and for human dignity, were presented as Quebec values—Quebec was the single, constant reference point.

Nemni drew the conclusion from her analysis of the manual that the nationalists had imposed their vision and enforced it with public funds. The COFIs were obliged to teach "that Quebec is not a province but already a country, that we are not Canadian citizens but Québécois. Those who think otherwise, or who would prefer to teach something else, are forced to keep silent."

I have also made a few inquiries and studied the manual. Though the money for the training comes entirely from the federal government, there is no acknowledgment of that fact anywhere. No COFI displays a Canadian flag. The COFIs offer language training only in French, never in English. Nowhere are immigrants newly arrived in a country called Canada informed that Canada has two official languages, English and French, although it is Canada, not Quebec, that will bestow on them their citizenship. Many of the immigrants will not stay in Quebec—nearly half will move on to other provinces of Canada—but they are prepared only for living in an ethnocentric French Quebec. No history of Canada, however brief, is offered. Instead, in a section dealing with the "stages of the evolution of Quebec society," a stereotypical dichotomy is presented of "two societies" from 1760 to 1867, with the British society being "Anglo-Saxon, Protestant . . . a minority dominant politically and economically, with the will to assimilate and reduce to minority status [French Canadian society] through immigration." French Canadians comprise "a majority, dominated politically and economically."

There is not a word about the multitudinous links of neighbourhood and blood, the day-to-day co-operation that has built one of the freest, most peaceful, and most prosperous countries in the world. Nor was there any recognition of the contribution of people who came from all parts of the world to create a country that has sought to rise above ethnocentrism and committed itself to multiculturalism. Instead, immigrants are taught a blinkered history, a one-dimensional vision. Quebec is not part of the Western world, with values shared in common with many other countries. Quebec is not an integral part of a federation. Quebec is the centre of the universe; Quebec and only Quebec exists in splendid autarchy.

Current Quebec nationalism is "territorial" to the extent that French Quebec has appropriated all of the territory of Quebec as being French only. Through an interrelated cluster of myths, denials, and selective vocabulary, French Quebec and the territory have been made to seem synomymous. To buttress the claim to special powers on the basis of a supposed unique population, nationalists have invented and popularized the double concept of "la langue québécoise" and "la culture québécoise."

Nemni commented on the flap caused in Quebec's intellectual circles when a French firm brought out what was supposedly a dictionary of the "Québécois" language.[34] She noted that the publication of a dictionary of the "Québécois language" had long been called for by such official bodies as the Conseil de la langue française, on the assumption that an authentic, original language called "Québécois" actually existed. But when the prestigious publishing company Robert brought out the *Dictionnaire québécois d'aujourd'hui,* in 1992, it was greeted with anger or embarrassed silence in Quebec. Robert had taken francophone intellectuals literally and described as the Québécois language a wide range of familiar and even vulgar expressions from daily speech, but Quebec's intellectuals were insulted when this was presented as the very language of Quebec.

As Nemni explained, to speak of "Québécois" as a language is to follow the dictates of ideology rather than lexicography. There are words and expressions that are specific to Quebec (just as there are words and expressions specific to Marseilles). But, when one describes the standard language spoken by educated Quebecers, it is French, not an indigenous Quebec language.[35] To use "Québécois" as the subject of a dictionary is to suggest that it is like Italian or Japanese. And it suggests, erroneously, that the language spoken in Quebec is distinct from that spoken by Franco-Ontarians and Franco-Manitobans.[36] Not only does calling the language "Québécois" cut Quebec off from the rest of Canada, it also suggests that only one language is commonly spoken in Quebec. "Imagine if francophone Belgians or Swiss called their language Belgian or Swiss! Once again, slyly and symbolically, Quebec is liberated from *les Anglais*. . . . And that is how, by the very title of its dictionary, Robert symbolically liberated Quebec from its triple bonds: the domination of the French language, the tutelage of Canada, and English as a legitimate language of Quebec. At last, Quebec is truly *libre*."[37]

The same kind of appropriation was carried out with culture. Quebec nationalists speak constantly of "la culture québécoise," as though an original culture was developed in Quebec and was specific to Quebec. Premier Bourassa even tried to get this myth vested in the constitution, when Quebec's "distinct society" was defined by the Charlottetown accord as having "a unique culture."

In fact, as sociologists or anthropologists define culture, there is no more a Quebec culture than there is a Quebec language. "Culture" refers to the specifically human ways of thinking, speaking, and doing that are transmitted from one generation to the next in a society. In Quebec, almost none of the ways of thinking, speaking, and doing were developed locally—neither the language, the religious beliefs or rituals, the science or technology, the ways of obtaining food, clothing, and shelter, the political institutions, nor the genres of artistic expression—all these were invented elsewhere and are shared widely in Western civilization. There is, indeed, culture in Quebec, but to designate it as "la culture québécoise" is about as accurate as to speak of Quebec algebra, Quebec Catholicism, Quebec engineering, and so on. All these are found in Quebec, but their specifically Quebec character is marginal.

Quebec nationalists have used the vocabulary of "la culture québécoise" in their ideological discourse to suggest that Quebec is unique and thus cannot be part of the Canadian federation, and that all who live in Quebec must adopt a single "Quebec" culture. "The culture constitutes the foundation and the essence of a society," states the program of the Parti Québécois. "And so, québécois culture must enjoy the best possible support. Only in this way, can the personality of Quebec express itself with power and originality."[38]

Calling culture in Quebec "la culture québécoise" begs the ethnic question. It suggests that there is one indigenous Quebec standard of culture to which all in Quebec must conform. It becomes possible, then, to demand that immigrants adapt to "Quebec" values. This was implied by Bernard Landry, vice-president of the Parti Québécois, when he told members of the Conseil des Citoyens d'Origine Haïtienne that his party rejected the idea of multiculturalism. He proposed, instead, what he called "la culture québécoise." He then explained himself to reporters:

Quebec is already multi-ethnic, with people from various backgrounds from all over the planet, and that sort of melting pot is a guarantee of tolerance and a guarantee of liberty and democracy. But as far as culture is concerned, the public, common culture of Quebec is Québécois culture. We have the duty, using influxes from everywhere, to build that common culture.[39]

Some sense of the meaning of the "common culture of Quebec" was conveyed by Louise Laurin, president of the Mouvement National des Québécoises et Québécois,[40] when she appeared before the Standing Committee on Citizenship and Immigration, which was studying the elements of a new Citizenship Act, in June of 1994. Laurin rejected Canada's two official languages and the policy of multiculturalism: "My compatriots do not recognize themselves either in official bilingualism or in multiculturalism, considered fundamental values of Canadian society," Laurin told the parliamentarians.[41] Instead, Laurin proposed, in tortuous language, her idea of a "common culture." It involved the affirmation that "Quebecers have their very own identity." To express what that identity was, she quoted a letter written in 1971 by Premier Bourassa to Prime Minister Trudeau: "While the federal government takes on general obligations toward all the cultures found in Canada, Quebec owes it to itself to take on the role of primary responsibility on its territory for the permanence of the French language and culture."

She repudiated what she called "a mosaic where all live one beside the other, rather than one with the other." Instead, she proposed what she called a "common public culture" to which all Quebecers must integrate. And this "common culture," as she made clear, was simply the culture of the dominant francophones. She called it the "heritage made up of a history, a common language, a set of values, laws, and institutions. This heritage unites all Quebecers, whatever their culture of origin. In this sense, the learning of French remains, for Quebec, a condition of obtaining citizenship."

Quebec nationalists view multiculturalism as a plot by the federal government to deny or weaken the French "identity" of Quebec. The two are seen as antithetical, because Quebec is defined by them as purely French. So it was that Claude Corbo, rector of the Université du Québec à Montréal, denounced multiculturalism as a policy developed by the Trudeau government in its fight against Quebec nationalism. "Canadian multiculturalism is apt to worsen the 'minorization' or trivializing of the Quebec identity, which becomes just one particularism among others," he told a roundtable on multiculturalism in Montreal.[42]

A Bloc Québécois MP, Madeleine Dalphond-Guiral, echoed in the Commons Corbo's suggestion that the policy of multiculturalism was intended to attack Quebec's "identity." "This policy, which dates back to the Trudeau era, has failed in two ways. Indeed, on the one hand, it has not helped integrate minority groups, while on the other hand it has failed, in spite of the unspeakable objectives of its architects, to rob the Quebec identity of its originality."[43] "Quebec identity," in the minds of nationalists, means exclusively a francophone identity. Anything which suggests that Quebec has a pluralist identity—such as two official languages and multiculturalism—is indignantly repudiated. It's the same old story: *le Québec aux Québécois!*

After appropriating "Quebec" for the French language and culture, the third stage of appropriation is to consider all of Quebec to be, simply, French Quebec. English is officially nonexistent as a general, public language. It is in this sense, and in this sense alone, that Quebec nationalism can be considered "territorial" and not ethnic: once the existence of ethnicities other than that of the French majority is blanked out, hidden from sight by law, purged of legitimacy by ideological language, French Quebec and the territory of Quebec are made one and the same. All non-francophones are required to live and work in French, and remain under the stringent restrictions of the law, with their numbers controlled. That is the "non-ethnic, non-discriminatory" nationalism that exists today in Quebec, defended by the intelligentsia and enforced by both major political parties.

This is also the exclusivist notion of "Quebec" that was projected in the Bloc Québécois's first manifesto, published on 25 July 1991. In outlining the Bloc's "mission" in Ottawa, it stated, "Our national allegiance is to Quebec. The territory to which we belong is Quebec, heartland of a people that is French by culture and language, and whose sovereignty we intend to promote."

It is in this sense that nationalists can speak of "two nations," and designate Quebec and English Canada. Quebec has become a French nation by dint of eliminating from public significance its English dimension. The repudiation of Anglos is expressed by their virtual exclusion from Quebec's public service and from Crown corporations. People whose first language is English account for 0.7 per cent of Quebec civil servants. In contrast, Franco-Ontarians make up 7.4 per cent of Ontario's civil servants. In other words, Franco-Ontarians, though far less numerous than Anglo-Quebecers, are ten times as present in their provincial civil service as are Anglo-Quebecers in theirs.

All the evidence points to the same conclusion: the objective of current Quebec nationalism is, as it was in the 1960s, the creation of an ethnic state of Quebec.

Far from being a "non-ethnic" nationalism, current Quebec nationalism militantly uses state power and ideological language to expunge from consideration any ethnic group except one, striving forcefully to identify Quebec, all of Quebec, with its French majority. The best indication that ethnic nationalism still thrives in Quebec is the very strength of separatism. Canada is not a country that oppresses Quebecers; in fact, Canada was declared by the United Nations in 1994 to be the best country in the world in terms of "human development."[44] Why would many Quebecers be willing to forfeit the rest of Canada as a country for themselves and their children? What would they gain? Why would they be willing to risk all the dangers of secession? There can only be one explanation: the desire to separate from the English-speaking majority of Canada in order to establish a fully independent French ethnic state.

Notes

1. "L'attrait du séparatisme. Entretien avec Lucien Bouchard conduit par George Tombs," *Politique internationale,* 63 (Spring 1994): 334–45.
2. *Globe and Mail,* 30 Apr. 1994.
3. Michael Ignatieff, *Blood and Belonging: Journeys Into the New Nationalism* (New York: Farrar, Straus & Giroux, 1994), p. 123.
4. Francis Fukuyama, "The War of All Against All," in *The New York Times Book Review,* 10 Apr. 1994, p. 7.
5. Parti Québécois, *Des idées pour mon pays. Programme du Parti Québécois Édition 1994* (Montreal: Parti Québécois, 1994).
6. Ibid., p. 1.
7. Ibid., p. 159.
8. Ibid., p. 159.
9. "A government of the Parti Québécois commits itself . . . to impose unilingual French signage, both inside and outside every establishment, private or public, so as to endow Quebec with an essentially French face." Ibid., p. 156.
10. Ibid., p. 155.
11. Ibid., pp. 155 and 162.
12. CEGEP is an acronym for Collèges d'enseignement général et professional.
13. Parti Québécois, *Des idées,* p. 157.
14. Ibid.
15. George Tombs, "Péquiste policy would knock the wind out of English universities," *The Gazette,* 17 May 1994, p. B-3.
16. Ibid.
17. Parti Québécois, *Des idées,* p. 162.
18. Ibid., p. 153.
19. Ibid.
20. Ibid., p. 154.
21. Ibid., p. 162.
22. Ibid., p. 157.
23. Ibid.
24. Ibid., p. 132.
25. Ibid., p. 156.
26. Ibid., p. 158.

27.Ibid. Emphasis added.
28.Ibid., p. 156.
29.Ibid., p. 155.
30.Lionel Groulx, "Notre doctrine," *L'Action française*, 5 (Jan. 1921): 25–26.
31.Ibid., p. 30.
32.Ibid., pp. 29–30.
33.COFI is an acronym for Centre d'Orientation et de Formation des Immigrants.
34.Monique Nemni, "Le Dictionnaire québécois d'aujourd'hui ou la description de deux chimères," *Cité libre*, 21, no. 2 (Apr.-May 1993): 30–34.
35.Ibid., p. 34.
36.Ibid., p. 32.
37.Ibid.
38.Parti Québécois, *Des idées*, p. 144.
39.Alexander Norris, "PQ opposes multiculturalism Haitians told. Landry says Quebec needs a single common culture," *The Gazette*, 1 May 1994.
40.An umbrella group for fifteen nationalist societies, including several Saint-Jean-Baptiste societies, with a combined membership of nearly 200,000.
41.Standing Committee on Citizenship and Immigration, Issue no. 17, 2 June 1994.
42."Le multiculturalisme banaliserait l'identité québécoise," *Le Devoir*, 13 June 1994, p. 3.
43.*Hansard*, 13 June 1994, p. 5206.
44.Julian Beltrame, "Canada is the best place to live: UN," *The Gazette*, 28 May 1994, p. A8.

CHAPTER TWENTY-THREE

A Right to Secede from Canada?

From the start of the Quiet Revolution, Quebec's provincial leaders assumed that they had the right to demand, and could expect to get, whatever powers they chose for the Quebec government. They had this right because they spoke in the name of a nation rather than as premiers of a province. If the changes they demanded were not forthcoming, Canada would no longer be a legitimate state. And they assumed that they had the right to secede from Canada as a last resort.

With remarkable presumption, they took it for granted that secession was the right of French-speaking Quebecers, and that the premier of Quebec could threaten it at will. Jean Lesage made the threat in oblique terms: if he did not get what he wanted, the rest of Canada would be responsible for Quebec's secession. Daniel Johnson made it explicit in the very title of his book: *Égalité ou indépendance*. No room for ambiguity there. When Pierre Trudeau was prime minister, Robert Bourassa was cautious about making threats but, from the time the Meech Lake accord seemed to be in trouble, Bourassa dropped transparent hints that if it did not pass, he would not guarantee that Quebec would remain in Canada. And, when Meech actually failed, he often repeated that Quebecers were henceforth free to choose whatever constitutional status they wanted, inside Canada or out. That was also the presumption of the Allaire report, the Bélanger-Campeau report, the law setting up a 1992 referendum on sovereignty, and just about all Quebec politicians who spoke on the subject.

In its 1994 official program, the Parti Québécois presents secession as simply a "normal" course, one followed routinely by all the peoples of the earth. "Because we want to see the emergence of a Quebec society that is more free, more just, and more prosperous, we have chosen as our chief goal to see the appearance of Quebec as a country—that is, that Quebecers should become fully responsible for their decisions before themselves and before the community of nations. This is a normal progression, one taken by peoples everywhere on the earth. The sovereignty of Quebec is part of the modern evolution of peoples."[1]

To make secession seem more normal and routine, the Parti Québécois and the Bloc Québécois have carried out a propaganda campaign to convince everyone that choosing to secede is as simple as voting for one political party rather than another. Jacques Parizeau has often used the simile that achieving sovereignty is like a hockey game: in the first period, the Bloc Québécois elected fifty-four members from Quebec in the federal elections of 1993. The second period, in 1994, brings the election of a PQ government. The third period is the referendum, which must lead quickly to independence. Just like that: one, two three. Parizeau spoke confidently to his troops of Quebec's independence following the referendum within "weeks," or, at the most, "very, very much less than a year."[2]

Lucien Bouchard, for his part, asked a trick question of Jean Chrétien in the House of Commons: "My question is whether the prime minister of Canada, of this country, respects Quebec democracy. Will the prime minister tell us clearly, and I will repeat my question, as head of state and prime minister, whether or not he recognizes Quebec's right to self-determination?"[3] The implication was that, if Chrétien "respects Quebec democracy" and "recognizes Quebec's right to self-determination," he would acknowledge Quebec's right to secede from Canada by referendum.

Chrétien fell partway into the trap: in parts of his answer, he seemed to accept Bouchard's premise. His only problem seemed to be with whether the referendum question was an honest one: "I want a referendum with a very clear question, not playing on words to try to confuse people, not talking about sovereignty, not talking about sovereignty-association, but talking about the real thing: the separation of Quebec from Canada."

Under repeated questioning, Chrétien spoke on both sides of the issue of Quebec's right to separate. "In 1980, we allowed a referendum on the question of the separation of Quebec." That seemed to imply a yes. But he also recalled Parizeau's saying the previous week that Quebec's borders were inviolable, according to the legal opinion submitted to Quebec's National Assembly by a panel of international law experts. The same experts, Chrétien pointed out, had also said that Canada's borders were inviolable. "In international law, Quebec can't separate from Canada without Canada's consent." That seemed to repudiate Quebec's right to secede. But, again, Chrétien doubled back. "We allow a vote on the question, and it's what we did in 1980. I was the one who worked for the federal government in a democratic vote, and Quebecers decided to remain in Canada."

Bouchard insisted on a clear answer to his question. He accused Chrétien of waffling on whether Quebec has a right to self-determination: "How can he reconcile this ambiguous attitude with his own behaviour and that of his leader, Pierre Elliott Trudeau, in 1980, when they were both very much involved in the Quebec referendum campaign and they agreed to abide by the outcome of this democratic process?" Bouchard was obviously attempting to establish the legitimacy of a referendum as a licence for Quebec to separate. Parizeau took the same approach the next day. He joined the attack on Chrétien's "ambiguity" about accepting the results of a Quebec referendum on secession. "The quite noted participation of the federal authorities, in money and in person, notably Messrs Chrétien and Trudeau, in the referendum of 1980, serves as a precedent and establishes the legitimacy of the process," he said in the National Assembly.

The following day, Premier Johnson agreed with the two separatist leaders. "It seems to me extremely clear that in Quebec . . . we already exercised in 1980 the right to self-determination. So I don't see why, all at once, it would have disappeared." And even the deputy prime minister, Sheila Copps, stated in the Commons that freedom of speech and democracy in Canada included "the right to separate."[4]

So, for more than three decades, Quebecers have been told that they have a right to secede, and that to exercise this right, all they have to do is hold a referendum and vote 50 per cent plus one in favour. Nothing could be simpler or more normal. Then, of course, the rest of Canada would fall into line and Quebec would start its new life as an independent country.

Separatist leaders have asserted that secession will be peaceful because it is in Canada's best interests to maintain economic ties with Quebec. This is Bouchard's constant, reassuring message. When he spoke before the Calgary Chamber of Commerce on 3 May 1994, he exuded a secession-is-normal urbanity. "A year from now, we will most probably be absorbed in the nuts and bolts of the future relations between Canada and Quebec, the accent being on the *how* rather than the *why* of sovereignty."

Even *La Presse* columnist Lysiane Gagnon predicted a peaceful separation, if it came to that, because Canada is too civilized to act otherwise: "If a majority of Québécois voted OUI, who can seriously believe that Canada would send the army to Quebec? Or that it would refuse to enter into negotiation with its legitimate government? Or that it would submit the question to a Canada-wide vote, which obviously would mean drowning the Quebec vote in the majority vote?"[5]

Gagnon assumed that Canada would choose one of two alternatives: send in the army, or negotiate secession. However, the course of events would hardly be as tidy as this short list would suggest. A thousand and one other courses, all unanticipated, would be far more likely. Since the 1992 referendum on the Charlottetown accord, elite accommodation has ceased to be the way of dealing with ultimate questions of national interest. The people must now have their say. Even if a prime minister of Canada wanted to negotiate secession with Quebec, he would be unable to do so: he would lack the constitutional power, and the people of Canada would not let him act against their deep convictions, just as they did not let Brian Mulroney have his way with the constitution to accommodate nationalist Quebec. The entire legal system would be thrown into chaos. Any attempt by the Quebec government to supplant the national government and violate its jurisdiction would necessarily be met by Ottawa exercising its great powers of reserve or disallowance, not invoked for decades, but still intact in the constitution. Quebec would submit or its actions would be challenged in the courts. Individual Canadians and provincial premiers would intervene. What constitution, what laws, would the courts of Quebec uphold? Would it abide by the rule of law, or venture into the no-man's-land where the law of the jungle rules?

There are already signs that a confrontation with a Quebec attempting to secede would be nasty. British Columbia premier Michael Harcourt was blunt. "Frankly, the position I'm taking is that Quebec and B.C. are natural allies in a renewed Canada and would be the best of friends," he told the *Globe and Mail.* "But if they decided to separate, we wouldn't be the best of friends; we'd be the worst of enemies. The anger that would be felt by British Columbians to the people of Quebec wanting to break up and destroy this great country would be immense."[6]

Harcourt predicted a dispute over Quebec's northern territories, which the province received after Confederation. There would also be hard bargaining over Quebec's share of the debt and the assets it would take with it. He called Parizeau a "pied piper" for suggesting that the breakup could be amicable. "Oh, it would be terrible consequences for everybody. They think it's going to be logical and civilized. Forget it, it won't be. There will be great bitterness and a nasty split. And they'll suffer, not just economically but they'll suffer every which way, the people of Quebec. And it'd do harm to Canada."

Indian-affairs minister Ron Irwin pinpointed one likely area of confrontation if secession were attempted: the fate of aboriginals living in Quebec. "They are part of Canada. If they want to stay in Canada, that's their choice," Irwin said in Quebec City, where he attended a federal-provincial meeting on native self-government. "I don't think Indians are chattels for the separatists to decide on. They've been here for 10,000 years."[7] Anyone remembering the 1990 confrontation at Oka over a pine grove by a golf course, which cost Quebec hundreds of millions of dollars in policing expenditures, will know that a confrontation between a secessionist Quebec and natives in the James Bay area could quickly destroy the multi-billion dollar hydro-electric dams, generating plants, and transmission pylons. Quebec's power supply would be indefensible. The cost, even without the intervention of the Canadian army, could be incalculable.

Other, usually moderate voices have also given warning. *The Toronto Star,* in an editorial on 7 May 1994, laid down conditions that Quebec must fulfill for secession. "First, the issue must be decided by an explicit referendum question on independence. Weasel words, such as sovereignty, will be meaningless." (Parizeau indicated that same day that the referendum question would use the word sovereignty.) Second, "Canadians must agree to any final partition agreement or Quebec will be treated as a rogue republic in the diplomatic and financial world." Third, "if Quebecers can leave Canada, then the Cree and Inuit of Ungava can leave Quebec, if they so choose." Bouchard said in Vancouver that very week, "There is no way that any Quebecer would accept that a square inch of that territory be extracted from Quebec." He suggested that even mentioning a partition of Quebec "would be the beginning of very nasty things."

The *Globe and Mail* also published a carefully worded editorial on the subject, on 29 March 1994. It also rejected unilateral secession. "Every citizen of this country is a citizen of the whole of this country, and should not be expected to stand and watch while a part of it is wrenched away." The *Globe*, like the *Star*, expected that an independent Quebec would have different borders. "What of the self-determination of the Cree, of the anglophones, of federalists of every stripe? What of the self-determination of the Canadian nation?"

Former Saskatchewan premier Allan Blakeney, in a speech at York University on 14 June 1991, also foresaw different Quebec borders. "If there is a basis for separation, it cannot be that the Canadian province of Quebec with its existing boundaries has any status to separate. There is no basis for such a position in either domestic or international law." Clearly, a Quebec claiming independence would begin with a serious border dispute.

Other voices raised in warning were those of *Toronto Star* columnist Richard Gwyn,[8] *Financial Post* columnist Diane Francis,[9] and Peter Newman, who wrote, "Instead of playing by Robert's Rules of Order let's tackle Bouchard on his own terms. Let's leave no doubt in his mind that our will to survive as one nation is at least as strong as his intention to turn himself into the first president of a socialist republic straddling the St. Lawrence Seaway."[10]

There is a gulf between the benign secession scenarios of Quebec separatists and the glowering predictions of English-speaking moderate opinion. In that gulf lies the likelihood of tragic miscalculations and, yes, violence. These are not fanciful terrors. The attempt to break up a country would unleash powerful forces of anger and anarchy. That is why peaceful secession within a mature democratic state is unheard of.[11]

The point of these warnings is not that Quebecers must be cowed into submission, but that they must realize that attempted secession would likely have terrible consequences, precisely because it is illegitimate, unprotected by Canadian or international laws. It violates the consensus of civilized countries. Once secession is attempted, no one can predict or control the course of events developing outside the law.

Canadians, including Quebecers, are moderate legitimists. They respect precedents and they respect the law as a guide to solving problems. That is why the two separatist parties try so hard to create a presumption that a referendum is a decisive means of creating a right to secede. But, contrary to the nationalist propaganda, in international law, Quebec does not have the right to secede, referendum or no referendum.

This was made crystal clear in the legal opinion given to the Quebec government in May of 1992 by the panel of five international experts referred to by Parizeau and Chrétien.[12] The National Assembly was studying the implications of Quebec's "acceding to sovereignty," as proposed by the Bélanger-Campeau commission, and the committee involved put to the experts two questions dealing with the borders of a newly sovereign Quebec. The committee did not ask whether Quebec had a right in international law to secede: it seemed to take that for granted, as had Bourassa and the Bélanger-Campeau commission.

The experts chosen for a joint opinion were tops in the field of international law. Christian Tomuschat, of Germany, was chairman of the United Nations Commission on International Law. The Frenchman, Alain Pellet, was a member of the United Nations Commission on International Law and a professor of international law at the Université de Paris and the Institut d'Études politiques. The American, Thomas Franck, was the editor-in-chief of the *American Journal of International Law*. Rosalyn Higgins was professor of international law at the London School of Economics and a member of the United Nations Committee on Human Rights. Malcolm N. Shaw, law professor at the University of Leicester, represented the United Kingdom at the 1990 United Nations Conference on Human Rights at Kiev.

The panel addressed a question that it had not been asked, stating, unanimously, categorically, and repeatedly, that in international law, Quebec did not have a right to secede from Canada. What Quebec—or French Canadians—did have, they said, was the right to self-determination; the right to self-determination, however, was not a right to secede: "The right of peoples to self-determination is a very general principle, which has as a consequence always and everywhere the right for the community involved to participate in its future, but this does not suffice to provide a basis for the right of a people to accede to independence, to the detriment of the state to which it is attached, except in colonial situations."[13]

The right to self-determination, they also said, "implies the right for minorities to have their identity recognized, and since the right to self-determination is a principle protecting human rights, the right for each of the members of a minority to have its sense of belonging to it recognized. At the same time, the Commission [of Arbitration on Yugoslavia] excludes the right of minority peoples to independence."[14]

Over and over, the panel made the same point: only colonies can claim a right to become independent under international law, and Quebec is not a colony. So they brushed aside with a summary rejection the pretensions of Quebec separatists and law professors Daniel Turp (chairman of the Bloc Québécois's policy commission) and Jacques Brossard, who claim, against the overwhelming consensus of legal opinion, that Quebec does have a right to secede.[15] Brossard stated that the Québécois constituted a people and that this people enjoyed the right to self-determination, because it fulfilled all the conditions which, according to him, were required: a "political dimension"—a territory and its own structures; a viable future as a state; acceptance of the principles of the Charter of the United

Nations and of international law; a will to be independent. The panel commented, "In any case, one cannot reasonably maintain that it is a colonial people, nor that it is deprived of the right to its own existence within the Canadian whole, nor to participate in democratic life. The very existence, which can scarcely be questioned, of the first criterion set out by Professor Brossard is enough to attest to the opposite."

After turning Brossard's own argument against him, the panel explicitly rejected Quebec's right to secede. "And therefore," it concluded, "the Quebec people effectively exercises its right to self-determination within the framework of the Canadian whole and is not legally well founded to invoke it to justify a future accession to independence."[16] Furthermore, "The right to secession does not exist in international law." Even the right of a colony to independence is not strictly speaking a right to secede, since the colony was never a true part of the state from which it wishes to become independent.[17]

The panel pointed out that chaos would result if the principle of secession on demand were accepted internationally, if every state could be dismembered at any time by the vote of a passing majority in one of its parts. "The generalization of the right to self-determination, understood as the right for a people to establish a state, would have dramatically destabilizing effects, which obviously cannot be countenanced by an international society made up in the first place of sovereign States."[18] One of its members was quoted to confirm its opinion: "It can be concluded that the view that all peoples, in the sociological sense, are entitled under international law in the last resort to create independent states is clearly unacceptable as a matter of practice."[19]

Furthermore, Chrétien, Bouchard, Parizeau and Johnson all misinterpreted the meaning of the 1980 referendum. It did not establish a precedent for Quebecers choosing whether or not to secede; the question put to Quebecers was not about secession, but about a "mandate to negotiate." Secession was to be the object of a subsequent referendum, which was never held.

The precedent established in 1980 was not that Quebec can secede just by voting to. If anything, the 1980 referendum established that the federal government did not recognize a referendum result as legitimating secession—nor did the provincial premiers. There lies a gulf between the reassuring propaganda of leaders in Quebec that secession by referendum is normal and simple and the contrary views of leaders in the rest of Canada. In that gulf of misunderstanding lies the possibility of tragic miscalculations.

Notes

1. Parti Québécois, *Des idées pour mon pays* (Montreal: Parti Québécois, 1994), p. 1.
2. Reported by Robert Mackenzie in *The Toronto Star*, 8 May 1994.
3. *Hansard*, 24 May 1994.
4. "Separatism called part of hard-won freedom," *Toronto Star*, 7 June 1994.
5. *La Presse*, 28 May 1994, p. B-3.

6.Miro Cernetig, "Harcourt hardens on Quebec," *Globe and Mail*, 17 May 1994.

7.Ottawa Sun, 18 May 1994.

8. "Canadians in no mood to appease Quebec," *Toronto Star*, 11 May 1994.

9."The severe storm that lies ahead," *Maclean's*, 16 May 1994, p. 9.

10.Peter Newman, "The Faustian deal of Lucien Bouchard," *Maclean's*, May 1994.

11.The PQ program refers to the secession of Norway from the Crown of Denmark in 1905. However, Norway and Denmark were two countries united by a single crown; even before the separation, they had different monetary systems and imposed custom duties against each other's imports.

12.Thomas M. Franck, Rosalyn Higgins, Alain Pellet, Malcolm N. Shaw, and Christian Tomuschat, "L'intégrité territoriale du Quebec dans l'hypothèse de l'accession à la souveraineté," in Assemblée nationale, Commission d'étude des Questions afférentes à l'accession du Quebec à la souveraineté, *Exposés et études*, vol. 1, *Les attributs d'un Quebec souverain* (1992), pp. 377–452.

13.Ibid., p. 383.

14.Ibid., p. 424.

15.Ibid., p. 425.

16.Ibid.

17.Ibid., pp. 428–29.

18.Ibid., p. 422.

19.Ibid.

CHAPTER 24

Conclusion:
The End of an Illusion

For more than three decades, Quebec's political life has been driven by an astounding syndrome of illusions and mythology. The country is battered and more than a little torn by the consequent prolonged polemics and dialectics, the confrontations, the ultimatums, the identity crises, the rumours of referendums, the threats of secession. Canada's history has been turned into a soap opera, with melodramas and intrigues leading to intrigues and melodramas. Or so it has seemed so far. Enough. It is time to break the cycle.

What does Quebec want? The answer is simple: Quebec does not know what it wants. Quebec, caught in contradictions, cannot resolve its ambivalences. Torn between the opposed appeals of liberalism and nationalism, of modernity and atavistic ghosts that still haunt the living, the people of Quebec are not free and will never be free until they have emancipated themselves from the myths that hold them in thrall.

Despite all the speeches, conferences, conventions, commissions, forums, accords, and referendums that have searched for a political settlement, the root cause of Quebec's discontent in Confederation has never been political. It was and is ideological—or, more accurately, mythological. Therefore, no mere political solution, however ingenious, generous, or dramatic, could ever assuage Quebec's discontents and restore stability to the federation. If a political solution could have been found, it would have been some time during these decades of ferment, with leaders of such outstanding ability as Jean Lesage, Pierre Trudeau, and René Lévesque making it their highest priority. Instead, enormous political capital and vast sums of money were invested in the national-unity industry. All the proposals for decentralization, special status, associate states, sovereignty-association, recognition of a distinct society, sovereignty without association, separation, and independence were nothing but so many illusions when offered as a cure for the *mal québécois* and the alienation that undermines Canada. No resolution is yet in sight, nor will Quebec be freed from its ambivalences until the underlying mythology is exorcised. For more than thirty years, a myriad of

illusions, making up this mythology, have inspired Quebec nationalism, driven Quebec's provincial politics, and set the political agenda for all of Canada. Here is a partial list:
- The Quiet Revolution was about "national liberation."
- The enemy to be overcome was *les Anglais*.
- French Canada was surrounded by a menacing sea of Anglo-Saxons.
- A French ethnic state of Quebec would best serve the interests of French-speaking Quebecers.
- There is a fundamentally different vision between separatists like René Levesque, Jacques Parizeau, and Lucien Bouchard and "federalists" like Robert Bourassa.
- Stability can be restored to Canada by granting the government of Quebec more powers and a distinct status.
- A referendum on Quebec independence can settle the instability in Canada, either by leading to secession or by putting an end to separatist pressures.
- An independent, or at least a national, state of Quebec is the normal and inevitable terminus of French-Canadian history.
- French-speaking Quebecers will be diminished human beings, their culture kept ethnocentric and pathological, until and unless Quebec becomes independent.
- The right to self-determination of a francophone "nation" of Quebec includes the right to secede from Canada or to choose freely any other constitutional arrangement and impose it unilaterally on the rest of Canada.
- A referendum with a 50 per cent plus one vote in favour of secession would legitimate Quebec's secession from Canada.
- A secession could be carried out quickly, with little opposition and no violence and a minimum cost or disruption involved in the transition.
- The secession of Quebec will ever take place.

Confused by endless repetition of the mythology by the intelligentsia, and yet attached to Canada, which 90 per cent agree is "the best country in the world,"[1] Quebecers are caught in a permanent aboulia, a chronic arrested state of repeating *non*. They cannot say *oui* to federalism, or to secession; they cannot say *oui* to a revised constitution, or to a suspension of constitutional negotiations. They cannot say *oui* to their own long-established English-speaking community, or to the immigrants, whom they need to make up for their own infertility: instead, they co-exist with them in aggressive anxiety, inventing new laws to restrict their freedom. They cannot say *oui* to the more than 300,000 English-speaking Canadians in other provinces who are studying in French and preparing a major future contribution to French culture in Canada. Nor can they say *oui* to French Canadians in other parts of Canada, together with whom, using their immense political influence, they could build a stronger, richer, more diverse French space in Canada, a *Francophonie* with a national network, still to be invented, of French institutions for education, health and welfare, culture, and even the economy. They cannot say *oui* to themselves, as they really are, with their complex history, which began in New France and continued through British control to emerge, eventually, as part of a free federation with two official languages that are the pride of this country and its unrivalled entrée into a multitude of other countries throughout the world. Instead, Quebec leaders compulsively deny the English dimension of Quebec's history and identity, and invent a complex Orwellian vocabulary to hide the reality: words like a "common public culture," the "French face" of Quebec, a "territorial nationalism," behind which lies the coercive power of the state to enforce the façade of an all-French society.

For three decades, politics has played out the fevered memories of a tribalist past, incongruously taking a place at the Cabinet table along with the preoccupations of a modern liberal society. Even while Quebec opened itself to religious pluralism, to sexual *laissez-faire*, to urban tolerance of differences, it passed laws to censure the sight and sound of English, and it told terrifying bedtime stories about the English bogeyman that would carry away francophone children and steal their identity and culture.

For three decades, Quebec's provincial leaders have shared a common political vision: Quebec as a French ethnic state. And, because of that vision, those leaders shared a notable characteristic, whether they ended up as federalists or as separatists: all were unstable and volatile in their demands for more powers to be wrested from Ottawa and transferred to the Quebec government. None could ever provide a definitive list of what these powers were, short of total independence. And whatever each leader demanded initially, it was soon not enough; demands were superseded by new demands. For those whose political vision began with the premise of the ethnic state, there was no limit short of full sovereignty, because any powers forfeited to another government weakened Quebec's claim to be and act as the full expression and the defender of the francophone nation.

That vision, which requires the state and the dominant ethnic group to reflect the same identity, is intrinsically incompatible with surrendering essential powers to a federal government in which francophones will forever be a minority. So, as long as the ethnic state continues to be accepted as the ideal by Quebec's political leaders, stability cannot return to Quebec or to Canada. The prospect of more powers will lure leaders to attempt new pressure campaigns, engage in blackmail, and threaten secession if they don't get what they want. And the ordinary people of Quebec will be pulled along by some leaders who demand secession and by other leaders who, while not advocating secession, regularly denounce the federation and libel it constantly as a technique for getting more powers. Separatists and supposed federalists play exactly the same game, with the latter using the threat of the former to extort more powers from the federation.

THE END OF AN ILLUSION

The rest of Canada would be foolish to co-operate with this game in the hope of buying peace and stability, although this is what some federal and provincial leaders have done, with the backing of right-thinking elites. It has never worked, and it has brought Canada to the brink of a major crisis between 1987 and 1992. Only Elijah Harper, the common sense of the people, and a good deal of luck deflected the country from the disastrous course on which it had embarked. Our leaders had failed to learn the lesson taught by Pierre Trudeau that a constitutional settlement with Quebec will be impossible as long as Quebec's political class is governed by the vision of the ethnic state. To attempt to come to terms with that vision can lead only to destroying Canada as a means of saving it—an altogether absurd course. No settlement is better than a self-destructive settlement. Constitutional negotiations cannot be reopened with the slightest hope of success until Quebec's leaders abandon their current ideological stance and are guided, instead, by pragmatic objectives inspired by the principles of liberal democracy rather than nationalistic utopias.

In Canada, we have seen the high cost to the entire country of Quebec's pursuit of the ethnic state and its assumption of a right to secede in that pursuit. It provoked two referendums and countless constitutional debates, as expensive as they were futile. The bill, still mounting up, could include the costs of past terrorism, as well as the risk of future terrorism if a referendum on secession resulted in a deadlock. The assumption of a right to secede, if it continues to guide Quebec politics, will bedevil all of our futures: Jacques Parizeau has stated that if the PQ loses a referendum, it will hold another, and another, until it wins. This raises the prospect of a permanent cycle of self-laceration in the pursuit of illusion, diverting national energies and investment from such real issues as job creation, economic development, child care, eradication of poverty, the construction of a richer French space across Canada, and the promotion of artistic creation. The lost opportunities of our endless and futile national-unity debate simply place an additional mortgage on the future of our children, who have already been impoverished by our follies.

The secessionist dream of a Jacques Parizeau or a Lucien Bouchard, like the dream of a French ethnic state of Quebec within a Canadian common market advocated by a Robert Bourassa, are reactionary diversions within Quebec's political life. They accomplish nothing concrete, yet they polarize the energies of the country around a utopian enterprise, never to be achieved, but always to be pursued. Bourassa failed three times to impose his ideas on Canada. The Parti Québécois failed once and will fail again. But their obsessions are neither innocent nor innocuous.

The nightmare scenario could come true: it is one in which the PQ holds a referendum on secession and wins a majority of votes. With no provision for secession in the constitution of Canada, no negotiations on secession could take place without an enabling amendment, and that would be impossible to attain.

What seven—let alone ten—provincial governments would consent to an amendment that would allow Quebec to leave the federation? The stage would be set for regional and ethnic clashes, confrontations in which no law or precedent could maintain a civilized procedure. Canada would be at risk of replacing the rule of law with the law of the jungle.

All these risks, all these costs, have been and will remain essentially unproductive. The people of Quebec do not really want to separate from Canada, and it is unlikely that they ever will, despite all the whipping up of nationalist passions by the leaders. The people have too much common sense to launch into an adventure for no better motive than the creation of a New Jerusalem on the St. Lawrence and a historic destiny imagined by the intellectuals.

A Léger & Léger poll published in June 1994 showed that 52 per cent of Quebecers would vote against the sovereignty of Quebec in a referendum, and that even among those who would vote in favour, 18 per cent were really opposed to Quebec's sovereignty.[2] Thus, even to reach a bare majority for sovereignty seems very unlikely. And what if a majority were, in fact, carried off? What then? An Angus Reid poll, also in June of 1994, showed that only 25 per cent of Quebecers believed that a bare majority could be the basis for declaring independence; in the rest of Canada, only 10 per cent thought so. In fact, 71 percent of Quebecers believed that independence would require a majority vote of between 60 per cent and 80 per cent. In the rest of Canada, six in ten called for an overwhelming consensus of 80 per cent if independence was to be considered legitimate. Does anyone believe that such a high level of support for secession is ever likely to be achieved?[3]

It will not be easy for the people of Quebec to recognize that they have been misled, taken down several garden paths for these more than thirty years. So much disinformation, so many illusions propagated over so many years have consequences. And yet, reality must sooner or later be faced. Otherwise, Quebec will endlessly repeat the cycle of wrenching, insoluble debates on whether or not to remain in Canada. The debates will achieve nothing except higher levels of frustration.

In 1831, when Alexis de Tocqueville was visiting Lower Canada and reflecting on its future, he interviewed the superior of the Montreal Seminary, Father Quiblier, who had originally come from France. De Tocqueville asked, "Do you think that this colony will soon break away from England?" "I don't think so," the priest replied. "The *Canadiens* are happy under the present regime."[4]

The leaders who thought that the people of Quebec were eager for revolutionary change were always disappointed. So it was in the 1830s and in 1980, and so it is today, and so it will be whenever the question is put to a real test. The allure of secession, always beckoning though never attained, has seduced a whole generation of intellectuals, writers, artists, teachers, and politicians. Many have invested heavily in the myth of the ethnic state: they have given of their time,

THE END OF AN ILLUSION

their passion, their imagination, their money, and their careers. Many imagined the ethnic state following secession to be the normal fulfilment of Quebec's history. It was presented as progressive, forward-looking, visionary, an idealistic goal to be pursued by the generous young and the less corrupted old. Secession has been the cause that, far more than any other, has channelled many of the best talents and energies that Quebec has produced.

There is a tragic irony in this, that the best and the brightest have pursued a goal that is rooted in reactionary and anti-social sentiments, in tribal anglophobia and ethnocentric exclusivism. The only powerful justification for secession, with all its risks and costs, is the goal to create a state wholly controlled by francophones, freed of having to share sovereignty with a federal government in which *les autres* outnumber them. It is the same ethnocentric principle which is causing havoc in Eastern Europe, in Kashmir, and many parts of Africa. It is a principle of dissolution, because every separatist enclave will breed its own separatist movement within itself. When the box of ethnic discord is opened, no one knows what horrors will fly out.

The myth of the ethnic state, so carefully cultivated by every Quebec government since 1960, does not bring peace or prosperity to Quebec's society. Quebec invests in young people, only to have thousands of them take their dynamism elsewhere. Quebec is bleeding, and it will continue to bleed as long as it maintains its commitment to a state in which the francophone majority keeps all other groups tightly controlled to ensure its own dominance. The bleeding will accelerate with each new nationalist shock: the election of a PQ government, a solemn declaration by the National Assembly that Quebec is commited to sovereignty, the announcement of another referendum on separation and, above all, a serious attempt at secession. Each shock will bring more exile and poverty, poverty and exile, which has been Quebec's vicious cycle since its ethnic revolution accelerated in the 1970s.

Will this hemorrhaging never stop? Whatever the rationalizations, the myth of the Quebec ethnic state arises ultimately from the long tradition of anglophobia, which urges French-speaking Quebecers to reject a civic partnership with English-speaking Canada. A true liberation of Quebecers from myth can be brought about only when Quebecers themselves at last confront, demystify, and reject the anglophobic tradition that has been so central to their intellectual life.

Quebecers need to free themselves from the collective illusion that their cultural security and their identity depend on creating and maintaining an ethnocentric society. The opposite is true: Quebecers have more to gain by accepting true pluralism, liberalism and federalism than by maintaining the authoritarian, separatist, and hegemonic society that nationalists have implemented and propose to intensify.

Quebec society experienced only a partial Quiet Revolution in the 1960s, when it freed itself from the tyranny of an anti-modern religion and anti-democratic educational institutions. But many archaic attitudes survived the regenerative ferment, including anglophobia, which was quickly married to the vision of the ethnic state to become provincial Quebec's official ideology. The true liberation that Quebecers still await is the liberation from reactionary anglophobia and the reactionary ethnic state. When the day comes that Quebec frees itself at last from these shackles of the past, then will be the time to shout: *Vive le Québec libre!*

Notes

1.According to a Decima Research poll published in *Maclean's*, 1 July 1994.
2.Poll reported in the *Journal de Montréal*, 17 June 1994.
3.The poll was carried out between 30 May and June 1 1994. *The Gazette*, 4 June 1994, p. A 13. The poll also showed that a majority outside Quebec believed that an independent Quebec would have a smaller territory than the province has at present.
4.Alexis de Tocqueville, *Oeuvres complètes. Édition définitive publiée sous la direction de J.-P. Mayer*. Vol. 5, *Voyages en Sicile et aux États-Unis* (Paris: Gallimard, 1957), p. 78.

INDEX

Liberal Party of Canada 80-2, 91, 96, 133, 161-2, 164, 189, 193, 214, 226-8, 250, 254, 257, 260, 286, 296, 307, 331, 349
Liberal Party of Quebec 13, 19-21, 24-26, 46-7, 55-6, 58, 67-71, 74, 83, 100, 133, 164-5, 167, 195, 207, 230, 233, 259, 267, 277, 279, 298, 324, 374-5, 384-6
Libman, Robert 223, 368, 376
Lincoln, Clifford 221, 228
Lisée, Jean-François 280, 291, 310, 344
Loiselle, Gilles 176, 347-50
Long, John 350
Lortie, Jean-Claude 188, 198
Loubier, Gabriel 133, 140
Lougheed, Peter 178-9, 181, 190, 303-4, 310, 315, 335
Lussier, Doris 250
Lyon, Sterling 177, 179,

M

MacDonald, Finlay 130
Macdonald, Flora 130
Macdonald, John A. 37, 129, 193, 375
Machiavelli, Niccolo 376
MacDougall, Barbara 235, 348
MacLean, Vincent 301
MacLean's 334, 404
Macnaughton, Alan 81
Maheu, Pierre 47-9
Maintenant 102
Maîtriser l'avenir 207
Major, André 48
Manning, Earnest 85
Manning, Preston 292, 331, 342, 354, 358-63
Marchand, Jean 15, 80-1, 94, 267, 376
Maria Chapdelaine 16, 19
Maria Chapdelaine, ou le Paradis retrouvé 371, 377
Marquette, Père Jacques 167
Marsolais, Claude-V. 367-8, 377
Martel, Pierre 216,
Martin, Paul (Sr.) 61
Martin, Paul Jr. 227
Marx, Herbert 221

Masse, Marcel 65, 142, 203-4, 215, 223, 227, 312, 321, 347-50
Ma traversée du Québec. 156
Masson, Claude 218-9, 322
McDonald, Donald 304
McDonough, Alex 301
McKenna, Frank 224, 231-2, 239, 243-7, 330, 374
McLaughlin, Audrey 228, 258, 260, 286, 354, 363
McRoberts, Kenneth 344
Memmi, Albert 13, 46, 48
Memoirs of the Right Honourable Lester B. Pearson 97
Menaud, maître-draveur 42, 43, 46, 49, 53, 278
Mercier, Honoré 166
Mercredi, Ovide 290, 305, 309, 343-5
Mes Premiers Ministres 105
Métis National Council 318
Meynaud, Jean 52, 75
Michaud, Yves 125
Miron, Gaston 48, 123,
Miville-Deschênes, Julie 298
Monahan, Patrick 344
Monde diplomatique, Le 75, 103-5
Monnet, Jean 256-7, 260
Mon Oncle Marcel qui vague vague près du métro Berri 372-3, 378
Montreal Herald 368
Montreal Star 67
Morin, Claude 80, 100, 105, 165, 177, 180, 182-3, 186, 190, 201,
Morin, Jacques-Yvan 141, 161,
Morin, Rosaire 138
Mouton noir, Le 374-7
Mouvement Souveraineté-Association 74, 103,
Mulroney, Brian 15, 100, 129-136, 139-40, 143, 175, 180, 188, 192-249, 254-8, 263-4, 276-7, 280-7, 292-4, 297-9, 317, 319-22, 330-1, 336, 339, 341-4, 346-50, 352-5, 358-9, 363, 385
Mulroney: The Politics of Ambition 143
Multilateral Ministerial Conference on the Constitution 309-10, 315-6, 320-1
Munro, John A. 75